COLD
RIVALS

COLD RIVALS

THE NEW ERA OF US-CHINA STRATEGIC COMPETITION

Evan S. Medeiros, Editor

Georgetown University Press / Washington, DC

The publisher is not responsible for third-party websites or their content.
URL links were active at time of publication.

Library of Congress Cataloging-in-Publication Data

Names: Medeiros, Evan S., editor.
Title: Cold rivals: the new era of US-China strategic competition / Evan S. Medeiros, editor.
Description: Washington, DC: Georgetown University Press, [2023] |
Includes bibliographical references and index.
Identifiers: LCCN 2022037013 (print) | LCCN 2022037014 (ebook) | ISBN 9781647123581
(hardcover) | ISBN 9781647123598 (paperback) | ISBN 9781647123604 (ebook)
Subjects: LCSH: Competition—China. | Competition—United States. | United States—
Foreign relations—China. | China—Foreign relations—United States. | United States—Foreign
economic relations—China. | China—Foreign economic relations—United States. | China—
Military relations—United States. | United States—Military relations—China.
Classification: LCC E183.8.C5 C64 2023 (print) | LCC E183.8.C5 (ebook) |
DDC 327.51073—dc23/eng/20220815
LC record available at https://lccn.loc.gov/2022037013
LC ebook record available at https://lccn.loc.gov/2022037014

∞ This paper meets the requirements of ANSI/
NISO Z39.48-1992 (Permanence of Paper).

24 23   9 8 7 6 5 4 3 2 First printing

Printed in the United States of America

Cover design by Pam Pease
Interior design by Paul Hotvedt

Dedicated to:
Harry Harding and Wang Jisi
Mentors, friends, and pioneers in the study of US-China relations

Contents

Illustrations

Tables

Figures

Introduction: A New Strategic Reality

Evan S. Medeiros

As the US-China relationship enters its fifth decade, profound changes are afoot. In the last five years alone, the relationship has experienced one of its most significant evolutions since normalization in 1979. Tensions are rising, differences are expanding, and interactions are more complex. US-China ties are now commonly and frequently described as a "strategic competition," a "great power struggle," and even a "new cold war." Gone are the days of policymakers referencing the virtues of dialogue, communication, and cooperation. Even the talk of balancing cooperation and competition is now outdated, if not obsolescent.[1] US president Joe Biden, in February 2021, just one month after his inauguration, referred to US-China interactions as "extreme competition," and his administration has continued using similar characterizations since then. For his part, China's president, Xi Jinping, is reported as saying in an internal meeting, "The biggest source of chaos in the present-day world is the United States. . . . and the United States is the biggest threat to our country's development and security."[2]

This shift in rhetoric has corresponded with a steady stream of criticism from both Washington and Beijing about each other's policies and behaviors as well as a rapid decline in both official government dialogues and unofficial business, civil society, and educational interactions. Of course, the rolling global pandemic that began in 2020 has made all of this worse; it both broadened and deepened the deterioration in perceptions and interactions. As of 2023, US-China ties stand between a gradual decline and a precipitous deterioration that produces a crisis or even a confrontation. Washington and Beijing may be one crisis away from a very different reality in US-China ties, evocative of the US-Soviet contest of the 1950s.

The deeper currents in the relationship are even more worrisome. Each nation's negative images of the other are pervasive and hardening, linked not just

1

to current tensions but the internal politics and external ambitions of each country.[3] The idea of a US-China ideological competition has moved from the fringe to the core of the debate. The relationship is also experiencing a structural shift from one in which both sides' national interests are compatible in some arenas to one in which differences are expanding and intensifying in multiple arenas, and the few remaining arenas of seeming compatibility are crowded out by the growing number of differences. As of this writing, American and Chinese national interests diverge more than they converge, and on a broader set of issues: economic, diplomatic, political, technological, and on questions of values and governance.[4]

Policymakers, business leaders, scholars, and analysts in both countries are struggling both to understand the changing nature of US-China ties in this new context and its future trajectory and to determine what to do about it. US debates about whether this is a "new cold war" are now widespread. US and Chinese scholars and analysts have devoted significant time and energy to understanding the similarities and differences between the prior era and the present day, and the appropriateness of the old term to the new context.[5] From the vantage point of 2023, and especially after the Russian invasion of Ukraine, many American strategists view this turn toward strategic competition as enduring rather than ephemeral. The last few years have revealed a growing number of differences in interests, values, and outlooks that form the basis of a long-term rivalry. China's alignment with Russia in February 2022, just twenty days before Russia's invasion of Ukraine, had a substantial impact on US perceptions of Chinese intentions and ambitions, just as Nancy Pelosi's trip to Taiwan in August 2022 had a major impact on Chinese perceptions of US intentions toward China.

However, scholars and analysts differ about why this change in US-China dynamics has occurred. Some attribute it to classic power transition ideas in which the narrowing of the relative power gap has led Washington to become more focused on Beijing's capabilities.[6] This line of argumentation is common in China, with some even attributing a number to it: Once the Chinese economy became 70 percent of the US economy, the relationship was bound to become more contentious.[7] Others in the United States and China see this downward trend as linked to domestic politics in both countries and the hardening perceptions of elites and publics.[8] A common view in China is that the United States is a declining superpower that needs an external threat to justify its hegemony and high defense expenditures to keep a decaying economy moving, especially after the devastation of the coronavirus.[9] A third perspective grounds the shift in the relationship to the ascension of Xi Jinping: his statist repressive actions at home combined with assertive and coercive behaviors abroad have put China on a trajectory toward long-term discord with US interests and values.[10]

Across these and other explanations run a set of common questions: Was the shift inevitable? Are the United States and China destined for long-term rivalry or confrontation? US and Chinese assessments of the current state of the US-China relationship are replete with speculation about the future. Predictions range from the moderate to the dire, with the possibilities narrowing toward the latter in recent years as relations have deteriorated. For some, conflict is inevitable due to China's growing ambitions and capabilities and American unwillingness to tolerate the diversity of challenges from China. Others see the situation as manageable, reflecting a belief that some combination of leadership, interdependence, and the high costs of conflict will prevail.[11] Of course, the risk of an accident or miscalculation that triggers a negative spiral is ever-present, though some argue that this risk is rising as dialogue and interaction decline.[12]

Most of these forecasts are equally logical (i.e., the causal links are clear and often historically grounded) and have a reasonable probability of materializing. Given the flux in the structure of the current international system, especially as unipolarity fades, perhaps the best way of looking at the future of the US-China relationship is as a Rorschach test. One's view of the future of the US-China relationship reflects one's views of how the world works: the relative restraint imposed by economic interdependence and nuclear weapons, the nature of US power, Chinese ambitions as a rising power, the type of international order we live in, and the importance of regime type in shaping a country's ambitions and actions.

Thus, as of this writing it is exceedingly difficult to predict with great precision how the US-China relationship will evolve in the next few years, let alone in the following decades. This book does not claim to do so, but it offers some directions and guideposts. Neither Beijing nor Washington say meaningful things about the future beyond bland rhetoric about seeking peace, stability, prosperity, and respect. A central premise of this book is that the relationship will be shaped, at least in part, by events that have yet to occur—events within both countries, around them, and, importantly, between them.

For the United States, the degree of domestic economic and political revitalization will matter as much in its competition with China as, and perhaps more than, its ability to generate and sustain international coalitions to shape Chinese behaviors. For China, the next decade will be momentous for its economic and political development, with Xi taking several bets about the success of his authoritarian and statist vision. Domestically, will China rebalance its growth model, exit the middle-income trap, and avoid the economic challenges posed by its imposing demographic challenges? Externally, Xi is betting on China's economic gravity, diplomatic presence, and military prowess to reduce external pressure and increase China's freedom of action in Asia and globally. Of course, then there is the momentous question of when Xi will turn over the reins to the next generation of political leaders and how they will manage China's ties with America.

Finally, the interaction between the United States and China—the people, the trade, the behaviors—is one of the most important and often underappreciated factors in determining the future of the relationship. If history teaches us anything about the relationship, it is that these interactions shape the perceptions, the politics, and, in some cases, the policies that collectively constitute and motivate the US-China relationship. These interactions, when combined with the other factors, underscore the highly contingent nature of the relationship.

This edited volume seeks to contribute to this debate about the current character and future trajectory of US-China ties. It seeks to do so by opening the aperture on this new era of strategic competition in US-China relations. The volume does so by examining the origins, manifestations, and implications of this shift in the relationship toward persistent and pervasive competition. It strives to answer several pivotal questions. First, how and why did this era emerge? How deep are its roots? What are its attributes? Was it inevitable? Second, what kinds of behaviors and dynamics will competition produce and to what extent will they differ, depending on the issue? Third, what are the implications for the future of US-China relations, including outside of Asia and on global issues? As competition evolves, is confrontation inevitable, and what issue or set of issues will drive it in that direction? The core goal of this collection of essays is to understand the nature of this generalized shift from an era marked by dialogue, interaction, management, and cooperation to one defined by disagreement, friction, disengagement, and competition. Why did this happen? What does it mean now? How will it manifest? Is it enduring?

A central premise of this edited volume is that there is little that is inevitable in the US-China relationship. History has proven that it is a highly contingent relationship whose trajectory has been shaped by domestic capabilities and political events in both countries, regional events in Asia, global events, and, importantly, the interactions between the two countries. Thus, it is the interplay of these large variables that helps us understand the emergence of this new era of competition and where relations might go in the future. The chapters in this volume look at competition from both a historical and a contemporary perspective in order to understand the roots of diverging interests as well as the factors that helped the two countries manage differences in the past and may constrain them in the future.

Framing and Explaining US-China Competition

The chapters in this volume examine and analyze from several angles the evolution of competition in US-China relations since normalization in 1979. Some chapters are historically oriented, and others are contemporary. The chapters, written by prominent specialists from both countries, incorporate both US and Chinese perspectives. Specifically, the chapters explore US-China competition from a diversity of functional perspectives: history, politics and economics, defense and security concerns, questions of technology, and the future of the relationship. The edited volume is structured into five sections corresponding to these issues.

Among the authors, there is broad agreement that competition has long been a feature of the relationship but that its drivers, character, intensity, and manifestations have evolved substantially. While the authors uniformly agree that competition today has become the core dynamic in the relationship, many argue that this outcome was not inevitable, and neither is the drift from competition to confrontation. However, the authors differ in their assessment of which dynamics—security, economics, technology, or ideas—have been the main contributors to this new era. There are differing assessments of the historical pathway competition has taken and its attributes today. There is a notable divide between US and Chinese authors about Chinese perceptions and contributions to this era of competition, with Chinese specialists putting less emphasis on competitive dynamics in the evolution of China's policymaking and more on China's defensive motives in the face of increasing US pressure over many decades.

A Conceptual and Historical Framework

The first section of this volume looks at US-China competition from a conceptual and a historical perspective: What does the concept of competition mean when applied to US-China relations, and what can history teach us about the evolution of competition in US-China interactions? In chapter 1, "Explaining and Understanding Competition in US-China Relations," Evan Medeiros argues that the concept of competition is undertheorized in the field of international politics and in US-China relations. To address this, his chapter seeks to define the meaning of competition—what kinds of behaviors do and do not constitute competition—and then apply these ideas to the history of US-China interactions. Drawing on recent studies of competition in great power politics, Medeiros argues that competition requires at least three conditions: perceived contention, an effort to gain mutual advantage, and the pursuit of some outcome or good that is not generally available. This definition applies to a state's pursuit of power, influence, status, and/or material goods when others seek the same things and the supply of them is limited; thus, competition exists when gaining access to some of these scarce items would confer a relative advantage of one state over another. In this sense, Medeiros argues that competition is different from conflict, which is a more intense varietal, and different from "disagreement or contestation," which is less intense and implies merely a difference of views. Moreover, Medeiros maintains that competition between and among states can be over specific goals, such as who controls a piece of land or maritime feature, as well as broader ones, such as regional leadership, a dominant economic position, and/or global status.

Based on this approach to competition, Medeiros's chapter then applies this definition to the forty-year history of US-China interactions since normalization. He argues that perhaps the most defining feature of the relationship over the past four decades has been the persistence of divergent perceptions and interests amid a shared desired to pursue common economic interests and, at times, diplomatic goals. In this sense, while competition has existed for much of the past forty years, it also has been bounded by both sides for the sake of common interests, even short-lived ones. The interventions of US and Chinese leaders to steady the relationship at critical times was an important source of ballast, for example. However, Medeiros continues that, over time, differences in perceptions, interests, and capabilities expanded and, as a result, the nature and scope of bilateral competition intensified. In surveying the last forty-plus years and especially the last five, Medeiros argues that one of the most significant drivers of competition has been the coercive nature of the economic, diplomatic, and military policies used by both sides, which has had the practical effect of intensifying the perceptions of disagreement, divergence, and, ultimately, contention. At the same time, the sources of stability in the relationship and the buffers against seeing the other as an inevitable rival began to fade away. This, in turn, accelerated the real contention at the heart of the bilateral competition—a broader set of clearly diverging interests—which then produced the era of "strategic competition."

In chapter 2, "Old Cold War and New," Richard Betts compares the features of the "old" US-Soviet Cold War to US-China relations today, which he calls a "new cold war." Betts argues that the similarities outweigh the differences in comparing the two situations, offering insights into how to understand US-China competition today.

Betts argues that the core similarity is a bipolar structure of the international system, based on his belief that structure drives outcomes. While appreciating the debate about such a stark claim, Betts's core argument is that "there was no third country in the same league of overall national power as the United States and the USSR then, and despite Russian belligerence there is no other state now in the same league as the United States and the PRC." Drawing on this conception of order, Betts further develops his argument by noting that in both instances the "stakes, power, and motives" are concentrated in the three dimensions of military, economic, and political power, albeit in differing configurations today in US-China interactions. In his account, the old Cold War was driven most intensely by political divisions over ideology, next by military confrontation, and third and least by economic competition. Today, between the United States and China, the order of these drivers in the new cold war is reversed: economics, military, and then ideology. Betts argues that "the biggest question" is whether economic or military competition will dominate. Betts's chapter then systematically compares US-Soviet and US-China dynamics in all three domains, with important insights about the differences and similarities in each category.

Drawing on his analysis of competition in these three arenas, Betts argues that unlike during the Cold War, the main risk of conflict in the US-China context today is not a deliberate military action but rather an accident or miscalculation. Betts concludes that the new cold war is likely to deepen as competition in all three arenas intensifies and the risk of inadvertent conflict grows. This risk is especially pronounced in the early stages of the new cold war, as the boundaries of competition have not yet been set. Betts notes that ambiguity may help reinforce deterrence now, such as regarding Taiwan, but it could also be the source of a miscalculation going forward. Optimistically, he adds that the latter conclusion has an underlying positivity because it implies neither Washington nor Beijing has an interest in launching a deliberate conflict due to an awareness of the high costs.

In this first section on historical perspectives, Harry Harding and Wang Jisi take a different approach from Betts, both focusing exclusively on US-China dynamics. They respectively examine the evolution of Chinese and US views on the rise of competition.

In chapter 3, "The United States and China," Harding takes a similar approach to Wang by tracing the evolution of the last forty years of US-China interactions and America's China policy to draw lessons for our understanding of competition. However, he tells a very different story about the evolution of differences, distrust, and antagonism. Harding begins by describing a relationship that was stable but also challenged, even "fragile," during the golden era of the 1980s. Bilateral ties were then severely disrupted by Tiananmen in 1989 and never regained their footing. In the 1990s, Washington and Beijing were able to find a stable basis for their relationship based on China's contributions to regional and global challenges and its desire—indeed, its need—for continued and expanded access to US markets, capital, and technology to reach its ambitious development goals. Importantly, these Chinese goals resonated with the broader US strategy to shape and socialize China into a constructive rising power. This basic and implicit modus vivendi for US-China ties then extended into the 2000s. Harding writes that in the 1990s and 2000s tensions were not far below the surface because none of the previous differences, like Taiwan or market access, had been resolved, and new ones crept onto the agenda.

Beyond this narrative history, Harding's chapter looks at analytic questions such as why and how the US pursued a paradigm of "engagement," why it ultimately produced a new paradigm of strategic competition, and where US policy and US-China relations will go from here. Harding argues that the engagement tool kit included a bevy of policies including promoting dialogue, building personal relationships, offering reassurance, fostering interdependence, building negotiation mechanisms, integrating China into international organizations, and articulating an aspirational framework for relations. Yet the application of all of these tools was fraught with challenges and ultimately failed due to differing interests and goals for the relationship. Harding argues that there was a superficial quality to these approaches in which both sides created the facade of a friendship amid growing differences in perceptions, policies, and interests. Many Americans, in his account, were never sold on the idea that the relationship was primarily cooperative, but US policy persisted nonetheless based on the hope that the United States could socialize China. Harding sees the emergence of strategic competition as a gradual shift and not the result of an external event, such as the global financial crisis or Tiananmen. Rather, he writes, it was the result of an accumulation of differences and concerns on the US side combined with the arrival of US president Donald Trump and a group of advisers composed of both national security hawks and economic nationalists who saw China as the primary threat to the United States. Trump's aggressive economic actions against China combined with his tough rhetoric led Chinese leaders to conclude that US policy had shifted fundamentally.

Harding attributes this sharp shift in US policy to several variables. As the gap in relative capabilities expanded, the lack of any kind of binding force, such as a common threat or track record of cooperation, accelerated US perceptions of competition. In particular, the differences in values and views of domestic governance contributed to a US view of China as not only increasingly different but as challenging to US interests. Harding adds to the list factors such as differing visions of international order, China's growing ambitions, a Chinese sense of victimization, and America's desire to lead global rulemaking at the very time China wanted a greater voice and influence. Ultimately, Harding sees the US-China relationship as a tragedy in which the policymakers in Beijing and Washington valiantly but futilely fought against an unavoidable fate: strategic competition. Harding concludes that the US-China relationship moving forward will be a shifting and evolving mix of cooperation, coexistence, competition, and confrontation, with the latter two being dominant features of bilateral interactions.

In chapter 4, "From Reluctant Cooperation to Assertive Competition," Wang Jisi frames his historical account (from 1979 to 2022) as China's reaction to "the strategic pressure of the United States." He argues that in the early stage of bilateral ties following normalization, China saw itself as a partner in cooperating with the United States to resist Soviet expansion in the world. However, by the end of the Cold War, he notes, China "reinforced its strategy" by opposing what it referred to as US hegemonism, and this strategy steadily evolved into "a more comprehensive and deliberate approach to compete with the United States in global affairs." Wang says that China's strategic goals have been threefold—a combination of sovereignty, security, and development over the past forty years. China's approach was about protecting and defending these interests, with a particular focus on preventing the United States from interfering in China's internal politics, including taking actions to prevent Washington from destabilizing China. According to Wang, as US-China interactions on these three issues—sovereignty, security, and development—changed, so did the nature of competition.

Wang argues that two fundamental drivers over the past forty years "have moved China steadily onto a road of strategic competition with the United States." The first is the concentration and consolidation of the power of the Chinese Communist Party (CCP), which the United States has consistently challenged. Wang states that the Chinese leadership "has every reason to view the United States as the major and increasingly deadly menace" to China's stability, security, and sovereignty. In Wang's account, US-China competition intensified after Xi came to power, as external security competition became linked to political security at home. He notes that over the last four decades, China's defensiveness about its domestic stability has evolved into an acute fear and a deliberate effort to insulate itself from US political and ideological influences. The second driver is China's effort to increase its material power, especially economic and military power. The pursuit of material gains initially involved cooperating with the United States but has now morphed into competing with America, even as Wang notes that Chinese leaders are conscious of the remaining power gap and the apparent need to maintain cooperation with the United States.

Looking forward, Wang identifies several features of US-China relations in the future. Given that "the United States is seen not only as the principal external political and ideological threat but also as a long-term internal challenge," he argues that disagreements about issues like Hong Kong, Xinjiang, and Tibet will only grow. China will support countries that also resist the United States by working with developed and developing countries sympathetic toward China. These policies, combined with triumphalism about China's relative position in the world and Xi's various entreaties to "struggle," have led to both a national interest competition and a "propaganda" war in which Beijing is even less willing to make compromises. Wang writes that "in the areas of economics, nontraditional security, technology, and humanitarian exchanges, a new pattern of competition and cooperation may emerge." He further argues that "the Chinese realize that a certain amount of trade and financial relations with America is indispensable" for China. Wang concludes that the United States and China will work together on various transnational challenges but that the potential for cooperation will be overshadowed by distrust, political disputes, and "ideational competitions" occurring in both countries.

Contemporary Dynamics

The second section of this volume explores contemporary bilateral political and economic dynamics. It is focused less on historical questions and more on the contemporary features of US-China competition. In chapter 5, "China's Management of Strategic Competition with the United States," Fudan University professor Wu Xinbo provides a Chinese perspective on US-China strategic competition. He explores the following questions: How does China perceive the strategic contest with the United States? How has China executed the contest, and what kind of instruments does it employ? What factors abet or constrain the rivalry? What might future scenarios look like, and what lessons can be drawn from the process so far?

Wu begins by noting that competition is certainly not a new feature of bilateral ties and has its roots in previous administrations, notably President Obama's pursuit of the Asia pivot strategy. Yet Wu focuses on President Trump's China's policy as the main driver of not just the emergence of the era of strategic competition but, more importantly, the intense and comprehensive nature of Trump's policies. Wu argues it was the comprehensive nature of Trump's actions against China, including the trade war and the multiple speeches drawing stark ideological differences, that led to this new level of distrust and acrimony: "The US maneuvering against China in economic coercion, technological blockade, diplomatic rivalry and political-ideological confrontation has intended to advance multiple goals of America's China strategy: gaining more economic benefits, weakening China's political system, thwarting China's rising power and expanding international influence, and preserving the US hegemony." As a result, in Wu's account, Beijing came to new and more severe assessments of US intentions, including the conclusion that they would persist beyond Trump due to political polarization in America.

Wu then examines the nature of China's response to Trump's pursuit of strategic competition to explain the resulting bilateral dynamics. Wu argues that Beijing pursued several approaches: seeking discursive power; counterattack; deterrence; bargaining, negotiation, and compromise; reducing vulnerability; divide and rule; and winning over third parties (in the United States and internationally). In Wu's account, all of these added to tensions and distrust, but of particular importance was the Trump administration's unwillingness to recognize that China sought to find a way back to stable relations. In assessing China's pursuit of these strategies, Wu maintains that China sought to execute a careful balancing act: fight back without jeopardizing the entire relationship. According to Wu, Beijing maintains that competition is "inevitable and likely to intensify, but a catastrophic, head-on confrontation and Cold War–style antagonism should be avoided"; still, others in China think that Beijing needs to resist the United States even more to deter further actions.

Wu concludes with a sober assessment about the future. He sees strategic competition as only intensifying due to two factors: the narrowing gap in relative capabilities and domestic politics in both countries that are feeding the sense of rivalry. Nonetheless, Wu also sees some factors that may moderate the competition, including competition that is more social and economic than political and military, the high degree of economic interdependence, and China's support for the prevailing international order and opportunities for the United States and China to cooperate within the international system. Wu finishes the essay by noting that, despite the acrimony of the new era, the two countries are far from confrontation and both sides should work to prevent such an outcome, a period he calls a "critical juncture." He sees the Taiwan issue and ideological competition as the two issues that could further destabilize the current situation.

In chapter 6, "The Evolution of America's China Policy," Elizabeth Economy looks at a similar set of issues, but from a US perspective. She sees the emergence of strategic competition as more evolutionary and less of a stark and quick shift in US thinking and policymaking, as Wu argues. In short, she believes the competitive dynamics were long in coming and may have been inevitable. In Economy's account, the security hedge aspects of US policy had been gradually growing, as US elites became more disillusioned with engagement as an overriding strategy.

Economy's analysis, in stark contrast to Chinese accounts, begins by pointing out the changes in Chinese behavior, at home and internationally, that led to a US disillusionment and anxiety. She highlights the growing restrictions on basic rights in China (beginning under former president Hu Jintao), the expansion of the state sector and indifferences to market reforms, and China's growing confidence in its international position (relative to the United States) and related assertiveness on its periphery. Economy gives special attention to the arrival of Xi, asserting that his statements and actions accelerated the shift in US thinking about China as a long-term competitor. She states, "President Xi transformed Chinese domestic and foreign policies in ways that raised fundamentally new questions about the country's commitment to domestic political and economic reform as well as to the rules-based order." In response, she argues, the Obama administration shifted from an approach of "engage but hedge" to one of "hedge but engage."

Economy goes on to say that Trump's election was also a major moment in the arrival of strategic competition, informed by his "America First" agenda and driven by his hawkish and nationalistic advisers. She notes that Trump's actual implementation of a coherent China policy was challenged by his own mixed motives—such as wanting a trade agreement and cooperation on North Korea—and a chaotic policymaking process on China. She argues that, as Trump focused on trade and North Korea in his China policy, a collection of his advisers were crafting a more confrontational approach to China focused on economic decoupling, technology competition, and ideological divides. Beyond policy issues, Economy highlights the negative shifts in not only elite but also US public opinion toward China, both seeing China as a threat to American values beyond narrow trade issues. This precipitated Trump's adoption of a "whole-of-government" approach that touched many different aspects of US society. Economy sees the COVID-19 pandemic as more of an accelerant than a determinant of the arrival of strategic competition.

Economy concludes that in the last decade and across administrations, US policymakers have gradually but also fundamentally rethought, recalibrated, and reset US policy toward China. US policy is not going back to the days of dialogue and engagement. America, she writes, will struggle with its economic interdependence with China and its need to cooperate with China on global issues, but the character of US policies and perceptions about China today and in the future have changed and will continue to change in fundamental ways.

Arthur Kroeber's chapter 7, "The Economic Origins of US-China Strategic Competition," looks at bilateral economic dynamics for clues to the origins and trajectory of US-China competition. He argues that several economic trends converged to cause US policy to shift from enabling China's rise to constraining it. He frames this shift as a "gradual disillusionment" on the part of US political and business elites with the benefits of China's economic rise. He highlights the following trends as causes: China grew bigger and faster than most anticipated; its industries became more directly competitive with (rather than supportive of) high-value industries in the United States; its technological progress spurred security concerns; its model of authoritarian, state-led capitalism proved more durable than expected, putting pressure on global governance systems built around market economies; and the unpaid political bills for the domestic dislocations caused by China's rise came due.

Kroeber also argues that there were and are countervailing trends. For some companies, a presence in China is not optional; it is vital to ensuring their continued global competitiveness. The US business community, which is unhappy with various aspects of Chinese regulation, still views China far more as an opportunity than as a threat. Looking ahead, Kroeber concludes that US policymakers will struggle to define a practical approach to economic relations with China, between the poles of the unsustainable (a wish to restore the relationship to its prior state of mutually beneficial exchange with limited competition) and the unachievable (a desire to "decouple" two economies that are tightly bound together).

The third section of this volume examines the national security and military dimensions of US-China competition. Phillip Saunders and Li Chen explore US and Chinese perspectives on military and defense issues relevant to bilateral competition. James Mulvenon looks at the role of nontraditional security issues, such as espionage and cybersecurity, in adding to distrust and, ultimately, competition.

Phillip Saunders's chapter 8, "The Military Factor in US-China Strategic Competition," assesses both the China factor in US military modernization and the US factor in Chinese military modernization to understand the relative contribution of security competition. He argues that US concerns about Chinese military modernization—and vice versa—have been central to the evolution of US thinking about China as a long-term strategic competitor. He maintains that US-China competition is seen in the United States as strategic and intensifying—as opposed to moderate and manageable—precisely because each side is focused on developing military capabilities aimed at degrading the other and pursuing influence at the other's expense. He implies that this is the most competitive dimension of the relationship, which carries with it zero-sum attributes.

In assessing the US factor in Chinese military modernization, Saunders points to a series of external events from 1989 to 1999 that led to a hardening of Chinese threat perceptions toward the US military, such as the mid-1990s Taiwan Strait crisis and the 1999 Belgrade bombing. Moreover, he argues that as preventing Taiwan independence became the central driver for People's Liberation Army (PLA) modernization in the 1990s, countering US intervention became a core task for the Chinese military. This drove PLA efforts to acquire or develop capabilities that might deter, delay, or defeat US military forces intervening in a conflict over Taiwan. For US policy, "as PLA modernization has produced new capabilities that erode the US military's technological edge and threaten its ability to operate near China, the United States has begun to treat China *as a strategic challenge to US regional dominance and to the US-led global order* [emphasis added]." The US shift to seeing China as the dominant threat driving US defense planning was a gradual one, by Saunders's account, delayed by the post-9/11 global war on terrorism and the conflicts in Iraq and Afghanistan. By 2018, China had finally become the dominant threat driving US military modernization. Saunders's chapter then chronicles the evolution of the US military's thinking about China.

Li Chen's chapter 9, "National Security and Strategic Competition between China and the United States," focuses on Chinese threat perceptions about the United States (and especially about the US military) and their relative contribution to PLA thinking. Li agrees with Saunders that defense and security competition has been the principal driver of a more contentious relationship. Li argues that US-China military competition is less intensive than US-Soviet military competition and is mainly focused on a contested maritime space as opposed to being global. Yet US-China military competition is growing in scope and intensity, and the risks of accidents and miscalculations are accumulating. Li agrees with Saunders that the military competition has its roots in the 1990s due to events like the Gulf War, US actions such as the Belgrade bombing, and, perhaps most importantly, China's growing concerns about Taiwan after the 1995–96 crises. Li points out that China's leaders and the PLA saw all of their actions as purely reactive and defensive, suggesting that they viewed the United States as the driver of competition per se. In the late 2000s, the US involvement in maritime disputes in East Asia further heightened PLA perceptions that the US military sought to constrain China in the region, viewing maritime issues, especially those with US allies, as a way to put additional pressure on the Chinese military.

Looking forward, Li characterizes US-China defense competition as a classic security dilemma; both sides feel increasingly targeted by the other's military and thus more vulnerable, which drives their overall military posture in Asia. This is being accentuated by advances in military technology on both sides because of the speed and lethality of new weapons systems. Li points out that defense competition is now spilling over into the type of military cooperation that the United States and China offer to third countries. Li stresses that both the CCP and PLA assessments of US strategic intentions hardened under the Trump administration, which intensified their desire to use the military to protect Chinese interests.

Li concludes with a series of projections for the future of US-China military competition. Chinese leaders will put even more emphasis on building "a world class military," viewing it as more of a necessity than a luxury. Chinese military planners may think more about their reach outside of Asia. The need for crisis management will grow, but the long-standing challenges to it will persist, such as China's ambivalence to such mechanisms. The PLA may become more open to confidence-building measures with regional militaries in an effort to offset US influence and what Li calls a "multi-front struggle" in Asia. Li calls for a shift on both sides from crisis management to competition management in order to prevent the current situation from drifting toward a highly militarized long-term rivalry.

In chapter 10, "Nontraditional Security Competition," James Mulvenon examines an entirely distinct but important set of national security issues in US-China relations: espionage and cybersecurity. Mulvenon's chapter begins with the important premise that competition is growing in these arenas and generating the same type of distrust and acrimony as in the defense arena—even though much of this competition is not public and often doesn't get as much attention as other arenas. He argues that "even the fragmentary public record clearly shows that espionage is now playing an increasingly central role in the nontraditional security competition between Washington and Beijing." Mulvenon's chapter provides a unique and useful typology of Chinese espionage that ranges from traditional state-directed collection efforts against US government targets to myriad forms of economic espionage against US companies to a diversity of cyberattacks involving the former. The chapter provides impressive detail and data on the expanding scope and frequency of economic and technology espionage by China, including its various manifestations across US society, which adds to US concerns about threats emanating from China.

Mulvenon argues that the expansion of Chinese espionage activities, both vague and diffuse in nature, are having the practical effect of intensifying US perceptions of security competition. He stresses that Chinese spies operate through government agencies but also through other quasi-official and private Chinese actors, which substantially complicates the United States' ability to locate, track, and target these groups for the purposes of disruption. Of particular note, Mulvenon addresses China's use of "nontraditional collection" methods—talent recruitment, academic collaboration, and supply chain access—all of which add to the US sense of vulnerability to Chinese espionage. Mulvenon then details the various US policy responses to Chinese espionage, such as naming and shaming, expanding US counterintelligence efforts, expulsions of Chinese officials, and even the closing of consulates. These and other tactics have fostered a negative action-reaction cycle of actions that have heightened tensions in US-China relations.

This unique and important chapter concludes with sobering notes about the trajectory of espionage issues and their contribution to the dynamics of competition. He states, "Espionage is a central, if discreet, battlefield of nontraditional great power competition. In the US-China relationship, the gloves have clearly come off in this realm." The action-reaction cycle in the espionage arena is accelerating as each side sees the other as both a target of opportunity for collection and an intelligence threat requiring enhanced response. Mulvenon admits that while much of this is in the shadows, it is very much an influence on how policymakers in both countries perceive the other and thus drive competition in an already fraught relationship.

The fourth section of this volume examines technology as a source of, and venue for, competition. Paul Triolo's chapter 11, "China's Rise as a Technology Power and US-China Technology Competition," assesses China's thinking about technology and how Beijing's policies resulted in an intensifying competition over technology dominance. In chapter 12, "From Backwater to Near-Peer," Helen Toner looks at US policy toward technology issues in US-China ties.

Triolo begins by examining the trajectory of China's technology rise from "innovation laggard" to "serious challenger" over the last decade, arguing that information and communications technology (ICT) has now become a focal point of US-China strategic competition. Triolo challenges the conventional wisdom both on how this happened and why it happened so fast. His chapter traces how China's technology rise became one of the most important points of tension in the bilateral relationship, with a focus on the issues of forced technology transfer, IP theft, industrial subsidies, and market access.

Triolo argues that Beijing has long viewed achieving technology parity with the West as critical to China's modernization and the CCP's survival. In the digital age this became an even higher priority because the CCP experienced an erosion of control over information. The vulnerability of connected systems posed new and existential threats to the Chinese Communist Party, which it reacted to by focusing on technology issues. This fear translated into new policies for fostering globally competitive technology companies, but the success of Chinese tech companies has resulted primarily in raising fears in the United States that they will ultimately do Beijing's bidding and represent a growing national security threat to the United States and like-minded allies around the globe. As a result, major US technology policy decisions are now designed primarily to slow or derail the perceived march of Chinese companies toward some sort of world domination in their respective sectors.

In assessing the future trajectory of US-China technology competition, Triolo argues that the United States and China appear to be headed toward a bifurcated technology stack, with China and its authoritarian partners and countries involved in the Belt and Road Initiative (BRI) pursuing one technology development track while the United States and like-minded Western democracies gradually remove most or all Chinese-origin technology from their critical infrastructure and supply chains. Under this messy and complicated scenario, Triolo concludes that Chinese digital technology companies, which have succeeded and have for the most part embraced global value chains, will now be faced with a variety of Western restrictions that complicate these Chinese firms' ability to expand and become global players, forcing them more deeply under the influence of the party/state and thus into supporting the party/state development priorities.

Toner's chapter also explores these issues, but mainly from a US perspective. Her chapter traces the growing range and scope of technology issues in the relationship, culminating in the current era of strategic competition. In the 1980s, discussions of technology primarily arose in military and strategic contexts, against the backdrop of US competition with the Soviet Union. In the 1990s and 2000s, China emerged as a major commercial market, and dual-use technologies—which have both civilian and military applications—grew in importance, leading to a push and pull between security and commercial interests. In the last ten years, the use under Xi Jinping of digital tools for social control has added human rights to the technology policy agenda, and China has risen as a science and technology force to be reckoned with.

Toner argues that technology competition lagged behind the evolution of a more contentious bilateral relationship, but it eventually caught up. In the 1980s, Washington did not remotely perceive China as a technological competitor given the chasm in capabilities between China and the West. Indeed, back then, technology cooperation held the prospect of accelerating China's economic development, which the United States would benefit from. As China's capabilities developed through the 1990s and 2000s, it became clear that China might someday challenge US interests. Today, Chinese companies and government practices directly challenge US ability to dominate key technologies in such sectors as quantum computing, artificial intelligence, life sciences, and others. For the United States, Chinese technology policies and practices are also seen as undermining US national security interests and US values, especially with China's use of technology to facilitate repression at home.

She concludes that the United States is struggling to find the right tools to compete with China, arguing that its current tool kit relies on outmoded means—such as export controls—in such a highly integrated global economy. She states, "Many US measures rest on the assumption that it is feasible to cut off or significantly slow down China's access to a given technology. In the vast majority of cases . . . this is unlikely to work." She maintains that a successful US response cannot be based on restrictions alone but must include close collaboration with allies to develop—and enforce—a proactive vision of what liberal democratic norms for these new technologies could look like, expressed through global scientific cooperation.

Looking toward the Future

The final section of the book is focused on the future of US-China competition and seeks to provide the reader with a framework for thinking about the future. In chapter 13, "Time Horizons and the Future of US-China Relations," David Edelstein seeks to answer two very specific questions: Where is the US-China relationship headed next, and what factors are likely to determine if the relationship develops in a more cooperative or confrontational direction?

To answer these questions, Edelstein draws on his previous work on the time horizon dimension of power transitions. He explains, "a declining power's dilemma is between acting now to try to prevent the continuing growth of a rising power with uncertain long-term intentions or waiting until later to act once the rising power's ambitions are clearer." A rising power's "now-or-later dilemma" involves "acting now to assert new interests or waiting until later to do so," and each option possesses its own risks and benefits. In explaining US policy toward China, he maintains that "declining powers generally prefer to procrastinate and address rising great powers later rather than in the present" because they lack the resources to address a potential long-term threat. Edelstein goes on to say that US policy toward China in recent years has reflected the caution induced by both uncertainty of China's intentions and irreversibility (e.g., strategies that would have foreclosed opportunities for mutually beneficial cooperation).

For Edelstein, rising powers like China take a different approach. Patience is a virtue for them, and they tend to avoid provocative action if they can. He argues that cooperation with other great powers may help fuel a rising power's growth. Moreover, rising powers have an incentive to maintain uncertainty about their future intentions. When their interests do expand, rising powers are inclined to do so through "salami tactics," expanding incrementally so that others do not uniformly sound alarms about their intentions. Yet, in Edelstein's account, rising powers like China sometimes lose patience and act aggressively when it would seem premature to do so, driven by a combination of domestic politics, more resources, and perceptions of regional provocations.

Drawing on his focus on time horizons in US-China interactions, Edelstein offers four scenarios for the future. In the first, Beijing backs away from its effort to capture short-term gains vis-à-vis the United States and returns to a more forward-looking perspective, and the United States focuses on short-term threats to its security rather than any potential long-term threats. In a second scenario, US time horizons extend into the future, and China's time horizons remain focused on the short term, which ends up leading to a highly unstable relationship defined by intensifying competition. In a third scenario, both Beijing and Washington adopt long time horizons. While this might help avoid short-term competition, it might also set the stage for a sustained long-term relationship that is neither friendly nor conflictual—a new cold war. In a fourth scenario, both the United States and China have short time horizons focused on more immediate costs and benefits while significantly discounting the future. This produces a highly competitive relationship in which any disagreement, even a minor one, could escalate into a dangerous conflict. Edelstein believes the final scenario to be the most likely.

In chapter 14, "Parsing and Managing US-China Competition," David Shambaugh sees the future as far less contingent. Rather, he sees the trajectory of the relationship as one of "indefinite comprehensive competitive rivalry," with each one of these terms serving as important descriptors of the future of the relationship. For Shambaugh, "It is now primarily a *competitive* relationship in which the existing elements of cooperation are far outweighed by the competitive ones, in which each side seeks to strengthen itself vis-à-vis the other and takes actions and counteractions against the other; it is *comprehensive* in that it stretches across virtually all functional issue areas and all geographic regions of the world, even into outer space; it has become a classic great power *rivalry* whereby each increasingly contests the other's presence and influence worldwide . . . and it is not time-bound and can be expected to last *indefinitely* into the future [emphasis added]."

In developing his projection, Shambaugh begins with an insightful discussion of the nature of competition in global affairs and in the US-China context. Shambaugh tempers his rather dire projections for the future by noting that "competition is not inherently negative and not intrinsically zero-sum. It is often a stimulus for improvement and can bring out the best in various actors." He adds, "nor is competition to be thought of as the opposite of cooperation. They can, and do, coexist. . . . Thus, when we say that the US-China relationship is primarily competitive, by no means does that imply that there is no scope for pragmatic cooperation." Shambaugh sees the best-case scenario for the future being one of "competitive coexistence." For him, the future of the relationship will be defined by a relative mix of both cooperation and competition in bilateral dynamics and not the exclusion of one over the other. In that context, Shambaugh sees the central challenge for the future as one of building a series of "guardrails," "buffers," and "off ramps" to "bound" the competition so that it does not evolve toward an adversarial relationship.

Shambaugh then devotes the remainder of his chapter to examining the variables which will "condition the relationship" in the future, including variables not entirely in the control of US and Chinese leaders. Shambaugh breaks them into five domains: ideological and political competition, bureaucratic competition, societal competition, regional competition in Asia, and global competition. His assessment of the substantial and growing differences in all five areas leads him to the conclusion that the US-China relationship exhibits an action-reaction dynamic that exhibits some zero-sum attributes in key arenas. Shambaugh finishes with a call for sober-minded thinking about both sides to dampen this action-reaction dynamic and manage this competition through better dialogue, more communication, and expanded use of confidence building and crisis-management tools.

Notes

1. White House, "National Security Strategy," February 2015, https://obamawhitehouse
.archives.gov/sites/default/files/docs/2015_national_security_strategy_2.pdf.

2. Demetri Sevastopulo, "Biden Warns China Will Face 'Extreme Competition' from US," *Financial Times*, February 7, 2021, https://www.ft.com/content/c23a4e67-2052-4d2f-a844-e5
c72a7de214; on Xi's statements, see Chris Buckley, "'The East Is Rising': Xi Maps Out China's

Post-Covid Ascent," *New York Times*, March 3, 2021, https://www.nytimes.com/2021/03/03/world/asia/xi-china-congress.html.

3. William A. Galston, "A Momentous Shift in US Public Attitudes toward China," Brookings Institution, March 22, 2021, https://www.brookings.edu/blog/order-from-chaos/2021/03/22/a-momentous-shift-in-us-public-attitudes-toward-china/; for Chinese attitudes, see Michael Cerny, Haifeng Huang, and Yawei Liu, "Chinese Public Opinion on the War in Ukraine," US-China Perception Monitor, April 19, 2022, https://uscnpm.org/2022/04/19/chinese-public-opinion-war-in-ukraine/.

4. Evan S. Medeiros, "The Changing Fundamentals of US-China Relations," *Washington Quarterly* 42, no. 3 (2019): 93–119. See also Orville Schell and Susan L. Shirk, eds., *Course Correction: Toward an Effective and Sustainable China Policy*, Task Force Report (New York: Asia Society, February 2019), https://asiasociety.org/sites/default/files/inline-files/CourseCorrection_FINAL_2.7.19_1.pdf.

5. Avery Goldstein, "US-China Rivalry in the Twenty-First Century: Déjà Vu and Cold War II," *China International Strategy Review* 2, no. 1 (2020): 28–62; Thomas J. Christensen, *No New Cold War: Why US-China Strategic Competition Will Not Be like the US-Soviet Cold War* (Seoul: Asan Institute for Policy Studies, September 2020), https://en.asaninst.org/wp-content/themes/twentythirteen/action/dl.php?id=50349; Wu Xinbo, "轮中美战略竞争" [On US-China Strategic Competition], *World Economics and Politics* 34, no. 5 (2020): 96–130; Liu Jianhua, "中美'亚冷战': 特征、成因及中国的应对" [US-China "Sub-Cold War": Characteristics, OrOigin, and China's Responses], *Contemporary International Relations* 32, no. 11 (2012): 35–43.

6. Robert S. Ross, "It's Not a Cold War: Competition and Cooperation in US-China Relaetions," *China International Strategy Review* 2 (2020): 63–72; Graham Allison, *Destined for War: Can America and China Escape Thucydides's Trap?* (Boston: Houghton Mifflin Harcourt, 2017); Rush Doshi, *The Long Game: China's Grand Strategy to Displace American Order* (Oxford: Oxford University Press, 2021); Oriana Skylar Mastro, "The Stealth Superpower: How China Hid Its Global Ambitions," *Foreign Affairs* 98, no. 1 (2019): 31–39.

7. Zhu Feng, "中美战略竞争与东亚安全秩序的未来" [US-China Strategic Competition and the Future of East Asian Security Order], *World Economics and Politics* 27, no. 3 (2013): 4–26; Zhao Minghao, "Is a New Cold War Inevitable? Chinese Perspectives on US–China Strategic Competition," *Chinese Journal of International Politics* 12, no. 3 (2019): 371–94; "中国经济总量已达美国七成，美国因此而焦虑" [Chinese Economy Reaches 70% of US Capacity, America Is Becoming Worried], China Internet Information Center, March 19, 2021, http://www.china.com.cn/opinion/think/2021-03/09/content_77290810.htm.

8. Kevin Rudd, "China Has Politics Too," Asia Society Policy Institute, December 9, 2020, https://asiasociety.org/policy-institute/china-has-politics-too; Weixing Hu, "The United States, China, and the Indo-Pacific Strategy: The Rise and Return of Strategic Competition," *China Review* 20, no. 3 (2020): 127–42; Wang Jisi and Hu Ran, "From Cooperative Partnership to Strategic Competition: A Review of China–US Relations 2009–2019," *China International Strategy Review* 1 (2019): 1–10.

9. Zhao Kejin, "'软战'及其根源" ["Soft War" and Its Roots], *Chinese Journal of American Studies* 34, no. 3 (2020): 9–34; Fang Changping, "美国抹黑中国的新表现与新特点" [New Display and Characteristics of America's Smear Campaign], *People's Tribunal* 27, no. 16 (2020): 16–19.

10. Robert D. Blackwill and Kurt M. Campbell, *Xi Jinping on the Global Stage: Chinese Foreign Policy under a Powerful but Exposed Leader* (Washington, DC: Council on Foreign Relations, 2016); Robert Sutter, "Barack Obama, Xi Jinping and Donald Trump—Pragmatism Fails as US-China Differences Rise in Prominence," *American Journal of Chinese Studies* 24, no. 2 (2017):

69–85; Elizabeth C. Economy, "China's Imperial President: Xi Jinping Tightens His Grip," *Foreign Affairs* 93, no. 6 (2014): 80–91.

11. Ryan Hass, "The 'New Normal' in US-China Relations: Hardening Competition and Deep Interdependence," Brookings Institute, August 12, 2021, https://www.brookings.edu /blog/order-from-chaos/2021/08/12/the-new-normal-in-us-china-relations-hardening -competition-and-deep-interdependence/; David Shambaugh, "Dealing with China: Tough Engagement and Managed Competition," *Asia Policy,* no. 23 (2017): 4–12; Liu Feitao, "美国强化对华竞争及中美关系的走势" [US Strengthening Competition with China and the Future of US-China Relations], *International Studies* 58, no. 1 (2016): 49–62; Li Wei and Zhang Zhexin, "战略竞争时代的新型中美关系" [New Model of US-China Relations in the Era of Strategic Competition], *Quarterly Journal of International Politics* 11, no. 1 (2015): 25–53.

12. For an assessment of these risks in various scenarios, see Evan S. Medeiros, *Major Power Rivalry in East Asia* (New York: Council on Foreign Relations, April 2021), https://cdn.cfr.org /sites/default/files/report_pdf/medeirosdp_final-no.-3.pdf.

PART I

1

Explaining and Understanding Competition in US-China Relations

Evan S. Medeiros

Deciphering Competition

A basic and nagging question lies at the heart of this volume: What does competition in the US-China context mean, in theory and in practice? Few would question the application of the term "competition" (or "strategic competition") to the US-China relationship today. Yet the *meaning* of competition—in both global politics and the US-China relationship—varies widely among scholars, analysts, and policymakers. Some treat competition as part of linear scale with cooperation at the other end on a spectrum. Others see competition as a midpoint on the way to confrontation or even as virtually synonymous with it. Some treat US-China competition as mainly focused on national security issues, with all other arenas of US-China interaction as more of a dynamic mix of cooperation and competition. The upshot is that competition in the US-China context means many things to many people and thus demands further inquiry given its dominance in the national discussion about the current state and future trajectory of this relationship.

In preparing this volume, it became clear there was a lack of systematic thinking about competition in the US-China relationship. Indeed, competition is one of the most undertheorized terms in the discipline of international politics, not just in US-China studies. The literature on competition is surprisingly thin, with many scholars assuming a reflexive understanding among readers about the types of behaviors that result from differing national interests under a condition of anarchy. This raises an assortment of important questions: What behavior actually constitutes competition, what form does competition take, what does bilateral competition imply for global politics, and how is all of this most relevant to US-China relations? These questions are relevant not only to this volume but to international relations and US foreign policy studies more broadly, given the accepted views among policymakers that the United States and China have entered a new era *defined by* competition.

Given these various ambiguities in the current literature, a first step is to define the meaning of competition in global politics. A survey of recent research on the issue of competition in international politics suggests at least three core attributes.[1] First, competition requires some degree of perceived contention, material or symbolic, that extends beyond a basic level of disagreement. There must be some degree of antagonism between two parties, which can vary in scope and intensity. Second, for a condition of competition to exist there needs to be a contest in which parties are focused on maximizing their relative power or at least one actor is focused on enhancing its power and influence relative to the other. In other words, two parties need something to compete over, such as land or status. Third, although not all competitions are zero-sum in nature and focused on relative gains, a competitive situation tends to involve a circumstance in which there is either "(1) scarcity in the object of the competition or (2) a significance to getting more of that object than someone else."[2]

A RAND report on great power competition nicely summarizes competition this way: "In the international relations context, competition can be understood as a state of antagonistic relations short of direct armed conflict between actors, which reflects the three basic distinguishing factors noted earlier: perceived contention, an effort to gain mutual advantage, and pursuit of some outcome or good that is not generally available. This implies a common pursuit of power, influence, prosperity, and status at the same time when others are also seeking those things and when supply is limited."[3]

Our understanding of competition is further clarified by comparing it to related terms such as "conflict" or "contestation." Conflict should be treated as a subset of competition, a high-end variant of sorts. While the term "conflict" can be described as a struggle between and among actors over opposing "needs, ideas, beliefs, values or goals," most uses of conflict imply a state of explicit combat and warfare. In this sense, conflict is a special and intensive manifestation of competition. There are boundaries around this conception of competition as well. As the RAND study concludes, "Whether in sports, the business world, or creative fields, competition usually involves the pursuit of relative success in a framework that has some degree of rules or norms" short of conflict. It is less clear, however, how this condition applies to competition in global politics given the condition of anarchy.[4] Another way to understand competition is to contrast it with the less-intense ideas of "disagreement" and "contestation." People and countries can disagree and contest each other's perspectives, interests, or objectives but still have stable and amicable relations; friendly countries often do so in negotiations, such as over trade issues. Yet contesting issues between states doesn't necessarily imply a situation of competition (though it can); it is more of an amicable disagreement over ways, means, or ends rather than one involving antagonism and pursuit of relative advantage, as the RAND report argues.[5]

Two additional points are worth making about the nature of competition in interstate affairs. First, competition between and among states can be over specific goals, such as who controls a piece of land or maritime feature, as well as broader ones such as regional leadership, a dominant economic position, and/ or global status. In other words, competition is not only over material goals— military or economic—but also nonmaterial ones such as prestige and status. Second, competition will manifest in different behaviors for each state depending on that state's objectives and capabilities. Accordingly, the competitive strategies of various states can change over time. The objectives of the competition and the tools used to compete—economic, military, ideational—can and often do evolve.

These latter two points are especially important in the US-China context. As argued in this edited volume, divergent perceptions and policy disagreements—large and small, lasting and ephemeral—have been at the heart of US-China relations since 1979. These differences have varied over time and by issue, with new ones emerging even today. At the same time, the two countries have managed their differences and cooperated in multiple ways in the last four decades. In retrospect, a core feature—perhaps a defining attribute—of the past forty-plus years has been the ability of Washington and Beijing to manage disagreements and bound differences in furtherance of some basic mutual interests, notably expansion of economic interests and avoiding armed conflict. This raises important questions about the nature of competition today as a phenomenon in US-China relations. What has changed to fuel broader and more intensive competition? How has competition evolved for both sides, not only in terms of the goals of competition but also the tools? What might the answers to these questions reveal about the trajectory of the relationship going forward? This chapter now explores these themes to set the foundation for the remainder of the volume.

Competition in the History of US-China Relations

The 1980s: Connections More Than Competition

The first decade of US-China relations after normalization in 1979 is a unique one in the history of bilateral competition, and not just because it was the first one. In the 1980s, there was minimal competition (drawing on the definition given earlier), even as the many differences between the two governments, economies, societies, and cultures became readily apparent to both sides. In fact, many of these differences were starkest in this period because China was just emerging from the excesses of Maoism. In many ways, US-China interaction in this decade is the exception that proves the rule about nature and scope of bilateral competition.

In the 1980s, the relationship was characterized by two basic dynamics. On the one hand there was a substantial alignment of several material interests, which mitigated impulses toward competition even as bilateral disagreements were numerous and varied. First, there was the convergence of overall security interests: balancing Soviet power. This was the original binding force that facilitated rapprochement in 1972 and which remained important—but not overriding—during the first decade after normalization in 1979. This alignment produced modest but important defense and intelligence cooperation throughout the decade, including sales of millions of dollars' worth of US weapons systems and technologies to the People's Liberation Army (PLA) and a joint signals intelligence collection program. Even as Chinese concerns about the Soviet threat lessened in the 1980s (and Beijing pursed rapprochement with Moscow), many Chinese leaders still viewed the United States as critical to Chinese military modernization, adding to the convergence of US and Chinese security and technological interests.[6]

Second, there was the convergence of China's domestic economic agenda—Chairman Deng Xiaoping's "reform and opening" and his "Four Modernizations"—and US economic and diplomatic objectives. China's desire—indeed, its imperative—to gain access to US capital, technology, and expertise were essential to the success of Deng's economic and S&T (science and technology) modernization agenda. For the United States' part, Washington wanted to encourage Chinese economic reforms, American companies wanted access to China's market (facilitated by the former goal), and US policymakers wanted to moderate China's external behavior, such as by pulling China more into international organizations and toward global rules and norms. In fact, this arena of US-China convergence served as the most persistent and consistent binding force in US-China relations.

Third, the US-China power gap—on military, economic, and technological fronts—was so stark that it was hard for competition to manifest. There were few Chinese actions that would have put it at an advantage relative to the United States or really threaten the United States. In other words, there were plenty of Chinese actions that Washington disliked, such as China's minimalist proliferation controls, but these were not about competition for relative economic or geopolitical gain.

On the other hand, the absence of competition was nevertheless accompanied by persistent differences and reoccurring disagreements that often destabilized this nascent relationship. In his seminal study *A Fragile Relationship*, Harry Harding calls this period "an oscillating pattern of progress and stagnation, crisis and consolidation."[7] In the early part of the 1980s, just after normalization and its associated political and societal euphoria, an array of problems led to an early disillusionment on both sides. This was driven by a mix of issues: Chinese dumping of textiles in the US market, US restrictions on technology transfers to China, US arms sales to Taiwan, high-profile Chinese defections to America, and unresolved financial issues left over from the Chinese civil war.[8]

Even as these early issues were resolved, new ones appeared. Chinese sales of sensitive nuclear weapons–related materials and technologies and missiles and missile-related technologies to countries in the Middle East and South Asia emerged as a source of substantial disagreement. Chinese restrictions on US companies' ability to invest in China aggravated matters as Beijing struggled with political barriers to greater foreign presence. This prompted frustration and distrust on all sides; in particular, the lack of transparency for US companies operating in China emerged as a pervasive problem.[9] For its part, Beijing was consistently opposed to US arms sales to Taiwan. A similar Chinese frustration resulted from the slow US approval of military cooperation with the PLA and the limited scope of US defense assistance; China wanted far more than Washington was willing to provide.[10] The shared frustrations—on top of the occasional human rights case—gradually accumulated, reflecting fundamental differences in political systems, outlooks, and priorities.

However, these disagreements and the underlying differences—security, economic, and political—collectively did not amount to outright competition in the sense of two antagonists seeking unilateral gain at the expense of the other. While there was clear distrust and frustration on both sides, the distrust and the slow process of engagement reflected two very different countries negotiating the process of connection and integration. In addition, there were substantial and enduring binding forces in the relationship that provided incentives for both sides, at times, to moderate behavior for the sake of the stability of the overall relationship. The high-profile disagreements over issues such as Taiwan and weapons proliferation resulted in policy adjustments to preserve the relationship. China adjusted more than the United States, however, such as by adopting basic arms sales restrictions and agreeing to a framework that allowed for continued arms sales to Taiwan (i.e., the 1982 communique). US policymakers—then and now—viewed these as a normal adjustment by China toward becoming part of the international community, including adhering to international rules and norms. These bilateral accommodations, from the US perspective, represented the costs of membership into groupings that China benefited from. One wonders now whether China viewed such adjustments with a sense of deep and enduring resentment, creating a bilateral balance sheet of grievances, rather than as the price of membership. Notably, China's adjust-ments focused more on security and economic issues and far less on human rights as its domestic restrictions continued. In this era, the line between in-tensive disagreement and competition is admittedly a thin one, but when the events of the 1980s are contrasted with the US-China relationship in the 1990s, the nature of competition in US-China relations becomes much clearer, largely by dint of the issues of distrust, antagonism, and relative advantage.

The 1990s: Dawn of a Competitive Era

US-China dynamics changed fundamentally in the 1990s, and not in a salutary manner. Today's competitive dynamics can trace their roots to the events of the 1990s. There were three events that notably deepened mutual distrust and pro-duced competitive dynamics. They were the collapse of the Soviet Union and the end of the Cold War, the Tiananmen massacre in 1989, and the Taiwan Strait crisis of 1995 and 1996. As a result of these events, US and Chinese perceptions of each other shifted, the domestic politics of the relationship evolved, and the national interests at the heart of the relationship changed in a manner that made bilateral ties more contentious and acrimonious.

It has become common, but also a bit trite, to argue that the end of the Cold War changed the US-China relationship, removing the common threat of the Soviet Union that was the proverbial strategic glue between these two very dif-ferent countries. It is commonly argued that this singular event unmoored the relationship at a time when basic geopolitical questions of polarity and order were in deep flux in 1989. In retrospect, the history of the relationship reveals that the Soviet threat was far less important as a binding force than is generally assumed and that other factors played a larger role.

Beginning as early as 1982, just three years after normalization, Deng articu-lated an independent foreign policy line, and China began pulling away from hard alignment with the United States and beginning the process of repairing relations with Moscow, with normalization occurring only seven years later, in May 1989. To be sure, Chinese concerns about the Soviet threat persisted in the 1980s, but China's experience was that US-China military cooperation was a challenged process and produced fairly modest US assistance to PLA moderniza-tion. China wanted more and faster liberalization of technology controls, both military and dual-use, but Washington was reluctant to offer it. Moreover, Chi-na's dabbling in the world of nuclear and missile proliferation undermined US trust in China's worldview, fearing a persistent undercurrent of Maoist revision-ism.[11] Bilateral intelligence cooperation materialized and focused on monitoring Soviet nuclear and missile sites. This was important to both sides—and strate-gically significant—but was sufficiently compartmentalized and subterranean in the relationship that it had little impact on the broader bilateral dynamics. There is little evidence it served as some kind of hidden source of ballast or even lubrication in the relationship.

By contrast, the impact of the end of the Cold War on US-China relations is better seen through the disorienting external implications for China. In one year alone, China witnessed the collapse of the Communist world of Eastern Europe, producing a fear that perhaps China was next. With the fall of the Berlin Wall in November 1989 occurring just a few months after Tiananmen, Chinese leaders felt besieged and threatened by the capitalist world. Whereas the events of June 4 challenged the legitimacy of Chinese Communist Party (CCP) leadership, the events of November 1989 made it appear as if the political headwinds to the CCP were both domestic *and* external—and perhaps global.[12]

This moment of global reordering fundamentally altered the US-China relationship. Chinese leaders immediately viewed the United States as a threat because it presented itself as the democratic victor in a struggle against socialism and communism. The unilateral and US-led multilateral sanctions against China after Tiananmen contributed to this view as well as augmenting domestic austerity. Moreover, in the wake of the end of the Cold War and the identity crisis facing China, the United States emerged as a hyperpower, with both a large and advanced economy and the world's most advanced and effective military. The Gulf War against Iraq in 1991 put a fine point on this by demonstrating the vast limitations of Soviet-style military capabilities and operations and the striking advances of the US military, both technological and operational. In short, it was not just that the Cold War ended but the way it ended and the resulting global order which challenged both CCP power and legitimacy. And the main source of that challenge was the strongest nation in the world. This course of events rapidly injected a degree of animosity, distrust, and, ultimately, competition into US-China interactions that did not exist previously.[13]

The second major event of the 1990s that changed US-China relations was the Tiananmen massacre in June 1989. It redefined relations in multiple ways. Most fundamentally, it further adjusted each side's perceptions of the other as well as the domestic politics of US-China interactions. For Chinese leaders, the threat to China's political stability, the US support for both protesters and democracy, and the resulting US and international sanctions led Beijing to view the United States as a direct threat to CCP legitimacy. In contrast to the 1980s, the difference in political systems was no longer a problem to be managed—or one that could be managed—but rather a core source of mistrust. For the United States, Americans were shocked by the violence, and this rapidly disabused both policymakers and the public of their expectations of reform in China. These shifts in US perceptions fundamentally changed domestic political debates and made them far more acrimonious. Following Tiananmen, it was far easier for policymakers in both countries to interpret the actions of the other as a challenge to the interests and ambitions of the other, if they accurately perceived the other's interests and ambitions at all.

The third major grouping of events in the 1990s that changed the competitive dynamic was the Taiwan Strait crisis of 1995 and 1996. The sequence of events, which began in fall 1995 and led to a major military deployment by the US Navy in 1996, precipitated a shift in the US-China security relationship. For the first time since normalization, US policymakers and defense officials had to consider and plan for a US-China conflict, one in which the US military assisting Taiwan was the central scenario. As a result, China became an emerging security threat to the United States and its allies. For China, responding to US military support for Taiwan, which was newly embracing democracy, became the core mission for the PLA. The United States thus became the PLA's main obstacle to using military force to achieve reunification. Due to the weaknesses these crises revealed in PLA capabilities, the PLA embarked on a broad comprehensive and multidecade modernization effort in which preventing US military intervention in a Taiwan crisis was the core task. The PLA became almost exclusively focused on developing capabilities that could target and disrupt US efforts to come to Taiwan's assistance. This initial modernization program lay the groundwork for a broader modernization effort two decades later.[14]

In short, in the 1990s the United States and China were clearly competing over the future of Taiwan following the events of 1995 and 1996. This, then, shaped domestic debates in the United States in which "the China security threat" became a dominant theme, with various and sundry issues attached to it. These included not just links to Chinese nuclear and missile proliferation but also the theft of nuclear and missile secrets from US defense companies. These were then used for political advantage, and the "Blue Team" of China hawks emerged as a voice in US debates on China.[15] Notably, the congressional investigation known as the Cox Committee Report in the late 1990s over alleged theft of nuclear and missile technologies created a toxic political climate in Washington that delayed US support for China's accession to the World Trade Organization (WTO) and echoes today in debates about technology competition.

The 2000s: A Mixed Picture

Competition evolved in a curious way in the first decade of this century. It operated at two levels in the 2000s: subdued and subterranean on the one hand and present and persistent on the other. Leaders and policymakers in both countries were mindful of their gradually diverging foreign policy differences after the experiences of the 1990s, especially regarding Taiwan. Yet Washington and Beijing ended up being aligned on Taiwan during most of this decade due to the politics in Taiwan. At the same time, American and Chinese policymakers—for different reasons—were also either distracted or preoccupied (or both) with other geopolitical endeavors. From the vantage point of 2023, the first decade of the 2000s was an interlude before the emergence of a relationship of peer competitors.

Competition was largely subdued and subterranean for much of the 2000s. Despite President George W. Bush's naming China as a "strategic competitor" during the 2000 election campaign,[16] US policy for the majority of this decade treated China as anything but that, and consistently so. The best explanation for the sharp shift from the acrimony of the 1990s is that US foreign and national security policy was decidedly focused on priorities other than China, namely, fighting global terrorism and fighting two wars in Afghanistan and Iraq. Asia and China were, at best, secondary interests (if not tertiary ones). The bulk of the US national security establishment—especially the US military—had fundamentally reoriented themselves to focus on the Middle East as a region, counterterrorism as a global priority, and counterinsurgency as the mission driving US military operations and planning (as opposed to preparing for a distant conflict with a peer competitor in Asia).

As a result, America's China policy was less focused on threats from Beijing and the competition for regional influence in Asia or over Taiwan. Instead, US policy toward China was more focused on growing economic links (now that China had entered the WTO), managing disagreements, and working with China on common problems like North Korea. Taiwan was perhaps the central challenge in US-China interaction, but the 2000s were a unique period because Beijing and Washington were largely aligned in their effort to constrain the provocative Taiwan president Chen Shui-bian, who notoriously had a bad relationship with Washington. Similarly, on North Korea, Bush and Chinese president Hu Jintao jointly agreed to work together to find a negotiated solution, which resulted in the Six-Party process and modest constraints on the North Korea nuclear programs (before Pyongyang walked away from them in 2009).

In the 2000s, the United States and China began bumping into each other in regions beyond Asia, such as in Africa, where Chinese companies were newly active in search of access to energy and raw materials. This suggested an incipient geopolitical competition. Yet Washington and Beijing were able to find ways to work together—to stop the genocide in the Darfur region of Sudan, for example. The mix of US aspirations for China and US apprehension about China's expanding global presence in the 2000s is nicely captured in the now-iconic phrase of then Deputy Secretary of State Robert Zoellick, who in 2005 called for China to become a "responsible stakeholder"—to take actions that would not only benefit China's narrow interests but also support the system of rules, norms, and institutions that China would benefit from.

A final point about the 2000s is the expanding importance of trade and investment to both countries, which opened a new and more intensive phase of bilateral economic integration and globalization. US policy and perceptions of China during the 2000s changed following China's WTO accession in 2001. US exports to China grew rapidly and substantially, exceeding the growth of US global exports. For many American multinational firms, this development put China at the center of their global supply chains and, as a result, at the center of their global business strategies. For China, the 2000s also represented a significant economic turning point as it enjoyed another decade of double-digit growth and deep integration with economies all over the world. By 2010, China surpassed Japan to be the second-largest economy in the world, based on market exchange rates.

During the first decade of the twenty-first century, the evolution in China's US policy mirrored US moves. After the multiple bilateral dramas of the 1990s, notably the 1999 Belgrade bombing, Chinese strategists harbored deep concerns about US intentions and the direction of US-China relations.[17] The attacks on September 11, 2001, and the wars in Afghanistan and Iraq immediately changed the context in which these Chinese perceptions resided, but it did not eliminate them. After 9/11, China's top leaders saw the opportunity presented by the US strategic preoccupation with counterterrorism, the Middle East, and, ultimately, the two wars. Chinese president Jiang Zemin was one of the first foreign leaders to call Bush after 9/11 and offer help, as modest as it was. Chinese nationalists' carping about 9/11 aside, Chinese leaders understood the significance of 9/11, especially after the US-China spy plane crisis in April 2001 that posed a risk of a spiral downward into long-term enmity.[18] Jiang famously and publicly declared in 2002 at the Sixteenth Party Congress that China now enjoyed "a strategic window of opportunity" (*zhanlue jiyuqi*),[19] arguing that China now possessed twenty years of a relatively benign external environment such that it could continue to focus on its own development.

Following a stable leadership transition from Jiang Zemin to Hu Jintao in fall 2002, Hu persisted with an essentially Dengist approach to foreign policy—keeping a low profile and biding his time, and also seeing the future as a strategic window of opportunity. Still, this guiding foreign policy approach, coupled with China's expanding global footprint and capabilities, further altered US-China dynamics by putting more US and Chinese economic, diplomatic, and military interests in greater proximity. For Hu, the external requirements of domestic development were expanding, meaning that the United States and China were bumping up against one another in regions all over the world. China's leadership of the Six-Party process on North Korea was a major evolution of its foreign policy. In Asia, China was effectively pursuing a charm offensive to build deeper roots across the region and gain further access to markets and resources while seeking to defuse concerns about a rising China. Hu Jintao was notably concerned about generating antibodies to China's rise in Asia and globally. This was all done in the context of a US-China relationship in which China prioritized preserving stability so that Hu could focus on domestic development. For Hu, and his outspoken premier Wen Jiabao, this task remained daunting, with economic inequality growing and some 300 million people still living in poverty.

This narrative for US-China relations in the 2000s existed alongside a more distrustful and contentious one, in both countries and in different ways. Following the tumult of the 1990s, Jiang and Hu were able to put US-China ties on stable footing, but distrust, frustration, and, at times, antipathy were quite present. In fact, the CCP highlighted and manipulated perceptions of such external threats to bolster its legitimacy. In this sense, the party/state apparatus needed to see the United States as both a threat and an opportunity. Diplomatically, the Chinese promoted ideas such as multipolarity and democracy in international relations that were fundamentally about constraining US power as Beijing became more aligned with Russia while simultaneously cooperating with US foreign policy. At this time, Beijing's strategy was less about implementing a grand vision of displacing the United States globally and more about building and sustaining relationships, especially with the United States, that could ensure access to the much-needed inputs for development while minimizing US efforts to constrain China, in Asia and globally.

US suspicion about China as a security threat was a gathering storm in the 2000s. The US national security establishment became increasingly concerned about PLA modernization as it racked up gains. Beginning in 1998, the Pentagon's annual report on PLA modernization highlighted both the successes in PLA modernization and the myriad ways it could frustrate US power projection in Asia. By the late 2000s, the US military had lost its operational sanctuary in the western Pacific. Notably, China deployed an array of ballistic missiles that could hold at risk most US military bases in Asia as well as US aircraft carriers. Following the EP-3 spy plane incident in 2001, the Pentagon under Secretary of Defense Donald Rumsfeld froze all interactions with the PLA, and these didn't resume until Rumsfeld's ouster in 2004. Even when bilateral military conversations resumed, they did little to lessen distrust and emerging military competition. Bilateral military dialogues have limped along for much of the last two decades, contributing little to managing misperception and misunderstanding.

Similarly, US concerns about increasingly direct Chinese economic competition picked up in this decade, even as bilateral exports and investment continued to grow. By the mid-2000s, the WTO-induced reforms started slowing, and Hu and Premier Wen Jiabao allowed state-run entities to ascend in China's domestic market. China created a complex array of industrial policy, subsidies, nontariff barriers, and preferential policies that undermined the market share and profits of US firms invested in China. The roots of US-China economic com-petition lay in this period when the state began asserting itself more in the Chi-nese marketplace and US companies were left with few response options.

The global financial crisis (GFC) in the late 2000s was another inflection point in the US-China relationship. Notably, the crisis recalibrated Chinese perceptions of the US role in the world. The GFC led many Chinese to reevalu-ate their belief in US economic primacy and the virtues of the US form of cap-italism, with its highly developed financial sector and capital markets. Many in China also saw the GFC, given its relatively modest impact on China, as a moment where the Chinese economy became even more important and central to economies globally. The CCP's narrative was that China's massive domestic stimulus package helped save the world from a global recession by propping up global demand. In retrospect, Chinese analysts now look back at the GFC and view it as a critical turning point for China's global role. China became even more important and respected globally as questions about the US economy and economic management grew.[20]

The 2010s: Intensification and Clarification

The 2010s were a key decade in the evolution of competition in US-China rela-tions. Both US and Chinese views of each other's long-term strategic intentions hardened. This shift toward strategic competition also emerged in official US nomenclature in 2018. By the end of the decade, competition gained full ex-pression in the perceptions and policies of both countries—and across most di-mensions of the relationship. For some in the United States, this was an obvious conclusion; for others, it was a reality reluctantly embraced. There are at least three important dimensions to the evolution of competition in this decade.

First, the shift in the thinking of both sides to framing the relationship *as defined by* competition was a gradual one and occurred for several different rea-sons. For the United States, the shift was gradual based on the desire, at least initially, to preserve the space for a more cooperative relationship and the belief that Washington could still shape Chinese perceptions and behaviors. Mean-while, for China, it was about preventing a relationship that could derail Chi-na's top objectives.

From the beginning of the decade, the Obama administration, while under-standing China's growing importance, was fundamentally focused elsewhere: fighting two wars, rebuilding the US economy (including the signature domes-tic initiative of health care reform), and addressing immediate external chal-lenges such as Iranian and North Korean nuclear programs and climate change. Obama officials acknowledged the growing sources of bilateral competition, including by saying so publicly, but were reluctant to treat competition as the relationship's defining aspect. The Obama administration spoke in terms of striking a balance between cooperation and competition as a way of finding a stable and mutually productive equilibrium. A common US reframe became: compete where we must but also cooperate where we can.

US strategy and policy, for at least the first half of the decade, was very much focused on shaping Chinese perceptions and policies in this emerging competition and doing so by working with China when possible and creating a strategic environment in Asia that limited Chinese choices. This approach sought multiple goals: deterring Chinese coercive behaviors, encouraging China to help solve global problems, and avoiding a rivalry with careful management. The Obama administration struggled to find the right mix. To be sure, there were internal debates about US strategy due to China's gradual assertiveness, including on maritime issues, and its intransigence to resolve lingering bilateral economic problems.

For China's part, the evolution in its perceptions and policies was similarly mixed in the 2010s. On the one hand, Chinese leaders remained deeply distrustful of US motives and specifically perceived US policy in Asia as an effort to destabilize China internally and constrain it externally. Chinese leaders also viewed events such as the Arab Spring in 2012 and the color revolutions in Central Europe as direct results of US actions, which could be directed at China in the future. Even under the leadership of a moderate Hu Jintao, political freedoms were substantially tightened. Externally, Hu continued to take actions, such as the formation and operationalization of the BRICS, that sought to limit US influence and counter US efforts to constrain China.

On the other hand, Chinese policymakers still sought to avoid an outwardly hostile relationship with the United States. The balance was aptly captured in the Chinese phrase, used under both Hu and Xi Jinping, for its America policy: "Struggle but not break." China sought to resist real and perceived US pressure while at the same time avoiding an outright rupture in bilateral relations, as such a rupture could derail many of China's top national objectives. In this sense, whereas China's distrust of US motives and its sensitivities to the competitive aspects of relations were more commonly accepted, there was also a reluctance to see the relationship as locked into a rivalry given its implications for China's economy and foreign policy.

Second, the arrival, ascension, and behavior of Xi Jinping, beginning in fall 2012, were central to the evolution of competition in US-China relations. Xi's domestic political actions combined with his external behavior reflected his substantial distrust of US intentions and a desire to push back against US actions. Xi's specific actions—cracking down at home and being more assertive externally—changed US perceptions of China's ambitions and capabilities. That is not to say that some of Xi's foreign policies did not have deeper roots in Chinese thinking. Rather, Xi gave unique expression to these in his willingness to tolerate risk and friction, which then steered the bilateral relationship in a fundamentally more competitive direction.[21]

From his earliest days, Xi's statements reflected substantial concerns about internal stability and foreign threats in Hong Kong, Xinjiang, and Tibet, and the CCP believed that most of these threats emanated from the United States. This insecurity led China to take a series of actions to assert more political control at home, under the banner of Xi's national security concept. Externally, one year into his first term, Xi began to take assertive actions to advance Chinese positions in the East China Sea and South China Sea (SCS); these reflected a desire to consolidate China's position at the expense of long-standing US interests and principles. The degree of Chinese diplomatic activism also steadily rose under Xi with a series of new policies, such as land reclamation in the South China Sea in 2014 and the launch of the Belt and Road Initiative (BRI) in 2013. These were, at least in part, part of an effort to grow China's power and influence relative to the United States', in Asia and beyond.

For the United States, the process of reaching the conclusion that this relationship had crossed a Rubicon into a long-term strategic competition also began under Xi. For many in the United States, trends in both domestic and external behavior gradually led to new assessments about Chinese intentions and, thus, US-China relations. Xi's rapid consolidation and centralization of power, his harsh anti-corruption campaign, his crackdown on civil society, his empowerment of the party apparatus, and his injection of Marxist-Leninist ideology back into social and economic life—all enabled by modern technology—had had a strong negative impact on US perceptions of China's domestic trajectory. These actions evoked images of a new breed of technology-enabled authoritarianism that drew a stark contrast with democratic principles and support for a liberal, rules-based international order.

For many US policymakers and analysts, Xi's overall approach to foreign policy reflected a confidence, ambition, and activism unseen in the reform period. This behavior appeared to many in the United States as a clear evolution, if not outright rejection, of Deng's model of adopting a low-key approach to foreign policy. Xi's assertions on maritime issues in Asia (especially in the SCS), his expanding use of economic sanctions against South Korea and other economies, his grand initiatives like the Asian Infrastructure Investment Bank (AIIB) and the BRI, and his affinity for Putin and Russia led to an escalating set of concerns and then countermoves on the part of the United States under President Donald Trump.[22]

In the late 2010s, US concerns about China's rise were palpably building, just as elites began questioning and debating past US policy toward China, implying mismanagement, if not failure. The wave of US concern about China as a rising power began cresting in the latter half of the decade. Xi's statements and actions during and after the Nineteenth Party Congress in fall 2017 had a catalytic impact on US perceptions: his public declaration of global ambitions, his promotion of "the China option" (*Zhongguo fangan*) as a model of development, and his moves within the party/state to remove barriers to remaining in power in perpetuity. In early 2018, the Trump administration gave expression to the emerging bipartisan consensus about China: competition in multiple arenas was now the core of the relationship, and US policy needed to adjust accordingly.

A third dimension to the rise of strategic competition in the last decade was the election of Donald J. Trump. The Trump administration's approach toward China led to the crossing of several critical thresholds in the evolution of competition in US-China dynamics. Most basically, the Trump team called China a "strategic competitor" for the first time in the December 2017 National Security Strategy, which not only changed the lexicon for the relationship but opened the floodgates to a bipartisan discussion about China in far more competitive terms.[23]

Strategic competition arrived in both word and deed. In addition to its tough rhetoric, the Trump administration also took a series of actions against China that dramatically accelerated the acrimony in the relationship.[24] Trump initiated a trade war involving imposing tariffs on some $350 billion in Chinese imports, many of which remain in place today. Trump also imposed harsh and heretofore unused sanctions on Chinese technology companies: first ZTE and then Huawei, which many in China saw as directed at crippling its flagship technology companies and as proof positive that the United States was now focused on containing China. Some Trump officials openly called for a full economic decoupling from China to reduce US economic exposure to China, perceiving the economic linkages as a national security vulnerability. Toward that end, the White House adopted a series of executive orders that restricted Chinese firms from accessing US capital markets and technologies. Furthermore, the administration dramatically reduced bilateral dialogue and cooperation with China, viewing them as a waste of time. And in their final year, ahead of the 2020 US election and with coronavirus raging globally, senior US officials went after the CCP in calling for the people of China to break away from the Communist Party; such a regime change approach was a first for any administration since normalization (let alone rapprochement).

China's response to Trump's prosecution of strategic competition was initially quite restrained. Hoping to avoid provoking Trump and to find a solution, Chinese reactions left open ample space for negotiations. Chinese rhetoric was similarly constrained, even in the face of much confrontational rhetoric coming out of Washington. Without much progress, Chinese restraint gradually withered beginning around 2019. Chinese officials concluded that US views about China had fundamentally shifted and there was little to be gained from restraint. China then adopted a more focused response of countermeasures and pushback as well as efforts to reduce its vulnerability to US actions. The emergence of COVID-19 then served as a major accelerant of Chinese frustration, distrust, and acrimony, especially in response to constant US criticism of China unleashing the virus on the world, as America struggled with even the most basic containment of it. By the latter half of 2020, the changes in the perceptions and policies of both Beijing and Washington appeared locked in place, even as the US presidential election loomed.

Joe Biden's victory over Trump in the 2020 US presidential election did not fundamentally change the prior trajectory of relations. The Biden administration embraced the language of strategic competition, with the new president even calling it "extreme competition"[25] at one point and continuing with this terminology as of this writing. The administration highlighted the ideological component of competition (such as calling the repression in Xinjiang a "genocide") while keeping in place many of Trump's prior decisions, such as the import tariffs and technology controls. In the first year, the Biden team's dialogues with China were minimal and so were the examples of meaningful cooperation. In short, the basic edifice of strategic competition endured. Where the Biden team diverged from Trump in strategic competition with China was in the investment at home, revitalizing alliances, recommitting to multilateral organizations, and prioritizing democracy. The track record of operationalizing the latter was impressive, with an early 2021 summit of the Asian Quad leaders (held virtually and then in person), followed by Biden's June trip to Europe, in which China was a centerpiece of the G7, NATO, and US-EU summits, and then a new defense-sharing agreement among the United States, the United Kingdom, and Australia. The unifying theme of these initiatives was to encourage other allies to appreciate the diversity of challenges from China and coordinate with the United States in addressing them—to present a united front, of sorts, in the face of a stronger and more active China. Not only were these and other initiatives sustained into 2022, but most of them were expanded. Both the Russian invasion of Ukraine and the Chinese strategic alignment with Russia some three weeks before the invasion created an enabling global strategic environment for the Biden administration to expand the scope of its initiatives to constrain Chinese power. The growing tensions over Taiwan, especially following Nancy Pelosi's August 2022 trip, put a fine point on the trajectory of US-China strategic competition by reminding the entire world that conflict over Taiwan was not only possible but increasingly probable.

Characteristics of US-China Competition

This review of the last four decades suggests that US-China competition—its evolution, its many manifestations, and its current expression—has, at minimum, the following four characteristics.

First, substantial and growing distrust of each other's immediate and long-term motives is at the heart of the bilateral competition. While the origins, nature, and manifestations of this distrust changed over the past four decades, it still lies at the heart of the competition. In the 1980s, when competitive dynamics (as defined in this chapter) were *de minimis*, there was distrust, but it was mainly due to the chasm of cultural, linguistic, historical, and economic differences following decades of alienation. This dynamic was reflected in the Chinese campaigns against spiritual pollution as well as American critiques of Chinese opacity, mendacity, and political controls. Yet, back then, the United States didn't fear Chinese power, mainly because China had so little of it. At the same time, Chinese leaders seldom feared US containment, and they *needed* engagement with the United States to realize their prime goal of economic and technological rejuvenation.

Bilateral distrust evolved rapidly and significantly in the 1990s, and it took on a sharper edge for both countries. In retrospect, this may have been the seminal moment, sowing the seeds of what has grown into today's broad-spectrum competition between two great powers. Of course, the Cold War's end removed the modest binding force of anti-Soviet cooperation, but that is only part of the story. It was the collapse of communism in Europe combined with the CCP's extreme violence against the Chinese people in June 1989 (and the US reaction to it) that fundamentally rewired the perceptions and incentives of policymakers *in both countries* about each other.

For Beijing, Tiananmen was the ultimate political crisis that led the CCP to perceive constant threats from the democratic world and focus on new and greater vulnerabilities to its political stability and legitimacy. At once, the CCP feared constant pressure from the United States to evolve politically but was also cognizant of its need for trade and investment from the United States to ground its legitimacy. It is no coincidence that stoking and manipulating nationalism with a focus on external threats became a central feature of CCP political campaigns in the 1990s. For the United States, the hardening of its distrust of China had less to do with Tiananmen per se and more with a creeping divergence in interests; in retrospect, US disgust and disillusionment from the events of 1989 served more as an accelerant than a determinant of US distrust of China. The Taiwan Strait crisis of the mid-1990s marked China's emergence as a proximate threat to US security interests in Asia. For many in the United States, these events opened the door, as China's military modernized and its economy expanded, to seeing China as a rising power that threatened a diversity of US interests: economic, security, diplomatic, and technological.

Second, the evolution in these competitive dynamics was a nonlinear process. It did not result from the gradual and steady accumulation of mistrust, diverging interests, and shifts in material capabilities. Rather, this process unfolded in response to major events, with some acting as accelerants and others as constraints, and it occurred in fits and starts over several decades. As argued earlier, several global events in the 1990s led to competition by accentuating mistrust, antagonism, and a focus by both countries on relative capabilities. For China's part, the events of 1989 were a major turning point. Not to be discounted, the Belgrade bombing in May 1999 and the EP-3 spy plane incident probably broadened and deepened Chinese antagonism toward the United States, or at least provided the CCP with an opportunity for promoting antagonism by stoking nationalist responses to both events.

Major events also had a salutary impact—or at least a dampening effect—on the evolution of competition. The events of 9/11, the two Middle East wars, and the reorientation in US defense strategy in the 2000s took the focus off a rising China. More instrumentally, in the 2000s, US and Chinese policymakers managed to cooperate on counterterrorism, North Korea, and even Taiwan in the Chen Shui-bian era. China's WTO accession in 2001, as challenging as it was to get there, reinforced US hopes for convergence of US and Chinese economic goals, if not political ones. The latter also provided many US companies with historic opportunities to expand their businesses. These moments of cooperation and convergence added to the sense of breathing room in US-China relations. At minimum, US exports to China were growing faster than US exports to the world, fostering a positive climate for managing concerns about Chinese external behaviors. Hu Jintao's essentially Dengist approach to foreign affairs, his moderate approach to Taiwan, and his desire to have a positive relationship with the United States amid the growing antagonism similarly helped moderate US concerns about diverging interests and relative gains.

Major macrolevel events—such as the GFC, continued US wars in the Middle East, the rise of global populism, and the Western mismanagement of the COVID outbreak in 2020—also eroded Chinese expectations that the United States would remain the dominant power for at least the first part of the twenty-first century. These events, combined with the ascension of Xi Jinping, fueled competitive dynamics. Xi was more confident in China's relative capabilities in the current era of global politics. As a result, he sought to explore the boundaries of Chinese power even when such actions would bring China into direct conflict with the United States and its allies in Europe and Asia.

A third feature is that leaders and domestic politics have mattered enormously in the evolution of competitive dynamics. Deng Xiaoping and President George H. W. Bush notably moderated the emergence of competition in the early 1990s, which could have developed faster and manifested in more intense ways. While Deng engineered China's re-embrace of reform and a nonconfrontational foreign policy, Bush prevented a rapid and sustained deterioration after

Tiananmen. Presidents Bill Clinton and Jiang Zemin were unable to fundamentally reorient the relationship in the 1990s, but they also sought to put it on a more stable and sustainable pathway through high-profile summits and agreements on Taiwan and nonproliferation.

In the 2000s, George W. Bush's strong views on China precluded it from becoming the domain of conservative national security thinkers. After 9/11, Jiang Zemin and Hu Jintao leaned into the shift in US strategy to find a new basis for the relationship, premised on shared problem-solving of global challenges. President Obama sought to extend this logic and embraced a similar approach as China's global presence and influence grew. In particular, Obama sought to avoid a strategic rivalry with China, viewing rivalry and confrontation as neither inevitable nor desirable while also expanding US efforts to hedge against negative outcomes. Xi's arrival is the exception that proves the rule. His ascension, beginning in 2012, further opened the aperture on bilateral competition by fomenting domestic mistrust of the West and the United States and using Chinese power to advance its diplomatic and economic interests even when it involved using aggression and coercion against other states.

Fourth, the growth of China's material capabilities and the expansion of its global presence and influence were central to the elevation of competition in bilateral relations. As argued earlier, and based on the three elements of competition, the baseline distrust in the relationship and the mutual focus on relative gains have been a part of the relationship since at least the 1990s, although its scope and intensity have varied over time. However, competition moved to the center of the relationship as China's economy grew, its military modernized, its diplomatic presence and influence expanded, and, importantly, Chinese leaders decided to explore their newfound capabilities. The last aspect of this is perhaps the most important one. It was the changes in Chinese behavior in the 2010s, facilitated by China's capabilities and a leader willing to use them, that produced an intensification of US-China competition. Xi Jinping's ambitions, sense of urgency, assessment of the West's relative weakness, and proclivity for external risk accelerated the process that led to the arrival of the era of strategic competition.

In retrospect, China's growing capabilities and the Chinese leadership's confidence to use them—including assuming risk and absorbing friction—played a significant role in competition becoming the defining feature of US-China interactions. To be sure, this is not to say that China was the only protagonist in the great power drama. The United States clearly played its role in taking actions China perceived as undermining Chinese interests, but the United States in the first two decades of the 2000s also created opportunities for a political modus vivendi for US-China ties which Beijing failed to fully grasp.

Notes

1. Michael J. Mazarr, Jonathan S. Blake, Abigail Casey, Tim McDonald, Stephanie Pezard, and Michael Spirtas, *Understanding the Emerging Era of International Competition: Theoretical and Historical Perspectives* (Santa Monica, CA: RAND Corporation, 2018); Michael J. Mazarr, "The Essence of the Strategic Competition with China," *PRISM* 9, no. 1 (2020): 3–22; Kathleen Hicks, interview with Michael Mazarr, Oriana Skylar Mastro, Christopher Preble, and Kori Schake, "Great Power Competition," *Defense 2020* (podcast), January 15, 2020, http://cs is.org/analysis/great-power-competition; Michael Mazarr and Hal Brands, "Navigating Great Power Rivalry in the 21st Century," War on the Rocks, April 5, 2017, http://warontherocks .com/2017/04/navigating-great-power-rivalry-in-the-21st-century.

2. Mazarr et al., *Understanding the Emerging Era.*

3. Mazarr et al.

4. Mazarr et al.

5. Mazarr et al.

6. For a wonderful examination of US-China military interactions in the 1980s, see Yitzhak Schichor, "Proxy: Unlocking the Origins of Military Sales to China," *Asia Papers*, no. 3, Center for International and Regional Studies, Georgetown University Qatar, 2020, https://cirs.qatar .georgetown.edu/publications/proxy-unlocking-origins-israels-military-sales-china/.

7. Harry Harding, *A Fragile Relationship: The United States and China since 1972* (Washington, DC: Brookings Institution Press, 1992), 5.

8. Harding, 107–37.

9. Harding, 107–37.

10. Harding, 125–38. Also see Schichor, *Proxy.*

11. Harding, 125–38; Schichor, *Proxy.*

12. M. E. Sarotte, "China's Fear of Contagion: Tiananmen Square and the Power of the European Example," *International Security* 37, no. 2 (Fall 2012): 156–82.

13. For a new and important assessment of the hardening of Chinese views about the United States in this period, see Rush Doshi, *The Long Game: China's Grand Strategy to Displace American Order* (New York: Oxford University Press, 2021).

14. M. Taylor Fravel, *Active Defense: China's Military Strategy since 1949* (Princeton, NJ: Princeton University Press, 2019), 217–35.

15. For examples of this, see Bill Gertz, *Betrayal: How the Clinton Administration Undermined American Security* (Washington, DC: Regnery Press, 1999); Edward Timperlake and William C. Triplett II, *Year of the Rat: How Bill Clinton and Al Gore Compromised U.S. Security for Chinese Cash* (Washington, DC: Regnery Publishing, 2013).

16. Thomas W. Lippman, "Bush Makes Clinton's China Policy an Issue," *Washington Post,* August 20, 1999, A9.

17. Paul H. B. Godwin, "Decisionmaking under Stress: The Unintentional Bombing of China's Belgrade Embassy and the EP-3 Collision," in *Chinese National Security: Decisionmaking under Stress*, ed. Andrew Scobell and Larry M. Wortzel (Carlisle, PA: United States Army War College Press, 2005); Peter Hays Gries, "Tears of Rage: Chinese Nationalist Reactions to the Belgrade Embassy Bombing," *China Journal*, no. 46 (2001): 25–43.

18. Godwin, "Decisionmaking under Stress."

19. Jiang Zemin, *Build a Well-Off Society in an All-Round Way and Create a New Situation in Building Socialism with Chinese Characteristics*, report at the Sixteenth National Congress of the Communist Party of China, November 8, 2002.

20. Doshi, *Long Game*, 159–68.

21. Elizabeth C. Economy, *The Third Revolution: Xi Jinping and the New Chinese State* (New York: Oxford University Press, 2018). On Xi's external behavior, see Robert D. Blackwill and Kurt M. Campbell, *Xi Jinping on the Global Stage* (Washington, DC: Council on Foreign Relations, 2016).

22. Ryan Hass, "Lessons from the Trump administration's Policy Experiment on China" (working paper, Penn Project on the Future of US-China Relations, Washington, DC: Brookings Institution, September 2020), https://www.brookings.edu/research/lessons-from-the -trump-administrations-policy-experiment-on-china/; see also Ryan Hass, "U.S.-China Relations: The Search for a New Equilibrium" (Washington, DC: Brookings Institution, February 2020), https://www.brookings.edu/wp-content/uploads/2020/02/FP_2020026_us_china_rel ations_hass.pdf.

23. It is often forgotten that this 2017 document was published only a few weeks after Trump's lavish state visit to China, dubbed "state visit plus."

24. For a narrative of the evolution of US-China trade tensions, see Bob Davis and Lingling Wei, *Superpower Showdown: How the Battle between Trump and Xi Threatens a New Cold War* (New York: Harper, 2020); for a more conceptual analysis, see Hass, "US-China Relations."

25. Demetri Sevastopulo, "Biden Warns China Will Face 'Extreme Competition' from US," *Financial Times*, February 7, 2021.

2

Old Cold War and New

Richard K. Betts

Russia's invasion of Ukraine shocked conventional wisdom into facing the return of great power conflict to center stage in the world. At the same time, the enormity of Russia's breakout overshadowed the West's growing preoccupation with the rise of Chinese power. But the United States and China had already ambled into a new cold war, though one that was soft-pedaled and as of yet unmarked by any dramatic announcement like Churchill's Iron Curtain speech or Kennan's long telegram. So big differences from the old Cold War, especially in its ideological and economic aspects, led many to reject that image when it came to China.[1]

If the Cold War meant much, however, it meant prolonged and dangerous rivalry just short of direct combat between two major states and their allies. By that standard, today's similarities with the old Cold War are quite salient, especially in the distribution of power in the international system between the two countries, the importance of a third country's changeable alignment, smoldering territorial disputes, indirect or quasi combat via covert action, the shadow of hot war in the background of everything else, and the remarkable convergence of opinion in American politics, at least outside the confines of the foreign policy elite, on punishing the adversary. The war in Ukraine shifted attention to Russia as the main antagonist in this contest, but before that, and in the longer term, China is the main event. It is reasonable to say that along with constraining climate change and stabilizing cybersecurity, avoiding real war between the United States and China is one of the top three priorities in all of international politics.

The biggest difference from the old Cold War is the entanglement of economic and strategic interests, the first demanding cooperation and the second fueling conflict. In the old Cold War this was no issue. Both sides then were nearly insulated from each other economically. Soviet and Chinese trade with the West was negligible, and the Communist powers' weight in the global economy was weak. Today the situation is entirely different. Far more than before, economic sanctions provide significant leverage against Moscow—and also entail pain in the West. But the impact of interrupting commerce with Russia diverted attention from the fact that economic interdependence is greater between the West and China—which means that the United States is by some nontrivial measure *dependent* on China. Unwinding dependence would risk American prosperity, while not unwinding it may risk national security. Nevertheless, despite this crucial difference with the old Cold War and the material disincentives to conflict between the United States and the People's Republic of China (PRC), even before the Ukraine war their relationship had become "defined by the proliferation of flash points, the downward spiral of hostility, the rise in zero-sum thinking, and the breakdown of mediating and mitigating institutions."[2]

From the old Cold War to the new one, US policy toward China evolved through three phases, each lasting a little over twenty years: first antagonism, then amity, then ambivalence. In the first phase of antagonism, until the early 1970s, the Soviet Union was the main enemy because of its capabilities, but China was seen as more radical and aggressive in its intentions. In the second phase, until the Cold War ended, common interests in opposing Moscow united the United States and the PRC in a shocking new marriage of convenience. In the third phase, after the old Cold War, with no common enemy facing the two, a long period of ambivalence reflected the conflicting American interests in cooperation and containment. For two decades after the old Cold War cooperative interests prevailed, but since then conflict has come to dominate.

One similarity between the old Cold War and today is the fundamental structure of the international system: bipolarity, this time with the second pole being China instead of the old USSR. To many this idea still seems premature, especially since the Russian onslaught against the much weaker country of Ukraine confused impressions of how major states rank in the global roster of power. For long after the Soviet collapse in the old Cold War the world was seen as unipolar, and from one angle it still is. Because of the dramatic speed of China's economic growth, its limitations and fragility have been overlooked and America's relative decline exaggerated.

In terms in which the old Cold War was measured, however, these points are not contradictory. The West was much further ahead of the Soviet Union in many indices of power than it is vis-à-vis China today, yet we do not hesitate to think of the old Cold War as bipolar. At the same time, China then played a big, disruptive role via the Korean War and promotion of revolution in the Third World. Such Chinese activism notwithstanding, the point is that there was no third country in the same league of overall national power as the United States and the USSR then, and despite Russian belligerence there is no other state now in the same league as the United States and the PRC.[3] Bipolarity has crept back in the twenty-first century, with no cataclysm to reveal it starkly in the way the end of World War II did. The new cold war has crept up in tandem, in fits and starts, since the Taiwan Straits flap of 1996 and the EP-3 incident of 2001. It became clear with the Trump administration when, despite being on the verge of civil war over most other issues, Democratic and Republican parties converged on hostility toward the PRC.

Will bipolarity prove stable? Neorealist theorists like Kenneth Waltz and John Mearsheimer have thought so, inspired by the long peace of the old Cold War, although Mearsheimer's optimism faltered when he contemplated China.[4] The more traditional realists' view, mindful of the records of Athens and Sparta or Rome and Carthage that contradict that of Washington and Moscow, is fearful. Although restraints against the outbreak of a third world war did become recognized by the mid-1960s, after several crises had raised the specter of nuclear conflict, the earlier phase of the old Cold War was quite dangerous. Moreover, bipolarity is both rough and complex, with the various elements of power unevenly distributed. This makes it conducive to miscalculation, as either side may misestimate its capacity to defeat the other.[5] For those who focus on basic international power structure as central, the critical question becomes the *passage* from unipolarity to and through bipolarity, as uneven growth generates ambition in the rising power and incentives for preventive war in the declining one—the risk of a so-called war of hegemonic transition.[6] This is what makes recognizing the emergence of a new bipolarity crucial.

Stakes, power, and motives in both cold wars are concentrated in three dimensions: military, economic, and political. The old Cold War was driven most intensely by political divisions over ideology first, next by military confrontation, and third and least by economic competition. The order and intensity of these drivers in the new cold war is reversed. Ideological conflict was more or less absent until the surge of deglobalization and populism after 2016 discredited the notion of Western liberalism as the inevitable wave of the future. The embarrassment of democracy under US president Donald Trump, Indian prime minister Narendra Modi, Brazilian president Jair Bolsonaro, Turkish president Recep Tayyip Erdoğan, Hungarian prime minister Viktor Orbán, and company has given President Xi Jinping's authoritarian growth model some currency as a wider alternative, but the ideological dimension of competition is less clearly defined than the old contest between Marxism and liberalism and still far behind the other two in material significance. The biggest question now is which of those two—economic or military—will dominate the other as choices they pose become harder to avoid.

In the near term, the economic dimension has priority because its effects are salient every day. Dependence on trade is constant and its importance is always immediate; combat remains a longer-term hypothetical risk—until it isn't. To paraphrase former assistant secretary of defense for international security affairs Joseph Nye, security is like oxygen: you don't think about it until you don't have it, and then it's all you think about.[7] While economic interests and leverage dominate the competition until there is a crisis, military power remains the ultima ratio regum.

The Military Dimension

In the old Cold War, American and Soviet armed forces, both conventional and nuclear, dwarfed all others. Of course, this did not mean that others were impotent—China and the United States did fight a war for three years in Korea, and Vietnamese Communists held American and allied forces at bay for a decade. Rather, it meant simply that the two superpowers, the United States and the USSR, could threaten each other's very existence. The strategic situation in the twenty-first century differs significantly from the old Cold War in the United States' deep entanglement in a third theater of conflict not subsumed by great power competition—the Middle East and Southwest Asia. These are at best indirectly related to the US-PRC rivalry, but they have diverted attention from it. Preoccupation with the Middle East was energized by counterterrorism after September 11 and enabled by the long post–Cold War holiday from great power conflict after the Soviet collapse, and Washington's efforts to disengage militarily from the region accelerated as tensions with Moscow and Beijing reemerged.

Two differences between the old and new cold wars mark the military dimension of great power conflict in the twenty-first century: geography and technology.

Geography

First, Asia is a higher priority than it was a half century ago. The crucial military arena then was the one in which war never went from cold to hot: central Europe. There, NATO and the Warsaw Pact arrayed huge forces unprecedented in peacetime. East Asia then was the secondary theater despite the fact that it was where Washington fought two midsize "proxy" hot wars. Europe was more militarily stable because the superpowers invested huge amounts in dense capabilities that maximized deterrence. The Korean War occurred largely because Washington did not even attempt to deter North Korea before June 1950, instead withdrawing US forces from South Korea and announcing a defense perimeter that did not include it. In Southeast Asia, agricultural societies were also more susceptible than industrial Europe to revolutionary movements and unconventional warfare. Today the economic and political stakes in Asia are far weightier than in the old Cold War and now at least equal American stakes in Europe.

Second, in technical military terms, the US-Soviet competition was primarily continental, while today's US-China competition is primarily maritime. In the old Cold War, the fundamental priority was the NATO central front in Germany. If the Soviet Army could drive to the English Channel, Moscow could win World War III, while what happened at sea or in Asia would have been sideshows. The Soviet Army was then larger than the US Army and positioned in the middle of the continent, in control of the eastern half of it. This continental standoff mandated mobilization unprecedented in peacetime: 6 to 9 percent of GDP allocated to military expenditures in the United States, more than 15 percent in the USSR, and conscription on both sides.

Between the old and new cold wars, the tables in Europe turned. Today, the Russian army is far weaker relative to NATO, standing alone against a vastly larger alliance, and is positioned much further back instead of in the middle of Germany, no longer in striking distance of the English Channel. The war in Ukraine might seem to belie this deflation of Russian military standing, but it should be seen as roughly analogous to the Korean War. No combat occurred in Europe while that conflict raged, but Europe remained the priority for American armed forces' planning.

The invasion of Ukraine paused the priority of US military planning against China but does not reverse it. Despite the clash in Europe, the main power competition in the world today is not with the old, larger USSR but between the United States and the PRC, and militarily between their forces at sea. Unlike Germany and France in the old Cold War, the territories of most crucial significance as strategic stakes or catalysts are not on the mainland but benefit militarily from water buffers (Japan and Taiwan) or, situated on a peninsula with a short front like South Korea, are more easily defensible by land forces than were the major countries of western Europe. These geographic conditions dampen competition in the size of forces deployed on land, although the Ukraine war did partly brake this reorientation. The greater importance of the maritime aspect, however, also means that the limits of probing in Asia are less starkly demarcated, and redlines are more uncertain. Moreover, the intermingling of naval forces operating at sea raises the odds of accidents in confrontations and outbreaks of unplanned crises.[8]

Technology

In this century, cybersecurity is not only a new arena of conflict but potentially among the most important. First, evolving cyberconflict in espionage and sabotage resembles what most typified the old Cold War: secret probes, covert action, political grand larceny, indirect damage, war in the shadows. This was first dramatically symbolized by Chinese hackers' ransacking of US Office of Personnel Management records. Second, modern military forces have become utterly dependent on computers for all functions, and cyberhacking that compromises command, control, and communication systems could revolutionize the dynamics of combat and determine war outcomes in ways yet unpredictable. Similarly, artificial intelligence, robotics, and precision targeting are the cutting edge of contemporary conventional military capabilities.

Intertwining of these economic and military innovations highlights the question of which realms will determine general net advantage. Will the crucial technological ingredients in competition prove to be TikTok or the F-35, WeChat or ballistic missile defense? Along with these concerns on the technological frontier, however, a technology now three-quarters of a century old is likely to loom larger than it has since the old Cold War: nuclear weapons. In the old Cold War, nuclear weapons and expectations about escalation in the event of hot war were at the center of strategists' concerns, ideas, and policy initiatives. Debates about military requirements and plans or schemes for arms control in those days began and ended with the nuclear element. After the old Cold War, concern with nuclear weapons shifted to their proliferation to smaller "rogue" states. Between the United States and the PRC there is less attention to nuclear strategy, less sensitivity to the lore of nuclear deterrence among political and military elites than in the old days, and less clarity about the risks nuclear capabilities pose or about which region's conflict presents the most danger of mass destruction. But as friction between the major states has grown at the same time that China's rise provides it more resources, old issues about nuclear strategy are coming back.

For more than forty years, NATO relied on the threat of nuclear escalation to counter perceived Soviet superiority in conventional forces and wrestled with the logical inconsistency of this doctrine with the stability of mutual nuclear deterrence between the superpowers. Nuclear strategy then was less central in the secondary conflict between Washington and Beijing. Today, the nuclear relationship is different in both theaters. It remains more important in what is now the secondary theater, the NATO-Russia conflict, than it is in the now-main theater, Asia, but in reverse fashion from the old Cold War. With the tables turned in the balance of conventional military power, it is now Moscow that has the stronger incentive to rely on the threat of nuclear first use to deter NATO. (American analysts who don't remember the old days now sometimes characterize the Russian idea of "escalating to deescalate" as if it is novel adventurism, forgetting that it echoes old NATO strategy.[9])

Asia has presented a stark contrast. In the old Cold War, extended deterrence—the reliance of US allies on US defense coverage and deterrent threats to protect them—was the main problem bedeviling military strategy. This was because western European countries were highly vulnerable to invasion and American threats to retaliate with first use of nuclear weapons seemed the necessary way to maximize Moscow's disincentives to launch a conventional attack. Today the credibility of extended deterrence remains a political issue, especially for Japan's and South Korea's confidence (and perhaps Taiwan's) in Washington's intention to fight for them. It is not a serious issue for military strategy, however, because war plans need not bank on being the first to fire nuclear weapons, plans that were the essence of extended deterrence and a howling dilemma for NATO in the old Cold War.

In contrast to the NATO-Warsaw Pact confrontation, there is no potential battleground in Asia that would require Beijing or Washington to rely on nuclear threats to hold significant territory. As a result, neither side has been preoccupied with nuclear strategy. China has had a nuclear no-first-use policy and for decades fielded only a small nuclear force appropriate for minimum deterrence. Unfortunately these geographic and technological differences made many strategists in both China and the United States complacent about the prospects for control of escalation in a potential US-China war. Most observers saw Chinese doctrine as assuming that mutual nuclear deterrence was ineluctable given capacity to destroy a limited number of population centers in the homelands, so a war could unfold with escalation varying only within the confines of conventional combat.[10] US planners as well focused on conventional war.

Downplaying the danger of nuclear escalation weakens mutual deterrence at the conventional level and raises the odds of limited war,[11] which in turn raises the odds of nuclear escalation. Moreover, since 2020 Beijing has moved toward major expansion of its nuclear force and appears to be reconsidering reliance on simple minimum deterrence. The focus of strategic concern is evolving in Asia in reverse fashion from the old Cold War. Through the 1950s, American planners assumed that combat with the USSR or the PRC would be nuclear.[12] In the 1960s, anxiety about relying on catastrophic escalation led to greater emphasis on conventional defense (the "flexible response" doctrine). In the early years of the new cold war, however, both the PRC and the United States seemed overconfident that they would be able to assault each other in intense combat without lurching over the nuclear threshold. Chinese strategists were especially overconfident in the ability to control conventional escalation.[13] The assumption of a simple and absolute firebreak between conventional war and nuclear apocalypse, however, is wobbly. Actual Chinese planning appears to take more account of possible limited nuclear war, and doctrinal exceptions to "no first use" as Western observers understand the concept may be greater than official Chinese rhetoric suggests.[14]

North Korea's nuclear weapons inject alarm into scenarios of limited war—or catalytic involvement of major powers in local war—in a way that has no clear parallel in the old Cold War. The main danger is that Pyongyang would miscalculate that its nuclear force not only makes retaliation (and thus deter-rence) credible but also provides a shield behind which conventional aggression can proceed safely. (The rationale could resemble Pakistan's probing attacks on Indian forces in the Kargil War of 1999 and is reflected in the Western consensus against countering Russian aggression in Ukraine with military action on Russian territory.) Nevertheless, North Korean nuclear as well as conventional military capabilities would still represent a fraction of what Soviet and Chinese capabilities were in the old Cold War, and decision-makers in the north would have to move from high-risk to nearly insane thinking to undertake first use of nuclear weapons in wartime. In contrast to North Korea, a China that comes to regard itself as a superpower could be a different story.

Strategizing for hot war in the Pacific is a fast-moving train, but as of 2022 it is unclear that dominant planning assumptions in either Beijing or Washington have taken sufficient account of the potential for *inadvertent* nuclear escalation. A particular problem in raising this concern is China's intermingling of conventional and nuclear missile forces. This organizational arrangement means that in a hot war American strikes aimed at attrition of Chinese conventional forces would not have the option of assuredly sparing nuclear delivery systems. Successful US conventional operations could have the by-product of whittling down the Chinese nuclear deterrent, which might provoke Beijing to revoke its no-first-use doctrine under the pressure to "use 'em or lose 'em."[15]

Geographic and technological conditions reinforce each other in the risk of inadvertent combat. Both the old and new cold wars involve sovereignty disputes, suspended but not ended, over territories of no material significance but outsize symbolic import. In the 1950s the Eisenhower administration twice tip-toed toward war over the minor offshore islands of Quemoy and Matsu. In the twenty-first century the PRC claims the even less significant Diaoyu/Senkaku islands administered by Japan. The other new, tiny artificial islands constructed by Beijing in the South China Sea are also a provocation to the countries that reject PRC claims to maritime jurisdiction in the area. As Christensen points out, both sides in the evolving conflict in the western Pacific believe they are the defenders rather than revisionists, which is psychologically a worst-case situation for avoiding a game of chicken where neither one swerves: "lack of agreement on the legitimate status quo in maritime Asia makes the region potentially more volatile than the Central European theater during the Cold War."[16]

The Economic Dimension

War is the most important risk in the new cold war, but it is in the background. Until a crisis puts it on the table, the economic aspect of competition buffets relations every day. The two countries' economic power relative to each other and the deep integration of China in the world trading system is the overwhelming difference from the twentieth century.

The concept and relevance of national economic power are controversial in the West. In the military realm, power is entirely a matter of relative capability, and economic resources are convertible to such capability, so those concerned with national security see relative economic resources and productivity as what count in international politics. Economists more often see absolute rather than relative gains and economic efficiency rather than political effects as the prime rational motives for economic policy. To most economists, trade is something to be maximized, so that specialization according to comparative advantage can optimize prosperity for all. Strategists who focus on security more than prosperity, in contrast, see benefits in limiting dependence on trade to avoid vulnerability to interruption of vital supplies. Thus, for national security, economic power does not vary directly with economic profit margins.

Economic Power

In the old Cold War, economic power was all on one side. In Europe, the Atlantic alliance was far richer and more productive than the Warsaw Pact, and in Asia, the United States and Japan outclassed China by an even wider margin. Bipolarity was essentially measured by military forces, with the West estimated to have an advantage in their technical quality and the Communists in their quantity due to their large population bases and willingness to dedicate more of their economies to military production.

GDP is a simplistic index of national economic power. Beckley suggests that a better back-of-the-envelope measure is GDP multiplied by GDP per capita— by which the disposable resources Beijing has to convert into force that can be directed externally are less impressive.[17] While it is questionable *how* significant the increase in Chinese GDP is, it is still stunning and at least reflects the trend of relative strength. The fact that by measures of purchasing power parity the Chinese economy may already be first in the world also reflects the magnitude of change.

Even if less than many assume, China has developed more economic power relative to the United States than the old Soviet Union had. The significance for national security depends on two factors: how long and at what level Chinese growth will continue and whether it will move more into the value-added stages of innovation. If China's growth rates decline but still remain higher than America's, the PRC will overtake a good part of the economic advantage to which the West was long accustomed. In the early years of the old Cold War, Soviet economic growth was impressive and reinforced the West's anxiety at the time of the Sputnik shock, but it was the reversal of that trend and the relative

Soviet economic decline in later years that drove the end of that cold war. Unless Chinese growth reverses in the same way, bipolarity will intensify.

Trade

In the old Cold War there was scant trade between East and West; interdependence and globalization were more or less limited to the noncommunist world. This changed as the old Cold War ended, the Western order expanded, and the PRC joined it as the Soviet Union collapsed. By the time the new cold war was emerging, interdependence had broadened and deepened, welcomed by liberals as a pacifying as well as profitable development. The questions this change raised for national security policy were only dimly recognized until the Trump administration. Then the one-two punch of the Huawei controversy and the disruption of supply chains by the coronavirus highlighted the second, negative edge of interdependence—dependence on an adversary.

The Huawei controversy arose because the Chinese company's jump on offering the 5G system to reconfigure worldwide communications illustrated two fundamental differences between the old and new cold wars. First, China's proffer for 5G infrastructure was a jolting bid to control the underpinning of civilian information technology, which is the linchpin of high-tech innovation and material progress in the twenty-first century. Reminiscent of Sputnik, it shocked those who assumed that the natural order of things was for the United States to be always at the forefront of modernization. American scientific hegemony was shaken in a category crucial not just for military applications, as Sputnik was, but for absolutely all activities in contemporary society. Divisions among Western allies about whether to accept or reject Huawei's bid, which would leave a new system vulnerable to demands the Chinese government might make on the company to manipulate the system, showed that economic interests could override security concerns. (This occurred in the old Cold War as well, with the dispute between the Reagan administration and European allies over construction of the Soviet gas pipeline.) Second, the Huawei controversy reflected the overwhelming strategic importance of cybersecurity for virtually everything, civilian and military activity alike. This huge and pervasive issue did not even exist during the old Cold War.

Following hard on Trump's trade war, Huawei and the coronavirus reflected the breaking wave of economic cooperation between the two major powers. In many respects, such as reliance on Chinese components for electronic equipment, dependence had emerged beyond what most strategists had grasped. Domestic opposition to free trade had been growing even longer in the United States as manufacturing employment declined. Trump's election empowered it, the Huawei issue linked economic and security interests in a more unstable mix, and the coronavirus's interruption of supply chains highlighted US vulnerability.

In the old Cold War the United States and its allies did not have to worry about economic dependence until the energy crisis of the 1970s, but then the adversaries were Middle Eastern oil producers, not the major Communist powers in Moscow or Beijing. The economic world then was already one of American primacy, the significance of which was lower only because of military and political bipolarity. For almost two decades after the Cold War, that economic dominance persisted. The process by which China's growth and outreach eroded it was gradual.

For a long time, most observers in the West considered that process benign because economic development is a positive-sum game. Moreover, national enrichment was also widely assumed to foster political liberalization, another pacifying force. The "democratic peace" theory became conventional wisdom among politicians. As the Chinese model increasingly appeared to confute the notion that economic progress would spur democratization, and Chinese muscle-flexing in the South China Sea grew, optimism wobbled. Nevertheless, the idea that interdependence prevents war because it gives both sides too much to lose remained strong. For example, Lyle Goldstein titled a book chapter "Mutually Assured Dependence," a play on words from the old Cold War idea that capability for "mutual assured destruction" kept the superpower nuclear standoff stable.[18]

This now stands as the principal question in the third decade of the century: Will interest in maximizing economic profit trump nationalist and territorial conflict, or the reverse? At this writing, a big test case is unfolding as the West undertakes economic warfare against Moscow over Ukraine. The challenge of balancing benefits and costs in that case highlights the question of whether and how the challenge could arise with China. Some believe that the idea of America "decoupling" from China is by now impossible, because economic integration has gone too far to turn back without devastating consequences or because Western capitalists are too greedy to give priority to strategic concerns. The political linkage of strategic fear with labor constituencies' opposition to free trade, however, makes backpedaling on interdependence and subsidy of security-related elements of the domestic economy as plausible as renewed integration.

The Political Dimension

Military and economic interactions are concrete, and trends are comparatively measurable by hard data. Political aspects of conflict and cooperation are easy to sense but harder to measure. These involve murky issues of national values and objectives as well as processes for pursuing them through negotiation. These may have less impact than the hard processes. The obvious record of the old

Cold War and observations from the recent record, however, highlight the continued importance of ideology, diplomacy, and internal politics that determine particular leaders and policies.

Ideology

What made the East-West conflict of the old Cold War starker than traditional great power rivalry was the titanic struggle over which form of social organization would come to dominate the world. To an extent hard for post–Cold War generations to grasp, Marxism-Leninism was a vibrant transnational force, with organized revolutionary movements and varying degrees of mass appeal in dozens of countries. The old Cold War was a moral as well as material competition, and the moral underwrote the material via its capacity to motivate and mobilize political and military action. With the collapse of communist regimes in 1989–91, however, ideology slid from sight as a major issue in world order. In the old Cold War it was front and center; in the new one it is, while not utterly absent, an underlying or even unconscious motive and different in form.

There are two ideological issues now. One is how far either government will go in projecting its society's political values or regime character outward. How vigorously will the United States advocate human rights, democratization, and regime change in China? Or, if the United States is seen to be in obvious decline, will the PRC be more interested in exporting its governance model of digital authoritarianism, or even join and lead the drift of antidemocratic regimes toward forming a new transnational opposition to the model of liberal universalism?[19] The other issue is about the institutional organization of countries' external relations: whether the American-led Western economic and political order that seemed triumphant after the old Cold War will continue to shape national interactions in business and diplomacy, with China participating equally, or a more powerful and frisky China will demand a different kind of international order in tune with its interests or culture.[20]

Diplomacy

In the old Cold War, the United States negotiated periodically with Moscow, but it did not negotiate directly at all with the PRC for more than twenty years. Then, after those two decades, it was diplomacy that inverted the alignments of the Cold War. The interplay from ping-pong exchanges to Kissinger's secret trips to formal recognition in the Carter administration engineered a geopolitical revolution for the rest of the twentieth century.

Relations with formal allies have changed less across time. From the beginning the United States has had far more allies in Asia than the PRC. What pass for Beijing's local allies, North Korea and perhaps Myanmar/Burma, have been net liabilities more than benefits. This disadvantage makes the variation in

Beijing's collaboration with Moscow all the more important. In the early Cold War, the clear alliance of China and the Soviet Union helped the PRC substantially, not only through material support but by deterring the United States from operations against the Chinese homeland during the Korean War. (The Truman administration feared that such escalation could bring the Soviets into the war and possibly trigger invasion of western Europe.) In the late phase of the old Cold War, in contrast, the enmity between the two major communist states helped the West, flipping the challenge of planning for a two-front World War III from Washington to Moscow.

The import of this stark change of geopolitical alignment in the old Cold War indicates how crucial the question of China-Russia relations became as the two grew closer again in the new cold war. Optimists in the West either were oblivious to the logic of realpolitik or assumed that deep conflicts of interest and distrust between Beijing and Moscow would prevent them from moving back to military cooperation. In recent times, however, the American camp gave both countries incentives to subordinate their animosities to their common interest in resisting pressure from the West. For those attuned to realpolitik, a Nixonesque-Kissingerian American strategy would reverse the old Cold War strategy for upending the global balance, now repairing US relations with Moscow in order to face Beijing with a two-front challenge. Trump's ham-handed sucking up to Vladimir Putin, Moscow's meddling in American elections, and, most dramatically, Russian action against Ukraine damaged the possibility of sensible adaptation. The geopolitically suicidal Russian venture in Ukraine, however, also severely complicated China's option for building an alliance with Moscow. If the dust settles on those disruptions, more adept American efforts to cooperate with Russia would be no more politically unthinkable than rapprochement with China seemed in 1970.

The United States' long-standing advantage of numerous and strong allies provides not just aggregate capabilities for deterrence but political leverage on China as well. In Asia, Japan is the most vital partner. In the early Cold War, Tokyo's demilitarization limited its clout. Because of the difference in strategic geography from the continental confrontation in Europe, the United States did not need to mobilize Japanese military power for defense of the most important territory as NATO was compelled to do with West Germany. Washington's ability to keep Japan's military role in Asia limited gives it a high card to play with China, where anti-Japanese sentiment and suspicion are intense.

A major difference in US diplomatic strategy that has endured in both cold wars is the development of a highly institutionalized multilateral alliance in Europe—NATO—contrasted with bilateral "hub and spoke" alliances in Asia. (The one exception, in theory though not in practice, has been in Korea, where the 1950–53 war was fought in principle by the United Nations and where an official UN Command has formally existed in South Korea ever since. The latter is utterly unnoticed outside, however, and Washington has neglected the chance to exploit it as a symbol of legitimacy and publicize it for propaganda purposes.) There are grounds for this bilateral—as opposed to multilateral—difference in alliance formatting, due to Asia's greater variety of cultures, colonial histories, and the lesser need for joint preparation and coordination of defense in peacetime required by maritime as opposed to continental conflict. Moreover, the one experiment in mimicking NATO—the Southeast Asia Treaty Organization (SEATO)—was a flop, defunct by 1977, never having functioned effectively during its twenty-two years of nominal existence. As long as the new cold war remains low-key and potentially reversible, it is also politic to refrain from formalizing what Beijing already sees as hostile encirclement.

The more the new cold war comes to seem definite and containment of China is admitted as an objective, however, the more sense military multilateralism—which can take a range of forms from subtle to formal—would make. First, more official regional solidarity under Washington's aegis would alleviate individual countries' anxiety about reliability of collective defense and American staying power. Second, it might constrain defection when allies wobble, as with Rodrigo Duterte's government in the Philippines. Third, multilateral alignment—in combination with endorsement of international court rulings—would raise both the legitimacy and strength of opposition to China's excessive maritime jurisdiction claims. Apart from provoking China, the dominant economic force in the region, the biggest major disincentive to pushing for an explicit multilateral alliance is the related urge to prevent intensification of the new cold war.

Leadership

Great tidal forces of economic, ideological, or cultural change channel national policy choices but do not necessarily determine them. Domestic political processes can produce leaders who are dragged along by trends, or who resist, override, or redirect them. Consider the differences between Leonid Brezhnev and Mikhail Gorbachev, Mao Zedong and Deng Xiaoping, or Barack Obama and Donald Trump.

There may be disagreements among Chinese politicians over how aggressively the country's rise in the international arena should be pushed, but potent political forces promoting retreat are not evident. The same cannot be said of the United States. Trump's stance was incoherent, arguing for retraction of American commitments because of allies' exploitation of US largesse while at the same time maintaining a general stance of chest-thumping belligerence on behalf of American dominance. The countercoalition of neoconservative and liberal interventionists of the first two decades after the old Cold War diminished in influence among the opposition to Trump, and domestic issues eclipsed foreign policy in American political contests since fear of terrorism ebbed. The impulse to activism, however, has been resilient since 1945, faltering for a decade after the Tet Offensive in Vietnam, bounding back until setbacks in Iraq and Afghanistan, then surging again with Ukraine. There are no solid grounds to assume a secular trend in either general direction—activism or retrenchment. The constituency for cooperation with China, however, concentrated so far among the business community and liberals as it has been, is unlikely to grow.

It is hard to imagine a presidential candidate of either party recommending rapprochement at the price of freer trade or territorial concessions. Even the cosmopolitan elements of the Democratic Party capitulated to economic nationalism when Hillary Clinton had to repudiate the Trans-Pacific Partnership in the 2016 presidential campaign. President Biden remains a mainstream Democrat and reflects the long-standing grievances of American labor against globalization and job losses. China's economic dynamism is the emblem of globalization's dark side. Biden's political instincts buttress his foreign policy instincts, and in his first year in office he did not rush to undo Trump's policies on China as he did with almost everything else. In that first year Biden twice outran the foreign policy establishment in articulating a definite defense commitment to Taiwan. The Afghanistan and Ukraine disasters reinforced incentives to project strength in US-PRC relations.

Stakes and Flashpoints

The point of departure in speculating about danger of war between the United States and China is to understand that the task is *not* to figure out what makes war *probable*. For odds makers in Las Vegas the chances of great power war over the next couple of decades are low, even given the warning of war on Ukraine, because statesmen recognize that war would be an epochal disaster. But this is usually true. War generally seems improbable until some steady trend or unplanned event changes the odds. This can happen so gradually that the change is unappreciated until some catalyst highlights it, or so abruptly that adaptation is frantic. Either such development is plausible in Asia.

Korea is the biggest continuity between the old and new cold wars. The border in the divided country is about the most densely militarized in the world, North Korea is about the most erratic and vicious American adversary apart from stateless terrorist groups, and no other country poses equal odds of aggression against an official American ally. (These points are not sufficiently accepted in Washington, where many incorrectly assess Iran's government and behavior as equal or greater on the "craziness" scale.) Compared with the old Cold War, nevertheless, US and South Korean conventional deterrence of a North Korean invasion seems almost as stable, though less than perfect as that stability has always been since 1953. Differences in the new cold war are that North Korea now has nuclear weapons, Russia is no longer a materially effective supporter, and China has less patience with its recalcitrant client in Pyongyang.

The differences raise the odds of inadvertent US-China war. If the regime in the north believes that its nuclear weapons deter counterattack against its territory, it may feel freer to gamble on military action against the south, even without the military backing from China that it got after 1950. The potential collapse of the Pyongyang regime could also prompt South Korean or US intervention in the north. Without prior consultation and coordination with Beijing, this could trigger Chinese counterintervention and a clash that neither side wants. Detailed advance discussion of how to coordinate response to a North Korean collapse, however, is a diplomatic bridge too far. Therefore, the most prudent policy to avoid war with China in the event of North Korea's disintegration is for the United States to foreswear introduction of American forces across the DMZ, communicate promptly the limits of South Korean humanitarian intervention, and entertain negotiations about limiting American presence in the country if it is reunified under the Seoul regime.

The other venues susceptible to inadvertent war are the South China Sea, where Beijing asserts legal jurisdiction not recognized by other nations, and the Diaoyu/Senkaku Islands, where it asserts sovereignty against Japan's claim. In the South China Sea, the main risk is accidental combat arising from potential Chinese harassment of US air or naval forces deemed to be trespassing (similar to the EP-3 incident of 2001, in which the American plane lacked self-defense capability that other US combat aircraft or ships would have in a future incident). In the Senkakus, the possibility of accident is matched by a possibility of miscalculation if a more risk-prone government in Beijing at some point decided that Tokyo and Washington would not dare forcibly counter a coup de main / fait accompli that landed Chinese troops to occupy the islands. For the United States the value of deterring such a hypothetical decision by presenting a less ambiguous commitment to military defense of the islands conflicts with the diplomatic price of ratcheting up tension.

The biggest danger is miscalculation over Taiwan. Since the wake-up call from the PRC's squeeze on Hong Kong, followed by the Ukraine war, the American foreign policy elite has shed some of its complacency about the indefinite durability of the Taiwan status quo. The Chinese government long enabled such complacency by not pressing the question of how the renegade province will be reincorporated in the People's Republic, but it has made quite clear that the question is when, not whether, that will happen. If Beijing's patience lasts yet another seventy-odd years, the issue is an academic question, as foreign policy issues go. Witnessing world reaction to the invasion of Ukraine may reinforce PRC caution. But why expect that China's patience will not wither as its power grows? By the time bipolarity seems evident to all, how low will the odds be that the Chinese government will say that it has been very patient, that it has offered more than one generous political solution to ease reunification (for example, one country / two systems), and that the time to resolve the island's status has come? Effective military coercion short of direct invasion like Russia's—for example, blockade—may seem less provocative. Moreover, Taiwan does not enjoy the sovereign status in international law or diplomatic recognition that Ukraine did and cannot count on the same breadth and depth of outrage and support from the international community. Indeed, it is unclear that any other country at all would join the United States in committing armed forces directly to combat against the PRC over Taiwan.

In the old Cold War, protecting Taiwan was no problem. In the first phase, Washington was unambiguously committed to defending the island. In the second phase, Beijing put the question on the back burner in order to exploit the tacit alliance with the United States against the USSR, and Washington fudged the question, abrogating the formal defense pact with Taipei but taking other initiatives implying that it would still defend the island. For most of the post–Cold War era the two major powers had other fish to fry. If the new cold war takes root and becomes as bitter as the old one, confidence in the status quo has to falter.

The Ukraine war's effect on Russian standing may restrain Beijing. Otherwise, the main danger lies in the ambiguity of the US position. To Americans, ambiguity may seem strong enough to deter, but to Chinese in a future crisis it could seem anemic enough to challenge. Most pertinently, the Taiwan question has not yet risen to the level of wide public debate in the American political arena. There is no evidence that if it does voters will endorse fighting a war with a nuclear-armed power over a stake that is more important to it than to Americans, any more than they wanted to go to war over Ukraine. If avoiding war were the only concern, there would be something to say for a decisive clarification—either reverting to the old Cold War's clearer commitment to defend Taiwan, in order to maximize deterrence, or embracing a clearer priority for accommodation with China by declaring that Taiwan is on its own. But avoiding war is not the only concern, and the costs of decisively going to either extreme of belligerence or appeasement are too high for politicians to bear as long as they don't have to.

After Ambivalence

The structure of the international system now resembles the old Cold War in one way and diverges in another. On one hand, it is roughly bipolar, with the primary and secondary adversaries of the early Cold War reversed in both power and behavior. Now "Russia is a rogue, not a peer [and] China is a peer, not a rogue."[21] Evolving bipolarity is the most fundamental consideration for those worried about a war of hegemonic transition. The alignment that could alter the military balance is not the US-China entente of the 1970s but reversion to the Russia-China alliance of the 1950s. On the other hand, the international system is far more economically integrated than the world of the twentieth century, and money talks. This combination of similarity in military structure and difference in economic structure underwrites persisting ambivalence in American policy even as relations have moved back toward antagonism.

Of course there is the possibility that dominant economic trends are misperceived and will avert harder choices for the United States. It is easy to forget that in the old Cold War there was a period of hand-wringing in the 1970s about a trend of American decline and Soviet ascendancy, and another decade of debate about whether the United States had to compromise with Moscow or could defeat it, only to be followed by Gorbachev's amazing surrender. If the Beckley view is confirmed, the specter of Chinese strength could dissolve. There is far less agreement among analysts about unviability of China's economy than there was about the USSR's, however, so Beijing's continued narrowing of the power gap with the United States remains a safer bet.

If so, for the new cold war to dissolve and the contestants to move back to amity, without a powerful common enemy as incentive, would probably require two shifts in direction: American accommodation via military retreat in Asia, and economic reglobalization. The first shift would be out of character, even for Trumpists who, for all their whining about ending allies' free riding, still cannot resist the urge to show other countries who's boss. The second shift seems hardly more likely than its opposite: further deglobalization and reduction of US-China economic linkages. At the height of the pandemic, Republican president Trump's closest adviser declared, "After this, we'll be putting in place very strong strategies to make sure that America doesn't have to rely on any other countries for critical supplies in the future."[22] Democrats' labor constituency has pressed even longer for limits on trade, and the bipartisan national security establishment now worries about insulating high-tech military equipment from malign suppliers. These urges sound more like the economic nationalism that destabilized the world of the 1930s than the West's cooperative institution-building in the old Cold War. The trend could prove a hiatus before a détente dampens the new cold war and free traders bounce back. Otherwise, more economic conflict, combined with US resistance to PRC territorial claims, is a recipe for both a clearer new cold war and increased risk of inadvertent combat.

In one sense, emphasis on this danger of thoroughly recognized cold war reflects optimism: it suggests that deliberate, considered decisions by either of the two powers to launch war in full awareness are hard to imagine. Moreover, "inadvertent" implies ignition by accident, which must be differentiated from miscalculation. Accident means unintentional crisis due to technical malfunctions and standard operating procedures of military forces not understood or anticipated by political decision-makers (such as the 2001 EP-3 incident) or catalysts beyond their control that trigger an unintended chicken game (such as the assassination of Franz Ferdinand in 1914). Miscalculation means a decision to launch war that is deliberate and intended but which flows from ignorant judgments or mistaken predictions of success (such as the second American war against Iraq). Accidents are common, yet they seldom overwhelm political circuit breakers enforcing restraint. Miscalculation, however, is common to most war outbreaks.[23] World War I flowed from both, a rare example of accidental precipitant escaping control; it is no accident that the 1914 case obsesses theorists of war avoidance.

In the old Cold War, it took fifteen years of crises over Berlin, Cuba, Korea, and the Chinese offshore islands to clarify the risks of miscalculation and the acceptable bounds of competition and probing. In the new cold war, it is still early. Washington and Beijing have so far avoided confrontations as dangerous as those that happened through 1962. If the United States wants to avoid a damaging choice between amicable trade and diplomatic relations on one hand and militant containment on the other, continuing ambivalence makes sense; a measure of ambiguity in the limits of commitment to use force is the path of least resistance in the short term. But while ambiguity supports peace now, it increases the chance of miscalculation over time.

Notes

1. Thomas J. Christensen, "No New Cold War: Why US-China Strategic Competition Will Not Be like the US-Soviet Cold War," Asan Report (Seoul: Asan Institute for Policy Studies, July 2020); Joseph S. Nye, "There's No Cold War with China," *New York Times*, November 6, 2021, A20; David E. Sanger, "Don't Call It a Cold War: U.S. Labors to Name China Rivalry," *New York Times*, October 18, 2021, A1, A8.

2. Jude Blanchette, quoted in Edward Wong and Ana Swanson, "Washington Takes Hard Line against Beijing during the Pandemic," *New York Times*, May 2, 2020, A8.

3. Compare the detailed contending arguments and data in Øystein Tunsjø, *The Return of Bipolarity in World Politics: China, the United States, and Geostructural Realism* (New York: Columbia University Press, 2018), and Michael Beckley, *Unrivaled: Why America Will Remain the World's Sole Superpower* (Ithaca, NY: Cornell University Press, 2018).

4. Kenneth N. Waltz, *Theory of International Politics* (Reading, MA: Addison-Wesley, 1979), 161–63, 170–76; John J. Mearsheimer, *The Tragedy of Great Power Politics*, 2nd ed. (New York: W. W. Norton, 2014), 336–41, 344, 346, 356, 358–59; John J. Mearsheimer, "The Inevitable Rivalry: America, China, and the Tragedy of Great-Power Politics," *Foreign Affairs* 100, no. 6 (November/December 2021).

5. Geoffrey Blainey, *The Causes of War*, 3rd ed. (New York: Free Press, 1988), 109–14, 122.

6. Robert Gilpin, *War and Change in World Politics* (New York: Cambridge University Press, 1981), chapter 5.

7. A different rendering is in Joseph S. Nye, "The 'Nye Report': Six Years Later," *International Relations of the Asia-Pacific* 1 (2001): 95–96.

8. Avery Goldstein, "US-China Rivalry in the Twenty-First Century: Déjà Vu and Cold War II," *China International Strategy Review* 2 (June 2020): 48–62.

9. The situation today is mixed because of the unique strategic problem NATO faces for defending its newest members, the Baltic states. NATO now enjoys overall theater-wide conventional military superiority in Europe, but the Baltics are geographically isolated from the alliance's main logistical lines, and they face local Russian military superiority. If NATO wants to stop a Russian invasion of these exposed members, the old NATO doctrine of threatening to resort to tactical nuclear weapons regains some appeal.

10. Thomas J. Christensen, "The Meaning of the Nuclear Evolution: China's Strategic Modernization and US-China Security Relations," *Journal of Strategic Studies* 35, no. 4 (August 2012): 451.

11. Glenn Snyder, "The Balance of Power and Balance of Terror," in *Balance of Power*, ed. Paul Seabury (San Francisco: Chandler, 1965), 185–201; Tunsjø, *Return of Bipolarity*, 127.

12. Richard K. Betts, *Nuclear Blackmail and Nuclear Balance* (Washington, DC: Brookings Institution, 1987), 54–62, 68–79.

13. Fiona S. Cunningham and M. Taylor Fravel, "Dangerous Confidence? Chinese Views on Nuclear Escalation," *International Security* 44, no. 2 (Fall 2019): 75–76.

14. James Samuel Johnson, "Chinese Evolving Approaches to Nuclear 'War-Fighting': An Emerging Intense US-China Security Dilemma and Threats to Crisis Stability in the Asia Pacific," *Asian Security* 15, no. 3 (2019): 219, 221, and passim; Christensen, "Meaning of the Nuclear Evolution," 475–76, 478, 480.

15. Caitlin Talmadge, "Would China Go Nuclear? Assessing the Risk of Chinese Nuclear Escalation in a Conventional War with the United States," *International Security* 41, no. 4 (Spring 2017); Christensen, "Meaning of the Nuclear Evolution," 453. On the general problem, see Barry R. Posen, *Inadvertent Nuclear War* (Ithaca, NY: Cornell University Press, 1991).

16. Christensen, "Meaning of the Nuclear Evolution," 452. The fact that Beijing and Washington restrained themselves in previous confrontations may make them "more likely to stumble into a dangerous crisis." Avery Goldstein, "First Things First: The Pressing Danger of Crisis Instability in US-China Relations," *International Security* 37, no. 4 (Spring 2013): 60.

17. The problem with GDP as a measure of power is that "a $100 million gulag shows up the same as a $100 million innovation center." Beckley, *Unrivaled*, 14–18.

18. Lyle J. Goldstein, *Meeting China Halfway* (Washington, DC: Georgetown University Press, 2019).

19. See Robert Kagan, *The Strongmen Strike Back*, policy brief (Washington, DC: Brookings Institution, March 2019).

20. For example, Tunsjø cites the PRC as seeking a revised regional security order (*Return of Bipolarity*, 134), while Johnston argues that it has accepted and acted within the existing Western economic and diplomatic order (Alastair Iain Johnston, "China in a World of Orders," *International Security* 44, no. 2 [Fall 2019]). Chinese commentators refer often to China's "soft power," although they seem to conceive it differently from the concept advanced by Joseph Nye. There is also an argument that moral leadership is a critical element of national power and that China has overtaken the United States in this. See Yan Xuetong, *Leadership and the Rise of Great Powers* (Princeton, NJ: Princeton University Press, 2019), 9–24.

21. Attributed to the RAND Corporation in Lyle J. Goldstein, "The Fate of the China-Russia Alliance," *The National Interest*, online ed., January 25, 2020.

22. Jared Kushner, quoted in Wong and Swanson, "Washington Takes Hard Line," A8.

23. Blainey, *Causes of War*, 144–45.

3

The United States and China: From Partners to Competitors in America's Eyes

Harry Harding

The normalization of US-China relations in 1979 offered the promise of a mutually beneficial relationship, based not only on the two nations' common security interest in opposing the rise of Soviet power in Asia and around the world but also on the commercial benefits that could be gained from the complementarities inherent in the sizes of their economies and their different levels of economic development. Nonetheless, the rapid accumulation of contentious issues, including Chinese arms exports to troubled regions, the two countries' growing bilateral trade imbalance, the United States' extensive residual relationship with Taiwan, and continuing American disappointment with China's human rights situation, meant that Sino-American ties remained tenuous.[1] Their fragile relationship was then severely disrupted by the Tiananmen Crisis of 1989, which led the United States to cut off economic aid, sever military-to-military relations, reduce the level of official contacts, and threaten to revoke China's most favored nation trade status. The latter threat was never carried out, due largely to resistance from the American business community and some of America's friends and allies, but only a few years later, in 1995–96, there was yet another crisis, resulting from Beijing's decision to fire missiles toward Taiwan in an attempt to influence the outcome of the island's first direct presidential election. Given the continuing American interest in Taiwan's security despite the termination of its mutual defense treaty with Taipei, the Taiwan Strait crisis demonstrated the possibility of a military confrontation between China and the United States, making the continued fragility of the relationship even more dangerous.

But the twin crises in Tiananmen Square and the Taiwan Strait did not lead to the collapse of the US-China relationship as many feared; instead they supported efforts to build more stable and cooperative ties. Although the collapse of the Soviet Union had eliminated the common security threat that had originally brought the two countries together, there were other compelling reasons to seek renewed cooperation. China's rapid economic growth meant that it would play a larger role both regionally and globally and would therefore be even more important for the United States than it had been as a card to be played in the final stage of the Cold War. For China, access to American capital, technology, markets, and institutions of higher education was essential to its ambitious program of economic development, structural reform, and scientific and technological modernization. And for the United States, China's "reform and opening" also revived the long-standing dream that China would eventually evolve in America's image, with a market economy and a democratic political system. For both governments, although each for its own reasons, the Sino-American relationship was too important to fail.

By the end of the 1990s, the United States had adopted a policy of "comprehensive engagement" with China, removing its restrictions on official dialogues and its narrow focus on human rights, and Beijing and Washington had formally agreed on the common goal of "building a constructive strategic partnership for the twenty-first century."[2] But despite that optimistic vision, the US-China relationship remained fraught, with none of the issues that had bedeviled the two countries resolved. By 2000, some Americans, including officials who would serve in the George W. Bush administration, had already concluded that a strategic partnership was unlikely and that the two countries would become strategic competitors. Yet today, almost three decades later, the two countries' interactions have become increasingly competitive and occasionally confrontational, characterized not only by continued contention over human rights, different political and economic systems, international security issues, and trade and investment concerns but also a growing rivalry over the balance of power in Asia, a race to dominate the development of advanced technologies from artificial intelligence to 5G telecommunications, and the worrying possibility of a military conflict in both the Taiwan Strait and the South China Sea. Chinese and American observers now talk more about mutual mistrust than about mutual benefit, and the American policy of seeking "partnership" has been replaced by a new paradigm of "strategic competition." Analysts in both countries warn that they may be entering a "new cold war," and some warn of the possibility of a hot one.

This chapter addresses three questions about these disturbing developments. First, it will describe the earlier policy paradigm, most commonly called "engagement" in the United States, that the two countries followed from the mid-1990s to the mid-2010s in their attempts to build the more stable and cooperative relationship they jointly envisioned. Second, it will ask why this paradigm failed to achieve the hoped-for results, leading instead to Washington's adoption of a different, far more competitive paradigm. And finally, it will ask, What happens now? What blend of cooperation, competition, and confrontation lies ahead? Are the two countries doomed to a new cold war, or will their relationship evolve in some other direction?

The Engagement Paradigm

The Chinese and American efforts to build a cooperative relationship over the last thirty years have been variations on what have become familiar themes: continuous dialogue to narrow differences and identify common interests, efforts to promote greater economic and societal interdependence, enmeshing both countries in international regimes and institutions that could regulate their interactions and manage their disagreements, defining a shared aspirational vision for the future of their relationship, and forging positive personal relations among civil and military officials so as to increase mutual understanding and reduce mistrust. Over time, the term "engagement" also came to include these other strategies, becoming in essence an enduring policy paradigm that incorporated the assumptions, goals, and strategies that the United States had adopted for dealing with China.

Continuous Dialogue

Of these strategies, the earliest and most persistent has been the reestablishment of official negotiations and unofficial dialogues, suspended after the Tiananmen Crisis, and their use to address the full range of issues in the relationship rather than focusing solely on China's human rights record. The various official negotiations, Track II dialogues, academic conferences, scholarly exchanges, and policy conversations that were part of comprehensive engagement are far too numerous to list here. The most important of these dialogues have of course been the summit meetings of Chinese and American leaders, starting with the twin summits exchanged by Bill Clinton and Jiang Zemin in 1997 and 1998 and continuing up to the exchange of visits between Donald Trump and Xi Jinping in 2017 and 2019. These have been supplemented by meetings of the top Chinese and American leaders on the sidelines of multilateral conferences, especially the Asia-Pacific Economic Corporation (APEC) economic leaders' meetings and the annual meetings of the UN General Assembly, as well as visits by the two countries' ministers of foreign affairs and national security advisors and their equivalents. These have been the most important channels through which much of the work of trying to build a cooperative relationship has been conducted. These have been complemented by numerous meetings at the ministerial level as well as the series of "strategic dialogues" on security and economic issues held from 2006 to 2016 that usually brought together several relevant ministers from both countries, often also including the president of the country in which the meetings were held.

Some of these meetings have been more successful than others in terms of making progress in managing major issues, launching cooperative and mutually beneficial projects on secondary issues, or simply establishing a personal relationship between the leaders participating in them. But on balance their results have been disappointing, especially to Americans but most likely also to Chinese as well. The various dialogues and negotiations may have produced greater understanding of each government's position but have not led to the permanent resolution of the most sensitive issues in the relationship or even to mutually agreed statements of the differences between the two countries, as the visits of Secretary of State Henry Kissinger and President Richard Nixon in 1971 and 1972 were able to achieve in the form of the Shanghai Communiqué. The Trump administration's demand for a shift to "results-oriented" dialogues is perhaps the clearest statement of the American disappointment in this aspect of engagement.

Promoting Economic and Societal Interdependence

In addition to ongoing dialogue and negotiation, another important strategy within the engagement paradigm has been the deliberate promotion of deeper economic and societal interdependence between China and the United States, building on the complementarities between a large developed country and a large developing country. In some ways, that goal has been extremely successful, given the growth in trade, investment, and societal ties that has occurred from the late 1970s at least until the recent trade war. But the broader consequences of interdependence have proven quite different, and less positive, than was expected.

The promotion of interdependence as a way of building a broader cooperative relationship reflected the assumption that social and economic interdependence would yield mutually beneficial outcomes that would increase support for the relationship from powerful stakeholders in both countries and thereby reduce the likelihood of war. But while interdependence may reduce the chances of war, it cannot eliminate them altogether, as both world wars in the twentieth century illustrated.[3] And even short of war, interdependence can create its own issues, particularly if it leads to unequal outcomes within and between the interdependent partners, as the previous tensions between the United States and Japan and the current tensions between the United States and China have shown. In recent decades, the United States has faced severe domestic problems such as stagnant wages, growing inequality, and economic insecurity, which have been attributed not only to domestic imbalances or the impersonal forces of globalization and technological change but also to an allegedly rapacious foreign actor, in this case China, which lured US-based companies to outsource their production at the expense of millions of American jobs.

In addition to these domestic grievances, one country in a notionally win-win relationship may believe it is benefiting less than the other. That has also been the fate of the interdependence between the United States and China. At a time when China is rising and America is declining, at least in relative terms, many American policy analysts and political leaders have blamed this on the lack of reciprocity in the relationship, charging that China has had more favorable access to the United States for its exports and investments than the United States has enjoyed in China. At an earlier stage a nonreciprocal relationship may have been acceptable, given the differences in level of development between the two countries. But over time, as China's economy rose and American incomes stagnated, the nonreciprocal and competitive aspects of their economic interaction caused considerable resentment in the United States and ultimately became politically unsustainable. As some cynical observers put it, what China calls a win-win relationship with the United States actually means "China wins twice."[4]

Nor has China's growing interdependence with the United States produced the more democratic China many Americans hoped for, at least by the common American definition of that word. To be sure, Chinese society is freer in many ways than it was in the 1990s, and the Chinese leadership is increasingly responsive to the material desires of its people, but China has not yet allowed the liberalization of its political and civic spheres, let alone the fully competitive elections that are so important to Americans. The assumption that interdependence would yield such results may never have been realistic, but it was part of the rationale given by the Clinton administration for China's admission to the World Trade Organization (WTO), which, it said, would provide further impetus to a democratic transition in China.[5] Many analysts outside the administration similarly believed that the pressures for democratization would increase as Chinese became wealthier and were more exposed to liberal values through their interactions with the West. These overly optimistic forecasts about domestic change in China were reinforced by the global wave of democratization during the latter part of the twentieth century and by the belief that the collapse of Soviet-style state socialism marked the "end of history": the conclusion of any serious debate over the most effective forms of political and economic institutions. The emergence of the Chinese models of governance that some call "consultative authoritarianism" or "meritocratic authoritarianism"[6] show that history has not ended but rather that ideological competition continues but with significantly different content.

Creating Mechanisms for Deeper Dialogue

Over time, the United States and China inaugurated additional mechanisms for dialogue to address the unresolved bilateral issues that interdependence was producing. The most ambitious of these was the Strategic Economic Dialogue (SED) launched during the second George W. Bush administration.[7] The SED was intended to identify and address not only the structural impediments to trade and investment but also the domestic imbalances in each country that were the underlying causes of their trade issues: that China invested too much and consumed too little while the United States saved too little, consumed too much, and raised insufficient tax revenues relative to government spending.[8] These imbalances not only produced serious and potentially unsustainable domestic consequences, including industrial overcapacity and nonperforming loans in China and burgeoning government budget deficits in the United States, but were also correlated with the two countries' trade imbalances, both globally and with each other. But while the SED identified and analyzed these structural issues at a very high level, it could not solve them, for solutions required difficult political decisions in both countries. While both took some steps to remedy their domestic imbalances—the United States to reduce government spending and China to increase domestic demand as shares of GDP—they have not been able to completely remove the structural factors that produced their trade imbalances.

Although the SED and its direct successors, the "senior dialogue" on security and the subsequent Strategic and Economic Dialogue (S&ED), were ended by the Trump administration in 2017, other channels of negotiation continued, including the "comprehensive dialogue" launched by presidents Trump and Xi after their meeting at Mar-a-Lago in April 2017, which also led to some progress in managing specific economic issues. But the results of dialogue came to be seen in Washington as unsatisfying relative to the time and effort involved. The Trump administration's insistence on results-oriented negotiations, as opposed to what it regarded as protracted and inconclusive dialogue for its own sake, reflected that frustration. As a result, since the onset of the trade war, the United States has suspended much of its official dialogue with China except on trade issues, and unofficial discussions between the two countries have also become far less frequent, especially as visas from both countries have become more difficult to obtain and the COVID pandemic has, until recently, made travel nearly impossible. A few virtual discussions and online conferences continue, but the channels for dialogue have become greatly attenuated. Nonetheless, the US State Department continues to see dialogue as an important means for achieving its now more modest vision for the relationship. While abandoning the references to "cooperation" and "partnership" from earlier years, it still asserts that "the United States seeks a constructive, results-oriented relationship with China" and that, "in addition to regular discussions between senior US officials and their Chinese counterparts, the United States uses a range of exchanges, dialogues, and people-to-people ties to pursue its goals."[9]

Integrating China into a Rules-Based International Order

Nor has another component of the engagement paradigm, integrating China into what the United States increasingly redescribes as a "rules-based international order," been the panacea that some expected. With American support, China has become a full participant in the postwar international system, with membership in virtually all international regimes and organizations. The most important example of this aspect of American China policy was Washington's support for China's accession to the World Trade Organization in 2001, albeit on strict "commercial" terms rather than on the more lenient "political" terms offered to other emerging economies. But even as China has joined the international order, it has questioned some of its norms and the distribution of power within it and has sought to reshape both to its own benefit. It understandably wants to be a rule maker rather than simply the rule taker that the United States envisioned. It also follows some rules more faithfully than others, gaming the system to its own advantage. It flatly rejected the ruling of an international tribunal that Beijing lacked a valid right to the rocks and reefs it claimed in the South China Sea and that China's construction of housing and other facilities on them did not transform them into habitable islands under international law. China has sought leadership positions in major international organizations, from Interpol to the World Health Organization to the World Intellectual Property Organization, which the United States has increasingly resisted.

In addition to seeking greater influence in existing international institutions, Beijing has also led or supported the establishment of new ones, especially to fill what are arguably gaps in the international order. It sponsored the creation of a new international financial institution, the Asian Infrastructure Investment Bank (AIIB), to help finance its Belt and Road Initiative (BRI), which the United States actively although futilely obstructed, and has promoted the Regional Comprehensive Economic Partnership (RCEP), a loose regional free trade agreement that, although led by the Association of Southeast Asian Nations (ASEAN), is seen by Beijing as an alternative to the more demanding Trans-Pacific Partnership that had been negotiated by the Obama administration but rejected by the Trump administration.

In addition to undertaking these institutional initiatives, China has challenged some of the intellectual assumptions on which the neoliberal economic order has been based, especially its faith in markets, private ownership, and free trade, instead advocating a greater role for state ownership and government interventions. Some have called this more mercantilist approach the Chinese Model or the Beijing Consensus, in contrast to the Washington Consensus. Given China's success in lifting millions of its citizens out of poverty and developing a modern technological and military base, its model has become increasingly attractive to emerging economies around the world.[10]

In response to some of these trends, the George W. Bush administration challenged China to become not simply a participant but what then deputy secretary of state Robert Zoellick called a "responsible stakeholder" in the international system,[11] a formula that Beijing rejected on the grounds that Washington should not have the right to define "responsible" behavior and then judge China's performance according to that definition. China also accused the United States of trying to use these international norms and institutions to contain China and prevent its rise. The Obama administration subsequently complained that Beijing had been a "free rider" in the international system, and, more recently, the Trump administration described it as a "revisionist" power, even if no longer a revolutionary one, trying to modify or undermine parts of the rules-based international order.

Defining an Aspirational Vision for the Relationship

The search for an aspirational formula to guide the relationship, a strategy especially favored by the Chinese, has been particularly frustrating. This strategy recalls China's efforts to secure agreement on basic principles at the beginning of any negotiation, as described in the classic analyses of Chinese negotiating behavior by Richard Solomon and Lucian Pye.[12] It is also reminiscent of the traditional Chinese concept of the "Rectification of Names," whereby assigning a name to a phenomenon serves not only to describe its present reality but also to shape its future evolution. But the aspirational formulas the two countries have proposed, even the ones they have agreed to, have not been able to establish a clear direction for the relationship, if only because Beijing and Washington have differed over the definition of the relationships they envisioned.

The first of these aspirational formulas, the construction of a "constructive strategic partnership," as agreed by Jiang Zemin and Bill Clinton, illustrated this problem.[13] To some observers in both the United States and Asia, it sounded too much like a military alliance, in part because of their understanding of the term "strategic." The subsequent idea of a G-2, advanced by C. Fred Bergsten shortly after the Asian financial crisis but never formally adopted by the United States, envisioned a greater role for China and the US-China relationship than either country, let alone the rest of Asia, was prepared to accept.[14] And the "new type of major power relationship," advocated by Xi Jinping in 2013, foundered on a key component: the premise that each country would agree to respect what the other defined as its core interests. Many American analysts viewed this formula as a blank check by which Beijing could announce more ambitious core interests as its power grew and then demand American deference.[15]

To the extent that the two countries could agree on an aspirational formula, they became more guarded, less ambitious, and more platitudinous over time, usually consisting only of strings of adjectives to describe the desired relationship. During the George W. Bush administration, the two countries agreed on the desirability of a "constructive, cooperative, and candid" relationship, thereby acknowledging both the hope for cooperation and the reality of growing differences ("candid" being a standard diplomatic euphemism for open disagreement in official discussions).[16] During the Obama administration, the formula changed slightly to the promotion of a "positive, constructive, and comprehensive" relationship, thus replacing "cooperative" with the more cautious "positive," but removing "candid" altogether. The Biden administration described the relationship in mixed terms, with Secretary of State Antony Blinken summarizing American policy toward China as one in which "we would cooperate where we could, compete where should, and confront where we must."[17] The main problem with the long search for common aspirational formulas was that while they may have embodied a positive vision for the US-China relationship, they did not specify how to get there. They communicated good intentions to both domestic and international audiences and to the leaders and publics of the other society, but they could not in themselves create common interests or define cooperative strategies where they did not exist. It was for this reason that the Qinghua University international relations scholar Yan Xuetong has called aspirational formulas little more than expressions of "superficial friendship" that have been able neither to promote cooperation nor to reduce mistrust.[18] Others have dismissed them as bumper stickers that carry little more than rhetorical value.

The Emergence of Strategic Competition as an Alternative Paradigm

The policy of seeking a primarily cooperative relationship with China was never completely accepted in the United States. Almost immediately, American analysts and politicians concerned by the ideological and policy differences between the two countries and the dangers posed by the rise of a more powerful and ambitious China considered a constructive strategic partnership to be an unrealistic vision. By the time of the 2000 presidential election campaign, an alternative paradigm was introduced, that of strategic competition. David Shambaugh of George Washington University published an article in *Survival* under the title "Sino-American Strategic Relations: From Partners to Competitors,"[19] which was followed closely by an article in *Foreign Affairs* by Condoleezza

Rice, then George W. Bush's foreign policy advisor and later his national security advisor, in which she listed the issues on which China and the United States
had significant differences, including Taiwan, human rights, the South China
Sea, and, more generally, China's desire to "reduce or constrain the role of the
US in the Asia-Pacific region," and concluded that those issues made China "a
strategic competitor, not a strategic partner."[20]

Neither Rice nor Shambaugh laid out a comprehensive policy for conducting
that strategic competition. And importantly, both supported continued efforts
at cooperation. "Cooperation should be pursued," Rice declared, "but we should
never be afraid to confront Beijing when our interests collide." She reiterated
that argument eight years later in the same journal under the title, "Rethinking
the National Interest: Realism for a New World," where she described the US-
China relationship, in what was becoming an increasingly familiar formula, as
a combination of competition and cooperation, stressing the need to work with
Beijing in order to deal constructively with both global and regional problems.[21]

Nonetheless, Beijing was sufficiently concerned about the possibility that
the constructive strategic partnership might be replaced by a new paradigm of
strategic competition that it sought clarification from knowledgeable Americans. Li Zhaoxing's memoirs reveal that, as ambassador to the United States,
he visited George H. W. Bush during the campaign to ask about the phrase. The
senior Bush replied, "I know my son better than anyone else" and assured Li
that this was only campaign rhetoric and would be dropped after the election
because W. wanted a positive relationship with China.[22]

If so, the younger Bush must have surprised his father by continuing to use
the phrase after he was elected and inaugurated. But just as the 1995–96 crisis in
the Taiwan Strait led the Clinton administration to return to the engagement
policy with China that it had criticized during the campaign, so, too, did the
EP-3 incident in April 2001, in which a Chinese fighter collided with an American naval aircraft conducting reconnaissance off the coast of China, leading to
the loss of the Chinese pilot and forcing the American plane to make an unauthorized emergency landing on China's Hainan Island. Once again, the risk of
military confrontation led Washington to reassess and revise its more negative
China policy. Moreover, 9/11, at least momentarily, gave the two countries a
major common interest—combating international terrorism—that they had
lacked since the collapse of the Soviet Union. In an awkward about-face, then
secretary of state Colin Powell described the United States and China as "strategic competitors but economic partners," reviving the language of partnership
without completely repudiating the characterization of China as a strategic
competitor.[23] One could argue that this short-lived alternative had things backward; it would have been more realistic to portray the two countries as potential
strategic partners in addressing some major global issues, particularly terrorism

and the North Korean nuclear program, but to acknowledge that they were increasingly becoming economic competitors as the Chinese economy continued to advance. But the Powell formula implicitly anticipated what would later become a major policy issue in the Trump administration: How could countries that were strategic competitors nonetheless maintain a robust economic partnership, especially in sensitive areas? The Trump administration would eventually answer that question in the negative—they couldn't.

The Bush administration not only backed away from explicitly describing China as a strategic competitor but ultimately agreed with Beijing, as already noted, on a new but more modest and more realistic aspirational vision: the desirability of a "constructive, cooperative, and candid" relationship.[24] Nevertheless, other aspects of its Asia policy suggested that the Bush administration continued to regard China as a strategic competitor even if it no longer said so. In the past, the main American security objective in Asia had been to prevent any other country or coalition from achieving hegemony in the region. The Bush administration went one step further by implying that the American goal should be to achieve and maintain that status for itself and to discourage any other party from seeking to become a peer competitor that could challenge American dominance in the region. If the engagement paradigm had been based on liberal conceptions of international relations, the Bush administration had clearly moved in a realist direction, as Condoleezza Rice's articles indicated. But with more specific regard to China policy the shift from cooperation to competition was not yet complete. Instead, as the articles by Shambaugh and Rice both implied, the Bush administration adopted an intermediate position between those two paradigms, describing a mixed relationship that combined elements of the older cooperative framework with aspects of the emerging competitive paradigm.

Trying to Save Engagement through Mutual Reassurance and Personal Relationships

The continued deterioration of US-China relations as the differences between the two countries increased was well recognized and produced growing concern in both countries. The problem was mainly defined as misunderstanding and mistrust, and a new set of engagement strategies was adopted to deal with both problems. The Obama administration's China policy moved along two tracks. In addition to agreeing with Beijing on yet another aspirational formula in 2009—striving for a future relationship that would be "positive, constructive, and comprehensive," thus removing both of the more extreme terms, "cooperative" and "candid," from the previous administration's version[25]—the United States also utilized additional channels for dialogue, including military-to-military exchanges, to promote greater transparency about capabilities and offer official reassurances about intentions. President Obama also placed special emphasis on building close personal relationships with his two Chinese counterparts, first Hu Jintao and then Xi Jinping, although apparently without much success, since neither Chinese leader was willing or able to depart from prepared talking points and engage in the free-flowing and honest exchange of views that Obama had hoped for. Also, some Chinese came to see the American efforts to increase transparency between two unequal military establishments as stratagems by which the stronger would try to intimidate the weaker by revealing its own strength and exposing the other's weaknesses.

Despite the president's best efforts, one Chinese analyst would later privately describe Obama as a "false friend," because his professions of friendship ran counter to the concrete policies his administration had adopted toward China. This description was almost certainly a reference to the second track of Obama's approach to China, which was to guard against the possibility that efforts to promote cooperation would fail by adopting a policy variously described as "hedging," "pivoting" to Asia, or "rebalancing" American military and diplomatic resources by moving them from what were now seen as lower-priority regions (such as the Middle East and Southwest Asia) to regions that deserved greater attention (especially the Asia-Pacific region).

In other words, the Obama administration's policies were walking on two legs—a combination of reassurance and resolve that was an understandable response to a complex situation but which was also almost certainly interpreted by the Chinese more as threat than reconciliation.[26] It was not surprising, therefore, that the attempts to restore mutual confidence were unsuccessful. Building or restoring trust in international relations requires concrete changes in policy that are more costly and therefore more meaningful than verbal assurances alone.[27] And neither China nor the United States was willing to pay a high enough price to convince the other of its benign intentions. Neither was willing to "meet the other halfway," as Lyle Goldstein proposed,[28] let alone completely eliminate the factors that had produced disagreement and mistrust. Their attempts to restore mutual confidence did not lead the United States to drop its residual security commitment to Taiwan, endorse unification, or completely set aside human rights as an issue in the US-China relationship. Nor did they lead China to adopt democratic values and institutions, adopt a less mercantilist trade and investment policy, or halt China's militarization of the South China Sea. In short, each side's expectations of the other remained largely unfulfilled.

Questioning Engagement

By 2015 the growing frustration in the United States with the unsatisfying results of the engagement paradigm led to what David Lampton described as a "tipping point" in American policy toward China.[29] While there was no single factor producing that shift toward pessimism—nothing comparable to the way in which the Tiananmen Crisis of 1989 caused a sudden and dramatic deterioration in American perceptions of China—the accumulation of frustrations and resentments produced, in the run-up to the 2016 presidential election, a widespread conclusion in the US policy community that America's China policy had failed and that it was time for a change, with most commentators advocating a tougher policy toward Beijing.[30] Donald Trump emphatically endorsed such views both during his election campaign and after his inauguration, not only in his harsh rhetoric about China but also in his implication that engagement had not been sufficiently results-oriented. Still, the Trump administration made a last effort to revitalize important elements of the engagement policy. Trump's meeting with Xi Jinping at Trump's Florida club, Mar-a-Lago, in April 2017 represented his attempt, like those of his predecessors, to build a warm personal relationship with his Chinese counterpart. After the meeting, Trump declared that he "liked" Xi and predicted that, while he had gotten "nothing, absolutely nothing" from Xi so far, "long-term, we are going to have a very, very great relationship and I look very much forward to it."[31] For at least a year thereafter, until the outbreak of the COVID pandemic, Trump would continue to lavish praise on Xi Jinping as his "friend." And, as already noted, the Mar-a-Lago summit also launched a new series of high-level dialogues to resolve outstanding trade issues—Trump's highest priority—but with the caveat that Washington expected "results" and not simply an exchange of views that would produce better understanding of positions without a narrowing of differences.

The failure of those dialogues to yield what Washington regarded as an adequate resolution of the bilateral trade issues resulted in Trump's decision in July 2018 to obtain a more "reciprocal" relationship with China by levying a total of $550 billion in tariffs, in several rounds, on Chinese imports, restricting Chinese investments in the United States, tightening controls on the export of advanced technology to China, and sanctioning Chinese firms alleged to have threatened US security. The tough Chinese response to these American measures—generally to impose tit-for-tat retaliatory measures, including $185 billion in tariffs on American goods[32]—pushed the relationship away from efforts at cooperation toward a blend of competition and confrontation.

The Adoption of the Competitive Paradigm

The full shift from a cooperative paradigm to a competitive one was also reflected in the Trump administration's reconceptualization of both the post–Cold War world in general and the US-China relationship in particular as dominated by competition rather than collaboration. In an important opinion essay in May 2017, then national security advisor H. R. McMaster and Gary Cohn, at the time the director of the National Economic Council, described the international order that had emerged after the Cold War not as the "global community" envisioned by liberals, with common norms and values that could provide the basis for cooperation, but as the realists' portrait of an "arena where nations, nongovernmental actors and businesses engage and compete for advantage."[33] As for US-China relations more specifically, one of the most revealing presentations of the change in American policy was given in a presentation by Matt Pottinger at a Washington, DC, event in October 2018 marking the sixty-ninth anniversary of the founding of the People's Republic of China. Pottinger, then the member of the National Security Council responsible for China policy and soon to become deputy national security advisor, declared that the Trump administration had "updated [America's] China policy to bring the concept of competition to the forefront." He went on to explain:

> To us this was really an example of what Confucius called "rectification of names" . . . In the *Analects*, Confucius said that "if names cannot be correct, then language is not in accordance with the truth of things; and if language is not in accordance with the truth of things, affairs cannot be carried on to success." And of course I think it's evident to everyone that the United States and China are engaging at some level in competition. To avoid acknowledgment of this fact would be to court misunderstanding and to invite miscalculation. So we've in some sense rectified the framing of our policy to reflect the reality of an evolution in our relationship.[34]

Other documents, especially the National Security Strategy issued in December 2017, elaborated on these themes by warning of countries that "challenge American power, influence, and interests, attempting to erode American security and prosperity," and that "control information and data to repress their societies and expand their influence."[35] Later, such countries, which were said to include Iran and North Korea but especially Russia and China, would be described more succinctly as "revisionist powers" against whom America's more competitive policy should be directed. The details of the new competitive American policy toward Beijing were then laid out in a comprehensive statement on China policy in May 2020, far broader and more specific than anything produced during the G. W. Bush administration, when the United States was beginning to view China as a strategic competitor. The document indicated that the United States now saw its relationship with China as a global competition, conducted in many geographic areas, covering many issues, and presumably persisting over a protracted period of time, that would require the United States to adopt a "whole-of-government" approach in response.[36] Moreover, this and other documents suggested that the US government worried that the balance of power in that competition had shifted in China's favor—a trend that was almost certainly exacerbated later by the continuing increase in China's military expenditures, the COIVID-19 pandemic and the fumbling US response to it, and further signs that the Trump administration was alienating some of its friends and allies by backing away from multinational institutions and earlier international agreements. It is no surprise, therefore, that the 2018 National Security Strategy was subtitled "Sharpening the American Military's Competitive Edge," implying that it had become blunted over time and that a more recent report to Congress by the Indo-Pacific Command, originally titled "Maintain the Advantage," was retitled "Regain the Advantage."[37]

These reports were followed by a coordinated series of speeches in 2020 by senior Trump administration officials—National Security Advisor Robert O'Brien, FBI director Christopher Wray, Secretary of Defense Mark Esper, Attorney General William Barr, and Secretary of State Mike Pompeo—who not only laid out a lengthy bill of particulars about a range of Chinese policies and behaviors but also defined America's rival not as "China" but as the Chinese Communist Party (CCP). Although intended to distinguish between the Chinese people, who were to be portrayed positively, and those who governed them, this formulation was widely seen, especially in China, as a call for regime change and certainly represented a major escalation of the dispute far beyond a trade war, a competition over technology, or even a strategic rivalry.

Just as there was controversy in the United States over its policy of seeking a strategic partnership with China, so, too, has there been a debate over the wisdom of the newer policy of strategic competition. Some analysts and former officials still call for the revival of engagement, describing it as the consensus policy that previous administrations may have criticized but to which they always returned. But they appear to be a shrinking minority. Some question not whether the relationship has become competitive but whether a new paradigm should portray China as a "competitor" (presumably on some issues), a "rival" (implying America's main competitor on all issues), an "adversary," or even an "enemy."[38] The Trump administration described China as an "adversary," posing a very serious, even existential threat to American interests, but not yet as an "enemy" (with whom a war is being waged).[39] By contrast, the Biden administration has consistently described China as a "competitor" and the relationship as "competition" (although with different modifiers such as "responsible competition," "managed competition," or, in Biden's own words, "extreme competition"). Other commentators ask whether this strategic competition will resemble the earlier Cold War with the Soviet Union, either as a model to be followed or a precedent to somehow be avoided.[40] But almost no one describes China as a potential "partner" any longer, except on a very limited range of issues. The paradigm shift in American China policy is therefore virtually complete.

What Went Wrong?

As we have seen, the rejection of engagement as the paradigm for American policy toward China was a response to problems with the specific elements of that broader policy. But there have been deeper structural issues as well. In fact, the question of why engagement failed seems easy to answer, if only because so many factors point in that direction and so many analysts have long predicted it. Ever since Thucydides offered his explanation of the Peloponnesian War in ancient Greece, scholars in the realist tradition have posited the dangers of an international power transition in which a previously dominant power faces an ambitious rising power that threatens to overtake and even supplant it. Although there is debate as to whether China and the United States have actually traded places yet, there is far more agreement that a power transition is underway, as indicated by China's rise in absolute terms, America's decline in relative terms, China's growing regional and global ambitions, and America's international retrenchment. As Harvard's Graham Allison has shown in his historical survey of power transitions, the relationship between the two countries in such a situation is likely to be difficult. Indeed, in his analysis, most power transitions have resulted in war, or at least in military preparations and confrontations that could have led to war.[41] Chinese and American efforts to build a more stable and cooperative relationship can therefore be interpreted as attempts to avoid another "Thucydides Trap," and, whatever the appropriateness of that analogy, officials and analysts in both countries have referred to it in their assessments of the US-China relationship.

Like others, Allison has identified a rare exception to this pattern that might have provided some reason for hope. The United States and Great Britain passed through their power transition relatively smoothly between the mid-nineteenth and mid-twentieth centuries, although not without discord and competition. Common values, a common language, and a successful partnership in two world wars, when both countries faced a severe common threat, made the difference. Unfortunately, the US-China relationship is not characterized by these rare favorable conditions. Their different values are seen in their contrasting definitions of human rights, with China focusing on economic and social rights and the United States emphasizing civil and political rights. Similarly, the value China places on harmony and order differs from the American celebration of pluralism and dissent. Chinese and English remain very different languages with different linguistic roots and many opportunities, as we have seen, for each country's policies and proposals to be misunderstood. Moreover, since the collapse of the Soviet Union, the two countries have been unable to identify a direct and imminent threat that could generate a closely coordinated response. They may agree that terrorism, climate change, and pandemics are common problems, but their differences over the strategies to deal with those issues and the allocation of the costs and benefits of doing so have obstructed cooperation, particularly in an atmosphere of mistrust.

The two countries also have different visions for the future of the international order. As we have seen, the Trump administration rejected the concept of an international community with common values and interests that can be governed by multinational institutions and norms and instead asserted that the world is an arena for international rivalry. In distinct contrast, the Biden administration has placed multilateral cooperation, international institutions, global governance, and the rules-based order at the top of its diplomatic agenda. Conversely, under Xi Jinping Beijing has replaced its earlier view of the international system as the arena for competition and confrontation between hegemonic and nonhegemonic powers with the concept of a global "community of common destiny." The ideational competition between cooperative and competitive views of international affairs therefore continues, but to some degree the two protagonists have switched sides, at least under their present leaders.

In addition, despite all the recent successes China has achieved through its integration into the existing international order, its historical narrative remains one of national humiliation by the United States and other imperial powers beginning in the nineteenth century. By comparison, America's narrative is one of reluctant engagement and then the creation of a benign hegemony after World War II that has inspired global admiration and gratitude. China's narrative of national humiliation provides a lens through which Chinese not only view their past but also interpret subsequent crises and problems in their relations with the United States. That narrative portrays an America that has consistently tried to negate Chinese values, foment instability, and block China's rise.[42] Conversely, the American narrative depicts a benevolent United States encountering an ungrateful China that constantly disappoints and denies America's contributions to China's development. Ongoing developments provide ample evidence to underscore the continued validity of those narratives.

Paradoxically, it is not just these differences between the two countries that complicate their relationship but also their similarities.[43] Both countries have adopted foreign policies that the Chinese scholar Yan Xuetong has characterized as "moral realism"—a competition for power, but one that is difficult to compromise because it is based on self-righteousness. Each country believes that its position is virtuous while insisting the other's is not. Both believe they are exceptional, although in different ways: Americans think their country is the exceptional embodiment of universal values; Chinese think their long history and unique culture shows that they can be an exception to those Western values whose universality they reject. Both countries think they are destined for international leadership and insist that their leadership will be accepted because their intentions are benign.

This paradoxical combination of similarities and differences, together with the shared frustration that the two countries have not been able to fully realize their hopes for the relationship, has made the vision of an essentially cooperative relationship based on equality and mutual respect extremely difficult, if not impossible, to achieve. In fact, if things had worked out differently, with differences managed and tensions avoided, the opposite question—Given their differences and the risks inherent in the power transition, why didn't the rise of China relative to the United States produce the competitive or confrontational relationship that so many had predicted?—would have been far more difficult to answer. In fact, it would have been seen as a triumph of diplomacy for which several Nobel Peace Prizes might have been awarded. Instead, the evolution of the US-China relationship since the mid-1990s can be interpreted as the kind of tragedy in which the protagonists struggle valiantly but futilely against an unavoidable fate, in this case an unwelcome outcome that many analysts, from different perspectives, have nonetheless regarded as inevitable.

What Happens Now?

What will be the future of this fraught relationship? Chinese analysts and officials have often asserted that there are only two possibilities, cooperation or confrontation—but they do not represent the only choices. There are, in fact, four possibilities: cooperation, coexistence, competition, and confrontation, with many variations within each. Of these, peaceful coexistence, as was advocated for the relationship between the United States and the Soviet Union during the Cold War and is supported by many Chinese analysts for China's relationship with the United States today, is actually unlikely. Coexistence implies two conditions: first, that each country will be indifferent to the other country's domestic systems, and second, that each country will accommodate to the other's core interests internationally. These conditions, intended to remove possible sources of conflict, will be hard for either country to accept. The mutual acceptance of each other's domestic arrangements will be difficult not simply because of America's claims to uphold the universal values that it sees China violating but also given that increasing numbers of Chinese and Americans live in the other country and more and more American companies are competing with Chinese firms in China's domestic market. How their companies and citizens will be treated in the other country will matter to both governments and to their publics as well. Coexistence might be possible if the two countries were mutually isolated, as was largely the case for the United States and the former Soviet Union, but that is not characteristic of their interdependent relationship today. Although further deterioration of US-China relations may cause some decoupling between the two countries, it is unlikely to go as far as to create the mutual indifference that peaceful coexistence would require.

Nor is it likely that either country will accept the other's core interests, as was originally proposed in the Chinese concept of a new type of major power relationship. Those core interests cross each other's red lines in too many places in the Asia-Pacific region, particularly in the Taiwan Strait and the South China Sea, and possibly on the Korean peninsula, as was evident in the past. They may increasingly cross each other in the rest of the world as well.

Alternatively, there may be some degree of Sino-American cooperation on specific issues, such as North Korea's nuclear program and the health of the global economy, and it will be important for the two countries to avoid falling into a rivalry that prevents the possibility of cooperation on such issues. But a comprehensive cooperative relationship—such as the strategic partnership the two countries once envisioned—remains unlikely for all the reasons that caused the search for it to fail. Only a common threat that both countries view as severe and imminent, and where cooperative responses can be agreed upon and adopted, could override these differences. So far, no conventional security threat or nonconventional security challenge has reached that level of severity. Even the COVID-19 pandemic has not produced the cooperation that many anticipated. Rather, there has been debate over the narratives describing the origins and evolution of the pandemic as well as competition over the search for diagnoses, vaccines, and treatments. The same appears true of climate change as well.

Conversely, confrontation on specific issues in the diplomatic, economic, and strategic spheres will continue to be part of the picture. These confrontations will be characterized by tests of strength (where one country tries to force the other to yield to its demands) and tests of capability (where one country denies resources to the other and challenges it to adapt or respond without retaliating or escalating). But escalation into military conflict is unlikely, largely because the two countries now have the capability for mutually assured physical destruction due to their nuclear capabilities. However, this reassuring statement is based only on an assessment of probabilities; as Allison and others have warned, the possibility of war by miscalculation or accident remains, and mutual assured destruction may be more able to deter nuclear war than conventional conflict. Moreover, maintaining mutual nuclear deterrence may engender an expensive and risky strategic competition, and even if it prevents direct military conflict between the two countries it may not prevent the emergence of proxy wars or grey-zone conflict, as was the case during the Cold War in countries ranging from Angola to Vietnam and more recently in Syria and Ukraine.

At the same time, the two countries have achieved a level of economic interdependence that threatens mutually assured economic destruction as well. There may be some decoupling of the two countries as their competition escalates, but a full decoupling would be extremely costly. Nonetheless, we should not forget that the two countries, also highly interdependent in the first half of the twentieth century, achieved nearly complete decoupling after the Communist revolution, such that, as Michel Oksenberg reminded us, before the US ping-pong team visited China in April 1971 in the early days of rapprochement, more Americans had set foot on the moon than had received the permission of the two governments to visit China. The issue is whether the level of interdependence today is sufficiently greater now than it was then so as to prevent that degree of decoupling from recurring.

If these assessments are correct, neither coexistence, cooperation, nor war will be the main characteristic of the relationship going forward. China and the United States may not be "destined for war," as some realists fear,[44] but neither will they be forced to cooperate, as some liberal analysts continue to hope. Instead, their relationship will primarily be competitive for the foreseeable future. We already see competition in a long list of arenas, including

- Ideas, particularly with regard to domestic political institutions, economic policies, development strategies, and historical narratives.
- Import and export markets.
- Advanced technologies, both civilian and military, and the creation of international technical standards that would favor the adoption of one country's technology over the other's.
- The establishment, reform, or control of major international regimes and institutions.
- Overseas aid and investment programs, such as China's BRI and America's new International Development Finance Corporation, which is also intended to finance infrastructure projects in emerging markets.
- Competition among nongovernmental actors, not only private or state corporations but increasingly academic institutions as well. Over time, perhaps this competition may come to involve Chinese and American civil society organizations operating abroad, espousing different values and different development strategies.

If wide-ranging competition seems nearly inevitable, the issue then becomes not how to prevent it but (as several chapters in this volume argue) how to *manage* it so that it does not produce purely zero-sum outcomes. As David Shambaugh also points out in chapter 14, competition is not inherently a bad thing. In fact, it is usually seen as positive and even essential in at least three areas: sports and comparable forms of human endeavor, economic markets, and pluralistic political systems. Competition in these arenas is believed to bring out the best in the competitors and therefore to achieve outcomes better than a noncompetitive environment. In these arenas competition is usually governed by rules that are intended to make the competition fair and constructive. But China and the United States may not always accept or honor those rules. And some of the arenas in which the United States and China are likely to compete have no rules, or they have rules that need to be updated to respond to new circumstances. Where there are rules, the two countries should abide by them. Where there are no rules, China and the United States will need to develop them, as in the areas of artificial intelligence and cybersecurity. Where the rules need to be updated, as may be the case with the WTO and international financial institutions, Beijing and Washington will have to agree on revisions. In all these areas, however, the two countries may find it difficult to reach consensus because of their increasingly competitive relationship.

Above all, the two countries should agree to limit the spread of competition from where it can be beneficial to where it will be costly and risky. This danger is clearest in the strategic realm, and one of the most neglected aspects of the US-China relationship is the possibility of arms control agreements on important weapons systems, whether nuclear, conventional, or nonconventional. This may be even more difficult for the United States and China than it was for the United States and the Soviet Union, whose military forces were more symmetrical. But the discussions need to begin.

The strategies the two sides have used in their attempt to create a cooperative relationship will continue to play a role in the new effort to manage a competitive one. Efforts to build trust, reduce misunderstanding, build personal relationships, and encourage interdependence will continue to be important parts of the picture. But China and the United States need to be more realistic about what they can accomplish and the conditions under which those accomplishments can be achieved. The overall aim should be to maximize the benefits of competition and minimize the costs and risks. The win-win cooperation both countries envisioned decades ago no longer describes the reality of their present relationship and is unlikely to be a feasible vision for their future relationship. Instead, peaceful competition, conducted fairly under mutually acceptable rules and resulting in positive-sum outcomes, may be the most plausible aspirational vision for their shared future.

Notes

1. Harry Harding, *A Fragile Relationship: The United States and China since 1972* (Washington, DC: Brookings Institution Press, 1992).

2. "Joint US-China Statement," October 29, 1998, https://1997-2001.state.gov/regions/eap/971029_usc_jtstmt.html.

3. Dale C. Copeland, *Economic Interdependence and War* (Princeton, NJ: Princeton University Press, 2014).

4. Rana Mitter and Elsbeth Johnson, "What the West Gets Wrong about China," *Harvard Business Review* 99, no. 33 (May–June 2021), 42–48. See also William P. Barr, "Remarks on China Policy," Gerald R. Ford Presidential Museum, July 16, 2020, Grand Rapids, MI.

5. This was one of the themes in a major speech in support of China's accession to the WTO given by President Clinton at Johns Hopkins University's School of Advanced International Studies. See "Full Text of Clinton's Speech on China Trade Bill," *New York Times,* March 9, 2000.

6. On consultative authoritarianism, see Jessica C. Teets, *Civil Society under Authoritarianism: The China Model* (Cambridge: Cambridge University Press, 2014). On meritocratic authoritarianism, see Daniel A. Bell, *The China Model: Political Meritocracy and the Limits of Democracy* (Princeton, NJ: Princeton University Press, 2015). See also Harry Harding, "Political Development in Post-Mao China," in *Modernizing China: Post-Mao Reform and Development*, ed. A. Doak Barnett and Ralph N. Clough (Boulder, CO: Westview Press, 1986), 13–37.

7. On the SED, see Henry M. Paulson Jr., *Dealing with China: An Insider Unmasks the New Economic Superpower* (New York: Twelve, 2015); and Thomas J. Christensen, *The China Challenge: Shaping the Choices of a Rising Power* (New York: W. W. Norton, 2015).

8. These imbalances are well analyzed in Stephan Roach, *Unbalanced: The Codependency of America and China* (New Haven, CT: Yale University Press, 2014).

9. Department of State, "Bilateral Relations Fact Sheet: U.S.-China Relations," accessed September 22, 2020, https://www.state.gov/.

10. These impressive achievements are often portrayed as the Chinese "economic miracle." On why that term is inappropriate, see Harry Harding, "Forty Years of Reform and Opening: From the 'Economic Miracle' to the 'Middle Income Trap,'" *Issues and Studies* 56, no. 1 (2020): 1–5.

11. Robert Zoellick, "Whither China? From Membership to Responsibility," remarks to the National Committee on US-China Relations, New York, September 21, 2005.

12. Lucian W. Pye, *Chinese Commercial Negotiating Style* (Cambridge, MA: Oelgeschlager, Gunn & Hain, 1982); and Richard H. Solomon, *Chinese Political Negotiating Behavior* (Santa Monica, CA: RAND Corporation, 1983).

13. Ministry of Foreign Affairs of the People's Republic of China, "China, U.S. Pledge to Build Constructive Strategic Partnership," accessed July 23, 2002, https://www.mfa.gov.cn/ce/ceus//eng/zmgx/zysj/zrjfm/t36212.htm.

14. C. Fred Bergsten, "A Partnership of Equals: How Washington Should Respond to China's Economic Challenge," *Foreign Affairs* 87, no. 4 (2008): 57–69.

15. David M. Lampton, "A New Type of Major-Power Relationship: Seeking a Durable Foundation for US-China Ties," *Asia Policy* 16 (2013): 51–68.

16. The phrase was used by Alan Holmer, the Treasury Department's envoy for the S&ED, as quoted in "US, China Should Build Up Cooperative, Constructive, Candid Relations," Xinhua News Agency, November 15, 2007, http://www.china.org.cn/international/opinion/2007-11/15/content_1231999.htm.

17. Blinken is quoted in Qi Ye, "Cooperation, Competition, or Confrontation?" *South China Morning Post,* July 15, 2021, https://www.scmp.com/presented/business/topics/international-trade/article/3140265/cooperation-competition-or.

18. Yan Xuetong, "The Instability of China–US Relations," *Chinese Journal of International Politics* 3, no. 3 (2010): 263–92.

19. David Shambaugh, "Sino-American Strategic Relations: From Partners to Competitors," *Survival* 42, no. 1 (2000): 97–115.

20. Condoleezza Rice, "Promoting the National Interest," *Foreign Affairs* 79, no. 1 (2000): 45–62. Condoleezza Rice, "Rethinking the National Interest: American Realism for a New World," *Foreign Affairs* (2008): 2–26.

21. Powell gave that description in his senate confirmation hearing; see "Confirmation Hearing by Secretary-Designate Colin L. Powell," January 17, 2001, https://2001-2009.state.gov/secretary/former/powell/remarks/2001/443.htm.

22. Zhaoxing Li, *Shuobujin de Waijiao* [Endless talk on diplomacy], (Beijing: CITIC Press Group, 2013).

23. "Secretary Colin L. Powell," interview on CCTV, Beijing, China, July 28, 2001, https://2001-2009.state.gov/secretary/former/powell/remarks/2001/4330.htm.

24. Bonnie S. Glaser, "Fleshing Out the Candid, Cooperative, and Constructive Relationship," *Comparative Connections* 4, no. 2 (July 2022), https://cc.pacforum.org/2002/07/fleshing-candid-cooperative-constructive-relationship/.

24. "Obama: US Has Positive, Constructive, Comprehensive Relationship with China," Xinhua, November 16, 2009, http://www.china.org.cn/world/obamas_asia_tour/2009-11/16/content_18897273.htm.

26. This was the approach that was later recommended by James Steinberg and Michael E. O'Hanlon in *Strategic Reassurance and Resolve: US-China Relations in the Twenty-First Century* (Princeton, NJ: Princeton University Press, 2014).

27. Andrew H. Kydd, *Trust and Mistrust in International Relations* (Princeton, NJ: Princeton University Press, 2007). A further study of the role of personal trust between national leaders by Nicholas J. Wheeler is more optimistic, concluding that personal trust increases the possibility that reassurances will be taken seriously but still reaffirming Kydd's insight that those reassurances must be costly to those providing them. See Wheeler, *Trusting Enemies: Interpersonal Relationships in International Conflict* (Oxford: Oxford University Press, 2018).

28. Lyle J. Goldstein, *Meeting China Halfway: How to Defuse the Emerging US-China Rivalry* (Washington, DC: Georgetown University Press, 2015).

29. David M. Lampton, "A Tipping Point in US-China Relations Is upon Us," *US-China Perception Monitor* 11 (2015).

30. See Harry Harding, "Has U.S. China Policy Failed?" *Washington Quarterly* 38, no. 3 (2015): 95–122.

31. Robert Delaney, "Trump Says He's Developed Friendship with Xi as First Day of US-China Summit Ends," *South China Morning Post*, April 7, 2017.

32. Dorcas Ong and Alexander Chipman Koty, "The US-China Trade War: A Timeline," *South China Morning Post*, updated August 25, 2020.

33. H. R. McMaster and Gary D. Cohn, "America First Doesn't Mean America Alone," *Wall Street Journal*, May 30, 2017.

34. Keegan Elmer, "US Tells China: We Want Competition . . . but Also Cooperation," *South China Morning Post*, October 1, 2018.

35. The White House, National Security Strategy of the United States of America, December 2017.

36. The White House, United States Strategic Approach to the People's Republic of China, May 2020.

37. National Defense Authorization Act (NDAA) of 2020, Section 1253 Assessment, "Regain the Advantage: U.S. Indo-Pacific Command's (USINDOPACOM) Investment Plan for Implementing the National Defense Strategy, Fiscal Years 2022–2026," Executive Summary.

38. Glaser, "Fleshing Out the Relationship."

39. For a summary of this terminological debate, see Paul Poast, "Competitors, Adversaries, or Enemies? Unpacking the Sino-American Relationship," War on the Rocks, October 14, 2020, https://warontherocks.com/2020/10/competitors-adversaries-or-enemies-unpacking -the-sino-american-relationship/.

40. The contributions to this debate include Hal Brands, "America's Cold Warriors Hold the Key to Handling China," Bloomberg, January 14, 2019; Melvyn P. Leffler, "China Isn't the Soviet Union. Confusing the Two Is Dangerous," *Atlantic*, December 2, 2019; and Walter Russell Mead, "Americans Aren't Ready for Cold War II," *Wall Street Journal*, June 10, 2019.

41. Graham Allison, *Destined for War: Can America and China Escape Thucydides's Trap?* (Boston: Houghton Mifflin Harcourt, 2017).

42. Zhen Wang, *Never Forget National Humiliation: Historical Memory in Chinese Politics and Foreign Relations* (New York: Columbia University Press, 2014).

43. Harry Harding, "Analyzing the U.S.-China Relationship: The Neglected Dimension," Distinguished Public Lecture, Rajaratnam School of International Studies, Nanyang Technological University, Singapore, April 20, 2015.

44. Allison, *Destined for War*; and John Mearsheimer, "Can China Rise Peacefully?" *National Interest* 25, no. 1 (2014): 1–40. Note, however, that neither Allison nor Mearsheimer argues that war between China and the United States is inevitable. Mearsheimer's pessimistic conclusion is that there is "considerable potential for war" between the two countries, and Allison's penultimate chapter is titled "Why War Is Not Inevitable." Still, both argue that war is highly likely and that it will take wise leadership on both sides to avoid military confrontations or, if they do occur, prevent them from escalating.

4

From Reluctant Cooperation to Assertive Competition: China's Reaction to US Strategic Pressure, 1979–2022

Wang Jisi

This chapter provides a historical account of the reaction of the People's Republic of China (PRC) to the strategic pressure of the United States since the two countries established diplomatic relations in 1979. In the early stage of their engagement during the four decades, the PRC was mainly a partner in cooperating with the United States to resist Soviet expansion in the world. After the end of the Cold War, however, China reinforced its strategy to oppose what it referred to as US hegemonism, and this strategy steadily evolved into a more comprehensive and deliberate approach to compete with the United States in global affairs.

In the whole period of China-US interaction from 1979 to 2022, China's strategic goals have been threefold—an integral combination of sovereignty, security, and development.[1] These three goals are also defined as China's core interests.[2] Sovereignty and security in China's context are largely overlapping.

The principle of sovereignty in the context of relations with the United States means preventing the United States from interfering in China's domestic politics or, more precisely, challenging the legitimacy and authority of the Communist Party of China (CPC) within the country. As former CPC general secretary Jiang Zemin put it, "We always insist on the Five Principles of Peaceful Coexistence in conducting international relations, especially noninterference of each other's domestic affairs, and oppose any form of hegemonism and power politics."[3] In the context of Chinese politics and foreign relations, sovereignty is an umbrella under which the CPC has the maximum right and power to rule the country and expel international intervention. As illustrated in the second part of this chapter, the PRC leadership has every reason to view the United States as the major and increasingly deadly menace to China's sovereignty.

The term "security" also carries special meanings in China. National security affairs, by definition, are led by the CPC instead of the government. In 2000, the Central Leading Group of National Security Work was founded, and its office was shared by the Central Leading Group of Foreign Affairs Work. From 2002 to 2012, then CPC general secretary Hu Jintao was the head of both Leading Groups. In November 2013, Xi Jinping announced the establishment of the National Security Commission of the Communist Party of China, of which he was the head. Xi put forward the "overall national security outlook" to cover the spheres of politics, territory, military, economy, culture, society, science and technology, information, ecology, and nuclear and natural resources. Xi emphasized in 2017 that "safeguarding national political security, especially security of the political power and system, should be put in the first place."[4] In 2018, Xi further stressed the need to "strengthen the CPC Central Committee's centralized and unified leadership over foreign affairs work."[5] Xi called for "insisting on the CPC's absolute leadership in national security work."[6] The current security and diplomatic issues between China and the United States, including those related to the South China Sea, Taiwan, and external military relations, should be seen in light of their connection with China's political security rather than simply as "national security" issues, as they are treated in the West.

Similarly, other geostrategic considerations, such as those related to Russia (after the disintegration of the Soviet Union), Yugoslavia (before its disintegration), Cuba, Venezuela, Zimbabwe, and North Korea, largely depend on their attitudes toward the United States and their political/ideological affinity with China. China's relations with developing countries at large have been driven partially by the expectation that they may side with China in fending off US and Western pressures on human rights debates.

"Development" as a core interest in contemporary China refers mainly to economic growth and prosperity. From China's decision to embark on reform and opening-up in 1979 until the beginning of the Trump administration's "trade war" with China in 2018, China's economic development depended increasingly on the American market, capital, and technology. For many years, Chinese leaders defined economic cooperation as the "ballast" and "propeller" in the overall China-US relationship.[7]

Meanwhile, China-US business ties and technological cooperation have functioned as a double-edged sword. On one hand, China has benefited enormously from US trade, investment, Treasury bonds, science and technology, and humanities exchanges. On the other hand, the deeper and broader China-US engagement goes in these areas, the more incompatibility the two sides may find in each other's political systems, values, and culture (including business culture). The PRC leadership fears that the United States is using bilateral cooperation as leverage to yield political and strategic concessions from China, and the United States sees the augmented Chinese presence in American society as a means to take advantage of American benevolence and influence its internal politics. A combination of nationalism and populism in both China and America has further diminished their mutual trust. To this extent, the decoupling of China-US engagement starting from 2017 should be seen as an unavoidable trend, not simply as a result of the Trump administration's action against China.

To put it simply, two fundamental drivers in the last four decades have moved China steadily onto a road of strategic competition with the United States. The first driver is concentration and consolidation of the power of the CPC, which has been challenged by the United States. Ever since the founding of the PRC in 1949, preserving the leadership of the CPC has been China's central goal in defending its sovereignty and security, and China's economic growth in large measure has served this goal as well. With China reaching out to the global economy and for global influence, strategic competition with the United States has to go outside of China and its peripheries to cover the whole world.

The second driver is the increase of the material power, in particular economic and military power, that the PRC has been accumulating in cooperating and competing with America. In 1979, China's GDP accounted for only 6.8 percent of America's; in 2021, China's GDP reached about 70 percent of America's. This progress was made possible by maintaining a stable relationship with America characterized by a combination of cooperation and competition. A head-on confrontation with the United States, the world's most powerful country, would disrupt the long haul of "realizing the great rejuvenation of the Chinese nation."[8] Chinese leaders have been very conscious of the power gap still existing between the two countries and the need to cooperate with America for China's modernization.

This chapter will first give a brief description of the historical evolution of the China-US strategic relationship. It will then examine, in some detail, the developments in political, security, international, economic, and technological fields. Finally, it will present a future outlook on China-US strategic competition.

Three Historical Stages

China-US relations between 1979 and 2022 may be divided into three stages. In the first stage, from 1979 to the Tiananmen storm in June 1989, the ties between Beijing and Washington were basically maintained by extrinsic values, namely, the common strategic grounds to counterweigh Soviet activities in international affairs and Vietnam's occupation of Cambodia that was seen as an extension of the Soviet expansion. Neither Beijing nor Washington gave much consideration to the other side's domestic politics, and there was little sense of strategic competition between the two countries.

Beijing's major concern about the United States at this stage was the potential risk of a definite tilt toward Washington in world affairs resulting in reduced bargaining power and maneuverability. Meanwhile, China's reform and opening led its leaders and elites to reevaluate Sino-Soviet ideological debates and military tensions in the Cold War era. In the 1980s, continuous domestic campaigns against what Deng Xiaoping called "bourgeois liberalization," which brought the purge of General Secretary Hu Yaobang in 1987, was reminiscent of Mao Zedong's warning of "peaceful evolution" toward capitalism. This domestic trend, together with the weakening of the Soviet Union and Western support of the Solidarity movement in Poland, had sown the seed of China-US political tensions that grew in later years.

In the second stage, after Tiananmen and before the US financial crisis in 2008, the key word of China's strategy toward the United States was "stability."[9] The three crises—Lee Teng-hui's US visit in 1995, NATO's bombing of China's embassy in Belgrade in 1999, and the Hainan Island incident in 2001 in which a Chinese jet fighter collided with a US surveillance aircraft—disrupted stability and triggered political and intellectual debates in China about US policy only temporarily. In November 2003, US Secretary of State Colin Powell and former Chinese vice premier Qian Qichen declared on the same platform that the bilateral relationship was in the best shape in history, and Qian added that it could and should be even better.[10] Bilateral economic cooperation grew rapidly after China's entry into the World Trade Organization (WTO) in 2001. The 9/11 tragedy in the same year provided new grounds to coordinate Chinese and US strategies. North Korea's nuclear program and its first nuclear test in 2006 gave rise to another common strategic objective.

On the domestic front, the CPC under the leadership of Hu Jintao put forward in 2004 the target of building up a "harmonious socialist society," which marked a drastic departure from Mao's theory of class struggle. Furthermore, to be consistent with the idea of "harmonious society" at home, Hu Jintao advocated in 2005 the construction of a "harmonious world," which contrasted sharply with the principle of fighting against "hegemonism and power politics," code words for US preponderance and behavior in world politics.[11] "Peaceful rise," or its variation, "peaceful development," became the motto of Chinese foreign policy in the mid-2000s. A white paper titled "China's Peaceful Development Road" was published in December 2005.[12]

In the third stage, from 2009 to 2022, two developments twisted China's attitude toward the United States and sharpened the consciousness of strategic competition, although the very concept of "competition" (*jingzheng*) is not usually applied in China's official statements. First, the 2008 financial storm wounded the US economy severely, whereas China recovered quickly from the turbulence. Then, in 2010, China's GDP surpassed that of Japan, making the PRC the second-largest economy in the world. This news boosted Chinese self-esteem immensely. The discourse of G2 and "Chimerica" became fashionable in China.[13]

In late 2010 and early 2011, Beijing indicated a subtle change in its foreign policy tone, which was not officially pronounced but was widely known to Chinese foreign affairs officials and specialists. The new guiding principle in China's foreign policy, especially pertinent to China-US relations, was defined as "persisting in keeping a low profile, and proactively making a difference."[14] This change of tone was based on the reassessment of the power balance between China and the United States tilting toward China, hence the more proactive Chinese behavior in global affairs in later years.

After Xi Jinping became the top leader of China in 2012, the emphasis in its foreign policy philosophy was further altered to reflect Xi's call for "maintaining a fighting spirit and strengthening the ability to struggle."[15] Since the Nineteenth CPC National Congress in 2017, in all of the four dimensions of China-US interaction described below, China's approach to the United States has been highlighted by a strengthened resolve of fighting against U.S policies and actions. The PRC's official line has encouraged nationalistic sentiments and triumphalism in social media unfavorable to the United States and discouraged people from voicing modest views. *Global Times* and other media acclaim China's "wolf warrior diplomacy," named after the 2015 patriotic action film and its 2017 sequel.[16] Those who are openly critical of such a diplomatic style run the risk of being attacked as traitors.

After Joe Biden assumed office in the White House in January 2021, despite frequent spats, the China-US relationship witnessed relative tranquility as compared to the drastic downward spirals between 2018 and 2020. Still overshadowed by the COVID-19 pandemic, Beijing and Washington were nonetheless able to hold several meaningful high-level talks, including a virtual meeting between President Xi Jinping and President Biden on November 16, 2021. Biden's virtual Summit for Democracy in December 2021 was obviously aimed at taking initiatives to "bolster democracy" around the world at the expense of China's expanding political influences. Partly in response to Western powers' joint efforts to isolate China, the CPC organized several international events to promote China's "whole-process people's democracy" and reveal the faults and pitfalls of Western democratization. The ongoing propaganda war between the two countries will probably intensify rather than subside in the coming years.

Safeguarding the CPC Leadership

China's struggles to prevent US interference in its internal affairs in defense of the leadership role of the CPC can be highlighted by thirteen episodes during the four decades.[17]

The Hu Na Incident

Hu Na was a teenage female tennis player who sought political asylum while attending a tournament in the United States in 1982, and her application was approved by the Reagan administration. It was the first incident of this kind known to the public after the normalization of China-US relations. The Chinese government reacted strongly, accusing intelligence officers from Taiwan and some malignant American individuals of inducing the young Chinese to defect.[18] The Chinese viewed this as a calculated political conspiracy to insult the PRC.[19]

US Support for the Dalai Lama in the 1980s

The Dalai Lama and his exiled community overseas made steady efforts in the 1980s to gain international support. In June 1987, the US House of Representatives adopted a bill that condemned "human rights violations"in Tibet.[20] A few days after the Dalai Lama gave a speech to Congress, Lhasa, the capital city of Tibet, witnessed the first riot in many years aimed at realizing Tibet independence. In 1989, after the Tiananmen incident, the Dalai Lama was awarded the Nobel Peace Prize. The PRC government indignantly denounced the US backing of the Dalai Lama and his cause as "rude political blackmail against China."[21] It is worth noting that Hu Jintao was the Communist Party secretary in Tibet from 1988 to 1992. Reportedly, Hu personally commanded the resolute measures to crack down on the riots in Lhasa, which won him the credit of being chosen as a member of the top leadership and becoming the general secretary of the CPC in 2002, ten years after his career in Tibet.[22] It should also be noted that martial law was declared in Lhasa in March 1989, two months prior to martial law being declared in Beijing, which triggered the Tiananmen tragedy.

The Tiananmen Incident in 1989

In what was first defined as a "political turmoil" and later as the "counterrevolutionary rebellion" in Beijing from April to June 1989, the CPC concluded that the United States and other Western countries were involved in staging the incident.[23] On July 2, 1989, the de facto paramount leader Deng Xiaoping told Brent Scowcroft and Lawrence Eagleburger, two special envoys sent clandestinely by President George H. W. Bush to Beijing, "This was an earthshaking event and it is very unfortunate that the United States is too deeply involved in it."[24] Beijing suspended or canceled a number of academic exchange and military programs with the United States. Meanwhile, Deng cautioned against radical reaction and called for China to "keep a low profile" in coping with US sanctions.[25]

Falun Gong

On April 25, 1999, more than ten thousand Falun Gong practitioners gathered around Zhongnanhai in Beijing, demanding official recognition of what was later referred to as an "evil cult." The sudden event was followed by an unforgiving cracking down on the movement and a lengthy ideological campaign against it. The US House of Representatives passed a resolution in November 1999 demanding that the PRC government "stop persecuting Falun Gong practitioners."[26] The PRC government was angered by the US position.[27]

The 2008 Lhasa Riots

The riot in Lhasa on March 14, 2008, was seen by the PRC as the result of the United States' long-term support and encouragement of the Tibetan separatists living overseas. President Hu Jintao denounced the Dalai Lama's "activities aimed at splitting the motherland" and sabotaging the upcoming Beijing Olympic Games.[28] Well before the Lhasa riot, in October 2007, the US Congress had bestowed its highest civilian honor on the Dalai Lama. President Barack Obama met with the Dalai Lama in the White House in February 2010.

The 2009 Xinjiang Riots

A series of violent riots starting on July 5, 2009, broke out in Urumqi, the capital city of Xinjiang. Beijing charged that the riots were planned and organized from abroad by the World Uyghur Congress (WUC) and its leader, Rebiya Kadeer, who lived in America. Beijing was convinced that Washington had been a "black hand" behind the Xinjiang riots.[29]

Liu Xiaobo and "Charter 08"

Liu Xiaobo, a dissident intellectual in Beijing, publicized an article on websites overseas in October 2008 titled "Charter 08," which demanded Western-type democratization in China and gathered 303 Chinese individuals to sign it. He was detained in December 2008 and sentenced in December 2009 to eleven years in prison.[30] In October 2010, Liu Xiaobo was awarded a Nobel Peace Prize. The US House of Representatives congratulated Liu and called on China to release him from jail. It is widely believed in China that US Secretary of State Hillary Clinton, among other American politicians, pushed the Norwegian Nobel Committee to award the prize to Liu.

The Google Incident in 2010

In January 2010, Google announced that the company had uncovered "attacks and surveillance" in China "to further limit free speech on the web" and that it was "discussing with the Chinese government the basis on which it could operate an unfiltered search engine within the law." Hillary Clinton stepped into the debate by expressing serious concerns.[31] In February, Google linked up with the US National Security Agency to look further into the origins of cyberattacks in China.[32] China's officials and media alleged that Google was closely associated with US intelligence agencies to wage a cyberwar against China.[33]

Wang Lijun's Defection and Chen Guangcheng's Entry into the US Embassy in 2012

On February 6, 2012, Wang Lijun, Chongqing's deputy mayor and former police chief, entered the US Consulate General in Chengdu for fear of being chased and persecuted by his boss, Bo Xilai, Chongqing's party secretary and a politburo member of the CPC Central Committee. The US side soon sent Wang back to Beijing to be prosecuted.

In late April 2012, Chen Guangcheng, a blind lawyer who was known in the West as a political dissident, was permitted to stay in the US embassy in Beijing for six days and finally flew to America, ostensibly to attend a law school. The incidents of Wang Lijun and Chen Guangcheng revealed how the US government could touch a nerve in China's internal politics and, in Wang's case, a very high-level political struggle inside the CPC.

The Occupy Central Movement in Hong Kong in 2014

A series of street protests, often called the Occupy Central movement or Umbrella Revolution, occurred in Hong Kong from September to December 2014. The movement began after Beijing issued a decision regarding proposed reforms to the Hong Kong electoral system. President Obama said in November 2014 that Washington would "encourage that the elections that take place in Hong Kong are transparent and fair and reflective of the opinions of people there."[34] The Chinese government condemned the US position of paying sympathy to the Hong Kong protesters.[35]

US Congressional Acts Related to Tibet in 2018–20

On December 20, 2018, President Trump enacted the Reciprocal Access to Tibet Act, which requires the State Department to punish Chinese officials who bar American officials, journalists, and other citizens from going freely to Tibetan areas in China. As expected, the Chinese Foreign Ministry reprimanded these acts.[36]

US Reproach over China's Management of Xinjiang in 2019

US human rights groups charged in 2019 that China had engaged in the arbitrary detention, surveillance, and torture of Uyghurs and other Muslim minorities and that Chinese authorities had detained at least one million people in camps in the Xinjiang region. The US House of Representatives overwhelmingly approved the Uyghur Human Rights Policy Act of 2019 on December 4, 2019, which required the Trump administration to toughen its response to China's crackdown on the unrest in Xinjiang. These US decisions drew swift condemnation from Beijing.[37]

The United States "Instigating" the Political Storm in Hong Kong in 2019–20

In February 2019, the government of the Hong Kong Special Administrative Region (HKSAR) proposed the Fugitive Offenders amendment bill. The bill would have allowed the extradition of wanted criminal fugitives to territories with which Hong Kong did not currently have extradition agreements, including the Chinese mainland and Taiwan. The proposal triggered a series of protests in Hong Kong. The Trump administration and US Congress quickly made announcements to deprecate the Hong Kong government's actions. The 2019 Hong Kong Human Rights and Democracy Act (HKHRDA), signed by President Trump, authorized sanctions on PRC and Hong Kong officials who were known to have committed "human rights abuses."[38] In response, the Chinese government on December 2, 2019, decided to suspend reviewing requests of US military vessels and aircraft to visit Hong Kong and impose sanctions on nongovernmental organizations (NGOs) that played an "egregious role" in Hong Kong.[39]

Trend of China-US Political Battles and Pattern in China's Reponses

In addition to the thirteen episodes discussed above, there were numerous political happenings in China that involved the United States in such areas as religious freedom, human rights, and intelligence work. The above account evidently indicates an intensification of political battles between the two countries in the last decade.

A four-pronged pattern can be identified in China's responses to US interference in its internal affairs. First, all of these cases involved a PRC citizen or citizens who were in one way or another encouraged and supported by the United States (with the exception of the case of Wang Lijun).[40] These citizens were branded as America's "stooges" and "political tools" colliding with anti-China forces in the United States. Second, none of these cases were seen in China as accidental or isolated. Rather, all of them were, in Chinese eyes, part of an integrated US strategy to westernize (*xihua*) and split up (*fenhua*) China and prevent it from rising into a greater power. Third, the PRC government and official media would not openly recognize the distinctions between the US executive branch, Congress, the media, and NGOs. American institutions and individuals were viewed as reinforcing each other in well-planned, well-organized, and ill-intentioned actions against China. Fourth, the reactions to US interference were not confined to rhetorical protests only but included measures to take tighter control over relevant people and information exchange at home and abroad.

The vigilance against US challenges to the CPC's legitimacy, popularity, and authority inside China has contributed to a comprehensive, long-term strategy to safeguard the CPC leadership. This strategy in the last decade has manifested itself in the passing and enforcing of a number of laws like the Counterespionage Law (2014), the State Security Law (2015), the Law on the Administration of Activities of Overseas Nongovernmental Organizations within the Territory of China (2016), the National Intelligence Law (2017), and the Cyber Security Law (2017). These laws have allegedly restricted and affected Americans' and other foreigners' activities in China, including Hong Kong. China has also greatly strengthened its political education and propaganda work. Increased Chinese "political influence activities" in the United States have caused American concerns about the United States' own domestic politics and security.

In sum, the last four decades have witnessed the growth of China's defensiveness of its domestic stability into deliberate and effective efforts to fend off US political and ideological influences. These efforts are expected to be more aggressive and serve as part of the strategic competition between China and the United States on the global stage.

National Security Concerns

This part of the chapter recounts issues of China's national security concerns that are not directly related to the PRC leadership's domestic authority or China's economic development but have bearings on China-US relations. These issues include Taiwan as well as territorial disputes in the South China Sea (SCS) and East China Sea (ECS).

The Taiwan Issue

The PRC always refers to the "three communiques" as the guidance for China-US relations. The third communique, also known as the Joint Communique on Arms Sales to Taiwan, was issued on August 17, 1982. In this document, the United States declared that it would not pursue a policy of "two Chinas" or "one China, one Taiwan." The US government made a commitment in this communique to "reduce gradually its sales of arms to Taiwan, leading over a period of time to a final resolution."[41] The two governments, however, had different interpretations of this commitment. Washington insisted that the reduction and ending of its arms sales to Taiwan were conditioned on China's peaceful intentions to solve the Taiwan issue. Since the August 17 communique of 1982,

US arms sales and other forms of military relations with Taiwan have triggered numerous disputes and crises between the two countries.

In 1995, Taiwan's leader Lee Teng-hui was issued a US visa to visit Cornell University, his alma mater, where he gave a political speech that irritated the PRC. In reaction, China conducted three consecutive military exercises near Taiwan. Washington sent two aircraft carrier battle groups to the area to "monitor Chinese military actions." The US military action reminded many in China that Washington remained the foremost obstacle to reunifying Taiwan. The event augmented the United States' status as China's foremost adversary and justified China's adopting a hostile policy toward the United States.[42]

However, the moderation of US policy toward Taiwan after the 9/11 tragedy in 2001 defused a possible conflict when Taiwanese leader Chen Shui-bian unfolded some proindependence plans. President George W. Bush opposed "any unilateral decision by either China or Taiwan to change the status quo," and Bush's warning seemed intended partly to thank Beijing for its crucial cooperation in defusing the North Korea nuclear crisis.[43]

During the Ma Ying-jeou administration in Taiwan between 2008 and 2016, the US role in cross-strait relations was not protruding. Beijing's attitude toward Taipei hardened again after 2016 when Democratic Progressive Party (DPP) leader Tsai Ing-wen took power and was reelected in 2020. President-elect Trump received a phone call from Tsai in December 2016 to congratulate his being elected.

Although Trump did not seem to be particularly friendly to Taiwan, his China policy team took a number of actions restating the Six Assurances given to Taiwan by the Ronald Reagan administration and threatening to revoke the third China-US communique.[44] The Taiwan Travel Act was signed into law by President Trump on March 16, 2018. This allowed high-level officials of the United States to visit Taiwan, and vice versa. More than a dozen other Taiwan-related bills have been introduced in Congress since then. The Biden administration has encouraged a number of former high-ranking US officials to visit Taiwan, including former chairman of the US Joint Chiefs of Staff Mike Mullen's tour to Taipei in March 2022. In the same month, Mike Pompeo, who served the Trump administration as secretary of state, proposed in Taipei that the United States should diplomatically recognize Taiwan as "a free and sovereign country."[45] These tours and statements, accompanied by Washington's increased military support to Taiwan, have further convinced Beijing of the United States' intentions to prevent China from achieving national reunification.

Looking back at the history of the Taiwan issue in overall China-US ties since 1979, both Beijing and Washington initially pushed aside their differences over the status of Taiwan in the interest of larger strategic concerns. Again, when Washington was preoccupied with the war on terror after 9/11, the two sides managed the issue cautiously. But the amended mutual understanding between Beijing and Washington over the Taiwan issue proved to be short-lived.

Two considerations, both related to the United States, have driven China to be increasingly assertive and impatient toward Taiwan. First, with the growth of China's economic leverage and military superiority over Taiwan, the mainland has gradually become more confident, hoping that Taipei will "yield surrender" to the PRC. Second, the mainland Chinese have noticed a change in the identity of Taiwanese people, especially the younger generation, which has much less attachment to China. President Xi Jinping's statement to the effect that the Taiwan issue cannot be allowed to fester indefinitely may reinforce the notion in some circles that the only way to get Taiwan back to China is by using armed force.[46] The Taiwan issue has definitely added a strong catalyst in China-US strategic competition.

National Security and Territorial Disputes

After the military face-off between China and the United States over the Taiwan Strait in 1995 and 1996, both sides stepped up their military activities vis-à-vis each other. While China's defense capabilities were evidently bolstered, more frequent US reconnaissance around China's coastal areas resulted in bitter quarrels.

On April 1, 2001, a US Navy EP-3 surveillance plane collided with a Chinese jet fighter above China's claimed two-hundred-mile exclusive economic zone (EEZ). The EP-3 made an emergency landing at Lingshui Airfield on Hainan Island. China detained the twenty-four-member US crew. After a tense stand-off, China released the crew and returned the aircraft, and President George W. Bush expressed regret over the death of a Chinese pilot and the landing of the US plane.[47] The aftermath of the EP-3 incident was a series of Chinese retributions and strong reactions to US military presence in the SCS. In an apparent fallout from the incident, in May 2001 China barred a US warship from visiting Hong Kong.[48]

China always insisted on resolving disputes with Southeast Asian countries in the SCS through bilateral negotiations, initially with individual countries only and now including China-ASEAN dialogues. The United States is regarded as an outsider that has no right to meddle with these negotiations. Tensions in the SCS started to build up in 2009 and escalated after 2012. It was widely believed in China that it was the Obama administration's "Asia-Pacific rebalance strategy" that accelerated the tensions and made the issue more complicated.[49]

The China-US arguments on maritime issues soon extended to issues of the East China Sea (ECS). In November 2013, China declared the establishment of the East China Sea air defense identification zone (ADIZ). A press release marked the zone's outer boundaries some two hundred nautical miles beyond China's

territorial sea, which created overlaps with existing ADIZs of Japan, South Korea, and Taiwan. The United States criticized Beijing's declaration as a "destabilizing attempt to alter the status quo."[50]

In January 2013, the Philippine government initiated an arbitration case
against the PRC allegedly in accordance with the dispute settlement provisions
of the United Nations Convention on the Law of the Sea (UNCLOS). Beijing
refused to participate in the arbitration process and completely rejected the
decisions of the tribunal by the Permanent Court of Arbitration (PCA) in The
Hague.[51] It was a strong view in Beijing that the entire process and ruling were
created and manipulated by the United States.[52]

Meanwhile, the United States continued to conduct "freedom of navigation"
(FON) operations in the SCS. In 2013, China launched reclamation projects on
its controlled Nansha (Spratly) Islands. China rapidly turned eight low-lying
reefs and rocks into artificial inlands. The United States refused to recognize the
legitimacy of these island reclamations. Both countries dispatched warships to
this area to challenge each other's position.[53] After President Trump took office
in early 2017, the frequency of US FON exercises seemed to be higher.[54]

In Chinese eyes, the Biden administration's Indo-Pacific strategy is more
ominous than that carried out by the Trump administration. State councilor
and foreign minister Wang Yi commented in March 2022 that the Indo-Pacific
strategy "ha[d] brought no gospel but a scourge disturbing regional peace and
stability." He referred to the strategy as a combination of "five, four, three, and
two," meaning the Five Eyes alliance (the United States, the United Kingdom,
Canada, Australia, and New Zealand), Quad (the United States, Japan, Australia,
and India), AUKUS (Australia, the United Kingdom, and the United States), and
the bilateral military alliances.[55]

Geopolitical Strategy around the World

After the normalization of China-US relations and until the late 1980s, the
PRC's geopolitical thinking was dominated by concerns of the Soviet Union's
expansion in the world, including the expansion of Vietnam, viewed in Beijing as a Soviet "pawn," in Indochina. China attacked Vietnam as a "self-defense
counter-attack"[56] in February 1979, seeking to "teach a lesson" to Hanoi.[57] This
war erupted one month after China and America established diplomatic relations. The two countries coordinated policies toward the Soviet Union, Indochina, Afghanistan, and other international issues.

In the 1980s, the mutual hostility between China and the USSR steadily
abated. The ideological struggle with the Soviets, which had seemed irreconcil-
able in the Mao Zedong years, became increasingly irrelevant. Meanwhile, the
balance of power in the PRC-US-USSR strategic triangle shifted in favor of the
United States after Ronald Reagan assumed office in the White House in 1981.

The Twelfth National Congress of the CPC, held in September 1982, announced the "independence foreign policy of peace," which distanced China's position away from the United States. In June 1985, Deng Xiaoping said at an internal meeting, "In view of the threat of Soviet hegemonism, over the years we formed a strategic line of defense—a line stretching from Japan to Europe to the United States. Now we have altered our strategy, and this represents a major change."[58] The China-Soviet rapprochement culminated with a summit between Deng Xiaoping and the Soviet leader Mikhail Gorbachev in Beijing in May 1989. A month later, the Tiananmen incident precipitated China-US relations into a grave crisis.

The collapse of the Soviet Communist Party, plus the post-Tiananmen Western sanctions on China, aggravated the Chinese fear of "peaceful evolution" that might bring about drastic political transformation at home. With increased worries, Beijing saw the United States assert itself aggressively in both Asia and Europe. The US-Japan decision in 1996 to revise defense guidelines, which would subsequently allow Japan to assist the United States in a Korean peninsula or Taiwan Strait contingency, alarmed the Chinese.

In the mid-1990s, China forged its security relationship with Russia by supporting Russia's Chechnya war. The China-Yugoslavia alignment was crystallized in the 1990s as both countries came under fire from the West for their refusal to grant more independence to autonomous regions under their control and for alleged human rights abuses toward minority communities. Chinese support for Slobodan Milošević, Yugoslavia's president, became especially prominent and substantial during the 1999 NATO bombings of Kosovo. Noting that the United States was reinforcing its global supremacy by the war in Kosovo, Beijing and Moscow joined hands in harshly criticizing the United States and NATO.

The NATO missile attack on the Chinese embassy in Belgrade on May 8, 1999, was a devastating blow to the China-US relationship. A wave of anti-American protests spread across China. The attack tapped into a deep vein of anti-Western, anti-American sentiment in China dating back a hundred years earlier, when the Eight-Power Allied Forces occupied Beijing in 1900 during the Boxer Uprising. Chinese people viewed the attack as yet another humiliation imposed by the Americans.[59] In an open address to the nation broadcast by China Central Television (CCTV) on May 10, 1999, the PRC's vice president Hu Jintao called the embassy bombing a "criminal," "brutal," "barbaric act" that "violate[d] international law and the norms of international relations."[60]

Despite the Clinton administration's apologies and interpretation that the NATO bombing was an unintentional "terrible mistake,"[61] the mainstream thinking in China was dominated by conspiracy theories. The tragedy triggered serious debates among China's political elites regarding the nature of US foreign policy in general and US policy toward China in particular.[62]

Founded in June 2001, the Shanghai Cooperation Organization (SCO), from a Chinese perspective, has functioned as a forum to strengthen confidence and neighborly relations among member countries. One of the primary objectives from the beginning has been to promote cooperation on security-related issues, especially combating the "three evils" of terrorism, separatism, and extremism.[63] Meanwhile, the SCO was also expected to be a shield against possible "color revolutions" instigated by the United States.[64]

Although China in principle backed the US war on terror after the 9/11 tragedy and did not try to obstruct US invasions of Afghanistan and Iraq, America's counterterrorism efforts were viewed in Beijing as a means to expand US spheres of interest around the world. Another aspect of the war on terror that China noticed as particularly dangerous was the US strategy of preemption, which entailed using force to respond to an imminent threat that might be seen from China. In addition, the war on terror was linked to the US advocacy of "regime change," and this policy tied in quite well with the wider Western export of liberal democracy and human rights worldwide. The regime change policy and US support for the Arab Spring in 2011 in the eyes of the Chinese could be traced back to the Cold War strategy of peaceful evolution.[65]

In the post–Cold War era, China's policies toward other countries around the world have been heavily influenced by concerns that the United States may topple the governments that they denounce as despotic rulers. These countries, such as North Korea, Cuba, Venezuela, Zimbabwe, and Iran, are essentially "anti-American" in their foreign policy orientation.

Beijing's apprehensions about Washington's regime change strategy were vividly manifested in the Chinese attitude toward North Korea. Despite Beijing's opposition to North Korea's nuclear weapon development, the CPC still regarded the Democratic People's Republic of Korea (DPRK) as a socialist country and called the North Korean leaders "comrades."[66]

Cuba is recognized by China as the only "socialist country" outside of Asia.[67] The China-Cuba relationship has been officially described as one of "good friends, good brothers, and good comrades" and has remained so under the leadership of Fidel Castro's successor and brother Raul Castro.[68]

China's relationship with Venezuela has also been very special. Venezuela has made the ideal trade and investment partner for Beijing. Politically, former Venezuelan president Hugo Chávez openly declared, "I have been very Maoist all my life."[69] Since Nicolas Maduro's rise to power in 2013, China has been carrying the burden of Venezuela's economic collapse as that country's biggest creditor.[70]

Over Robert Mugabe's thirty-seven-year rule in Zimbabwe, Chinese support for him never wavered despite considerable international pressure. After the death of Mugabe, President Xi Jinping said China had "lost an old friend and a good friend" and wanted to foster cooperation with Zimbabwe.[71]

With regard to Iran, the PRC was at times careful in its deals with the Islamic Republic of Iran while simultaneously trying not to antagonize China's relationship with the United States or its growing relations with Israel.[72] However, Beijing was more open in its sympathy toward Tehran when tensions arose in both Iran-US and China-US relations in recent years.[73]

On top of strengthening relations with the foreign governments that the United States loathes, China has rapidly escalated its strategic cooperation with Russia under Vladimir Putin. In an interview with Russia's state TASS news agency, Xi said, "I have had closer interactions with President Putin than with any other foreign colleagues. He is my best and bosom friend. I cherish dearly our deep friendship."[74] Since the 2010s, China and Russia have been enjoying close partnership militarily, economically, politically, and culturally.[75] China, Russia, and Iran held a series of unprecedented joint naval drills between them, which took place in the Indian Ocean and the Sea of Oman in December 2019.[76] In February 2022, Putin went to Beijing to attend the Winter Olympics and met with Xi Jinping. On February 4, Beijing and Moscow signed a significant joint statement, which declared that they "oppose[d] further expansion of NATO and urge[d] NATO to discard its Cold-War ideology."[77] Soon after, the Russia-Ukraine war broke out. Beijing blamed NATO's expansion as the original cause of the conflict and showed great sympathy with Moscow. Chinese and Russian foreign ministers expressed determination for stronger ties at a meeting on March 30, 2022, and reiterated that "China-Russia cooperation has no limits."[78]

In sum, the past forty-three years, between 1979 and 2022, have witnessed a gradual transformation of China's approach to the United States, from cooperation against Soviet expansionism to limited coordination in coping with issues like international terrorism and North Korea's nuclear menace, and finally to a series of robust and extensive challenges to US-led alliances and arrangements.

Economic and Technological Engagement

Trade and economic cooperation had been frequently referred to by Chinese leaders as the stabilizer and the ballast in China-US relations until their trade war broke out in 2018.[79] In fact, the bilateral trade and economic interactions cannot be separated from politics and have also created bumps in the road of China-US ties since 1989.

The United States first granted China most favored nation (MFN) status in 1980, which made trading with China more attractive by lowering tariffs on goods imported to the United States. The status was subject to annual renewal. After the Tiananmen incident in June 1989, negotiating MFN status became a political football. Under pressure from Congress and American public opinion, President George H. W. Bush declared a series of sanctions including suspending economic aid and loans to China.

The dominant issue of China-US ties in 1990–94 was the linkage between China's human rights record and its MFN status. The annual renewal of China's MFN became a highly contentious political issue in the United States. The Chinese government gradually shifted from denial and silence over the Tiananmen "massacre" to a head-on approach, launching an intense media campaign on the human rights issue.

The linkage between China's MFN status and human rights record was a fruitless attempt. For the PRC to join the WTO, US congressional action was needed to grant permanent normal trade relations (PNTR) to China. China's MFN status was made permanent in December 2001 and China joined the WTO in the same year.

During the negotiations over China joining the WTO, a few cases concerning China's alleged stealing of US technology surfaced. The US-China Economic and Security Review Commission (USCC) was created in October 2000. The purpose of the USCC was to monitor, investigate, and report to Congress on the national security implications of the bilateral trade and economic relationship. The commission adopted a broad interpretation of national security in evaluating how the US-China relationship affected the state of US economic and security interests and influence in Asia.

Among other reports, the 2007 USCC Annual Report censured China for its commerce and trade policy as well as its lack of intellectual property rights (IPR) protection and calling China a threat to US security. In response, Beijing commented, "Turning a blind eye to China's political, economic, and social progress and achievements in other fields, the Commission clings to its biased position, grossly interferes in China's internal affairs and vilifies China. Their attempt to mislead public opinion and set obstacles for China-US extensive cooperation will lead nowhere."[80]

After China's entry into the WTO, the decline in US manufacturing jobs accelerated. In the same period, trade imbalance between the two partners soared. In 2006, the US trade deficit with China exceeded $350 billion and was the United States' largest bilateral trade deficit. In addition, the US side pointed to the undervaluation of the renminbi relative to the US dollar. To address those problems, China and the United States agreed to hold regular high-level talks about economic issues and other mutual concerns by establishing the Strategic and Economic Dialogue (S&ED), beginning in July 2009 and ending in June 2016.

The Trump administration terminated the S&ED. But in Xi Jinping's first meeting with Donald Trump at Palm Beach, Florida, in April 2017, the two leaders decided to conduct four high-level dialogues between the two governments. All of them—the diplomatic and security dialogue, the China-US Comprehensive Economic Dialogue, the social and people-to-people dialogue, and the dialogue on law enforcement and cybersecurity—were held between June and October 2017. However, there were no reported follow-ups after the four inaugural meetings. The one-hundred-day economic cooperation plan that Xi and Trump agreed on during their first meeting also came to naught.

To succeed the China-US Comprehensive Economic Dialogue, a new round of high-level China-US economic and trade consultation began in February 2018. China's vice premier Liu He led the Chinese delegation, and his counterparts were then US Trade Representative Robert Lighthizer and Treasury Secretary Steven Mnuchin. Until October 2019, thirteen rounds of consultation rotated in Beijing and Washington between the two sides. The end result was a Phase One economic and trade agreement formally signed on January 15, 2020, with Chinese vice premier Liu He and US president Donald Trump inking the papers in the White House.

This Phase One trade deal required structural reforms and other changes to China's economic and trade regime in the areas of intellectual property, technology transfer, agriculture, financial services, and currency and foreign exchange. The Phase One agreement also included a commitment by China that it would make substantial additional purchases of US goods and services in the coming years. Importantly, the agreement established a strong dispute resolution system that ensured prompt and effective implementation and enforcement. In return, the United States agreed to modify its Section 301 tariff actions in a significant way and was expected to withdraw at least some of the tariffs it had imposed on China after the trade war started in 2018.

China has not totally rejected these US dissatisfactions as illegitimate. On the one hand, many Chinese officials and analysts have admitted that making some of the US-requested changes in Chinese policies and practices would be beneficial to China as well, but these changes should be made at China's own pace and suiting its national conditions. On the other hand, the rise of nationalism and the consolidation of the power of the CPC in recent years have given impetus to more strenuous resistance to US pressure.

Meanwhile, economic issues are being politicized and securitized (in the sense of undergoing national security scrutiny). Both the Trump and Biden administrations took steps to restrict inbound Chinese investment and curb high-technology exports to China. Alarmed by the mounting technological competition from China, the Biden administration and many members of US Congress have called for more government intervention to bolster strategic sectors such as semiconductors, drones, and artificial intelligence. The United States has imposed extensive human rights–related sanctions on hundreds of Chinese individuals and entities. In response, the PRC has introduced laws and regulations related to national security and sanctioned a number of US officials and organizations that infringe on China's sovereign rights. The most serious and long-term struggles are waged in high-tech fields where Americans want to keep their edge and Chinese attempt to surpass them.

A few themes and points have been particularly assertive in China's official statements and media that bear strategic implications. First, it is widely believed that economic and trade frictions are only a manifestation of the geostrategic competition between the United States and China. America's true intentions were said to be containing China and maintaining US hegemony.[81]

Second, there has been increased awareness in China that economic and trade disputes with the United States are centered on rules and regimes in the Western-dominated international economic order. Since joining the WTO, China has been under increased Western reprimands on state-owned enterprises, subsidies to exported goods, and other forms of government intervention in the economy. From a political perspective, these requests must be rejected. As Xi Jinping insisted, "State-owned enterprises are an important material base and political base of socialism with Chinese characteristics, and are the backbone of socialist economy with Chinese characteristics."[82] The promotion and establishment of BRICS, the Belt and Road Initiative (BRI), and the Asian Infrastructure Investment Bank (AIIB), among other efforts, exemplify what kind of world order and economic rules China wants to promote and how China will compete with the West on international economic rules and regimes.

Third, China's economic success has given rise to stronger confidence in its development pattern, political system, and values. Now the CPC is proudly introducing its experiences abroad. As Xi Jinping stated in his report to the Nineteenth CPC National Congress, "The path, the theory, the system, and the culture of socialism with Chinese characteristics have kept developing, blazing a new trail for other developing countries to achieve modernization. It offers a new option for other countries and nations who want to speed up their development while preserving their independence; and it offers Chinese wisdom and a Chinese approach to solving the problems facing mankind."[83]

Fourth, China has drawn enough lessons in its history about the need to advance science and technology toward "making China a country of innovators."[84] A report by the Research Office of the State Council in 2008 complained that in the majority of industrial sectors core technologies had been controlled by foreign companies, and "with intensifying international competitions, core technologies cannot be bought with money."[85]

Fifth, a constant theme during the past four decades in Chinese publications and media discussing international economic affairs has been the "US dollar hegemony." The consensus in these discussions is that US superiority in global economics and politics is related to the domination of the US dollar in the global monetary system, and this domination should and will be rejected.[86] China's government officials have been more subtle in expressing their reservation about the US dollar's domination.[87]

In retrospect, since China's entry into the WTO, with increasing frictions over trade, investment, monetary, and technological issues, and with the upgrading of China's economic and technological prowess, Chinese leaders, businesspeople, and elites have developed a clearer realization that the difficulties in these areas are deep-rooted not only in the two nations' different economic interests but also in their respective political structures. Consequently, as long as China insists on "socialism with Chinese characteristics" (or what some Americans call "state capitalism") and refuses to make fundamental political changes, it must be prepared to engage in a long-term strategic competition with the United States.

Future Outlook for Strategic Competition with America

Considering the two drivers of China's relations with the US discussed at the outset of this chapter—resisting US political influences in order to strengthen the CPC leadership at home and seeking US cooperation to increase China's power—the following prospects may be discerned.

In the CPC's endless pursuit of authority and power, the United States is seen not only as the principal external political and ideological threat but also as a long-term internal challenge, as a percentage of Chinese intellectuals and citizens are allegedly "pro-American." Beijing will persistently carry out and defend its policies toward Hong Kong, Xinjiang, Tibet, and other domestic issues and tighten internal political control by traditional and new techniques. In foreign relations, Beijing will continue to support those countries that also resist US pressures and foster forces in both developing and developed countries that may be sympathetic to China.

The popular perception in China that US power has been steadily declining while China will soon succeed the United States as number one in the world has diminished the appeal of adhering to Deng Xiaoping's advocacy of keeping a low profile in the 1980s and 1990s. The consolidation of the CPC power will need stronger "spirit of struggle" and more triumphalism to boost people's confidence and loyalty. China's propaganda war with the United States will endure not only between the two countries but also worldwide. Chinese officials will be ready to talk to their US counterparts, but they are not going to make substantive compromises over sensitive bilateral issues.

Over Taiwan and territorial issues, a large-scale military engagement is unlikely, but saber-rattling and military pressures are certain to increase. In both China and the United States, their strategic relationship is increasingly seen as a zero-sum game driven by the "iron logic of power." In political and geostrategic arenas, China-US interaction will display intensifying competition.

The over five million ethnic Chinese currently living in America, including those who were born in mainland China after 1949, may face an identity problem as their loyalty and affinity may be in doubt when the two political entities are competing for their affiliation. The ethnic Chinese community in America is divided within itself when US politics is being polarized. This issue may surface in the next few years and become an irritant when China-US ties are strained.

In the areas of economics, nontraditional security, technology, and humanitarian exchanges, a new pattern of competition and cooperation may emerge. Economic and technological decoupling between China and America, an initiative taken by the United States in the Trump years, will persist. On one hand, bilateral trade and investment will likely diminish in volume. Student and cultural exchanges, joint scientific research, and tourism will not be restored to pre-2018 levels in the foreseeable future, partly because of the deteriorating political relations and partly due to the COVID-19 pandemic. The US government's sanctions of Chinese companies like Huawei and TikTok for national security reasons will further convince the Chinese of the necessity to speed up their independent innovation efforts and reduce dependence on US technology. Now there are more incentives to move Chinese production chains, trade, and investments back to China or to other countries and away from America. The BRI, which is Xi Jinping's signature venture, along with China's efforts to be more active and vocal in international institutions, will be met with US resistance.

On the other hand, the Chinese realize that a certain amount of trade and financial interaction with America is indispensable. It would be costly to try to replace American products from soybeans to Boeing aircraft, and keeping US Treasury bonds will continue to be normal practice. China will curry favor with US businesses to offset some US politicians' attempts to push them to leave China. For this and other reasons, the Chinese will conduct economic reforms in such areas as IPR, policy transparency, labor rights, government subsidies to export, and reciprocity in market access. The effectiveness of these reforms will help shape the contour of China-US economic ties. Meanwhile, competitions in cybersecurity and other areas related to national security will be increasingly intense.

Finally, China and the United States are expected to work together in climate change, environmental protection, public health, public security, drug trafficking, and other nontraditional security areas. However, these potential areas of cooperation are overshadowed by political disputes and public sentiments in both countries. Their quarrels over the origin of the COVID-19 virus do not bode well for policy coordination.

In every field of China-US interaction, there are ideational competitions going on in both countries as well as in the world—globalism versus nationalism, universal values versus parochial outlooks, progressive thinking versus fatalism, foresight versus shortsightedness, radicalism versus toleration, integration versus fragmentation, and democratic ideas versus absolutism. The future outlook for China-US strategic entanglement depends largely on the unfolding of these ideational competitions.

Beijing has consistently rejected the prospect of a "new cold war" and denounced what it refers to as the "Cold War mentality." If the Cold War between the Soviet Union and the United States was defined by geostrategic competition (not only bilaterally but also around the world), ideological rivalry, and an arms race then, a new cold war has already been taking shape between China and America. However, the current China-US contention is different from the Cold War in three dimensions. First, the economic development and technological advancement of the two countries are intertwined to such a degree that complete separation between the two economies and societies is impossible. Second, neither China nor the United States is capable of building up a bloc of countries against the other like the Soviet Bloc and the Western Bloc during the Cold War. Third, while the endgame of the Cold War involved the disintegration of the Soviet Bloc and the collapse of the Soviet Union itself, it is difficult to imagine the downfall of either the PRC or the United States in the foreseeable future.

The two giants are therefore likely to coexist for a long period of time, probably even longer than the forty-plus years of the Cold War. It is not so certain that the power balance between them will continue to tilt toward China, but it remains an important variable. Global political developments, particularly the disturbances in Eurasia, will make a strong impact. The more decisive variable in shaping the direction of China's US policy is Beijing's strategic choice contingent on its internal political transformation.

Notes

1. For a comprehensive discussion of China's grand strategy and its evolution, see Wang Jisi, "China's Search for a Grand Strategy: A Rising Great Power Finds Its Way," *Foreign Affairs* 90, no. 2 (2011): 68–79.

2. 习近平: 不要指望我们会吞下损害我国主权、安全、发展利益的苦果 [Xi Jinping: Don't expect us to swallow the bitter fruit that will harm our interests of sovereignty, security and development], *China National Radio*, July 1, 2016, http://www.cnr.cn/zgzb/jd95zn/zy/2016 0701/t20160701_522551506.shtml.

3. He Ping and Liu Siyang, '希望寄托在你们身上——江泽民总书记关怀青年一代纪事 ["The hope rests on you," Secretary General Jiang Zemin takes care of the younger generation], *People's Daily*, May 4, 1998.

4. 习近平: 要把维护国家政治安全特别是政权安全、制度安全放在第一位 [Xi Jinping: Safeguarding national political security especially regime security and system security should be put in the first place], *Xinhua*, January 13, 2017, http://www.globalview.cn/html/zhongguo /info_15774.html.

5. 习近平: 加强党中央对外事工作的集中统一领导，努力开创中国特色大国外交新局面 [Xi Jinping: Strengthening the CPC Central Committee's centralized and unified leadership

over foreign affairs work, and strive to create a new situation in the diplomacy of major countries with Chinese characteristics], *Renmin Ribao* [People's daily], May 16, 2018, http://cpc.people.com.cn/n1/2018/0516/c64094-29992657.html.

6. 习近平主持会议强调以总体国家安全观为指导，坚决维护国家核心和重大利益，政治局通过国家安全战略纲要，坚持中国共产党对国家安全工作绝对领导，坚持集中统一高效权威的领导体制 [Xi Jinping presided over the meeting and emphasized that a holistic approach to national security should be used as the guide to resolutely safeguard the core and major national interest], *CPC News*, January 24, 2015, http://cpc.people.com.cn/big5/n /2015/0124/c87228 -26441781.html.

7. 习近平应约同美国总统特朗普通电话 [Xi Jinping holds phone call with US president Trump], *Renmin Ribao* [People's Daily], May 9, 2018, http://politics.people.com.cn/n1/2018/0509/c1024-29973099.html.

8. 高举邓小平理论伟大旗帜，把建设有中国特色社会主义事业全面推向二十一世纪——江泽民在中国共产党第十五次全国代表大会上的报告[Hold high the great banner of Deng Xiaoping theory and push forward the cause of building socialism with Chinese characteristics into the twenty-first century – report by Jiang Zemin at the fifteenth CPC National Congress], Central People's Government of the People's Republic of China, September 12, 1997, http://www.gov .cn/test/2007-08/29/content_730614.htm; 高举中国特色社会主义伟大旗帜，为夺取全面建设小康社会新胜利而奋斗——胡锦涛在中国共产党第十七次全国代表大会上的报告 [Hold high the great banner of socialism with Chinese characteristics and strive for new victories in building a moderately prosperous society in all respects – report by Hu Jintao at the seventeenth CPC National Congress], Central People's Government of the People's Republic of China, October 15, 2007, http://www.gov.cn/ldhd/2007-10/24/content_785431.htm; Xi Jinping, 决胜全面建成小康社会，夺取新时代中国特色社会主义伟大胜利——在中国共产党第十九次全国代表大会上的报告 [Secure a decisive victory in building a moderately prosperous society in all respects and strive for the great success of socialism with Chinese characteristics for a new era – delivered at the nineteenth National Congress of the Communist Party of China], *Xinhua*, October 18, 2017, http://www.xinhuanet.com/english/download/Xi_Jinping's_report_at_19th_CPC_National_Congress.pdf.

9. Wang Jisi, "Searching for Stability with America," *Foreign Affairs* 84, no. 5 (2005): 39–48.

10. Jiang Daoli,"中美关系处于最好时期" [China-U.S. Relationship Is in the Best Period], Global Times, November 14, 2003.

11. 国家主席胡锦涛在联合国首脑会议上发表重要讲话 [President Hu Jintao delivered important speech for a harmonious world at the UN summit], Central People's Government of the People's Republic of China, September 16, 2005, http://www.gov.cn/ldhd/2005-09/16/content_63867.htm.

12. "China's Peaceful Development Road," State Council Information Office of the People's Republic of China, December 22, 2005, http://www.china.org.cn/english/2005/Dec/152669.htm.

13. The Group of Two (G-2 or G2) was originally initiated in 2005 by the economist C. Fred Bergsten as primarily an economic relationship between China and the United States. It became a popular notion recognizing the centrality of the China-US relationship near the beginning of the Obama administration. Its prominent advocates included former US national security advisor Zbigniew Brzezinski and historian Niall Ferguson. "Chimerica" was a concept coined by Niall Ferguson, among others, describing the symbiotic relationship between China and the United States. See Niall Ferguson and Moritz Schularick, "'Chimerica' and the Global Asset Market Boom," *International Finance* 10, no. 3 (2007): 215–39, https://doi.org/10.1111/j.1468-2362.2007.00210.x.

14. Yang Shilong,"坚持韬光养晦，积极有所作为"[Persisting in Keeping a Low Profile, and Proactively Making a Difference], Outlook Weekly, no. 45 (2010): 34–35.

15. "Xi emphasizes 'struggles' to achieve national rejuvenation," *People's Daily Online*, September 4, 2019, http://en.people.cn/n3/2019/0904/c90000-9611854.html

16. Wang Wenwen, "West Feels Challenged by China's New 'Wolf Warrior' Diplomacy," *Global Times*, April 16, 2020, http://www.globaltimes.cn/content/1185776.shtml.

17. The Taiwan issue, also viewed in China as a domestic affair, is discussed in the second part of this chapter as an issue of national security and territorial integrity. The major difference between the Taiwan issue and other domestic matters is that Taiwan is a political entity not practically under the administration of the PRC.

18. Stuart Taylor Jr., "Chinese Tennis Player Gets Asylum in U.S.; Peking Aide Protests," *New York Times*, April 5, 1983, https://www.nytimes.com/1983/04/05/world/china-tennis-player -gets-asylum-in-us-peking-aide-protests.html.

19. Allen S. Whiting, "Assertive Nationalism in Chinese Foreign Policy," *Asian Survey* 23, no. 8 (1983): 923, https://doi.org/10.2307/2644264.

20. Representative Daniel Mica introduced amendments to H.R. 1777 that dealt with the Tibet issue in June 1987. See H.R. 1777, Foreign Relations Authorization Act, fiscal years 1988 and 1989, 100th Cong. (1987–88), https://www.congress.gov/bill/100th-congress/house-bill /1777?s=4&r=1777.

21. Huan Xiang, 一年来的中美关系 [Sino-US relations over the past year], *Outlook Weekly*, no. 2 (1988): 22–23.

22. Richard Daniel Ewing, "Hu Jintao: The Making of a Chinese General Secretary," *China Quarterly* 173, no. 1 (2003): 17–34, https://doi.org/10.1017/S0009443903000032.

23. Michel Oksenberg, Lawrence R. Sullivan, and Marc Lambert, eds. *Beijing Spring, 1989: Confrontation and Conflict; The Basic Documents* (New York: Routledge, 1990), 56–88.

24. Henry Kissinger, *On China* (New York: Penguin Books, 2011), 418–20.

25. Kissinger, *On China*, 438.

26. "Cult Leader Becomes Anti-China Tool," *People's Daily*, April 18, 2000, http://en.peo ple.cn/english/200004/18/eng20000418_39145.html.

27. "Cult Leader."

28. "President Hu Jintao Holds Telephone Talks with His U.S. Counterpart Bush," Embassy of the People's Republic of China in the United States of America, March 28, 2008, http:// www.china-embassy.org/eng/xw/t419280.htm.

29. Qiu Yongzheng et al., 美国民主基金会扶植热比娅，出力张罗反华团队 [The U.S. National Endowment for Democracy backs Rebiya and helps establish an anti-China team], *Huanqiu shibao* [Global Times], August 12, 2009, https://world.huanqiu.com/article/9CaKrnJmhnS.

30. Liu Xiaobo reportedly died of liver cancer in July 2017.

31. Tania Branigan, "Google to End Censorship in China over Cyber Attacks," *Guardian*, January 13, 2010, https://www.theguardian.com/technology/2010/jan/12/google-china -ends-censorship.

32. Bobbie Johnson, "Google Stops Censoring Chinese Search Engine: How It Happened," *Guardian*, March 22, 2010, https://www.theguardian.com/technology/blog/2010/mar/22 /google-china-live.

33. Li Yunlu, Wang Jianhua, and Yan Hao, 中国拒绝"政治的谷歌"与"谷歌的政治"" [China refuses a political Google and Google's politics], State Council Information Office of the People's Republic of China, March 19, 2010, http://www.scio.gov.cn/wlcb/llyj /Document/579155/579155.htm.

34. Kwong Man-ki and Ng Kang-chung, "US Has No Involvement in Fostering Occupy

Protest, Obama Tells Xi," *South China Morning Post*, November 12, 2014, https://www.scmp.com/news/hong-kong/article/1638128/us-has-no-involvement-fostering-occupy-protest-obama-tells-xi.

35. Hua Yiwen, "Why Is the United States So Keen on 'Color Revolutions'?" *People's Daily Overseas Edition*, October 10, 2014, http://en.people.cn/n/2014/1011/c98649-8793283.html.

36. "Foreign Ministry Spokesperson Hua Chunying's Remarks on the US House of Repreesentatives Passing the Tibetan Policy and Support Act of 2019," Ministry of Foreign Affairs of the People's Republic of China, January 29, 2020, https://www.fmprc.gov.cn/mfa_eng/xwfw_665399/s2510_665401/2535_665405/202001/t20200129_697011.html.

37. "Foreign Ministry Spokesperson Hua Chunying's Remarks on the US House of Repreesentatives Passing the Uyghur Human Rights Policy Act of 2019," Ministry of Foreign Affairs of the People's Republic of China, December 4, 2019, https://www.fmprc.gov.cn/mfa_eng/xwfw_665399/s2510_665401/2535_665405/t1721334.shtml.

38. "Foreign Ministry Spokesperson Geng Shuang's Remarks on the Passing of the Hong Kong Human Rights and Democracy Act in the US Congress," Ministry of Foreign Affairs of the People's Republic of China, September 26, 2019, https://www.fmprc.gov.cn/mfa_eng/xwfw_665399/s2510_665401/2535_665405/t1708170.shtml.

39. "Foreign Ministry Spokesperson Hua Chunying's Regular Press Conference on Decemeber 2, 2019," Ministry of Foreign Affairs of the People's Republic of China, December 2, 2019, https://www.fmprc.gov.cn/mfa_eng/xwfw_665399/s2510_665401/2511_665403/t1720852.shtml.

40. The Dalai Lama with his followers and some individuals in Hong Kong may not consider themselves citizens of the PRC.

41. "Text of U.S.-China Communique on Taiwan," *New York Times*, August 18, 1982, https://www.nytimes.com/1982/08/18/world/text-of-us-china-communique-on-taiwan.html.

42. Robert S. Ross, "The 1996 Taiwan Strait Crisis: Lessons for the United States, China, and Taiwan," *Security Dialogue* 27, no. 4 (1996): 463–70, https://doi.org/10.1177/09670106960027004010.

43. Brian Knowlton, "Bush Warns Taiwan to Keep Status Quo: China Welcomes U.S. Stance," *New York Times*, December 10, 2003, https://www.nytimes.com/2003/12/10/news/bush-warns-taiwan-to-keep-status-quo-china-welcomes-us-stance.html.

44. Joseph Bosco, "Scrap the Third Communique with China, Keep the Six Assurances to Taiwan," *The Hill*, October 12, 2018, https://thehill.com/opinion/international/410931-scrap-the-third-communique-with-china-keep-the-six-assurances-to-taiwan. As cited in this comment, the Six Assurances are that the United States would not (1) set a date for termination of arms sales; (2) amend the Taiwan Relations Act (TRA); (3) consult with China regarding US arms sales; (4) mediate between Taiwan and China; (5) alter its position that Taiwan's future be decided peacefully between the parties, or pressure Taiwan to negotiate; or (6) recognize Chinese sovereignty over Taiwan.

45. Lawrence Chung, "US Should Recognize Taiwan as 'Free and Sovereign' Nation, Mike Pompeo Says," *South China Morning Post*, March 4, 2022, https://www.scmp.com/news/china/diplomacy/article/3169320/us-should-recognise-taiwan-free-and-sovereign-nation-mike.

46. "Xi's Speech Sets Course for Taiwan Affairs Work: Mainland Official," *Xinhua*, January 2, 2019, http://www.china.org.cn/china/Off_the_Wire/2019-01/02/content_74335005.htm.

47. Tang Jiaxuan, 劲雨煦风 [Heavy storm and gentle breeze: A memoir of China's diplomacy] (Beijing: World Knowledge Publishing House, 2009), 266–80.

48. 中国拒绝美国军舰访问香港 [China denies US warship visit to Hong Kong], *BBC Chinese*, May 29, 2001, http://news.bbc.co.uk/hi/chinese/news/newsid_1357000/13579351.stm.

49. Fu Ying and Wu Shicun, "South China Sea: How We Got to This Stage," *National Interest*, May 9, 2016, https://nationalinterest.org/feature/south-china-sea-how-we-got-stage-16118.

50. Chico Harlan, "China Creates New Air Defense Zone in East China Sea amid Dispute with Japan," *Washington Post*, November 23, 2013, https://www.washingtonpost.com/world /china-creates-new-air-defense-zone-in-east-china-sea-amid-dispute-with-japan/2013/11/23 /c415f1a8-5416-11e3-9ee6-2580086d8254_story.html.

51. Michael D. Swaine, "Chinese Views on the South China Sea Arbitration Case between the People's Republic of China and the Philippines," *China Leadership Monitor*, no. 51, August 24, 2016, https://carnegieendowment.org/files/CLM51MS.pdf.

52. "Yang Jiechi Gives Interview to State Media on the So-Called Award by the Arbitral Tribunal for the South China Sea Arbitration," Ministry of Foreign Affairs of the People's Republic of China, July 15, 2016, http://www.fmprc.gov.cn/mfa_eng/zxxx_662805/t1381740 .shtml.

53. "South China Sea Dispute: The Three Chinese and US Ships Involved in the Escalating Row," *South China Morning Post*, October 28, 2015, https://www.scmp.com/news/china/diplo macy-defence/article/1873116/south-china-sea-dispute-three-chinese-and-us-ships.

54. Kai He and Mingjiang Li, "Understanding the Dynamics of the Indo-Pacific: US-China Strategic Competition, Regional Actors, and Beyond," *International Affairs* 96, no. 1 (2020): 1–7, https://doi.org/10.1093/ia/iiz242.

55. 王毅: "印太战略" 是企图搞印太版 "北约" [Wangyi: "Indo-Pacific strategy" is intended to establish Indo-Pacific "NATO"], Ministry of Foreign Affairs of the People's Republic of China, March 7, 2022, https://www.mfa.gov.cn/web/wjbzhd/202203/t20220307_10648866.shtml.

56. 保卫我国边疆和平安定 [Safeguard the peace and security of our country's border], *Jiefangjun bao* [PLA Daily], February 19, 1979.

57. Yan Wu and Xiong Zhengyan, 铁证如山——河内当局赖不掉的事实 [Irrefutable evidence – facts that the Hanoi authorities cannot deny], *Xinhua*, March 5, 1979.

58. Deng Xiaoping, 在中央军委扩大会议上的讲话 [Speech at an enlarged meeting of the Military Commission of the Central Committee of the Communist Party of China], June 4, 1985, in 邓小平文选第三卷 [Selected Works of Deng Xiaoping, vol. 3] (Beijing: People's Publishing House, 1993), 128.

59. Kyle Mizokami, "In 1999, America Destroyed China's Embassy in Belgrade (and Many Chinese Think It Was on Purpose)," *National Interest*, January 21, 2017, https://nationalinterest .org/blog/the-buzz/1999-america-destroyed-chinas-embassy-belgrade-many-chinese-19124.

60. Gregory J. Moore, "Not Very Material but Hardly Immaterial: China's Bombed Embassy and Sino-American Relations," *Foreign Policy Analysis* 6, no. 1 (2010): 23–41, http://www.jstor .org/stable/24909876.

61. John Sweeney and Jens Holsoe, "NATO Bombed Chinese Deliberately," *Guardian*, October 17, 1999, https://www.theguardian.com/world/1999/oct/17/balkans.

62. Wu Baiyi, "Chinese Crisis Management during the 1999 Embassy Bombing Incident," in *Managing Sino-American Crises: Case Studies and Analysis*, ed. Michael D. Swaine, Zhang Tuosheng, and Danielle F. S. Cohen (Washington, DC: Carnegie Endowment for International Peace, 2006), 364–70.

63. Jing-Dong Yuan, "China's Role in Establishing and Building the Shanghai Cooperation Organization (SCO)," *Journal of Contemporary China* 19, no. 67 (2010): 855–69, https://doi.org /10.1080/10670564.2010.508587.

64. Wu Dahui, 美国在独联体地区策动 "颜色革命" 的三重诉求——兼论中俄在上海合作组织 架构下抵御 "颜色革命" 的当务之急 [On the triple-interest appeal of the US-instigated "color revolution" in CIS region: Concurrently on the urgency of China-Russian resistance of "color

revolution" within the SCO framework], *Eluosi zhong ya dong'ou yanjiu* [Russian, Central Asian and East European Studies], no. 2 (2006): 1–8.

65. Russell Ong, "China and the U.S. War on Terror," *Korean Journal of Defense Analysis* 18, no. 2 (2006): 95–116, https://doi.org/10.1080/10163270609464108.

66. Kenneth Lieberthal and Wang Jisi, "Addressing U.S.-China Strategic Distrust," Brookings Institution, March 2012, https://www.brookings.edu/wp-content/uploads/2016/06/0330_china_lieberthal.pdf.

67. The other countries remaining "socialist" in the definition of the CPC are the DPRK, Vietnam, and Laos with which communist party-to-party relations are maintained.

68. 中古 "三好" 关系进入新阶段 [The China-Cuba "three-good relationship" enters a new stage], Xinhua, September 28, 2016, http://news.sina.com.cn/o/2016-09-28/doc-ifxwermp4100915.shtml.

69. Roger F. Noriega, "Chávez and China: Challenging U.S. Interests," American Enterprise Institute, August 18, 2010, https://www.aei.org/research-products/report/chavez-and-china-challenging-u-s-interests/.

70. Cristina Guevara, "China's Support for the Maduro Regime: Enduring or Fleeting?" *Atlantic Council*, January 13, 2020, https://www.atlanticcouncil.org/blogs/new-atlanticist/chinas-support-for-the-maduro-regime-enduring-or-fleeting/.

71. Jevans Nyabiage, "China Mourns Zimbabwe's Robert Mugabe after Years of Unwavering Support," *South China Morning Post*, September 7, 2019, https://www.scmp.com/news/china/diplomacy/article/3026159/china-mourns-zimbabwes-robert-mugabe-after-years-unwavering.

72. Erica Downs and Suzanne Maloney, "Getting China to Sanction Iran: The Chinese-Iranian Oil Connection," *Foreign Affairs* 90, no. 2 (2011): 15–21.

73. Joel Wuthnow, "Will China Strengthen Iran's Military Machine in 2020?" *National Interest*, January 16, 2020, https://nationalinterest.org/blog/middle-east-watch/will-china-strengthen-iran%E2%80%99s-military-machine-2020-114681.

74. David Ho, "The Other Special Relationship: China's Xi Visits Russia," *Al Jazeera News*, June 5, 2019, https://www.aljazeera.com/economy/2019/6/5/the-other-special-relationship-chinas-xi-visits-russia.

75. Ho, "Other Special Relationship."

76. Syed Fazl-e-Haider, "The Strategic Implications of Chinese-Iranian-Russian Naval Drills in the Indian Ocean," Jamestown Foundation, January 17, 2020, https://jamestown.org/program/the-strategic-implications-of-chinese-iranian-russian-naval-drills-in-the-indian-ocean/.

77. "Joint Statement of the Russian Federation and the People's Republic of China on the International Relations Entering a New Era and the Global Sustainable Development," President of Russia, February 4, 2022, http://en.kremlin.ru/supplement/5770.

78. Evanne Yu, "China Says 'No Limits' in Cooperation with Russia," *South China Morning Post*, March 31, 2022, https://www.scmp.com/video/china/3172475/china-says-no-limits-cooperation-russia.

79. Xi Jinping made this reference when he welcomed Donald Trump in Beijing in November 2017. See 习近平同美国总统特朗普举行会谈 [Xi Jinping and Trump held talks], Xinhua, November 9, 2017, http://www.gov.cn/xinwen/2017-11/09/content_5238327.htm. See also 习近平：经济是中美关系 "压舱石"" [Xi Jinping: Economy is the "ballast" in China-US relations], *Renmin ribao* [People's daily], March 20, 2013, http:/ theory.people.com.cn/n/2013/0320/c49150-20849001.html.

80. "Foreign Ministry Spokesman Liu Jianchao's Comments on the US-China Economic and Security Review Commission Annual Report," Embassy of the People's Republic of China

in the Republic of Estonia, November 20, 2007, https://www.fmprc.gov.cn/ce/ceee/eng/jbwz lm/ztlm/fyrth/t382671.htm.

81. Ren Ping, 美国挑起贸易战的实质是什么？ [What is the nature of the trade war started by the United States?], *Renmin Ribao* [People's Daily], August 10, 2018, http://opinion.people.com.cn/n1/2018/0810/c1003-30220231.html.

82. Li Jin, 专家谈: 国有企业是中国特色社会主义经济的 '顶梁柱' [Experts talks: State-owned enterprises are the "backbone" of Socialism with Chinese characteristics], China National Radio, January 23, 2018, http://views.ce.cn/view/ent/201801/23/t20180123_27868024.shtml.

83. "Full Text of Xi Jinping's Report at 19ᵗʰ CPC National Congress," *China Daily*, November 4, 2017, https://www.chinadaily.com.cn/china/19thcpcnationalcongress/2017-11/04/content_34115212.htm.

84. Xi Jinping, 为建设世界科技强国而奋斗——在全国科技创新大会、两院院士大会、中国科协第九次全国代表大会上的讲话 [Strive to build a top science and technology power in the world – speech at the national science and technology innovation conference, the academician conference of the Chinese Academy of Sciences and the Chinese Academy of Social Sciences, and the ninth national congress of the China Association for Science and Technology], *Xinhua*, May 31, 2016, http://www.xinhuanet.com//politics/2016-05/31/c_1118965169.htm.

85. 如何增强自主创新能力？ [How to Enhance Capacity for Independent Innovation?], Central People's Government of the People's Republic of China, March 19, 2008, http://www.gov.cn/2008gzbg/content_924032.htm.

86. Wang Cong, "Revolt Brews against Dollar Hegemony," *Global Times*, December 5, 2019, https://www.globaltimes.cn/content/1172327.shtml.

87. Zhou Xiaochuan, 关于改革国际货币体系的思考[Thinking on the reform of the international monetary system], *Zhongguo Xinwen Wang* [China News], March 26, 2009, https://www.chinanews.com.cn/cj/kong/news/2009/03-26/1618790.shtml.

PART II

5

China's Management of Strategic Competition with the United States

Wu Xinbo

From 2018 to 2022, expanding and intensifying strategic competition between China and the United States has produced an unprecedented negative impact on bilateral relations: political ties are now tenser and more antagonistic than at any other time since Nixon's visit to China in 1972, while economic ties have suffered from the largest scale of tariff war in human history and the strictest US ban on technological transfer to China in decades. The outbreak of novel coronavirus in early 2020 didn't turn into an opportunity for two countries to cooperate and coordinate in dealing with a common challenge, but only further soured the mood and strained the ties between Beijing and Washington. Indeed, as the downward spiral in bilateral relations gained more and more momentum in 2022, people around the world wondered how far and fast the political, economic, and social decoupling between the two countries may go and whether a "new cold war" is going to befall Sino-US relations.

It is the strategic competition with China launched by the Trump administration, and continued and broadened in many ways by the Biden administration and Beijing's response to it, that has combined to shape the contour of bilateral relations since 2018. To help understand China's counterstrategy vis-à-vis the United States, this chapter will, from a politico-economic perspective, explore the following questions: How does China perceive the strategic contest with the United States, including the rationale and dynamics of the Trump and Biden administrations' China policy as well as its competitive tactics, the impact of strategic competition, and its future development? How has China executed the contest, and what kind of instruments have been employed? What are the factors that may abet or constrain the rivalry? What might the future scenarios look like? So far, what lessons can be drawn from the process?

Understanding Strategic Competition in Bilateral Relations

Sino-US strategic competition didn't start with the Trump administration. In 1999, George W. Bush announced in his presidential campaign that China was not America's "strategic partner" but its "strategic competitor."[1] Shortly after entering the White House in January 2001, Bush jump-started a series of policy adjustments aimed at pursuing a strategic contest with China. However, as the 9/11 terrorist attack on the United States brought the war on terror to the forefront of its National Security Strategy (NSS), concern over the China challenge had to be put to the back burner. As Beijing extended support to Washington in its efforts to fight terrorism and deal with the Democratic People's Republic of Korea (DPRK) nuclear issue, Sino-US ties gradually improved and even witnessed some significant progress during Bush's second term. On the other hand, throughout the Bush administration, the Pentagon had kept close eyes on the People's Liberation Army's (PLA) modernization drive, and bilateral military rivalry of some sort had persisted in the western Pacific, standing as a major manifestation of strategic rivalry between the two countries. Overall, the Bush administration started with an agenda preoccupied with strategic competition with China but ended up with a relationship characterized by more comprehensive cooperation and tempered competition.

President Obama came into office amid the 2008 financial crisis, and his administration started with a cooperation-oriented China policy. Yet as the United States moved out of the crisis and tensions arose around issues like Taiwan, Tibet, and regional security in Sino-US relations, Washington launched the Rebalance to Asia strategy in 2011 as a major US endeavor to compete with China. Aimed at checking China's rising power and influence in the Asia-Pacific region, this strategy sought to wrestle with China on both security and economic fronts. Meanwhile, the Obama administration also managed to expand bilateral economic, social, and cultural ties and promote cooperation and coordination with China on multilateral issues such as Iran and climate change, manifesting an effort to keep a balance between competition and cooperation in the overall relationship. To some extent, the Obama administration brought geopolitical rivalry with China in the Asia-Pacific to an unprecedented level, yet the two sides also expanded their substantive cooperation both bilaterally and multilaterally.

The Trump administration turned a new page in US strategic competition with China. Vowing to redress the unfair trade relations with China during his presidential campaign, President Trump maintained relatively stable relations with China during his first year in office, partly because he wanted to secure Beijing's cooperation in dealing with the DPRK nuclear program. In this period, Beijing's US approach was characterized by extending more help on the DPRK issue, making gradual concessions on economic issues, and developing a close personal relationship between Chinese president Xi Jinping and Trump. During Trump's state visit to Beijing in November 2017, China offered him a "state plus" reception as well as a package deal of trade and investment worth over $200 billion. Having been shown respect and gaining remarkable economic interests during his China trip, Trump, Beijing assumed, would continue to pursue a pragmatic China policy, and Sino-US ties could thus remain on a relatively stable path. However, the signal of major change came in December 2017 when the Trump administration released an NSS report that announced the return of major power competition and named Beijing as America's arch strategic competitor. China, it asserted, not only challenged US security and prosperity but also threatened to erode the prevailing international order that the United States had helped craft and lead.[2] The document went on to outline a blueprint to engage China in a comprehensive strategic contest with a strong economic focus.

China's understanding of the Trump administration's competitive strategy evolved as bilateral relations embarked on an unprecedented, turbulent course. Shortly after the release of the NSS report, the Trump administration threatened to launch a trade war with China by imposing extra tariffs on certain imported Chinese products, suggesting that it was serious about getting tough on China. Somewhat surprised by Trump's about-face in his attitude toward China, Beijing attributed these actions to a combination of two major factors. One was the general concern among the US political elite over the relative decline of the United States' hegemonic position against the background of China's rapid rise, and the other was the particularly strong concern harbored by the Trump administration over US economic interests, which deemed economic security as national security. Given this judgment, Beijing assumed that the Sino-US contest would persist over a relatively long period of time, and competition and confrontation would inevitably intensify. Beijing also noted that Trump's competitive strategy had both economic and political/strategic components, aimed at not only extracting more economic benefits from China but also slowing down and even disrupting China's pace of ascendance.

Beijing's concern over malign US political/strategic intentions was aggravated by a series of developments. In October 2018, US vice president Mike Pence delivered a major speech on China in which he lambasted Beijing in an all-around way, from its alleged violations of human rights and freedoms at home to its expansive foreign policy abroad, with a particular accusation directed at China's interference in America's domestic politics.[3] Pence's remarks alerted Beijing to the fact that the Trump administration did not just seek economic interests in relations with China but that it also had a strong political agenda: containing the expansion of Chinese power and influence as well as challenging China's political and economic system.[4] The relentless efforts by the United States in bilateral trade negations to pressure China to promise to significantly alter its economic system further accentuated Beijing's vigilance. In fact, it was the concern over the possible political fallout from a deal requiring China to make significant structural changes that prompted Chinese leaders to decide in April 2018 to withhold China's previous concessions and adopt a tougher stance. Beijing concluded that as Washington appeared determined to pursue a strategy of containing, weakening, and changing China, it had to be prepared for a long-term and severe strategic contest with the United States. Beijing's hardening of attitude stoked a wave of strong anti-American sentiment in China, escalated bilateral trade frictions, and further strained relations between two countries. When the trade negotiation resumed in the fall, Beijing made sure that any concessions China made would not compromise its political and economic system. It was against this background that the Phase One trade agreement was reached in December 2019.

Against the backdrop of intensified Sino-US rivalry, Beijing sought to gain a more insightful and nuanced understanding of the dynamics behind US China policy. Chinese analysts suggested that there existed a broad economic and political coalition on China within the Trump administration. The economic team, which was largely responsible for recalibrating Trump's China policy and launching a trade war with China, was composed of three different schools representing divergent economic thinking and policy preferences. The first school was economic nationalism, which cared about trade imbalance and unemployment caused by the relocation of manufacturing bases overseas, sought to maximize US economic interests, and favored protectionism and unilateralism. It advocated for redressing China's long-held unfair trade practices by all means, including trade war. The second school was economic realism, which intended to make sure that economic exchanges did not serve to enhance the key capabilities of its adversary, particularly in the field of technology, and would not help narrow the power gap between them. Thus, it sought relative rather than absolute gains in economic relations with others. This school pushed to tighten the control of technology flow to China as well as China's direct investment in the United States. The third school was economic liberalism, which viewed economic relations with others in the context of globalization and placed a premium on multilateralism. In economic relations with China, it sought to increase US access to the Chinese market, particularly in the service sector, and addressed its economic concerns in both bilateral and multilateral settings.[5]

Overall, economic nationalists and realists dominated Trump's China policy and kept pushing a coercive and confrontational approach toward China. Meanwhile, they were joined by national security hawks from the military, the intelligence community, and the National Security Council. It was this coalition of economic and security hard-liners that fomented the strategic competition with China and drove Sino-US relations to an abrupt downward turn beginning in early 2018. More broadly, this group echoed and played on various negative sentiments against China prevailing in US society: worry over the rise of China and its more assertive external behavior after the 2008 financial crisis, such as the large scale of reclamation in the South China Sea and military deployments on those islands; complaints about China's business environment, which had been deemed as becoming less favorable toward foreign investment; anxiety over the perceived tightening political atmosphere within China after 2012; frustration over the US failure to "change" China through engagement; the fury over China "stealing" American jobs and technologies; and other concerns.[6]

As the Sino-US rivalry has evolved, so has Beijing's perception of US competitive tactics. The Trump administration pledged to pursue a "whole-of-government" approach to competing with China. It employed multiple instruments at its disposal and engaged with China in a wide range of areas: trade, technology, finance, law enforcement, cultural and educational exchanges, diplomacy, ideology, and others. The extra tariffs imposed on imported Chinese products brought the two countries into a trade conflict on an unprecedented scale. Harsh measures were taken to tighten the control of technology transfer to China. More and more sanctions were launched against Chinese individuals and entities. The Chinese telecom giant Huawei became the main target of a US-led global witch hunt. Bilateral cultural and educational ties were brought under greater restrictions, and many collaborative projects in science and technology were terminated. Diplomatic engagements shrank and almost all the major dialogue mechanisms stalled, while geopolitical rivalry extended from the Asia-Pacific to South Asia, Europe, Africa, and Latin America. Bilateral quarrels over Taiwan, Tibet, Xinjiang, and Hong Kong heated up and became inflammable at some points. Perhaps the most notable development of all was that Washington launched a sharp attack on the Chinese Communist Party (CCP) and its top leader Xi Jinping, trying to differentiate them from the Chinese people. This was reminiscent of the toxic ideological fight during the Cold War. Overall, the US maneuvering against China in economic coercion, technological blockade, diplomatic rivalry, and political-ideological confrontation has intended to advance multiple goals of America's China strategy: gaining more economic benefits, weakening China's political system, thwarting China's rising power and expanding international influence, and preserving US hegemony.[7]

As Trump's new China policy unfolded, Beijing came to a more severe assessment of the consequences of strategic competition. When Washington kicked off the tariff war in early 2018, some liberals in China suggested that this might not necessarily be a bad thing, as it would push Beijing to undertake more serious and strident steps in opening up and reforming the Chinese economy, which in the long term would benefit China's socioeconomic development.

Others took the more alarmist view that the US moves were intended to disrupt China's advancement to catch up with and overtake the United States economically. As the frictions intensified and spread into many other areas, more grave and wide-ranging concerns emerged in China's policy and academic circles. Although the complete decoupling of China's and America's economies is unlikely, some degree of decoupling, particularly in the technology sector, will be inevitable. Educational and cultural links, which flourished over decades since normalization of Sino-US ties and have been regarded as an important foundation of the bilateral relationship, are being eroded. Pursuit of the Indo-Pacific Strategy by the Trump administration has threatened to aggravate geopolitical rivalry and raise tensions in the South China Sea and the Taiwan Strait, increasing the risk of intended or unintended conflict. It has also posed greater challenges to China's Belt and Road Initiative (BRI), especially in Southeast and South Asia. US involvement in Hong Kong, Xinjiang, and Tibetan affairs confounds Beijing's efforts to pursue its agendas in those areas. And finally, the political and ideological assault orchestrated by the Trump administration has brought to bear more pressure on the Chinese Communist Party and tarnished its image at home and abroad. The worst-case scenario for the Sino-US rivalry, as some in China have speculated, would be a new cold war, which may not be exactly the same as the last Cold War between the United States and the Soviet Union but would bear some of its main features: an arms race, geopolitical rivalry, ideological antagonism, and alliance creation or expansion.[8] Should this happen, economic ties between two countries may not entirely evaporate but would shrink drastically to the lowest-possible level.

The Biden administration inherited from the Trump administration its definition of China and line of thinking on US China policy. It regarded China as "the most serious competitor" to US prosperity, security, and democratic values as well as the only competitor "potentially capable of combining its economic, diplomatic, military, and technological power to mount a sustained challenge to a stable and open international system."[9] During its first year in office, the Biden administration formulated a China policy anchored in competition and supplemented by necessary confrontation and possible cooperation. In practice, it vigorously seeks to pressure, constrain, and confront China across the board.

Politically, at this writing, Washington describes Sino-US rivalry as one between autocracy and democracy, and it is exerting pressure on Beijing on issues like Xinjiang, Tibet, and Hong Kong. Economically, President Biden maintains the extra tariffs imposed by Trump on imported Chinese products, has further tightened the technology blockade against China, and seeks decoupling from China in certain production chains and key technologies.

Diplomatically, the administration works hard to align with allies and partners in Europe and Asia to counter China: promoting transatlantic coordination, strengthening US-Japan-Australia-India (the Quad) cooperation in the Indo-Pacific, and forging the US-Britain-Australia security pact (AUKUS). Although the Biden administration has resumed diplomatic contacts with China, lessened visa restrictions on Chinese students studying in the United States, allowed Huawei CFO Meng Wanzhou to return to China, and sought Chinese cooperation on climate change, Afghanistan, and Iran, the overall relationship has been fraught with tension and frictions, and the negative dynamics driving bilateral ties remain strong and robust.

When Biden took office, Beijing, originally expecting an alteration of Trump's China policy and an amelioration of Sino-US relations, quickly felt disappointed and frustrated. It switched from calling on the Biden administration to bury Trump's legacy on China and bring bilateral ties back on track to a stance of firmly fighting with its perceived bully. Instead of advocating for expanding cooperation and exchanges between the two sides, China turned to urge the United States to address its political, economic, and security concerns and prevent the two countries from entering into serious conflicts, intended or not.

As Biden pursues an antagonistic China policy and bilateral ties sour, Chinese analysts have concluded that Biden's harsh attitudes toward China reflect a broad bipartisan consensus in the United States. In fact, in a highly polarized political context, China seems to be the only area where Democrats and Republicans can find common ground. Biden not only needs to get tough on China in order to shield himself from attacks from Republicans but also chooses to use China as a trade-off with Republicans in pursuing his own political agenda. Moreover, from the Chinese perspective, the Biden administration is adding Cold War flavor to the intensifying Sino-US contest by casting it as one between two political systems and attempting to build the widest possible coalition against China. If this trend continues, what is likely to emerge between two countries is a quasi–cold war, if not a replica of the last Cold War. Although the Biden administration has expressed the hope that Sino-US competition should not veer into conflict and has suggested a need to build a guardrail for bilateral ties, its poor handling of US house speaker Nancy Pelosi's visit to Taiwan in August 2022 alarmed Beijing. From the Chinese perspective, a trip to the island by the highest-level US government official in twenty-five years not only marked a major breach of Washington's promise of maintaining only unofficial relations with Taipei after establishing diplomatic ties with Beijing in 1979 but also revealed the inability on the part of the Biden administration to manage US domestic politics as it impacted China-US relations. Beijing's strong reactions, from suspending military exchanges and diplomatic contacts between two countries to holding large-scale military exercises in the air and sea around the Taiwan island, highlighted the high risk of conflict between China and the United States over the Taiwan issue.

China's Responses to US Competitive Strategy

China's responses to US competitive strategy were developed step-by-step during the period of 2018–19, as the trade conflict escalated and frictions spread into political, security, and other areas, prompting Beijing to formulate a set of comprehensive countermeasures based on its evolving assessment of US approaches and intentions. From early 2018 to April 2019, Beijing dwelled more on the economic dimension. Initially it tried to prevent the occurrence of the trade war through negotiation and concessions. When this effort failed to work, it decided to launch a war of resistance by imposing retaliatory tariffs on imported US products, aimed at forcing the Trump administration to return to the negotiation table. As the opportunity emerged in late 2018, Beijing proposed a truce in the tariff war and a possible deal for negotiation. From May 2019, however, Beijing was not only prepared for long-term economic frictions with the United States but also inclined to view the rivalry with Washington more and more from political and strategic perspectives. Toward late 2019 and early 2020, China seemed to have formed a set of sophisticated approaches to the US strategic offensive.

Seeking Discursive Power

The Trump administration stressed the notion of major power competition in its national security concept and proactively planned and executed strategic competition with China in practice. This deviated from the previous US China policy, which promoted both cooperation and competition with China. Faced with this new reality, Beijing altered its usual behavior of evading talking about competition with the United States and tried to come up with its own narrative about competition. Acknowledging that competition and differences would always exist between these two countries, Beijing called for benign rather than vicious competition; in other words, competition should be fair and guided by rules, both sides should seek win-win rather than zero-sum outcomes, and cooperation should not exclude necessary cooperation. It stressed that "China and the United States can have competition but should not view each other with a Cold War mentality. Nor should they slip into the trap of a zero-sum game."[10] These narratives reflected China's attempt to guide Sino-US rivalry in a healthy direction. Noticing a strong concern expressed by the Trump administration over China's overtake of America's primary position, Beijing made repeated efforts to reassure Washington that China had no such intentions.[11]

After the Trump administration kicked off the trade war, Beijing portrayed it as a serious threat to the global industry chain and value chain, stating, "The multilateralism, free trade and rules-based order are now pit against unilateralism, protectionism and power games. China will join hands with the international community to stand on the right side of history and champion multilateral trading system and rules."[12] As Washington waged more vocal and fierce rhetorical attacks on China, especially the CCP, Beijing fought back with more targeted and sharper counterattacks. For instance, in 2019 and 2020, the *People's Daily* carried several strongly worded articles refuting US Secretary of State Mike Pompeo for his harsh remarks on China. The war of words between the two sides culminated in the summer of 2020 as National Security Advisor Robert C. O'Brien, FBI Director Chris Wray, Attorney General William Barr, Mike Pompeo, and Secretary of Defense Mark Esper delivered a series of belligerent speeches against China.

Counterattack

Counterattack stands as a significant component of China's approaches. After Washington started the first round of tariff hikes on imported Chinese products, Beijing responded immediately by imposing the same rate of extra tariffs on the same amount of imported US products. This tit-for-tat pattern went through the whole period of the trade war. The tactic of counterattack has also been applied in other fields of Sino-US rivalry. For instance, in 2019, after Washington imposed new restrictions on the activities of Chinese diplomats stationed in the United States, Beijing did the same to US diplomats assigned to China. In December 2019, to punish the United States for its involvement in Hong Kong unrest, China denied requests for two US Navy ships to make port visits to the city and imposed sanctions on related US NGOs.[13] In early 2020, in response to US moves to tighten rules on China's state media operating in the United States, China expelled US journalists working for the *New York Times*, the *Washington Post*, and the *Wall Street Journal*. Overall, the tit-for-tat strategy is intended to demonstrate China's resolve and impose costs on the United States for its actions against China.

Deterrence

In addition to counterattack, China also tries to pose credible deterrence to the United States with leverage at its disposal. In May 2019, after Sino-US trade negotiation stalled and Washington threatened to heat up the battle with China in trade and technology, Chinese president Xi Jinping paid a visit to a rare earth company in Jiang Xi province, signaling that China might limit its export of rare earths—a group of seventeen prized elements broadly used in modern high-tech products from smartphones to high-precision missiles—to the

United States. Given the United States' heavy reliance on the Chinese market for the supply of the critical minerals, a ban or reduction in Chinese exports would surely generate a fatal impact on the latter's semiconductor sector. Three months later, the Association of China Rare Earth Industry issued a statement indicating that China might slow down its rare earth shipments to the United States. The fact that Chinese rare earth exports to the United States dropped 11.3 percent year-over-year during the first half of 2019 made the deterrence more credible.[14]

In mid-May 2019, the US Department of Commerce placed Huawei and its dozens of affiliates around the globe on an entity list of companies, essentially preventing them from buying American-provided microchips, software, and other parts and technologies without seeking special licenses from the US government. Shortly thereafter, some large US technology companies and organizations indicated they would stop supplying Huawei or cut off their business cooperation with the company. On May 31, China's Ministry of Commerce (MOFCOM) announced that China would release its "Unreliable Entity List" (UEL), a list that would include any foreign companies, organizations, and individuals that "damage[d] the legitimate rights and interests of Chinese companies by disobeying market rules, breaking their promises and blocking or cutting off supply to Chinese companies on non-commercial grounds."[15] This move stood apparently as a tit-for-tat counterstrike against action taken by the Trump administration and was intended to deter US companies from following the US government's instructions. Although the Trump administration kept up the pressure on Huawei and put more and more Chinese entities on the sanction list in the ensuing period of more than one year, Beijing didn't come up with provisions on the UEL until September 2020,[16] and the list has yet to be released, suggesting Beijing would like to keep it in hand as a deterrent rather than shoot out the bullet.

Negotiation and Compromise

Bargaining has been an important approach for China to deal with the tariff war initiated by the Trump administration. Over the years, Beijing has accumulated rich experiences in managing Sino-US economic frictions through dialogue and consultation. During the eras of George W. Bush and Obama, the two countries conducted high-level economic dialogue, which played an important role in facilitating the expansion of bilateral economic ties and addressed various associated problems and concerns, although dissatisfaction also existed on both sides over its efficacy. After Trump entered office and pledged to push China hard on the economic front, Beijing proposed to set up the Comprehensive Economic Dialogue as a mechanism to discuss and deal with bilateral economic issues. Although the US side accepted this idea at first, the dialogue didn't go far as Trump, who, probably influenced by hawkish aids such as Peter Navarro and Robert Lighthizer, was eager to see fast progress in China's addressing US concerns. When he threatened to impose extra tariffs on imported Chinese products in early 2018, Beijing deemed it as largely a bluff to extract concessions from China and decided to forestall the trade war through negotiation. This led to a series of negotiations between the two sides from May to June, during which Beijing agreed to accommodate some of the US concerns in areas such as market access, trade imbalance, and protection of intellectual rights. However, much to Beijing's surprise, Washington decided to kick off the tariff war in spite of the progress achieved. Frustrated and angered, Beijing was determined to stand up and fight back, so the trade conflict ensued and escalated from July to November 2018.

As Trump became impatient with the protracted trade war (he initially thought the US could win the battle quickly and easily), he reached out to President Xi in November. Beijing interpreted this as a sign of the United States being willing to return to the negotiation table and decided to grasp the opportunity to bring an end to the war through reopening negotiation. When Xi and Trump met on the sideline of the G20 summit held in Buenos Aires, Argentina, in early December, Xi proposed a package deal as well as a road map for future negotiation, to which Trump consented. The negotiation resumed in January 2019 and moved forward through intense interactions between two sides. While Beijing tried its best to accommodate US demands in the hope of ending the trade war, Washington viewed China's flexibility as a great opportunity to extract the most concessions, not only in the sum of China's extra purchase of US products but also on structural changes in China's economic policy and system.[17] Washington's excessive push backfired as Chinese leaders decided in April 2019 to reject the concessions made in the prior four months, thus stranding the talks. Beijing turned to a tougher stance toward the US, vowing neither to succumb to extreme US pressure nor compromise on major principles,[18] while Washington moved to impose more tariffs on Chinese products and laid restrictions on Huawei and other Chinese high-tech companies.

After over one month of a stormy standoff between the two countries, Xi and Trump met on June 29 during the G20 summit held in Osaka, Japan, where they agreed to restart the talks and suspend further tariff measures. The resumed negotiation did not lead to a breakthrough until the US side agreed to a Chinese proposal for a phased approach; that is, instead of striking a comprehensive deal covering all the issues of concern at one time, the two sides would first seek to reach an agreement on the low-hanging fruits while leaving more difficult issues for the second and third stages of talks, and once the Phase One agreement was achieved, both sides would start to roll back some of the extra tariffs already imposed. Since both sides found a more pragmatic and feasible approach, particularly because Trump desired to strike a deal with China as the presidential election year neared, the Phase One agreement was finally nailed down in December 2019. China made concessions to the United States in areas of intellectual property, technology transfer, agriculture, financial services, and currency and foreign exchange, and agreed to make additional purchases of US goods and services worth $200 billion in the following two years. A dispute resolution system was also established to ensure prompt and effective implementation and enforcement. The United States agreed to suspend further tariff imposition on Chinese products and curtail some of the extra tariffs already in place.[19] This hard-earned deal suggests that negotiation, although a very tortuous course, stood as an important approach to Sino-US economic disputes, and Beijing was able to make concessions that were both politically and economically feasible.

Reducing Vulnerability

Trump's competitive strategy toward China gave top priority to economic competition, which centers on trade and technology. After the trade war broke out, China, in addition to fighting back by imposing retaliatory tariffs on US products, also sought to reduce its reliance on the US market by expanding trade with other markets, such as Southeast Asia, Europe, and countries participating in the BRI. In 2018, the European Union (EU), the United States, and the Association of Southeast Asian Nations (ASEAN) stood as China's top three trading partners. China's trade with them increased by 5.7 percent, 7.9 percent, and 11.2 percent, respectively, compared with the previous year, yet trade with the EU and ASEAN grew faster than with the United States.[20] In 2019, as compared with 2018, China's trade with the EU and ASEAN grew by 8 percent and 14.1 percent, respectively, while trade with the United States fell by 10.7 percent and ASEAN overtook the United States as China's second-largest trading partner.[21] Also compared with 2018, China's exports in 2019 to the EU and ASEAN grew by 9.6 percent and 17.6 percent, respectively, whereas exports to the United States fell by 8.7 percent.[22]

Beijing's market diversifying strategy has worked to some extent, in spite of the fact that the rapid growth in China-ASEAN trade is partially due to China's use of ASEAN, particularly Vietnam, as a base for reexport to the United States. The response to the US trade war has led to more fundamental adjustments in China's economic development strategy. In May 2020, the Chinese leaders, taking into consideration the adverse developments in China's international environment for the foreseeable future, urged the country to "fully bring out the advantage of its super-large market scale and the potential of domestic demand to establish a new development pattern featuring domestic and international dual circulations that complement each other."[23] The concept of "dual circulations" calls for efforts to establish a new model of development in which domestic and external demand complement one another while the domestic market plays a more important role. This implies a decreasing reliance on the external market, particularly the United States.

Aside from trade, technology became the next major battle front in the Sino-US economic contest. In 2015, China launched an ambitious national plan, "Made in China 2025," aimed at improving its manufacturing competitiveness through technological indigenous innovation. The Trump administration regarded this initiative as a major challenge to the US technological lead and was determined to obstruct China from achieving its goal. On April 16, 2018, when the US Department of Commerce announced a ban forbidding American firms from doing business with ZTE, a major Chinese telecommunication company selling smartphones and telecommunications equipment around the world, Beijing was shocked and realized that Washington was going to make technology another focal point in the cross fire. The US pressure however, only made China more deeply convinced of the necessity and urgency of technological autonomy and more firmly committed to advancing its objective. Ten days later, on April 26, 2018, President Xi visited two high-tech research institutions in Wuhan, Hubei province, where he stressed that core technologies that are important to the country should always be fully mastered by the country itself and encouraged researchers and developers to "break away from illusion" and fight on their own.[24] In this way, Xi sent an overt and strong signal that China would speed up its efforts in pursuit of technological advancement. Since then, Beijing has pumped in more resources and extended more preferential policies to facilitate progress in the high-tech sector, with particular stress on artificial intelligence (AI), 5G telecommunication, and robots, among others.[25] As the US takes more comprehensive and vigorous measures to tighten the flow of important technologies to China, there is an emerging consensus among Chinese analysts that tech war and decoupling in the high-tech sector is the long-term trend in Sino-US relations; therefore, China has no choice but to work even harder to achieve technological progress on its own so as to reduce its strategic vulnerability vis-à-vis the United States.[26]

Divide and Rule

Beijing understands that there exist in the United States various interest groups in relations with China and that they hold somewhat divergent policy preferences. This offers China opportunities to exploit the internal differences in the United States so as to counter and check Trump's offensive. For instance, US multinational companies usually favor a stable bilateral relationship, as it helps boost their business in the Chinese market; US financial and high-tech sectors represented by Wall Street and Silicon Valley tend to endorse strong ties with

China, as it contributes to their commercial expansion; US state and local governments view relations with China more from an economic than a national security lens, and they welcome trade with and investment from China. Based on this understanding, Beijing has utilized a wide array of instruments to win the support of these groups for robust China-US economic ties and incentivize them to exert pressure on Washington.

Since the outbreak of the trade war, the Chinese government has vowed repeatedly to further open-up and reform so as to improve its investment environment.[27] Beijing has taken steps to widen market access for foreign investors, especially the financial sector for Wall Street; adopted more measures to enhance intellectual property rights (IPR) protection; lifted restrictions on foreign investment; and increased the import of foreign products through lowering import tariffs and holding the annual China International Import Expo in Shanghai. Meanwhile, China has reached out actively to state and local governments in the United States to promote links in trade, investment, education, culture, and other areas through such platforms as the Governors Forum, the Business Forum, and sister province/state and sister city connection. In addition, given the fact that US agriculture states were Trump's main political base, and they relied heavily on exporting soybeans and wheat to the Chinese market, Beijing targeted the US agricultural products in imposing the first round of retaliatory tariffs. In Beijing's calculation, this tactic threatened to undermine US farmers' support for Trump and would force him to hit the brakes on the trade war.

On another front, as the Trump administration moved to curtail bilateral ties in the fields of culture, education, and science and technology in an attempt to prevent China from expanding its influence in the United States and benefiting from access to US universities and research institutions, Beijing decided not to respond likewise. Instead, it took such measures as visa facilitation to encourage Sino-US cultural and people-to-people exchanges. In March 2019, President Xi met with visiting president of Harvard University Lawrence Bacow and expressed a willingness to conduct more extensive exchanges and cooperation with US educational and research institutions.[28] As China continued to become an important market for US higher education and Chinese scholars continued their long pursuit of robust and productive collaboration with their US partners, Beijing sought to work with US educational and academic institutions to resist attempts by the Trump administration to limit and scale back bilateral cultural and educational exchanges.

Winning over the Third Parties

In the contest with the United States, China also casts its eyes on third parties in an attempt to strengthen ties with them, winning their support, or preventing them from tilting toward the United States. Russia, the European Union, India, Japan, and ASEAN are some important third-party actors that China seeks to work with. Confronted with mounting pressure from Washington, Beijing has deepened political, economic, and security ties with Moscow. In relations with the EU, China has pledged to stick to such principles as multilateralism, free trade, and global governance, which resonate with the Europeans. Meanwhile, it seeks to forge concrete cooperation with the EU by coping with climate change within the framework of the Paris Agreement, negotiating a bilateral investment treaty, and promoting links in trade, investment, culture, education, and people-to-people exchanges. As Washington did its utmost to press the EU to exclude Huawei from participating in building their 5G infrastructure, Beijing worked hard to ensure that EU countries would not bow to US pressure. Caught between China and the United States, Britain changed its mind and decided to boycott Huawei. Germany resisted US pressure and insisted that it wouldn't exclude a company simply for its nationality, while some other European countries hesitated. Since 2018, Beijing also has managed to ameliorate ties with India and Japan, two of its major neighbors that Washington has attempted to draw to its side in its tug-of-war with China, and Sino-Indian and Sino-Japanese relations witnessed some improvement during the period of 2018 and 2019. However, Sino-Indian ties suffered from a serious setback in 2020 due to a border clash, while Sino-Japanese ties cooled down due to the impact of the COVID-19 pandemic on Japan.

In relations with ASEAN, China promoted bilateral cooperation on the one hand through initiatives like the BRI and the Lancang-Mekong Cooperation mechanism, and on the other, it pressed ahead the negotiation of the Code of Conduct (COC) in the South China Sea. As the Trump administration vehemently pursued economic nationalism and trade protectionism, China attached more significance to regional and subregional cooperation. Beijing actively participated in the talks over the Regional Comprehensive Economic Partnership (RCEP), a free trade agreement (FTA) involving China, Japan, the Republic of Korea (ROK), ten ASEAN member states, Australia, New Zealand, and India.[29] It also expressed enthusiasm in pushing forward the ongoing negotiation of a trilateral FTA among China, Japan, and the ROK. On the other hand, as Canada, at Washington's request, arrested Meng Wanzhou, a top executive and the daughter of the founder of Huawei, and threatened to extradite her to the United States, Beijing arrested two Canadian citizens for alleged illegal activities conducted in China. Similarly, as Australia fanned anti-China sentiment at home and actively danced to Washington's tune on issues like Huawei, the South China Sea, and COVID-19, Beijing responded by laying restrictions on the import of some Australian agricultural products. These punitive and retaliatory actions certainly sent a strong signal to other countries as well.

From 2018 to 2019, China developed its counterstrategy toward the strategic competition waged by the Trump administration. In this process, Beijing tried to cope with three sets of dynamics: the technical need to counter Trump's tariff war and the strategic need to preserve Sino-US economic ties, the short-term challenge to resist Trump's offensive and the long-term need to preserve bilateral relations, and the external pressure from the United States for structural and nonstructural changes and the internal demand for further opening-up and reform. Overall, China's strategy was reactive, restrained, and resourceful. Confronted with unprecedented economic warfare initiated by Washington, Beijing responded in tit-for-tat fashion by imposing extra tariffs on US products; however, as some hawks in the Trump team pushed for decoupling between the two economies, Beijing acted to encourage coupling. As the Trump administration launched an offensive against China in trade, technology, investment, diplomacy, security, and politics, Beijing sought to fight back without jeopardizing the entire relationship, as guided by the principle of *dou er bu po* (struggle without breaking). Beijing maintained that competition was inevitable and likely to intensify, but a catastrophic, head-on confrontation and Cold War–style antagonism should be avoided.[30]

In the trade negotiations, the US side compelled China to make a wide range of adjustments in its economic policies and practices, yet it turned out that some of the US requirements overlapped with China's internal need for further opening-up and reform. Therefore, Beijing incorporated certain US demands into its reform agenda, facilitating a more transparent, open, rules-based, and market-oriented economic environment. Beijing's counterstrategy drew on various sources (domestic, bilateral, and multilateral) and multiple means (political, economic, and security, among others), lending China more leeway and resources in the contest. Although there exist different ideas among various party, state, and military agencies about the nature of competition with the United States and the ideal way to deal with it, and senior Chinese leaders may not agree with each other on those issues all the time, President Xi has played the key role in the decision-making process by building consensus and giving the final say.

To some extent this strategy has worked reasonably well. The Phase One agreement was reached while more difficult issues were left for future negotiations. A series of substantive reform and opening-up measures have been adopted to help make China's business environment more attractive to foreign investors, including the US business community.[31] According to a survey released by the American Chamber of Commerce in Shanghai in September 2020, despite a rise in US-China tensions and a slowing economy in 2019, American businesses in China remained profitable, with 78.2 percent of companies reporting profits, marginally ahead of recent years. Companies remained committed to the China market, with 78.6 percent of companies reporting no change in their investment allocations, a 5.1 percentage point increase compared to 2019.[32] Meanwhile, as China eases restrictions on its financial sector, financial institutions from the US and other countries have substantially increased their presence in China.[33] Moreover, China's insistence on multilateralism and free trade has also won international sympathy and plaudit. For instance, in September 2020, the World Trade Organization (WTO) ruled that the US tariffs imposed on more than $350 billion worth of Chinese products under its so-called Section 301 of the domestic Trade Act violated global trade regulations.[34]

On the other hand, Beijing's strategy failed to prevent Washington from ratcheting up pressure on China in a wide range of areas, and bilateral ties have taken a turbulent nosedive since 2018. As a result, there exists a strong opinion among Chinese elite as well as the public that Beijing's counterstrategy was neither powerful enough to stop the Trump administration from further provoking China nor effective in stabilizing bilateral relations. Entering the year of 2020, several major developments, accidental or not, had worked to complicate China's efforts to manage its strategic contest with the United States. The spread of COVID-19 and the heavy cost it inflicted on human life and the economy in the United States shadowed Trump's bid for reelection, filling him with full rancor and outrage against China. The hawks on his team got a free hand to pursue their long-awaited agenda, slashing the tree of Sino-US ties with all strength and inflicting as much damage as possible. In addition, Beijing's decision to pass and implement the National Security Law in Hong Kong aroused widespread concern among US allies, causing them to toughen their attitude toward China. By the end of the Trump era, Sino-US relations had fallen to their nadir since normalization, covered in a toxic atmosphere of strong distrust and antagonism.

As the Biden administration continued and intensified competition with China, Beijing, drawing on its experiences in dealing with the Trump administration, formulated and executed an upgraded counterstrategy. The first step was taking initiative. China sought to actively guide US China policy and set the agenda for bilateral relations. For instance, in February 2021, Chinese foreign minister Wang Yi called on the Biden administration to establish dialogue mechanisms with China, remove Trump's tariffs on Chinese goods, lift its unilateral sanctions on Chinese companies and research and educational institutes, and terminate its restrictions on Chinese educational and cultural groups, media outlets, and institutions for overseas Chinese affairs in the United States.[35] In July 2021, as Washington dragged its feet in cleaning up the mess left by Trump, China proposed to the American side two lists specifying areas and cases where Beijing demanded changes. One dealt with US policies and allegations concerning China, and the other was a list of key cases concerning Chinese officials and people in the United States. This was the first time that China presented to the United States a long to-do list. Meanwhile, Wang Yi also underlined in his meeting with a senior US State Department official three basic demands for effectively managing differences and preventing China-US relations from getting out of control.[36]

The second step was to adopt a more combatant posture vis-à-vis the United States. Beijing sought to undermine US discursive power in bilateral relations by refuting US rhetoric. For instance, Chinese officials argued that the US definition of its China policy as competitive, collaborative, and adversarial was "a thinly veiled attempt to contain and suppress China," and the US side's so-called rules-based international order was "an effort by the United States and a few other Western countries to frame their own rules as international rules and impose them on other countries."[37] Confronted with continued sanctions and pressure from the Biden administration, China launched a counterattack. In June 2021, China's National People's Congress passed the Anti-Foreign Sanctions Law as an attempt to "counter the hegemonism and power politics of some Western countries,"[38] which provided a legal basis for China to deter, undermine, and retaliate against US sanctions targeting Chinese entities and individuals. After Washington announced the sanctioning of some Chinese officials on the issues of Xinjiang and Hong Kong, Beijing acted to impose sanctions against related US individuals. When the United States leveled accusations against China concerning coronavirus origins tracing, China demanded an investigation of the biolab at the University of North Carolina for its poor safety record as well as the US Army Medical Research Institute of Infectious Diseases and the Integrated Research Facility at Fort Detrick for their involvement in research on high-risk viruses and coronaviruses.[39] As the Biden administration drew closer to Taiwan, China stepped up its military activities in the vicinity of the island as a warning to both Washington and Taipei.[40] Overall, faced with a more confrontational United States, China has demonstrated that it "dares to fight and knows how to fight (*ganyu douzheng, shanyu douzheng*)," a spirit that has been advocated by Chinese president Xi Jinping in recent years.[41]

The third step was to intensify cooperation with Russia and Iran as part of its tactics to compete with the United States for these third parties. For instance, to enhance the China-Russia comprehensive strategic partnership of coordination, the Chinese and Russian militaries held the joint exercise ZAPAD/INTERACTION-2021 (*Xibu Unity*-2021) in China's northwest region in August 2021, the first time that the Russian army or any foreign army was invited by China to participate in the PLA's strategic exercises in China. In October 2021, the Chinese and Russian navies conducted their first joint cruise in the western Pacific. When Russian president Vladimir Putin visited China in February 2022 to attend the opening ceremony of the Twenty-Fourth Olympic Winter Games held in Beijing, Presidents Xi and Putin agreed to further boost bilateral ties, and a joint statement was issued outlining the two sides' shared views on international affairs and their commitment to mutual support and cooperation on the world stage. The two countries also signed a series of documents regarding cooperation in the fields of food, energy, navigation satellite systems, information technology, and digital sectors, among others.[42]

In early 2021, China and Iran concluded a twenty-five-year comprehensive cooperation plan which aimed to strengthen bilateral cooperation in energy, infrastructure, production capacity, science and technology, and medical and health care; expand cooperation in agriculture, fisheries and cybersecurity; and deepen cultural and people-to-people exchanges and promote tripartite cooperation.[43] In September 2021, Iran became a full member of the Shanghai Cooperation Organization (SCO), thus opening a new venue for China-Iranian cooperation in regional security. In January 2022, China, Russia, and Iran held their second joint naval exercises in the Gulf of Oman. Needless to say, Beijing's efforts to enhance cooperation with Moscow and Tehran were intended to constrain US strategy toward China.

During Biden's first year in office, Beijing moved quickly to adapt to America's approach to China and deployed a set of more effective tactics in dealing with the United States. China appeared to be firmer and more resolute in fighting with Washington in both words and deeds. It also sought to get the United States to address China's major concerns more effectively, including freeing Meng Wanzhou, reaffirming the US government's long-standing One China policy, and reassuring Beijing that Washington did not seek to change China's system, the revitalization of its alliances was not anti-China, and the United States had no intention of stoking a conflict with China.[44] Although Beijing pays more attention to what Washington does than it says, such reassurances marked a gesture somewhat different from the Trump administration. Moreover, as the Biden administration categorizes its China policy into competition, confrontation, and cooperation, and assumes it can pursue the three elements simultaneously, Beijing frustrates Washington by demonstrating that it is just impossible to seek China's cooperation while stoking it as an adversary.

The Future of Sino-US Competition

As discussed earlier, the Sino-US strategic contest didn't start with the Trump administration. However, it was the Trump administration that rendered competition so overwhelming, comprehensive, and intense and made competition so confrontational. The Biden administration carries on Trump's China policy centered around competition, while intensifying rivalry with China in technology, geopolitics, and values. Looking into the future, the rivalry will very likely intensify as a result of the coalescing of two major elements. One is the structural factor in international politics. As China's comprehensive national power continues to grow and further narrows the power gap with the United States, Washington, out of concern over its primacy, will do its utmost to slow down and retard China's advancement. Moreover, with its rich experiences of wrestling with a peer competitor during the Cold War, the United States may be somewhat tempted to turn strategic rivalry with China into a new cold war.[45] The other element is domestic politics on both sides. In the United States, there emerges a broad consensus across the political spectrum that a tougher China policy is needed as Beijing becomes more powerful, ambitious, and assertive. In China, there arises a common belief among both the elite and the general public that it should be prepared to struggle with greater resolve, braveness, and perseverance to resist and confound the US attempt to contain China's rise. Domestic politics on both sides may reinforce each other and heighten the momentum of rivalry, leading up to occasional confrontation and even structural antagonism between the two countries.

The occurrence of major events on the world stage may also shape the contour of Sino-US relations. The outbreak of the Russia-Ukraine crisis in early 2022 and its consequences could produce long-term impacts on the dynamics between Beijing and Washington. One possibility is that, pressed by the rigorous sanctions of the West, Russia will nudge further toward China and Beijing will provide stronger support to Moscow in economic and other fields. This will cause the United States, along with its allies—particularly European ones—to adopt a harsher stance toward China, and alignment confrontation will escalate. Another possibility is that Washington, out of the need to engage in long-term and significant security confrontation with Russia in Europe, will have to temper its impulse to rival China, and such an adjustment will cause Beijing to adopt a more reconciliatory and cooperative posture toward Washington. This may help reduce tension and contribute to stability in bilateral ties. The contest between the two sides will surely continue to unfold, though it will be less intense and antagonistic.

On the other hand, some significant constants may work to constrain and moderate Sino-US competition. First and foremost, the essence of the contest between China and the United States is social-economic, not political-military.[46] It differs from the US-Soviet Cold War, which was largely political-military by nature. Political-military rivalry tends to be sharp and antagonistic, while social-economic contest runs a lower risk of military conflict.

Second, the high degree of economic interdependence between China and the United States has embedded a win-win element in the relationship. Even though the economic link turns out to be a major source of contention between the two countries, decoupling it is neither desirable nor feasible. In fact, as China's market opens wider to US goods, services, and capital, economic interdependence will somehow further grow, even though the bilateral technological link is likely to shrink.

The third factor is the existing international system/order. China does not seek to overthrow the current system, nor does it attempt to create a separate one. Beijing views itself as a major beneficiary of the prevailing order and is willing to sustain it, although it also maintains that some reform is needed to improve the order's inclusiveness, representativeness, and efficiency.[47] Meanwhile, the United States has crafted the current international system and supervised its operations, and the system has served US national interests reasonably well in spite of Donald Trump's statements. To preserve the system, Washington can expect more and more assistance from Beijing as China's influence increases. Therefore, the need to maintain the existing system will work to constrain the competitive behavior of both countries.

Theoretically, there exist several scenarios regarding the future of the Sino-US strategic contest. One is benign competition. Two countries pursue competition while also seeking cooperation/coordination as necessary. As they compete, they abide by a set of common rules, and both parties want to prevent competition from degenerating into confrontation. As a result, bilateral ties are largely stable and predictable. Another is mixed competition. Competition is benign in certain areas while malign in others, frictions and conflicts occur from time to time, and bilateral relations operate like a roller coaster. The third is disruptive competition. As two sides neither abide by a set of common rules nor try to avoid confrontation, competition is largely malign, driving bilateral ties toward structural antagonism.

From the Chinese perspective, a common understanding is that Sino-US competition will be a long-haul venture, sometimes accompanied by fierce confrontation and conflict unseen over the last several decades since normalization. However, China and the United States have not entered a period of all-out confrontation or a major showdown. Their relationship has just crossed the threshold to a bumpier course, yet American China policy is not completely locked up; adjustments are likely a result of changes in US domestic and international circumstances. In fact, China itself stands as a major factor shaping America's China policy as well as Sino-US interactions. Based on this understanding, Beijing believes that it is worthwhile to make relentless efforts to strive for benign competition and avoid disruptive competition.[48] Simply put, the Chinese concern over a new cold war or a quasi–cold war is rising, yet Beijing is still trying its best to forestall such a possibility.

In a sense, both sides stand at a crucial juncture to shape bilateral interactions down the road. The worrisome and dangerous tendency, as manifested in Sino-US competition during the Trump administration, reveals how nasty the rivalry could become, and the trend prevailing in early Biden administration policies related to bilateral ties suggests that a quasi–cold war scenario could emerge between the two countries, both of whom underscore the urgency of managing the future race. From the political perspective, Beijing and Washington will need to always stay in good communication with each other, not only to keep the channel open under any circumstances but also to ensure quality exchanges. It is extremely unhelpful to suspend all major dialogue mechanisms simply because they are not delivering instant results, or turn to microphone diplomacy when exchanges are not satisfactory. Consistent and serious dialogue and quiet diplomacy should always be encouraged.

Meanwhile, some red lines must not be crossed. Should Washington continue to demonize the CCP and its top leader and imply a preference for regime change in China, as occurred during the Trump years, confrontation and conflict are almost guaranteed. Likewise, the impulse to fundamentally reshape US Taiwan policy—to abandon the "One China" policy and adopt a "one China, one Taiwan" formula—would be catastrophic. It is one thing for Washington to play the "Taiwan card" against Beijing as it usually does; it is quite another to subvert the existing framework of managing the Taiwan issue, which will only facilitate the collapse of the entire relationship between China and the United States. Also, it is desirable that the two countries avoid putting ideology at the forefront.[49] Playing the ideological card may serve the purpose of domestic mobilization,[50] but it warps the nature of Sino-US competition and, more seriously, makes it all the more difficult to manage.[51] From the economic angle, each side should not resort to unilateral actions—imposing sanctions or collecting extra tariffs—to punish the other, nor should they weaponize technology or rare earth elements that will snarl the global supply chain. More broadly, they should not wrestle with each other at the expense of multilateral institutions and rules that have underpinned the current international system in which both sides have developed huge stakes.

Notes

1. Thomas W. Lippman, "The Tables Turn as a Bush Criticizes Clinton's Policy toward China," *Washington Post*, August 20, 1999, https://www.washingtonpost.com/archive/politics/1999/08/20/the-tables-turn-as-a-bush-criticizes-clintons-policy-toward-china/4f9f7aad-ca6d-49ea-9838-9fc02d8541fe/.

2. *National Security Strategy of the United States of America*, December 2017.

3. Mike Pence, "Remarks by Vice President Pence on the Administration's Policy toward China," Hudson Institute, October 4, 2018, Washington, DC, https://trumpwhitehouse.archives.gov/briefings-statements/remarks-vice-president-pence-administrations-policy-toward-china/.

4. Commentator of Xinhua News Agency, "Renghe dui zhongguo de eyi dihui doushi tout lao" [Any malicious slander of China is futile], *People's Daily*, October 12, 2018, 3; Commentator

of Xinhua News Agency, "Shui dedaoduozhu, shui shidaoguazhu" [Who attracts more support for just cause and who finds little for an unjust one?], *People's Daily*, October 18, 2018, 3.

5. Wu Xinbo, "US Competitive Policy toward China and Transformation of China-US Relations," *China International Studies*, no. 4 (2019): 26–27.

6. For a summary of America's growing and widespread dissatisfaction with China, see Harry Harding, "Has U.S. China Policy Failed?" *Washington Quarterly*, no. 3 (2015): 96–99.

7. Zhang Wenzong, "Meiguo duihua quanmian jingzheng zhanlve ji zhongmei guanxi xinx bianju" [The US strategy to compete with China in a comprehensive way and the new changes in China-US relationship], *Heping yu Fazhan* [Peace and development], no. 2 (2019): 3–7; Wu, "US Competitive Policy," 15.

8. According to a survey conducted among one hundred Chinese scholars in June 2020, 62 percent believe that the United States is indeed waging a new cold war against China, yet more than 90 percent believe that China is capable of coping well with the new cold war offensive by the United States. "China Can Deal with the US: Scholars," *Global Times*, July 7, 2020, http://www.globaltimes.cn/content/1193707.shtml.

9. Joe Biden, "Remarks by President Biden on America's Place in the World," US Department of State Headquarters, February 4, 2021, Washington, DC, https://www.whitehouse .gov/briefing-room/speeches-remarks/2021/02/04/remarks-by-president-biden-on-americas -place-in-the-world/; The White House, Interim National Security Strategic Guidance, March 2021, 8.

10. Cao Desheng, "Wang Yi: China, US Should Not Dwell on Frictions," *China Daily*, January 18, 2019, https://www.chinadailyasia.com/articles/140/196/50/1547786431632.html; "China's Foreign Minister: U.S., China Must Avoid 'Cold War Mentality,'" *China Daily*, September 27, 2018, http://www.ecns.cn/news/politics/2018-09-27/detail-ifyyknzp7230278.shtml.

11. For instance, during the second round of the China-US Diplomatic and Security Dialogue held in November 2018 in Washington, DC, the Chinese side stressed that everything China was doing was intended to contribute to the well-being of the Chinese people and the rejuvenation of the Chinese nation, not to challenge or replace anyone. See "Dierlun zhongmei waijiao anquan duihua zai meiguo huashengdun juxing" [The second round of China-US Diplomatic and Security Dialogue was held in Washington DC], Ministry of National Defense of the People's Republic of China, November 10, 2018, http://www.mod.gov.cn/topnews/20 18-11/10/content_4829114.htm.

12. "China's Ministry of Commerce (MOFCOM) Spokesman Comments on the US' Tariffs on US$34 Billion Worth of Products Imported from China," Ministry of Commerce, People's Republic of China, July 8, 2018, http://english.mofcom.gov.cn/article/newsrelease/policy re leasing/201807/20180702766205.shtml; "Foreign Ministry Spokesperson Hua Chunying's Regular Press Conference on July 11, 2018," Ministry of Foreign Affairs of the People's Republic of China, July 11, 2018, https://www.fmprc.gov.cn/ce/cglagos/eng/xwfb/fyrth/t1576325.htm.

13. "China Warns US with Sanctions on NGOs," *Global Times*, December 3, 2019, http:// www.globaltimes.cn/content/1172163.shtml.

14. "Industry Association Indicates Chinese Rare Earths Shipment to US May Slow Down," *Global Times*, August 8, 2019, http://www.globaltimes.cn/content/1160741.shtml.

15. "Regular Press Conference of the Chinese Ministry of Commerce," Ministry of Commerce, People's Republic of China, June 6, 2019, http://english.mofcom.gov.cn/article/news release/press/201906/20190602873158.shtml.

16. "MOFCOM Order No. 4 of 2020 on Provisions on the Unreliable Entity List," Ministry of Commerce, People's Republic of China, September 19, 2020, http://english.mofcom.gov .cn/article/policyrelease/questions/202009/20200903002580.shtml.

17. The author was briefed by a senior official in the Chinese Foreign Ministry, May 2019.

18. Zhong Sheng, "Zhongguo buhui qufu yu renhe jixian shiya" [China will never succumb to any extreme pressure], *People's Daily*, May 11, 2019, 3.

19. "United States and China Reach Phase One Trade Agreement," Office of the United States Trade Representative, December 13, 2019, https://ustr.gov/about-us/policy-offices/press-office/press-releases/2019/december/united-states-and-china-reach.

20. Chen Liubing, "China's Foreign Trade up 9.7% in 2018,"*China Daily*, January 14, 2019, http://www.chinadaily.com.cn/a/201901/14/WS5c3bee95a3106c65c34e43a1_1.html.

21. Chu Daye and Ma Jingjing, "China's Foreign Trade Expands 3.4% in 2019 Despite Trade Tensions with US," *Global Times*, January 14, 2019, http://www.globaltimes.cn/content/1176745.shtml.

22. Data are based on the statistics from China's General Administration of Customs: http://www.customs.gov.cn/customs/302249/302274/302276/2278778/index.html; http://www.customs.gov.cn/customs/302249/302274/302277/302276/2851260/index.html.

23. Xin Zhiming, "'Dual Circulation': A New Mode for Development," *China Daily*, August 14, 2020, https://www.chinadailyhk.com/article/140142.

24. Zhang Yunbi, "President: Strive for High-Tech Self-Reliance," *China Daily*, April 28, 2018, http://www.chinadaily.com.cn/kindle/2018-04/28/content_36112207.htm.

25. In August 2020, China's State Council unveiled a series of preferential policies aimed at further optimizing the development environment of the integrated circuit industry and the software industry. See "China Stresses High-Quality Development in Integrated Circuits and Software," State Council, People's Republic of China, August 4, 2020, http://english.www.gov.cn/policies/latestreleases/202008/04/content_WS5f2956b4c6d029c1c26373f1.html.

26. Li Zheng, "Meiguo tuidong zhongmei keji 'tuogou' de shenceng dongyin ji changqi qushi" [Motivations and long-term trends of the U.S. technology decoupling strategy], *Xiandai Guoji Guanxi* [Contemporary international relations], no. 1 (2020): 33–40; Zhu Qirong and Wang Yuping, "Telangpu zhengfu qianghua dui zhongguo jishu chukou guanzhi de jingji yingxiang: Jiyu 'quanqiu maoyi fenxi moxing' de pinggu" [On the economic impact of Trump administration's strengthening control of the US technology export to China: Assessment based on GTAP], *Dongbeiya Luntan* [Northeast Asia forum], no. 1 (2020): 54–68.

27. "China Vows to Further Open Up, Improve Investment Environment," *China Daily*, August 21, 2018, http://www.chinadaily.com.cn/a/201908/21/WS5d5d58b4a310cf3e35567241.html.

28. "President Xi Meets Harvard President," State Council, People's Republic of China, March 20, 2019, http://english.www.gov.cn/news/top_news/2019/03/20/content_28147657 1167688.htm.

29. The RCEP negotiations concluded in November 2019 with India deciding to stay away, but with the option to join at a later date if its concerns were satisfactorily addressed.

30. "Interview on Current China-US Relations Given by State Councilor and Foreign Minister Wang Yi to Xinhua News Agency," Ministry of Foreign Affairs of the People's Republic of China, August 5, 2020, https://www.fmprc.gov.cn/mfa_eng/wjdt_665385/zyjh_665391/t1804328.shtml.

31. Such measures include lowering tariff rates so as to boost import; broadening market access to the financial sector, service industry, manufacturing industry, agriculture, infrastructure, and other fields; further opening up the financial industry; accelerating the construction of free trade port and zones; and promulgating and implementing regulations of the Foreign Investment Law so as to strengthen intellectual property protection and create a market environment where domestic and foreign companies are treated equally and compete

on a level playing field. See "Vice Foreign Minister Zheng Zeguang Holds a Video Symposium with the Business Community of the United States (US)," Ministry of Foreign Affairs of the People's Republic of China, July 17, 2020, https://www.fmprc.gov.cn/mfa_eng/wjdt_665385 /wshd_665389/t1799274.shtml.

32. "AmCham Shanghai Releases 2020 China Business Report, " AmCham Shanghai, September 9, 2020, https://www.amcham-shanghai.org/en/article/amcham-shanghai-releases -2020-china-business-report. Similarly, a survey released by the US-China Business Council in August 2020 found nearly 70 percent of US firms expressing optimism about market prospects in China and 87 percent saying they had no plans to shift production out of China. US-China Business Council, Member Survey, 2020, 6–8, https://www.uschina.org/sites/default/files/us cbc_member_survey_2020.pdf.

33. Nicholas R. Lardy and Tianlei Huang, "Despite the Rhetoric, US-China Financial Decoupling Is Not Happening," PIIE, July 2, 2020, https://www.piie.com/blogs/china-economic -watch/despite-rhetoric-us-china-financial-decoupling-not-happening.

34. "WTO's China Tariff Ruling Warns US That Multilateralism Will Continue without It: Expert," *Global Times*, September 16, 2020, https://www.globaltimes.cn/content/1201026 .shtml.

35. Wang Yi, "Righting the Wrongs and Committing to Mutual Respect and Win-Win Cooperation," Ministry of Foreign Affairs of the People's Republic of China, February 22, 2021, https://www.fmprc.gov.cn/mfa_eng/wjb_663304/zzjg_663340/bmdyzs_664814/xwlb_6648 16/202102/t20210222_10409669.html.

36. "Wang Yi: Underline Three Bottom Lines of China's Relations with the United States," Ministry of Foreign Affairs of the People's Republic of China, July 26, 2021, https://www.fmp rc.gov.cn/mfa_eng/wjb_663304/zzjg_663340/bmdyzs_664814/xwlb_664816/202107/t2021 0727_9169400.html.

37. "Xie Feng: The Competitive, Collaborative and Adversarial Rhetoric Is a Thinly Veiled Attempt to Contain and Suppress China," Ministry of Foreign Affairs of the People's Republic of China, July 26, 2021, https://www.fmprc.gov.cn/mfa_eng/wjb_663304/zzjg_663340/bmd yzs_664814/xwlb_664816/202107/t20210726_9169403.html; "Xie Feng: The U.S. Side's So-Called 'Rules-Based International Order' Is Designed to Benefit Itself at Others' Expense, Hold Other Countries Back and Introduce 'The Law of the Jungle,'" Ministry of Foreign Affairs of the People's Republic of China, July 26, 2021, https://www.fmprc.gov.cn/mfa_eng/wjb_6633 04/zzjg_663340/bmdyzs_664814/xwlb_664816/202107/t20210726_9169404.html.

38. "Anti-Foreign Sanctions Law Necessary to Fight Hegemonism, Power Politics: Official," Xinhua, June 10, 2021, http://www.xinhuanet.com/english/2021-06/11/c_1310001370.htm.

39. "China Urges Probe into US Bio-Lab over Coronavirus 'Lab-Leak' Theory," China.org. cn, August 24, 2021, http://www.china.org.cn/world/2021-08/24/content_77710212.htm.

40. "PLA's Patrols around Taiwan Decisive Acts against 'Taiwan Independence' Separatist Forces: Defense Spokesperson," Ministry of Defense of the People's Republic of China, December 30, 2021, http://eng.mod.gov.cn/news/2021-12/30/content_4902054.htm.

41. "Xi Jinping jili nianqing ganbu fayang douzheng jingsheng" [Xi Jinping incentivizes young cadres to exercise fighting spirit], Dang Jian Wang Wei Pingtai [Micro platform at party-building website], September 9, 2021, https://m.gmw.cn/baijia/2021-09/09/35150338.html.

42. "President Xi Jinping Held Talks with Russian President Vladimir Putin," Ministry of Foreign Affairs of the People's Republic of China, February 4, 2022, https://www.fmprc.gov .cn/mfa_eng/zxxx_662805/202202/t20220204_10638923.html.

43. "Wang Yi Holds Talks with Iranian Foreign Minister Mohammad Javad Zarif," Ministry of Foreign Affairs of the People's Republic of China, March 28, 2021, https://www.fmprc.gov

.cn/mfa_eng/wjb_663304/zzjg_663340/xybfs_663590/gjlb_663594/2818_663626/2820_663
630/202103/t20210329_9168904.html; "Wang Yi Holds Talks with Iranian Foreign Minister
Hossein Amir-Abdollahian," Ministry of Foreign Affairs of the People's Republic of China, January 15, 2021, https://www.fmprc.gov.cn/mfa_eng/wjb_663304/zzjg_663340/xybfs_663590
/gjlb_663594/2818_663626/2820_663630/202201/t20220115_10496094.html.

44. "President Xi Jinping Had a Virtual Meeting with US President Joe Biden," Ministry
of Foreign Affairs of the People's Republic of China, November 16, 2021, https://www.fmprc
.gov.cn/mfa_eng/wjb_663304/zzjg_663340/bmdyzs_664814/gjlb_664818/3432_664920/34
35_664926/202111/t20211116_10448843.html.

45. See, for instance, Michael Lind, "Cold War II," *National Review*, no. 10 (2018): 24–29; Niall Ferguson, "The New Cold War? It's with China, and It Has Already Begun," *New York Times*,
December 2, 2019, https://cn.nytimes.com/opinion/20191204/china-cold-war/.

46. See, for instance, Henry Kissinger, *On China* (New York: Penguin Press, 2011), 525.

47. For a more detailed discussion of the impact of China's rise on international order,
see Wu Xinbo, "China in Search of a Liberal Partnership International Order," *International
Affairs*, no. 5 (2018): 995–1018.

48. Wu Xinbo, "Lun zhongmei zhanlve jingzheng" [On Sino-US strategic competition],
Shijie Jingji yu Zhengzhi [World economics and politics], no. 5 (2020): 96–130. In the summer of
2020, as the Trump administration took a series of actions to pressure and punish China and
drove bilateral ties to a new low, Chinese state councilor and foreign minister Wang Yi stated
that China would make a "cool-headed and sensible response to the impulsive moves and
anxiety of the US side," and it was ready to "restart the dialogue mechanisms with the US side
at any level, in any area and at any time." Beijing also proposed to Washington that the two
countries draw up three lists, respectively, on cooperation, dialogue, and issues that needed
proper management, and draw up a road map for future interactions. See "Interview on Current China-US Relations Given by State Councilor and Foreign Minister Wang Yi to Xinhua
News Agency," Ministry of Foreign Affairs of the People's Republic of China, August 6, 2020,
https://www.fmprc.gov.cn/mfa_eng/wjdt_665385/zyjh_665391/t1804328.shtml.

49. A speech made by National Security Advisor Robert C. O'Brien is especially illustrative
of efforts on the part of the Trump administration to highlight the ideological dimension of
rivalry with China. Robert C. O'Brien, "The Chinese Communist Party's Ideology and Global
Ambitions," June 24, 2020, Phoenix, AZ, https://trumpwhitehouse.archives.gov/briefings-st
atements/chinese-communist-partys-ideology-global-ambitions/.

50. It is worth noting that some US analysts suggest that Washington should cast its strategic competition with China in ideological terms because "historically what has moved [and]
motivated the American people is a recognition that the principles on which their systems
[are] founded are under threat." See Aaron L. Friedberg, "Competing with China," *Survival*,
no. 3 (2018): 10.

51. Elbridge Colby and Robert D. Kaplan, "The Ideology Delusion: U.S.-China Competition
Is Not about Ideology," *Foreign Affairs*, September 4, 2020, https://www.foreignaffairs.com/ar
ticles/united-states/2020-09-04/ideology-delusion.

6

The Evolution of America's China Policy: Rethink, Reset, Recalibrate

Elizabeth Economy

Introduction

From the late 2000s through 2022, the US approach to China transformed from one that sought to expand areas of cooperation and simultaneously reduce competition to one that accepted overt political, economic, and security competition and sought to manage it through discrete areas of cooperation. This evolution of US policy toward an embrace of strategic competition reflected a complex interplay of political change in both China and the United States. For decades, the United States had pursued a policy of "constructive engagement," in which the United States encouraged China's integration into the rules-based international order with the understanding that, over time, China would become a pillar of that order, or a "responsible stakeholder."[1] Many adherents of constructive engagement also believed that this process, when coupled with the rise of the Chinese middle class, would eventually lead China to liberalize its political and economic systems. The United States maintained a system of allies and partners in the Asia-Pacific as a hedge against the possibility that China might not proceed along this path, but the presumption of the US policymaking community was that China's trajectory would follow that of other previous rapidly growing authoritarian-turned-democratic nations, such as Japan, South Korea, and Taiwan.

Despite such optimism, China's path did indeed diverge from the expectations of many US policymakers. The 2008 global financial crisis and the advent of Xi Jinping as China's leader in 2012–13 ushered in changes to Chinese domestic and foreign policy that challenged the assumptions of constructive engagement. At home, Chinese political and economic reform stalled and even regressed. And on the global stage, China's ambition to be on par with, or even surpass, the United States crystallized and encouraged a far more assertive foreign policy. Even members of the US business community and civil society—traditionally mainstays of support for constructive engagement—questioned whether US policy was adequate to manage the relationship with China. Gradually, US policy evolved from an approach of "engage but hedge" to one more accurately described as "hedge but engage." In 2011, the United States "pivoted" or "rebalanced" to Asia, elevating the hedge element of its approach while still seeking cooperation with China.

The dramatic changes inside China were matched in 2016 by an equally consequential change in the United States: the transition in US leadership from Barack Obama to Donald Trump, and then in 2020, to Joe Biden. President Trump entered office with an "America First" agenda, a determination to reduce US commitments on the global stage, and a lack of strategic vision for the US relationship with China. The Trump administration China policy soon bifurcated: the president focused almost exclusively on bilateral negotiations with China over trade and North Korea, while much of the rest of his administration amplified and hardened the hedge component of the US approach. The Trump administration policy cohered into one that rejected engagement and centered on competing with, countering, and containing an ever-expanding number of perceived threats emanating from China. Its approach gained credibility when former Obama officials Kurt Campbell and Ely Ratner published an article suggesting that engagement had failed.[2] And the COVID-19 pandemic, which originated in China and engulfed the United States and much of the rest of the world during 2020, only confirmed for the White House the correctness of its approach. By the time the administration left office, observers in and outside the United States wondered whether China and the United States were on the precipice of a "new cold war."[3]

The perception of the threat posed by China to US economic and national security, as well as to democratic values, remained consistent when President Biden assumed power in January 2021; the new administration retained a number of the policies put in place by President Trump and rejected some others, such as an overt effort to weaken the Chinese Communist Party (CCP). The new administration, for example, enhanced significantly the priority placed on allied cooperation and US leadership on the global stage as a means of reinforcing US policy priorities and countering China. The administration also introduced the concept of guardrails in the US-China bilateral relationship—discrete areas of cooperation, such as climate change, for example—in an effort to prevent the relationship from devolving into kinetic conflict. Tensions remained high, however, and China's decision to offer tacit support to Moscow's invasion of Ukraine solidified and reinforced the sense of an emerging new cold war.

This chapter analyzes the interplay of factors in both China and the United States during the Obama and Trump administrations as well as during the first year of the Biden administration, which contributed to the transformation in US policy toward China from one of constructive engagement to managed competition. While the US-Soviet Cold War analogy—with competing economic, political, and security blocs—does not accurately reflect the current situation between the United States and China, policy choices by both sides have enhanced the likelihood of such an outcome.

A Changing China

As President Obama entered office in 2009, US policy was firmly grounded in the notion of constructive engagement. The president traveled to China during his first year in office and, together with Chinese president Hu Jintao, adopted a broad joint statement of potential areas of collaboration, including military-to-military relations as well as science, human rights, climate change, and health, among others.[4] President Obama also launched a Strategic and Economic Dialogue that expanded upon the previous Bush administration's Strategic Economic Dialogue and Senior Dialogue, which covered political and security issues; he also spoke about the US-China relationship as one that would "shape the 21st century."[5] In a burst of optimism, the Obama administration also announced an initiative to send one hundred thousand students to study in China during 2009–12.[6] Former senior US officials, such as C. Fred Bergsten, Henry Kissinger, and Zbigniew Brzezinski urged the president to elevate the US-China relationship even further by proposing a "G2" or special relationship with China (advice the president firmly rejected).

Yet China had already begun a public rethink of its relationship with the United States and its approach to the international order. The 2008 US-led global financial crisis caused a number of Chinese officials and scholars to question the long-accepted dominance of the US financial system and global leadership status. China's high savings rate, deep foreign currency reserves, and strict capital controls had enabled the country to weather the financial crisis far better than the United States. Several senior Chinese officials suggested that the US economy no longer deserved its model status. China's central banker Zhou Xiaochuan penned an article in which he advocated that the world move away from the dollar as the world's reserve currency.[7] And Vice Premier Wang Qishan famously told US Secretary of the Treasury Hank Paulson, "You were my teacher but look at your system, Hank, we aren't sure we should be learning from you anymore."[8] Even Premier Wen Jiabao warned the United States that it needed to ensure that Chinese savings in US treasuries remained safe.[9]

China also began to display greater assertiveness in its own backyard. In 2010, for the first time, People's Republic of China (PRC) diplomats referred to the South China Sea as a "core interest," a term that until then had included only Taiwan, Tibet, and Xinjiang. Their use of the term signaled that China would not compromise on its expansive claim of sovereignty in the South China Sea; China's claim encompasses approximately 80 percent of the South China Sea, but its assertion is contested in part or in whole by Vietnam, Malaysia, Taiwan, and the Philippines. In discussing issues related to the South China Sea, Chinese officials adopted a bullying and coercive approach. Foreign Minister Yang Jiechi, for example, threatened Singapore, stating, "China is a big country and other countries are small countries, and that's just a fact."[10] And in response to the US assertion that freedom of navigation, including in the South China Sea, was a US national interest, Yang accused the United States of plotting against China.[11] That same year, a Chinese fishing trawler collided with two Japanese patrol ships near the Japanese-administered, but disputed, Diaoyu/Senkaku islands, leading to a diplomatic standoff between China and Japan.

This new Chinese assertiveness contributed to a significant evolution in US policy. In 2011, in her article "America's Pacific Century,"[12] Secretary of State Hillary Clinton suggested that the United States would "pivot" to Asia. The "pivot"—or "rebalance," as it was later termed—signaled a shift in the United States' center of gravity away from the Middle East and Europe to the Asia-Pacific. It reinforced America's commitment to its formal allies and suggested enhanced partnerships with other countries in the region, such as Singapore, Malaysia, and India. The Obama administration had already taken steps to increase its engagement in the region by announcing in November 2009 that the United States would participate in negotiations initiated by New Zealand to establish a Trans-Pacific Partnership (TPP), a high-standard trade agreement with eleven other countries in Asia and the Americas that represented 40 percent of global GDP.[13] The agreement, while not directed against China, was viewed by some members of the US administration as an opportunity to signal China that its failure to make progress on economic reform had costs.[14] (Others also argued that the TPP could be used by economic reformers in China to push for greater opening.[15]) As part of the pivot, the United States pledged to move 60 percent of its military forces to the Asia-Pacific by 2020.[16] And in 2011, the United States also joined the East Asian Summit, a regional economic and security forum that China had hoped to lead.[17] In formal government documents describing the rebalance, China was identified separately, and primarily in the context of helping to solve global challenges. The Obama administration also noted that Beijing should not believe that it could "wield influence while opting out of international norms."[18]

The Xi Factor

Even more significant than the global financial crisis in transforming US policy toward China was the selection of Xi Jinping as General Secretary of the Chinese Communist Party in 2012 and president of China in 2013. Structural changes in the economic and military power of China relative to that of the United States certainly held the potential for greater conflict. Economic competition between the United States and China, for example, was almost certain to intensify as China's economy moved up the value chain, no matter the selection of Chinese leader. Moreover, Chinese rhetoric concerning its sovereignty claims in the South China Sea had begun to intensify prior to Xi's ascension, contributing to growing security tensions in the region.

However, President Xi transformed Chinese domestic and foreign policies in ways that raised fundamentally new questions about the country's commitment to domestic political and economic reform as well as to the rules-based order.[19] Major economic initiatives such as Made in China 2025[20] and new restrictive laws around cybersecurity created an uneven playing field for multinationals and threatened their ability to compete effectively. These policies, along with a lack of progress on issues such as market access, government subsidies for Chinese firms, and intellectual property theft, weakened US business support for a traditional engagement approach. Xi also reduced opportunities for Chinese nongovernmental organizations (NGOs) to interact with their foreign counterparts through the highly restrictive January 1, 2017, Law on the Administration of Activities of Overseas Nongovernmental Organizations in the Mainland of China. The law mandated onerous registration and operational conditions on foreign NGOs. As a result, the number of foreign NGOs operating in China fell from over 7,000[21] in 2016 to 420 in 2020.[22] This lack of civil society engagement also eroded support within the United States for the idea that "engagement" was yielding success.

Under Xi Jinping, China also assumed a more expansive role on the international stage in ways that challenged both the norms of the liberal international order and US global leadership. In June 2013, at the Obama-Xi Sunnylands summit, Xi proposed a "new model of major country relationship"[23] that elevated the US-China relationship above others and carried with it an implicit message of equality in China's and the United States' status on the global stage. Beijing's announcement of its One Belt, One Road infrastructure connectivity initiative that same year greatly overshadowed the Obama administration's modest 2011 "New Silk Road" initiative in Central Asia[24] and ultimately laid the foundation for the spread of Chinese economic, political, and security influence globally.[25] China also succeeded in attracting scores of countries—including many US allies—in support of its Asian Infrastructure Investment Bank, despite US efforts to counsel countries not to participate, at least until the bank's operational principles became clear.[26] In the security realm, China unilaterally declared an air defense identification zone over the East China Sea[27] and dramatically raised the stakes in the South China Sea by constructing and militarizing seven artificial features[28] (despite President Xi's promise to President Obama in September 2015 during a state visit to Washington that China did not "intend to pursue militarization" of the Spratly Islands[29]).

Across the Pacific, the Obama administration struggled to account for the shifting political winds in China and their broader implications for the US-China relationship. As the direction of Xi's reforms solidified, concern mounted in some parts of the US policymaking community that US policy was failing to protect, much less advance, US interests. China appeared to be laying the groundwork for a fundamental transformation in the regional—if not global—balance of power. Serious debates emerged over the CCP's intentions toward issues like the South China Sea, economic reform, and the CCP's ambitions in East Asia, among others.[30] The administration further strengthened the hedge element of its strategy by bolstering its commitment to regional security. The US supported the Philippines in pursuing its (winning) case in the International Permanent Court of Arbitration against Chinese claims in the South China Sea,[31] lifted the ban on the sale of lethal weapons to Vietnam, and pledged that US patrols in the South China Sea in defense of freedom of navigation would be a regular occurrence.[32] At the same time, the administration remained committed to pursuing concrete cooperation with China on issues it believed were critical to US security. Together the United States and China forged an agreement in 2014 that helped jump-start the international climate change negotiations and ultimately resulted in the 2015 Paris climate accord.[33] And the United States and China also signed a US-China cyberagreement in 2015 that resulted in a decline in the absolute number of Chinese cyberattacks (although experts argued that while the absolute number declined, the sophistication of the attacks increased).[34]

Ultimately, the Obama-era "engage but hedge" and "hedge but engage" approaches to China achieved discrete successes in both tangibly reengaging the United States in the Asia-Pacific and achieving important agreements with China on climate change and cybersecurity. Chinese domestic political and economic reform, however, stalled. And the administration did not effectively constrain Chinese ambition in areas such as the South China Sea. Instead, as one senior Obama official neatly summed up the situation at the end of the administration's tenure, "An increasingly assertive China under the bold and powerful leadership of Xi Jinping has posed an undeniable challenge to American regional leadership and prevailing international principles."[35]

The Trump Administration: A Revolution Begins

The election of Donald Trump as president of the United States in 2016 presaged the end of the "engage but hedge" approach. Both President Trump's broad strategic framework and his priorities with regard to China were at odds with traditional US engagement policy. Campaigning under the banner of "America First," President Trump argued that the United States had sacrificed its own interests in support of others—that it had borne an unfair share of the burden of global security and fallen victim to unequal trade deals that disadvantaged the country.[36] He dismissed the value of allies and multilateralism, viewing them as constraints on American interests and power.[37] And he embraced a new priority on sovereignty in US foreign policy that suggested the United States would no longer seek to influence the domestic political choices of others.[38] The president's style of diplomacy also transformed US policy. He introduced a transactional, personalistic, and unpredictable approach to diplomatic engagement and opened a fresh page in America foreign policy in which everything appeared open to negotiation.

The president's America First platform had important implications for US policy toward China. He identified only two priorities as central to the interests and security of the American people: redressing the bilateral trade deficit and dealing with North Korea.[39] Trade with China had been an important talking point on Trump's presidential campaign trail, where he railed against Chinese "illegal activities" and suggested that he would impose a 45 percent tariff on Chinese exports to the United States.[40] At the same time, the president wanted China's help in making progress on the denuclearization of the Korean peninsula.[41] A skeptic on multilateral institutions and arrangements, he focused more on withdrawing the United States from international institutions rather than drawing China into the rules-based order.

Yet the president's America First framework and narrow agenda with China represented only one element of his administration's China policy. Rather than constraining the US agenda with China, the president's focus on trade and North Korea—and relative lack of interest in the broader array of bilateral and global concerns—ultimately allowed others in his administration to pursue a much more expansive foreign policy. Many of the president's foreign policy advisers viewed China not only as an economic competitor but also as a revisionist power bent on undermining the rules-based order. The 2017 National Security Strategy directly challenged traditional notions of US engagement: "For decades, U.S. policy was rooted in the belief that support for China's rise and for its integration into the post-war international order would liberalize China." Instead, the report noted, "China seeks to displace the United States in the Indo-Pacific region, expand the reaches of its state-driven economic model, and reorder the region in its favor."[42] The president's national security and foreign policy team believed that the United States should lead in upholding the current rules-based order and, in this context, placed a much higher value on US relations with allies and partners than the president. Moreover, they embraced a much broader agenda for US-China policy, including human rights, technology competition, Taiwan, and Chinese influence activities, among others. The Trump administration's China policy, therefore, reflected both a strong emphasis on trade and North Korea as well as the adoption and amplification of the Obama administration's hedging strategy. Missing in this policy constellation, however, was a determined effort to continue trying to engage China.

"America First," Trade, and North Korea to the Fore

"America First" quickly translated into actual policy. On just his third day in office, President Trump withdrew from the end-stage negotiations around the Trans-Pacific Partnership, the twelve-nation trade deal that would have been the largest regional trade accord in history.[43] In addition, he suggested that he would consider withdrawing troops from Japan and South Korea if they did not increase their financial share of maintaining the alliance.[44] For both China and US partners, these announcements appeared to signal a retreat from the Obama administration's rebalance and commitment to regional leadership.

At the same time, President Trump early on telegraphed his new diplomatic style. Immediately following his election, he angered Beijing by accepting a congratulatory phone call from Taiwanese president Tsai Ing-wen, becoming the first president to have direct contact with a Taiwanese leader since President Jimmy Carter in 1979.[45] He also indicated that he would be willing to reconsider the One China policy, noting, "I don't know why we have to be bound by a One China policy unless we make a deal with China having to do with other things, including trade."[46] Just one month later, however, during his first call with President Xi Jinping, President Trump recognized the One China policy as a foundational principle for the US-China relationship.

Securing a favorable trade deal with China quickly emerged as President Trump's top priority. During his first meeting with President Xi at Mar-a-Lago in April 2017, the two sides agreed to a ten-point economic action plan to be implemented over the course of one hundred days,[47] and they established a new framework for dialogue, the United States-China Comprehensive Dialogue, with four tracks: the Diplomatic and Security Dialogue, the Comprehensive Economic Dialogue, the Law Enforcement and Cybersecurity Dialogue, and the Social and Cultural Issues Dialogue.[48] At the same time, President Trump seemed to suggest a willingness to exchange a trade deal for a North Korea deal, remarking that if Beijing were to "solve the problem in North Korea" it would be "worth having deficits."[49] And in the aftermath of the meeting, he praised Xi

Jinping as a "good man."[50] The president's personal outreach to Xi only accelerated in the following months; when the two met in Beijing, Trump stated that Xi was a "great friend" and the "Chinese people should be proud to have him as their leader."[51]

Despite this seemingly auspicious beginning, both trade and North Korea became significant sources of contention rather than cooperation in the bilateral relationship. Both substantively and stylistically, the Trump and Xi administrations shared little common ground. In the trade negotiations, President Trump's demands for China to rectify the trade imbalance and undertake immediate systemic economic reform generated limited enthusiasm among Chinese policymakers (with the exception of some Chinese economic reformers who held out hope that pressure from the White House would force Xi Jinping to get back on track with economic reform and opening). Within only a few months of the meeting in Mar-a-Lago, the Trump administration initiated an investigation into China's alleged theft of intellectual property under Section 301 of the Trade Act of 1974, and, reflecting concern over China's hollowing out of the US semiconductor industry, the president also blocked the purchase of Lattice Semiconductor by a Chinese-backed investor.[52] It marked only the fourth time in over twenty-five years that a US president had made such a decision.[53] Less than a year later, in the face of China's failure to make progress on his demands, President Trump levied tariffs on $34 billion of Chinese goods, precipitating a tit-for-tat series of progressively harsher tariffs over the course of 2018–19.[54] Ultimately, in October 2019, the two sides concluded a Phase One trade deal.[55] The deal fell well short of Washington's ambitions to force China to reform its economy, but it was generally assessed by outside observers as a relative win for the administration. One year later, however, China had fulfilled only 53 percent of the target, and, in fact, Chinese imports from the United States were lower than they had been prior to the trade deal (although some of the shortfall likely resulted from the COVID-19-related contraction in the Chinese economy during the first quarter of 2020).

President Trump also moved quickly to try to make progress on his second priority: working with China to reign in North Korea's nuclear program. After appearing to win an almost unprecedented level of cooperation from China in the early stages of his administration to sign on to and enforce sanctions on North Korea, however, the president soon became impatient with the lack of progress.[56] By his second year in office, the administration's policy and rhetoric toward China was noticeably more critical, castigating China for failing to fully implement sanctions while rejecting its "dual-track approach" to peace on the Korean peninsula.[57] President Trump also attempted to secure a deal independently with North Korea during a June 12, 2018, meeting with North Korean leader Kim Jong-Un in Singapore.[58] Despite Beijing's dismay at being excluded from the process, it ultimately viewed the deal as a win because the concessions President Trump made were in line with Beijing's "freeze for freeze" proposal—an initiative the United States had previously rejected.[59] China and the United States continued to hold discussions on North Korea but never regained the early momentum of the first year.[60] Together with Russia and North Korea, China called for easing UN sanctions on North Korea[61] and twice blocked US efforts in the United Nations to declare North Korea in breach of sanctions (in July 2018 and in June 2019).[62] The United States, in turn, sanctioned Chinese shipping companies and banks for allowing ship-to-ship transfer of sanctioned North Korean oil and coal in the Yellow Sea.

President Trump's efforts on trade and North Korea fell significantly short of his objectives, and his negotiating style produced a brinksmanship that roiled markets and threatened a rupture in the relationship. Nonetheless, his approach won plaudits from many in the US business and security communities who had long been frustrated with China's ongoing failure to reform its economy and/or use its leverage to pressure North Korea.[63] Even within some segments of the American farming community, which was among the hardest hit by the president's tariff war, his efforts commanded support for attempting to level the playing field.[64]

The Rise of the Rest: Reinforcing the Rules-Based Order

While President Trump's high-profile diplomatic wrangling with China on trade and North Korea captured global headlines, much of the rest of his administration worked to sustain important elements of the more traditional US hedging strategy toward China. Senior administration officials and members of Congress stressed to allies that the United States placed a high value on its strategic partnerships and that the US was committed to strong and historical alliances with other Asian countries. They traveled widely throughout Asia reiterating calls for a rules-based order, freedom of navigation, free trade, and political freedoms.[65]

President Trump only rarely mentioned the importance of allies and the rules-based system. At the November 2017 APEC CEO Summit, however, he called for a "free and open Indo-Pacific" and referenced the need for all countries in the region to uphold the principles that had benefited everyone, such as "respect for the rule of law, individual rights, [and] freedom of navigation and overflight, including open shipping lanes." He went on to state, "These principles create stability and build trust, security, and prosperity among like-minded nations."[66] The speech was followed by a meeting of senior officials from the United States, Australia, Japan, and India, in what amounted to the revival of the Quadrilateral Security Dialogue—a 2007 initiative originally proposed by

Japan.[67] This grouping became the foundation for the administration's continued effort to hedge against an increasingly influential China.

The administration's contention that China was a "strategic competitor" and "revisionist power" opened the door to the mobilization of resources across government agencies to defend against a wide range of perceived threats including China's Belt and Road Initiative (BRI), activities in the South China Sea, and initiatives in the United Nations. In 2017, the administration followed through on President Trump's pledge to President Xi to send a delegation to the first Belt and Road Forum. By early 2018, however, senior administration officials, such as Secretary of State Rex Tillerson, were calling out the BRI for its predatory loan policies and weak governance standards.[68] The administration and Congress also collaborated to develop institutions and initiatives to compete with the BRI, such as the 2018 Build Act, which created the Development Finance Corporation to support private sector infrastructure investment in developing economies,[69] and the Asia Reassurance Initiative Act, which provided support for democracy promotion in the Indo-Pacific.[70] In 2019, the United States, Australia, and Japan announced the Blue Dot Network, a certification process for companies and countries seeking to ensure high-quality infrastructure projects.[71]

In the highly contested South China Sea, the administration publicized Chinese activities and ramped up its freedom of navigation operations (FONOPS) from three in 2017 to nine in 2019.[72] In addition, the United States worked closely with allies and partners, including Australia, Japan, Vietnam, the UK, France, and India, among others, to increase multilateral maritime patrols,[73] and it disinvited Beijing from the 2018 Rim of the Pacific exercise in retaliation for its continued militarization of the contested features in the Spratly islands.[74] Secretary of State Pompeo, upending decades of US neutrality around the validity of various nations' claims, also declared China's activities unlawful.[75]

Even in areas not considered high priority by President Trump, such as the United Nations, the administration pushed back against Chinese initiatives. President Trump denigrated the United Nations, calling it an "underperformer" and "not a friend of democracy," and he complained about the large share of the United Nations budget paid by the United States.[76] Most notably, he pulled the United States out of the UN Human Rights Council, the Paris climate accord, and the World Health Organization. Nonetheless, his foreign policy team targeted the United Nations as an important arena in which to counter Chinese influence. In March and then again in September 2019, the Trump administration successfully fought off Chinese attempts to include language supporting the Belt and Road in the reauthorization resolution for the UN mission in Afghanistan, despite the fact that the reference had been included for the three years prior. Jonathan Cohen, acting US permanent representative to the United Nations, argued that China was "using Security Council resolutions as a platform for inappropriately promoting self-serving initiatives."[77] And in January 2020, the United States appointed veteran US ambassador Mark Lambert to serve as a special envoy responsible for "maintaining the integrity of multilateral institutions"—a position widely understood to be devoted to checking undue Chinese influence in the United Nations.[78]

Trade and the Trade-Off with Human Rights and Democracy

Human rights have traditionally occupied a considered, albeit rarely a central, role in US policy toward China, and Washington has often agreed to limit its criticism in exchange for Chinese compliance on other issues, such as trade. During the Trump administration, this battle became a defining feature of the administration's China policy.

In 2017–18, reports that Beijing had detained more than one million Uyghur Muslims in labor and reeducation camps in Xinjiang Uyghur Autonomous Region flooded the Western media.[79] President Trump reportedly supported the Chinese effort, telling Xi Jinping personally in two separate meetings in 2017 and 2019 that the Chinese government was doing the right thing in building the camps.[80] And in May 2019, as the United States worked toward a trade deal with China, Treasury officials successfully blocked the sanctions on individual Chinese officials that had been proposed by Congress over concerns that the move would undermine a trade deal.[81] Despite the president's reluctance, however, the administration did take action. In October 2019, after the trade deal had been concluded—albeit not yet signed—the United States put in place visa restrictions for CCP officials and their families involved in the detention of Muslim minority groups in China and blacklisted twenty-eight Chinese companies, government offices, and security bureaus for participating in human rights abuses in Xinjiang.[82] That same month, the administration joined twenty-two other countries at the United Nations calling on China to respect human rights and permit international monitors in Xinjiang,[83] and in October 2020 the United States again supported a German resolution criticizing China's actions in Xinjiang.[84]

President Trump displayed a similar reluctance in fall 2019 to risk the pending trade deal for the Hong Kong Human Rights and Democracy Act, a congressional bill that called on China to protect the freedoms promised Hong Kong under the Basic Law or risk the United States terminating the island's special economic status. The president commented, "We have to stand with Hong Kong, but I'm also standing with President Xi; he's a friend of mine."[85] Later, he made clear that his resistance to the bill stemmed from his concern that it

might derail the success of his trade deal. He also suggested that his administration might ignore provisions of the bill that interfered with the exercise of
his "constitutional authority to state the foreign policy of the United States."[86]
Congress secured the passage of the bill and President Trump signed it into law
in November 2019. Seven months later, in the wake of Beijing's implementation
of a new National Security Law in Hong Kong, Secretary of State Pompeo decer-
tified Hong Kong as sufficiently politically autonomous to merit independent
standing. In July, Hong Kong lost the special economic status that enabled it to
be treated separately from mainland China on issues related to trade and investment, visas, and other policies.[87]

By most measures, the Trump White House was a strong advocate for Taiwan
on the global stage. This support reflected not only the long-standing efforts of
the US Congress but also the interests of a constellation of Asia experts within
the Trump administration who themselves had deep ties to Taiwan. Congress advanced a number of new Taiwan-related initiatives, including the Taiwan Travel
Act, which encouraged senior US officials to travel to Taiwan,[88] and the Taiwan
Allies International Protection and Enhancement Initiative Act, which called,
among other things, for the United States to withhold funding from countries
that withdrew diplomatic recognition from Taiwan in favor of China.[89] In July
2019, members of Congress accused the administration of delaying the com-
pletion of an $8 billion arms sales package to Taiwan in July 2019 for fear of
undermining trade negotiations,[90] but the administration did approve parts of
the arms sales package the following month.

Chinese Influence and the American Public

One of the most significant shifts in US policy toward China during the Trump
administration was the extent to which officials portrayed China as a direct
threat to core American interests and values that extended well beyond unfair trade practices. Spurred in part by Congress, the administration called for
a "whole-of-society" response to the threat posed by Chinese efforts to influence the American public.[91] These influence activities included the presence
of Confucius Institutes and Chinese Student and Scholars Associations on
college campuses, unfettered Chinese media access to American citizens, and
Chinese government efforts to steal US technology and/or coerce US companies into aligning themselves with Chinese political values. The decision of
Beijing to sanction the NBA for a tweet posted by the general manager of the
Houston Rockets in support of democracy activists in Hong Kong was particularly important in bringing these issues into the consciousness of the broader
American public.[92] The administration expressed concern both over the lack
of reciprocity—or equivalent access for US actors in China—and the ability of

these Chinese actors to use their economic leverage and political influence to undermine US institutions.

The US Congress held multiple hearings to explore the issue of Chinese influence operations.[93] Once obscure programs, such as the Thousand Talents Program, which offered financial and other incentives for leading scientists outside China to partner with Chinese research labs, made media headlines as the Trump administration and Congress identified the program as a conduit for intellectual property theft.[94] Both the FBI and US attorneys general devoted significant resources to exposing the avenues of PRC technology theft, educating university and corporate heads, and prosecuting alleged perpetrators.[95] By 2020, there were one thousand investigations underway.[96] The Trump administration also took the unprecedented step of closing the Chinese consulate in Houston, accusing it of fraud and espionage.[97] These efforts to protect the United States from undue Chinese influence, while welcomed in some quarters, also raised serious concerns about the potential for students and scholars of Chinese descent to be targeted for discrimination or even attack.[98]

The COVID-19 pandemic, which originated in China and spread throughout the world in 2020, only heightened the sense of popular fear and distrust of China within the American public. The White House criticized the Chinese leadership for its lack of transparency at the outset of the pandemic and for allowing the virus to spread beyond the country's borders. As the virus devasted the US population, the administration did not mandate the strict policies adopted in some other countries to control the virus's spread. Instead, the president continued to lay the blame squarely at the feet of Beijing, repeatedly calling the disease the "China virus." In his speech before the United Nations in September 2020, President Trump accused China and the World Health Organization of collusion, stating, "The Chinese government and the World Health Organization—which is virtually controlled by China—falsely declared that there was no evidence of human-to-human transmission. Later they falsely said people without symptoms would not spread the disease."[99]

The White House's message of Chinese culpability took hold within a wide segment of the US population. The Pew Research Center reported in October 2020 that 77 percent of Americans had no confidence that Chinese president Xi Jinping would do the right thing with regard to world affairs, a dramatic increase from 50 percent the year before. And a roughly equivalent number, 73 percent, saw China in a negative light.[100] China's own undiplomatic behavior in managing the coronavirus on the global stage undoubtedly contributed to the steep decline in US popular opinion with regard to China; however, the president's rhetoric certainly contributed to inflamed tensions. One result was a significant increase in verbal and physical assaults against Asian Americans.[101]

Revitalizing American Resilience and Responsibility

The advent of the Biden administration in January 2021 introduced a complex new mix of policies that reflected both Obama- and Trump-era preferences as well as new approaches to managing the challenges that surfaced as a result of COVID-19. The overarching approach moved away from the Trump-era "strategic competition" to the notion of "managed competition"—a clear recognition that the bilateral relationship was characterized by strategic competition across all domains coupled with the belief that such competition could be managed by intensive diplomacy. The US ability to manage strategic competition with China, in turn, rested on four pillars.

First, the administration stressed that for the United States to be competitive with China, it needed to focus on transforming the US political economy: investing more in research and development (R&D), strengthening supply chain resilience—whether on semiconductors or critical minerals—and redoubling efforts to incentivize corporations to locate advanced manufacturing facilities at home.

Second, the administration sought to counter unfair and malign Chinese political and economic behaviors. In so doing, it retained many of the punitive elements of the Trump administration's strategy that were designed to pressure China to change its behavior, such as the extensive tariffs on Chinese goods. The Biden team also expanded the number of sanctions and export controls levied against Chinese entities. President Biden further signed into law the Uyghur Forced Labor Prevention Act in December 2021, which forced companies that sourced from Xinjiang to prove that their goods were not produced by forced labor.[102]

Third—and the most significant shift in US policy from the Trump to the Biden administrations—was the clear priority of working with democratic allies and other partners and reengaging with multilateral institutions as a means of changing the strategic environment in which China operated. The administration also cast much of its work with allies and multilateral institutions as values-based diplomacy, drawing a sharp distinction between the United States and its allies and an autocratic China. In December 2021, for example, it held a Summit for Democracy with well over one hundred countries in attendance.

US cooperation with regional partners also flourished. In March 2021, for example, the administration worked with the Quad to expand the writ of the institution by launching a Quad Vaccine Partnership and a set of new cooperative ventures around critical and emerging technologies, climate change, semiconductor supply chains, and cybersecurity.[103] In addition, it established a new defense pact with Australia and the UK, AUKUS. The Biden team worked particularly diligently to reestablish positive relations with the European Union and the UK. President Biden referred to the transatlantic relationship as "the cornerstone of all that we hope to accomplish in the 21st century,"[104] reaffirmed US support for NATO, resolved several outstanding trade disputes, and, together with European partners, established the Trade and Technology Council to foster cooperation on issues such as technical standards, supply chains, and export controls.

Beyond reasserting the importance of working with allies to shape China's external environment, the Biden administration also distinguished itself from its predecessor by a renewed focus on US leadership of international agreements and institutions. It reclaimed leadership on climate change; stood up a new initiative around global infrastructure development, Partnership for Global Infrastructure Investment; rejoined the UN Human Rights Commission; and put forward a US nominee for leadership of the International Telecommunication Union, a UN body that had been headed by a Chinese official for eight years.

The fourth pillar of the Biden administration's China strategy was continued bilateral engagement with China. Presidents Xi and Biden, as well as their senior-most foreign affairs officials, US National Security Advisor Jake Sullivan and Secretary of State Antony Blinken and their Chinese counterparts State Councilor Yang Jiechi and Foreign Minister Wang Yi, maintained a consistent stream of political dialogues. Equally consistently, however, these dialogues served more to underscore rather than help bridge the growing diplomatic, economic, and security divide between the two countries.[105] Taiwan, trade, and human rights as well as differing conceptions of the "rules-based order," among other issues, all emerged as points of discord. Moreover, the two sides laid bare a vast disconnect in how they preferred to approach their diplomatic engagement moving forward. The Chinese officials called for an improved overall environment in the bilateral relationship before negotiating individual issues, while the US officials stressed the need for negotiations on a set of critical and unique issues—later referred to as "guardrails"—such as military-to-military relations or climate change, that would help prevent the competitive relationship from devolving into kinetic conflict. Even the calls between presidents Biden and Xi appeared to result more in clarifications of differences than success in ameliorating tensions.

Nonetheless, bilateral diplomacy did achieve some notable successes. In line with the fall 2021 United Nations Climate Change Conference in Glasgow, China and the United States signed a framework agreement to work together to reduce methane emissions and protect forests.[106] In addition, cooperation among environmental, energy, and economic bureaucracies continued to move forward, with negotiations on trade, capacity building on intellectual property rights protection, and dialogues on macroeconomic strategy. In addition,

China supported a US-led initiative to release strategic oil reserves in November 2021 to help control prices.

Conclusion

Over the past decade, US policymakers have rethought, recalibrated, and reset US policy toward China. The Obama administration began the process of re-assessing the bilateral relationship as China's stalled economic and political reform at home and more assertive behavior on the international stage raised questions about the adequacy of constructive engagement for managing the US-China relationship. Still, even as the administration strengthened the hedge element of its China policy, it retained a belief that engagement with China was both useful and necessary to address the range of global challenges shared by the two countries.

The Trump administration continued the Obama effort to strengthen relations with allies in the Asia-Pacific but discerned little value in engaging China beyond President Trump's efforts to achieve agreement on trade and North Korea. Despite the president's lack of interest in the wider sweep of US-China policy, the administration successfully identified and attempted to push back against a wide range of Chinese initiatives and perceived threats. Without presidential leadership, however, US policy assumed a highly reactive and defensive character; there was no articulation of a proactive or positive narrative of US leadership. The Trump administration also introduced issues of Chinese influence operations in ways that contributed to a new and overwhelmingly negative perception of China within the American public—a perception that was exacerbated by the pandemic and the administration's associated rhetoric.

The Biden administration reasserted a more traditional form of US leadership on the global stage, working with allies and seeking to forge a broader shared narrative around democratic values that stood in stark contrast to China's increasingly authoritarian regime. At the same time, the US administration did not shy away from using its economic leverage in the form of extensive tariffs, sanctions, and export controls to try to pressure China to change its behavior with regard to trade and human rights abuses. It also developed a new effort to develop resilient supply chains in concert with allies and partners. Unlike the Trump administration, it acknowledged the value of cooperation with China, albeit on a narrow set of issues rather than a broad-based strategic level.

The future of the US-China relationship is a challenging one as sources of strategic competition grow. During the February 2022 Winter Olympics held in Beijing, President Biden, along with leaders of several other major market democracies, exercised a diplomatic boycott in protest over China's continued detention of Uyghur Muslims in labor and reeducation camps in Xinjiang. For his part, Xi Jinping used the occasion to stand side by side with Russian president Vladimir Putin to criticize Western alliances and claim that the Russia-China relationship was "superior to political and military alliances of the Cold War" and that there were no "forbidden areas of cooperation."[107] Just days after the Olympics ended, Russia invaded Ukraine in late February 2022; in response, China not only refused to condemn the invasion—or even call it one—but also blamed the United States and NATO for provoking Russia's action.[108]

Russia's invasion of Ukraine was an important litmus test for China's interest in improving relations with the United States and the world's other market democracies. While the long-term benefits and costs for China of its decision to provide at least tacit support to Russia are still to be realized, its refusal to acknowledge Russia's culpability has had serious near-term consequences for broader considerations of US-China policy. The decision has increased the credibility of those who argue that a new cold war between the world's democracies and autocracies is at hand, enhanced other countries' mistrust of China, and reinforced the drive by the United States and other countries toward economic decoupling. It has also brought renewed attention to Taiwan as a vulnerable democracy. National Security Advisor Sullivan stated in October 2021 that the United States' objective with China was coexistence, "not containment," and "not a new cold war."[109] Xi Jinping may well agree, but his choices are contributing to precisely the opposite outcome.

Notes

1. "Responsible stakeholder" became a term of art in September 2005 as a result of a speech by Deputy Secretary of State Robert Zoellick before the National Committee on US-China Relations. Robert Zoellick, "Whither China? From Membership to Responsibility," remarks to the National Committee on US-China Relations, September 21, 2005, https://www.ncuscr .org/wp-content/uploads/2020/04/migration_Zoellick_remarks_notes06_winter_spring.pdf.

2. Kurt M. Campbell and Ely Ratner, "The China Reckoning," *Foreign Affairs*, March/April 2018, https://www.foreignaffairs.com/articles/china/2018-02-13/china-reckoning.

3. Jeffrey A. Bader, "Avoiding a New Cold War between the US and China," Brookings Institution, August 17, 2020, https://www.brookings.edu/blog/order-from-chaos/2020/08/17 /avoiding-a-new-cold-war-between-the-us-and-china/.

4. "US-China Joint Statement," White House Office of the Press Secretary, November 17, 2009, https://obamawhitehouse.archives.gov/realitycheck/the-press-office/us-china-joint-st atement.

5. Mark Memmot, "Obama: U.S.-China Relationship Will 'Shape the 21st Century,'" NPR, July 27, 2009, https://www.npr.org/sections/thetwo-way/2009/07/obama_uschina_relations hip_wil.html.

6. "U.S.-China Joint Statement," White House Office of the Press Secretary, November 17, 2009, https://obamawhitehouse.archives.gov/realitycheck/the-press-office/us-china-joint -statement.

7. Jamil Anderlini, "China Calls for New Reserve Currency," *Financial Times*, March 23, 2009, https://www.ft.com/content/7851925a-17a2-11de-8c9d-0000779fd2ac.

8. Tom Mitchell, Gabriel Wildau, and Henry Sender, "Wang Qishan: China's Enforcer," *Financial Times*, July 24, 2017, https://www.ft.com/content/d82964ba-6d42-11e7-bfeb-33fe0 c5b7eaa.

9. Michael Wines, Keith Bradsher, and Mark Landler, "China's Leader Says He Is 'Worried' over US Treasuries," *New York Times*, March 13, 2009, https://www.nytimes.com/2009/03/14 /world/asia/14china.html.

10. John Pomfret, "U.S. Takes a Tougher Tone with China," *Washington Post*, July 30, 2010, https://www.washingtonpost.com/wp-dyn/content/article/2010/07/29/AR2010072906416 .html.

11. Pomfret, "Tougher Tone."

12. Hillary Clinton, "America's Pacific Century," *Foreign Policy*, October 11, 2011, https://fo reignpolicy.com/2011/10/11/americas-pacific-century/.

13. "Overview of TPP," Office of the United States Trade Representative, https://ustr.gov /tpp/overview-of-the-TPP.

14. Ian F. Fergusson, Mark A. McMinimy, and Brock R. Williams, "The Trans-Pacific Partnership (TPP) Negotiations and Issues for Congress," Congressional Research Service, March 20, 2015, https://fas.org/sgp/crs/row/R42694.pdf.

15. Zhang Yuanan, Chen Lixiong, and Chen Qin, "Closer Look: How Agreements like the TPP Press China to Reform," *Caixin*, October 30, 2013, https://www.caixinglobal.com /2013-10-30/closer-look-how-agreements-like-the-tpp-press-china-to-reform-101013996 .html.

16. David Alexander, "U.S. Rebalance to Asia-Pacific Gaining Steam, Pentagon Chief Says," Reuters, May 2013, https://www.reuters.com/article/us-security-asia-usa/u-s-rebalance-to-as ia-pacific-gaining-steam-pentagon-chief-says-idUSBRE95002820130601.

17. Mohan Malik, "The East Asia Summit," *Australian Journal of International Affairs* 60, no. 2 (June 2006): 207–11, https://www.tandfonline.com/doi/abs/10.1080/10357710600696134 ?journalCode=caji20.

18. "FACT SHEET: Advancing the Rebalance to Asia and the Pacific," White House Office of the Press Secretary, November 16, 2015, https://obamawhitehouse.archives.gov/the-press-off ice/2015/11/16/fact-sheet-advancing-rebalance-asia-and-pacific.

19. "Xi Highlights National Goal of Rejuvenation," *China Daily*, November 2012, https:// www.chinadaily.com.cn/china/2012-11/30/content_15972687.htm.

20. "The Made in China 2025 Initiative: Economic Implications for the United States," Congressional Research Service, April 2019, https://crsreports.congress.gov/product/pdf/IF /IF10964/4.

21. Edward Wong, "Clampdown in China Restricts 7,000 Foreign Organizations," *New York Times*, April 2016, https://www.nytimes.com/2016/04/29/world/asia/china-foreign-ngo-law .html.

22. Jessica Batke, "'The New Normal' for Foreign NGOs in 2020," China NGO Project, January 3, 2020, https://www.chinafile.com/ngo/analysis/new-normal-foreign-ngos-2020.

23. "Remarks by President Obama and President Xi Jinping of the People's Republic of China," White House Office of the Press Secretary, June 7, 2013, https://obamawhitehouse.ar chives.gov/the-press-office/2013/06/08/remarks-president-obama-and-president-xi-jinping -peoples-republic-china-.

24. "President Xi Jinping Delivers Important Speech and Proposes to Build a Silk Road Economic Belt with Central Asian Countries," Ministry of Foreign Affairs of the People's Republic

of China, September 2013, https://www.fmprc.gov.cn/mfa_eng/topics_665678/xjpfwzysiesg
jtfhshzzfh_665686/t1076334.shtml.

25. "The United States' 'New Silk Road' Strategy: What Is It? Where Is It Headed?" Departp
ment of State, September 2011, https://2009-2017.state.gov/e/rls/rmk/20092013/2011/1748
00.htm.

26. Tom Mitchell, "China-Led AIIB Attracts Rush of Applicants," *Financial Times*, April
2015, https://www.ft.com/content/94728d96-d82f-11e4-ba53-00144feab7de.

27. Michael Green et al., "Counter-Coercion Series: East China Sea Air Defense Identificai
tion Zone," Asia Maritime Transparency Initiative, June 2017, https://amti.csis.org/counter
-co-east-china-sea-adiz/.

28. Derek Watkins, "What China Has Been Building in the South China Sea," *New York
Times*, October 2015, https://www.nytimes.com/interactive/2015/07/30/world/asia/what
-china-has-been-building-in-the-south-china-sea.html.

29. Ankit Panda, "It's Official: Xi Jinping Breaks His Non-Militarization Pledge in the Spratp
lys," *Diplomat,* December 16, 2016, https://thediplomat.com/2016/12/its-official-xi-jinping
-breaks-his-non-militarization-pledge-in-the-spratlys/.

30. Austin Wright, Bryan Bender, and Philip Ewing, "Obama Team, Military at Odds over
South China Sea," *Politico*, July 31, 2015, https://www.politico.com/story/2015/07/barack
-obama-administration-navy-pentagon-odds-south-china-sea-120865.

31. Barack Obama, "Remarks by President Obama at U.S.-ASEAN Press Conference," An"
nenberg Retreat at Sunnylands, Rancho Mirage, CA, February 2016, https://obamawhite
house.archives.gov/the-press-office/2016/02/16/remarks-president-obama-us-asean-press
-conference.

32. "Obama Says Will Ensure Freedom of Navigation in South China Sea," Reuters, May 24,
2016, https://www.reuters.com/article/us-vietnam-obama-southchinasea/obama-says
-will-ensure-freedom-of-navigation-in-south-china-sea-idUSKCN0YF0IJ.

33. Joanna Lewis, "The U.S.-China Climate and Energy Relationship," Center for Strategic
and International Studies, September 22, 2017, https://www.csis.org/us-china-climate-and
-energy-relationship.

34. Adam Segal, "The U.S.-China Cyber Espionage Deal One Year Later," Net Politics, Coun€
cil on Foreign Relations, September 28, 2016, https://www.cfr.org/blog/us-china-cyber-espio
nage-deal-one-year-later.

35. Kurt M. Campbell, *The Pivot: The Future of American Statecraft in Asia* (New York: Twelve,
2016), 212–13.

36. Ryan Teague Beckwith, "Read Donald Trump's 'America First' Foreign Policy Speech,"
Time, April 2016, https://time.com/4309786/read-donald-trumps-america-first-foreign-poli
cy-speech/.

37. Steven Erlanger and Jane Perlez, "America's Allies Fear That Traditional Ties No Longer
Matter under Trump," *New York Times*, December 2018, https://www.nytimes.com/2018/12
/21/world/europe/trump-jim-mattis-syria.html.

38. Donald Trump, "Remarks by President Trump to the 74th Session at the United Nations
General Assembly," United Nations Headquarters, New York, NY, September 24, 2019, https://
trumpwhitehouse.archives.gov/briefings-statements/remarks-president-trump-74th-session
-united-nations-general-assembly/.

39. "Read Donald Trump's Speech on Trade," *Time*, June 2016, https://time.com/4386335
/donald-trump-trade-speech-transcript/.

40. Maggie Haberman, "Donald Trump Says He Favors Big Tariffs on Chinese Exports," *New*

York Times, January 7, 2016, https://www.nytimes.com/politics/first-draft/2016/01/07/donald-trump-says-he-favors-big-tariffs-on-chinese-exports/.

41. Gerald F. Seib, Jay Solomon, and Carol E. Lee, "Barack Obama Warns Donald Trump on North Korea Threat," *Wall Street Journal*, November 22, 2016, https://www.wsj.com/articles/trump-faces-north-korean-challenge-1479855286.

42. *National Security Strategy of the United States of America*, December 2017, 25, https://trumpwhitehouse.archives.gov/wp-content/uploads/2017/12/NSS-Final-12-18-2017-0905.pdf.

43. Peter Baker, "Trump Abandons Trans-Pacific Partnership, Obama's Signature Trade Deal," *New York Times*, January 23, 2017, https://www.nytimes.com/2017/01/23/us/politics/tpp-trump-trade-nafta.html.

44. Choe Sang-Hun and Motoko Rich, "Trump's Talk of U.S. Troop Cuts Unnerves South Korea and Japan," *New York Times*, May 8, 2018, https://www.nytimes.com/2018/05/04/world/asia/south-korea-troop-withdrawal-united-states.html.

45. Anne Gearan, "Trump Speaks with Taiwanese President, a Major Break with Decades of U.S. Policy on China," *Washington Post*, December 3, 2016, https://www.washingtonpost.com/world/national-security/trump-spoke-with-taiwanese-president-a-major-break-with-decaes-of-us-policy-on-china/2016/12/02/b98d3a22-b8ca-11e6-959c-172c82123976_story.html.

46. Mark Landler, "Trump Suggests Using Bedrock China Policy as Bargaining Chip," *New York Times*, December 11, 2016, https://www.nytimes.com/2016/12/11/us/politics/trump-taiwan-one-china.html.

47. The plan included opening the Chinese market to electronic payment services, credit ratings agencies, and US beef; for the US part, it agreed to open its market to Chinese poultry imports, export liquefied natural gas, and support China's Belt and Road Initiative by sending an official delegation to the BRI summit in May 2017.

48. "US and China Sign Trade Agreement," BBC, May 12, 2017, https://www.bbc.com/news/business-39894119; "US-China Comprehensive Economic Dialogue," Department of the Treasury, https://www.treasury.gov/initiatives/Pages/china.aspx.

49. Gerard Baker, Michael C. Bender, and Carol E. Lee, "Trump Says He Offered China Better Trade Terms in Exchange for Help on North Korea," *Wall Street Journal*, April 12, 2017, https://www.wsj.com/articles/trump-says-he-offered-china-better-trade-terms-in-exchange-for-help-on-north-korea-1492027556.

50. Ben Blanchard and Philip Wen, "Asia Weighs Risk and Reward in Trump 'Bromance' with China's Xi," Reuters, April 28, 2017, https://www.reuters.com/article/us-usa-trump-xi-analysis-idUSKBN17U1M5.

51. Matthew Carney, "Donald Trump Heaps Praise on Xi Jinping, Makes No Breakthrough on North Korea or Trade," ABC News, November 10, 2017, https://www.abc.net.au/news/2017-11-09/donald-trump-makes-no-breakthrough-on-north-korea/9135796.

52. "USTR Announces Initiation of Section 301 Investigation of China," Office of the United States Trade Representative, August 18, 2017, https://ustr.gov/about-us/policy-offices/press-office/press-releases/2017/august/ustr-announces-initiation-section.

53. "Trump Blocks China-Backed Lattice Bid," Bloomberg, September 13, 2017, https://www.bloomberg.com/news/articles/2017-09-13/trump-blocks-china-backed-bid-for-chip-maker-over-security-risk.

54. Weizhen Tan, "Trade War Begins: US and China Exchange $34 Billion in Tariffs," CNBC, July 5, 2018, https://www.cnbc.com/2018/07/06/trade-war-worries-us-china-tariffs-to-kick-in-on-friday.html.

55. China agreed to purchase $200 billion of US goods over two years, institute intellectual property protection measures, and suspend retaliatory tariffs, while the United States agreed to halt 15 percent tariffs on consumer goods, which were supposed to go into effect on December 15, and reduce tariffs implemented in September by one-half. See "Economic and Trade Agreement between the Government of the United States of America and the Government of the People's Republic of China Text," Office of the United States Trade Representative, https://ustr.gov/countries-regions/china-mongolia-taiwan/peoples-republic-china/phase-one-trade-agreement/text.

56. Dan Merica, "Trump to China: Thanks for Trying with North Korea," CNN, June 21, 2017, https://www.cnn.com/2017/06/20/politics/trump-china-north-korea/index.html.

57. David Brunnstrom and David Ljunggren, "Nations to Consider More North Korea Sanctions, U.S. Warns on Military Option," Reuters, January 16, 2018, https://www.reuters.com/article/us-northkorea-missiles-diplomacy/nations-to-consider-more-north-korea-sanctions-u-s-warns-on-military-option-idUSKBN1F528B?feedType=RSS&feedName=newsOne.

58. "Joint Statement of President Donald J. Trump of the United States of America and Chairman Kim Jong Un of the Democratic People's Republic of Korea at the Singapore Summit," White House, June 12, 2018, https://trumpwhitehouse.archives.gov/briefings-statements/joint-statement-president-donald-j-trump-united-states-america-chairman-kim-jong-un-democratic-peoples-republic-korea-singapore-summit/.

59. Tarun Chhabra, "A Slushy 'Freeze-for-Freeze': The Deal China and North Korea Always Wanted," Brookings Institution, June 2018, https://www.brookings.edu/blog/order-from-chaos/2018/06/12/a-slushy-freeze-for-freeze-the-deal-china-and-north-korea-always-wanted/.

60. Stephen Biegun, "Remarks on DPRK at Stanford University," January 31, 2019, Palo Alto, CA, https://www.state.gov/remarks-on-dprk-at-stanford-university/.

61. Lee Jeong-Ho, "China, Russia, North Korea Call for Adjusted Sanctions ahead of Denuclearisation," South China Morning Post, October 10, 2018, https://www.scmp.com/news/china/diplomacy/article/2167931/china-russia-north-korea-call-adjusted-sanctions-ahead.

62. Edith M. Lederer, "Russia, China Block UN from Saying NKorea Violated Sanctions," Associated Press, June 19, 2019, https://apnews.com/cb6be1337d2a48ecbde14dac590be083.

63. Kevin Breuninger and John W. Schoen, "US-China Trade War Is Hurting Farmers, but They're Sticking with Trump," CNBC, August 7, 2019, https://www.cnbc.com/2019/08/07/us-china-trade-war-is-hurting-farmers-but-theyre-sticking-with-trump.html.

64. Qu Shuyang et al., "Midwest Crop Farmers' Perceptions of the U.S.-China Trade War," Iowa State University Center for Agricultural and Rural Development, October 2019, https://www.card.iastate.edu/products/policy-briefs/display/?n=1294.

65. Gardiner Harris, "Tillerson Hails Ties with India, but Criticizes China and Pakistan," New York Times, October 18, 2017, https://www.nytimes.com/2017/10/18/us/politics/tillerson-india-china-pakistan.html.

66. Donald Trump, "Remarks by President Trump at APEC CEO Summit in Da Nang, Vietnam," Ariyana Da Nang Exhibition Center, November 10, 2017, White House, https://trumpwhitehouse.archives.gov/briefings-statements/remarks-president-trump-apec-ceo-summit-da-nang-vietnam/.

67. Ankit Panda, "US, Japan, India, and Australia Hold Working-Level Quadrilateral Meeting on Regional Cooperation," Diplomat, November 13, 2017, https://thediplomat.com/2017/11/us-japan-india-and-australia-hold-working-level-quadrilateral-meeting-on-regional-cooperation/.

68. Tripti Lahiri and Kari Lindberg, "From Asia to Africa, China's 'Debt-Trap Diplomacy'

Was under Siege in 2018," *Quartz*, December 28, 2018, https://qz.com/1497584/how-chinas-debt-trap-diplomacy-came-under-siege-in-2018/.

69. Build Act of 2018, S. 2463, 115th Cong., introduced in Senate February 2018, https://www.congress.gov/bill/115th-congress/senate-bill/2463.

70. Asia Reassurance Initiative Act of 2018, S. 2736, 115th Cong., introduced in Senate December 31, 2018, https://www.congress.gov/bill/115th-congress/senate-bill/2736/text.

71. "Blue Dot Network: Frequently Asked Questions," Department of State, https://www.state.gov/blue-dot-network/.

72. David B. Larter, "In Challenging China's Claims in the South China Sea, the US Navy Is Getting More Assertive," *Defense News*, February 5, 2020, https://www.defensenews.com/naval/2020/02/05/in-challenging-chinas-claims-in-the-south-china-sea-the-us-navy-is-getting-more-assertive/.

73. Mackubin Thomas Owens et al., "Dangerous Waters: Responding to China's Maritime Provocations in the South China Sea," *National Interest*, December 20, 2019, https://nationalinterest.org/feature/dangerous-waters-responding-china%E2%80%99s-maritime-provocations-south-china-sea-107746?page=0%2C1.

74. Megan Eckstein, "China Disinvited from Participating in 2018 RIMPAC Exercise," USNI News, May 23, 2018, https://news.usni.org/2018/05/23/china-disinvited-participating-2018-rimpac-exercise#:~:text=The%20US%20military%20has%20disinvited,a%20Defense%20Department%20spokesman%20announced.&text=As%20an%20initial%20response%20to,the%20Pacific%20(RIMPAC)%20Exercise.

75. Michael R. Pompeo, "U.S. Position on Maritime Claims in the South China Sea," US Department of State, July 13, 2020, https://2017-2021.state.gov/u-s-position-on-maritime-claims-in-the-south-china-sea/index.html.

76. "Factbox: What Trump Has Said about the United Nations," Reuters, September 17, 2017, https://www.reuters.com/article/us-un-assembly-trump-comments-factbox/factbox-what-trump-has-said-about-the-united-nations-idUSKCN1BS0UO.

77. "Chinese Envoy Criticizes 'Prejudice' against BRI at UNSC," *China Daily*, March 16, 2019, http://www.chinadaily.com.cn/a/201903/16/WS5c8cbf01a3106c65c34eefab.html.

78. "U.S. Tasks Official to Counter China's 'Malign Influence' at U.N.," Reuters, January 23, 2020, https://www.reuters.com/article/us-usa-un-china/u-s-tasks-official-to-counter-chinas-malign-influence-at-u-n-idUSKBN1ZM2Y3.

79. Chris Buckley and Austin Ramzy, "'Absolutely No Mercy': Leaked Files Expose How China Organized Mass Detentions of Muslims," *New York Times*, November 16, 2019, https://www.nytimes.com/interactive/2019/11/16/world/asia/china-xinjiang-documents.html.

80. David Choi and Sonam Sheth, "Trump Told China's President That Building Concentration Camps for Millions of Uighur Muslims Was 'Exactly the Right Thing to Do,' Former Adviser Says," *Business Insider*, June 17, 2020, https://www.businessinsider.com/trump-china-detention-camp-xinjiang-2020-6.

81. Alan Rappeport and Edward Wong, "In Push for Trade Deal, Trump Administration Shelves Sanctions over China's Crackdown on Uyghurs," *New York Times*, May 4, 2019, https://www.nytimes.com/2019/05/04/world/asia/trump-china-uighurs-trade-deal.html.

82. Jennifer Hansler, "US Announces Visa Restrictions on China for Xinjiang Abuses," CNN, October 9, 2019, https://www.cnn.com/2019/10/08/politics/xinjiang-visa-restrictions-state-department/index.html.

83. Karen Pierce, "Joint Statement on Human Rights Violations and Abuses in Xinjiang," UK Foreign and Commonwealth Office, October 29, 2019, https://www.gov.uk/government/speeches/joint-statement-on-xinjiang.

84. Christoph Heusgen, "Joint Statement on the Human Rights Situation in Xinjiang and the Recent Developments in Hong Kong, Delivered by Germany on Behalf of 39 Countries," United States Mission to the United Nations, October 6, 2020, https://usun.usmission.gov /joint-statement-on-the-human-rights-situation-in-xinjiang-and-the-recent-developments -in-hong-kong-delivered-by-germany-on-behalf-of-39-countries/.

85. David J. Lynch, "Trump Says He Might Veto Legislation That Aims to Protect Human Rights in Hong Kong because Bill Could Affect China Trade Talks," *Washington Post*, November 22, 2019, https://www.washingtonpost.com/business/2019/11/22/trump-says-he-might-veto -legislation-that-aims-protect-human-rights-hong-kong-because-bill-would-impact-china -trade-talks/.

86. Paul LeBlanc and Steven Jiang, "Trump Signs Hong Kong Human Rights Act as China Blasts 'Plainly Bullying Behavior,'" CNN, November 27, 2019, https://www.cnn.com/2019/11 /27/politics/trump-hong-kong-human-right-democracy.

87. The President's Executive Order on Hong Kong Normalization, White House Press Office, July 14, 2020, https://trumpwhitehouse.archives.gov/presidential-actions/presidents -executive-order-hong-kong-normalization/.

88. Taiwan Travel Act, H.R. 535, 115th Cong., introduced in House March 16, 2018.

89. Taiwan Allies International Protection and Enhancement Initiative Act of 2019, S. 1678, 116th Cong., introduced in Senate March 26, 2020.

90. Eric Schmitt and Edward Wong, "Lawmakers Accuse Trump and Aides of Delaying F-16 Sales to Taiwan," *New York Times*, July 30, 2019, https://www.nytimes.com/2019/07/30/world /asia/trump-taiwan-arms-china-trade-.html.

91. "The China Threat," Federal Bureau of Investigation, accessed December 3, 2022, https://www.fbi.gov/investigate/counterintelligence/the-china-threat.

92. Jonathan Oatis, "Fans, U.S. Politicians, Others React to NBA's China Controversy," Reuters, October 7, 2019, https://www.reuters.com/article/us-china-basketball-nba-reaction -factbox/factbox-fans-us-politicians-others-react-to-nbas-china-controversy-idUSKBN1 WM1RU.

93. *China's Impact on the U.S. Education System, Homeland Security and Government Affairs Permanent Subcommittee on Investigations Hearing*, February 28, 2019, https://www.hsgac.sena te.gov/subcommittees/investigations/hearings/chinas-impact-on-the-us-education-system.

94. Jeannie Baumann, "Scientists Hiding Foreign Ties Prompt Concerns from White House," Bloomberg Law, February 27, 2020, https://news.bloomberglaw.com/pharma-and -life-sciences/scientists-hiding-foreign-ties-prompt-concerns-from-white-house.

95. See, for example, "Harvard University and Two Chinese Nationals Charged in Three Separate China Related Cases," Department of Justice Press Release, January 28, 2020, https:// www.justice.gov/opa/pr/harvard-university-professor-and-two-chinese-nationals-charged -three-separate-china-related.

96. Kevin Johnson, "Chinese Espionage, Tech Theft Is 'Greatest Long-Term Threat to U.S. Economy,' FBI Director Says," *USA Today*, February 6, 2020, https://www.usatoday.com/story /news/politics/2020/02/06/fbi-director-1-000-open-investigations-into-chinese-technology -theft/4677384002/.

97. "Briefing with Senior U.S. Government Officials on the Closure of the Chinese Consulate in Houston, Texas," Department of State, July 24, 2020, https://2017-2021.state.gov/brie fing-with-senior-u-s-government-officials-on-the-closure-of-the-chinese-consulate-in-hous ton-texas/index.html.

98. Elizabeth Redden, "Stealing Innovation," Inside Higher Ed, April 29, 2019, https://www

.insidehighered.com/news/2019/04/29/fbi-director-discusses-chinese-espionage-threat-us
-academic-research.

99. Scott Neuman, "In U.N. Speech, Trump Blasts China and WHO, Blaming Them for Spread of COVID-19," *National Public Radio*, September 22, 2020, https://www.npr.org/sections/coronavirus-live-updates/2020/09/22/915630892/in-u-n-speech-trump-blasts-china-and-who-blaming-them-for-spread-of-covid-19.

100. Laura Silver, Kat Devlin, and Christine Huang, "Unfavorable Views of China Reach Historic Highs in Many Countries," Pew Research Center, October 6, 2020, https://www.pewresearch.org/global/2020/10/06/unfavorable-views-of-china-reach-historic-highs-in-many-countries/.

101. "Reports of Anti-Asian Assaults, Harassment and Hate Crimes Rise as Coronavirus Spread," Anti-Defamation League, June 18, 2020, https://www.adl.org/blog/reports-of-anti-asian-assaults-harassment-and-hate-crimes-rise-as-coronavirus-spreads.

102. Antony J. Blinken, "The Signing of the Uyghur Forced Labor Prevention Act," US Department of State Press Release, December 23, 2021, https://www.state.gov/the-signing-of-the-uyghur-forced-labor-prevention-act/.

103. "Fact Sheet: Quad Leaders' Summit," White House, September 24, 2021, https://www.whitehouse.gov/briefing-room/statements-releases/2021/09/24/fact-sheet-quad-leaders-summit/.

104. "Fact Sheet: NATO Summit: Revitalizing the Transatlantic Alliance," White House, June 13, 2021, https://www.whitehouse.gov/briefing-room/statements-releases/2021/06/13/fact-sheet-nato-summit-revitalizing-the-transatlantic-alliance/.

105. Justin McCurry, "US and China Publicly Rebuke Each Other in First Major Talks of Biden Era," *Guardian,* March 18, 2021, https://www.theguardian.com/world/2021/mar/19/us-china-talks-alaska-biden-blinken-sullivan-wang.

106. Valerie Volcovici, William James, and Jake Spring, "U.S. and China Unveil Deal to Ramp Up Cooperation on Climate Change," Reuters, November 11, 2021, https://www.reuters.com/business/cop/china-us-make-joint-statement-cop26-climate-summit-2021-11-10/.

107. "Joint Statement of the Russian Federation and the People's Republic of China on the International Relations Entering a New Era and the Global Sustainable Development," President of Russia, February 4, 2022, http://en.kremlin.ru/supplement/5770#sel=1:21:S5F,1:3 7:3jE.

108. Evelyn Cheng, "China Refuses to Call Russian Attack on Ukraine an 'Invasion,' Deflects Blame to U.S.," CNBC, February 24, 2022, https://www.cnbc.com/2022/02/24/china-refuses-to-call-attack-on-ukraine-an-invasion-blames-us.html.

109. Sravasti Dasgupta, "US Is Seeking Coexistence with China, Not Cold War, Says Jake Sullivan," *Independent*, November 9, 2021, https://www.independent.co.uk/asia/china/us-china-coexistence-jake-sullivan-b1954090.html.

7

The Economic Origins of US-China Strategic Competition

Arthur R. Kroeber

The shift in the consensus view of US elites toward China policy from "constructive engagement" to "strategic competition" since about 2015 has many sources. This chapter will first examine the economic factors that contributed to this shift. It will then analyze the ways in which the bilateral economic relationship has changed since 2015 in response to these pressures, and sketch a framework for understanding how the economic relationship could evolve in the coming decade, as pressure builds to push it further toward "decoupling" or even a new cold war.

The general story is that (a) China grew bigger and more quickly than most anticipated; (b) its industries became more directly competitive with (rather than supportive of) high-value industries in the United States; (c) its technological progress spurred security concerns; (d) its model of authoritarian, state-led capitalism proved more durable than expected, putting pressure on global economic governance systems built around market economies; and (e) the unpaid political bills for the domestic dislocations caused by China's rise came due.

These factors combined to cause the US government to shift its basic objective from enabling China's economic rise to constraining it. This policy shift is in tension with the interests of the US business community, which is unhappy with various aspects of Chinese regulation but still views China far more as an opportunity than as a threat. Partly because of this tension, and partly due to the peculiar nature of the Trump administration, execution of the new, more adversarial official policy in 2017–21 was both robust and haphazard. The Biden administration accepted Trump's basic strategic competition framework but tried to make it more systematic, and it increased coordination with allies.

Looking ahead, US policymakers will struggle to define a practical approach to economic relations with China, between the poles of the unsustainable (a wish to restore the relationship to its prior state of mutually beneficial exchange with limited competition) and the unachievable (a desire to fully "decouple" two economies that are tightly bound together). Analogies to the Cold War are unhelpful because of China's close integration with the global economy, technology supply chains, and US companies. US-China policy will need to find a balance between security and economic interests that will inevitably look very different from the Cold War policy toward the Soviet Union.

Economic Sources of the US-China Rivalry

The US-China economic relationship is complicated, and so are the reasons for the gradual disillusionment of American elites with its benefits. US policymakers in the late 1970s bet that closer economic engagement with China was in the national interest, despite the gulf in values and ideology between the two countries. They renewed this bet in the early 1990s, even though the collapse of the Soviet Union eliminated the original geopolitical rationale for the US-China rapprochement, and the suppression of the 1989 Tiananmen Square protests made clear that the Chinese Communist Party (CCP) had little interest in allowing China's political system to evolve toward more openness.[1]

US policy for several decades after 1980 was to support China's economic development, encourage China's inclusion in global economic institutions, and foster greater integration between the US and Chinese economies. The high-water mark of this approach was China's accession to the World Trade Organization (WTO) in December 2001, after fifteen years of tortuous negotiations. China's full entry into the global trading system prompted a surge of investment by international (including American) companies, who hoped to use China as a production base and gain access to its fast-growing markets.

In the past few years, US elites have questioned this policy and in general no longer subscribe to the idea that enabling China's economic development is in the US national interest. Many specific discontents have contributed to this shift. We may divide these into clusters that relate to three broad sets of issues: the shift of manufacturing activity from the United States to China, Chinese industry becoming more directly competitive with the United States, and China's international economic activities.

The Shift of Manufacturing Production and Jobs to China

After China's WTO entry, global manufacturers started shifting production to China en masse to take advantage of its low production costs (including cheap labor), good logistics, and economies of scale. Manufacturers around the world faced increasing pressure to compete with an ever-lower "China price," which often meant closing higher-cost plants in the United States and Europe and

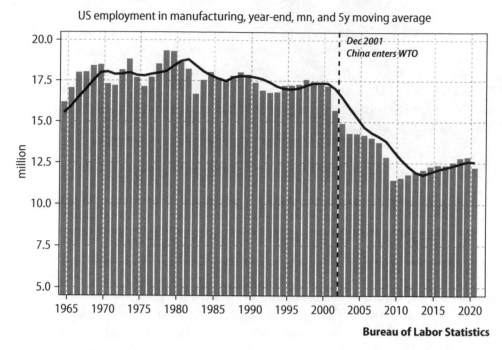

Figure 7.1 US manufacturing employment plummeted after 2002. (Kroeber)

either opening factories in China or becoming distributors for China-produced goods.[2]

One supposed impact of this shift was a massive, and evidently permanent, loss of manufacturing jobs in the United States. Between 1965 and 2000, US manufacturing employment steadily averaged close to 18 million persons, with a variation of less than 10 percent up or down during booms or recessions. Between 2000 and 2009, manufacturing employment plummeted by one-third, or 5.7 million jobs (see figure 7.1). Several factors contributed to this fall, including technological changes such as a sharply lower cost of automation. And about one million manufacturing jobs were lost as a result of the Great Recession of 2008–09. Overall, about 85 percent of the manufacturing job losses in the decade after 2000 were probably due to technological changes, and only about 15 percent were due to import competition from low-labor-cost countries such as China.[3]

Still, in the minds of many, China was the chief reason for the huge and unprecedented loss of manufacturing jobs. More important was the fact that by the presidential election of November 2016, manufacturing employment was still about a third lower than in 2000, having barely grown in the seven years after the Great Recession began. Manufacturing job losses were concentrated in the industrial Midwest, in states including Pennsylvania, Ohio, Michigan, and

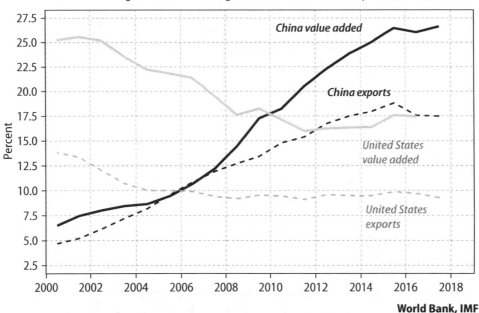

China / US share of global manufacturing value added (solid) and exports (dashed), %

World Bank, IMF

Figure 7.2   China has surpassed the United States as the world's biggest manufacturer. (Kroeber)

Wisconsin. These states were crucial parts of the electoral coalition that elected Donald Trump, whose campaign pledges included the imposition of huge tariffs on imports from China and other measures to bring manufacturing jobs back to the United States. Politically, the perceived harm caused by the loss of jobs to China proved more potent than the substantial but diffuse benefits US consumers derived from the relationship with China, including cheaper prices for a wide range of consumer goods and lower interest rates.

Another impact was that the United States ceded to China its long-standing position as the world's biggest manufacturing producer and exporter. In 2000, the United States accounted for a quarter of global manufacturing value and 14 percent of world manufacturing exports. China's shares of both manufacturing value and exports were less than a third of the US totals. But in 2006, China surpassed the United States in manufactured exports, and in 2010 it became the world number one in total manufacturing production. By 2015, the two countries' positions had virtually reversed from what they had been fifteen years before. China accounted for 26 percent of global manufacturing production and 19 percent of manufactured exports, compared to 17 percent and 10 percent, respectively, for the United States (see figure 7.2).

Of course, these stark figures concealed a more complex reality. China's outsize manufacturing figures only partly represented the activities of Chinese companies. About half of China's exports and two-thirds of its technologically advanced exports were produced by foreign companies. In some of the biggest and most visible categories, virtually all of the value chain for goods produced in China was controlled by foreign firms. The outstanding example was the iPhone, which was manufactured in China by a Taiwanese company according to American designs, with components largely sourced from the United States, Japan, South Korea, and other Asian countries.[4]

Nonetheless, the shift in the physical location of so much manufacturing from the United States to China gave rise to many complaints. Smaller companies, which found it harder to relocate than big multinationals, argued that they were being undercut by Chinese competitors who benefited from state subsidies and an undervalued exchange rate. There were also concerns that the hollowing-out of the US manufacturing base could, in the long run, create a national security threat by making it harder for the United States to produce critical equipment in times of crisis or war.

China Moves from Complement to Competitor

A second cluster of issues revolved around China's industrial policies and regulatory environment. The underlying issue was that China's economy gradually shifted from being complementary to the US economy to being a direct competitor in many sectors. This shift gave rise to operational challenges for US businesses in China, anxieties about the national security implications of China's technological advance, and fears that global economic governance institutions, notably the WTO, were inadequate to regulate China's "predatory" or "unfair" policies.

A key part of the calculation behind constructive engagement was that China's vast market would become ever more open for US firms, which would enjoy a strong competitive position there. Broadly, this has happened: China's market is much more open to foreign companies now than at any point in the past, and US firms occupy large and often highly profitable positions in many sectors.

Despite this, US businesses voiced steadily rising complaints about the terms under which they could enter and operate in the Chinese market. An important turning point came in 2006. Under the terms of its WTO accession agreement, China had pledged to a schedule of tariff reductions and market openings over a five-year period ending in December 2006. It met these requirements (in letter if not always in spirit), and during that period foreign companies, including those from the United States, enjoyed rapidly expanding market access in a booming market.

Once the schedule of required openings ended, however, Chinese economic policy took a decidedly more nationalist turn. The pace of market opening slowed. Over a period of more than a decade, there was little increase in market

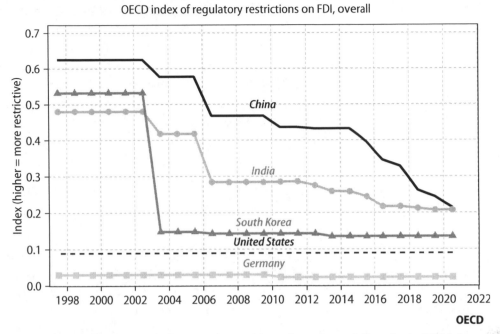

OECD index of regulatory restrictions on FDI, overall

Figure 7.3 China's restrictions on inward investment are falling, but still high. (Kroeber)

access for foreign companies in service sectors where the United States was strongly competitive, notably finance, retail, and professional services. By international standards, China's barriers to inbound foreign direct investment (FDI) remained high (see figure 7.3). And companies that were already in China faced a rising tide of regulations and policies whose cumulative effect was to create structural competitive advantages for domestic firms. These included

- Large subsidy programs which seemed disproportionately to benefit domestic firms.
- The passage of an anti-monopoly law which did little to curb the monopoly power of large state-owned enterprises but was used to block foreign acquisitions of prominent Chinese companies.
- Successive technology-focused industrial plans that more or less explicitly targeted the creation of powerful domestic companies in a host of high-value sectors.
- Efforts to mandate the use of unique Chinese technical standards; for example, in wireless networks, encryption, and network security.[5]

By far the biggest source of concern was China's technology policies. Since the 1970s, Chinese leaders had been open about their desire to raise China's technological level and foster large numbers of technologically advanced Chinese firms that could supply most of the country's equipment needs and, eventually, compete in global markets. For many years Chinese firms were technological laggards, and the main concern of foreign companies was China's notoriously lax enforcement of intellectual property rights (IPR) laws protecting patents, copyrights, and trademarks. This enabled Chinese companies to launch knock-off versions of imported products, use pirated versions of US-produced software, and so on. China's unwillingness to enforce strict IPR protections was a major irritant in US-China commercial relations from the early 1990s onward. Yet for most technology-intensive companies the lack of IPR protection was a risk to be managed rather than a deal breaker, and it did not prevent them from massively increasing their presence in China.

Concerns rose with the Medium- and Long-Term Program for Science and Technology Development, published in 2006, which laid out a fifteen-year strategy for enhancing China's domestic technological capabilities and introduced the term "indigenous innovation" (*zizhu chuangxin*).[6] Exactly what this meant has been hotly debated. But many foreign companies and governments came to believe that it was code for efforts to develop Chinese-owned companies that could compete directly with international firms—compelling, where possible, foreign companies to transfer key technologies to Chinese companies, or to comply with unique Chinese technology standards that would force them to buy equipment or software from Chinese vendors.[7] This plan was followed by the "strategic emerging industries initiative" of 2010, which identified seven (later expanded to eight) high-tech industries for priority support.

The results of these technology development plans were mixed at best. In some areas—notably telecoms network equipment and infrastructure sectors such as high-speed rail systems, electrical power generation and distribution, and wind and solar power equipment—Chinese companies developed world-leading positions and clearly did so with the aid of support from the state. In other areas—notably semiconductors—tens of billions of dollars of state funds were spent with little to show for it in terms of manufacturing capability, although fabless chip design companies did make significant gains.[8] And in one of the hottest growth sectors—the Internet—successful Chinese companies emerged mainly as the result of intense competition and with little direct support from industrial policy. (They did, however, benefit substantially from state controls on the Internet—both domestic censorship policies and the "Great Firewall" that blocked sensitive content from abroad—which made it difficult for foreign Internet companies to compete effectively.[9])

Against this backdrop, in 2015 Beijing launched its "Made in China 2025" initiative. This shared many elements with previous technology development blueprints, but three factors made it more alarming to foreign companies and governments. First, it came with explicit domestic and global market share targets for Chinese companies in many high-tech sectors, typically in the range of 40–70 percent.[10] Second, it was supported by a plethora of "government guidance funds" organized by the central and local governments, which aimed to raise hundreds of billions of dollars to subsidize Chinese firms in the targeted sectors. And finally, the plan had greater credibility than previous ones because of the demonstrably rapid progress of Chinese companies in many technology-intensive sectors and the increasing acceptance that Chinese companies were no longer just copycats but were significant innovators in their own right.[11]

We should not overstate the present level of threat to US firms. Various studies have shown that while China has made rapid progress in many technology-intensive industries, it remains heavily reliant on imported components, equipment, and know-how, and the success of industrial policy in building globally competitive leading-edge industries is spotty.[12] The market share targets accompanying the Made in China 2025 policy are best understood as aspirational directional signals rather than achievable goals. And outside of semiconductors, both the size and the likely effectiveness of government guidance funds have been greatly exaggerated. More than two thousand funds have been set up since 2014, with combined fundraising targets of around $1 trillion. Yet spot checks suggest that the total amount of funds amassed has been a small fraction of that target, and in many cases local governments use these funds to support infrastructure and real estate projects.[13]

Semiconductors are an important exception: two central government integrated circuit (IC) funds have mobilized about $50 billion and have financed several start-ups to produce memory chips, of which two were in operation by early 2020. Memory chips lie at the least technologically sophisticated end of the semiconductor spectrum, and most industry analysts are skeptical that China is close to becoming competitive in more complex segments such as logic, graphics, and artificial intelligence chips; high-end fabrication; or the production of chip-fabricating tools.

But this sector is critical to understanding the increasingly strained US-China economic relationship. Leadership in semiconductors is seen as an essential part of the United States' national competitive advantage, and specialized chips are essential to many defense systems. Maintaining a strong lead in semiconductor technology, as well as a large domestic production base, is viewed by policymakers as a high priority for both commercial and national security reasons. The rise of Japanese semiconductor makers was a major issue in the US-Japan relationship in the 1980s, and it led to Japan acceding to quota limitations on its chip exports in 1986 and to industrial policy efforts in the United States to support its domestic industry.[14]

The capabilities of Chinese semiconductor firms today are well below those of Japanese firms in the 1980s, but the issue is even more contentious. This is in large part because China is an independent geopolitical actor rather than a US ally, like Japan. The United States has national security concerns both about how success in semiconductor development could boost China's military capabilities and about how competition from China could weaken the US industry and hence the US military's own supply chain.

It is also because the chip industry sits at the convergence of a variety of US concerns: China's technological ambitions, subsidies, IPR theft, and forced technology transfer. A neat example of this convergence is Fujian Jinhua Integrated Circuit Co. Ltd. This was one of the memory chip fabs created via the government integrated circuit guidance fund: it received $5.6 billion in start-up capital from the IC fund and the Fujian provincial government. In November 2018 the United States put it on an export-control blacklist because it was found to have colluded with a Taiwanese chip fabricator, UMC, to steal designs from Micron Technologies, the leading US memory chip maker. Unable to source equipment and components, Fujian Jinhua was forced to shut down.[15]

A final source of technology-related concerns was a rapid rise in Chinese direct investment in the United States, beginning around 2012. Until that year Chinese direct investment in the United States was minimal, but inflows averaged nearly $15 billion a year in 2013–15 and then surged to $45 billion in 2016. A relatively small share of these investments was in technology fields, but the absolute numbers were still substantial (see figure 7.4). Moreover, at around the same time there was a big pickup in Chinese participation in venture capital (VC) rounds for US start-up companies: from almost nothing in 2010–13, Chinese investors participated in an average of 250 VC funding rounds a year in 2014–17, including dozens in exciting new fields such as artificial intelligence.[16]

Surges in direct investment from non-European nations are reliable precursors of anxiety in the United States. A sudden rise in investment by newly rich oil-producing countries in the 1970s prompted the creation of the Committee on Foreign Investment in the United States (CFIUS) to vet such investments for national security risks. A big increase in investments by Japanese companies in the 1980s spurred a strengthening of CFIUS legislation in 1989 via the Exon-Florio Amendment. And, as discussed below, the surge in Chinese investment led quickly to a further beefing up of the CFIUS rules in 2018. In China's case, the usual concerns about important national assets being sold off to foreigners were intensified by the recognition that China was a serious geopolitical rival and by the suspicion that Chinese investments (even those by private companies) were enabled by state subsidies and were part of a state-coordinated plan to siphon off US technology for the benefit of China's own technological development.

The last component of the cluster of concerns about China-as-competitor relates to global economic governance institutions, specifically the WTO. As described above, in the decade following the 2006 end of China's commitments

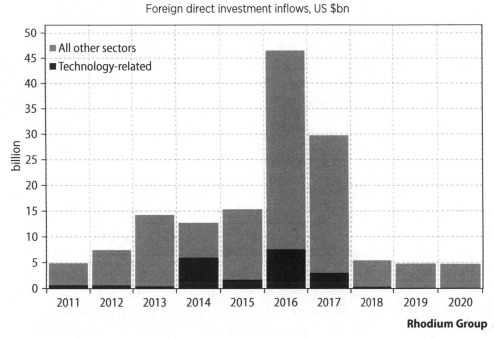

Figure 7.4 China's foreign direct investment (FDI) into the United States surged before 2016, then collapsed. (Kroeber)

for WTO entry, US companies and the US government increasingly came to the following conclusions:

- Market access for US companies was not expanding as fast as expected, especially in service sectors where US firms had strong competitive advantages.
- US companies operating in China faced increasingly onerous regulatory requirements and increased pressure to transfer technology as a condition for market access.
- China's technological capabilities were rising much faster than anticipated, creating potential future competitive challenges for US companies.
- China's technological advance was aided by a number of nonmarket forces, including subsidies, state coordination, and policies to accelerate the transfer of technology from foreign firms to Chinese ones.

These concerns boiled down to the complaint that China was an increasingly powerful global competitor, that it was competing in unfair ways, and that this unfair competition threatened American industrial health and national security. In this story, China exploited the open global system to export and invest freely around the world, subsidizing its companies so they could sell their goods more cheaply and put in the highest bids for investment deals. At the same time, Beijing set up barriers that made it hard for American and other foreign companies to compete in China and enabled the Chinese government to exact a toll—in the form of technology transfers—as the price of market access.[17]

In an ideal universe, complaints of this kind would be submitted to a global competition regulator. In reality, the world does not have such a regulator. The closest thing to it is the WTO, which has a commercial dispute resolution process. But in recent years US officials have grown skeptical of the WTO's ability to restrain what they see as China's predatory and unfair behavior. Cases take a long time to conclude, which means that companies damaged by unfair competition could be out of business by the time they receive a favorable judgment. WTO enforcement provisions are weak, rendering judgments sometimes meaningless.

A notable example was the WTO's 2012 ruling that China violated WTO rules by requiring that all debit and credit card transactions go through its homegrown China UnionPay network. This effectively barred Visa, Mastercard, and other foreign payment networks from the China market. After the ruling, it took China five years to establish application procedures for foreign networks to enter the market, and by 2019 it had still refused to recognize the applications filed by Visa and Mastercard.[18] It did approve an application by American Express, but Amex operated through a joint venture with a Chinese firm, whereas Visa and Mastercard were applying to set up wholly owned subsidiaries.

Finally, some Chinese practices are impossible for the WTO to address under current rules. The most important is subsidies. WTO rules prohibit subsidies to promote exports but say nothing about subsidies aimed at the domestic market. Most of China's subsidies are ostensibly domestically oriented, even though their follow-on impact may be to create companies with such economies of scale and dominant positions in their home market that they enjoy advantages in export markets. (Arguably this has occurred in the wind and solar power equipment markets.) There are also questions as to whether the WTO, established under the leadership of market-oriented democracies, is able to adequately police the pervasive state intervention and coordination activities in China's unique authoritarian state-led economy.[19] In any event, the WTO's efficacy has been rendered moot by the Trump administration's decision to block the appointment of new members to its appellate body, preventing it from achieving the quorum needed to issue judgments. The Biden administration has continued to block these appointments.[20]

Anxiety Along the Belt and Road

The third cluster of issues has to do with the ways in which China's economic rise began to translate into growing geopolitical influence, thanks to both the natural effects of trade and investment flows and deliberate policy by Beijing.

This led to concerns that Chinese firms would compete with American firms for resources and markets, and to worries that China's economic clout would enable it to gain global political power at the expense of the United States.

In the 1980s and 1990s China was almost entirely focused on internal development, and its companies had little presence abroad. This began to change after President Jiang Zemin announced a "Going Out" policy in 2000, which provided official sanction for Chinese firms to seek international opportunities. The mandate was vague, and for several years the international activities of Chinese companies had only modest impact. Over time, however, two trends emerged. One was that Chinese state-owned companies aggressively sought investments in resource assets such as oil fields and iron ore and copper mines, in order to secure sources of supply for the commodity demand generated by China's extraordinary construction boom that began in the early 2000s.

This led to charges that Chinese state firms, backed by subsidies and cheap financing from state-run banks, were bent on "locking up" supplies of critical resources.[21] In reality, of course, most of the world's existing resource base was already "locked up" by Western multinationals and national resource companies, so late-to-the-table Chinese firms mainly took on higher risk projects in less stable regions.

The second trend was a steady increase of Chinese firms building infrastructure in developing countries. Some of this was road, rail, or pipeline infrastructure directly related to resource investments by Chinese companies; much of the rest was in general projects such as electric power plants, dams, and telecoms networks. Chinese investments in global resource projects rose and fell with global commodity prices, but infrastructure-building activities rose at a very steady pace. The overseas revenues of Chinese construction and engineering firms climbed from virtually nothing in the early 2000s to over $100 billion a year by 2013.

In September 2013 Xi Jinping put a name to all this activity by announcing what was ultimately called the Belt and Road Initiative (BRI).[22] The initial stated aim was to enhance prosperity in Central and Southeast Asia by building infrastructure (roads, rail lines, pipelines, and ports) that would connect these regions with western and southern China, respectively. The description rapidly grew to encompass pretty much any Chinese investment in infrastructure anywhere in the world.

The initiative was supported by the creation of dedicated financing mechanisms. These included the Silk Road Fund, a $10 billion facility led by the People's Bank of China, and the Asian Infrastructure Investment Bank (AIIB), a Beijing-based multilateral lender modeled closely on the Asian Development Bank and the World Bank. AIIB now has about sixty nations as shareholders, although China is the largest with a 26 percent shareholding and effective veto power over key decisions. In reality, these funds have played a marginal role in financing BRI projects, most of which are funded by China's policy banks— China Development Bank and China Exim Bank—or by Chinese commercial lenders.

It was clear from the outset that, in addition to its economic functions, the BRI also housed a political agenda. It was a way to use China's economic strengths (deep financial pockets, expertise in infrastructure projects) to build up geopolitical influence. A subtler aim was to build international approbation around China's model of state-directed, infrastructure-led economic development as an alternative to the model of market-led capitalism championed by the United States and its allies.

As such, the BRI represented a potential challenge to the dominant, US-led world economic order, although Chinese officials were always careful to present it as complementary rather than competitive. The initiative became the subject of much anxious analysis in Washington, the worry being that any increase in China's economic influence would inevitably erode the geopolitical position of the United States.[23] These concerns are reasonable, but we should also not exaggerate either the BRI's concrete impact or the nature of its challenge to existing arrangements. To a significant degree, the BRI was an advertising slogan pasted on a preexisting pattern of activity. Despite all the hoopla and breathless media reports about a trillion dollars of new projects, its announcement had basically no impact on the trend in overseas construction and engineering revenues of Chinese companies.

Similarly, China's outward direct investment (ODI), which had been growing steadily for years, continued to grow at a somewhat more rapid pace. By 2014 China was the world's second-largest provider of ODI (behind the United States), and since 2019 it has been the largest, with annual flows of over $100 billion a year (see figure 7.5). Much of this investment focused on technology and consumer markets in rich countries rather than roads and railways in poor ones. A spike in ODI in 2015–16 owed more to capital flight by private investors than to state-led infrastructure spending. Both overseas construction revenues and Chinese ODI started to decline in 2018, reflecting the fact that financial returns on many BRI projects were disappointing, Beijing was becoming more parsimonious in starting new projects, and capital controls imposed in 2016 to stem capital flight made it harder to finance ODI (see figure 7.6).

Nevertheless, the image of well-financed Chinese state companies roaming the world, buying off governments with gaudy projects, contributed to the perception among US policymakers that China's growing economic power had negative implications for US global interests. The focus of concern also shifted to China's role as a provider of debt finance to developing countries, which rose even as China's direct overseas investments moderated. There were prominent

Annual outward direct investment, US$ billion

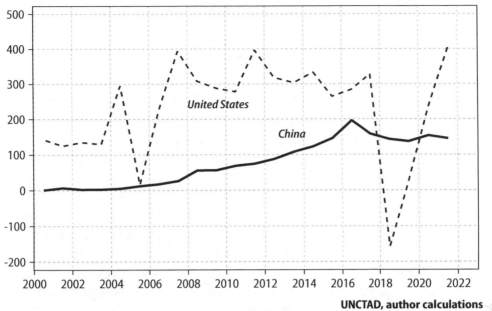

UNCTAD, author calculations

Figure 7.5 China is now the world's leading provider of FDI. (Kroeber)

Chinese outward direct investment and foreign construction revenues, monthly, US$ billion

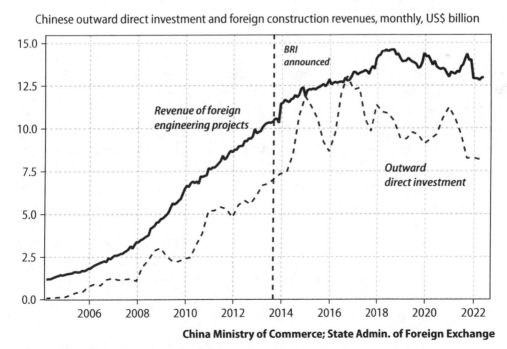

China Ministry of Commerce; State Admin. of Foreign Exchange

Figure 7.6 China's outward push has slowed. (Kroeber)

fears that excessive provision of Chinese credit to countries with shaky finances would lead those countries into unhealthy dependency.[24]

US Policy Responses

The US policy of constructive engagement with China that prevailed until about 2015 was partly built around a set of economic calculations, principally the bet that American national interests were better served by a prosperous, growing China that was well-integrated with the global system in general and the US economy in particular than they were by a China that was isolated from the rest of the world.[25]

This bet, in turn, rested on some key assumptions. One was that China's economy was likely to grow quite quickly for a long time regardless of whether or not it was fully integrated into the global system, thanks to its abundant natural advantages and a leadership that clearly put a high priority on economic growth. This being the case, China's market would be a huge opportunity for US firms, and integrating China into the global system would make it easier for US companies to cash in on this opportunity.

A second assumption was that China's authoritarian state-capitalist model was intrinsically unsustainable, and to keep growing quickly China would, over time, be forced to rely more on market forces and progressively reduce the state role in the economy. This was not because China's Communist leaders were closet neoliberals but simply because they would gradually discover that only market-led methods would reliably deliver the high growth required to sustain the CCP's legitimacy. A specific rationale for orchestrating China's entry into the WTO (on terms far more onerous than for any prior entrant) was that it would accelerate the processes of market-oriented reform and strengthen the hands of economic reformers in the party and government. As a result, economic or commercial frictions between the United States and China could be managed because both sides were committed to roughly the same "rules of the game."[26]

By the middle of the 2010s, conviction around this second assumption began to crumble. It was increasingly clear that China's leaders—and in particular Xi Jinping, who assumed power in 2012–13—were not committed to the kind of rapid market-oriented reforms envisaged back in 2001. Instead they had embraced a state capitalist model with a large and enduring role for state-owned enterprises, state-directed finance, and state-directed industrial development. And while China's growth was slowing from the stratospheric double-digit rates of 1980–2010, it was not collapsing. China appeared to have created a sustainable form of state-led capitalism.[27]

The second term of the Obama administration saw steadily rising frustration with China's unwillingness to accelerate market reforms, open up more to foreign investment, or abide fully by WTO rules. In response, the administration focused on two mechanisms. One was a bilateral investment treaty (BIT), which would have codified terms of market access for Chinese and US firms in each other's countries. China was eager to negotiate a BIT because a handful of major Chinese investments in the US had been blocked by CFIUS or by political opposition in Congress, and Chinese leaders foresaw that many other investment opportunities would be lost without more formal legal protection. The United States sought to use this leverage to compel China to eliminate many of its market access barriers, especially in services. Despite substantial progress, a BIT was never concluded. China did, however, accept a number of key provisions of the BIT, notably the "negative list" concept (under which investments are presumptively approved unless they are in sectors that are restricted for specific reasons), and the phasing out of joint venture requirements in several sectors.

The second initiative was the Trans-Pacific Partnership (TPP), a free trade agreement that the United States had begun to negotiate with eleven other countries on both sides of the Pacific Ocean in 2005. In addition to broad tariff cuts, the TPP incorporated strict provisions on intellectual property protection, subsidies, state-owned enterprises, and other issues where the deficits of WTO governance had become clear.

China was not a party to this agreement, but the TPP's relevance to China was obvious. As a new high-standard free trade zone encompassing about one-third of the world's GDP, the TPP would present China with a choice. It could apply for membership, at the price of eliminating or modifying the subsidies, discriminatory practices, and market access barriers that the US government and companies found obnoxious. Or it could preserve its system and stay out—at the potential cost of losing a wealth of economic opportunities. The TPP was signed by the member states in 2016, but the Obama administration failed to secure its ratification by Congress. On his first day in office in January 2017, President Trump theatrically withdrew the United States from the agreement, setting the tone for a new, more confrontational, and unilateral approach to trade policy.

Under Trump, economic policy toward China was both adversarial and incoherent. This reflects both the idiosyncrasies of decision-making in the Trump administration and the complexity of the forces at play in the US-China relationship. It was easy to agree that the old policy framework of constructive engagement had passed its sell-by date. It was hard to come up with a new framework that satisfied all the interests involved. This difficulty persisted in the first year of the Biden administration, which promised a careful review and recalibration of Trump-era policies, but in practice left all those policies in place. By late 2022, the Biden team's strategy had coalesced around a concept of "invest, align, and compete."[28] "Invest" refers to large-scale industrial policy investments; "align," to increased coordination with allies; and "compete" mainly to increased export controls, targeting technologies (notably semiconductors) with potential military applications.

Objectively, the main interests of the United States in its economic relationship with China include:

1. Strengthening the US industrial base, at least in part by reducing the incentives to move production in key sectors to China.
2. Improving the market access conditions for US companies in China. This objective conflicts with the first. More market access for American companies in China reduces their incentives to move investments back from China to the United States.
3. Protecting the US technology base from unfair competition by Chinese companies or from efforts by China to get hold of US technology by IPR theft, forced technology transfer, or mergers and acquisitions.
4. Reforming global economic governance so that there are more constraints on China's ability to tilt the competitive playing field, or gain political influence, through subsidies, industrial policy support for favored domestic companies, or state-led investments at home and abroad.

The pursuit of these various interests is complicated by the overlapping agendas of various interest groups. Simplifying greatly, three main groups seek to influence US economic policy toward China. One is economic nationalists, who believe that China's entry into the WTO—along with other policies aimed at increasing cross-border financial and investment flows—damaged American workers and the country's manufacturing base and weakened the US economic structure.[29] Another is the national security community, which seeks to maintain US strategic superiority over China by choking off flows of technology and finance from the United States to China. The third is the business community, which has enormous investments in China and seeks to improve the terms of its participation in that market.

Economic policy toward China under Trump was driven largely by economic nationalist concerns, especially in the first two years of the administration, and increasingly by national security concerns beginning in 2019. The business community mainly played defense, pushing back with some success against extreme measures that they feared would hurt their prospects in China.

Economic nationalists supported the use of tariffs to punish China for its allegedly unfair practices, raise the cost of goods coming from China, encourage American manufacturers to relocate production in the United States, and pressure China to accede to a regime of managed trade under which it would import more goods from the United States. Between July 2018 and September 2019, the administration imposed four tranches of tariffs on around $300 billion of Chinese exports to the United States, raising the average effective tariff on goods coming in from China from 3.8 percent to 19.3 percent.[30]

These tariffs were effective in getting China to agree to a "Phase One" trade deal in January 2020, under which it pledged to increase its imports of American goods and undertake some modest domestic reforms.[31] But much of the economic impact of the tariffs was offset by a (completely predictable) depreciation of the Chinese currency, and China retaliated by cutting off purchases of US agricultural products, causing those exports to plummet from $23.8 billion in 2017 to $9.1 billion in 2018.[32] By late 2020 it was clear that the tariffs had failed either to reduce the overall US trade deficit, substantially influence China's economic policies, or engineer an exodus of American firms out of China. China's purchase commitments under the Phase One deal were seen as wildly unrealistic and in fact were not met: although it increased its imports of some US products, China fell short of its commitments by $200 billion.[33] The main uses of the trade deal were political, not economic. For the Trump administration, some deal was needed to prove that the costly tariff policy of the prior two years had been worth it, while for Beijing the agreement was useful in buying some breathing space until after the 2020 US presidential election.

Moreover, the economic nationalist agenda also included actions against other countries and institutions: tariffs on steel and aluminum imports from numerous countries, including allies like Japan, South Korea, Canada, and Germany, and efforts to hobble the WTO by vetoing the appointments of judges to the appellate panel. This reflected a belief that the United States would do better by downgrading multilateral arrangements and negotiating trade deals one-on-one with individual countries, with tariffs as the means of choice to bring them to the negotiating table. But this also makes it harder for the United States to join up with its allies to launch concerted action against China's illiberal policies.

The national security agenda is no less problematic. The basic concern is that China is now a geopolitical rival, and it is not in the interests of the United States to provide flows of technology and finance that will enable China to become a more rich, powerful, and technologically able rival. This concern was outlined in a 2017 Defense Department report, which sounded the alarm over Chinese investments in the US tech sector and called for tighter controls on Chinese investment, exports of technology goods to China, and visas for Chinese nationals wishing to study or work in tech fields in the United States.[34]

Controls on technology investments and exports were swiftly embodied in two pieces of legislation passed with bipartisan support in Congress in August

2018: the Foreign Investment Risk Review Modernization Act (FIRRMA), which strengthens CFIUS, and the Export Control Reform Act (ECRA), which widens the scope of export controls.

The key common feature of FIRRMA and ECRA is that they broaden the standard of review from national security (for investment) or dual-use technology (for export controls) to a more general technology standard. Previously, to block an investment or an export, one had to show a national security risk or prove that a product could be used for military purposes. Under the new laws, all one has to show is that the investment or export involves a technology that is on a government list of "foundational" and "emerging" technologies. In principle, this would greatly expand the US government's ability to restrict Chinese acquisitions of US technology firms and products. In practice, FIRRMA has already contributed to a near cessation of Chinese direct investment in the United States and the virtual elimination of Chinese funding from the venture capital industry—not because CFIUS has rejected a lot more deals but because Chinese investors have concluded that the United States is a hostile environment and are staying away (see figure 7.4).

Export controls are a different matter. In order to make them effective, the Department of Commerce's Bureau of Industry and Security (BIS) must devise the lists of emerging and foundational technologies. By early 2023, after more than four years of deliberation, BIS had yet to release comprehensive lists and instead had selected only a small handful of narrowly defined sectors for control.[35] It is caught between the demands of national security policymakers to make the lists as expansive as possible and the demands of the US technology industry to make them as narrow as possible, so as not to cut too deeply into the revenues of companies that rely on customers in China for anywhere from 20 to 70 percent of their business.

There are other mechanisms for export controls beyond the expanded powers under ECRA. Chief among these is the BIS "entity list"—effectively an export blacklist. American firms are prohibited from selling products or services to companies on this list without a license from the Commerce Department, which is unlikely to be granted. This tool was used to bring down Fujian Jinhua, and in an exceptionally aggressive move, China's leading telecommunications equipment maker, Huawei Technologies, was put on the entity list in May 2019. Because Huawei depends heavily on imported components—chiefly semiconductors—from US suppliers, the export ban threatened to cripple the company severely or even destroy it. Subsequently, several dozen other Chinese companies were put on the entity list, for reasons including US national security concerns, their role in building China's surveillance state, and helping with the suppression of the Uyghur minority in Xinjiang.

The Huawei case illustrates the conflicts between the economic nationalist, national security, and business agendas. The US national security community has long worried about Huawei. Its equipment is embedded in many telecoms networks around the world, and the company is a leader in the technology for 5G mobile networks, which will connect many more devices to the Internet at high speeds. The principal worry is that Huawei could install back doors into its network equipment, enabling China to surveil the US and its allies and potentially disable key communication, electricity, and other networks in the event of conflict.

In May 2019 China backed away from a trade deal that the US side thought was fully negotiated, and an angry Donald Trump was looking for a way to retaliate. Members of his national security team suggested putting Huawei on the entity list, and Trump took the suggestion. The move was opposed by trade negotiator Robert Lighthizer, who feared it would make his negotiations more difficult.[36] And US technology companies, which relied on Huawei as a major customer, were distressed by the potential loss of a key source of revenue.

A tug-of-war ensued over the next sixteen months as the national security wing of the Trump administration sought progressively to tighten the ban on selling to Huawei, while the company's US suppliers sought, with initial success, to circumvent the ban by continuing to supply Huawei from overseas factories. In an odd twist, one effort to make the export controls more stringent stalled in February 2020, when the Defense Department vetoed it out of concern that depriving US semiconductor firms of a big source of revenue would reduce their capacity for research and development, thereby imperiling the US military's own supply chain for advanced chips.[37]

President Trump also publicly intervened against restrictions on US technology sales to China, tweeting that such controls were "ridiculous" and an impediment to US businesses.[38] The administration crystallized around a maximally hard-line stance on Huawei only after Trump decided that the rising health and economic toll of the COVID-19 epidemic made it impossible for him to run for reelection as the president who forged a great trade deal with China, and instead forced him to run as the president who was tough on China in all ways.

The key lesson from the Huawei saga is that forming a new strategy for US economic relations with China will be made very difficult by the intricate triangular battle between the economic nationalists, the national security community, and the business community. The national security community would like to choke off sales of advanced technology to China but is constrained from pushing for a full ban by the dependence of the US military's own technology suppliers on China as a source of revenue to finance their research and development

(R&D). It also recognizes the need for the United States to exploit its many alliances and partnerships around the world in countering China's influence.

Economic nationalists want to discourage US companies from outsourcing more manufacturing to China, but they are also happy to increase China's role as a destination for US exports. They thus agree with the national security community on the need to constrain US investments in China but also align (to a degree) with the business community on the need to keep vibrant commercial relations between the two countries. They also favor a unilateral approach, which puts them at odds with the national security community focus on alliances.

Finally, many businesses have pushed back hard against efforts by both the economic nationalists and the national security establishment to make it harder for them to do business in China and with Chinese companies. Yet they also favor hardball tactics to pressure Beijing to relax its limits on market access and its efforts to compel transfer of advanced technology as the price of market access. President Trump's erratic positions, driven almost entirely by his moment-to-moment political calculations, made this confusing situation even harder to read. But even an administration that pursues a more disciplined and strategic course will have a tough time coming up with a strategy that satisfies all relevant interests.

This was made clear in the first year of the Biden administration, which basically continued Trump's economic policies toward China. It left all tariffs in place and expanded sanctions on people and companies involved in political crackdowns in Xinjiang and Hong Kong or who were deemed to be involved in China's "military industrial complex."[39] It strengthened export controls, notably with a draconian set of semiconductor restrictions which are likely to severely retard the growth of China's chip industry.[40] It beefed up China-focused security arrangements—the "Quad" that includes the United States, India, Japan, and Australia, and the AUKUS alliance with the UK and Australia, anchored by the sale of nuclear submarines to Australia. But it has not devised an international economic strategy. It has launched no economic dialogues with China, and a vague Asian regional initiative, the Indo-Pacific Economic Framework (IPEF), specifically excludes increasing market access in the United States for Asian countries, meaning they have little incentive to participate.[41]

Meanwhile, Congress is pushing ahead with efforts to restrict financial flows to China. The Holding Foreign Companies Accountable Act of 2020 requires the delisting from US stock markets of any firm unable to fully comply with US audit oversight requirements for three years. The legislation targets Chinese companies, which are prevented by Chinese national security law from full audit compliance. If fully implemented, it could result in the expulsion of dozens of firms with a combined market capitalization of over $1 trillion—mostly private companies in sectors with few if any national security implications for the United States.[42] At the time of writing it appears that a deal between US and Chinese regulators will avert these delistings, but the reliance of Chinese firms on US capital markets is sure to decrease. Another probable action is legislation or an executive order that would set up a mechanism, similar to CFIUS, to screen investments by US companies in China for national security risks. Whatever the scope of the initial mechanism, it is likely to expand over time.

The Future: Between the Unsustainable and the Unachievable

US economic policy toward China is being remade, but the outcome is far from clear. It will be hard to reconcile the desires of national security policymakers who want to reduce flows of technology and finance to the China market and work with allies to constrain China's rise; economic nationalists who disdain alliances and want to re-shore manufacturing, sometimes against economic logic; and US companies that view further engagement with the China market as indispensable to their future growth but also welcome US government pressure on China to reduce regulations they find obnoxious.

The making of the new policy sausage will be messy and lengthy. This chapter concludes its analysis with a few observations about the basic conditions of the relationship and some recommendations for policy.

First, there is no going back to the old stance of constructive engagement, with its hopeful assumption that China's political-economy arrangements would converge with Western norms. China's authoritarian state-led capitalist economy is secure, and the tensions between it and the market-oriented systems of the United States and Europe will endure. And the geopolitical rivalry between the United States and China is acute enough that it makes sense for both countries to reduce their dependence on the other in certain areas, notably in technology. Some "decoupling" is already visible in reduced trade and investment flows. A continuation of the old path of maximal interdependence is unsustainable.

It is notable that the move to a tougher stance toward China is fully bipartisan, as evinced by the broad support for both ECRA and FIRRMA in 2018 as well as a swath of China-related bills in Congress in 2019–20.[43] US public opinion toward China has grown sharply more negative.[44] As in the era of constructive engagement, changes of administration may lead to shifts in tactics or emphasis, but the overall stance toward China—cooperative in the past, competitive now—is likely to remain stable.

Equally, however, the dream of full "decoupling" is achievable only at gigantic cost. Although some in Washington talk of the need for a "new cold war" with China, the economic relationship between the United States and China bears no resemblance to that between the United States and the Soviet Union or its successor states. In trade volume, it is much closer to the relationship with Japan in the 1980s (see figure 7.7). And, in fact, it is far deeper than the relationship with Japan because years of patient work have enabled US companies to build up huge positions in China's domestic market. The subsidiaries and affiliates of US companies in China generated $573 billion in revenues in 2019, more than triple the value of goods and services exported from the United States to China (see figure 7.8).

Even these figures understate the nature of the interdependence. Many big US companies consider a presence in China essential not just because it is a large market but because it offers an efficient large-scale production base; possesses an abundant pool of both factory labor and skilled engineering, financial, and managerial talent; and is the site of an increasing share of the world's innovation. For these companies, a presence in China is not optional; it is vital to ensuring their continued global competitiveness. This perspective is evident in surveys showing that US businesses have no particular plans to reduce their presence in China.[45] The lack of realistic business alternatives to China was pithily expressed by a country manager for a major US technology firm, who said in a recent interview, "Our plan B for China is China."[46]

It is certainly possible for companies to execute a "China plus one" or "China plus two" diversification strategy where continued presence in China is complemented by production bases in other locations (most likely other emerging Asian economies such as India or Vietnam rather than the United States). It is not plausible for them to abandon China altogether.

Aside from being unrealistic, the "decoupling" idea is analytically unhelpful because it construes the choice as binary: either the United States and China are "coupled" or they are "de-coupled." This is a false choice. Short of all-out war, the United States and China are bound to remain deeply interdependent. The question is not whether or not to decouple but which elements of dependency must be reduced to serve national interests, and at what cost.

Framing the problem this way, let us return to our earlier definition of US national economic interests vis-à-vis China. These were strengthening the country's industrial base, improving the market access conditions for US companies in China, protecting the US technology base from unfair competition from China, and strengthening international economic governance to constrain China's illiberal behavior. It is perfectly possible to address these interests, and satisfy to a reasonable degree the demands of the national security, economic nationalist, and business lobbies, without resorting to the excessive, headstrong, and often harmful tactics of the Trump administration.

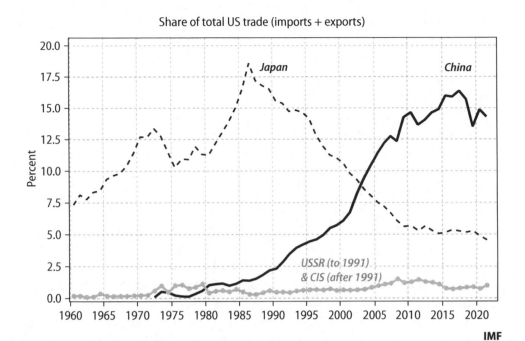

Figure 7.7 US trade with China: more like Japan than the USSR. (Kroeber)

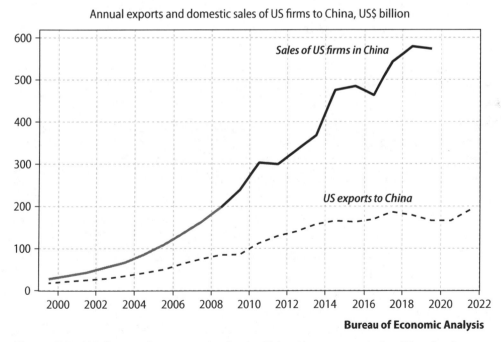

Figure 7.8 US firms rely more on sales in China than on exports. (Kroeber)

To strengthen the American industrial base, the main tools should be things that improve the investment environment at home, not efforts to pry US companies out of what they believe to be indispensable positions in China. These should include increased government investment in education and basic R&D, selective industrial policy to promote manufacturing capacity and discourage offshoring in a few key sectors, and a liberal immigration policy for students and skilled workers to ensure that the United States can continue to attract the best minds from around the world, including China.[47] The year 2022 saw two promising developments in this direction. One was the passage of two pieces of industrial policy legislation: the Chips and Science Act, which mobilized $50bn in federal support for semiconductor production, and the Inflation Reduction Act, which created an estimated US$260 billion in tax credit for clean energy investments. The other was the ending of the Trump-era "China Initiative," a poorly designed program for rooting out Chinese industrial espionage that functioned more as a tool of intimidation against researchers of Chinese descent or with China ties.[48]

Applying pressure on China to improve market access conditions, protecting US technology from unfair competition, and promoting better international economic governance all require a combination of direct unilateral pressure and coordinated international action, with more emphasis on the latter. Trump's tariffs failed to achieve any of their aims: decreasing the US trade deficit, increasing US exports to China, or boosting US manufacturing.[49] Now that they are in place, though, they should be removed in exchange for specific actions by China to reduce discriminatory regulations and subsidies that favor Chinese firms over foreign ones. ECRA and FIRRMA can be useful tools and should be applied more as scalpels than as meat cleavers to protect clearly specified US sectors and companies. They, and other mechanisms such as the entity list, should not be used to try to destroy Chinese companies. In general, a strategy that focuses mainly on building up US strengths, and not on the fantasy of crippling China's own development, best serves American interests.

In part this is because any US strategy must realistically account for China's responses. China reacted to the Trump administration's pressure in three main ways. First, it launched a carefully calibrated set of retaliatory tariffs (mainly on agricultural products) designed to inflict as much political damage on Trump as possible while keeping overall trade disruption to a minimum.[50] Second, it doubled down on efforts to create domestic replacements for technology now imported from the United States, including semiconductors.[51] Third, it undertook a charm offensive to reassure multinational companies that they would enjoy good treatment and increased market access, and it accelerated the timetable for opening up the financial sector, leading to large inflows of portfolio capital.[52] China's strategy continues to be one of selective market reform, generally increased openness, and industrial policy that may involve considerable wasted resources but is also likely to foster new industries. The United States has little ability to push China off course, so its best response is a comparable program of self-strengthening.

Moreover, US allies and countries throughout Asia will not go along with a strategy of crushing China: they simply have too much to gain from China's economic growth. An intelligent effort at multilateral coordination is essential. The United States should set a priority on reentering the TPP successor agreement, the Comprehensive and Progressive Agreement for Trans-Pacific Partnership (CPTPP). If this proves politically impossible, then the IPEF should be upgraded to include large material incentives for regional partners: improved access to US markets and significant infrastructure funding. The United States should also prioritize the creation of plurilateral agreements to forge rules and standards for digital commerce, embodying broadly market-based principles and designed to resist influence from China's illiberal state capitalist model. All international agreements should be open to any country regardless of political system.[53]

The US-China economic relationship is almost certain to remain an uneasy combination of rivalry and interdependence for many years to come. On the US side, it will require careful management, under a well-thought-out strategy governed by dispassionate assessment of national interests rather than posturing or wish-fulfillment fantasies, and with a full awareness of the costs and trade-offs involved in any course of action.

Notes

1. A good account of the logic behind the engagement strategy is Alastair Iain Johnston, "The Failures of the 'Failure of Engagement' with China," *Washington Quarterly* 42, no. 2 (Summer 2019): 99–114. Johnston rejects the now-popular narrative that supporters of engagement naively believed that integrating China into the global order would lead to political reform and democratization. The calculation was, rather, that China's behavior on a wide range of issues would be more constrained, and more subject to influence, if it had a stake in the global economic system. See also Robert Zoellick, "Whither China: From Membership to Responsibility?" Department of State, September 21, 2005, https://2001-2009.state.gov/s/d/former/zoellick/rem/53682.htm.

2. Alexandra Harney, *The China Price: The True Cost of Chinese Competitive Advantage* (New York: Penguin Books, 2008).

3. The finding that 85 percent of US manufacturing job losses were due to technology is in Michael J. Hicks and Srikant Devaraj, *The Myth and the Reality of Manufacturing in America*, (Muncie, IN: Ball State University Center for Business and Economic Research, June 2015), https://conexus.cberdata.org/files/MfgReality.pdf. Supporting evidence is that productivity growth in US manufacturing after 2000 was extremely high, suggesting effective use of automation: Robert Z. Lawrence, "Recent Manufacturing Employment Growth: The Exception

That Proves the Rule," (working paper 24151, National Bureau of Economic Research, December 2017), http://www.nber.org/papers/w24151.

A paper by MIT labor economist David Autor is often cited to support the argument that competition from China was the main source of manufacturing job loss: David H. Autor, David Dorn, and Gordon H. Hanson, "The China Syndrome: Local Labor Market Effects of Import Competition in the United States," *American Economic Review* 103, no. 6 (2013): 2121–68. But this paper's empirical finding is that import competition, mainly from China, accounted for around one million manufacturing job losses in the United States, a finding consistent with the Hicks and Devaraj research. A valid conclusion from this paper is that trade flows can have nonnegligible impacts on employment and that these impacts should be taken seriously by policymakers. For other treatments of this issue, see David H. Autor, "Trade and Labor Markets: Lessons from China's Rise," IZA World of Labor (2018), 431; Matthias Flueckiger and Markus Ludwig, "Chinese Export Competition, Declining Exports and Adjustments at the Industry and Regional Level in Europe" (MPRA paper no. 48878, August 2013).

4. Chinese companies accounted for less than 4 percent of the wholesale value of an iPhone produced in 2009. By 2018, that figure rose to 25 percent. These estimates apparently attribute to China the value of assembly by Foxconn, a Taiwanese company. Yuqing Xing, "How the iPhone Widens the Trade Deficit with China: The Case of the iPhone X," VoxEU, November 11, 2019, https://voxeu.org/article/how-iphone-widens-us-trade-deficit-china-0.

5. For an early litany of complaints about the increasingly onerous nature of China's regulatory regime and favoritism toward state-owned enterprises, see James McGregor, *No Ancient Wisdom, No Followers: The Challenges of Chinese Authoritarian Capitalism* (Westport, CT: Prospecta Press, 2012).

6. "国家中长期科学和技术发展规划纲要" State Council Information Office, People's Republic of China, February 9, 2006, http://www.gov.cn/jrzg/2006 -02/09/content_183787 .htm. English translation at https://www.itu.int/en/ITU-D/Cybersec urity/Documents/National_Strategies_Repository/China_2006.pdf. A good early analysis is Cong Cao, Richard P. Suttmeier, and Denis Fred Simon, "China's 15-Year Science and Technology Plan," *Physics Today* (December 2006): 38–43. An excellent comprehensive review of China's various science and technology plans is Tai Ming Cheung et al., *Planning for Innovation: Understanding China's Plans for Technological, Energy, Industrial and Defense Development* (US-China Economic and Security Review Commission, July 28, 2016), https://www.uscc.gov /sites/default/files /Research/Planning%20for%20Innovation%20-%20Understanding%20China's%20 Plans%20for%20Tech%20Energy%20Industrial%20and%20Defense%20Development 072816.pdf.

7. James McGregor, *China's Drive for "Indigenous Innovation": A Web of Industrial Policies*, (United States Chamber of Commerce, July 28, 2010), https://www.uschamber.com/sites/de fault/files/documents/files/100728chinareport_0_0.pdf.

8. James A. Lewis, "Learning the Superior Techniques of the Barbarians: China's Pursuit of Semiconductor Independence," Center for Strategic and International Studies, July 2019, https://www.csis.org/analysis/chinas-pursuit-semiconductor-independence.

9. Kai-Fu Lee, *AI Superpowers: China, Silicon Valley, and the New World Order* (Boston: Houghton Mifflin, 2018), 51–80, has a good description of the cutthroat market competition that led to the rise of China's successful Internet companies.

10. "Made in China 2025: Global Ambitions Built on Local Protections," United States Chamber of Commerce, March 2017.

11. For a comprehensive history of Chinese industrial policy, which spells out the

continuities of Made in China 2025 with previous policies and its innovations, see Barry Naughton, *The Rise of China's Industrial Policy, 1978–2020* (Academic Network of Latin America and the Caribbean on China, 2021). For a respectful treatment of China's technological innovation, see "The China Issue," *MIT Technology Review* 122, no. 1 (January/February 2019).

12. Jonathan Woetzel et al., "China and the World: Inside the Dynamics of a Changing Relationship" (McKinsey Global Institute, July 2019), 1–15; Scott Kennedy, "The Fat Tech Dragon: Benchmarking China's Innovation Drive," Center for Strategic and International Studies, August 2017.

13. Lance Noble, "Paying for Industrial Policy," Gavekal Dragonomics research note, December 4, 2018, https://research.gavekal.com/article/paying-industrial-policy.

14. Douglas A. Irwin, "Trade Politics and the Semiconductor Industry" (working paper 4745, National Bureau of Economic Research, July 1, 2003), https://papers.ssrn.com/sol3/papers.cfm?abstract_id=420309#.

15. Kathrin Hille, "Trade War Forces Chinese Chipmaker Fujian Jinhua to Halt Output," *Financial Times*, January 28, 2019.

16. Official data in both China and the United States substantially understate the actual value of bilateral direct investment flows between the two countries. The data set compiled by the Rhodium Group from individual deal announcements is more comprehensive. Data on Chinese participation in venture capital deals is from Michael Brown and Pavneet Singh, *China's Technology Transfer Strategy* (Defense Innovation Unit Experimental, January 2018).

17. This indictment is summarized in *Findings of the Investigation into China's Acts, Policies, and Practices Related to Technology Transfer, Intellectual Property, and Innovation under Section 301 of the Trade Act of 1974,* Office of the United States Trade Representative, March 22, 2018, https://ustr.gov/sites/default/files/Section%20301%20FINAL.PDF.

18. Gabriel Wildau, "China's Central Bank Delays Market Entry for Visa and Mastercard," *Financial Times*, January 13, 2019, https://www.ft.com/content/8dee4b22-13ef-11e9-a581-4ff78404524e.

19. Mark Wu, "The 'China Inc.' Challenge to Global Trade Governance," *Harvard International Law Journal* 57, no. 2 (2016): 261–324.

20. Bryce Baschuk, "Biden Picks Up Where Trump Left Off in Hard-Line Stances at WTO," *Bloomberg*, February 22, 2021, https://www.bloomberg.com/news/articles/2021-02-22/biden-picks-up-where-trump-left-off-in-hard-line-stances-at-wto.

21. *National Security Strategy*, March 2006, https://nssarchive.us/national-security-strategy-2006/.

22. Originally, "One Belt, One Road" (OBOR), which is a literal translation of the initiative's Chinese name, *yi dai yi lu*.

23. See, for instance, Nadège Rolland, *China's Eurasian Century? Political and Strategic Implications of the Belt and Road Initiative* (National Bureau of Asian Research, 2017), https://www.nbr.org/publication/chinas-eurasian-century-political-and-strategic-implications-of-the-belt-and-road-initiative/.

24. The strong form of this fear, that China was creating a "debt trap" for countries in order to foreclose on strategic assets, has been thoroughly debunked. The weaker form, holding that Chinese debt contracts differ importantly from those of traditional Paris Club international lenders and lack transparency, accountability, and recourse, is a serious issue. See Kevin Acker, Deborah Brautigam, and Yufan Huang, "Debt Relief with Chinese Characteristics" (working paper 39, China-Africa Research Initiative, 2020); and Anmar A. Malik et al., *Banking on the Belt and Road*, AidData policy report, 2021, https://www.aiddata.org/publications/banking-on-the-belt-and-road.

25. A classic exposition of the logic behind the engagement strategy is Thomas J. Christensen, *The China Challenge: Shaping the Choices of a Rising Power* (New York: W. W. Norton, 2016).

26. Edward S. Steinfeld, *Playing Our Game: Why China's Rise Doesn't Threaten the West* (Oxford: Oxford University Press, 2010).

27. Expressions of disappointment over China's lack of "convergence" with Western norms include Kurt M. Campbell and Ely Ratner, "The China Reckoning: How Beijing Defied American Expectations," *Foreign Affairs* (March/April 2018): 60–70; and Daniel H. Rosen, "A Post-Engagement US-China Relationship?" Rhodium Group, January 19, 2018, https://rhg.com/research/post-engagement-us-china-relationship/.

28. Antony Blinken, "The Administration's Approach to the People's Republic of China," May 26, 2022, US Department of State, https://www.state.gov/the-administrations-approach-to-the-peoples-republic-of-china/.

29. A concise summation of the economic nationalist agenda under Trump is Robert E. Lighthizer, "The Era of Offshoring U.S. Jobs Is Over," *New York Times*, May 11, 2020.

30. Chad Bown, "US-China Trade War Tariffs: An Updated Chart," Peterson Institute for International Economics, February 14, 2020, https://www.piie.com/research/piie-charts/us-china-trade-war-tariffs-date-chart.

31. An excellent blow-by-blow account of the US-China trade negotiations is Bob Davis and Lingling Wei, *Superpower Showdown: How the Battle between Trump and Xi Threatens a New Cold War* (New York: Harper Business, 2020).

32. Data from Department of Agriculture, https://www.fas.usda.gov/regions/china.

33. Chad Bown, "US-China Phase One Tracker," Peterson Institute for International Economics, March 11, 2022, https://www.piie.com/research/piie-charts/us-china-phase-one-tracker-chinas-purchases-us-goods; Chad Bown, "Unappreciated Hazards of the US-China Phase One Deal," Peterson Institute for International Economics, January 21, 2020, https://www.piie.com/blogs/trade-and-investment-policy-watch/unappreciated-hazards-us-china-phase-one-deal; Scott Kennedy, "Mystery Math: The U.S.-China Phase-1 Purchase Figures Do Not Add Up," Center for Strategic and International Studies, March 10, 2020, https://www.csis.org/analysis/mystery-math-us-china-phase-1-purchase-figures-do-not-add.

34. Brown and Singh, *China's Technology Transfer Strategy*.

35. Thomas M. deButts, Nicholas Klein, and Thomas Reynolds, "First Emerging Technologies Identified and Controlled for Export in the EAR," DLA Piper International Trade Alert, June 26, 2020, https://www.dlapiper.com/en/us/insights/publications/2020/06/first-emerging-technologies-identified-and-controlled-for-export-in-the-ear/.

36. Davis and Wei, *Superpower Showdown*, 25–26.

37. Dan Wang, "Tech War, Meet Trade Deal," Gavekal Dragonomics research note, March 10, 2020.

38. Donald J. Trump (@realdonaldtrump), Twitter thread, February 18, 2020, https://twitter.com/realDonaldTrump/status/1229790099866603521.

39. "OFAC Sanctions Eight Firms as Part of the Chinese 'Military-Industrial Complex,'" Comply Advantage, December 29, 2021, https://complyadvantage.com/insights/ofac-sanctions-eight-firms-as-part-of-the-chinese-military-industrial-complex/. See also "Issuance of Chinese Military-Industrial Complex Sanctions," Department of the Treasury, February 15, 2022, https://home.treasury.gov/policy-issues/financial-sanctions/recent-actions/20220215.

40. Gregory C. Allen, "Choking Off China's Access to the Future of AI," Center for Strategic and International Studies, October 11, 2022, https://www.csis.org/analysis/choking-chinas-access-future-ai.

41. Bob Davis, "Biden Promised to Confront China. First He Has to Confront America's Bizarre Trade Politics," *Politico*, January 31, 2022, https://www.politico.com/news/magazine/2022/01/31/biden-china-trade-politics-00003379.

42. In March 2022 the Securities and Exchange Commission notified the first five compaonies that could be delisted under the act. These included the company that operates Kentucky Fried Chicken and Pizza Hut fast food restaurants in China, along with four biotech and tech hardware companies. Aaron Nicodemus, "SEC Notifies Five Chinese Companies of HFCAA Noncompliance," Compliance Week, March 11, 2022, https://www.complianceweek.com/regulatory-enforcement/sec-notifies-five-chinese-companies-of-hfcaa-noncompliance/31452.article.

43. In the 2019–20 congressional session, 474 bills mentioning China were introduced, up from an average of around 150 in the previous ten congressional sessions. Data from https://www.govtrack.us/.

44. In the summer 2021 Pew Global Attitudes Survey, 76 percent of Americans expressed an unfavorable view of China, compared to just 20 percent with a positive view. Moreover, 70 percent of Americans supported promoting human rights in China, even at the cost of worsening economic ties. Aidan Connaughton, "Fast Facts about Views of China Ahead of the 2022 Beijing Olympics," Pew Research Center, February 1, 2022, https://www.pewresearch.org/fact-tank/2022/02/01/fast-facts-about-views-of-china-ahead-of-the-2022-beijing-olympics/.

45. In its 2020 survey of member companies, the US-China Business Council found that 83 percent of companies listed the China market as one of their top five global priorities, 68 percent expressed optimism about the five-year business outlook there, and 87 percent said they had no plans to move operations out of China. Only 4 percent said they had plans to move operations from China back to the United States, the same as the average for the previous five years. US-China Business Council, Member Survey 2020, https://www.uschina.org/sites/default/files/uscbc_member_survey_2020.pdf.

46. Author interview in Shanghai, November 10, 2021.

47. A more detailed elaboration of these recommendations is in Peter Cowhey, ed. *Managing Risks, Investing in Leadership and Preserving Openness: An American Strategy for U.S.-China Science and Technology Competition* (Working Group on Science and Technology in US-China Relations, November 2020).

48. Margaret K. Lewis, "Criminalizing China," *Journal of Criminal Law and Criminology* 111, no. 1 (2021): 145–224.

49. Chad Bown, "Anatomy of a Flop: Why Trump's US-China Phase One Trade Deal Fell Short," Peterson Institute for International Economics, February 8, 2021.

50. Davis and Wei, *Superpower Showdown*, 340.

51. Yoko Kubota, "China Sets Up New $29 Billion Semiconductor Fund," *Wall Street Journal*, October 25, 2019.

52. Wei He, "Flows Favor the Renminbi," Gavekal Dragonomics research note, October 5, 2020.

53. A more expansive blueprint for reimagining the US-China relationship across all dimensions, not just economics, in which I participated as a coauthor, is Orville Schell and Susan L. Shirk, eds. *Course Correction: Toward an Effective and Sustainable China Policy* (Task Force on U.S. Policy toward China and The Asia Society, February 2019), https://asiasociety.org/sites/default/files/inline-files/CourseCorrection_FINAL_2.7.19_0.pdf.

PART III

8

The Military Factor in US-China Strategic Competition

Phillip C. Saunders

Thirty years ago, China's military, the People's Liberation Army (PLA), was an insular, ground-dominated force equipped with obsolete weapons and operating almost exclusively within China's borders. Extensive modernization efforts have transformed the PLA into a modern military with a regular air and naval presence throughout the Asia-Pacific and a periodic presence in other parts of the world.[1] China's objective of building a military that can "fight and win" informationized wars is attached to a timeline of "basically completing" modernization by 2035 and building a "world-class military" by midcentury.[2]

The US military has played an important role in PLA modernization, both as a threat and as a model for the PLA to emulate. As PLA modernization has produced new capabilities that erode the US military's technological edge and threaten its ability to operate near China, the United States has begun to treat China as a strategic challenge to US regional dominance and to the US-led global order. This manifested in the Obama administration's 2011 Rebalance to Asia and in the Trump administration's December 2017 National Security Strategy, which described China as a revisionist power seeking to "challenge American power, influence, and interests, attempting to erode American security and prosperity."[3] The Biden administration has continued this approach, describing democratic nations as "under siege" and singling out China as "the only competitor potentially capable of combining its economic, diplomatic, military, and technological power to mount a sustained challenge to a stable and open international system."[4] The Biden administration's 2022 National Military Strategy labels China "our most consequential strategic competitor and the pacing challenge for the Department [of Defense]."[5]

US-China relations are increasingly characterized by strategic competition, with each side developing military capabilities aimed at the other and pursuing influence at the other's expense. Given the resources and focus Washington and Beijing are bringing to the task, this competition is likely to continue and intensify, and may even develop into a new cold war marked by global competition for power and influence.[6] This chapter begins by examining how the United States and China moved from a quasi alliance against the Soviet Union in the 1970s and 1980s to become strategic competitors, with an emphasis on how and when each side came to view the other as a military threat. The evolution of US-China strategic competition will have a major impact on US and Chinese military modernization, and that military competition, in turn, is likely to weigh on the broader bilateral relationship. This chapter examines these interactions and considers factors that might increase or dampen military competition as a subset of the broader strategic competition.

The Road to Rivalry

The US opening to China in the early 1970s and the subsequent quasi alliance against the Soviet Union were driven by realpolitik motives. After the Sino-Soviet split in 1960, China was in the difficult position of confronting both superpowers simultaneously. The Soviet Union was the larger and more proximate threat; rapprochement with Washington could improve China's external security environment and potentially gain US support against the Soviets. For Washington, an improved relationship with China could help extract the United States from Vietnam and change the strategic balance with Moscow, including by tying down Soviet military forces in the east. This strategic logic, coupled with domestic political imperatives on both sides, allowed President Nixon and Chairman Mao to overcome the Korean War legacy and great differences in ideology and political systems to pursue rapprochement.

The US Factor in Chinese Military Modernization

Military modernization was one of the Four Modernizations Deng Xiaoping announced in December 1978, but China's need to build overall economic and technological capacity relegated it to the lowest priority. The Chinese defense industry responded to the decline in military orders by reorienting production for commercial and export markets to survive. China hoped that strategic cooperation with the United States might enable access to Western military technology; US policymakers were sympathetic to the need to improve the PLA's ability to resist a Soviet invasion. The United States created a new category in multilateral export controls in April 1980 that allowed Western arms sales to China on a case-by-case basis, and the United States eventually approved deals to sell Mark-46 torpedoes, artillery counterbattery radars, and avionics upgrades for Chinese F-8 interceptor planes. Some of these sales were completed before military technology cooperation came to an end following the June 1989 Tiananmen massacre.[7]

Improved relations with the Soviet Union in the late 1980s reduced Chinese fears of a Soviet invasion and eventually enabled PLA access to modern weapons that its own defense industry could not produce. In the early 1990s the PLA was able to procure a number of advanced Soviet/Russian systems, including Su-27 fighters, *Kilo*-class diesel submarines, S-300 surface-to-air-missiles, and Sovres menny destroyers equipped with advanced anti-ship cruise missiles, which helped the Chinese military gain experience operating and maintaining modern weapons systems. These systems were initially procured in small quantities, with the hope that the Chinese defense industry could use access to them to improve its own design and production capabilities. The arms relationship survived the collapse of the Soviet Union, which made the Russian defense industry dependent on the China market. It also provided opportunities for China to acquire advanced defense technology and expertise from Russia and former Soviet states to accelerate its defense modernization.[8]

The twin developments of Tiananmen and the dissolution of the Soviet Union in 1991 transformed China's security environment. On the one hand, the Soviet collapse removed a major security threat as Russian military capabilities eroded and China established diplomatic relations with the former Soviet states, including resolution of border disputes. On the other hand, Tiananmen and the collapse of communism in the Soviet Union and Eastern Europe heightened Chinese Communist Party (CCP) concerns about internal stability and shifted US attitudes toward China in a sharply negative direction,[9] despite President George H. W. Bush's efforts to preserve bilateral relations with Beijing. The Soviet collapse removed a common enemy that had facilitated US-China strategic and military cooperation and allowed both countries to look past their political differences. The combination of China's post-Tiananmen domestic political turmoil and strategic vulnerability to superior and now less-constrained US power made Chinese leaders highly suspicious of US hostile political and military intentions and eventually sparked efforts to convert China's economic wealth into military power.[10]

Several developments led CCP leaders to accelerate the measured pace of PLA modernization. First, US military success in the 1991 Gulf War shocked PLA leaders. The United States and its allies were able to use precision-guided munitions and advanced intelligence, surveillance, and reconnaissance (ISR) capabilities to take apart the Iraqi military (the fourth largest in the world) in weeks, while suffering few casualties. US success demonstrated the critical role information played in modern war and showed that China's military—much less well equipped than Iraq's—was equally vulnerable.[11] Second, the March 1996 Taiwan Strait crisis—during which the United States sent two carriers toward

Taiwan following PLA exercises and missile launches intended to influence Taiwan elections—convinced CCP leaders that the threat of Taiwan independence
was growing and that the US military might intervene on Taiwan's behalf.
Chinese leaders responded with increased military budgets and accelerated
modernization efforts, while PLA planners began studying how to deal with
US military forces that might intervene in a future crisis. Third, the accidental
US bombing of China's embassy in Belgrade during the 1999 Kosovo conflict
was interpreted by Chinese civilian and military leaders as a deliberate action
to intimidate China. Although Chinese leaders ultimately sought to stabilize
relations with Washington, the bombing reinforced suspicions about US hostile
intentions and led to additional funding for PLA modernization.[12]

These factors increased the priority of military modernization, and the PLA's
budget grew at a double-digit rate for almost two decades. Chinese threat perceptions also changed, with the "main strategic direction" shifting from the Soviet
threat in the north to the threat of Taiwan independence and maritime challenges in the southeast.[13] Preventing Taiwan independence became the central
driver for PLA modernization, which also required preparing for possible US intervention in a conflict. This produced a corresponding shift in modernization
priorities, which benefited the Navy, Air Force, and missile forces at the expense
of the ground forces. This was explicitly stated in the 2004 People's Republic of
China (PRC) defense white paper and symbolized by adding the Navy, Air Force,
and Second Artillery commanders to the Central Military Commission (CMC),
the top military decision-making body, in 2004.[14] Chinese defense white papers avoid referring to specific adversaries by name, but PLA concerns about the
United States are evident in their descriptions of worrisome military trends and
criticisms of US military and alliance actions.

These changes produced increased PLA efforts to acquire or develop capabilities that might deter, delay, or defeat US military forces intervening in a conflict over Taiwan. In such a conflict, the PLA would benefit from home field
advantage while US forces would have to deploy from bases in Japan, Guam,
Hawaii, or the continental United States. The PLA invested in an array of anti-
access/area denial (A2/AD) capabilities intended to raise the costs and risks for
US forces operating near China. These included advanced diesel submarines,
which could attack US naval forces deploying into the western Pacific; surface-
to-air missiles such as the Russian S-300, which could target US fighters and
bombers; increasingly accurate ballistic missiles and land-attack cruise missiles
that could target the bases and ports the US military would employ in a conflict
with China; anti-ship cruise missiles optimized to attack US aircraft carrier battle groups; and an innovative anti-ship ballistic missile designed to attack US
aircraft carriers from above. China sought to exploit US military dependence
on space systems by developing a range of anti-satellite (ASAT) capabilities that
could degrade, interfere with, or directly attack US satellites and their associated

ground stations. It also invested in cyber capabilities to collect intelligence and attack the US military's logistics and command and control systems in a crisis or conflict. Collectively, these investments represented an asymmetric effort to degrade US military advantages in order to give a less-capable PLA force a chance of success in a conflict. PLA strategists hoped that the ability to inflict significant casualties on US forces coming into range of its various A2/AD systems would deter US intervention.

PLA modernization involved more than weapons. Chinese strategists also sought to harness the advantages of US- and Russian-style joint operations, which integrated multiple services to achieve synergistic effects. This was a major conceptual shift for the ground-force-dominated PLA, which had previously viewed naval and air forces mostly as supporting ground force operations. In 1993, the PLA promulgated a new military strategy that prioritized preparations for high-tech regional conflicts and described joint operations as the "main form" of future operations. A 2004 doctrinal revision placed even more emphasis on what became known as "integrated joint operations," which highlighted the need for deeper cooperation between services.[15] These high-level efforts to define the nature of future warfare were matched by efforts to develop operational joint campaign doctrine detailing *how* the services should work together to accomplish specific tasks as well as a series of joint exercises intended to improve the ability of the services to work together.[16]

At the same time, PLA theorists emphasized the importance of information in advanced warfighting and sought to emulate US "network-centric warfare." If accurate information about enemy forces could be passed quickly to commanders and field units, military forces could gain the initiative and reap operational synergies that would dramatically increase their effectiveness. Conversely, attacks on adversary intelligence, communications, and command and control systems could produce paralysis and force individual units to fight in isolation, at a huge disadvantage.[17] In 2004, PLA doctrine shifted to a stress on the need to fight and win "local wars under conditions of informationization" (changed in 2015 to "informationized local wars").[18]

This doctrinal change implied a shift away from emphasizing asymmetric means of giving the weaker PLA a chance to prevail against a stronger US military and toward a more symmetric approach where the PLA would attempt to replicate and adapt aspects of US military concepts, systems, and organization. This required the ability to compete effectively in the traditional warfighting domains of land, sea, and air as well as the newer nuclear, space, cyber, and electromagnetic domains. However, efforts to implement jointness and informationized warfare were hindered by ground force dominance of the PLA and the lack of a joint command and control system to allow forces from all services to work together.

China's early 2016 military reforms, launched by Xi Jinping, involved an extensive and unprecedented reorganization of the PLA intended to enhance its political reliability and improve its ability to conduct integrated joint operations.[19] The reforms jettisoned the old Soviet military organizational template—which had guided the PLA for seven decades—in favor of an American-style joint command and control system. The reforms abolished the powerful general departments in favor of an expanded CMC staff under Xi Jinping's direct supervision and moved from seven army-dominated military regions to five joint theater commands with control over all ground, naval, air, and conventional missile forces within their area of responsibility. Each theater was given responsibility for a specific set of cross-border or maritime contingencies, while the postreform role of the military services shifted from operational command to "force building" (e.g., "plan, train, and equip" functions). Each service headquarters was now responsible for developing military equipment, recruiting and training personnel, setting training requirements, and providing trained and equipped forces to the joint theater commands.

The China Factor in US Military Modernization

The US intelligence community and various think tanks tracked China's military modernization as the PLA took delivery of Russian systems and the Chinese defense industry began to produce more capable weapons. Although US defense officials regularly criticized China for a lack of transparency about its military capabilities, testimony by US defense and intelligence officials, congressional hearings, annual public reports by the Department of Defense, and open-source publications provided extensive analysis of Chinese military developments and documented gradual but significant improvements in PLA capabilities from the mid-1990s to the present.[20]

The policy question was the extent to which improving PLA capabilities constituted a threat that required changes in US defense budgets, policies, modernization priorities, doctrine, and force deployments. By 2018, China had become the dominant threat driving US military modernization, but this shift happened gradually and was delayed as the United States focused on other priorities, especially the post-9/11 global war on terrorism and the conflicts in Iraq and Afghanistan. PLA actions that might have sparked dramatic responses, such as the 1995–96 missile tests, the April 2001 accidental collision between a US Navy reconnaissance plane and a Chinese fighter, and the 2007 direct-ascent anti-satellite (ASAT) test, instead produced modest and limited adjustments in US threat perceptions and military modernization efforts.

The relative frequency of terms in US congressional testimony and strategic documents is a reasonable proxy for how much attention the United States paid to specific strategic challenges at any given moment. Figure 8.1 captures the number of references to China, Russia, and the Middle East/terrorism in annual testimony by the US Pacific Command (USPACOM) commander. The data

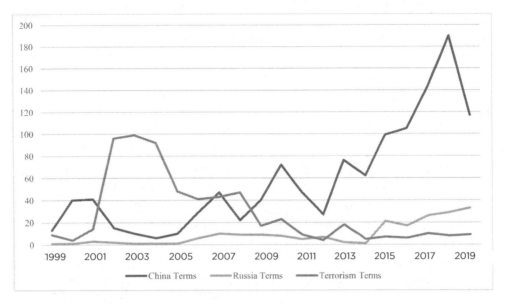

Figure 8.1   Terms in USPACOM posture statements. (Saunders)

show a spike in mentions of China after the 1995–96 Taiwan Strait crisis, and again in 2000 and 2001. However, the 2002 testimony has a dramatic increase in terrorism-related terms, as Pacific Command sought to demonstrate its relevance in the global war on terrorism. The 2001 statement begins with a focus on regional security developments, while the 2002 statement starts with "Combating terrorism in the Asia-Pacific region," which is described as "USPACOM's top priority." USPACOM contributions to the war on terrorism remained the lead item until 2009. A spike in mentions of China is evident in 2009 and 2010, corresponding to increased Chinese assertiveness in the South China Sea. From 2013 to 2018, mentions of China increase in each successive testimony.[21] Similar patterns are evident in US strategic documents and annual worldwide threat briefings by senior US intelligence officials.[22]

What explains the delayed US response to Chinese military modernization? In addition to the impact of 9/11 and the wars in Iraq and Afghanistan, key factors include US assessments of PLA relative military capabilities, PLA aggressive military behavior, and the PLA's role in justifying US military procurement priorities.

The 9/11 Attacks and the Wars in Iraq and Afghanistan

The shift in threat perceptions and budgetary priorities caused by the 9/11 terrorist attacks was arguably the most important factor delaying US responses to improvements in Chinese military capabilities. The Bush administration responded to the threats posed by terrorism and rogue states pursuing weapons of mass destruction (WMD) by invading Iraq and removing President Saddam Hussein from power. The initial rapid US military victory was followed by the emergence of a violent insurgency that required maintaining large numbers of US ground troops in Iraq. Deepening US involvement in Iraq allowed the Taliban to reconstitute its forces and seize control of large portions of Afghanistan, mounting attacks against the Afghan government and the US and NATO forces deployed to assist it. The United States found itself waging twin counterinsurgency campaigns that imposed heavy operational demands on US military forces, required huge amounts of resources, and consumed the attention of US defense officials and military leaders. In May 2008, then Secretary of Defense Robert Gates explicitly acknowledged the trade-offs, arguing that the United States needed to focus on winning current wars even if this meant deferring force modernization for future conflicts.[23]

US Assessments of PLA Relative Military Capabilities

Differences in missions, overall military proficiency, and the technical capabilities of weapons complicated US efforts to assess the significance of improving PLA capabilities. The US and Chinese militaries have very different missions, with the US military focused on power projection to fulfill global responsibilities and the PLA historically focused on land border and maritime contingencies within Asia. Today's PLA still lags well behind the US military in overall technological capacity, the ability to project and sustain power over long distances, and the ability to conduct sophisticated joint operations that fully leverage space and cyber capabilities. Most PLA weapons systems and munitions are less capable than their US equivalents, although the most recent generation of Chinese weapons systems has narrowed the gap in performance and now exceeds US capabilities in some areas such as conventional missiles.[24] China's goal of building a "world-class military" (e.g., one equivalent to the US military) by 2049 is an implicit acknowledgment that the PLA has a long way to go to catch up with the United States.

However, as Thomas Christensen wrote in 2001, China did not necessarily need to match US capabilities across the board to pose a strategic challenge.[25] US assessments gradually shifted from emphasizing the PLA's weaknesses to assessing what it could do against the US military in specific scenarios. These assessments judged PLA offensive capabilities against US defenses (and vice versa), often in the context of a conflict over Taiwan, and found that PLA A2/AD capabilities imposed significant constraints on US ability to deploy air and naval power into the western Pacific and conduct combat operations.[26] Limitations in PLA power projection capabilities were less significant in the context of a campaign against Taiwan, less than one hundred miles off the Chinese coast. An influential 2015 RAND study assessed US and Chinese relative military capabilities in South China Sea and Taiwan scenarios and found that many US military advantages had eroded. The study argued that "the PLA [was] not close to catching up to the US military in terms of aggregate capabilities, but it [did] not need to catch up to the United States to dominate its immediate periphery."[27] This shift in the basis for comparison of military capabilities produced a greater sense of urgency for US defense planners.

PLA Aggressive Military Behavior

Another important factor shaping US threat perceptions was aggressive PLA behavior. China's 1995–96 missile tests, which Beijing viewed as necessary to deter Taiwan independence, and actions to seize and construct a facility on Mischief Reef in the South China Sea in November 1994 prompted numerous writings highlighting China's growing nationalism and asking whether China posed a military threat to the Asia-Pacific region.[28] China responded by decrying the "China threat theory" but also sought to improve relations with the United States and its neighbors via a range of diplomatic, military, and economic assurance measures.[29] This charm offensive from 1998 to 2008 was predicated on a patient approach to territorial disputes and restraint in employing military force (even as PLA modernization accelerated).[30]

In 2009, however, a more assertive Chinese posture emerged on a wide range of international issues.[31] Chinese diplomatic bullying, assertive military and paramilitary actions in the South China Sea and East China Sea, and disregard for foreign reactions undid many of the gains from Beijing's charm offensive.[32] For the US military, Chinese interceptions and harassment of US military ships and planes operating inside China's exclusive economic zone (EEZ) posed a risk to safety and a challenge to the principle of freedom of navigation. One incident with particular impact on US military views was the March 2009 harassment of the USNS *Impeccable*, an unarmed ocean surveillance ship, by two Chinese fishing trawlers, two Chinese paramilitary ships, and a PLA Navy intelligence ship. Other Chinese actions included using paramilitary ships to seize control of Scarborough Shoal from the Philippines (April 2012), the initiation of maritime patrols near the Diaoyu/Senkaku islands (September 2012), unilateral declaration of an air defense identification zone in the East China Sea (November 2013), and extensive land reclamation and subsequent militarization of China-occupied land features in the South China Sea (2013–16).[33] Although China sought to limit the negative consequences of these actions by avoiding the use of lethal force, its use of "grey zone" military and paramilitary tactics to expand its control of disputed territories heightened US and regional perceptions of a growing China threat.

The PLA and US Procurement Priorities

Another factor delaying the US response is that the PLA initially served as a poor justification for the capabilities the US services wanted to procure. Although the Chinese military's purchases of Russian fighters, submarines, destroyers, and surface-to-air missiles in the 1990s constituted a leap forward in PLA capabilities, these systems were based on 1980s technology and were procured in small quantities; Chinese-built weapons were even further behind in technical capability. These systems did little to justify the advanced stealth fighters, aircraft carriers, Aegis destroyers and cruisers, and other systems at the top of the US Navy and Air Force procurement list. This situation persisted until the US services began to focus on the new challenges posed by PLA A2/AD capabilities. By 2010, US services and combatant commands were openly citing China as justification for increased funding and doctrinal innovation. The US Air Force and Navy announced a new "AirSea Battle" operational concept in 2010 intended to improve their ability to operate in an A2/AD environment.[34] This concept tied funding justification for new aircraft, ships, and submarines directly to the China military threat. The marines and army, who bore the heaviest burden in the wars in Iraq and Afghanistan, also looked to Asia and the China threat to justify funding and a "recapitalization" of the ground forces. The marines fought for a role in AirSea Battle, which eventually evolved into the Joint Operational Access Concept (JOAC) issued in January 2012.[35] China worked less well as a justification for US Army procurement, since one lesson accepted throughout the US military was "never fight a land war in Asia." The need to justify military budgets became more acute as US troops were withdrawn from Iraq in 2011 and budget sequestration began to impose mandatory cuts on defense spending in 2013.

These factors all came together around 2014 and 2015 as concerns about terrorist threats eased, the cumulative gains from PLA modernization became more widely acknowledged, assertive Chinese military behavior increased, and the US military began looking for persuasive justifications for military spending. The unclassified version of the 2015 National Military Strategy, issued by the chairman of the Joint Chiefs of Staff, gave voice to military concerns, arguing that "China's actions are adding tension to the Asia-Pacific region" and decrying "aggressive land reclamation efforts that will allow it [China] to position military forces astride vital international sea lanes."[36] These concerns about the Chinese military threat were shared inside and outside the military and produced a widespread sense that a tougher approach to China was necessary. This would eventually manifest in the Trump administration's declaration in the December 2017 National Security Strategy that China was a revisionist power that sought to displace the United States in the Indo-Pacific and a January 2018

National Defense Strategy that singled out China as the principal focus of renewed great power competition.

With brief interruptions, the PLA and the US military conducted military diplomacy throughout this period, including regular high-level visits; recurrent dialogues at the operational, policy, and strategic levels; and functional exchanges focused on nontraditional security cooperation, crisis avoidance and management, and military education.[37] Military-to-military contacts gave each side a better understanding of the interests and security concerns but did not generate much trust or alleviate suspicions. China's push from 2011 to 2013 to establish a "new type of great power relationship" with the United States included a parallel effort to build a "new type of military-to-military relationship." In practice, however, this was predicated on US willingness to accommodate Chinese interests and change its policies on issues such as arms sales to Taiwan and US reconnaissance activities inside China's EEZ. Military-to-military talks did produce some useful confidence-building measures, including secure voice and video links useful for crisis management and 2014–15 bilateral agreements on rules of behavior for air and maritime encounters.[38] However, they did not alter the trend toward military competition, probably because neither side was prepared to make significant concessions to accommodate the other's interests and concerns.

The Future of Sino-US Military Competition

Today, US strategic competition with China manifests itself in an ideological competition of political systems, a regional competition for influence and military dominance, and a global competition over international rules, norms, and influence. The military competition is evident in US and Chinese operational actions in the Asia-Pacific, conventional force modernization to gain an edge in a potential conflict over Taiwan, and development of nuclear and nonnuclear strategic capabilities, including a struggle for space and cyber dominance and the modernization of each side's nuclear, missile, and ballistic missile defense forces. US and Chinese weapons are increasingly designed to attack and defend against each other's systems; the two militaries increasingly plan and train for conflicts against each other. This section considers the extent to which developments in specific areas are likely to sustain US-China military competition and potentially affect broader US-China bilateral relations.

Operational Encounters in the Indo-Pacific Region

US military aircraft and ships routinely perform reconnaissance activities and conduct freedom of navigation operations inside China's EEZs, which China regards as a violation of its sovereignty. Chinese military forces routinely respond to US flights by deploying fighter aircraft to intercept US aircraft and sending China Coast Guard or Chinese naval vessels to intercept US ships and tell them to leave Chinese waters. Chinese military and paramilitary forces have sometimes engaged in dangerous maneuvers to try to disrupt US operations. The potential for accidental or deliberate collisions is real, as the April 2001 EP-3 incident and the March 2009 *Impeccable* incident illustrate.

These US operations are likely to continue, partly because they serve the additional functions of demonstrating US commitment to the region and the US military's will to operate throughout the Indo-Pacific. The US military is also increasing its exercises and deployments in the region, both to reassure allies and deter potential Chinese adventurism. The May 2020 deployment of B-1 bombers to Guam to practice conventional strike missions against land and maritime targets and the June 2020 simultaneous deployment of three US carrier battle groups to the Indo-Pacific are examples that are likely to be repeated regularly in the future.[39] The Chinese military and Chinese research institutes track US military activity in the Indo-Pacific and interpret it as evidence of a strengthened US military focus on China, "which poses increasingly high risks of China-US friction and conflict in the air and at sea."[40]

PLA air and naval activity is also increasing throughout the region, both inside the first and second island chains and into the Indian Ocean. China's deployment of a counterpiracy task force in December 2008 marked the beginning of a continuous naval presence in the Gulf of Aden, which the PLA has used for military diplomacy and to conduct operational missions such as the evacuation of Chinese citizens from Libya in 2011. The PLA Navy is pursuing a maritime strategy of "near seas defense and far seas protection," and the PLA Air Force has increased its training and operations over water.[41] This activity includes increasing PLA intelligence collection flights and patrols into Japan's EEZ as well as military patrols and exercises designed to strengthen China's effective control over disputed land features and waters.[42] Although not usually aimed directly against US forces, these grey zone activities place military pressure on Taiwan and US allies and thus contribute to Chinese efforts to erode support for the US military presence in the region.

The two sides have made efforts to develop mutually understood rules for air and maritime encounters that would reduce the risks of collisions and to develop crisis communications and management equipment and protocols that could de-escalate a crisis if an accident occurs.[43] The best case would be that these types of military operations are understood to be making symbolic political points and are met with ritualized responses that minimize operational risks.[44] However, rules of behavior may sometimes be deliberately violated in order to try to exploit the other side's risk aversion and deter it from operational behavior that damages one's security interests. Chinese military academics have acknowledged that this logic sometimes explains the PLA's willingness to deliberately engage in risky behavior.[45]

As the two militaries increasingly treat each other as adversaries, these operational encounters may become both more frequent and more dangerous. If conducting military operations and exercises to demonstrate political will becomes a key feature of the US-China military competition, both militaries will have incentives to take risks in order to send stronger signals of commitment. This dynamic also increases the risk of an incident escalating into a broader confrontation, even though both militaries typically operate under strict rules of engagement designed to limit escalation risks. A future collision or exchange of fire would likely have a serious and enduring impact on each military's view of the other as an adversary, especially if there is significant loss of life. Such an incident might also have wider political consequences that affect the broader bilateral relationship.

Conventional Force Modernization and Taiwan

As discussed earlier, the US military has long played a central role in PLA force modernization, both as a potential adversary and as a model. The PLA is now widely viewed by US military leaders as the principal US military challenge.[46] A potential conflict over Taiwan has become the key planning scenario for both militaries. Chinese leaders describe Taiwan as a "core interest," meaning that they are prepared to fight to prevent Taiwan independence and are potentially willing to use force to achieve unification. The United States does not have a formal treaty obligation to defend Taiwan, but the 1979 Taiwan Relations Act states that it is US policy to maintain the capacity to resist force or coercion against Taiwan. Taiwan constitutes a "hard case" for the US military's ability to project power in the face of Chinese A2/AD systems and to defeat an increasingly capable PLA. As a result, US military leaders are focused on developing capabilities, doctrine, and plans for conflict with the PLA over Taiwan. Other potential conflict scenarios with China are considered "lesser included cases" because China's military advantages would not be as strong.

US military concerns about a potential conflict with China over Taiwan are partly based on the fact that China would enjoy "home field advantage" in operating from its own territory while the United States would have to deploy forces from distant locations and operate from a limited number of regional bases and ports or from aircraft carriers vulnerable to Chinese attack.[47] This raises the possibility that China might initiate a conflict and hope to win a quick victory before the United States can fully deploy its forces to the theater, thereby presenting the United States with a hard-to-reverse fait accompli.[48] The Department of Defense is working to adapt US weapons and operating concepts to fight the PLA in an A2/AD environment, including forward deployment of forces and supplies to overcome the "tyranny of distance." This thinking is evident in the 2018 National Defense Strategy and in the joint concept of "globally integrated operations," which seeks to leverage information and US global capabilities to achieve decisive strategic effects in regional contingencies. The Biden administration's 2022 National Defense Strategy stresses integrated deterrence, which "entails developing and combining [US] strengths to maximum effect, by working seamlessly across warfighting domains, theaters, the spectrum of conflict, other instruments of U.S. national power, and [the United States'] unmatched network of Alliances and partnerships."[49]

At the request of Congress, US Indo-Pacific Command commander Adm. Philip Davidson developed the Pacific Deterrence Initiative (PDI), a six-year, $20 billion investment program for the US military to "regain the advantage" over China in the Indo-Pacific. Congress has funded the first three years of the request and appears likely to continue funding.[50] The US services all have active efforts underway to adapt systems and doctrine to meet A2/AD threats, with a clear focus on China. For the US Navy, this involves efforts to disrupt the "kill chain" necessary for Chinese missiles to locate and target US carriers, and to develop the ability to operate and reload ship armaments from a diverse set of nontraditional port facilities. For the US Air Force, this involves efforts to develop both standoff and penetrating platforms[51] and to improve the service's ability to conduct expeditionary, distributed operations from austere airfields with reduced logistics and maintenance requirements, which the service calls Agile Combat Employment.[52] The US Army has created new Multi-Domain Task Forces", which combine artillery and precision strike capabilities with a range of cyber, electronic warfare, space, and intelligence capabilities to operate within and degrade an adversary's A2/AD capabilities. The initial pilot program was conducted under the US Army Pacific, and the first operational task force was established at Joint Base Lewis-McChord, which is aligned to the Indo-Pacific theater.[53] The US Marine Corps has made a major shift in its force modernization plans to adapt its forces to meet the China challenge and improve its ability to conduct Expeditionary Advanced Base Operations (EABO) in contested environments.[54]

US military strategists, operators, and force developers are now heavily focused on how to defeat the PLA in a conflict over Taiwan or elsewhere in the Indo-Pacific, just as Chinese operators, theorists, and force developers have been focused on the US military for the past twenty-five years. Other aspects of conventional force development and planning are likely to reinforce US and Chinese mutual threat perceptions. US weapons developers will focus on optimizing the performance of US offensive systems against Chinese defenses and US defenses against Chinese offensive systems; their Chinese counterparts will do the same. This will entail increased intelligence efforts to understand the technical capabilities of adversary weapons and increased counterintelligence efforts to protect one's own secrets. Each side is likely to cite expected improvements in the technical capabilities of the other's advanced weapons systems as justification for funding new systems to counter them. Each side is likely to look at the other military's force structure to argue for increased procurement; this arms race dynamic is already evident in advocacy for a larger US Navy.[55] Moreover, as the cost of developing, operating, and maintaining high-tech weapons systems increases, there will be increasing interservice and interbranch competition for scarce dollars and yuan, which will strengthen incentives for actors on both sides to exaggerate threats to justify budgets and programs.

Strategic Capabilities and Defenses

This section briefly sketches the likely dynamics of US-China military competition in the space and cyber domains, in developing new artificial intelligence and autonomous weapon technologies that point the way toward future intelligentized warfare, and in conventional and nuclear-armed missiles and missile defense. There is not sufficient space for a full treatment or net assessment of relative capabilities, so the emphasis will be on the nature and intensity of the competition in each area.[56]

Space and Cyber Competition

US-China military competition is increasingly characterized by competition for dominance in the space and cyber domains. Both militaries believe that information is critical to winning modern wars. The Chinese 2015 defense white paper argued, "Outer space and cyber space have become new commanding heights in strategic competition among all parties."[57]

China has sought to exploit US military dependence on space systems by developing a range of ASAT capabilities that could degrade, interfere with, or directly attack US satellites and their associated ground stations. At the same time, China has also invested significant resources in developing space-based ISR, communications, and global positioning satellites to support its own ability to fight informationized war. Both countries are engaged in an intense competition to develop the capability to attack or deny the use of the other's satellites in a conflict and to protect their own satellite capabilities or have the ability to reconstitute them if they are attacked (which the US military calls "operationally responsive space"). The importance both countries place on space is evident in China's decision to concentrate space and cyber capabilities in a new Strategic Support Force in 2016 and the US decision to form the Space Force in 2020. Space is likely to remain an area of intense and expensive competition, since both sides view it as a critical enabler for conventional warfighting and now have independent institutional bodies to advocate for space and counterspace capabilities.

The United States has long enjoyed advanced cyberintelligence and cyberattack capabilities; their importance for modern war is symbolized by the establishment of US Cyber Command as an independent combatant command in 2018. The PLA has made significant investments in building a capable cyberforce (now integrated into the Strategic Support Force). Cyberspace appears to be an offense-dominant domain where it is easier to attack than to defend networks against capable nation-state entities. China has demonstrated an impressive capability to penetrate US military, government, and defense contractor networks and extract large amounts of useful data. The US military and intelligence establishment has also demonstrated a significant capability to collect cyberintelligence and mount cyberattacks. Many of the emerging US military efforts to operate within the Chinese A2/AD envelope, such as US Army Multi-Domain Task Forces, appear to rely heavily on cyber and electronic warfare operations to degrade Chinese sensors and command and control networks. Given the importance of information and computer networks to how each military wants to fight, the cyber domain is likely to remain an area of intense competition and jockeying for advantage.

Artificial Intelligence and Autonomous Weapons Competition

Artificial Intelligence (AI) is "the ability of a computer system to solve problems and to perform tasks that would otherwise require human intelligence."[58] AI has a variety of potential military applications. At the weapons level, its applications include optimizing the performance and accuracy of missiles, improving the ability of weapons platforms and missiles to defeat defenses and countermeasures, and increasing the effectiveness of cyberattacks and cyberdefenses. A second set of applications involves improvements in sensor and image recognition technology that could make it more difficult for systems such as nuclear submarines, mobile missiles, and stealth aircraft to survive undetected on the modern battlefield, thereby potentially eroding strategic stability by making deterrent forces vulnerable to a first strike. Another set of applications involves the use of AI in autonomous or unmanned systems, either acting independently, in swarms, or to augment manned systems. A fourth set of applications involves the use of AI in command and control systems, either to develop and plan alternative courses of action for human commanders or execute operations without human involvement.

The US military is engaged in efforts to leverage advances in artificial intelligence and autonomous systems to produce sustained military advantage, which the Obama administration called a "third offset strategy." The US Congress set up a National Security Commission on Artificial Intelligence in 2018 to provide recommendations on how the United States can compete more effectively in this field. In 2017, the Chinese government announced an ambitious AI development plan that sought to catch up with leading countries by 2020 and become "the world's leading artificial intelligence innovation center by 2030."[59] The PLA is currently pursuing a wide range of military applications for AI, and Chinese military theorists speak of a potential shift from today's "informationized" warfare to tomorrow's "intelligentized" warfare.[60] Artificial intelligence and related technologies such as quantum information and big-data analysis are emerging areas of military competition with the potential to produce significant military advantages. The Chinese military reorganized its military research institutes under the Academy of Military Sciences in 2017 to pursue synergies between military technology and doctrinal development.

Early fruits of US efforts to develop unmanned systems were evident in US operation of unmanned reconnaissance and attack systems in the conflicts in Iraq and Afghanistan, but more advanced air and naval systems are intended to have greater autonomy and produce advantages in fighting against sophisticated military adversaries. The Chinese 2019 defense white paper argued, "New and high-tech military technologies based on IT are developing rapidly. There is a prevailing trend to develop long-range precision, intelligent, stealthy or unmanned weaponry and equipment."[61] The PLA is investing significant resources in developing unmanned air and naval systems, and Chinese defense enterprises have exported unmanned combat aerial vehicles to a variety of customers in the Middle East and Africa. This is a growing area of military competition that is likely to become more important in the future as unmanned systems play critical roles as sensors and shooters. Competition in the areas of artificial intelligence and unmanned/autonomous systems is not simply a matter of technological innovation; it also involves experimentation, doctrinal development, and the ability to adapt military organizations and doctrines to use these systems to full advantage.

Conventional and Nuclear-Armed Missiles and Missile Defense

Until recently, conventional and nuclear missiles have had relatively limited impact on US-China military competition. Partly due to US conventional force advantages and partly due to China's "no-first-use" nuclear policy, there was a considerable separation between conventional systems likely to be used in a conflict and nuclear forces primarily intended to deter adversary use of nuclear weapons. This conventional-nuclear separation and the relative stability it supported has eroded over the last decade. One reason is the growth in China's regional missile capabilities. In recent years China has deployed more than 2,200 short- and medium-range ballistic and cruise missiles that can target Taiwan and US bases in Japan and Guam.[62] By contrast, from 1987 to 2019 the United States was prevented by the Intermediate-Range Nuclear Forces (INF) treaty with Russia from deploying ground-based ballistic and cruise missiles with ranges from 500 to 5,500 kilometers. The US military is now focused on closing what it believes is a significant gap in theater missiles that could disadvantage US forces in a conflict. An emerging feature of the missile competition is the advent of hypersonic missiles, which travel at very high speeds and follow less predictable flight paths, making them more difficult to intercept than traditional ballistic and cruise missiles.

Another factor is changing offense-defense dynamics related to nuclear weapons and missile defenses. In the past, China appeared willing to live with a smaller nuclear force so long as Beijing was confident that its "lean and effective" arsenal could maintain a secure second-strike capability and thereby deter a nuclear attack.[63] Chinese strategists worried about the potential impact of expanded US missile defenses or potential breakthroughs that would allow the United States to locate and target Chinese mobile missiles. This theoretical concern seems more concrete today. China has been modernizing its nuclear forces to deploy a second generation of land- and sea-based nuclear missiles that will strengthen confidence in its ability to retaliate against a US first strike that could be enabled by improved US missile defense capabilities. US officials have consistently argued that its defenses are not sized or configured to negate China's (or Russia's) strategic nuclear deterrent, and the United States has tolerated China's nuclear expansion while seeking a dialogue to discuss how to maintain strategic stability in a more complex environment.

However, Washington is increasingly suspicious of Beijing's nuclear ambitions. Modernization of Chinese ground-based nuclear missiles, deployment of sea-launched ballistic missiles on nuclear submarines, and the deployment of air-launched nuclear weapons are leading to a major expansion of deployed Chinese nuclear weapons. The Department of Defense projects that the PRC may have seven hundred deliverable warheads by 2027 and one thousand warheads by 2030, a major increase over previous estimates.[64] For the first time, China's nuclear forces have become a significant factor in the US calculus about its own nuclear forces, at a time when the United States is engaged in an expensive effort to field a next-generation nuclear triad to replace its Cold War–era nuclear delivery systems.[65] US policymakers have expressed concerns about a possible Chinese "sprint to nuclear parity" and have sought to include China in arms control negotiations with Russia concerning the New START treaty and possible follow-on agreements.[66] China has held to its position that it will not discuss nuclear arms control until the United States and Russia reduce forces to its level. At present, there are no official nuclear arms control negotiations between the

United States and China, and previous semi-official "Track 1.5" dialogues appear to be on hold.

As a result of these trends, there is much more strategic interdependence between Chinese and US conventional missile developments, US missile defenses, and nuclear modernization. As China's conventional missiles have grown in numbers and sophistication, US strategists increasingly view this arsenal as a major threat to the survivability of US bases and ports in the region and the US ability to prevail in a conventional war against China. In addition to deploying its own missiles in the region, the United States increasingly highlights the importance of missile defenses to counter China's missile arsenal.[67] US policymakers are less inclined to give much weight to Chinese concerns that regional missile defenses to support conventional warfighting might erode the credibility of the Chinese strategic nuclear deterrent.

These conditions are ripe for security dilemma dynamics, where actions one side views as reasonable and defensive are viewed by the other as offensive actions that undermine its security. US deployments of missile defense to help protect regional air bases and ports in a conventional conflict are likely to be viewed by Beijing as efforts to erode the credibility of China's nuclear deterrent and potentially enable a US nuclear first strike. The situation is further exacerbated by China's deployment of the DF-26 intermediate-range ballistic missile, which can carry either conventional or nuclear warheads, raising the risk that US retaliation against Chinese conventional missile strikes might inadvertently degrade China's nuclear deterrent.[68] China may respond to this perceived threat by increasing alert rates on its deployed nuclear missile force and flushing its ground-based and sea-based missiles in the early stages of a crisis, thus potentially weakening crisis stability.[69] The bottom line is that Chinese conventional missiles, US missile defenses, and the US and Chinese nuclear arsenals, which previously had been loosely coupled so that changes in one area did not prompt major changes in other areas, appear to be becoming more interdependent and tightly coupled. This suggests that increased—and more complex—competition is likely, and developments in nonnuclear forces (conventional missiles and missile defenses) may affect the other side's nuclear force posture.

This section has focused primarily on likely competitive dynamics in operational encounters between the two militaries, conventional force modernization in the context of a Taiwan scenario, and the development of various types of nuclear and nonnuclear strategic capabilities and defenses. It is worth posing the larger question of how this competition may affect the likelihood of a US-China conflict. It is generally assumed that nuclear powers will exercise a high degree of caution in dealing with each other due to fear that a conflict will escalate to the nuclear level and impose damage far out of proportion to the original stakes. Chinese nuclear doctrine and military writings appear consistent with this assumption.[70]

However, the US and Chinese militaries are preparing for a high-end conventional conflict employing advanced capabilities. Both US and Chinese doctrine for information warfare involves efforts to target adversary sensors and command and control networks to disorient the adversary and force him to fight with individual weapons and units rather than as an integrated, networked force. Both emphasize the importance of seizing the initiative in a conflict to achieve decisive impact. At the same time, both militaries hope to leverage advanced sensors, command and control networks, and precision strikes to achieve synergistic and often cross-domain effects for their own forces. Although some of these systems have been employed against less-capable militaries, there are no real-world examples of advanced militaries using the full suite of capabilities against equally capable adversaries. The lack of real-world experience and the expectation that informationized warfare will produce synergistic effects suggests a high potential for overestimating one's own capabilities and underestimating the adversary's. The significant risk of misperceiving the balance of capabilities and the likely outcome of a military conflict suggests that intensifying military competition could be far less stable than many assume.

Conclusion

This analysis suggests that military competition is increasingly evident across the US and Chinese militaries and is likely to persist. Both militaries are likely to advance a suspicious view of the other side and advocate measures to reduce security risks by reducing economic interdependence, technology transfer, and educational exchanges that might benefit the other side's military modernization. Military competition is likely to have a negative impact on the overall bilateral relationship and reinforce impulses toward economic decoupling and limits on US-China economic, cultural, and educational exchanges. It is too early to tell whether this will produce a US-Soviet–style cold war, but the relationship is headed in that direction.[71] To the extent that there is a mutual interest in crisis avoidance and management mechanisms to reduce escalation risks, intensified military competition may produce stronger incentives for military-to-military relations.[72] However, this is likely to be a careful dialogue between adversaries on limited issues of common interest rather than broader contacts than can spark improvements in the overall relationship. In truth, this has been the state of military-to-military contacts for the last five years.

Several exogenous factors could alter the dynamics of US-China military competition. First is the regional and global security environment. Both the United States and China are competing for influence in the Indo-Pacific region, and the attitudes of regional countries are the political battlefield for this competition. The willingness of US allies to provide US military forces access to bases on their territories and the willingness of Indo-Pacific countries to engage in security cooperation with the US military are the US strategic center of gravity in the Indo-Pacific.[73] China's importance as an economic partner means that countries do not want to be forced to choose between the United States and China. This political environment may impose some constraints on US-China military competition in the region. For example, US allies may be reluctant to host US ballistic and cruise missiles targeted against China. Alternatively, developments in North Korea could spark a regional confrontation that neither Beijing nor Washington wants. Some of the same dynamics are evident in other regions, especially in Europe, where the United States has been pushing European Union and NATO member states to regard China as a threat to common values and shared economic and security interests. Russia's invasion of Ukraine, coupled with China's tacit support for Moscow, may translate into increased European willingness to cooperate with Washington against both Russia and China.

A second factor is economic constraints as both countries deal with growing national budget deficits in a post-COVID global economy. Producing and fielding large numbers of expensive weapons (and the trained personnel to maintain and operate them effectively) will strain military and national budgets. The ability of China or the United States to afford these costs over the long term depends on continuing economic growth and a domestic political consensus that high military spending is strategically necessary, even at the expense of other national priorities. A prolonged economic downturn or crisis could delay the production and fielding of high-end capabilities, which would constrain military modernization. The negative impact of COVID-19 on the US and Chinese economies may have a dampening effect on near- and mid-term military budgets, although this has not been evident so far. Even absent a crisis, lower growth rates are likely to slow military modernization and heighten interservice competition for resources and missions.[74]

A third factor is domestic stability in China. Serious domestic turmoil could shift resources and the direction of PLA modernization toward capabilities useful for internal stability, such as ground forces, the People's Armed Police, strategic airlift, and counterterrorism forces. Sustained domestic unrest would reduce the PLA's ability to invest in high-end capabilities aimed at the United States and focus on overseas missions and power projection capabilities. This could ease competitive pressures.

A fourth question is the extent to which China's growing overseas interests, fueled by investment under the Belt and Road Initiative (BRI), will stimulate a more permanent PLA military presence outside Asia and the development of a blue water navy, additional overseas bases, and expeditionary capabilities. In

2021, the US Department of Defense reported, "The PRC is seeking to establish a more robust overseas logistics and basing infrastructure to allow the PLA to project and sustain military power at greater distances . . . [which] could both interfere with US military operations and support offensive operations against the United States."[75] A parallel question is whether the United States will retain the political will to be actively engaged to pursue US global interests with military means. The answers may shape whether US-China military competition remains focused in the Indo-Pacific or whether it extends to other regions as well.

The extent to which US-China military competition can be "managed" and balanced by cooperation on trade, global governance, and nontraditional security challenges is unclear, but the signs are not encouraging. China continues to call for a bilateral relationship based on "peaceful co-existence" and "win-win cooperation" but argues that this must rest on a foundation of mutual respect for each other's core interests, including strict US adherence to a One China policy.[76] The Biden administration has stated that the US relationship with China "will be competitive when it should be, collaborative when it can be, and adversarial when it must be. The common denominator is the need to engage China from a position of strength."[77] While officials on both sides acknowledge the potential benefits of bilateral cooperation, both governments appear more focused on gearing up for long-term competition. One observer of the US-China relationship argues that the two countries are now engaged in a full-spectrum competition and that the "Biden administration has thus moved to place long-term strategic competition with China at the center of its grand strategy."[78] China rejects a definition of the US-China relationship focused solely on competition but is also gearing up for long-term competition.[79]

Intensified strategic competition could accelerate Chinese development of advanced weapons systems, heighten US-China competition for regional and global influence, and spur PLA efforts to extend the range of its power projection and counterintervention capabilities. The US and Chinese rivalry is likely to continue, reducing the space for cooperation on areas of common interest and increasing the pressure on Indo-Pacific countries and global and regional powers to choose between the United States and China. US-China military competition may also produce increasingly expensive conventional and nuclear arms races. This would be suboptimal for China, the United States, the Indo-Pacific region, and the world but appears the most likely outcome given current trends.

Notes

* Phillip C. Saunders is director of the National Defense University's Center for the Study of Chinese Military Affairs and a distinguished research fellow at the NDU's Institute for National

Strategic Studies. The views expressed are his alone and do not necessarily reflect those of the National Defense University, the Department of Defense, or the US government. The author thanks Joel Wuthnow, David C. Logan, Paul Bernstein, T. X. Hammes, Frank Hoffman, Evan S. Medeiros, Margaret Baughman, Jonah Langan-Marmur, and two anonymous reviewers for comments on previous drafts.

1. Joel Wuthnow et al., eds., *The PLA beyond Borders: Chinese Military Operations in Regional and Global Context* (Washington, DC: National Defense University Press, 2021), https://ndu press.ndu.edu/Publications/Books/PLA-Beyond-Borders/.

2. "Full Text of Xi Jinping's Report at 19th CPC National Congress," *Xinhua,* November 3, 2017, www.xinhuanet.com/english/special/2017-11/03/c_136725942.htm. For a discussion of what China means by a "world class military," see M. Taylor Fravel, "China's 'World-Class' Military Ambitions: Origins and Implications," *Washington Quarterly* 43, no. 4 (Spring 2020): 85–99, https://doi.org/10.1080/0163660X.2020.1735850.

3. *National Security Strategy of the United States of America*, December 2017, 2, https://trump whitehouse.archives.gov/wp-content/uploads/2017/12/NSS-Final-12-18-2017-0905.pdf.

4. *Interim National Security Strategic Guidance*, March 2021, https://www.whitehouse.gov /wp-content/uploads/2021/03/NSC-1v2.pdf.

5. "Fact Sheet: 2022 National Defense Strategy," Department of Defense, March 28, 2022, https://media.defense.gov/2022/Mar/28/2002964702/-1/-1/1/NDS-FACT-SHEET.PDF.

6. See Thomas F. Lynch III, ed., *Strategic Assessment 2020: Into a New Era of Great Power Competition* (Washington, DC: National Defense University Press, 2020), https://ndupress.ndu .edu/Publications/Books/Strategic-Assessments-2020/.

7. Kevin L. Pollpeter, *U.S.-China Security Management: Assessing the Military-to-Military Relationship* (Arlington, VA: RAND Corporation, 2004), 10–11.

8. Bates Gill and Taeho Kim, *China's Arms Acquisitions from Abroad: A Quest for "Superb and Secret Weapons"* (New York: Oxford University Press, 1995); Stephen J. Blank, *The Dynamics of Russian Weapons Sales to China* (Carlisle, PA: Army War College Strategic Studies Institute, 1997).

9. See David Shambaugh, *China's Communist Party: Atrophy and Adaptation* (Berkeley: University of California Press, 2008).

10. Rush Doshi, *The Long Game: China's Grand Strategy to Displace American Order* (New York: Oxford University Press, 2021).

11. Dean Cheng, "Chinese Lessons from the Gulf Wars," in *Chinese Lessons from Other Peoples' Wars*, ed. Andrew Scobell, David Lai, and Roy Kamphausen (Carlisle, PA: Strategic Studies Institute, 2011), 153–200.

12. David M. Finkelstein, *China Reconsiders Its National Security: The Great Peace and Development Debate of 1999* (Alexandria, VA: CNA, 2000).

13. M. Taylor Fravel, "Shifts in Warfare and Party Unity," *International Security* 42, no. 3 (Winter 2017/2018): 37–83.

14. *China's National Defense in 2004* (Beijing: State Council Information Office, December 2004).

15. Fravel, "Shifts in Warfare," 73–80.

16. James Mulvenon and David Finkelstein, eds., *China's Revolution in Doctrinal Affairs: Emerging Trends in the Operational Art of the Chinese People's Liberation Army* (Alexandria, VA: CNA, 2005).

17. The PLA calls this "systems attack" or "systems confrontation." See Jeffrey Engstrom, *Systems Confrontation and System Destruction Warfare: How the Chinese People's Liberation Army Seeks to Wage Modern Warfare* (Arlington, VA: RAND Corporation, 2018).

18. Fravel, "Shifts in Warfare," 79–80.

19. See Phillip C. Saunders et al., eds., *Chairman Xi Remakes the PLA: Assessing Chinese Military Reforms* (Washington, DC: National Defense University Press, 2019).

20. These included annual testimony by defense officials and the USPACOM commander to Congress about the defense authorization bill, annual unclassified briefings by the director of central intelligence/director of national intelligence beginning in 1994, congressionally mandated reports on Chinese military modernization by the US-China Economic and Security Review Commission and the Office of the Secretary of Defense beginning in 2002, and annual PLA conferences organized by Taiwan's Council of Advanced Policy Studies (CAPS), RAND, and the National Defense University, and by the US Army War College and the National Bureau of Asian Research.

21. The 2019 testimony is by a new commander and is significantly shorter than the 2018 testimony, so the drop in mentions of China is not necessarily significant.

22. This data is available from the author.

23. Robert M. Gates, "Remarks to the Heritage Foundation," Colorado Springs, CO, May 13, 2008, https://www.airforcemag.com/PDF/DocumentFile/Documents/2008/gates_heritagespch_051308.pdf.

24. Office of the Secretary of Defense, *Annual Report to Congress: Military and Security Developments Involving the People's Republic of China 2020* (Washington, DC: Office of the Secretary of Defense, 2020): 38.

25. Thomas J. Christensen. "Posing Problems without Catching Up: China's Rise and Challenges for US Security Policy," *International Security* 25, no. 4 (Spring 2001): 5–40.

26. An important early study was Roger Cliff et al., *Entering the Dragon's Lair: Chinese Antiaccess Strategies and Their Implications for the United States* (Santa Monica, CA: RAND Corporation, 2007), https://www.rand.org/pubs/monographs/MG524.html.

27. Eric Heginbotham et al., *The U.S.-China Military Scorecard: Forces, Geography, and the Evolving Balance of Power, 1996–2017* (Santa Monica, CA: RAND Corporation, 2015), xxxi, https://www.rand.org/pubs/research_reports/RR392.html.

28. Samples include Denny Roy, "Hegemon on the Horizon? China's Threat to East Asian Security," *International Security* 19, no. 1 (Summer 1994): 149–68; and Richard Bernstein and Ross H. Munro, *The Coming Conflict with China* (New York: Alfred A. Knopf, 1997). For a contemporaneous survey of regional views and strategies, see Alastair Iain Johnston and Robert S. Ross, eds., *Engaging China: The Management of an Emerging Power* (New York: Routledge, 1999).

29. See Phillip C. Saunders, "China's Role in Asia: Attractive or Assertive?" in *International Relations of Asia*, 2nd ed., ed. David Shambaugh and Michael Yahuda (Lanham, MD: Roman and Littlefield, 2014), 147–72.

30. M. Taylor Fravel, *Strong Borders, Secure Nation: Cooperation and Conflict in China's Territorial Disputes* (Princeton, NJ: Princeton University Press, 2008).

31. See Jeffrey A. Bader, *Obama and China's Rise: An Insider's Account of America's Asia Strategy* (Washington, DC: Brookings Institution Press, 2012), chap. 7; Michael D. Swaine, "Perceptions of an Assertive China," *China Leadership Monitor* 32 (2010).

32. Michael D. Swaine and M. Taylor Fravel, "China's Assertive Behavior—Part Two: The Maritime Periphery," *China Leadership Monitor* 35 (2011).

33. See Michael Green et al., *Countering Coercion in Maritime Asia: The Theory and Practice of Gray Zone Deterrence* (Washington, DC: Center for Strategic and International Studies, May 2017), https://csis-website-prod.s3.amazonaws.com/s3fs-public/publication/170505_Green M_CounteringCoercionAsia_Web.pdf.

34. The original public mention of the concept, Andrew F. Krepinevich, *Why AirSea Battle?* (Washington, DC: Center for Strategic and Budgetary Assessments, February 19, 2010), was explicit about China as the main focus; Department of Defense statements were sometimes more discreet.

35. *Joint Operational Access Concept (JOAC)*, Department of Defense, January 2012, https://dod.defense.gov/Portals/1/Documents/pubs/JOAC_Jan%202012_Signed.pdf.

36. *National Military Strategy of the United States of America*, 2015, https://www.jcs.mil/Portals/36/Documents/Publications/2015_National_Military_Strategy.pdf.

37. Pollpeter, *U.S.-China Security Management*.

38. Phillip C. Saunders and Julia G. Bowie, "US-China Military Relations: Competition and Cooperation in the Obama and Trump Eras," in *Reshaping the Chinese Military: The PLA's Roles and Missions in the Xi Jinping Era*, ed. Richard A. Bitzinger and James Char (Abingdon, UK: Routledge, 2019), 88–108.

39. Oriana Pawlyk, "B-1 Bomber May Become the New Face of US Military Power in the Pacific," Military.com, May 20, 2020, https://www.military.com/daily-news/2020/05/20/b-1-bomber-may-become-new-face-us-military-power-pacific.html; Lolita C. Baldor, "U.S. Naval Buildup in Indo-Pacific Warning to China," Associated Press, June 12, 2020.

40. South China Sea Strategic Situation Probing Initiative (SCSPI), *An Incomplete Report on US Military Activities in the South China Sea in 2021* (Beijing: SCSPI, March 2022), http://www.scspi.org/sites/default/files/reports/an_incomplete_report_on_us_military_activities_in_the_south_china_sea_in_2021.pdf.

41. See Defense Intelligence Agency, *China Military Power: Modernizing a Force to Fight and Win* (Washington, DC: Defense Intelligence Agency, 2019); and Asia Maritime Transparency Initiative, "Chinese Power Projection," Center for Strategic and International Studies, https://amti.csis.org/chinese-power-projection/.

42. See Shinji Yamaguchi, "China's Air and Maritime ISR in Coastal Defense and Near Seas Operations," in Wuthnow et al., *PLA beyond Borders*, 127–50.

43. "Memorandum of Understanding between the Department of Defense of the United States of America and the Ministry of National Defense of the People's Republic of China Regarding the Rules of Behavior for Safety of Air and Maritime Encounters," Department of Defense, November 9–10, 2014, https://archive.defense.gov/pubs/141112_MemorandumOfUnderstandingRegardingRules.pdf.

44. One such example is cross-strait artillery fire between the Taiwan-occupied island of Kinmen and the Chinese mainland in the 1960s and 1970s; this eventually evolved into a ritual display of shelling on alternate days with little risk of causalities.

45. Mark E. Redden and Phillip C. Saunders, *Managing Sino-U.S. Air and Naval Interactions: Cold War Lessons and New Avenues of Approach*, China Strategic Perspectives 5 (Washington, DC: National Defense University Press, September 2012).

46. Colin Clark, "SecAF Says B-21 'On Schedule' as China Rises to Air Force's Top Threat," *Breaking Defense,* February 14, 2018, https://breakingdefense.com/2018/02/secaf-says-b-21-on-schedule-as-china-rises-to-air-forces-top-threat/; David H. Berger, "Notes on Designing the Marine Corps of the Future," Headquarters Marine Corps, December 6, 2019, https://www.marines.mil/News/News-Display/Article/2033629/notes-on-designing-the-marine-corps-of-the-future/.

47. See Heginbotham et al., *U.S.-China Military Scorecard*.

48. For an assessment of PLA ability to execute various military campaigns against Taiwan, see Joel Wuthnow et al., eds., *Crossing the Strait: China's Military Prepares for War with Taiwan* (Washington, DC: National Defense University Press, 2022).

49. "Fact Sheet: 2022 National Military Strategy," Department of Defense.

50. Mallory Shelbourne, "INDOPACOM Wants $20B over the Next Six Years to Execute National Defense Strategy," Inside Defense, April 2, 2020, https://insidedefense.com/daily -news/indopacom-wants-20b-over-next-six-years-execute-national-defense-strategy; Tony Bertuca, "White House Report on China Sets Stage for New Indo-Pacific Investments," Inside Defense, May 21, 2020, https://insidedefense.com/daily-news/white-house-report-china -sets-stage-new-indo-pacific-investments; Jim Inhofe and Jack Reed, "The Pacific Deterrence Initiative: Peace through Strength in the Indo-Pacific," War on the Rocks, May 28, 2020, https://warontherocks.com/2020/05/the-pacific-deterrence-initiative-peace-through-strength -in-the-indo-pacific/.

51. Alex Grynkewich, "The Future of Air Superiority, Part III: Defeating A2/AD," War on the Rocks, January 13, 2017, https://warontherocks.com/2017/01/the-future-of-air-superiori ty-part-iii-defeating-a2ad/.

52. Brian M. Killough, "The Complicated Combat Future of the U.S. Air Force," National Interest, February 9, 2020, https://nationalinterest.org/feature/complicated-combat-future-us -air-force-121226.

53. Sean Kimmons, "Army to Build Three Multi-Domain Task Forces Using Lessons from Pilot," Army News Service, October 15, 2019, https://www.army.mil/article/228393/army_to _build_three_multi_domain_task_forces_using_lessons_from_pilot.

54. Berger, "Notes on Designing"; "Expeditionary Advanced Base Operations (EABO)," Headquarters U.S. Marine Corps, August 2, 2019, https://www.marines.mil/News/News-Dis play/Article/2708120/expeditionary-advanced-base-operations-eabo; Michael R. Gordon, "Marines Plan to Retool to Meet China Threat," Wall Street Journal, March 22, 2020, https:// www.wsj.com/articles/marines-plan-to-retool-to-meet-china-threat-11584897014.

55. Jon Harper, "Eagle vs Dragon: How the U.S. and Chinese Navies Stack Up," National Defense, March 9, 2020, https://www.nationaldefensemagazine.org/articles/2020/3/9/eagle -vs-dragon-how-the-us-and-chinese-navies-stack-up/.

56. For a fuller analysis, see Phillip C. Saunders and David C. Logan, "China's Regional Nuclear Capability, Non-nuclear Strategic Systems, and Integration of Concepts and Oper- ations," in China's Strategic Arsenal: Worldview, Doctrine, and Systems, ed. James M. Smith and Paul J. Bolt (Washington, DC: Georgetown University Press, 2021), 125–57.

57. China's Military Strategy, State Council Information Office (Beijing, May 2015), http:// eng.mod.gov.cn/Press/2015-05/26/content_4586805.htm.

58. National Security Commission on Artificial Intelligence, Interim Report (Washington, DC: National Security Commission on Artificial Intelligence, November 2019), 7.

59. Paul Mozur, "Beijing Wants A.I. to Be Made in China by 2030," New York Times, July 20, 2017.

60. For an overview of PLA thinking and research lines of effort, see Chinese Military Inno- vation in Artificial Intelligence, Testimony before the US-China Economic and Security Review Com- mission Hearing on Technology, Trade, and Military-Civil Fusion, June 7, 2019 (testimony of Elsa B. Kania).

61. China's National Defense in the New Era (Beijing: State Council Information Office, July 2019), https://www.globalsecurity.org/military/library/report/2019/china-national-defense -new-era_20190724.pdf.

62. Douglas Barrie, Michael Elleman, and Meia Nouwens, "The End of the Intermediate Range Nuclear Forces Treaty: Implications for Asia," in Asia-Pacific Regional Security Assess- ment 2020: Key Developments and Trends (London: International Institute for Strategic Studies, 2020) 27–38.

63. See M. Taylor Fravel and Evan S. Medeiros, "China's Search for Assured Retaliation: Explaining the Evolution of China's Nuclear Strategy," *International Security* 35, no. 2 (Fall 2010): 48–87.

64. Office of the Secretary of Defense, *Annual Report to Congress: Military and Security Developments Involving the People's Republic of China 2021* (Washington, DC: Office of the Secretary of Defense, 2021), 90–94.

65. *2022 Defense Posture Review*, included in *2022 National Military Strategy*, Department of Defense, October 27, 2022, https://media.defense.gov/2022/Oct/27/2003103845/-1/-1/1/2022-NATIONAL-DEFENSE-STRATEGY-NPR-MDR.PDF#page=33.

66. Paul Sonne and John Hudson, "Trump Orders Staff to Prepare Arms-Control Push with Russia and China," *Washington Post*, April 25, 2019, https://www.washingtonpost.com/world/national-security/trump-orders-staff-to-prepare-arms-control-push-with-russia-and-china/2019/04/25/c7f05e04-6076-11e9-9412-daf3d2e67c6d_story.html.

67. Office of the Secretary of Defense, *2019 Missile Defense Review* (January 2019), https://www.defense.gov/Portals/1/Interactive/2018/11-2019-Missile-Defense-Review/The%202019%20MDR_Executive%20Summary.pdf.

68. See Caitlin Talmadge, "Would China Go Nuclear? Assessing the Risk of Chinese Nuclear Escalation in a Conventional War with the United States," *International Security* 41, no. 4 (2017): 50–92; David C. Logan, "Are They Reading Schelling in Beijing? The Dimensions, Drivers, and Risks of Nuclear-Conventional Entanglement in China," *Journal of Strategic Studies* (November 12, 2020), 5–55, https://doi.org/10.1080/01402390.2020.1844671.

69. See Wu Riqiang, "Living with Uncertainty: Modeling China's Nuclear Survivability," *International Security* 44, no. 4 (Spring 2020): 84–118.

70. Fravel and Medeiros, "China's Search"; Fiona S. Cunningham and M. Taylor Fravel, "Dangerous Confidence? Chinese Views on Nuclear Escalation," *International Security* 44, no. 2 (Fall 2019): 61–109.

71. For a partial evaluation of some of these dynamics, see Avery Goldstein, "US-China Rivalry in the Twenty-First Century: Déjà Vu and Cold War II," *China International Strategy Review* 2 (2020): 48–62, doi:/10.1007/s42533-020-00036-w.

72. See Joel Wuthnow, "U.S.-China Military Relations in an Era of Strategic Competition" (working paper, Penn Project on the Future of U.S.-China Relations, Spring 2021), https://cpb-us-w2.wpmucdn.com/web.sas.upenn.edu/dist/b/732/files/2021/04/Joel-Wuthnow_US-China-Military-Relations_Updated.pdf.

73. See Thomas F. Lynch III, James Przystup, and Phillip C. Saunders, "The Indo-Pacific Competitive Space: China's Vision, the Post–World War II American Order and Implications," in Lynch, *Strategic Assessment 2020*, 185–218.

74. *A "World-Class" Military: Assessing China's Global Military Ambitions*, Testimony before the U.S.-China Economic and Security Review Commission, June 20, 2019 (statement of Phillip C. Saunders, director, Center for the Study of Chinese Military Affairs, National Defense University), https://www.uscc.gov/sites/default/files/Saunders_USCC%20Testimony_FINAL.pdf.

75. Office of the Secretary of Defense, *Military and Security Developments Involving the People's Republic of China 2021* (Washington, DC: Office of the Secretary of Defense, 2021), 130–31.

76. Wang Yi, "Wang Yi Delivers an Address at the Meeting in Commemoration of the 50th Anniversary of the Shanghai Communiqué," February 28, 2002, https://www.fmprc.gov.cn/eng/zxxx_662805/202202/t20220228_10646417.html.

77. Antony J. Blinken, "A Foreign Policy for the American People," speech, March 3, 2021, Ben Franklin Room, Washington, DC, https://www.state.gov/a-foreign-policy-for-the-american-people/.

78. G. John Ikenberry, "Systemic Rivals: America's Emerging Grand Strategy toward China," *Global Asia* 16, no. 4 (December 2021): 14–18.

79. Ryan Hass, "Beijing's Response to the Biden Administration's China Policy," *China Leadership Monitor* 71 (Spring 2022), https://www.prcleader.org/hass-1.

9

National Security and Strategic Competition between China and the United States

Li Chen

The defense and security competition between China and the United States has deep roots. These include a changing balance of power characterized by diminished US primacy, structural conflicts of interests, and a related US-China security dilemma in East Asia. The defense and security competition between China and the United States that features heavily in today's international environment began far before the current narrative of strategic competition or the trade war.

The current security competition remains relatively moderate compared to Cold War military competition, but the challenge going forward is daunting given the prospect for this competition to intensify. While the Cold War featured the emergence of nuclear parity and a rough balance in conventional military capabilities thanks to the efforts of both sides to keep up with each other, the current gap in military power between China and the United States remains skewed in favor of the latter. Absent a corresponding and explicit Chinese aspiration for military parity and the restraining fears of nuclear war, the trajectories of the current competition are more uncertain, and miscalculation and escalation may easily occur as a result.

The expansion of security competition to realms beyond military capabilities may also exacerbate the risks of confrontation in US-China relations. Recent competition has also featured extensive political, military, and diplomatic mobilization of both sides, in combination with a trend toward economic decoupling that has expanded the scope of bilateral security competition to nonmilitary domains. These developments, especially in economic and technology policy, provide greater means and space for security competition but also undermine the forces that constrained previous crises and confrontations.

This chapter assesses the origins and implications of the security competition between China and the United States in six parts. The first section traces the recent origins of the security competition, identifying events in the 1990s as the catalysts for the broadening bilateral strategic competition in motion today. The second describes an initially reluctant and restrained Chinese response to an intensified competition. The third section characterizes new perceptions and other changes that have driven a more robust Chinese response since 2019. The fourth section focuses on structural analysis, identifying major components of current and future security competition, and the fifth section sketches out possible Chinese approaches to longer-term competition with the United States. Finally, the chapter concludes with recommendations for more effective management of strategic competition between China and the United States.

Origins of US-China Security Competition

Although the overall competition between China and the United States has intensified in recent years, the origins of the security competition date back to the 1990s. Generations of Chinese decision-makers have long regarded stable relations with the United States as a priority in order to secure a favorable external environment to grow the Chinese economy and implement overall modernization. Chinese decision-makers and scholars pursued a long-term strategy of economic modernization, with foreign and security policy contributing to this overall objective by defending critical national interests and shaping an international environment favorable to economic development at home. Accordingly, Chinese political institutions also adhered to this development-oriented grand strategy; in the Chinese system both the Communist Party of China's (CPC) leadership and Chinese central government play a larger role than the US federal government in social and economic development.

What Chinese leaders initially viewed as a necessary military modernization in response to security threats and the People's Liberation Army's (PLA) inability to successfully mitigate them has since contributed to a broader, much more expansive strategic and security competition with the United States. The Chinese strategic community has traditionally paid substantial attention to the continuities of Chinese strategic evolution but remains sensitive to changes on the US side; compared to the active interventions in foreign affairs that frequently appear in US foreign policy, the Chinese are convinced that their own strategy is not only moderate but also keeps the possibilities of friction and conflicts with others to a minimum. The Chinese military buildup of the 1990s and 2000s that emerged from this strategic culture became the genesis of the current strategic and security competition.

The 1990s: A Buildup Motivated by Inadequacy

The current security competition between China and the United States has its roots in the 1990s. The era was characterized by relative strategic calm but also a dramatic disparity in military capabilities between China and the United States as well as intermittent but serious security challenges. These challenges ultimately drove China to remediate the aforementioned gap in its military capabilities, a trend that exacerbated the security dilemma that underlies the current competition between the two countries.

At the strategic level, neither China nor the United States adopted strategies explicitly to confront each other between 1990 and 2010, but both countries realized they had to cope with security challenges emanating from the other. Long-standing conflicting security interests stemmed from such issues as the US-led alliance system in East Asia and Chinese sovereignty issues—but on balance, these were also manageable in the 1990s. While US contingency planning and military presence in the Asia-Pacific took China into account, the overall national security strategies of the Clinton and Bush administrations did not prioritize a security challenge from China.[1] For its part, while China was frustrated with US policy toward Taiwan and the huge gap in military power with the United States, it well understood that an armed showdown with the United States over Taiwan was a worst-case scenario that could be avoided if all parties wished to maintain the status quo. Under those conditions, China gradually carried out its military modernization to reduce the gap with the United States.

Despite these mutually nonconfrontational strategic postures, the United States did pose security challenges to China in the post–Cold War era, and these seemed to intensify as the 1990s evolved and into the 2000s. The outcome of the Persian Gulf War demonstrated a generational gap between US and Chinese military power arising from the United States' successful military modernization (the revolution in military affairs) and US primacy after the collapse of the Soviet Union. Other events illuminated security challenges at hand for China. The third Taiwan Strait crisis between 1995 and 1996, the accidental 1999 US bombing of the Chinese embassy in Yugoslavia, and the 2001 EP-3 incident each highlighted to Chinese leaders the prospect of US neutralization of Chinese military power and unacceptable damage to Chinese national interests. Together, these events motivated an accelerated Chinese military modernization that began in earnest in 1995 with a three-phase overall plan aimed at achieving military modernization by the mid-twenty-first century, along with the development of advanced weapons systems that could generate adequate deterrence in the 2000s.[2] In the context of US primacy, Chinese strategists viewed these modernization efforts as necessary and purely reactive and defensive.[3]

The procurement decisions underpinning this post–Cold War Chinese military modernization were largely meant to meet the immediate challenge of defeating Taiwan's military, but this modernization also affected the military balance with the United States in the region and set the stage for an exacerbated security dilemma. Taiwan's armed forces, in particular its air force and navy, had access to advanced US and some state-of-art European combat platforms by the late 1990s. Taiwan's military boasted more than two hundred F-16 and Mirage 2000 fourth-generation multipurpose fighter aircraft, E-2 early warning aircraft, *Perry*-class and French stealth frigates, and Patriot PAC-2 surface-to-air missile systems. By comparison, most of the PLA's contemporary combat systems were based on early and mid–Cold War technologies, which could not meet the demands of a large-scale PLA operation against Taiwan's military that could include power projection operations requiring both long-range precision strike and amphibious landing capabilities.

Worst-case scenarios for conflict in the Taiwan Strait also included the possibility of US military intervention, and the PLA recognized that it might have to not only defeat Taiwan's military but also confront regional US forces with more advanced capabilities directly. The PLA's modernization was complemented by changing doctrine and reorganization as its strategists worked to develop technologies and operational concepts against US technologies like cruise missiles and stealth aircraft. Senior commanders also frequently called for exploiting vulnerabilities of militarily superior rivals.[4] These moves, perceived by the Chinese leaders and the PLA as defensive actions, gradually eroded comparative US military superiority in the Asia-Pacific.

Continued Military Modernization

Even as China undertook long-term military modernization to address the gap in capabilities, US security strategy was focused elsewhere. Both the revolution in military affairs and military buildup of the Reagan administration enabled the United States to sustain supremacy in the 1990s and well into the 2000s, and the emphasis on the "peace dividend" and challenge of regional conflicts or civil wars after the end of the Cold War reduced US military spending[5] and slowed down future force modernization, in particular the development of new generation major combat platforms.

At the strategic level, the global war on terror transformed the China policy of the Bush administration from strategic competition to strategic cooperation, as the United States shifted its priorities toward conflicts in the Middle East. This focus on national security threats from terrorism came with concomitant reductions of burden in Asia, even resulting in the outsourcing of leadership opportunities on some regional security issues to China, as the Chinese hosted both the three-party and then the Six-Party talks on the denuclearization of the Korean peninsula.[6]

Despite this US willingness to maintain stability in Asia and even defer a more active Chinese role in some areas of regional security, cross-strait relations began to sour with the election of pro-independence Democratic Progressive Party (DPP) leader Chen Shui-bian to office in Taiwan, precipitating a continued Chinese military buildup.[7] As a result, the Chinese leadership decided to continue the long-term program of military modernization with an emphasis on an armed contingency in the Taiwan Strait. In December 2005, Hu Jintao stated in a Central Military Commission meeting that neither an expensive military modernization nor an arms race was realistic but that the PLA should only carry out its modernization according to demands of national security and unity as well as "preparation for military struggle."[8]

The Chinese approach to military modernization—at the time—mainly foe cused on replacing outdated weapons based on early Cold War technologies as well as introducing a few conventional deterrence capabilities in scenarios such as Taiwan rather than overwhelming the United States. Under such circumstances, as long as the United States made the right choices about force structure and technology modernization, its military primacy would not diminish easily. Still, progressive Chinese military modernizations in the 1990s and 2000s, especially the increasing production and deployment of conventional short- and medium-range ballistic missiles, acquisition of fourth-generation combat aircraft, and greatly improved intelligence, surveillance, and reconnaissance capabilities in its immediate periphery not only led to the upgrade of PLA combat systems to the standard of revolution in military affairs in 2010s but also gradually reshaped the military balance in the Asia-Pacific by eliminating overwhelming and unchallenged US military supremacy in the region.[9]

It is worth noting that the United States also contributed to the gradual change in the Asia-Pacific military balance, even as the post–Cold War peace was interrupted by the global war on terror. Counterinsurgency operations in the 2000s exhausted the US military and further delayed its modernization. Even as the United States began to perceive the changes wrought by China's steady and continued military buildup and began to respond with the Rebalance to Asia, as described in the following section, world events conspired to divert the attention of US strategists and policymakers from air and naval combat with a major regional power such as China.

The Rebalance and an Expanded and Intensified Security Competition

The long wars in Afghanistan and Iraq, as well as the 2008 financial crisis, led to a more anxious and less confident United States. The Obama administration intended to terminate long wars in the Middle East and cope with the rise of China in Asia-Pacific security, although it wished to maintain and expand cooperation with China on global issues. To those ends, the Obama administration pursued a new strategy in the Rebalance to Asia, intended to refocus US strategic attention toward a rising China and an Asia-Pacific region viewed as increasingly vital to US national security interests. Chinese strategists were attentive to and concerned about this shift in US strategic focus and resources.

The Asia-Pacific rebalance served as a wake-up call to the Chinese in three ways. First, Beijing saw that amicable China-US relations were no longer the most important pillar of the US security strategy toward the Asia-Pacific: the rebalance had transformed the role of China from stakeholder to threat. According to the memoir of Ash Carter, the last secretary of defense in the second Obama administration, he was proud of his tough line toward his Chinese counterpart over differences in regional security.[10] Second, the United States made the decision to deploy more than half of its total naval and air forces to the Asia-Pacific. Although the US military assets redeployed according to this shift would not restore the military balance of the 1990s, it demonstrated that the United States had begun to take China's military modernization seriously and was responding with a transformation of its long-term military posture. Third, the United States began to adopt a more assertive role in maritime territorial disputes and other security issues in the region.

In reaction, Chinese strategists concluded that the United States had shifted its strategic intentions, revised its military posture, and begun carrying out operations around major security flashpoints against China. In retrospect, the Chinese analysis of the US military strategy transition at the time was accurate: according to Michael Green, "They saw unambiguously particularly after 2010, 11, that China was a strategic competitor. They just weren't allowed to say it."[11]

Despite the rising tensions in geopolitical competition, on the strategic level, Chinese leaders remained optimistic in their engagement with the Obama administration. According to Dai Bingguo, the most senior Chinese diplomat who oversaw the running of China's foreign policy between 2003 and 2013, when cochairing the 2012 China-US Strategic and Economic Dialogue with Secretary of State Hillary Clinton, he elaborated in detail to the latter why conflict between China as a rising power and the United States as the established power was not inevitable and why a new type of major power relationship was a realistic option.[12] Between 2010 and 2016, the security competition intensified in the western Pacific, when China and the United States regarded each other as major security challenges. Nevertheless, they could still maintain a broad range of security cooperation under the mutual desire to further develop and improve bilateral relations.

To Chinese strategists and policymakers, the incrementally greater security challenges posed by the rebalance burst into the forefront of Sino-US relations during the Trump administration. Once the Trump administration took office in early 2017 and launched its National Security Strategy and National Defense Strategy a year later, the China-US security competition not only continued but was also integrated within the larger framework of strategic competition between the two sides.

A Reluctant and Restrained Chinese Response to Competition, 2017–19

As strategic competition between China and the United States deepened under the Trump administration, the Chinese response to the US great power competition strategy throughout the Trump administration can be characterized by two main phases. The first phase, between 2017 and early 2019, was marked by reactive and reluctant Chinese perceptions and responses to the emerging competition for a variety of different reasons.

Inertia toward a New Administration

First, Chinese leadership and China's strategic community were more familiar with the previous framework and process of bilateral relations with the United States, and it took some time for them to conclude that trends had changed and business as usual was not an option. Trump's victory in the 2016 presidential election surprised the whole world, including the Chinese. Chinese decision-makers and strategists likely presumed some degree of confusion and even friction in China-US relations as the new administration took office, as may have been the case with past US presidential transitions. For Chinese leaders, historical experience had demonstrated that the rhetoric of a candidate was one thing, but the policy of a president was quite another. Patience normally led to improvement and stability after transitions.[13]

As a result, Trump's early statements on China and his brief postelection phone call with Taiwan's president Tsai Ing-wen did not immediately undermine Chinese efforts to engage with the new administration. As Trump was a nontraditional president that lacked political experience and had taken an unconventional path to the White House, some considered that he might change his mind on his China policy later.[14]

Indeed, while Trump's "America First" policy seemed to signal the possibility of increased hostility toward China, the Trump administration's first forays into China-related security policy initially gave China's foreign policy and security professionals a glimmer of hope that the strategic competition would not escalate. The bilateral summit in April 2017 and the establishment of new high-level exchange mechanisms, including a foreign policy and security dialogue, helped assuage initial fears of an immediately hostile strategic posture.[15] Though the Trump administration appeared to spurn most forms of nontraditional security cooperation with its "America First" policy, it also withdrew from the Trans-Pacific Partnership that had troubled Chinese strategists in the waning years of the Obama administration, and it prioritized the Korean peninsula nuclear issue, which relied on active Chinese participation (and cooperation) rather than confrontation.

Balance between Chinese Domestic and Foreign Policy Agendas

Second, the Communist Party of China's whole-of-government approach to strategic planning, as well as the domestic agenda confirmed by its Nineteenth Party Congress in October 2017, generated strong initial constraints in escalating the strategic competition. The Party Congress Work Report emphatically exhorted party cadres to "secure a decisive victory in building a moderately prosperous society in all respects."[16] Chinese grand strategy would continue to balance domestic development and foreign policy and stress domestic development, as the party had emphasized.

When the Trump administration published both the National Security Strategy and National Defense Strategy in early 2018, focusing on great power competition with China and Russia, the new documents caught the attention of the Chinese strategic community,[17] but some analysts argued that overreaction would accelerate competition and affect domestic development. For instance, trade negotiations in particular appeared to dominate the agenda of bilateral relations in 2018 and early 2019, and although many practitioners and observers clearly understood the complexity of the relationship at this stage, they still expected serious trade talks to be mutually beneficial and, at minimum, provide a brake to the deterioration of the overall relationship.[18]

Relative Continuity of US Security Policy in the Asia-Pacific

Third, the Trump administration appeared to mainly accelerate and strengthen military programs originated by the Obama administration rather than introduce novel policy shifts, and where novelty was involved it did not yield much headway for the United States; sometimes it even damaged alliance cohesion through its America First policy orientation. For instance, the year 2018 marked a real shift in China-US security relations. With the support of China, South Korea, and other regional actors, the Trump administration changed its approach toward North Korea, leading to a summit between Kim Jong-Un and President Trump on the prospects for the improvement of bilateral relations and management of the nuclear crisis. These developments reduced tensions and the risk of military conflict but also showed the real limitations of diplomacy. Neither side appeared prepared to make the genuine concessions that any meaningful breakthrough would have required.

As novelty wore off and progress toward denuclearization on the Korean peninsula stagnated, the air of competition again dominated China-US security relations. But the Trump administration's America First approach created opportunities for China: when President Trump coerced US allies on trade and burden sharing, China managed to improve relations with many maritime neighbors, including key US allies like South Korea, Japan, and the Philippines.[19] Under such circumstances, the Trump administration's early emphasis on maritime security and more frequent freedom of navigation operations were interpreted as continuations of Obama-era policies that would yield little in the way of strategic changes.

China's Response to US Strategic Pressure Intensifies, 2019–20

The second phase of the recently intensified strategic competition, however, began around 2019. The anticipated smooth transition between American presidential administrations failed to materialize, and friction between China and the United States became protracted and intensified. The changes detailed in the following section have helped precipitate a shifting Chinese view of strategic competition, from a previously comparatively passive and moderate approach to an increasingly robust, hardened stance today.

Expanding Confrontation in Bilateral Ties

Increased US domestic and international mobilization against China generated a new consensus that China-US relations no longer contributed to the rise of China, making it difficult, if not impossible, to save the relationship from an eventual breakdown.

Events outside the security realm played crucial roles in this mobilization. Trade and people-to-people exchanges had previously been regarded as bipartisan Washington shibboleths, immune to the vagaries of US domestic politics. Sudden escalation of tensions in these sectors seriously undermined prospects for stabilizing bilateral relations. Major setbacks in trade talks in late 2018 and early 2019, and continuous US efforts to undermine Huawei and other Chinese high-technology businesses, proved that the United States was determined to securitize bilateral economic ties as part of a strategic competition. Chinese scholars and students in US universities and research institutions, especially those studying science and technology, mathematics, and engineering, also became targets of US law enforcement agencies as part of a widened campaign against so-called Chinese industrial and economic espionage.[20]

Other aspects of bilateral ties deteriorated as well, closing off possible channels for informal communication. Since 2018, many Chinese foreign policy experts from universities and think tanks were also affected by US pressure on people-to-people exchanges. US law enforcement agencies questioned Chinese scholars upon arrival in the United States for academic conferences or Track II dialogue on bilateral relations. Some Chinese scholars, including contributors to the discussion of bilateral relations and crisis management on both sides of the Pacific, had their visas canceled.[21] These occurrences sent a strong signal to emerging Chinese debates on the transformation of US policy toward China: the US government held a dim view of the importance of bilateral dialogue.[22]

Bilateral military ties between China and the United States also began to suffer. Systematic criticisms of China dominated the public policy statements of defense leaders—in particular admirals Harris and Davidson, the two successive commanders of the Pacific/Indo-Pacific Command. These critiques implied that the US military was less interested in the stability of bilateral relations in general and military and security relations in particular.[23] US defense and military leaders worked to reduce military-to-military relations to narrowly defined crisis management through curtailing daily exchanges among senior leaders, military units, and military academies.[24] The last-minute revocation of China's invite to the 2018 RIMPAC multilateral exercises due to its continued militarization of the South China Sea also alarmed the Chinese, as the United States appeared to prioritize competition with China in the South China Sea over military exchanges and confidence-building measures.[25] The US government also sanctioned the PLA's Equipment Development Department in 2018 over purchases of Russian military equipment, a move that was viewed as an attempt to undermine Chinese military modernization and China-Russia military ties.[26] Military-to-military relations based on difference management, confidence building, and practical cooperation began to gradually collapse.

The US mobilization for strategic competition with China also went international. When dealing with third parties or multilateral occasions, US leaders, senior diplomats, and commanders not only frequently raised long-standing differences between the United States and China, like geopolitical flashpoints, political institutions, and human rights, but also tried to prevent third parties from cooperating with China in its Belt and Road Initiative (BRI) and the introduction of Chinese high-technology brands such as Huawei.[27] Tough US countermeasures against the BRI and Huawei suggest that the United States is expanding the competition to a global level and is determined to confront a rising China's international influence and the success of its high-technology industries.

Based on the above perceptions, Chinese leaders have apparently arrived at a new consensus in the policy debate. In January 2019, the Central Party School organized a seminar for senior officials on preventing and addressing major risks, during which President Xi Jinping gave a speech stressing high alertness to cope with a deteriorating international environment.[28] In September of that same year, he gave another speech at the Central Party School, calling for preparation to "struggle against unprecedented challenges."[29] Together, these speeches seem to suggest that both the framework and process of China-US relations are lurching in an unfavorable direction and will have critical negative impacts on Chinese domestic development and the international environment. A moderate and restrained approach to this challenge is increasingly less likely to return the relationship to the right track and defend Chinese interests, and passive responses only invite more US pressures. The new consensus has encouraged preparation for worse scenarios and calls for determination to defend Chinese interests.

Upgraded Military Tools

While Chinese decision-makers are adjusting their assessments amid the intensified competition, the decades of sustained PLA modernization efforts have yielded upgraded military tools and means of competition for Chinese leaders. These new capabilities and institutions increase options for Chinese leaders and may buoy their confidence in competing with the United States.

In the realm of traditional security competition, the PLA appears increasingly able to employ and test the achievements of its long-term military modernization and reform in the burgeoning strategic competition. By 2012, major military platforms that reached the standard of the revolution in military affairs were available to the PLA, thanks to the military modernization efforts of the 1990s and 2000s. As the security competition with the United States deepened, the PLA not only had to continue technological innovation but also better transform military assets into joint combat power.

Sweeping organizational reforms beginning in 2016 aimed to build a stronger joint force and improve the PLA's effectiveness amid the anticipated challenges of modern warfare.[30] The reorganized components of the Central Military Commission highlight strategic command, training, long-term assessment and planning, and technology innovation. Service-level reforms terminated the traditional army-centric organization and established a Strategic Support Force for cyber and space domains as well as a Joint Logistic Support Force to improve logistics for more complex military operations. Theater Commands replaced the army-centric military region headquarters and focused on joint operations command, more capable of commanding joint maritime and air operations. In recent years, navy admirals and air force generals have commanded these new Theater Commands, and with the commission of a new generation of combat, command and control, and support platforms, the combat units of all the services have also embraced joint warfare.[31]

No longer dominated by army officers and responsibilities, the Theater Commands with maritime responsibilities have more openly committed themselves to the preparation and conduct of maritime competition. According to the *PLA Daily*, in autumn 2017, the Southern Theater Command organized a joint maritime exercise in which its commanders tested new operational concepts by abandoning the previous naval-centric approach to maritime operations and assigning a major role to the party's strategic missile forces, the PLA Rocket Force.[32] In January 2018, the PLA's Eastern Theater Command published an article in *Qiushi*, the CPC Central Committee journal, highlighting preparations for military struggles on maritime directions.[33] Since the end of 2018, the spokesperson of the Southern Theater Command has taken over responsibility for public statements on US naval operations in the South China Sea from the spokesperson of the Ministry of National Defense, suggesting that the Theater Commands play a more important role in dealing with maritime contingencies.[34]

Although Chinese leaders and analysts are aware of the shortcomings of the PLA, they also realize that they have more available options to cope with different scenarios arising from the security competition, especially those within the First Island Chain. Improved PLA capabilities can enable the Chinese response to US military challenges to evolve from passive to reactive.

Intensified Grey Zone Competition

Aside from military tools, China has also steadily integrated nonmilitary tools into its security strategy, and these nonmilitary fronts of competition have afforded China's leaders more opportunities to shift China's overall strategic response to competition from a passive stance to a more reactive one. Perhaps the most obvious example of these "grey zone" scenarios is China's construction of artificial islands in the South China Sea, which Chinese strategists regard as a relatively low-stakes means of competing with the United States. In the last half century, maritime territorial disputes generated very few armed conflicts: most of the time, all the claimants used a broad range of nonlethal approaches to address the issue. In particular, although disputes are long-standing, they must be subordinated to domestic and overall foreign policy priorities, and keeping the disputes under the threshold of conflict is normal.

After 2010, as the maritime territorial disputes in the East and South China seas intensified, the action-reaction mechanism also became more complicated. The US rebalance strategy led to more active involvement in these disputes and more support to those claimants that are its allies and partners. Under such circumstances, China has mobilized and acted to consolidate its position, ostensibly to defend its interests. Chinese officials view Chinese coastal guard patrols and island construction in both the East and South China seas as defensive and appropriate, but they also realize that, due to the size and resources mobilized by China, these efforts send strong signals and shock others within and outside the region.[35] These shocks generate new rounds of reactions that further shape the course of events. In their debates on the grey zone competition between 2014 and 2016, the US strategic communities focused on both maritime territorial disputes in Asia and the ongoing Ukraine crisis. Overestimating similarities between the two cases might affect analytic frameworks and policy prescriptions.

The Biden Administration Upgrades US Competition Strategy

Regardless of the outbreak and continuation of the Russia-Ukraine conflict, the United States still regards China as its central threat, which it now calls the "pacing threat." Although the Biden administration is more serious about competition management and maintaining communication channels, it will not make concrete efforts to stabilize and de-escalate current competition. The Biden administration pays more attention to nonmilitary aspects of the competition than its predecessor, but it does not ignore security and military competition. It prioritizes innovation, security alliance, and partnerships as well as Taiwan Strait contingencies. The Chinese response includes enhancing deterrence, especially with regard to the Taiwan issue, shaping the security environment regionally and globally, and continuing competition management with the United States.

The Russia-Ukraine conflict motivates further mobilization for US-China military competition on the US side, and this might lead the United States to doubt the Chinese military's effectiveness and political determination. China has to accelerate military modernization and preparation for all scenarios to enhance deterrence. The US emphasis on security ties with Taiwan will lead to more PLA deployment and operations for the sake of deterrence and preparation for more challenging scenarios. As General Wei Fenghe, minister of national defense, emphasized in his prepared remarks for the June 2022 Shangri-La Dialogue, "If anyone dares to secede Taiwan from China, we will not hesitate to fight. We will fight at all costs and we will fight to the very end. This is the only choice for China."[36]

When the United States actively mobilizes international partners to shape China's international and security environment, China cannot sit idle. China has to maintain strategic and security cooperation with Russia, even if differences exist on the Russia-Ukraine conflict. Given that most third parties are still cautious toward taking sides, and those taking the US side are also not prepared to cut off ties with China, China can shape its security environment through confidence building and cooperation. One advantage for China is that its objectives are limited. It pursues security ties to reinforce foreign policy rather than to form an alliance against the United States. The new Chinese global security initiative, introduced in April 2022, seeks to explore an international security framework beyond traditional military alliance.[37]

China does not share the US public framing of bilateral relations as strategic competition and calls for more stabilization and cooperation, but it understands the importance of managing competition with the United States. Top leaders of both sides highlight great power responsibility of avoiding confrontation in their virtual meetings and phone calls. Foreign policy heads talk with each other on management of bilateral relations and international security issues. In the Shangri-La dialogue in 2022, Chinese and US defense leaders did mention differences in bilateral meetings and speeches, but they also identified bottom lines and called for further exchanges on crisis management.[38]

Major Components of Recent and Future Competition

The security competition precipitated by the expanded bilateral competition is characterized by developments in four main areas: evolving strategies and operational doctrines; adaptation to new, transformative military technologies; military posture and operations in the western Pacific, especially those around the First Island Chain; and military activities in support of foreign policy objectives. Changes in each of these three areas will greatly impact the intensity of the strategic competition between China and the United States.

Neither China nor the United States is interested in achieving overall military parity with each other, but both nations are working hard to adapt to the opportunities and challenges presented by the advent of a new military technology revolution. The United States has arguably lost its primacy in military power, but it still takes the lead and works hard to maintain as much superiority as possible to enhance deterrence and support its strategic objectives. For their part, China's strategists agree on the priority of domestic development and thus regard overall military parity with the United States as too expensive, unrealistic, and unnecessary. Despite a shrinking gap with US military power and continued emphasis on domestic stability and economic development, however, China remains determined to continue its military modernization to secure its great power position.[39]

Evolving Strategies and Operational Doctrines

Changing US and Chinese strategies and doctrines regarding the western Pacific will have a dramatic impact on the nature of future competition between the two powers. The western Pacific is the primary theater for security and military competition between China and the United States given their respective strategic interests and military postures. Strategically, the competition focuses on the evolution of a security order in the region that could better serve interests of either China or the US-led alliance system. The most recent articulations of US perceptions of the regional order are articulated in its February 2022 Indo-Pacific Strategy,[40] while China has also gradually developed its own vision of Asia-Pacific security in its own documents, namely a 2017 white paper on China's security cooperation policy in the Asia-Pacific, among others.[41] Competitive perceptions and pressures neglect possible security architectures and frameworks that might effectively accommodate and integrate the security interests of both China and the United States. The two competitors may pay more attention to winning instead of mutual understanding or the active support of regional actors throughout the competition.

Operationally, both China and the United States have developed their operational systems to enhance conventional deterrence and cope with worst-case scenarios, focused primarily on major security contingencies within the First Island Chain like the Taiwan Strait, the South and East China seas, and the Korean peninsula. The US Defense Department was keenly aware of the anti-access/area denial challenge at least as far back as the early 2000s. By 2009, the Department of Defense had announced its systematic operational concept development for the western Pacific in the AirSea Battle concept, although the United States continued to update its operational plans for the Korean peninsula.

This doctrinal evolution has continued apace for both China and the United States. Nearly all the US military services continue to develop their own doctrine and operational concepts for worst-case scenarios of competition with China; recent versions include Distributed Maritime Operations, Multi-Domain Operations, and Agile Combat Employment. In spring 2020, the Indo-Pacific Command also revealed its operational concept of the Joint Fires Network.[42] The PLA, for its part, did not stand still on this front either: between the 1990s and the 2000s, the PLA called for "preparations for military struggle" concentrated on Taiwan Strait contingencies.[43] In its 2015 white paper on military strategy, China's leaders made clear that the PLA's efforts should evolve toward a broader "maritime direction."[44]

Technological Innovation and the Changing Nature of Warfare

A second factor that will influence the character of future competition is a new wave of technological innovations with military applications. Technological innovation in these fields generates significant uncertainty about the military balance in the long run and intensifies the security dilemma between China and the United States. Both sides predict that artificial intelligence (AI), 5G, hypersonic weapons, and other emerging and disruptive technologies will transform warfare. Successful application of these new technologies might generate strategic and operational initiative, while failure to do so would reduce military effectiveness. Perhaps the most profound lesson that Chinese strategists learned through the 1990s was that technologically inferior militaries were bound to be marginalized at the hands of other great powers.[45] The United States also understands that a failure to adapt would further close the gap in military capabilities with China, but a successful mastery of these emerging technologies might enlarge the gap again.[46]

Successful military transformation using these technologies is not simply a matter of military affairs. Technology innovation, the upgrade of a nation's defense industrial base, military organizational reform, and doctrinal innovation will determine success or failure in adoption of these transformative technologies and profoundly shape the future military balance. The importance of these technologies is not lost on either China or the United States, as both nations use nonmilitary policies to secure their prospects of successful development. For instance, China's elevation of military-civil fusion to the level of a national strategy in 2015 is meant to funnel civilian resources into the technological innovation needed to successfully master emerging technologies for military use.[47] US restrictions on science and technology exchanges and the struggle over 5G do not have simple economic explanations—rather, these actions are perhaps better understood through the lens of broader strategic competition, as these measures extend strategic competition beyond simply the military domain into broader economic and technological competition.

Military Posture, Disposition, and Operations in the Western Pacific

The respective dispositions of military forces arrayed by China and the United States in the western Pacific will also be a critical bellwether for the nature of future competition. Following the Obama administration's decision to deploy more air and maritime assets in the Asia-Pacific region, the Trump administration tabbed the theater as the most highly prioritized theater in its defense strategy and sped up both the modernization of forces within or assigned to the area and the development of new capabilities to meet the operational demands of the theater. Both the tyranny of distance and increasingly capable Chinese long-range precision strike weapons have forced the US military to revise its traditional deployment and logistic modes, including by working with allies and requesting more funding from Congress.[48]

On the theater level, the Chinese enjoy both homefield advantage and easier concentration of resources. First, beyond the western Pacific, China does not have to deal with other great power competitions and associated military or security contingencies that might call for high-intensity warfare, while the United States has defined its security interests more broadly, diverting its attention and resources to Europe, the Middle East, and, indeed, much of the globe. This prioritized asymmetry makes it easier for China to focus its expenditures and efforts on strategic competition within a single region, even as its global economic and military footprint continues to expand.

Second, China can rely on the strategic depth of its homeland to support operations in the western Pacific, while the United States mainly depends on the territories of its allies in the First Island Chain and a few other US possessions, like Guam. This strategic depth makes it easier for China to commit its available infrastructure and assets to a conflict in the region, especially land-based combat aircraft and missiles, with the notable caveat that doing so raises the possibility that China's cities and industrial centers may be attacked in a large-scale conventional conflict. Conversely, the United States must rely largely on the willingness of its allies to deploy forces into the western Pacific, which considerably increases the complexity of such an action.

The maritime environment is an enormous space for routine peacetime competition. Both sides are capable of frequently deploying military assets around maritime flashpoints in the Taiwan Strait, South China Sea, and East China Sea. Such deployments enhance presence, capabilities, and deterrence and frequently serve as signals during various contingencies. In carrying out these missions, frontline units like naval vessels and aircraft frequently encounter each other, and the PLA and the US military cannot rule out the possibility of accidents that could escalate to conflicts if not properly controlled.

Military Activities in Support of Broader Foreign Policy

A final component of recent and future security competition is the use of military activities in support of nonmilitary foreign policy objectives and initiatives. As both countries begin to regard each other's foreign policy with suspicion or even hostility, they oppose and even apply countermeasures against military participation in foreign policy initiatives in geographic regions beyond the Asia-Pacific.

The United States has increasingly sought to counter what it views as an expanded PLA role in China's foreign policy. The Obama administration regarded nascent PLA power projection outside the Asia-Pacific as providing potential opportunities of cooperation, due to shared interests in a broad range of global and regional issues.[49] The Trump administration, however, did not take the same view, instead seeing PLA activities around the globe as more of a security threat. In its apparent determination to escalate competition with China, the Trump administration reduced the frequency and scope of military cooperation and tried hard to mobilize other countries to oppose security ties with China.[50] Some indications of the changing attitude toward China's global military and security interests were made clear by US combatant commanders outside of the Indo-Pacific Command's area of responsibility, who addressed the challenge of China in their testimonies and other public statements.[51]

China has thus far avoided a symmetrical response to this expanded global pressure against military support for its foreign policy, likely because Chinese decision-makers understand that a global security competition with the United States does not serve Chinese interests. The PLA has, however, continued to engage in military diplomatic activities around the globe, including a continued naval anti-piracy presence in the Gulf of Aden, in part to demonstrate that the Chinese military is a responsible partner and supplier of public goods in the security realm.[52] These activities also serve to strengthen security ties with countries in other regions that also face US strategic pressure to counterbalance international mobilization efforts undertaken by the United States.

Even as the strategic competition between China and the United States accelerates in these major components of recent competition, both sides still regard armed conflict as a worst-case scenario of last resort, and the risk of direct military confrontation exists in only a few competition areas. Despite intensifying struggles over innovation and supply chains, competitions over military technological superiority focus on investment, development, and application within each country's own innovation, industrial, and military ecosystems.

Possible Future Chinese Approaches to Long-Term Competition

The long-term prospects of the US-China competition are uncertain and challenging. First, as the United States remains preoccupied with the competition in modernization and military posture, the long-term trajectory of the economic and military balance will be uncertain, but arms race dynamics will intensify. Second, China must cope with the choices of third parties in the long run. At the global level, the United States might reduce the intensity of competition with Russia and Iran and instead concentrate more resources in the Asia-Pacific, though the recent conflict in Ukraine may yet change this orientation. At the regional level, China must determine what continued US international mobilization could achieve with its major allies and new security partners. The strategic competition that results will shape Chinese defense and security policy in several ways.

Continued Military Modernization

First, the orientation of the PLA's modernization and force development is likely to focus more on innovation in both doctrine and technology. Between the 1990s and the 2010s, the Chinese military modernization was focused primarily on catching up with the revolution in military affairs and following the technological model of the US military. Today, in the context of US-China strategic competition, the Chinese military must navigate through uncharted waters with more emphasis on innovation and contingency and scenario-driven capability development. As a result, Chinese leadership has put more emphasis on strategic planning and management.[53] The Fourteenth Five-Year Plan guideline not only strongly emphasizes national security but also regards major progress in integrated development of a mechanized, informatized, and intelligentized military as a strategic objective by 2027, the one-hundredth anniversary of the founding of the PLA, given the unprecedented impact of new technologies and warfare.[54]

The objective of building a world-class military has become a necessity rather than a luxury. The current progress of Chinese military modernization is impressive but not sufficient to cope with the existing long-term competition. The PLA has learned lessons from both the Cold War and the post–Cold War era, including that modernizing hardware is one thing but using it effectively in relevant scenarios is another. While the US military has mastered joint operations for decades, the PLA only recently introduced its first joint operations doctrine, in November 2020.[55] Facing a US military mobilized for competition with China, China must sustain its current ambitions of military modernization as long as its domestic development permits.

Nevertheless, the competition is not yet a global military competition, and China does not need a global military strategy like that of the United States. PLA modernization will likely focus more on quality, such as access and resilience in new domains of cyber and outer space; limited but reliable nuclear deterrence; conventional deterrence vis-à-vis US joint forces inside the First Island Chain as well as power projection capabilities that could support high-intensity conflict scenarios in the western Pacific; and nontraditional security contingencies such as COVID-19, noncombatant evacuation operations, and disaster relief at home and abroad.

A Need for Improved Crisis Management

Second, the competition requires both appropriate and effective response to US challenges and a concomitant upgrade of conflict and crisis prevention and management. As a result, military and security relations with the United States are more important than before. Without strong social and economic interaction as a foundation for the bilateral relationship, security relations may bear more of the burden of crisis management. Some of this was apparent in October 2020, when China and the United States conducted a crisis communication working group video conference, but much more must be done.[56] Existing mechanisms of crisis management are based on a certain level of strategic trust and focus only on sporadic incidents. Such arrangements could not survive intensified competition after the collapse of strategic trust.

Technology innovations also pose new challenges for crisis management as the competition expands into cyber and space, while more and more stealth combat platforms, unmanned vehicles, and AI-enabled systems are deployed on the front line. In spite of the intensifying strategic competition, common security challenges such as COVID-19 can emerge globally, regionally, or locally, and security relations should not exclude coordination and cooperation to address these challenges.

Expanded Statecraft and Policy Changes

Third, the PLA will need to expand confidence-building and security cooperation efforts with other nations in order to offset the US-led international mobilization against China. Long-term strategic competition requires cost control. Escalation of tensions with others would not only impose a heavier burden but also invite US exploitation of those tensions. Confidence-building and security cooperation would prevent the emergence of a multifront struggle. Such efforts include security cooperation with Russia to balance against the United States, provision of public goods in the security realm, confidence building and security cooperation with neighbors to reduce local security dilemmas and devalue the US alliance system, and exchanges and cooperation with countries in other regions to demonstrate Chinese intentions and responsibilities and contribute to the protection of Chinese interests as well.

China also should and could employ economic statecraft appropriately in security competition. The rise of the Chinese economy and its integration into the regional and global economies can provide economic tools in Chinese foreign policy agendas, including on security issues. Long-term economic benefits from China would reduce the incentives of other countries, in particular Asian countries, to confront China. This is not without precedent: at the beginning of the Cold War, the United States introduced the Marshall Plan to stabilize western Europe and laid the foundation for the NATO alliance due to shared strategic interests and ideological affinity with western European countries.[57]

Because of historical, geopolitical, and ideological context, any systematic Chinese economic aid program today is unlikely to pave the way for a Chinese-dominated security architecture. Economic agendas, regardless of their importance to social welfare and national development, could neither replace political and security agendas nor terminate the nationalism and populism that would sustain a security-focused incentive structure. In addition, other actors might interpret signals conveyed with economic measures differently from their original intentions. As a result, economic statecraft in security contingencies like crises is unlikely to achieve the desired immediate results and can even backfire if mishandled. Use of economic statecraft is frequently as challenging as use of force.

One critical lesson China should learn from the Cold War strategic competition is that foreign and security policy was no less important than the military balance, especially in the primary theater. US popularity on both ends of the Eurasia continent was based on its role as a security balancer and broad provider of public goods. Soviet behaviors after the Second World War intensified the security dilemma and increased demand for US-provided security and other public goods.

China enjoys a more favorable position today than the Soviets did seventy years ago. China is able to provide international public goods, and it is more likely to be able to moderate the threat perceptions of its neighbors than the Soviets, with their long history of coercion and subversion to achieve and defend their security interests. Aside from the beneficial maritime geography in which China resides, Chinese behaviors will also strive to prevent the emergence of a NATO-like military alliance in Asia that is mobilized and prepared to confront China. A successful Chinese security policy in the end will also reduce the likelihood of an all-out arms race and the possibility of conflicts, as third parties can maintain their maneuvering space and constrain the US military presence in Asia as well as their military integration with the United States.

From Crisis Management to Competition Management

The COVID-2019 pandemic and President Biden's election in 2020 led to both opportunities within, and challenges to, the management of US-China security competition. The pandemic confirmed the level of determination in and mobilization for strategic competition on both sides. Nevertheless, both the United States and China, as well as other relevant actors, still face the immediate task of controlling the pandemic globally and the long-term task of economic recovery. Controlling strategic competition is a prerequisite for fulfilling these tasks.

The arrival of a new Biden administration staffed by more foreign policy professionals increased the scope of policy adjustment on China. Although this change will not alter the course of strategic competition, a more stabilized security competition is possible. However, the limited victory Democrats achieved precluded any swift and dramatic stabilization of competition. Before leaving office, the Trump administration's final wave of measures against China decreased the chances of positive initiatives by either China or the United States at the beginning of 2021. At home, the Biden administration must rely on the very few areas of bipartisan consensus within US public opinion, namely, a hard line on China, to push forward its own agenda. For their part, Chinese officials do not seem immediately inclined to reduce tensions: erstwhile Chinese ambassador to the United States Cui Tiankai indicated as much when he remarked in early December 2020 that he did not think that China "should just do something to please anybody here."[58] Therefore, even if both sides work hard, it will take some time to stop further escalation of the bilateral tensions.

Stabilization of competition requires long-term efforts. Both China and the United States have in the past relied on crisis management to cope with increasing tensions, but such an approach is probably outdated in the era of great power competition. Both sides must upgrade crisis management into competition management through the four approaches described below.

Address Deficiencies in Grand Strategy

First, both sides must address the grand strategy deficiency of the current competition. Security competition is more than action and reaction. The arrival of social media and accumulated domestic challenges increase the difficulties of debating and making grand strategies in the twenty-first century. Nevertheless, a strategic competition solely driven by emotions would almost certainly spiral out of control. In addition, the two sides must at least implicitly develop and share a framework of competition that defines limits and roles of the game. Management of competition demands more communication on the strategic level rather than less.

China and the United States also should communicate and work on a regional security order that could accommodate parts of the security interests from both sides and reduce the danger of competition over security flashpoints. In the Taiwan Strait, both sides developed rich mutual understanding and implicit rules of conduct after many crises in the Cold War and post–Cold War era. The Taiwan Strait remains the most sensitive area of China-US relations, and the escalation of tensions from their present level would cause unprecedented damage. The two sides should renew and upgrade existing understandings and rules rather than abandon them.

A new security order would ameliorate tensions in other areas of the western Pacific as well. The tensions in the South China Sea are one of the newest features of the strategic and security competition. A security order would ensure access to sea lines of communication, promote peaceful resolution of disputes, and reduce the risk of escalation and conflict. In northeast Asia, short-term diplomatic progress cannot replace a long-term security order to control security risks in both the Korean peninsula and the East China Sea.

Distinguish Red Lines from Grey Zones

Second, decision-makers and strategists in both China and the United States must obtain a better understanding of the core interests of both sides, distinguishing grey zone interests from red lines throughout an ongoing strategic competition. The status of the maritime grey zone originates from disparity of political and security interests. Both China and the United States have redlines in maritime security issues, but many grey zones in US perception are redlines in Chinese perception. Expansion of grey zone competition based on perceptions of illegitimacy of the other's strategic objectives might cross redlines, triggering domestic sensitivities to sovereignty issues and pushing decision-makers into a corner. Failure to prepare and respond would invite escalation or damage to Chinese interests and prestige.

Working together on building regional security orders, including maritime security institutions, will reduce the number and scope of grey areas where a lack of shared understanding of the situation and rules of the game may lead to conflict. As both mutual confidence and serious exchanges on security issues decline sharply between the two sides, miscalculations provide more opportunities to drive grey zone competition scenarios toward escalation.

Balance Reassurance with Pressure

Third, competition management requires balancing reassurance with pressure. Reassurance includes security cooperation based on shared interests and military exchanges. Both sides should resume security cooperation in nontraditional security sectors and security contingencies outside the Asia-Pacific where shared interests exist. Strategic competition does not eliminate the diversified and sometimes shared security challenges both countries face.

Once domestic and international mobilization for strategic competition reaches a maximum limit, resumption of security cooperation will be feasible and mutually beneficial. Daily military exchanges are also important for confidence building and avoidance of miscalculation, and they should not be ignored.

Reemphasize the Danger of Great Power Conflict

Finally, both sides should realize the limitations and risks associated with use of force. Nuclear weapons loomed large over the US-Soviet competition during the Cold War and will do the same for the current China-US strategic competition. The current generation of decision-makers and strategists has not personally experienced any great power conflict, and the literature on China-US strategic competition rarely highlights the specific dangers of nuclear war.

Additionally, both societies depend more and more on new strategic domains such as cyber and space, which will be extremely vulnerable in great power conflicts. The application of advanced AI and robotics in future warfare also raises issues weightier than simply their military effectiveness. At an operational level, real, perfect technological solutions to operational problems will still not be available, as both sides will remain capable of seriously damaging or even paralyzing the operational systems of the other side. As a result, even for war on paper, so-called theories of victory are not as convincing as many assume.

Accordingly, further militarization of the competition is costly and dangerous, and demilitarization is necessary in competition management. Both sides need to raise the threshold of using nonlethal and lethal force in a broad range of scenarios. Decision-makers, operators, and analysts must develop shared understandings through continuous dialogue regarding the challenges that new technologies pose to the stability of competition. Sooner or later, interlocutors from both sides will need to discuss what balance of military power is acceptable to both sides and how to achieve it.

Notes

1. University of Southern California US-China Institute, *China in U.S. National Security Strategy Reports, 1987–2017*, December 18, 2017, https://china.usc.edu/china-us-national-se curity-strategy-reports-1987-2017.

2. Zhang Wannian, *Zhang Wannian Junshi Wenxuan* [Zhang Wannian's selected works on military affairs], (Beijing: Jiefangjun chubanshe, 2008), 517.

3. For one contemporary example of their views of modernization, see "China's National Defense in 2002," People's Republic of China, State Council Information Office, May 26, 2005, http://www.gov.cn/zwgk/2005-05/26/content_1384.htm.

4. Zhang, *Zhang Wannian Junshi Wenxuan*, 507–15.

5. Hamid Davoodi et al., "Military Spending, the Peace Dividend, and Fiscal Adjustment," International Monetary Fund, July 1999.

6. For a Chinese account, see Fu Ying, "The Korean Nuclear Issue: Past, Present, and Future; A Chinese Perspective," Brookings Institution, April 2017, https://www.brookings.edu/wp -co ntent/uploads/2017/04/north-korean-nuclear-issue-fu-ying.pdf. For a US account, see Christopher R. Hill, *Outpost: Life on the Frontlines of American Diplomacy; A Memoir* (New York: Simon and Schuster, 2014), 205–90.

7. "Expert on the Taiwan Problem: Taiwan Passed the 'Referendum Law' to Leave Endless Hidden Dangers," Ministry of Foreign Affairs, People's Republic of China, February 27, 2004, https://www.mfa.gov.cn/ce/cebe//chn/sgxx/t68514.htm.

8. Hu Jintao, *Hu Jintao Wenxuan* [Selected works of Hu Jintao], vol. 2 (Beijing: Renmin chubanshe, 2016), 394.

9. Michael S. Chase et al., *China's Incomplete Military Transformation: Assessing the Weaknesses of the People's Liberation Army* (RAND Corporation, 2015), 13–24, https://www.rand.org /pubs/research_reports/RR893.html.

10. Ash Carter, *Inside the Five-Sided Box: Lessons from a Lifetime of Leadership in the Pentagon* (New York: Dutton, 2019), 282–83.

11. Elbridge Colby and Pat Buchan, "Plan Your Move: The NDS and the Chessboard," interview by Mike Green, *The Asia Chessboard* (podcast), Center for Strategic and International Studies, June 22, 2020, https://www.csis.org/analysis/plan-your-move-nds-and-chessboard.

12. Dai Bingguo, *Zhanlue Duihua* [Strategic Dialogues] (Beijing: Renmin chubanshe, 2016), 173–75.

13. Ma Wensheng, "Te lang pu shidai de zhong mei guanxi—zhuanfang cha ha er xuehui fu mishu zhang, zhongguo guoji guanxi xuehui lishi wang chong" [Sino-US Relations in the Trump era—interview with Wang Chong, deputy secretary general of the Charhar Institute and director of the China National Association for International Studies], *Gonggong waijiao jikan* [Public diplomacy quarterly] 24, no. 4 (Winter 2016): 70–75.

14. For one take, see Ni Feng, "Te lang pu 'bu an changli chu pai' dui zhong mei guanxi yeyou haochu" [Trump's 'unconventional play' also has benefits for Sino-American relations], *Shijie Zhishi* [World affairs] no. 14 (2017): 18.

15. Chen Jimin, "Te lang pu shiqi de zhong mei guanxi tixi" [An analysis of Sino-US relations in the Trump era], *Hepin yu fazhan* [Peace and development] no. 4 (2017): 26–42.

16. For the full text of Communist Party of China General Secretary Xi Jinping's Nineteenth Party Congress Work Report, see Xi Jinping, "Juesheng quanmian jiancheng xiaokang shehui duoqu xin shidai zhongguo tese shehui zhuyi weida shengli" [Win a decisive victory in building a moderately prosperous society in an all-round way and win the great victory of socialism with Chinese characteristics in the new era], October 18, 2017, http://jhsjk.people.cn/article/29613458.

17. Li Yan, "Te lang pu anquan zhanlue de tianzheng yu xiandu" [Adjustments and limits of Trump's security strategy], *Guoji anquan yanjiu* [Journal of international security studies] 36, no. 5 (2018): 54–72.

18. Zhang Zhen and Wang Jianbin, "Zhong mei maoyi moca: chengyin, yingdui cuoshi yu qishi" [Sino-US trade friction: Causes, countermeasures, and findings], *Jiangsu shehui kexue* [Jiangsu social sciences] 301, no. 6 (2018): 116–22.

19. For example, Chinese officials held various diplomatic meetings with South Korean officials routinely in 2019, even as President Trump demanded that South Korea pay more for US troops based on their soil. See "China-South Korea Relations," Ministry of Foreign Affairs, People's Republic of China, last updated August 2021, https://www.fmprc.gov.cn/web/gjhdq_676201/gj_676203/yz_676205/1206_676524/sbgx_676528; and Robert Burns, "Trump Demands Five-Fold Increase in Costs from South Korea to Keep US Troops, Reports Say," Associated Press, November 15, 2019, https://eu.usatoday.com/story/news/world/2019/11/15/trump-administration-demands-south-korea-pay-more-for-us-troops/4200210002/.

20. United States Department of Justice, "Information about the Department of Justice's China Initiative and a Compilation of China-Related Prosecutions Since 2018," updated November 19, 2021, https://www.justice.gov/archives/nsd/information-about-department-justice-s-china-initiative-and-compilation-china-related.

21. Jane Perlez, "F.B.I. Bars Some China Scholars from Visiting U.S. over Spying Fears," *New York Times*, April 14, 2019, https://www.nytimes.com/2019/04/14/world/asia/china-academics-fbi-visa-bans.html.

22. Zhu Feng, "Meiguo Guojia Anquan Jiqi Xianlu Zhengming Mianmu" [The US national security machine reveals a fierce face], *Huanqiu shibao* [Global times], May 23, 2019, https://opinion.huanqiu.com/article/9CaKrnKkFJA.

23. Texts of the speeches indicating these criticisms are available at US Indo-Pacific Command, "Speeches/Testimony," https://www.pacom.mil/Media/Speeches-Testimony/.

24. See Caitlin Campbell, *China Primer: U.S.-China Military-to-Military Relations* (Congressional Research Service, January 4, 2021), https://crsreports.congress.gov/product/pdf/IF/IF11712/3.

25. "Guofang bu jiu mei quxiao yaoqing zhongfang canjia huan tai jun yan fabiao tanhua" [Remarks by the Ministry of National Defense on the US cancellation of China's invitation

to participate in the Rim of the Pacific military exercise], *Zhongguo jun wang* [China military online], May 24, 2018, http://www.81.cn/jwgz/2018-05/24/content_8040905.htm.

26. "Meifang ni zhicai zhongguo zhongyang junwei zhuangbei fazhan bu waijiao bu hui-ying" [Response of the PRC Ministry of Foreign Affairs on the US intent to sanction the Central Military Commission Equipment Development Department], *Renmin ribao* [People's daily], September 21, 2018, http://world.people.com.cn/n1/2018/0921/c1002-30308531.html.

27. See "'Fed Up' of US Criticism of BRI, Says China," *Economic Times*, May 9, 2019, https://economictimes.indiatimes.com/news/international/business/fed-up-of-us-criticism-of-bri-says-china/articleshow/69253669.cms; and "China Asks United States to Stop 'Unreasonable Suppression' of Huawei," Reuters, May 16, 2020, https://www.reuters.com/article/us-usa-huawei-tech-idUSKBN22S0DE.

28. For a Chinese official summary of the speech, see "Xi jinping zai sheng bu ji zhuyao lingdao ganbu jianchi dixian siwei zhuoli fangfan huajie zhongda fengxian zhuanti yantao ban kai ban shi shang fabiao zhongyao jianghua" [Xi Jinping delivered an important speech at the opening ceremony of the special seminar for main leading cadres at the provincial and ministerial levels to adhere to the bottom-line thinking and focus on preventing and resolving major risks], Xinhua, January 21, 2019, http://www.xinhuanet.com/politics/leaders/2019-01/21/c_1124022412.htm.

29. For a Chinese official summary of the speech, see "Fayang douzheng jingshen zeng-qiang douzheng benling wei shixian 'liang ge yibai nian' fendou mubiao er wanqiang fen-dou" [Carry forward the fighting spirit and enhance fighting ability, and strive tenaciously for the realization of the "two centenary goals"], Xinhua, September 3, 2019, http://www.xinhuanet.com/politics/2019-09/03/c_1124956081.htm.

30. Joel Wuthnow and Phillip C. Saunders, "Chinese Military Reforms in the Age of Xi Jinping: Drivers, Challenges, and Implications," *China Strategic Perspectives* 10, March 2017, https://ndupress.ndu.edu/Portals/68/Documents/stratperspective/china/ChinaPerspectives-10.pdf.

31. For an official Chinese overview of the military reform, see "China's National Defense in the New Era," State Council Information Office, People's Republic of China, July 24, 2019, http://eng.mod.gov.cn/publications/2019-07/24/content_4846452.htm.

32. "Lianzhan Lianxun, Wo de Zhanwei zai Nali?" *Jiefangjun bao* [PLA daily], December 12, 2017, http://www.81.cn/hj/2017-12/12/content_7864115_2.htm.

33. Dongbu Zhanqu Dangwei [Eastern Theater Party Committee], "Lvxing Hao Xinshidai Zhanqu Shiming Renwu" [Fulfill the mission of the new era theater], *Qiushi* [Seeking truth], January 31, 2018, http://www.qstheory.cn/dukan/qs/2018-01/31/c_1122337127.htm.

34. "Nanbu Zhanqu Fayanren jiu Meijian Shanchuang Wo Xisha Linghai Fabiao Tanhua" [The spokesperson of the Southern Theater Command made a remark on the US warship tres-passing in our territorial waters of Xisha], *Zhongguo Jun Wang* [China military online], November 30, 2018, http://www.81.cn/jwgz/2018-11/30/content_9361424.htm.

35. "Realities in the South China Sea and China's Position," Ministry of Foreign Affairs of the People's Republic of China, Chinese Embassy in Germany, August 2, 2021, https://www.mfa.gov.cn/ce/cede/chn/sgyw/t1896942.htm.

36. Wei Fenghe, "China's Vision for Regional Order," transcript of speech delivered at the Nineteenth Regional Security Summit, the Shangri-La Dialogue, June 12, 2022, https://www.iiss.org/-/media/files/shangri-la-dialogue/2022/transcripts/p5/general-wei-fenghe-state-coun cilor-minister-of-national-defense-china-provisional-transcript.pdf.

37. Xi Jinping, "Rising to Challenges and Building a Bright Future through Cooperation,"

Transcript of speech delivered at the opening ceremony of the Boao Forum for Asia, April 21, 2022, https://www.fmprc.gov.cn/eng/zxxx_662805/202204/t20220421_10671081.html.

38. "Chinese Defense Minister Holds Talks with US Counterpart in Singapore," China Military Online, June 10, 2022, http://eng.mod.gov.cn/news/2022-06/10/content_4912693.htm.

39. "Jianchi zou zhongguo tese qiang jun zhi lu" [Persist in walking the path of a strong military with Chinese characteristics], *Renmin ribao* [People's daily], December 9, 2021, http://opinion.people.com.cn/n1/2021/1209/c1003-32303127.html.

40. *Indo-Pacific Strategy of the United States*, February 2022, https://www.whitehouse.gov/wp-content/uploads/2022/02/U.S.-Indo-Pacific-Strategy.pdf.

41. State Council Information Office, People's Republic of China, "Zhongguo de yatai anquan hezuo zhengce" [China's Asia-Pacific security cooperation policy], Xinhua, January 11, 2017, http://www.gov.cn/zhengce/2017-01/11/content_5158864.htm.

42. Phil Davidson, "Transforming the Joint Force: A Warfighting Concept for Great Power Competition," transcript of speech delivered at West 2020, San Diego, CA, March 3, 2020, https://www.pacom.mil/Media/Speeches-Testimony/Article/2101115/transforming-the-joint-force-a-warfighting-concept-for-great-power-competition/.

43. "2002 nian zhongguo de guofang" [China's National Defense in 2002], State Council Information Office, People's Republic of China, http://www.gov.cn/zwgk/2005-05/26/content_1384.htm.

44. "Zhongguo de junshi zhanlue" [China's Military Strategy], State Council Information Office, People's Republic of China, May 2015, http://www.scio.gov.cn/zfbps/ndhf/2015/Document/1435161/1435161.htm.

45. For a discussion, see Liu Guangming, "Bainian da dang junshi lilun chuangxin de jingyan yu qishi" [Findings and experiences of 100 years of party-army theory innovation], *Guangming ribao* [Guangming daily], June 6, 2021, http://www.qstheory.cn/qshyjx/2021-06/06/c_1127534865.htm.

46. For a discussion of these technologies and their possible impacts, see Kelley Sayler, "Emerging Military Technologies: Background and Issues for Congress," Congressional Research Service, updated April 6, 2022, https://crsreports.congress.gov/product/pdf/R/R46458/10.

47. "Xi jinping: Jiangjun min ronghe fazhan shangsheng wei guojia zhanlue" [Xi Jinping: Upgrade military-civil fusion to a national strategy], Xinhua, March 13, 2015, https://china.zjol.com.cn/system/2015/03/13/020550910.shtml.

48. Aaron Mehta, "Inside US Indo-Pacific Command's $20 Billion Wish List to Deter China—and Why Congress May Approve It," *Defense News*, April 2, 2020, https://www.defensenews.com/global/asia-pacific/2020/04/02/inside-us-indo-pacific-commands-20-billion-wish-list-to-deter-china-and-why-congress-may-approve-it/.

49. Barack Obama and Xi Jinping, "Remarks by President Obama and President Xi Jinping in Joint Press Conference," Obama White House Archive, November 12, 2014, https://obamawhitehouse.archives.gov/the-press-office/2014/11/12/remarks-president-obama-and-president-xi-jinping-joint-press-conference.

50. Patricia Zengerle, "U.S. Senators Alarmed If China Gets Control of Djibouti Port," Reuters, November 13, 2021, https://www.reuters.com/article/us-usa-china-congress-idUSKCN1NI2YM.

51. For an example, see "USEUCOM 2019 Posture Statement," US European Command Public Affairs, March 5, 2019, https://www.eucom.mil/article/39546/useucom-2019-posture-statement.

52. Zhao Lei, "People's Liberation Army Navy Fleet Sent for Gulf of Aden Escort Mission," *China Daily*, January 17, 2022, https://www.chinadaily.com.cn/a/202201/17/WS61e4aa16a3 10cdd39bc8152f.html.

53. "Xi Jinping dui quanjun zhanlue guanli jixun zuochu zhongyao zhishi" [Xi Jinping gives important instructions to the whole army's strategic management training], "Xuexi juntuan" weixin gongzhong hao ["Xuexi juntuan" WeChat account], June 18, 2020, http://www .81.cn/xue-xi/2020-06/18/content_9837673.htm.

54. "Zhonggong zhongyang guanyu zhiding guomin jingji he shehui fazhan di shisi ge wunian guihua he 2035 nian yuanjing mubiao de jianyi" [Suggestions of the Central Committee of the Communist Party of China on formulating the Fourteenth Five-Year Plan for National Economic and Social Development and the Vision for 2035), Xinhua, November 3, 2020, http://cpc.people.com.cn/gb/n1/2020/1103/c419242-31917562.html.

55. "Laogu li qi xin shidai beizhan dazhang zhihui bang" [Firmly erect the baton of war preparations for the new era], *Jiefangjun bao* [PLA daily], November 26, 2020, http://www.81 .cn/jfjbmap/content/2020-11/26/content_276709.htm.

56. Ministry of National Defense, People's Republic of China, "Regular Press Conference of the Ministry of National Defense on October 29," China Military Online, November 1, 2020, http://eng.chinamil.com.cn/view/2020-11/01/content_9928668.htm.

57. Benn Steil, *The Marshall Plan: Dawn of the Cold War* (New York: Simon and Schuster, 2018).

58. "Transcript of Ambassador Cui Tiankai's Dialogue with Professor Graham Allison at the Annual Conference of the Institute for China-America Studies," Annual Conference of the Institute for China-America Studies, Washington, DC, December 5, 2020, http://www.china -embassy.org/eng/zmgxss/t1838064.htm.

10

Nontraditional Security Competition:
The Espionage Realm

James Mulvenon

Introduction

This chapter examines the security competition between the United States and China in the espionage realm, including both traditional espionage against classified state secrets and Beijing's planetary-scale cyber and human espionage against technology as well as economic and trade targets. The strategic backdrop for this competition is the slow and steady slide of the bilateral relationship from the previous mix of cooperation and conflict to a "new Cold War," exhibiting many of the same features of the "shadow war" between the KGB and the CIA during the first Cold War. To explore the contours of the current intelligence battle, the scope of the analysis is intentionally broad, including both civilian and military intelligence services, ranging from the Ministry of State Security (MSS) to the Central Military Commission (CMC) Intelligence Department and the People's Liberation Army's (PLA) signals intelligence (SIGINT) organization, the Strategic Support Force. Despite the empirical problem of incomplete information about activity that by design works in the shadows, even the fragmentary public record clearly shows that espionage is now playing an increasingly central role in the nontraditional security competition between Washington and Beijing as it spirals downward into a new cold war.

Over the last twenty years, American government officials have warned of a serious and growing threat from China's intelligence services. Dave Szady, then assistant director of the FBI's counterintelligence division, told the *Wall Street Journal* in 2005, "China is the biggest [espionage] threat to the US today."[1] In the wake of the Chi Mak case in 2008, FBI spokesman William Carter declared, "The intelligence services of the People's Republic of China [PRC] pose a significant threat both to the national security and to the compromise of U.S. critical national assets. . . . The PRC will remain a significant threat for a long time as they attempt to develop their military capabilities and to develop their economy in order to compete in today's world economy."[2] This view was supported by current and former officials in an August 2010 *60 Minutes* story, in which former director of the Office of the National Counterintelligence Executive (NCIX) Michelle Van Cleave told the interviewer

> The Chinese are the biggest problem we have with respect to the level of effort that they're devoting against us, versus the level of attention we are giving to them. . . . Virtually every technology that is on the U.S. control technology list has been targeted at one time or another by the Chinese. . . . Sensors and optics . . . biological and chemical processes . . . all the things we have identified as having inherent military application. . . . I think we are a real candy store for the Chinese and for others.[3]

Van Cleave's successor at NCIX, Joel Brenner, also publicly seconded her remarks in 2007: "The Chinese are putting on a full-court press in this area. . . . They are trying to flatten out the world as fast as possible. . . . One of the ways they accelerate that process is economic espionage. If you can steal something rather than figure it out yourself, you save years. You gain an advantage."[4] Indeed, the view of senior counterintelligence officials has not changed with the passage of time but has become more concrete in terms of action and policy. In remarks to the Hudson Institute in July 2020, FBI director Chris Wray asserted, "The greatest long-term threat to our nation's information and intellectual property, and to our economic vitality, is the counterintelligence and economic espionage threat from China. It's a threat to our economic security—and by extension, to our national security."[5] In response to persistent criticism from Chinese advocacy groups and techno-globalists that the US government was fabricating or exaggerating the extent of the activity, Wray countered in November 2020, "The Chinese Communist Party's theft of sensitive information and technology isn't a rumor or a baseless accusation. It's very real, and it's part of a coordinated campaign by the Chinese government."[6] Wray upped the ante in late January 2022, asserting, "There is just no country that presents a broader threat to our ideas, our innovation, and our economic security than China."[7]

While quantifying the threat is difficult given the problem of nonreporting, credible estimates of the scale of the problem and its growth over time are available from authoritative government sources. As early as 2007, then head of the FBI's counterintelligence division Bruce Carlson told *USA Today* that "about one-third of all economic espionage investigations [were] linked to Chinese government agencies, research institutes or businesses"[8] and that between 2000 and 2005 "the total number of [economic espionage] charges [against Chinese] ha[d] grown by around 15% annually."[9] In response, the FBI increased the number of agents working Chinese counterintelligence issues from 150 in 2001 to 350 in 2007.[10] By 2018, the scope and scale of the activity had increased to the point where the Department of Justice (DOJ) launched a broad-ranging "China Initiative," the myths and realities of which are discussed later in this chapter. In his July 2020 speech to the Hudson Institute, FBI director Wray provided more detail about the scale of Chinese espionage than had been previously released, saying, "We've now reached the point where the FBI is opening a new China-related counterintelligence case about every 10 hours. Of the nearly 5,000 active FBI counterintelligence cases currently underway across the country, almost half are related to China. . . . We're conducting these kinds of investigations in all 56 of our field offices. And over the past decade, we've seen economic espionage cases with a link to China increase by approximately 1,300 percent."[11] Wray reiterated and confirmed this pace of counterintelligence case initiation in late January 2022, telling a public audience that the bureau opened a new counterintelligence case against China about twice a day.[12]

The next section creates a typology of Chinese espionage in order to improve analytic understanding of the problem and design more surgical responses.

A Typology of Chinese Espionage

Traditional State-Sponsored Espionage against Government and Military Targets

Spying is often described as the world's second-oldest profession, and traditional state-sponsored espionage by China has been a consistent feature of US-China relations since the founding of the PRC in 1949, though its intensity has waxed and waned because of domestic and foreign factors. China's human intelligence operations have been well-documented in other sources.[13] One increasingly popular and successful vector for Chinese state-sponsored espionage against government and military targets has been cyberespionage. Since the early 2000s, the Chinese government and military have been conducting a planetary-scale cyberespionage campaign against the United States and its allies. While the media began reporting rumors of large-scale intrusions in 2005,[14] US officials did not publicly acknowledge exfiltrations of data until August 2006, when the Pentagon asserted that hostile civilian cyber units operating inside China had launched attacks against the NIPRNet (Nonclassified Internet Protocol Router Network) and downloaded up to twenty terabytes of data.[15]

In March 2007, the then vice chairman of the Joint Chiefs, General James Cartwright, told the US-China Economic and Security Review Commission that China was engaged in cyberreconnaissance, probing computer networks of US agencies and corporations.[16] This view was seconded in the 2007 *China Military Power Report*, an annual Pentagon assessment mandated by the National Defense Authorization Act, which claimed "numerous computer networks around the world, including those owned by the U.S. government, were subject to intrusions that appear[ed] to have originated within" the People's Republic of China.[17] Former White House and Department of Homeland Security (DHS) cyber official Paul Kurtz told *BusinessWeek* that the Chinese activity was "espionage on a massive scale."[18] China's cyber intrusions reached a new level of seriousness in 2014 with the breach of the Office of Personnel Management (OPM), resulting in the exfiltration of approximately 21.5 million security background investigation files of cleared government employees and contractors as well as 5.6 million fingerprints.[19] According to Brenner, the OPM data represented "crown jewels material . . . a gold mine for a foreign intelligence service."[20] Former National Security Agency (NSA) and CIA director Michael Hayden emphasized the life cycle value of the data: "[OPM data] remains a treasure trove of information to the Chinese until the people represented by the information age off. There's no fixing it."[21] As Chinese cyberespionage activities continued at an intense pace throughout the Trump and Biden administrations, the latter rallied a coalition of allies (Australia, Britain, Canada, the European Union, Japan, and New Zealand) to condemn Beijing for cyberoperations around the world, and Secretary of State Antony Blinken publicly accused China's Ministry of State Security in July 2021 of fostering "an ecosystem of criminal contract hackers who carry out both state-sponsored activities and cybercrime for their own financial gain."[22]

Economic Espionage

If we step back and look at all of the cases of Chinese technology espionage over the last forty years as an analytical whole, it is helpful to systematically categorize different modes of economic and technology espionage. Peter Mattis identifies at least five forms involving varying degrees of government or intelligence service involvement:

1. Intelligence service collection of economic secrets for state-supported industrial development,
2. Intelligence service collection of technology for military intelligence and planning as well as strategic economic intelligence,
3. Government-sponsored, nonintelligence service collection for state-supported industry,
4. Economic actors stealing competitors' secrets for the actors's own benefit, and
5. Entrepreneurial individuals stealing economic secrets to sell to any of the above actors and/or go into business for themselves.[23]

Mattis argues that "cases conclusively linked to mainland China demonstrate all five modes of economic espionage and technology transfer."[24] First, in 1993, Wu Bin and two other Chinese nationals were prosecuted for smuggling export-controlled equipment to China at the direction of the MSS.[25] In the second category, two accredited Chinese diplomats in the United States— one an assistant military attaché reporting to Chinese military intelligence— were expelled in 1987 after attempting to purchase cryptographic materials in an FBI sting operation.[26] Third, the Chinese military owns or owned several import-export companies to facilitate the purchase of foreign dual-use technologies, such as Poly Technologies.[27] Combining the fourth and fifth categories, two Silicon Valley engineers, Ye Fei and Zhong Ming, were indicted in 2002 for the attempted theft of technical schematics from Sun Microsystems and Transmeta. Ye and Zhong wanted to start their own company in China. They also sought state funding through the national technical modernization program, the 863 Program, according to court documents.[28] Finally, in late 2005, Bill Moo was arrested prior to exporting General Electric's newest engine for the F-16. Moo reportedly stood to make a $1 million profit for selling the engine to the Chinese military.[29]

Like their activities against government and military targets, a primary vector for Chinese economic espionage has been in the cyber realm. As early as 2008, Robert Jamison, the top cybersecurity official at DHS, told reporters, "We're concerned that the intrusions are more frequent, and they're more targeted, and they're more sophisticated."[30] After the Operation Aurora intrusions against Google and other Silicon Valley companies in 2009 and 2010, officials worried that China was escalating its intrusions. Whereas previously the activities had been targeted at government and military networks, threatening US military advantage and government policies, the new intrusions went beyond state-on-state espionage to threaten American technological competitiveness and economic prosperity. Because the underlying evidence was classified, government and military officials could not provide detailed evidence of these allegations against the Chinese government and military, which naturally led to scrutiny of the specific attribution to China. In his confirmation testimony questions, then US Cyber Command (CYBERCOM) commander General Keith Alexander agreed that "attribution can be very difficult."[31] Former senior DHS cybersecurity official Greg Garcia told the *New York Times* in March 2009 that "attribution is a hall of mirrors."[32] With respect to China, Amit Yoran, the first director of DHS's National Cybersecurity Division, cautioned, "I think it's a little bit naive to suggest that everything that says it comes from China comes from China."[33] Yet other officials were more confident in the assessment of Chinese responsibility. Then director of the Director of National Intelligence (DNI) National Counterintelligence Executive, Joel Brenner, told the *National Journal* in 2008, "Some [attacks], we have high confidence, are coming from government-sponsored sites. . . . The Chinese operate both through government agencies, as we do, but they also operate through sponsoring other organizations that are engaging in this kind of international hacking, whether or not under specific direction. It's a kind of cyber-militia. . . . It's coming in volumes that are just staggering."[34]

From 2014 to 2018, Chinese state-sponsored hackers also infiltrated and stole almost 80 million personally identifiable information (PII) records from health care provider Anthem,[35] 1.1 million PII records from health care provider CareFirst BlueCross BlueShield,[36] and approximately 147.9 million names, Social Security numbers, birth dates, addresses, and driver's license numbers from consumer credit reporting agency Equifax.[37] Together with the OPM hack mentioned earlier, this unprecedented tranche of potentially compromising and enumerating information likely represents the greatest human and signals intelligence targeting database in the history of espionage. Damaging Chinese cyber intrusions have continued through the Trump and Biden administrations, most notably a large-scale enabling intrusion campaign by the MSS-linked Hafnium group against corporate and government Microsoft Exchange servers globally in 2021, which prompted the global condemnation described earlier.[38]

Nontraditional Collection

The final category is what experts and US counterintelligence officials call "nontraditional collection," which is aimed at helping the Chinese government achieve its ambitious technology-related industrial policies.[39] A June 2018 joint testimony by DOD officials before the House Armed Services Committee provides a solid framework for understanding the scope and the scale of the activity:

Foreign adversaries are scrutinizing public information, such as our own Department's innovation focus areas, to craft their investment strategies to overmatch our technology. Furthermore, the increasing ease of access to large amounts of unclassified or non-government data in the private sector offers opportunities for exploitation. Some of this data in aggregation can be as damaging as a breach of classified information. . . . The Department is seeing the technology transfer threat manifest through numerous nontraditional methods, including talent recruitment, academic collaboration, and supply chain access. Through numerous talent recruitment programs, such as the Thousand Talents Program, China is actively seeking the most talented engineers and scientists from around the world to work in or for Chinese private or public institutions. We have seen the Chinese target top talent in American universities, and research labs of the private sector, including Defense contractors, and the U.S. Government. Lastly, Chinese access to, and acquisition of, elements of the DoD supply chain—both inside and outside the United

States—has been a growing threat for the past decade. In some regards, the Chinese government could more easily understand the Department's supply chain through its relationships with sub-tier suppliers than the Department can understand its supply chain through its prime contractors.[40]

In his December 2018 congressional testimony, then assistant attorney general John Demers summarized the ultimate goals of this activity: "Rob the American company of its intellectual property, replicate the technology, and replace the American company in the Chinese market and, one day, the global market."[41]

With this typology of Chinese espionage in mind, let's pivot to examining the range of American counterespionage efforts.

American Counterespionage Efforts against China

Naming and Shaming

A notable feature of the Obama administration's response to Chinese cyberespionage was a greater willingness to "name and shame" the perpetrators, even when identified to be Chinese government or military personnel. The most prominent example was the published indictment of five Chinese military intelligence officers associated with Unit 61398,[42] which had been exposed in a Mandiant report as performing cyberespionage against US companies for the benefit of Chinese state-owned enterprises.[43] Specifically, the officers were charged with (1) conspiring to commit computer fraud and abuse; (2) accessing (or attempting to access) a protected computer without authorization to obtain information for the purpose of commercial advantage and private financial gain; (3) transmitting a program, information, code, or command with the intent to cause damage to protected computers; (4) aggravated identity theft; (5) economic espionage; and (6) theft of trade secrets. In another unprecedented move, the Justice Department identified victim companies, including Westinghouse; SolarWorld; US Steel; Allegheny Technologies Inc. (ATI); the United Steel, Paper and Forestry, Rubber, Manufacturing, Energy, Allied Industrial and Service Workers International Union (USW); and Alcoa. Previously, companies had been unwilling to be named for fear of threatening their business interests in China, but the scale and the brazenness of Chinese intelligence activity had finally crossed an unacceptable threshold.

The Obama Administration escalated its "name and shame" strategy in April 2015 with the promulgation of Executive Order (EO) 13694, "Blocking the Property of Certain Persons Engaging in Significant Malicious Cyber-Enabled Activities."[44] The EO declared that "increasing prevalence and severity of malicious cyber-enabled activities originating from, or directed by persons located, in whole or in substantial part, outside the United States constitute[d] an unusual and extraordinary threat to the national security, foreign policy, and economy of the United States." For our purposes, the EO targeted two key categories of person, including those

- "causing a significant misappropriation of funds or economic resources, trade secrets, personal identifiers, or financial information for commercial or competitive advantage or private financial gain" or
- "responsible for or complicit in, or to have engaged in, the receipt or use for commercial or competitive advantage or private financial gain, or by a commercial entity, outside the United States of trade secrets misappropriated through cyber-enabled means, knowing they have been misappropriated, where the misappropriation of such trade secrets is reasonably likely to result in, or has materially contributed to, a significant threat to the national security, foreign policy, or economic health or financial stability of the United States."

The prescribed penalty was sanctions against persons and property, with the concrete result of seizure of assets and the restrictions of international financial transfers and travel associated with being placed on the Interpol "red notice" list. The Chinese reaction to this EO was swift and intense, though not surprising given that it potentially implicated senior government officials serving as the heads of large, state-owned enterprises. Beijing dispatched Communist Party of China (CPC) Central Political and Legal Affairs Commission Secretary Meng Jianzhu to Washington in September 2015 for consultations ahead of Xi Jinping's state visit later that month, reportedly giving him unusually wide latitude to negotiate an arrangement that would preclude a set of public sanctions for commercial cyberespionage.[45] Chinese state media reported after the meeting that Meng reached an "important consensus" with the US and said China would punish domestic hackers, including cyber thieves that stole corporate secrets.[46] This commitment was then consummated with an "understanding" between Xi and Obama in a joint press conference, where they agreed that neither government would knowingly support cyber theft of corporate secrets or business information.[47]

The Trump administration followed suit in 2017 with an indictment of three Chinese hackers (Wu Yingzhuo, Dong Hao, and Xia Lei) employed by a Chinese government contractor company (Boyusec), charging them with "computer hacking, theft of trade secrets, conspiracy and identity theft directed at US and foreign employees and computers of three corporate victims in the financial, engineering and technology industries between 2011 and May 2017."[48] The specific named victim companies were Moody's Analytics, Siemens AG, and Trimble.

The (Former) Department of Justice "China Initiative"

The Department of Justice initiated its own "China Initiative" in 2018, designed to address a wide range of China-related legal issues in the United States. In January 2022 the department formally announced that it was reviewing the China Initiative, and then in February 2022 it announced a "new approach" focused more broadly on "countering nation-state threats."[49] Given this turn of events, it is imperative to assess the initiative as a policy instrument, particularly given the surprising number of myths that had been perpetuated by its critics and the seeming inability of the department to use the actual realities to change the narrative.

* * *

> **Myth:** The China Initiative is focused on espionage and trade secret theft, and recent attempts to add other issues like research integrity and visa fraud are evidence of mission creep or policy drift.

> **Reality:** The China Initiative was always broader than economic espionage, even from the launch.

A highly publicized study in the *MIT Technology Review* asserted that "the Department of Justice ha[d] no definition of what constitutes a China Initiative case," that "the initiative was supposed to focus on economic espionage, but it ha[d] increasingly charged academics with 'research integrity' issues," and as a result the initiative "ha[d] strayed far from its initial mission."[50] In fact, the China Initiative was launched with a clear definition and scope and began with the assumption that the scale of the issues of concern was much larger than just economic espionage. The China Initiative Fact Sheet that accompanied the launch described a much broader agenda than espionage, including influence operations, academic freedom, investment security, supply chain security, and the use of the Mutual Legal Assistance Agreement (MLAA) in cross-border crime. Its items included:

- Identify priority trade secret theft cases, ensure that investigations are adequately resourced; and work to bring them to fruition in a timely manner and according to the facts and applicable law;
- Develop an enforcement strategy concerning non-traditional collectors (e.g., researchers in labs, universities, and the defense industrial base) that are being coopted into transferring technology contrary to U.S. interests;
- Educate colleges and universities about potential threats to academic freedom and open discourse from influence efforts on campus;
- Apply the Foreign Agents Registration Act to unregistered agents seeking to advance China's political agenda, bringing enforcement actions when appropriate;

- Equip the nation's US attorneys with intelligence and materials they can use to raise awareness of these threats within their Districts and support their outreach efforts;
- Implement the Foreign Investment Risk Review Modernization Act (FIRMA) for DOJ (including by working with Treasury to develop regulations under the statute and prepare for increased workflow);
- Identify opportunities to better address supply chain threats, especially ones impacting the telecommunications sector, prior to the transition to 5G networks;
- Identify Foreign Corrupt Practices Act (FCPA) cases involving Chinese companies that compete with American businesses;
- Increase efforts to improve Chinese responses to requests under the Mutual Legal Assistance Agreement (MLAA) with the United States; and
- Evaluate whether additional legislative and administrative authorities are required to protect our national assets from foreign economic aggression.[51]

The China Initiative was first and foremost about providing focused priorities, direction, and oversight to FBI field offices and US attorney offices to pursue the above activities, codified in a series of classified memos to US attorneys around the country. The critics of the China Initiative often ignore this broader agenda and actively seek to blur the distinction between separate sub-initiatives, especially between the espionage cases and the research integrity cases. One virulent strain of this argument asserts without evidence that the government is using fraud in the research integrity cases as cover for a lack of evidence of economic espionage and trade secret theft because that conflation bolsters the racist persecution narrative, comparing the cases to the tax evasion charges against Chicago gangster Al Capone.[52] The mainstream media is complicit in this blurring, going for the easy story and lazily mixing the case types together without highlighting the distinctions. In nearly all cases, the prosecutors are deeply constrained in their ability to correct any of these narratives because of concern about compromising the integrity of the cases, even on appeal. While the Justice Department was right to try and stay above the politics of the issue, it meant it largely abandoned the public opinion battlefield.

* * *

Myth: The China Initiative was created by the US government because of internal dynamics that were disconnected from any actions by China.

Reality: China's published national industrial planning strategies, talent programs, and corresponding espionage activities compelled the creation of the China Initiative.

Critics of the China Initiative have a notable blind spot when it comes to China's "agency" in these issues. If it wasn't for the aggressiveness of China's more than five hundred national, provincial, and municipal talent programs, set against the backdrop of the massive open source science and technology (S&T) collection and processing apparatus, there would never have been a need for the China Initiative in the first place.[53] If anyone has unfairly exposed American scientists to scrutiny it is the Chinese authorities, especially when they make foreign researchers sign Trans-Pacific Partnership (TTP) contracts that specifically direct them to hide or obfuscate the scope and purpose of the agreement.[54]

* * *

Myth: China's efforts are no different than other country in the world seeking to attract technology and talent.

Reality: The scope and scale of the Chinese talent programs significantly dwarf any other comparable national effort.

Critics of the China Initiative like to refer to hoary historical facts, such as Samuel Slater's theft of textile technology from Great Britain to New England in the eighteenth century, to argue that every country's economic development involves technology espionage and China's state policies are simply the latest iteration of a "natural" process.[55] While the historical facts cannot be denied, the scope and scale of the Chinese government's foreign technology acquisition effort are unprecedented in human history, as described in tedious detail in my two previous coauthored books, *Chinese Industrial Espionage* and *China's Quest for Foreign Technology*.[56] Add to this more than five hundred national, provincial, and municipal foreign talent programs, distributing billions of dollars, and it becomes difficult to compare the scale of China's effort to any other country in the world.

* * *

Myth: Every government, including the United States, engages in commercial economic espionage, so this is all just hypocritical "sour grapes."

Reality: The United States government, probably alone among national governments, does not engage in commercial economic espionage on behalf of its companies.

Many countries around the world use their intelligence services to steal technology and secrets for the benefits of their domestic countries. Even if the US government wanted to steal commercial technology or trade secrets and provide them to American companies, it could not, admittedly for a very banal reason.

Hypothetically, if the NSA in the future were to steal Huawei's 9G tech, for instance, there would be no way to share it with US companies without falling afoul of US antitrust law. If the technology is given to Cisco and Juniper but not some networking start-up in Austin or Silicon Valley, that start-up has standing in federal court to sue for antitrust. As a result of this legal barrier, the US government does not steal commercial tech and share it with American companies. Chinese interlocutors are deeply skeptical of this argument, probably because of the structural differences between the two systems. When I explained it to Chinese participants in a cyber track 1.5 dialogue ten years ago, for example, one asked, "Well, why doesn't the USG [US government] just tell the courts what to do?" highlighting again a serious deficiency of US civics understanding on the Chinese side.

* * *

Myth: The Andrew Kim study shows racial bias in DOJ investigations and prosecutions.

Reality: The Kim study, along with the *MIT Technology Review* analysis, is deeply methodologically flawed.

The most common criticism of the US government's legal efforts against technology theft from China is that the program is driven by racial bias. The oft-cited example is the May 2017 study by Andrew Kim, whose statistical analysis is presented by the Committee of 100 as counterevidence of the pervasiveness of Chinese economic espionage and proof of ethnic bias in the prosecution system.[57] Yet Kim's study contains deep methodological flaws and is undermined by the absence of key data.

Methodologically, the authors say they have used "a random sample of cases charged under the Economic Espionage Act (EEA) from 1997 to 2015 (136 cases involving 187 individual defendants), using publicly available court documents drawn from the Public Access to Court Electronic Records system (PACER)."[58] First, this statement reflects a lack of understanding of the statistical meaning of a "random sample," which does not mean "publicly available court documents drawn from the Public Access to Court Electronic Records system (PACER)" found in a search. Moreover, given this small N, analyses of percentages within a given year are statistically unstable, averaging only ten per year over the period in question. It is therefore not surprising that one of the study's reviewers, Dr. David Harris, advises the reader to "recognize the limitations of these data."[59] Harris argues that from the data, "we cannot tell how many investigations under the EEA (as opposed to cases charged) took place during the study period, what ethnic groups the targets of those investigations came from (Chinese, Asian, or other), and the rate at which those investigations actually blossomed into charged cases."[60] This leads Harris to conclude that "the data presented in the study do not prove the existence of 'researching while Asian,'" which is the core argument of the entire document.[61] Kim actually asks the right question later in the conclusion, but his findings depend on knowing the answer.

These methodological problems undermine the study's main conclusions. For example, the author begins with an initial caveat that the findings are "not conclusive," which immediately gives the reader pause.[62] They continue with the very first summary statement, that "the percentage of people of Chinese heritage charged under the EEA has tripled since 2009, to 52%," but the reader is not given the corresponding increase in charges for the same crime against non-Chinese for comparison purposes.[63] This error is common in analyses of racial bias. The gold standard test for discrimination would be similar to the question of the proportion of Whites charged with the same crime as Blacks for selling the same kind of cocaine. If Blacks disproportionately are charged with more serious offenses for the same action, then there is evidence of some kind of discrimination. If the probability of being arrested for espionage is higher for Chinese than non-Chinese in the same conditions, then discrimination exists. But the author does not provide the necessary data to evaluate the situation.

Second, Kim expands the aperture of his analysis by asserting that "62% of EEA defendants charged since 2009 have been people of Asian heritage."[64] By including the undefined category of "people of Asian heritage," the author dilutes the strength of his conclusions since he does not provide data about the relative percentage of non-Chinese Asians arrested each year since 2009 and therefore cannot refute the supposition that Chinese themselves are not disproportionately being arrested. Moreover, the author does not provide a rationale for choosing 2009 as the starting point. Data provided later in the study show that if 2007 is used as a starting point, the percentage drops to 42 percent, and over the entire period since 1996 it is 25 percent. This is a classic statistical manipulation involving adjusting the numbers on the Y or X axis to exaggerate the seeming conclusion. In addition, the author asserts that "22% of people of Asian heritage charged with economic espionage were never convicted of espionage" but fails to provide the nonconviction rate for non-Asians.[65]

Additionally, the data cannot say whether Chinese are disproportionately charged if the underlying pool—the percentage of people working on sensitive technology—is not also known. In the tech secrets cases under discussion, the author needs to show the relative differential in the prosecution rates for Chinese and non-Chinese, adjusting for the percentages of each group in the overall pool of people engaged in similar work on sensitive technologies. One cannot use the population of the US as a metric since the relevant pool is people working in domains where the EEA could apply. According to the authors' data, for example, the "Western:Chinese" ratio of those accused of economic espionage is roughly 1.8:1, but we do not know the overall ratio of those two groups in the population of personnel working in EEA-relevant domains and therefore cannot really conclude disproportionate discrimination.[66]

Third, the author asserts that in almost half "(48%) of cases of economic espionage in the dataset, the alleged beneficiary of espionage was an American entity while [only] a third (34%) of cases involved a Chinese beneficiary."[67] But this statistical sleight of hand is meant to confuse the reader. The data from appendix 2 clearly show that Chinese perpetrators overwhelmingly were seeking data for a Chinese beneficiary, and in 57 percent of cases the beneficiary was a "foreign instrumentality" of the Chinese government.[68]

Fourth, the author insists that "the average sentence for Chinese and all Asian defendants convicted of espionage was 25 months and 22 months respectively, twice as long as the 11-month average sentence for defendants with Western names."[69] The problem with this analysis takes us back to the examples of Whites and Blacks charged with cocaine-related crimes. If Blacks disproportionately receive more severe punishments for the same crime than Whites, there is evidence of discrimination. But the author of this study does not break down the EEA violations by any measure of scope or scale, such as numbers of transfers or the financial value of the transfers, making it impossible to judge the relative differences. Also, a name alone may tell us little about a person.

Finally, the author claims as evidence of discrimination that "as many as 1 in 5 Asian people prosecuted as spies may be innocent, a rate twice as large as for other races."[70] Rather than point to discrimination, the data actually imply that Asians are twice as likely to be charged but ultimately not convicted, which might point to discrimination in charging thresholds but also could mean that the cases are weaker *or* that the evidence of espionage is more sensitive and they are convicted of other things (e.g., mishandling classified materials). While there is surely reputational and financial damage from these aborted prosecutions, they also perversely validate the independence and fairness of the American judicial system.

To summarize, the Kim study contains several methodological and empirical flaws. To make the study more methodologically sound, the author should answer four empirical questions:

- Were the crimes for which "Western"-named people and Chinese-named people were charged the same in terms of degree?
- What is the pool of people working in sensitive tech, and what is their distribution by ethnicity?
- What was the rationale behind the time frame of the evidence offered?
- What is the nationality of Chinese charged? Does the percent of PRC citizens go up after 2009 while the percent of US Chinese Americans charged remains

the same? If so, does this suggest nationality, not ethnicity, is driving the data?

The Kim study does not answer these key questions, which undermines its—admittedly cautious—conclusions that current DOJ prosecutions are motivated by racial bias.

* * *

> **Myth:** The China Initiative is a racist witch hunt aimed at anyone of "Asian," especially "Chinese" ethnicity or "heritage."
>
> **Reality:** Nationality, not ethnicity, is the key explanatory variable for indictments and convictions for economic espionage and trade secret theft cases that benefit a China-based entity (see table 10.1).

- A highly publicized critique of the China Initiative in the *MIT Technology Review* asserted that "early 90% of the defendants charged are of Chinese heritage,"[71] ironically using an inclusive definition of the "Greater China" diaspora that Beijing regularly abuses in its extraterritorial policies like rendition under operations Fox Hunt and Sky Net.
- Nationality, especially PRC origin, appears to be much more statistically significant than the ill-defined "Chinese" or "Asian" ethnicity highlighted by critics of the former China Initiative. Between 1998 and early 2022, 203 individuals were indicted by the Department of Justice for economic espionage or trade secret theft benefiting a PRC entity, resulting in 137 convictions (many are still pending).[72] PRC nationals or naturalized US citizens of PRC origin make up the majority of those indicted (63 percent) or convicted (67.1 percent) of economic espionage or trade secret theft from 1998 to early 2022.[73]
- The percentage of nonethnic-Chinese US citizens indicted (11.3 percent) or convicted (13.1 percent) has always been a relative minority of cases, in sharp contrast to the recent spike in nonethnic Chinese individuals (e.g., Gregg Bergersen, James Fondren, Benjamin Bishop, Glenn Duffie Shriver, Kevin Patrick Mallory) indicted or convicted of nontechnology espionage on behalf of the Chinese intelligence services.[74]
- The low percentage of Taiwanese citizens indicted (2.5 percent) or convicted (1.5 percent) has almost been a surprising outlier, which is notable because ethnic and linguistic compatibility as well as high levels of economic intercourse between China and Taiwan theoretically lowers the barriers to economic espionage or theft of trade secrets on behalf of the mainland.[75]
- Most telling, multigenerational Chinese Americans are completely absent in the data, again undermining the narrative that the key explanatory variable is "Chinese heritage."[76]

Table 10.1 Nationality of indictments/convictions for economic espionage or trade secret theft benefiting a PRC entity, 1998–2022.

	PRC National	Naturalized US Citizen (PRC Origin)	Naturalized US Citizen (Taiwan Origin)	Taiwan Citizen	US Citizen	Other National	UNK
Indictments 203	84 (41.3%)	44 (21.7%)	3 (1.5%)	5 (2.5%)	23 (11.3%)	11 (5.4%)	34 (16.7%)
Convictions 137	57 (41.6%)	35 (25.5%)	3 (2.2%)	2 (1.5%)	18 (13.1%)	5 (3.6%)	18 (13.1%)

* * *

Myth: The DOJ's focus on Chinese espionage was created and hyped by the xenophobic Trump administration and does not represent a long-term structural threat.

Reality: The number of convictions of China-based economic espionage cases was higher during the Obama administration, *before* the China Initiative was launched.

In fact, the figure below shows that the number of indictments for economic espionage or trade secret theft between 1998 and 2022 averaged over eight per year, peaking at nineteen indictments in 2012, while convictions averaged five per year, peaking in 2009 and 2013 at thirteen convictions.[77] The spikes in indictments and convictions both occurred during the Obama administration, which certainly belies the popular argument that the dramatic growth in these prosecutions started with the 2017 Department of Justice China Initiative under President Trump (see figure 10.1).

* * *

Myth: The espionage cases do not benefit "China" but instead benefit only greedy individuals.

Reality: More than 57 percent of economic espionage or trade secret theft cases between 2004 and 2019 benefited a "foreign instrumentality," which is statutorily defined as an "entity controlled by the government of a foreign country that performs a function the controlling government treats as its own."[78] Over 20 percent of economic espionage or trade secret theft cases between 1998 and 2022 benefited a private PRC commercial company, often a competitor of the US victim, though the incidence of nongovernment, commercial-focused espionage has increased

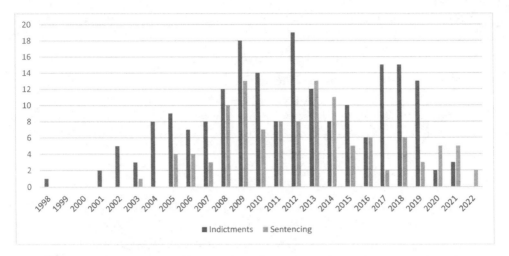

Figure 10.1 Indictments and convictions for economic espionage and trade secret theft benefiting a PRC entity, 1998–2022. (Mulvenon)

dramatically in 2018–19, surpassing foreign instrumentality cases for the first time.[79] Only 6 percent of economic espionage or trade secret theft cases between 1998 and 2022 benefited a company established in the PRC by the defendant for private commercial purposes.[80]

* * *

Myth: The China Initiative was focused on research integrity issues from the outset.

Reality: The focus on research integrity was an evolution that was driven by data, specifically clear evidence that hundreds of federal grantees had been awarded Chinese talent program money and had not reported the money on their disclosure forms.

The critics of the China Initiative strongly imply in their analysis that racist hysteria in the US government about China led the authorities to scrutinize universities for researchers with "Asian"-sounding names and then worked backward to charge them with minor offenses (wire and visa fraud) while they continued to search for evidence of espionage. In fact, the authorities at the National Institutes of Health (NIH) and the National Science Foundation (NSF) were first presented with Chinese talent program award data downloaded from (now deleted) official Chinese websites. When the Inspectors General of the NIH and NSF received evidence that hundreds of federal grantees were taking money from Chinese talent programs and obfuscating that fact, they had no choice but to investigate. In cases where wrongdoing was discovered, the NIH and NSF then coordinated with the Justice Department to pursue a range of administrative or criminal actions.

* * *

Myth: A study published in the *MIT Technology Review* concluded that the research integrity focus of the China Initiative has been a failure, resulting in a small number of botched prosecutions, and should have instead been dealt with through noncriminal administrative measures.

Reality: While there have been a relatively small number of prosecutions, *hundreds* of researchers have lost their academic jobs and/or been formally "debarred" by federal agencies from receiving future grants, using precisely the noncriminal administration measures recommended by critics, but privacy rules and disclosure gaps in the regulations have prevented the full empirical picture from emerging.[81]

The previously referenced study in *MIT Technology Review* asserted that "many of the cases concerned with research integrity have fallen apart" and "a significant number of research integrity cases have been dropped or dismissed."[82] The actual empirical reality is quite different. As a result of investigations by the NIH and NSF, hundreds of American researchers have lost their university or lab jobs or have been formally "debarred" from receiving any future federal grants. Prosecution was always judged to be the last resort, usually in cases where individuals were caught lying to federal investigators, and should never be the metric used to judge this problem. Universities have been understandably reluctant to publicize the firings because of a fear of backlash and human resources privacy concerns. The figures on the hundreds of federal debarments are currently not required to be publicly released under the law, although they could be released under congressional subpoena. Some of the data have come to light in the media, including a partial disclosure by the NIH to the *Washington Post* that it had opened 222 compliance reviews since 2018, resulting in the resignation, retirement, or firing of eighty-five scientists.[83] Even this fraction of the real data about the results of the research integrity cases demolishes the dismissive argument of the authors of the *MIT Technology Review*.

* * *

Myth: Many of the activities of US researchers involved in the Chinese talent programs are "legitimate," not illegal.

Reality: There are many aspects of the Chinese effort that are "legitimate," defined as the mutual pursuit of research and science, but it is not "legitimate" when the agreements require the recipients to violate their own country's laws. Thousand Talents Program contracts, for example, specifically require the recipients to sign nondisclosure agreements that prevent them from telling their home university or US government granting agencies about the award, which is where some of the problems arise.[84] Also, the talent programs are explicitly seen by the Chinese government tech acquisition community as a critical supplement to industrial and cyberespionage, providing critical contextual information with which to understand the intangible aspects of innovation.

* * *

Myth: The renaming of the "China Initiative" is the end of the activities of the China Initiative.

Reality: All of the main features of the former China Initiative will continue apace, though under a different named framework, the "Strategy for Countering Nation-State Threats."

The critics of the China Initiative, especially Maggie Lewis, were obsessively fixated on the word "China" in title, believing that it criminalized "Chinese-ness" rather than analyzing the specific details of cases.[85] As empirically shown above, however, the primary explanatory variable for indictment and conviction is nationality rather than ethnicity, so it probably would have been more accurate to call the previous policy the "DOJ (People's Republic of) China Initiative." Even as the Department of Justice formally ended the formal "China Initiative" in early 2022 in favor of the broader "Strategy for Countering Nation-State Threats," however, Assistant Attorney General Matthew Olsen made it clear to a George Mason University audience that China is still the primary focus because "the government of China stands apart" among other nation-states, threatening American interests "through its concerted use of espionage, theft of trade secrets, malicious cyber activity, transnational repression, and other tactics to advance its interests."[86]

Expelling of Suspected American and Chinese Intelligence Officers

In scenes that are redolent of classic Cold War clashes between the United States and the USSR, the American and Chinese governments have begun a pattern of expulsion of suspected intelligence officers. The recent tit for tats began in January 2016, when Chinese plainclothes security service officers seized a US consular official in Chengdu off the streets, interrogated him for hours, and then eventually released him to US custody for evacuation out of the country.[87] In fall 2019, the US government expelled two Chinese embassy officials after they drove on a sensitive military base in Virginia,[88] which marked the first US expulsion of Chinese intelligence officers since Hou Desheng and Zhang Weichu were sent home in 1987.[89]

Closing the Houston Consulate

In perhaps the most escalatory counterespionage move to date, the State Department on July 21, 2020, ordered the Chinese Foreign Ministry to close its Houston, Texas, consulate within seventy-two hours.[90] State Department spokesperson Morgan Ortagus declared, "The United States will not tolerate [China's] violations of our sovereignty and intimidation of our people, just as we have not tolerated [its] unfair trade practices, theft of American jobs, and other egregious behavior."[91]

China maintains an embassy in Washington and consulates in New York, Chicago, San Francisco, and Los Angeles, in addition to the one maintained in Houston.[92] In a formal press conference on July 22, Assistant Secretary of State David Stilwell described the action as "long overdue,"[93] given the "malign and criminal" activities emanating from the consulate and the overall "lack of reciprocity" in the relationship.[94] While the official announcement asserted that the closure was intended to "protect American intellectual property and the private information of Americans," a number of specific reasons were cited in subsequent remarks and documents:

- Consular officials provided the PLA researchers described earlier with "guidance on how to evade and obstruct [the] investigation."[95] Houston consular staff had also tried to hide their contacts with researchers in the city, telling them to stop using their work email addresses when communicating with the consulate.[96] The consul general and two other diplomats used fabricated documents to access a secure area of George Bush Intercontinental Airport, near the departure gate of an outbound Air China flight on May 31, to facilitate the exit of one of the researchers.[97]
- Consular officials were involved in the trade secret theft efforts of Shan Shi, a Houston-area businessman who was successfully convicted of stealing intellectual property from Trelleborg Offshore and was sentenced to sixteen months in prison.[98]
- Consular officials were linked to fifty examples between 2010 and 2020 of recruiting for PRC government talent programs, including extensive recruiting of nearby Texas A&M and University of Texas researchers for the PRC government's Thousand Talents Program.[99]
- Consular officials were linked to S&T espionage against COVID-19 vaccine research at MD Anderson Cancer Center.
- Consulates served as bases of operations for China's Operation Fox Hunt

personnel, whom the US government has accused of being rendition "snatch teams" under the public guise of law enforcement. One Houston consulate representative delivered a letter to a person in the South, allegedly from his father, imploring the person to come back to China.[100]

- Consulates infiltrated anti-China organizations and supported nationalist counterdemonstrators.

Because of diplomatic immunity and the Vienna Convention, none of the roughly sixty consular officials and staff were charged with any crimes, but they were expected to leave the country. Almost immediately, the Chinese Foreign Ministry announced the closure of the US consulate in Chengdu, citing similar accusations, though the earlier abandonment of the US consulate in Wuhan during the COVID outbreak meant that the US government was a net loser in the bargain.

Conclusions

Espionage is a central, if discreet, battlefield of nontraditional great power competition. In the US-China relationship, the gloves have clearly come off in this realm. On the US side, decades of Beijing-directed technology and cyber-espionage against the United States have been answered with a full-throated response, opening a new counterintelligence investigation every ten hours and closing the PRC consulate in Houston for its role in facilitating espionage. For its part, Beijing has responded with characteristic brutality, allegedly massacring between twelve and thirty American assets between 2010 and 2012, including a husband and his pregnant wife executed on internal China Central Television (CCTV) so their colleagues could receive the full measure of warning.[101]

These escalations, combined with China's continued planetary-scale cyber-espionage campaign against the United States and the dramatic increase in Chinese military capabilities, raise serious questions about the continued relevance or utility of certain longtime liaison activities with the Chinese intelligence services. Moreover, given China's emerging and evolving global ambitions, the current espionage tensions portend a "new cold war" between the American and Chinese services, reminiscent even of the US-USSR espionage competition around the world during the first Cold War. There have already been cases of the two intelligence communities bumping into each other in third countries, presaging a "spy vs. spy" grey war in every country around the globe.[102] These trends only elevate the importance of Washington strengthening the intelligence relationships with traditional partners in the Five Eyes and NATO and even some of the more mature third- and fourth-party relationships in Asia.

Notes

1. Jay Solomon, "FBI Sees Big Threat from Chinese Spies," *Wall Street Journal*, August 10, 2005, A1.

2. Joby Warrick and Carrie Johnson, "Chinese Spy 'Slept' in US for Two Decades," *Washington Post*, April 3, 2008, http://www.washingtonpost.com/wp-dyn/content/article/2008/04/02/AR2008040203952.html.

3. Michelle Van Cleave, "Caught on Tape: Stealing America's Secrets," interview, *60 Minutes,* August 25, 2010.

4. David Lynch, "Law Enforcement Struggles to Combat Chinese Spying," *USA Today*, July 23, 2007, http://www.usatoday.com/money/world/2007-07-22-china-spy-1_N.htm.

5. Christopher Wray, "The Threat Posed by the Chinese Government and the Chinese Communist Party to the Economic and National Security of the United States," remarks to the Hudson Institute, Washington, DC, July 7, 2020, https://www.fbi.gov/news/speeches/the-threat-posed-by-the-chinese-government-and-the-chinese-communist-party-to-the-economic-and-national-security-of-the-united-states.

6. "The China Initiative: Year-in-Review (2019–20)," Office of Public Affairs, Department of Justice, November 16, 2020, https://www.justice.gov/opa/pr/china-initiative-year-review-2019-20.

7. Christopher Wray, "China's Quest for Economic, Political Domination Threatens America's Security," remarks to the Ronald Reagan Presidential Library and Museum, Simi Valley, CA, January 31, 2022, https://www.fbi.gov/news/speeches/countering-threats-posed-by-the-chinese-government-inside-the-us-wray-013122.

8. David Lynch, "Law Enforcement Struggles to Combat Chinese Spying," *USA Today*, July 23, 2007, http://www.usatoday.com/money/world/2007-07-22-china-spy-1_N.htm.

9. Jay Solomon, "FBI Sees Big Threat from Chinese Spies," *Wall Street Journal*, August 10, 2005, A1.

10. David Lynch, "Law Enforcement Struggles to Combat Chinese Spying," *USA Today*, July 23, 2007, http://www.usatoday.com/money/world/2007-07-22-china-spy-1_N.htm.

11. Christopher Wray, "Threat Posed."

12. Wray, "China's Quest."

13. David Wise, *Tiger Trap: America's Secret Spy War with China* (Boston: Houghton Mifflin Harcourt, 2011), 158.

14. Tom Espiner, "Chinese Hackers US Military Defenses," *Silicon,* November 2005; and Bradley Graham, "Hackers Attack via Chinese Web Sites," *Washington Post*, August 2005.

15. Dawn Onley, Dawn and Patience Wait, "Red Storm Rising: DoD's Efforts to Stave Off Nation-State Cyber Attacks Begin with China," *Government Computer News*, August 2006.

16. See *U.S.-China Economic and Security Review Commission*, 110th Cong., 1st Sess., March 29–30, 2007 (statement of General James E. Cartwright, "China's Military Modernization and Its Impact on the United States and the Asia-Pacific," 90).

17. Shane Harris, "China's Cyber Militia," *National Journal*, May 2008, 31.

18. Brian Grow, Keith Epstein, and Chi-Chu Tschang, "The New E-spionage Threat," *BusinessWeek*, April 21, 2008, 32–41.

19. House of Representatives, *The OPM Data Breach: How the Government Jeopardized Our National Security for More Than a Generation*, 114th Cong., Committee on Oversight and Government Reform, September 7, 2016, https://republicans-oversight.house.gov/wp-content/uploads/2016/09/The-OPM-Data-Breach-How-the-Government-Jeopardized-Our-National-Security-for-More-than-a-Generation.pdf.

20. David Perera and Joseph Marks, "Newly Disclosed Hack Got 'Crown Jewels,'" *Politico*, June 12, 2015, http://www.politico.com/story/2015/06/hackers-federal-employees-security-background-checks-118954.

21. Dan Verton, "Impact of OPM Breach Could Last More Than 40 Years," FedScoop.com, July 12, 2015, http://fedscoop.com/opm-losses-a-40-year--problem-for-intelligence-community.

22. Zolan Kanno-Youngs and David E. Sanger, "U.S. Accuses China of Hacking Microsoft," *New York Times*, July 19, 2021, https://www.nytimes.com/2021/07/19/us/politics/microsoft-hacking-china-biden.html.

23. Peter Mattis, "Intelligence without Chinese Characteristics: A Critical Review of Western Perspectives on Chinese Intelligence," *Studies in Intelligence* (forthcoming). See also Peter Mattis, "Chinese Intelligence Operations Revisited: Toward a New Baseline" (master's thesis, Georgetown University, 2011).

24. Mattis, "Intelligence without Chinese Characteristics"; Mattis, "Chinese Intelligence Operations Revisited."

25. Select Committee on U.S. National Security and Military/Commercial Concerns with the People's Republic of China, *Report of the Select Committee on U.S. National Security and Military/Commercial Concerns with the People's Republic of China* (Washington, DC: Government Printing Office, May 1999), 69–70.

26. Nicholas Eftimiades, *Chinese Intelligence Operations* (Annapolis, MD: Naval Institute Press, 1994), 93–94; James Mann and Ronald Ostrow, "US Ousts Two Chinese Envoys for Espionage," *Los Angeles Times*, December 31, 1987.

27. Kan Zhongguo, "Intelligence Agencies Exist in Great Numbers, Spies Are Present Everywhere; China's Major Intelligence Departments Fully Exposed," *Chien Shao* (Hong Kong, January 1, 2006), 27; *Cox Report*, 65. It is unclear to what extent the forced military divestiture of commercial enterprises affected those companies used by the Chinese military to acquire technology. See Michael Chase and James Mulvenon, "The Decommercialization of China's Ministry of State Security," *International Journal of Intelligence and Counterintelligence* 15, no. 4 (November 2002): 481–95; and James Mulvenon, *Soldiers of Fortune: The Rise and Fall of the Chinese Military-Business Complex, 1978–1998* (Armonk, NY: M. E. Sharpe, 2001).

28. Terence Jeffrey, "Two Silicon Valley Engineers Indicted for Economic Espionage Aiding China," *Human Events*, January 13, 2003, 1, 8.

29. Simon Cooper, "How China Steals U.S. Military Secrets," *Popular Mechanics*, August 2006, http://www.popularmechanics.com/technology/military/3319656.

30. Harris, "China's Cyber Militia."

31. Keith Alexander, "Advance Questions for Lieutenant General Keith Alexander USA, Nominee for Commander, United States Cyber Command," submitted to the Senate Armed Services Committee, April 15, 2010, https://www.washingtonpost.com/wp-srv/politics/documents/questions.pdf.

32. Shaun Waterman, "Chinese Cyberspy Network Pervasive," *Washington Times*, March 30, 2009.

33. Harris, "China's Cyber Militia."

34. Harris.

35. Anna Wilde Matthews, "Anthem: Hacked Database Included 78.8 Million People," *Wall Street Journal*, May 4, 2020, https://www.wsj.com/articles/anthem-hacked-database-included-78-8-million-people-1424807364.

36. "CareFirst Says Cyber Attack Stole Data of 1.1 Million Users," Vox, May 20, 2015, https://www.vox.com/2015/5/20/11562828/carefirst-says-cyber-attack-stole-data-of-1-1-million-users.

37. "Equifax Identifies Additional 2.4 Million Customers Hit by Data Breach," *NBC News*, March 1, 2018, https://www.nbcnews.com/business/business-news/equifax-identifies-addi tional-2-4-million-customers-hit-data-breach-n852226.

38. Gordon Corera, "China Accused of Cyber-Attack on Microsoft Exchange Servers," BBC, July 19, 2021, https://www.bbc.com/news/world-asia-china-57889981.

39. These policies are summarized in *Findings of the Investigation into China's Acts, Policies, and Practices Related to Technology Transfer, Intellectual Property, and Innovation under Section 301 of the Trade Act of 1974*, Office of the US Trade Representative, March 22, 2018, 14–17.

40. *Military Technology Transfer: Threats, Impacts, and Solutions for the Department of Defense, House Armed Services Committee* (June 21, 2018) (Department of Defense joint testimony), https://docs.house.gov/meetings/AS/AS00/20180621/108468/HHRG-115-AS00-Wstate-Bing enK-20180621.pdf.

41. *Committee on the Judiciary, United States Senate, China's Non-Traditional Espionage against the United States: The Threat and Potential Policy Responses* (December 12, 2018) (statement of John C. Demers).

42. "US Charges Five Chinese Military Hackers for Cyber Espionage against US Corpora- tions and a Labor Organization for Commercial Advantage," Office of Public Affairs, Depart- ment of Justice, May 19, 2014, https://www.justice.gov/opa/pr/us-charges-five-chinese-mili tary-hackers-cyber-espionage-against-us-corporations-and-labor.

43. Dan McWhorter, "APT1: Exposing One of China's Cyber Espionage Units," Mandiant, 2014, https://www.mandiant.com/resources/apt1-exposing-one-of-chinas-cyber-espionage -units.

44. White House Office of the Press Secretary, Executive Order: 'Blocking the Property of Certain Persons Engaging in Significant Malicious Cyber-Enabled Activities,' April 1, 2015, https://obamawhitehouse.archives.gov/the-press-office/2015/04/01/executive-order-block ing-property-certain-persons-engaging-significant-m.

45. "Readout of Senior Administration Officials' Meeting with Secretary of the Central Po- litical and Legal Affairs Commission of the Communist Party of China Meng Jianzhu," White House Office of the Press Secretary, September 12, 2015, https://obamawhitehouse.archives .gov/the-press-office/2015/09/12/readout-senior-administration-officials-meeting-secretary -central.

46. Chen Weihua, "China, US Gradually Move to Manage Cyber Dispute," *China Daily*, September 14, 2015, http://usa.chinadaily.com.cn/opinion/2015-09/14/content_21849481 .htm.

47. Matt Spetalnick and Michael Martina, "Obama Announces 'Understanding' with Chi- na's Xi on Cyber Theft but Remains Wary," Reuters, September 25, 2015, https://www.reuters .com/article/us-usa-china-iduskcn0ro2hq20150926.

48. "US Charges Three Chinese Hackers Who Work at Internet Security Firm for Hacking Three Corporations for Commercial Advantage," Office of Public Affairs, Department of Jus- tice, May 19, 2014, https://www.justice.gov/opa/pr/us-charges-three-chinese-hackers-who -work-internet-security-firm-hacking-three-corporations.

49. Matthew Olsen, "Assistant Attorney General Matthew Olsen Delivers Remarks on Countering Nation-State Threats," Washington, DC, February 23, 2022, https://www.justice .gov/opa/speech/assistant-attorney-general-matthew-olsen-delivers-remarks-countering-na tion-state-threats.

50. Eileen Guo, Jess Aloe, and Karen Hao, "The US Crackdown on Chinese Economic Es- pionage Is a Mess. We Have the Data to Show It," *MIT Technology Review,* December 2, 2021,

https://www.technologyreview.com/2021/12/02/1040656/china-initative-us-justice-depart
ment/.

51. "Attorney General Jeff Session's China Initiative Fact Sheet," Department of Justice, November 1, 2018, https://www.justice.gov/opa/speech/file/1107256/download.

52. Ellen Nakashima and David Nakamura, "China Initiative Aims to Stop Economic Espionage. Is Targeting Academics over Grant Fraud 'Overkill'?" *Washington Post*, September 15,
2001, https://www.washingtonpost.com/national-security/china-initiative-questions-dismi
ssals/2021/09/15/530ef936-f482-11eb-9738-8395ec2a44e7_story.html.

53. Two hundred of the talent programs are identified in this report: *Threats to the U.S.
Research Enterprise: China's Talent Recruitment Plans*, Permanent Subcommittee on Investigations, Committee on Homeland Security and Governmental Affairs, United States Senate, November 18, 2019, https://www.hsgac.senate.gov/imo/media/doc/2019-11-18%20PSI%20Staff
%20Report%20-%20China's%20Talent%20Recruitment%20Plans%20Updated2.pdf. For
an excellent database of national programs, see Emily Weinstein, "Chinese Talent Program
Tracker," Georgetown University Center for Security and Emerging Technology, https://china
talenttracker.cset.tech.

54. These contractual issues are detailed at length in Permanent Subcommittee on Investigations, *Threats*.

55. Dan Wang, "China Hawks Don't Understand How Science Advances," *Atlantic*, December 18, 2021, https://www.theatlantic.com/ideas/archive/2021/12/china-initiative-intellectu
al-property-theft/621058/.

56. See William Hannas, James Mulvenon, and Anna Puglisi, *Chinese Industrial Espionage:
Technology Acquisition and Military Modernization* (New York: Routledge, 2013), especially chapters 2, 4 and 7; and William Hannas and Didi Kirsten Tatlow, *China's Quest for Foreign Technology: Beyond Espionage* (New York: Routledge, 2020).

57. Andrew Kim, "Prosecuting Chinese 'Spies': An Empirical Analysis of the Economic Espionage Act" (Washington, DC: Committee of 100, 2017).

58. Kim, "Prosecuting Chinese 'Spies,'" 7.

59. Kim, 12.

60. Kim, 12.

61. Kim, 12.

62. Kim, 6.

63. Kim, 6.

64. Kim, 6.

65. Kim, 6.

66. Kim, 7.

67. Kim, 9.

68. Kim, 9.

69. Kim, 10.

70. Kim, 6.

71. Guo, Aloe, and Hao, "US Crackdown."

72. Mulvenon database of China-related economic espionage cases in the United States,
19982022. Available upon request at mulvenonjames@gmail.com.

73. Mulvenon database.

74. Mulvenon database.

75. Mulvenon database.

76. Mulvenon database.

77. Mulvenon database.

78. Mulvenon database.

79. Mulvenon database.

80. Mulvenon database.

81. Interview with a senior official in the National Science Foundation Office of the Inspector General, November 2021.

82. Guo, Aloe, Hao.

83. Nakashima and Nakamura, "China Initiative."

84. *Threats to the U.S. Research Enterprise: China's Talent Recruitment Plans*, Committee on Homeland Security and Governmental Affairs, Permanent Subcommittee on Investigations, 116th Cong., November 19, 2019.

85. Lewis wrote the same article with the same argument many, many times in many different fora, so this list may not be complete. Margaret Lewis, "Criminalizing China," *Journal of Criminal Law and Criminology* 145 (2020), https://papers.ssrn.com/sol3/papers.cfm?abstract_id=3600580; Margaret K. Lewis, "Time to End the U.S. Justice Department's China Initiative," *Foreign Policy*, July 22, 2021, https://foreignpolicy.com/2021/07/22/china-initiative-espionage-mistrial-hu/; Juan Zheng, "Interview with Professor Margaret Lewis on China Initiative," *U.S.-China Perception Monitor*, July 27, 2020, https://uscnpm.org/2020/07/27/interview-with-professor-margaret-lewis-on-china-initiative/; Margaret K. Lewis, "The U.S. China Initiative: From Review to Reformulation," The China Story, December 14, 2020, https://www.thechinastory.org/the-u-s-china-initiative-from-review-to-reformulation/; Margaret Lewis, "The U.S. Department of Justice's China Initiative," *National Committee on U.S-China Relations*, June 9, 2020, https://soundcloud.com/ncuscr/us-doj-china-initiative; Margaret K. Lewis, appearing on National Committee on US-China Relations podcast on "Higher Education and U.S.-China Relations," May 21, 2021, https://www.ncuscr.org/event/higher-education-us-china-relations/; Margaret K. Lewis, "The DOJ' China Initiative," appearing on the USC U.S.-China Institute's webinar, June 12, 2020, https://www.youtube.com/watch?v=ZnKu9ptS6JQ; Margaret K. Lewis, discussion of ethnic profiling in the DOJ's China Initiative, appearing on the *SupChina* "Sinica" podcast, May 13, 2021, https://supchina.com/podcast/margaret-lewis-on-ethnic-profiling-in-the-dojs-china-initiative/.

86. Olsen, "Countering Nation-State Threats."

87. Ali Watkins, "China Grabbed American as Spy Wars Flare," *Politico*, October 11, 2017, https://www.politico.com/story/2017/10/11/china-spy-games-espionage-243644.

88. Edward Wong and Julian E. Barnes, "U.S. Secretly Expelled Chinese Officials Suspected of Spying after Breach of Military Base," *New York Times*, December 15, 2019, https://www.nytimes.com/2019/12/15/world/asia/us-china-spies.html.

89. Philip Shenon, "2 Chinese Depart in Espionage Case," *New York Times*, December 31, 1987, https://www.nytimes.com/1987/12/31/world/2-chinese-depart-in-espionage-case.html.

90. "Briefing with Senior U.S. Government Officials on the Closure of the Chinese Consulate in Houston, Texas," Department of State, July 24, 2020, https://2017-2021.state.gov/briefing-with-senior-u-s-government-officials-on-the-closure-of-the-chinese-consulate-in-houston-texas/index.html.

91. Ken Moritsugu and Matthew Lee, "US Orders China to Close Its Consulate in Houston," Associated Press, July 22, 2020.

92. Kate O'Keeffe, Aruna Viswanatha, and Chun Han Wong, "U.S. Orders China to Close Houston Consulate," *Wall Street Journal*, July 22, 2020.

93. O'Keeffe, Viswanatha, and Wong, "U.S. Orders China."

94. Department of State, "Closure of the Chinese Consulate."

95. Department of State.

96. O'Keeffe, Viswanatha, and Wong, "U.S. Orders China."

97. O'Keeffe, Viswanatha, and Wong.

98. "American Businessman Who Ran Houston-Based Subsidiary of Chinese Company Sentenced to Prison for Theft of Trade Secrets," US Attorney's Office, District of Columbia, Department of Justice, February 11, 2020, https://www.justice.gov/usao-dc/pr/american-busi nessman-who-ran-houston-based-subsidiary-chinese-company-sentenced-prison.

99. Department of State, "Closure of the Chinese Consulate."

100. Department of State.

101. For mainstream media accounts of these unconfirmed, lurid tales, see Zach Dorfman, "Botched CIA Communications System Helped Blow Cover of Chinese Agents," *Foreign Policy*, August 15, 2018, https://foreignpolicy.com/2018/08/15/botched-cia-communications-sys tem-helped-blow-cover-chinese-agents-intelligence/; Peter Mattis and Matthew Brazil, *Chinese Communist Espionage: An Intelligence Primer* (Naval Institute Press, 2019); and Mark Mazzetti et al., "Killing C.I.A. Informants, China Crippled U.S. Spying Operations," *New York Times*, May 20, 2017, https://www.nytimes.com/2017/05/20/world/asia/china-cia-spies-espi onage.html.

102. A recent example was the intentional luring and then Belgian extradition of Ministry of State Security Jiangsu State Security Department officer Yanjun Xu to trial in the United States. See "Jury Convicts Chinese Intelligence Officer of Espionage Crimes, Attempting to Steal Trade Secrets," Office of Public Affairs, Department of Justice, November 5, 2021, https:// www.justice.gov/opa/pr/jury-convicts-chinese-intelligence-officer-espionage-crimes-at tempting-steal-trade-secrets.

PART IV

11

China's Rise as a Technology Power and US-China Technology Competition: Assessing Beijing's Response

Paul Triolo

Technology competition between the world's two leading economic powers is now central to the bilateral relationship and a major driver of bilateral competition. A new technology "cold war" has been unfolding for the past five years, and just as in the case of the era of US-Soviet competition, technology competition and technology restrictions are central to the overall security competition. Going forward, as the terms of the overall strategic competition change under a Biden administration, the longer-term parameters of the struggle over the technologies of the future are also coming into clearer focus.

For its part, Beijing will accelerate its goal of achieving some level of technology self-reliance, this time with the private sector fully in tow following a sustained period of regulatory rectification and planning documents squarely placing priority on the "hard" and "core" technologies at stake in the intense technology competition central to the relationship. Beijing's competing vision of the future of the Internet, under Xi's concept of "making China into a cyber superpower," will continue to push the concept of data sovereignty, including state control of information flows, a strong preference for data localization, and further restriction of foreign company presence in critical information infrastructure. This will mean even more intense competition to dominate the technologies of the future, some of which are already here, such as artificial intelligence (AI), quantum computing, biotechnology, fintech, and the architecture over which they will operate, advanced mobile telecommunications. For both Beijing and Washington, it is game on in the technology arena. On the side of the United States and like-minded allies, there is an emerging sense that a new version of the Soviet-era Coordinating Committee for Multilateral Export Controls (COCOM) technology controls may now be needed to address the challenge of a rising China in the military and economic domains.

This chapter will examine the trajectory of the rise of China's technology sector from innovation laggard to serious challenger over the last decade and will explain how information and communications technology (ICT) has become the focal point of strategic competition between the United States and China. It will challenge the conventional wisdom both on how this happened and why it happened so fast. Finally, it will trace how China's technology rise has become the single most important point of tension in the bilateral relationship, from forced technology transfer to intellectual property (IP) theft to industrial subsidies to market access.

Beijing has long viewed achieving technology parity with the West as critical to China's modernization and the survival of the Chinese Communist Party (CCP). In the digital age this has become an even higher priority as the past two decades have seen an erosion of CCP control over information, and the vulnerability of connected systems pose new and existential threats to the party—which it has been so far successful in navigating. This has translated into new policies for fostering globally competitive technology companies, but the success of Chinese tech companies has resulted primarily in raising fears in the United States in particular that they will ultimately do Beijing's bidding and represent a growing national security threat to the United States and like-minded allies around the globe.

Finally, the chapter will examine the future trajectory of US-China technology competition. The "technology cold war" paradigm suggests that we are headed toward a bifurcated technology stack. That means China, Russia, and its authoritarian partners and countries along the Belt and Road pursuing one technology development track while the US and like-minded Western democracies gradually remove most or all Chinese-origin technology from their critical infrastructure and supply chains. Under this messy and complicated scenario, Chinese digital technology companies, which have succeeded and, for the most part, embraced global value chains, will now be faced with the prospect that US policymakers—driven by Western perceptions of both Beijing's ability and willingness to order them to do malicious things and Beijing's unwillingness to adhere to global best practices in areas such as data governance—will complicate these Chinese firms' ability to expand and become global players, forcing them more under the influence of the party/state and into supporting the party/state development priorities.

China's Rise as an Information Technology Power: The Struggle for Control of Core Technologies

Since the 1960s divorce from the Soviet Union, Beijing has long viewed reducing the heavy reliance of Chinese firms on key technologies available from strategic rivals, while achieving some level of parity with the West, as critical to China's modernization and the survival of the party and as a matter of prestige for Chinese science and innovation capacity. During the 1950s and 1960s, the focus of China's technology policy centered on nuclear weapons and intercontinental ballistic missiles—first with Russian assistance, then after the Sino-Soviet split, using its own research and development (R&D) resources. China was able to rapidly master all the technologies required for nuclear weapons and their delivery, successfully detonating its first fission device in late 1964, a successful nuclear-capable medium-range missile launch in late 1966, and a hydrogen fusion device test in the summer of 1967. Beijing was able to successfully mobilize a Soviet-style science and technology (S&T) system in this endeavor, and once the decision had been made at the top, the system responded to the challenge.[1]

The role of the military in this period was crucial, and the military continued to play a major role in technology programs going forward, from indigenous innovation, to large numbered programs such as 863 and 973, to long-term S&T programs and megaprojects, which included both civilian window (*minkou* 民口) and military window (*junkou* 军口) projects, the latter usually classified or with little public acknowledgment outside China's S&T community. Under this traditional S&T development system, major roles were played by state-backed research organizations, such as the Chinese Academy of Sciences (CAS) and its many subordinate research institutes, and military R&D was a major focus of technology developed in China, centered in large complexes mostly in the hinterland far from the border of the former Soviet Union—places like massive Mianyang north of Chengdu in Sichuan province, the Los Alamos of China.

In the digital/information age, however, China has confronted a new challenge, one not ideally suited to the type of massive system mobilization of the planned economy and state-controlled R&D system. The Chinese leadership realized even in the early stage of the information age, during the 1980s and 1990s, when telephone technology was developing, that it would need to foster domestic champions to avoid dependence on Western companies and potentially hostile governments. During the 1990s, after depending on US and European suppliers of stored program-controlled switches, China's leading industrial ministries, including the Ministry of Posts and Telecommunications (MPT), helped to foster the rise of alternative vendors by supporting emerging companies including Huawei and Zhongxing Telecommunications. It also fostered companies in other key information technology sectors, such as fiber optic cables, in some cases by spinning off government research arms into state-owned companies. By the time of the mobile telecommunications age and the Internet, these companies were already able to begin to compete domestically, and soon internationally, with their giant Western counterparts like AT&T, Siemens, and Alcatel.[2]

As it became clear that the Internet and mobile devices would carry vast quantities of information, fostering domestic players up and down the technology stack became an even higher priority for the planners in Beijing. The past two decades have seen a major reduction in the party's ability to control information flows; as mobile devices proliferated, a tech-savvy population figured workarounds to some control. Hence the conclusion that the vulnerability of connected systems poses new and existential threats to the party—threats that it has been so far successful in navigating. By the early 2000s, this had translated into a new set of policies and long-term strategies designed to foster globally competitive technology companies, but the ambitious nature of the approach and its heavy state backing also began raising concerns in Western countries about the trajectory of China's technology development and the role of the state in fostering alternatives to Western suppliers, skewing the playing field, restricting market access.

Indigenous Innovation and the Medium- and Long-Term S&T Plan

China's state-directed technology policies began to change as economic reforms reduced the role of the state in key nonmilitary sectors, including information and communications technology, in the early 2000s. While ICT goals were addressed to some degree in the annual Five-Year Plan process, over time other vehicles were developed to help drive more rapid indigenous capabilities in key areas where there was increasing overlap between military and civilian systems and priorities. At the same time, Beijing was freeing up its formerly captive defense industry to allow it to spin off ostensibly civilian companies in key technology areas where the defense industry had strong R&D capabilities, including telecommunications, semiconductors, and satellite systems.

Three critical developments related to China's evolving industrial policy for the digital age during this period would set the stage for the technology confrontation that began to accelerate in the Xi Jinping era. These initiatives came with differing resource levels and strategies.

Indigenous or Independent Innovation (自主创新)

The broad outlines of what became known as the indigenous innovation initiative, along with the standard set of slogans, were officially rolled out in 2006. It would take several years before the full impact of the initiative became clear to Western observers. The indigenous innovation theme over time came to be injected into supporting regulations that galvanized Chinese tech bureaucracy, ramped up government spending on S&T, and launched programs that led to the development of China's first largely indigenously developed passenger aircraft, satellite positioning system, and semiconductors as well as Chinese companies' push to participate in global standards-setting bodies based on having developed some level of independent intellectual property rights.[3] The zeitgeist of indigenous innovation underlies all subsequent major policy initiatives under President Hu Jintao and President Xi Jinping, of which there are many, such as Made in China 2025 and Xi's new industrial policies, which rolled out in 2020. The results of indigenous innovation for China's technological development are mixed, however.[4]

Medium and Long-Term Plan for S&T (MLP)

The major blueprint for implementing indigenous innovation was the sprawling Medium- and Long-Term Plan for the Development of Science and Technology (2006–20), or MLP.[5] A document distinctly different from traditional Five-Year Plans, the MLP was the first nationally promulgated document that expressed lofty aspirational goals and specific targets for China's technology sector, exhorting and propelling it to take a leading role on the world stage. Critically, the plan came with a series of more than a dozen "megaprojects," designed to turn S&T success into practical commercial applications, a major problem with previous efforts such as the 863 Program. The plan hit on 2020 as a target date by which China would become a technology powerhouse, which it has achieved to some degree in some areas driven by the megaprojects, such as the BeiDou satellite positioning system, plus other sectors such as high-speed rail. Importantly, the plan called for China to become a global leader by 2050. Other follow-on plans would call for similar aspirations, including ominous-sounding terms such as achieving "dominance" in some sectors by key dates. The growing number of these target dates, and, importantly, the corollary that there seemed to be government-driven metrics for achieving the aspirational goals, have been huge contributors to Western policymaker perceptions about China's intentions, regardless of how close Chinese companies and particular sectors are to achieving anything like the trumpeted goals, let alone dominance. The rhetoric in the case of the MLP, broadly speaking, has been well ahead of the reality on the ground.

Several aspects of both indigenous innovation and the MLP, however, have contributed to another by now-familiar narrative. The suspicion of foreign intentions and the goal to transform foreign technology into something that could be called "Chinese" runs through the myriad documents generated by these initiatives. These memes quickly gave rise to another counter-meme among Western companies and governments, that China was basically intent on using the theft of intellectual property, or forced technology transfer, to increase its ability to develop cutting-edge technology that could compete with and ultimately displace Western versions. Hence these programs fairly quickly gave rise to a meme currently running rampant on China, that Beijing's ultimate strategy is "techno-nationalism," along with corollaries such as "techno-authoritarianism."[6]

But the MLP and its ambitious core goals did not initially generate much international concern. Indigenous innovation, however, did, particularly as the language around it began to creep into areas such as government procurement tenders, particularly following the issuance of a State Council circular on accreditation of indigenous innovation products in 2009, followed by the adoption of a range of provincial guidelines and catalogs at the local government level, as the bureaucracy responded to signals from the center to try and use more products with more local content.[7] In response, the US International Trade Commission kicked off a Section 332 investigation of indigenous innovation,[8] including intellectual property protection, a dynamic that would be repeated during the later Section 301 investigation into what the US Trade Representative viewed as China's unfair trade practices; that investigation was much broader but focused on similar issues.

In a dynamic that would play out again nearly a decade later, under a much more toxic climate in Washington around bilateral relations, in 2011 Beijing promised to eliminate all indigenous innovation product catalogs at the May 2011 US-China Strategic and Economic Dialogue (S&ED). But this response, as well as the fact that many provincial and municipal governments did not drop the local catalogs of approved products meeting the criteria for indigenous innovation products, just added to what would become a long list of broken promises that would drive a more forceful response to the follow-on versions of indigenous innovation under Xi Jinping, as the concept of "secure and controllable" gained traction in the bureaucracy. Secure and controllable is a concept that developed out of concerns about foreign control or espionage linked to ICT supply chains as well as specific events like the 2013 Snowden revelations.[9]

Two other major themes that would prove to be crucial to the eventual US and broader Western backlash to China's rise as a technology power come from this era. One is the growing use of Chinese language around "core technology" and Beijing's emphasis on things like critical infrastructure. "Core technology" in Chinese parlance can be widely interpreted as anything critical to developing capabilities in a particular sector, but it has focused in the ICT sector, primarily around software and hardware, particularly semiconductors, where China has been and continues to be heavily dependent on Western suppliers.

The other key policy direction coming out of the MLP in particular was an increasing emphasis on the concept of military civilian integration/fusion (军民结合). MCF is simply the concept that the civilian sector and its technology advances should be available to the military as it modernizes. Chinese sources tend to claim that this concept is derived from the United States, which moved quickly from a more captive defense industrial sector to procurement based on fostering a thriving commercial sector in areas such as aviation, semiconductors, and advanced materials. China's military had also relied for a prolonged period on a captive and sprawling defense industrial base, in part an inheritance of the Soviet model and one whose ability to produce cutting-edge equipment began to wane in the 1990s, particularly as the digital age dawned.[10] The first stage of MCF was to allow defense industrial research institutes to spin off commercial arms, generate revenue, and be able to invest more in R&D. Over time, the People's Liberation Army (PLA) turned increasingly to the growing number of private sector companies that were developing advanced communications gear for the civilian sector—for example, Huawei and ZTE. Indigenous innovation and the replacement of foreign, particularly US, telecommunications equipment took place rapidly within China's military after 2000, as Chinese firms became more capable.

But MCF at its core is very different from the "spin on/off" concepts in the US defense industrial base. Over time, the concept has evolved from a more rhetorical exhortation for cooperation and integration into a much more coordinated process between civilian and military entities, explicitly fostered and encouraged by government ministries, and given new life with the establishment in 2017 of a high-level commission headed by Xi.[11] This event was key to the renewed US focus on the concept and its elevation under the Trump administration to one of the central points of focus for new export control measures and other executive actions against Chinese firms.[12]

The military-developed BeiDou system of satellites was then over time allowed to be used by civilian companies, providing a viable global alternative to both GPS and the Russian GLONASS system and eventually in later iterations becoming a big part of initiatives such as the Belt and Road Initiative (BRI) and its digital counterpart, the Digital Silk Road (DSR). Here, an MCF-related effort was successful in displacing a Western system, and this became part of the narrative that Beijing would use indigenous innovation as part of a long-term strategy to displace Western technology with technology with "Chinese characteristics." It also marked a major milestone in the separation of the two countries' technological foundations.[13]

The reality, of course, was that for the underlying hardware and software for virtually all success that China claimed for the MLP megaprojects or indigenous innovation, the guts of these systems still relied heavily on US semiconductors, enterprise operating systems, and database software. The core technology remained "in others' hands," as official Chinese documents frequently lamented.

The Xi Jinping Era: Large National Technology-Centered Programs and the Expansion of China's Global Digital Footprint

By the time Xi Jinping came to power in 2012, cyberspace, in all its manifestations, had become a priority for Beijing and the party, and that meant reasserting control over the digital domain. Xi clearly understood the importance of both controlling and securing cyberspace for the future of the regime and the primacy of the party and for driving economic growth in the expanding digital economy. Even as Xi set about regaining control of the online media, he appeared to firmly grasp that the party and government had to foster conditions so that Chinese companies could be in a position to both build the critical parts of cyberspace within China and become globally competitive. This would put China in a position to set international standards in the technology space and have a say in the governance of the Internet and other technology domains.

Structural Reorganization to Meet Challenges of the Digital Domain

Xi set about this in a methodical manner. One of his most important initiatives was to reorganize China's governmental structure around both cyberspace and the digital economy, or informatization. In early 2014 he announced the establishment of a Central Leading Group for Cybersecurity and Informatization, a superministerial body designed to oversee policy development for both emerging issues around the security of networks and, critically, the development of the digital economy and its technology stack.[14] The office of the Leading Group would become the Cyberspace Administration of China (CAC), a hybrid state and party organization that has played a critical role in China's technology development. The CAC was behind the 2017 Cybersecurity Law, key elements of which have caused major concern within the Office of the US Trade Representative (USTR) and the US government around critical issues such as sharing source code, disclosing other IP, and data governance, data localization, and data privacy.[15] The Leading Group was transformed in 2018 into the Central Commission for Cybersecurity and Informatization (CCCI), giving it more permanence within the system and the ability to continue to oversee and attempt to resolve the many bureaucratic rivalries that had plagued the system since the attempt to centralize control around cyber and ICT issues began in 2014.[16]

In addition, Xi embarked on a major effort to promote his vision of cyberspace and the digital economy and educate the senior leadership on key technology developments around which China and the party would need to be constantly vigilant and aware. This included several pillars. The first was the establishment of an annual conclave, the World Internet Conference (WIC), in the small town of Wuzhen east of Shanghai, to serve as an alternate platform for discussing Xi's evolving vision of cyberspace, and specifically of Internet and data sovereignty.[17] Another was Xi's annual detailed policy speeches around the digital economy and security, delivered at the Cybersecurity and Informatization Work Conference each April. One of the most important of Xi's speeches was the April 19 speech given in 2016.[18] In the speech, Xi outlined his view of the importance of core technology, highlighting the greatest hidden danger for the party, that this technology was controlled by others. Xi noted, "[If] the 'vital gate' of the supply chain is grasped in the hands of others, this can be compared to building a house on another person's foundation, however large or beautiful it is, it might not stand the wind or the rain, or might even collapse at the first blow."[19]

Xi Perfects the Language Defining How the Party Will Drive the Digital Age in China

Key to Xi's thinking on technology broadly, and the key role he believes the digital age will play in maintaining the party's leading role, is his concept of "building China into a cyber superpower" (网络强国). The four-character meme is a pithy formulation in Chinese that can be translated as "building China into a national power in cyberspace," but with an additional critical corollary, the implication that this should make China "on par with the United States" in cyberspace. With this critical strategic concept attached to it, the phrase ties together a series of concepts and initiatives that Xi has pushed in major speeches and the Chinese government has moved to enact, all of which have contributed and will continue to contribute to the US-China technology conflict.

By 2018, Xi's annual speeches at the Cybersecurity and Informatization work conferences had become even clearer about the task China faced. In 2018, Xi updated his guidance and goals for industrial policy, cybersecurity, and the sociopolitical aspects of the Internet, presenting his view that technology is an "important instrument of the state." In the 2017–18 time frame, Xi also both stepped up visits to high-tech facilities and began to hold more frequent politburo "study sessions" focused on key technology domains and how China's strategy of reducing foreign dependence was faring.

And in yet another development that showed how critical China's technological trajectory had become for the general secretary and the party, Xi launched politburo study sessions, likely starting in 2017, that focused on key technology issues, tackling semiconductors, artificial intelligence (AI), and blockchain, and likely other topics too. The fora provided an opportunity for leading Chinese technology advisers, senior academicians, and even technology company leaders to explain critical but complicated technology developments to the politburo.

Even as Xi remade the bureaucracy to be better positioned to lead China into the digital age and increase Beijing's influence, he also launched three critical national programs that would become key touchpoints for US concern over China's technology rise, starting late in the Obama administration and reaching a fever pitch under the Trump administration.

The National IC Investment Fund

The so-called Mother Fund, announced in June 2014, was both an acknowledgment that previous approaches to reducing China's dependence on semiconductors had failed and a huge and long-term commitment involving substantial funding from many sources to turning that around within a foreseeable time frame.[20] The new fund was led by former government officials, primarily from the Ministry of Industry and Information Technology (MIIT), and used funds from Chinese state-owned enterprises (SOEs) and state banks. To a growing number of Western observers, the fund was a deliberate attempt to sidestep the prohibition on state subsidies under China's World Trade Organization (WTO) commitments. It also included the novel use of some private investment managers to oversee where the fund would prioritize its financial support. Early attempts in 2015–16 by the fund to finance Chinese semiconductor acquisitions of US firms, including memory leader Micron, immediately ran into US government and industry concerns, sparking a regulatory reaction that refocused attention on the US foreign investment review process and the legal basis undergirding the Committee on Foreign Investment in the US (CFIUS).

Late in the Obama administration, the fund would also be the target of former commerce secretary Penny Pritzker's accusatory comment that the National IC Investment Fund represented nothing less than an attempt by China to "appropriate the global semiconductor supply chain."[21] Several major semiconductor company acquisitions would be shot down by CFIUS over the next several years, including a proposed deal for a fund-backed company to buy a European semiconductor firm. By the time the Trump administration took office in 2017, then, the writing was on the wall that no Chinese company would be able to buy or invest in a US semiconductor company. But semiconductors would become even more important in the US-China strategy struggle over technology as the Trump and Biden administration efforts to confront China gained steam.

Made in China 2025 (MIC2025)

Perhaps no Xi Jinping technology program, though, has had greater impact on the strategic competition between the United States and China than MIC2025. The program symbolizes and encapsulates both Beijing's long-term aspirations in the technology arena and all the concerns over China's rise as a technology power and how the West can or should confront it.

The MIC2025 program quickly became the centerpiece of Xi's new strategy to push forward indigenous innovation and make China a player across all the sectors of key traditional and emerging technology sectors. In some sense, it replaced the MLP as the focal point of China's industrial policies and the work of its industrial ministries. At its core, the MIC2025 program is a ten-year, comprehensive blueprint aimed at transforming the country into an advanced manufacturing leader. The plan, endorsed by Premier Li Keqiang and released in 2015, was the first action plan focusing on the broad promotion of technology-driven manufacturing—defined as including the most advanced sectors of the economy. The initiative covers 2016–25 and includes targets for 2020 and 2025, such as broadly raising domestic content in targeted sectors to 50 percent (2020) and 70 percent (2025). It is part of a broader three-stage plan designed to make China a leading manufacturing power globally by 2049, the centennial anniversary of the founding of the People's Republic of China and a key milestone for government officials. MIC2025 centers on reducing China's reliance of foreign companies for critical components (read "core technology") and also high-cost capital equipment, such as the array of complex systems used in semiconductor manufacturing.

Significantly, however, unlike other countries' manufacturing plans, such as Germany's Industry 4.0, MIC2025 appeared to provide preferential access to capital primarily to domestic firms to promote their indigenous R&D capabilities, support their ability to acquire technologies abroad, and enhance their overall competitiveness.[22] In concert with the Thirteenth Five-Year Plan, the Next-Generation Artificial Intelligence Development Plan, the Internet Plus Action Plan, and other state-led development plans, MIC2025 constituted a broader strategy to use state resources to alter and create comparative advantage in these sectors on a global scale. In this sense, MIC2025 arguably represented China's most far-reaching industrial policy on a continuum of such policies to develop not only national champions but global champions that could dominate the global market.[23] Hence it was not surprising that by the time the Trump administration had launched a major trade investigation into China's practices, MIC2025 was set to become the target of a broad US effort to target China's industrial policies and technology transfer approaches.[24] As Beijing realized the importance of the MIC2025 brand in generating a strong US response via trade and export control measures, the term was widely dropped from media stories about industrial policy starting in 2019.

The Belt and Road Initiative and the Digital Silk Road

Xi's BRI, launched in 2015, has become a key and central piece of China's strategic competition with the United States, with increasing focus on the technology domain. While initially the principal thrust of BRI projects financed by

Chinese state banks and the Asian Infrastructure Investment Bank (AIIB) was directed at large energy and transportation projects, by 2019 the digital portion of the BRI was beginning to dominate discussions around China's intentions for the BRI. Xi had brought the ICT sector to the forefront of economic growth in his work report to the Nineteenth Party Congress in 2017. In addition, by this time, the president's flagship foreign policy initiative, the BRI, had been enshrined in the Communist Party constitution. Two major components of the BRI—the Silk Road Economic Belt, from Central Asia to Europe, and the Maritime Silk Road, stretching from Southeast Asia to Africa and Europe—were well known to the West and beginning to generate concern around issues such as the increasing debt load taken on by some BRI countries.[25] But a third part of the initiative, the DSR, had received less attention. Yet this component would have an equal if not more significant impact for governments, as well as companies operating in countries along the BRI, than infrastructure projects such as ports, rail, and pipelines.

As it looks ahead at funding and advancing BRI projects, Beijing has come to increasingly believe that its firms have an advantage, particularly in areas such as next-generation infrastructure, including fifth-generation (5G) mobile and cloud services. Here, "Team China," including Huawei, ZTE, and over the top (OTT) players such as payment giants Alibaba and Tencent provide a major advantage but have also generated additional concern over growing Chinese company dominance in some areas, particularly 5G.[26] States along the BRI will be under pressure to include China's digital economy companies as partners in leading infrastructure projects that require regional and global connectivity—including for building new data centers, operating cloud services, and assisting with smart finance, smart customs, smart taxation, smart cities, and other ICT solutions.

Long-Term Strategies for Artificial Quantum Computing

A key addition to the strong technology and global ambitions brew that Xi was stirring were major new initiatives in fields traditionally dominated by the United States. The August 2017 release of the National AI Development Plan (AIDP), development for which started in the waning days of the Obama administration, was typical of China's new and seemingly unbridled tech ambitions and Xi's increasing emphasis on the need for China to play a leading role in developing key technologies and the regulatory systems that would form around them. The AIDP set off more alarm bells within the Beltway, as US officials realized that China had a plan for AI, even working to achieve "dominance" by 2030, as laid out in the text.[27]

Other major initiatives from Beijing included large funding increases for quantum computing and, broadly, quantum information sciences (QIS), a sector which Chinese officials believe they can compete in and have been investing in for more than a decade. A major step forward in the quantum field for China was the establishment of a $10 billion quantum research center launched in Hefei in late 2017 and due for completion in 2022. As the US-China technology rivalry has intensified, in addition to AI and semiconductors, Xi has also added quantum to the list of technologies where he sees China having some advantages—Xi called out China's quantum successes in a January 2018 address.[28]

As the Trump era dawned, Xi Jinping's ambitious and well-funded industrial policies and technology programs, coupled with his crackdown on dissent and the growing realization that he was taking China away from the opening and reform policies of his predecessors, had set the stage for a major strategic showdown with the United States. While the harder line view of Xi and China would expand into virtually every aspect of the relationship, the clash over technology dominance, supply chains, investments, and the use of advanced technologies would constitute the hallmark of US-China strategic competition as the new administration grappled with the challenge of China's technology rise.

Beijing Shifts to a Different Approach: The Race for Self-Reliance

By the time the Trump administration took office in 2017, the stage was already being set for a much broader technology confrontation between the two peer competitors, one that Beijing does not appear to have fully anticipated and prepared for. The technology rivalry centered on four major issues:

Trade-Related Technology Issues Centered on the Primary Concerns of the USTR Section 301 Investigation, Launched in August of 2017

The investigation,[29] ordered by President Trump, reflected a growing consensus in US policy circles and the business community that China had not lived up to its obligations under its accession to the World Trade Organization, and previous US efforts to engage Beijing about addressing US concerns had not been backed with workable enforcement mechanisms. These included subsidies, primarily focused on Made in China 2025; market access, including for technology and financial services companies; forced technology transfer; and cybertheft of intellectual property. The full report from the USTR, issued in March 2018,[30] provided detailed descriptions of China's practices in all these areas and would become the defining framework for the subsequent trade negotiations that culminated in a Phase One deal in January 2020.

Beijing, for its part, was clearly not ready to allow foreign companies free rein in sensitive areas such as cloud services, which includes content delivery and support for critical infrastructure companies, clearly touching on national security. With Washington increasingly shutting down Chinese technology company access to the US market and to US technology, Beijing was in no mood to make concessions in the digital realm.[31]

Supply Chain Dependence

In 2019 China hawks, centered at the Pentagon and White House, began to take new policy steps to reduce the dependence of both the Pentagon and US critical infrastructure suppliers on China. The May 2019 ICT supply chain executive order issued by President Trump was designed to provide a way for the US government enforce a ban on Huawei and ZTE gear in US networks and to give an interagency group the ability to nix any deal that involved Chinese-origin gear going into critical infrastructure networks.[32] The evolving White House policy on supply chains centered on China was to deleverage and reduce what some officials called a "hyperdependence" on China. There was no agreement, however, on what the right level of dependence should be and how much deleveraging would cost industry and consumers.

The Struggle for the Technologies of the Future, and Also Technologies of the Present

An overriding theme of US-China strategic competition by mid-2020 was an increasingly zero-sum view from Washington that the US and China were locked in a long-term competition around advanced technologies. A critical corollary of this argument was that Beijing had already shown it was willing to use these technologies, or planned to use them, in ways that Western democracies would find objectionable. Thus, the US-China tech competition at its root had become a struggle over values and how the two systems would not only compete for—and more importantly, use advanced technologies for—economic competition but also struggle for military dominance in Asia generally, now in other areas such as along BRI countries.

From Beijing's perspective, Huawei is the quintessential national champion, having risen from nowhere to compete with all comers globally at the cutting edge of telecommunications. At the same time, Huawei is also China's leading semiconductor firm, whose chip design arm HiSilicon can design chips on par with Western leaders like Apple, Qualcomm, Broadcom, and Samsung. Beijing views Huawei as key to its plans to push China's carriers to roll out 5G networks rapidly and allow Chinese firms to dominate the development of applications on top of those advanced networks. Beijing has been pushing in this direction since at least 2014, with a whole-of-government approach to 5G.[33]

China's emphasis on its military civilian fusion/integration initiative, driven from the top by Xi Jinping's frequent pronouncements on the need for China's PLA to work more closely with China's private sector tech companies to improve its military capabilities, had given China hawks in the Trump administration a hook for arguing for new measures; language on military civilian fusion was now routinely included in Department of Commerce export control–related language and in congressional bills proposing new limitations on Chinese tech companies.[34] The stage was set for the next stage of US-China strategic competition in the technology domain.

Beijing's Response to US Pressure: A New Approach to Industrial Policy

As the US-China tech cold war has crescendoed from mid-2019 to mid-2022, Beijing has faced two tough choices, both of which will determine the future direction of US-China tech competition. First, how should China react to the wave of US actions targeting virtually all of its leading technology companies? Second, how should China adjust internal policies to continue to assist its private sector firms in developing capabilities to further reduce their dependence on US technologies increasingly being held hostage by Washington?

The problem of how to react to US technology policy has been a complicated one for Beijing and Chinese industrial ministries. Beijing has been very disciplined in the face of action after action targeting its national champions—only the decision to run out the clock on the 2018 Qualcomm-NXP merger approval appears to have been designed as a retaliatory move. Chinese antitrust officials have instead continued to approach large mergers and acquisitions involving technology companies, attempting to avoid the charge of politicizing these types of decisions.[35]

In terms of its broader internal response, Beijing and key players such as the big four ministries—MIIT, the National Development and Reform Commission (NDRC), the Ministry of Finance (MOF), and the Ministry of Science and Technology (MOST)—began to fall back on a number of well-worn strategies, along with some new ones. Beijing's evolving industrial policy 2.0 for the digital age, where access to US technology and financial markets are likely to continue to contract, will include the following key elements.

Leveraging Domestic and Regional Capital by Encouraging and Facilitating Tech Company Listings in Hong Kong and on the New Shanghai High-Tech Market (STAR)

The new STAR Market, launched with unusual swiftness in the summer of 2019 (after an endorsement from Xi himself),[36] will help Beijing accomplish three of its strategic priorities. First, it will provide stable, long-term funding for Chinese tech unicorns, which are not well served by the traditional financial system. Second, it will place China's next generation of innovative firms under the control of domestic regulators instead of that of foreign regulators and shareholders—an urgent concern for Beijing amid rising US-China geopolitical tensions. This is also a reaction to the potential for major Chinese technology companies to be delisted from US exchanges as a result of long-standing US financial regulator concerns that Beijing refuses to allow the firms to be audited by an independent body, the Public Company Accounting Oversight Board (PCAOB).[37] Third, Chinese, rather than foreign, investors will obtain the lion's share of the potential wealth generated by China's future national champions. In addition, as the United States began to move in mid-2020 to potentially delist leading Chinese tech firms from US stock exchanges, many of these firms were looking at or had already pursued secondary listings in Hong Kong, including Alibaba, Tencent, JD, and Baidu.[38]

Revamping Government-Financed Technology Development Programs

The National IC Fund was given a second major injection in October 2019.[39] This second state-backed fund for semiconductors raised $29 billion from twenty-seven stakeholders including state-owned enterprises, local governments, and the Ministry of Finance. The second fund marked a notable upgrade from the original $21 billion in registered capital raised for its predecessor in 2014, the National IC Investment Fund, which had invested in twenty-three semiconductor companies to date. With local integrated circuit (IC) funds totaling another $24 billion for the first fund and an estimated $100 billion available via bank loans, Beijing continued to make huge sums of capital available to the sector, destined to become the most significant in the US-China technology competition.

At the National People's Congress (NPC) in May 2020, postponed because of the pandemic, a major new investment package for "new infrastructure" was rolled out. The NDRC had announced plans in March 2020 to boost investment in new infrastructure, including smart cities and 5G networks. Government efforts would focus on spurring private investment and accelerating the rollout of next-generation networks. The Ministry of Finance noted that $260 billion of local government bonds, including $182 billion of special bonds, had been allocated for infrastructure projects in 2020.

The focus on digital infrastructure—increasingly referred to clearly as "new infrastructure" in government and party statements—will occur in a sector that is more market-driven than many traditional Chinese industries. Beijing is increasing investment in digital infrastructure amid the economic downturn, driven by US-China tech tensions and the pandemic.

But in the wake of the major boost to China hawks and decouplers provided by the pandemic and Beijing's handling of the crisis, it increasingly appears that the future trajectory of US-China strategic technology competition will center on several major issues: the role of semiconductors and Taiwan (and how the island will continue to serve as a key piece of both "red" and "blue" technology supply chains) and how Beijing plans to leverage the Digital Silk Road portion of the BRI to develop markets for its technology companies and build a separate technology domain dominated by Team China.

Taiwan as Pivotal to US-China Strategic Clash, Tech Competition Goes Regional . . .

Several strategic trends are at work here. First, elements of the US government concerned about the long-term security of supply chains for advanced semiconductors used in military and sensitive civilian applications have stepped up efforts to ensure that the United States retains access to trusted manufacturers. The May 2020 announcement that Taiwan industry leader TSMC would invest up to $12 billion to build a new 5 nm manufacturing facility in Arizona was an important step forward in this.[40] Although TSMC's announcement did not explicitly state that the investment was intended to pave the way toward TSMC becoming part of the Pentagon's "trusted" supply chain—possibly due to sensitivities around how this would be perceived in Beijing—it is likely that this was one of the goals of the project.

Second, other hawkish factions in the Trump administration and certain US government agencies have zeroed in on Taiwan's importance as a supplier of cutting-edge semiconductors to Chinese companies as part of their campaign to cripple Huawei. On the same day that TSMC announced its new Arizona semiconductor factory, the United States issued a long-awaited foreign direct product rule designed to stop shipments of advanced chips to Huawei's HiSilicon chip subsidiary from TSMC.[41] The action succeeded in cutting off the flow of the world's most advanced chips to Huawei and has rendered Huawei's global business uncompetitive, dealing a major blow to Beijing's broader technology ambitions.

TSMC also supplies many US original equipment manufacturers, which build devices using other companies' components that are then marketed under their own brand names. US companies currently account for around 60 percent of TSMC revenue. Going forward, whether Taiwan is forced to choose to support the "red" or "blue" supply chain will be a key focal point of US-China tech competition.[42] This raises the potential for Taiwan and semiconductors to become new focal points of cross-strait tensions.[43]

. . . While the Digital Silk Road and the Future of the Internet Mean the Strategic Ground on Tech Competition Is Increasingly Spilling into Global Venues

In addition, US-China tech competition also appears to be coming to a head over the future of the Internet. Beijing's competing vision, under Xi's "make

China into a cyber superpower," also includes the concept of data sovereignty, meaning state control of information, strong preference for data localization, and further restriction of foreign company presence in critical information infrastructure. The thrust of these policies, coupled with the increasing emphasis on the digital portion of the BRI, the Digital Silk Road, suggests the US and China will remain in a slow-motion struggle for the future control of global cyberspace, and applications such as digital payments systems, data flows, 5G, and cyber norms of behavior.

For the last five years, Chinese firms such as Huawei have played a significant role in setting global technology standards for 5G and building out mobile infrastructure via bodies like the International Telecommunication Union (ITU).[44] Other Chinese firms are eager to follow suit and contribute more to the global standards-setting process, which would help advance Beijing's vision of a more China-influenced technology stack. But the US government and some data privacy advocates believe that greater involvement by Chinese companies in multilateral technology standards-setting efforts could materially alter the course of global norms in ways the United States and other democracies would not support. Effective global standard-setting that balances this tension with Beijing's stated ambitions of the DSR appears to be increasingly difficult, and it will get even more challenging as the bilateral relationship deteriorates and Beijing reacts to US actions restricting Chinese firms access to US technology and financial markets.

Instead, geopolitical trends brought about by the pandemic and Beijing's accelerating support for DSR-branded projects could, over time, put greater pressure on existing Internet governance frameworks and technology standards-setting processes at the ITU, including, in particular, for 5G standards at 3GPP.[45] As BRI countries look to boost digital infrastructure capacity, Team China's tech majors and conglomerates will enjoy significant support from Beijing to meet this demand as state organs seek to kick-start economic growth and bolster geopolitical influence.

Critically, US-China technology competition is increasingly spilling over into the financial services domain. China's central bank digital currency plans, for example, also neatly align with the DSR. Just as Chinese officials have ramped up criticism of existing Internet governance systems as excessively US-dominated, they have also targeted SWIFT—a Brussels-based communications network that facilitates interbank transfers. SWIFT is frequently identified as a cat's-paw of the United States in state media outlets, given the body's responsiveness to past US sanctions—and new packages targeting Russia over Ukraine—and reports that SWIFT messages have been surveilled by US intelligence agencies. Clearly, over time, in addition to reducing dependence on US technology, Beijing aspires to lead the development of a global, non-US-influenced payments system, although there are major political, economic, and technological hurdles facing this effort.

Technology Competition 2022: China United around a Strategy of S&T Self-Reliance

Finally, Beijing has not yet fully formulated a realistic long-term strategy for coping with the coming intensification of the US-China clash over technology and the future of cyberspace. However, the course of the Trump and early Biden administrations has highlighted China's dependence on core technologies, particularly semiconductors, semiconductor manufacturing equipment, and enterprise software, and by the end of 2020, as Beijing pushed toward formulation of a new industrial policy, the private sector in China was fully on board in a way it had not been during previous periods of exhortation on indigenous technology development and Made in China 2025.

First, Xi again delivered a major speech to set the tone of Beijing's new approach to technology and industrial policy going forward into 2021.[46] On September 11, 2020, Xi delivered a speech to a major group of science and technology workers. Xi's speech followed a major study session in which senior Chinese leaders listened to input from a range of scientists on how to deepen structural reform and innovation in the S&T domain, both issues of long-standing concern to Xi and the country's leadership. Xi linked S&T strength to ensuring industrial supply chain security and stability, a nod to US efforts to restrict access of Chinese technology firms to critical technical inputs via export controls and other measures.

Second, in late 2020, documents related to the Fifth Plenum of the Party Central Committee[47] and the Fourteenth Five-Year Plan emphasized the theme of self-reliance in science and technology (科技自立自强) as a strategic pillar of national development,[48] while pledging an estimated $1.4 trillion in funding to develop critical technologies up to 2025. While much of the rhetoric was not new, it fell on more fertile ground this time around: after four years of Trump administration policies targeting their technology supply chains, China's private sector companies were all now much more receptive to Beijing's exhortation to reduce dependence on US technology and fund and improve domestic alternatives. There was no turning back.

The newly coined term "self-reliance in science and technology" now describes Beijing's vision for a domestic-focused technology advancement agenda. It highlights party leaders' recognition of China's technological weakness under the pressure of US-China decoupling. As a result, the ambitious, outward-facing MIC2025 framework has been replaced by a more defensive posture, underpinned by the goal to achieve strategic technology breakthroughs to enable internal circulation/consumption and domestic growth, under an environment less susceptible to outside pressure. Vice premier and lead economic reform architect Liu He drove home the new approach in a major editorial on November 25, 2020, emphasizing that China needed to move faster toward technological self-reliance and that "accelerating scientific and technological self-reliance [was] the key to smoothing domestic circulation and shaping China's position taking the initiative in international circulation."[49]

Beginning in 2022, the Five-Year Plan (FYP) recommendations will begin to play a greater role in shaping Chinese tech firms' business plans. Telecom equipment makers and surveillance technology providers, heavily dependent on government entities and state-owned enterprises for revenue, for example, are likely to launch new R&D efforts in the areas of semiconductor design and other strategic technologies, including mobile operating system and enterprise software. Major Internet companies, including Alibaba,[50] Baidu, and Tencent—which have already made substantial initial investments in semiconductor design—could expand their projects with additional government backing. Major AI-driven computer vision companies such as SenseTime, Megvii, Yitu, and CloudWalk, will likely attract more investor interest as AI and smart city applications remain a critical priority area for channeling state support.

Despite the Ant IPO fiasco, the new industrial policy that will gain major momentum going forward has some significant differences from past government-led efforts. First and foremost, the tech self-reliance mantra is not something China's private sector companies and major domestic investors are now pursuing without the need for government exhortations; Huawei, in fact, has accomplished more in this regard via its drive to design out US technology in the face of export restrictions than have editorials by senior leaders in state media outlets. Aligning both the government and key private sector companies in China around the imperative of finding domestic alternatives to core technologies like semiconductors and software may be one of the most important outcomes of the Trump presidency.

Second, the year 2021, following the scuttling of the Ant IPO, saw the launching of a major domestic regulatory rectification campaign, which was still underway as of mid-2022 but had eased considerably in the run-up to the Party Congress in October as Chinese industrial planners believed major elements of the campaign had succeeded and economic growth concerns and pandemic management dominated policy decisions. This has revealed that Beijing is serious about changing the direction of technology development, platform business models, and investment flows in directions more in keeping with long-term strategy goals of technology competition. The goals of the campaign are varied and also caught up in the broader meme of "common prosperity," a party-generated slogan that has manifested in the technology domain as support for policies that improve the working conditions of workers, encourage technology companies to contribute to government-preferred charitable programs, and, in general, seek to reduce the harsher aspects of unbridled competition and financialization of the economy. The campaign also came with regulatory focus on keeping technology platforms more narrowly in lanes associated with their core business and tackling problems like data security and cross-border data flows.[51]

As of early 2022, the stock prices of leading Chinese technology firms had plummeted from all-time highs, and appeared headed down further, and the US Securities and Exchange Commission (SEC) had started to notify US-listed Chinese companies that they were not in compliance with auditing requirements, as called for in the 2020 Holding Foreign Companies Accountable Act.[52] The SEC and China Securities Regulatory Commission (CSRC) were continuing to discuss the issue, but it remained unclear whether there was sufficient political will on both sides to resolve the long-standing issue—US concern over China's support for Russia in the Ukraine conflict also put pressure on broader financial decoupling.

The potential impact of the loss of access to US and other Western capital markets for Chinese technology firms, and how this will force readjustment of Beijing's broader S&T goals, remains unclear. At a minimum it will reduce foreign investment in the sector, and it is not clear that China's still-immature capital markets, or smaller, mature ones such as Hong Kong, can absorb the return of large numbers of technology firms and substitute for the exposure and liquidity provided by US capital markets. As of late March 2022, Chinese officials attempted to calm markets, with Vice Premier Liu He suggesting that the rectification campaign would ease and CSRC and other financial sector officials suggesting that there was major progress on resolving the auditing issue with the SEC.[53] In late 2022, major progress had been made in resolving the auditing issues, as CSRC and US financial regulators signed a deal in August and completed pilot audits and Chinese regulators appeared to have made major concessions related to third-party auditing of listed Chinese companies.[54] This means that Beijing was concerned about the impact of S&T development on its technology firms, including many unicorns, and about a loss of the option to raise capital in US financial markets.

In late 2021 and early 2022, several developments also revealed the challenges Beijing will face in driving forward state-driven attempts to bolster domestic innovation, reduce reliance on foreign technology, and develop competitive global companies in priority technology sectors. In a major signal of how Beijing now views S&T development, in late December 2021 the CCCI released the Fourteenth Five-Year Plan for Informatization,[55] which contained detailed guidance for technology sectors and critical passages on how Chinese regulators will treat the role of market forces going forward. A close read of the document suggests that Beijing is stepping back from allowing market forces more leeway, in favor of a more active government role in guiding investment in, and focus on, "hard" technologies. The document is a fascinating read and look into the minds of industrial ministry and CAC officials, who now more than ever believe that they have a mandate from both the top, via senior political leaders including Xi himself, and from the bottom, in sync with public opinion on reining in big tech, to steer the technology sector toward a preferred version of informatization rather than allow a messy, unsupervised market to bring the ill effects of financialization, worker exploitation, and the inefficiencies of "disorderly capital."[56]

In addition, in February 2022, a summary of a detailed study by an element of Beijing University highlighting how far Chinese companies lagged behind their Western counterparts in key technology sectors, including semiconductors and AI, was pulled from the Internet, almost certainly because it cast China as much further behind than Beijing was comfortable with admitting. The incident raised a host of issues, as it contrasted with Western studies claiming that China would surpass the United States in these sectors—highlighting the issue of whether the United States has "right sized" the long-term challenge of competition from China and downplayed the benefits of collaboration and cooperation in the S&T domain, pursuing a policy dominated by confrontation and Cold War–style zero-sum thinking.[57]

Third, while government support and positive signals to the bureaucracy around enhancing preferential policies for domestic firms are important, the external environment is now the paramount driver of decisions in Chinese company boardrooms around long-term technology access plans. US actions targeting not just Huawei but a host of other Chinese firms have permanently galvanized companies that might otherwise have gone with the best available and mostly US technology to look elsewhere, either in Asia or Europe, and also be willing to gamble on perhaps second- or third-best domestic technology while also being willing to help domestic players improve their game. Huawei is already doing this with leading domestic foundry SMIC, for example. Getting leading domestic players such as Huawei, who are competitive globally, on board with the drive to boost domestic capabilities in the semiconductor industry will give the new push for self-reliance a major lift and the potential to succeed in ways a solely state-driven effort has been unable to achieve.

Finally, the new wrinkle to this equation, introduced in early 2022 by the West's response to China's response to the Russian invasion of Ukraine, has added a major new element to the decoupling narrative and the technology cold war meme. A strong Russia-China condominium in the political, economic, military, and technology domains will almost certainly lead to major new pressures on technology—decoupling in particular. US officials, working with European Union counterparts, have developed new tools that could be applied to China, including new versions of the Foreign Direct Product (FDP) rule, first applied to Huawei, Russia as a whole, and Russian firms added to the Entity List.[58]

Challenges and Headwinds Remain

The ultimate success of Beijing's new domestic and international approaches, including leveraging of markets, and policies such as dual circulation and technology self-reliance, will depend on a host of factors, many of them external. These will critically include how US policy and China technology policy develop under the second half of the Biden administration.

The domestic challenges to reducing dependence on US core technologies will be considerable, particularly for semiconductors and manufacturing equipment. Beijing is pushing for greater emphasis on open-source approaches, such as the RISC-V consortium for semiconductor design, but this will only help reduce dependence on US design tools at the margins for the near-term, for example. China's domestic software design tool and semiconductor manufacturing sector is five to ten years behind its Western counterparts, depending on the specific subsector.[59]

Under this messy and complicated scenario, with the United States pushing China on technology issues on all fronts, Chinese digital technology companies that have succeeded and have, for the most part, embraced global value chains will now be faced with the prospect that Western perceptions of both Beijing's ability and willingness to order them to do malicious things and unwillingness to adhere to global best practices in areas such as data governance will increasingly complicate their ability to expand and become global players. This will push those firms more deeply under the influence of the party/state and into supporting the party/state development priorities. Further isolation as a result of sanctions stemming from China's response to the Russia-Ukraine conflict will also influence this dynamic.

For Beijing and Xi in particular, this will mean dealing with a major new set of challenges in the technology arena. Chinese companies face the prospect of being shut out of investment in and acquisition of US and also European technology companies. Chinese companies will also continue to be cut off from US technology suppliers, and this will increasingly focus on semiconductors and semiconductor manufacturing tools and software as the United States under President Biden will continue to weaponize its technology advantages. A landmark package of export controls, for example, was released in early October 2022, targeting advanced semiconductors such as graphical processing units (GPUs) used for AI and high-performance computing and controls on manufacturing equipment and US persons supporting semiconductor manufacturing at specific technology levels for logic and memory.[60] President Xi told President Biden at the G20 summit in Indonesia that while China believed the move was bad for companies in both countries, China would rise to the challenge by doubling down on boosting domestic semiconductor manufacturing capabilities. The US Congress and the Biden administration as of April 2022 were also considering structuring an outbound investment review mechanism that would put further pressure on the ability of Chinese companies to attract foreign investment in key technology sectors and on the willingness of US companies to expand their China-based operations and investment in key areas such as R&D with Chinese partners. The sectors likely to be covered include semiconductors, AI, quantum computing, and biotechnology.

With Taiwan, semiconductors, and Xi's signature Belt and Road and its digital counterpart increasingly the focus of US-China technology competition and the evolving technology cold war, along with the technologies of the future—AI, quantum, and 5G/6G—the success of Beijing's domestic efforts to spur innovation will take time to mature, meaning continued areas of friction around trade and technology issues during the remainder of the Biden era.[61] The primary countervailing forces are the desire of most of Western technology sector companies to avoid a substantially bifurcated world, with different standards, messy interoperability, and higher costs for innovation. But it will take a lot of effort to rebuild trust and engage in nuanced policymaking on both sides, mixed with close cooperation with the industry and technological foresight to put the tech decoupling genie back in the bottle. But for China and Xi, the focus for 2022 and beyond will now be more on technology self-reliance and managing decoupling in ways that do not undermine that long-range goal.

Notes

1. Evan Feigenbaum, *China's Techno-Warriors* (Stanford, CA: Stanford University Press, 2003). Feigenbaum deftly weaves together four stories: Chinese views of technology since 1950, the role of the military in China's political and economic life, the evolution of open and flexible conceptions of public management in China, and the technological dimensions of the rise of Chinese power.

2. Paul Triolo, "The Telecommunications Industry in US–China Context: Evolving toward Near-Complete Bifurcation," Johns Hopkins Applied Physics Laboratories, 2020, https://www.jhuapl.edu/assessing-us-china-technology-connections/publications.

3. James McGregor, "China's Drive for 'Indigenous Innovation': A Web of Industrial Policies," Global Regulatory Cooperation Project, US Chamber of Commerce, 2010.

4. See, for example, Richard Applebaum et al., "Innovation in China: Challenging the Global Science and Technology System," *Science*, October 15, 2018.

5. Cong Cao et al., "China's 15-Year Science and Technology Plan," *Physics Today*, 2006, https://asu.pure.elsevier.com/en/publications/chinas-15-year-science-and-technology-plan.

6. McGregor, "China's Drive."

7. Eric Baark, "The Chinese Policies of Indigenous Innovation," East Asian Institute, National University of Singapore, 2019, https://www.researchgate.net/publication/330738277_The_Chinese_Policies_of_Indigenous_Innovation.

8. "China: Effects of Intellectual Property Infringements and Indigenous Innovation Policies on the U.S. Economy," US International Trade Commission, 2011, https://www.usitc.gov/publications/industry_econ_analysis_332/2011/china_effects_intellectual_property_infringement.htm.

9. Lauren Dudley et al., "China's Cybersecurity Reviews Eye 'Supply Chain Security' in 'Critical' Industries," *DigiChina* (blog), New America, April 27, 2020, https://www.newamerica.org/cybersecurity-initiative/digichina/blog/chinas-cybersecurity-reviews-eye-supply-chain-security-critical-industries-translation/.

10. Evan Feigenbaum, "Who's Behind China's High-Technology 'Revolution'? How Bomb Makers Remade Beijing's Priorities, Policies, and Institutions," *International Security* 24, no. 1 (Summer 1999): 95–126.

11. Audrey Fritz, "China's Evolving Conception of Civil-Military Collaboration," *Trustee China Hand* (blog), Center for Strategic and International Studies, August 2, 2019, https://www.csis.org/blogs/trustee-china-hand/chinas-evolving-conception-civil-military-collaboration.

12. "The Chinese Communist Party's Military-Civil Fusion Policy," Department of State, https://2017-2021.state.gov/military-civil-fusion/index.html.

13. See Eric Hagt, "China's Beidou: Implications for the Individual and the State," *SAIS Review of International Affairs* 34, no. 1 (2014): 129–40.

14. "Zhongyang wangluo anquan he xini hua lingdao xiaozu chengyuan mingdan 12 zhengfu guo ji jianzhi shen gaizu" [List of members of the central cyber security and informatization leading group], *Guancha*, February 24, 2014, https://www.guancha.cn/politics/2014_02_28_209672.shtml.

15. See, for example, *Findings of the Investigation into China's Acts, Policies, and Practices Related to Technology Transfer, Intellectual Property, and Innovation under Section 301 of the Trade Act of 1974*, Office of the United States Trade Representative, 2018.

16. Rogier Creemers et al., "China's Cyberspace Authorities Set to Gain Clout in Reorganization," *DigiChina* (blog), New America, March 26, 2018, https://www.newamerica.org/cybersecurity-initiative/digichina/blog/chinas-cyberspace-authorities-set-gain-clout-reorganization/.

17. For more detail on the WIC and its origins, see Paul Triolo, "China's World Internet Conference Struggles to Live Up to Its Name," *DigiChina* (blog), New America, November 6, 2018, https://www.newamerica.org/cybersecurity-initiative/digichina/blog/chinas-world-internet-conference-struggles-to-live-up-to-its-name/.

18. Xi Jinping, "Speech at the Work Conference for Cybersecurity and Informatization," April 19, 2016, https://chinacopyrightandmedia.wordpress.com/2016/04/19/speech-at-the-work-conference-for-cybersecurity-and-informatization/.

19. Xi, "Cybersecurity and Informatization."

20. "The National IC Industry Investment Fund Is Officially Launched," State Council, People's Republic of China, October 14, 2014, http://www.gov.cn/xinwen/2014-10/14/content_2764849.htm.

21. Penny Pritzker, "U.S. Secretary of Commerce Penny Pritzker Delivers Major Policy Address on Semiconductors at Center for Strategic and International Studies," November 2, 2016, https://2014-2017.commerce.gov/news/secretary-speeches/2016/11/us-secretary-commerce-penny-pritzker-delivers-major-policy-address.html.

22. Jost Wubbeke et al., "Made in China 2025. The Making of a High-Tech Superpower and Consequences for Industrial Countries," Merics Mercator Institute of China Studies, August 12, 2016, https://www.merics.org/sites/default/files/2017-09/MPOC_No.2_MadeinChina2025.pdf.

23. Jost Wubbeke, "China's High-Strategy Raises Heat on Industrial Countries," Mercaetor Institute of China Studies, December 14, 2016, https://www.merics.org/en/china-flash/chinas-high-tech-strategy-raises-heat-industrial-countries.

24. Office of the US Trade Representative, *Findings of the Investigation*. MIC2025 is referenced over one hundred times in the document.

25. See, for example, *China's Belt and Road Initiative in the Global Trade, Investment and Finance Landscape* (Paris: OECD Business and Finance Outlook, 2018), https://www.oecd.org/finance/Chinas-Belt-and-Road-Initiative-in-the-global-trade-investment-and-finance-landscape.pdf.

26. Paul Triolo and Robert Greene, "Will China Control the Global Internet via Its Digital Silk Road?" *SupChina* (blog), May 8, 2020, https://supchina.com/2020/05/08/will-china-control-the-global-internet-via-its-digital-silk-road/.

27. Graham Webster et al., "China's 'New Generation Artificial Intelligence Development Plan,'" *DigiChina* (blog), New America, August 1, 2017, https://www.newamerica.org/cybersecurity-initiative/digichina/blog/full-translation-chinas-new-generation-artificial-intelligence-development-plan-2017/.

28. For more, see Elsa Kania et al., "Quantum Hegemony? China's Ambitions and the Challenge to U.S. Innovation Leadership," Center for a New American Security, September 12, 2018, https://www.cnas.org/publications/reports/quantum-hegemony.

29. Office of the United States Trade Representative, *Federal Register* 82, no. 163 (August 24, 2017).

30. Office of the US Trade Representative, *Findings of the Investigation*.

31. For a detailed discussion of the trade negotiations, see Bob Davis and Lingling Wei, *Superpower Showdown: How the Battle between Trump and Xi Threatens a New Cold War* (New York: HarperCollins, 2020).

32. White House, Executive Order on Securing the Information and Communications Technology and Services Supply Chain, https://trumpwhitehouse.archives.gov/presidential-actions/executive-order-securing-information-communications-technology-services-supply-chain/.

33. Paul Triolo et al., "The Geopolitics of 5G," Eurasia Group, November 15, 2018, https://www.eurasiagroup.net/live-post/the-geopolitics-of-5g.

34. For Beijing's view, see Paul Triolo et al., "From Riding a Wave to Full Steam Ahead," *DigiChina* (blog), New America, February 28, 2018, https://www.newamerica.org/cybersecurity-initiative/digichina/blog/riding-wave-full-steam-ahead/; For the US view, see Michael Pence, "Vice President Mike Pence's Remarks on the Administration's Policy towards China," speech, Hudson Institute, Washington, DC, October 4, 2018, https://www.hudson.org/events/1610-vice-president-mike-pence-s-remarks-on-the-administration-s-policy-towards-china102018.

35. Davis and Wei, *Superpower Showdown*.

36. Evelyn Cheng, "China Kicks Off New Shanghai Board as It Tests New Ways to Improve Volatile Stock Market," CNBC, July 21, 2019, https://www.cnbc.com/2019/07/22/china-star-market-shanghai-kicks-off-new-nasdaq-style-tech-board.html.

37. As of late 2020, the US Securities and Exchange Commission was working on rulemaking around this issue, following the recommendation by an advisory board to President Trump in June 2020.

38. Miguel Cordon, "JD, Baidu, Other Chinese Tech Giants Reportedly Eye Hong Kong Listings," Tech in Asia, January 15, 2020, https://www.techinasia.com/jd-baidu-second-listing-hong-kong.

39. Yoko Kubota, "China Sets Up New $29 Billion Semiconductor Fund," *Wall Street Journal*, October 25, 2019, https://www.wsj.com/articles/china-sets-up-new-29-billion-semiconductor-fund-11572034480.

40. "TSMC Announces Intention to Build and Operate an Advanced Semiconductor Fab in the United States," TSMC, May 15, 2020, https://www.tsmc.com/tsmcdotcom/PRListingNewsArchivesAction.do?action=detail&newsid=THGOANPGTH&language=E.

41. United States Department of Commerce, Bureau of Industry and Security, "Export Administration Regulations: Amendments to General Prohibition Three (Foreign-Produced Direct Product Rule) and the Entity List," *Federal Register*, May 19, 2020, https://www.federalregister.gov/documents/2020/05/19/2020-10856/export-administration-regulations-amendments-to-general-prohibition-three-foreign-produced-direct.

42. Alex Capri, *Semiconductors at the Heart of the US-China Tech War* (Hinrich Foundation, January 17, 2020), https://www.hinrichfoundation.com/research/wp/tech/semiconductors-at-the-heart-of-the-us-china-tech-war/.

43. For more detail, see Paul Triolo, "Sino-American Technology Competition and the Asia-Pacific," in *Asia-Pacific Regional Security Assessment 2022* (London: International Institute for Strategic Studies, June 2022), https://www.iiss.org/publications/strategic-dossiers/asia-pacific-regional-security-assessment-2022/aprsa-chapter-7.

44. Paul Triolo and Kevin Allison, "The Geopolitics of 5G," Eurasia Group, November 15, 2018.

45. The 3rd Generation Partnership Project (3GPP) is an umbrella term for a number of standards organizations which develop protocols for mobile telecommunications, including for so-called fifth-generation (5G) networks.

46. Rogier Creemers et al., "Xi Jinping's Sept. 2020 Speech on Science and Technology Development (Translation)," *DigiChina* (blog), New America, September 22, 2020, https://www.newamerica.org/cybersecurity-initiative/digichina/blog/translation-xi-jinpings-sept-2020-speech-science-and-technology/.

47. See Communiqué of the Fifth Plenary Session of the Nineteenth Central Committee of the Communist Party of China.

48. See, for example, "Four Aspects of China's Deployment and Promotion of 'Science and Technology Self Reliance,'" *Xinhua News Agency,* November 3, 2021, http://www.gov.cn/zhengce/2020-11/03/content_5557101.htm.

49. Liu He, "Accelerating the Construction of a New Development Structure with Domestic Circulation as Primary and Mutually Promoting Domestic and International Dual Circulation," *People's Daily*, November 25, 2020, http://paper.people.com.cn/rmrb/html/2020-11/25/nw.D110000renmrb_20201125_1-06.htm.

50. See, for example, Paul Triolo, "Alibaba's Silicon Chip in the Age of Hypersonic Missiles," *SupChina* (blog), November 1, 2021, https://supchina.com/2021/11/01/alibabas-silicon-chip-in-the-age-of-hypersonic-missiles/.

51. For more, see Paul Triolo and Michael Hirson, "Didi Debacle Highlights Weaknesses in Regulatory Coordination, but It's Not Decoupling," *SupChina* (blog), July 12, 2021.

52. See Holding Foreign Companies Accountable Act of 2020 (HFCAA), https://www.sec.gov/hfcaa.

53. Tom Mitchell, Ryan McMorrow, William Langley, "China Makes Rare Intervention to Bolster Confidence after Market Rout," *Financial Times*, March 16, 2022, https://www.ft.com/content/8d6d1394-c10a-45e2-bcc4-374439fd6760; Tabby Kinder and Eleanor Olcott, "China

Plans Audit Concession in Face of US Threat," *Financial Times*, March 16, 2022, https://www.ft.com/content/0463c70d-4d24-4b9b-b7e5-ace22409d8e2.

54. "PCAOB Signs Agreement with Chinese Authorities, Taking First Step toward Complete Access for PCAOB to Select, Inspect and Investigate in China," PCAOB, August 26, 2022, https://pcaobus.org/news-events/news-releases/news-release-detail/pcaob-signs-agreement-with-chinese-authorities-taking-first-step-toward-complete-access-for-pcaob-to-select-inspect-and-investigate-in-china.

55. Rogier Creemers et al., "14th Five-Year Plan for National Informatization (translation)," *DigiChina* (blog), December 2021, https://digichina.stanford.edu/work/translation-14th-five-year-plan-for-national-informatization-dec-2021/.

56. Paul Triolo, "Analyzing China's 2021–2025 Informatization Plan: A DigiChina Foarum," *DigiChina*, February 2022, https://digichina.stanford.edu/work/analyzing-chinas-2021-2025-informatization-plan-a-digichina-forum/.

57. Paul Triolo, "Why Did a Peking University Paper on China's Tech Deficiencies Get Deleted?" *SupChina* (blog), February 25, 2022, https://supchina.com/2022/02/25/why-did-a-peking-university-paper-on-chinas-tech-deficiencies-get-deleted/.

58. "U.S. Department of Commerce and Bureau of Industry and Security Russia and Belarus Rule Fact Sheet," Department of Commerce, February 24, 2022, https://www.commerce.gov/news/fact-sheets/2022/02/us-department-commerce-bureau-industry-and-security-russia-and-belarus.

59. Paul Triolo et al., "The Geopolitics of Semiconductors," Eurasia Group, 2020.

60. For a more in-depth look at these issues, see Reva Goujon et al., "Freeze-in-Place: The Impact of US Tech Controls on China," Rhodium Group, October 21, 2022, https://rhg.com/research/freeze-in-place/.

61. For a more in-depth look at these issues, see Triolo, "Telecommunications Industry."

12

From Backwater to Near-Peer: Changing US Approaches toward China as a Technological Competitor

Helen Toner

Technology has become an essential part of strategic competition between the United States and China. Artificial intelligence (AI), 5G, gene editing, quantum computing, and other high-tech fields are front and center in contemporary discussions of the US-China relationship. How did this come to be?

On one level, the answer is simple: for the first time, China's level of technological development has begun to rival the United States', coinciding with a period when the bilateral relationship has become increasingly strained. By contrast, it would have made no sense to perceive China as a technological competitor in the 1980s, when the country was recovering from the Cultural Revolution's gutting of Chinese science and technology (S&T). As China grew and developed through the 1990s and 2000s, it became clear that its technological capabilities might someday draw level with the United States, but it wasn't until the last decade or so that this actually came to pass.

Digging in deeper, we can see how the role of technology in the bilateral relationship has shifted and evolved over time. Over the years, technology issues have reflected dynamics in the larger relationship. In some areas there have been total reversals: the 1980s US approach of deliberately transferring technology to aid the Chinese military would be unthinkable today. In other areas, underlying issues have remained constant, but the way the United States has interpreted and responded to them has evolved with the relationship. Chinese intellectual property (IP) theft, for instance, has been a grievance of US policymakers for decades. But where it once could be seen as part of a common—if irksome—pattern of behavior by emerging economies, it is viewed with a new level of urgency and aggravation now that the perpetrator represents a challenge to US global leadership.

This chapter traces the growing range and scope of technology issues in the US-China relationship, culminating in the current era of strategic competition. In the 1980s, discussions of technology primarily arose in military and strategic contexts, against the backdrop of US competition with the Soviet Union. In the 1990s and 2000s, China emerged as a major commercial market, and dual-use technologies—which have both civilian and military applications—grew in importance, leading to a push and pull between security and commercial interests. More recently, China has risen as an S&T force to be reckoned with, and the use of digital tools for social control under President Xi Jinping has added human rights to the technology policy agenda.

The present era is no exception to the pattern by which broader dynamics in the US-China relationship shape technology's place in it. Whether it is accurate to characterize the present situation as a "new cold war" has become a fashionable question in recent years. Clearly, comparing the current US-China relationship with the US-Soviet relationship of the Cold War years turns up some important similarities (a bipolar global system, significant ideological differences, growing mutual suspicion) along with important differences (far greater economic and social interconnection, a lack of clear ideological blocs, much less focus on the threat of nuclear war). It is thus a choice of framing, not of fact, to claim that we are facing a new cold war (despite some differences) or that we are not (despite some similarities). Either way, since the ascension of Xi Jinping as China's head of state, US technology policy toward China has increasingly drawn on Cold War–style tools of decoupling and denial. The final section of this chapter examines how the three US presidents who have overlapped with Xi have employed these tools, including trade controls, investment restrictions, and immigration bans, noting points of continuity and difference between administrations.

Technology in the Background: How We Got Here

In the period immediately following normalization in 1979, technology figured into US policy toward China primarily with regard to exports of military equipment. Given the intense Cold War climate and poor Sino-Soviet relations during this time, the United States saw strengthening China—for example, by transferring military technologies across the Pacific—as a way to balance against the Soviet Union. Policymakers' discussions of technology centered on the question of how to assist China in holding off the Soviets without increasing Chinese offensive capabilities against the United States and its allies, against the backdrop of a broader debate about what the newly normalized US-China relationship should look like.

Throughout the 1970s, different factions in Washington had fought over whether to promote or prevent the transfer of US technologies to the People's Liberation Army (PLA). Within the Carter administration, the argument revolved around how tighter military ties with China would affect the United States' relationship with the Soviet Union. National Security Advisor Zbigniew Brzezinski and Secretary of Defense Harold Brown argued that closer engagement with China would send a useful signal to the Soviet Union, while Secretary of State Cyrus Vance worried that it would jeopardize valuable US-Soviet diplomatic efforts, such as the SALT II disarmament talks.[1] Through 1979, the White House took Vance's view, pursuing an "evenhanded" policy toward China and the Soviet Union that included prohibition of military exports to both countries.[2]

This calculus changed abruptly with the Soviet invasion of Afghanistan in late December 1979, which put a serious dent in US optimism about the value of diplomacy with the Soviets. In the span of a few weeks between the invasion and the departure of Defense Secretary Brown on a visit to Beijing on January 4, 1980, the Carter administration's reluctance to permit military exports to China dissolved.[3] By September 1980, China had been moved into a new export control category—separate from the Soviet Union—and the United States had approved more than four hundred licenses for the export of nonlethal military hardware and electronic equipment.[4] These moves created an opening for China to access US technologies that were prohibited to the Soviets.

Despite this warm beginning, however, in practice the volume of technology exports across the Pacific during the remainder of the decade was modest, for two reasons. First, it was challenging for the US bureaucracy to agree which technologies would bolster China's defenses against the Soviets without increasing its offensive capabilities against the United States. As described by Secretary of Commerce Malcolm Baldrige, "Though the transfer of technology will prevent a widening of the military gap between the PRC [People's Republic of China] and the USSR," sales must "not alter the US-PRC strategic balance."[5] US officials also saw it as critical that technology sales did not increase the threat China could pose to US allies and partners in the region, especially Taiwan.[6] The task of determining which set of technologies could be exported to strike that balance was subject to a convoluted decision process involving Congress, executive branch agencies such as the departments of Defense, Commerce, and State, and an international body known as the Coordinating Committee for Multilateral Export Controls (CoCom), meaning that the bureaucratic hurdles to approve any given technology sale were high. A second reason sales were limited was that Washington's appetite for engagement with China generally, and for technology exports specifically, waxed and waned over the decade. The goal of

enabling China to serve as a "strategic counterweight"[7] to the Soviet Union had
to be pursued in the context of the larger Sino-American relationship, which
in the 1980s fluctuated between tentative optimism, stalemate, and mutual
resentment. The postnormalization momentum toward a closer relationship
was interrupted by the election of Ronald Reagan, whose staunch support for
Taiwan quickly became a major source of tension.[8] Beijing was suddenly suspicious of US offers to license technologies for export, fearing—with good reason—that accepting would be seen as acquiescence to ongoing US arms sales to
Taipei. As one official put it, "We would rather receive no US arms than accept
continued US interference in our internal affairs by selling arms to Taiwan."[9] By
1983, tensions over Taiwan had eased somewhat, but China's stance on nuclear
nonproliferation had become a new potential roadblock.[10] Then in 1987, an increase in Chinese sales of weaponry to the Middle East during the Iran-Iraq War
prompted Washington to halt export control liberalization altogether, resum-
ing only after China made assurances that it would reduce these sales.[11]

The net result was that the 1980s saw a meaningful—but not outsize—transfer of advanced technology from the United States to China. In 1982, China pur-
chased $630 million worth of US advanced technology; by 1988, that figure had
reached $1.72 billion.[12] In line with the aim of assisting China in keeping pace
with the Soviet Union without affecting the Sino-American strategic balance,
the bulk of these exports were computers, precision instruments, electronics,
and telecommunications equipment.[13] By contrast, off-limits areas included
nuclear weapons and delivery systems, electronic warfare, surface-ship antisub-
marine warfare, intelligence, power projection, and air superiority.[14]

Technology's place in US-China relations of the 1980s, therefore, largely reflected the dynamics of the larger relationship. By the end of the decade, the
counter-Soviet rationale that underlay US strategy in China was beginning to
look less solid, as President Mikhail Gorbachev made overtures to both Beijing and Washington.[15] This shift would likely have altered the terms of the
Sino-American relationship, and the place of technology in that relationship,
over time. In practice, of course, the events of June 1989 turned that gradual
realignment into a sharp break.

From Tiananmen to Xi Jinping: 1989–2012

The Tiananmen Square crackdown of June 4, 1989, and the collapse of the Soviet Union over the following two years acted as a one-two punch, shattering
the foundations of US engagement with China. Horrifying images of military
forces in Tiananmen Square gunning down students demonstrating for democracy and government reform sent US attitudes toward China—both among
policymakers and the general public—into a nosedive. Without the Soviet Union as an external foe, and with optimism about Chairman Deng Xiaoping's

campaign of "reform and opening-up" badly shaken after Tiananmen, the case for deliberately transferring some military technology to China crumbled.

The same was not true of the case for commercial engagement, which—at least according to US companies looking to access the burgeoning Chinese market—was as strong as ever. After a brief stutter in 1990, when US exports to China fell slightly in the aftermath of Tiananmen, the next two decades saw US-China bilateral trade balloon into one of the largest trading relationships in the world, facilitated by China's entry into the World Trade Organization (WTO) in 2001.[16] As a result, contention around how technology should figure into US policy toward China shifted from being primarily concentrated within the military-strategic domain to encompassing both the military and economic spheres. Where US policy toward China in the 1980s had primarily touched on technology in the context of balancing the strategic risks and benefits of strengthening Beijing militarily, technology-related tensions in the post-Tiananmen period arose from the need to balance commercial incentives in favor of high-tech trade against the security risks of assisting the PLA in its ongoing modernization campaign. Put simply, the business community wanted to do business, the security community wanted to prioritize security, and policymakers perceived technology primarily (though not exclusively) in terms of that struggle.

The crux of the issue was the fact that many of the fastest-developing technologies of the 1990s and 2000s were "dual use," meaning they were relevant in both civilian and military contexts. The computing, telecommunications, and aerospace industries all saw enormous financial opportunity in China's immature but increasingly accessible markets. AT&T, for example, leaped at the chance to be a part of the telecommunications industry's transition from a government-run monopoly (under which there was only one telephone line for every seventy people in the early 1990s) to a more competitive system.[17] While ultimately ill-fated—none of the company's attempted investments or partnerships ended up making real inroads in China—the mood at the time was one of great optimism. US industry groups such as the Computer Systems Policy Project, which included the CEOs of Apple Computer, Hewlett-Packard, Sun Microsystems, and other major computer companies, lobbied successfully for Cold War–era export restrictions to be loosened so they could get in on the action.[18]

To some in Washington, however, this blossoming of commercial activity was not an unalloyed positive. Members of Congress, in particular, sought to block deals where they saw any risk that technology sold to a supposedly civilian customer might wind up in military hands. Isolated cases of exactly that happening, as in the case of aircraft manufacturer McDonnell Douglas, reinforced these fears. In 1994, McDonnell Douglas was granted an export license to sell state-of-the-art machine tools as part of a billion-dollar deal to manufacture commuter aircraft in China. The company and its affiliates were later indicted on sixteen charges after it transpired that the equipment had been diverted instead to a military facility involved in producing missiles and fighter aircraft.[19] Then in 1995 and 1996, two attempted launches of US-built satellites on Chinese rockets both failed, prompting the companies involved to conduct a postmortem investigation of what had gone wrong.[20] When it came out in 1998 that unauthorized technical details were shared with Chinese partners as part of the postmortem process, simmering concerns within the US government boiled over into partisan warfare. The Republican-controlled Congress established a commission, chaired by Rep. Christopher Cox, to investigate the failures of the Clinton administration's export control policies. The Cox Commission's findings led Congress to legislate an overhaul of satellite export controls, seizing jurisdiction over the issue from the executive branch and making the United States the only country to treat satellites as a fully military (not dual-use) technology.[21] The computing and telecommunications industries managed to avoid similarly strict controls but were nonetheless subject to close scrutiny throughout the Clinton and Bush administrations.[22]

On the sidelines of this dispute over the trade-offs between commercial profits and national security, two complicating factors began to attract attention during this period. First, some representatives of both government and industry staked out the position that commercial engagement with China might be not only economically tempting but also militarily necessary. As Deputy Assistant of Defense Mitchel Wallerstein put it in his 1995 testimony before a Senate committee, "This situation requires that we be careful not to put U.S. exporters at any unnecessary competitive disadvantage, particularly when export revenues are an important contribution to profitability and to financing defense-related R&D [research and development]."[23] Adherents of this view pointed out that, in part due to the increasing importance of dual-use industries, state-of-the-art defense technology increasingly emerged from the private sector rather than from government-sponsored labs or contractors.[24] As the Department of Defense (DOD) came to rely on US companies for access to cutting-edge innovation, the existence of a vibrant and flourishing private sector therefore—according to this argument—became a matter of US national security. This contingent insisted that for sectors such as high-performance computing, semiconductors, and telecommunications, relatively liberal export policies supported both economic and security interests.[25]

A second, separate argument suggested the opposite: that engagement with China was bad for business as well as for defense. It was becoming clear that China was conducting coordinated campaigns to transfer US technology into China by illicit means—not only from the defense sector but also through targeting civilian or dual-use technologies such as computer chips,[26] telecommunications software,[27] and even paint formulas.[28] The Economic Espionage Act of 1996 was an early attempt to stymie efforts by China (among others) to steal US IP.[29] The gradual ramp-up of US concern from that point on is evident in the so-called Special 301 Reports produced annually by the Office of the US Trade Representative (USTR). In the 1990s, these reports—which document IP-related trade barriers the US faces globally—linked China primarily with pirated CDs and counterfeit consumer goods.[30] Over the next decade or two the focus gradually shifted toward illicit technology transfer, with the 2012 report describing "a recent alarming increase in cases involving the theft of trade secrets in China" as well as "policies intended to [. . .] coerce the transfer of IP [rights] from foreign rights holders to domestic entities."[31]

The basic ways in which US policymakers thought about technology and China during this period would continue to shape US policy in the years to follow: trade-offs between economic and security interests, the possibility that trade restrictions might harm national security, and frustration about IP theft. But as China became more able to compete with the United States technologically, and as US apprehension about China's goals grew, the level of concern and attention dedicated to these questions would increase significantly, and new questions would also enter the mix.

Technology Takes Center Stage: The Xi Era, 2012 to Present

Under Xi Jinping, China's technological capabilities have for the first time begun to rival those of the United States. This fact alone would have been enough to bring US policymakers into a competition mindset, as it was when Japanese semiconductor and automobile capabilities approached parity with American companies in the 1980s.[32] In the case of China, additional factors have raised the stakes of the competition. Technology has assumed a central role in Chinese Communist Party (CCP) efforts to control the population at home and pursue Chinese interests abroad, and consensus has grown in Washington that these efforts are inherently threatening to US interests and values. As a result, US leaders see China's growing technological prowess not only as a source of competition for US technology companies but as an intrinsic part of the CCP's plan to challenge the US-led world order.

The remainder of this chapter briefly outlines two major drivers of these US views: how Xi Jinping's China has become a major S&T power and how technological success undergirds the CCP's ambitions for domestic stability, military modernization, and international engagement. It then delves into how US policy has so far attempted to tackle this era of technology competition with China. This includes continued attention to old themes, such as shoring up US military advantage and preventing IP theft, as well as newer challenges such as military-civil fusion, digital authoritarianism, and the beginning of the 5G age.

Indigenous Innovation and Digital Authoritarianism under Xi

Xi sees global technological leadership as an essential part of China's national rejuvenation. He has continued and deepened earlier efforts to support the development of a vibrant S&T sector in China, elevating "indigenous innovation" (自主创新) to be one of China's central development priorities and referring repeatedly to the goal of becoming a "cyber superpower" (网络强国).[33] In Xi's view, technological progress is necessary not only to reduce China's dependence on foreign inputs (long a source of suspicion) or drive continued economic growth (a crucial source of CCP legitimacy). It is, more broadly, a way for China to regain its place as a great power on the world stage. Chinese leaders see their country as having missed the first three industrial revolutions (roughly: the steam engine, mass electrification, and the computer) and are determined to be at the vanguard of the fourth.[34]

The period since Xi took office has been one of remarkable success for Chinese S&T. Fostered by initiatives that predate his presidency as well as a slew of new planning documents, China has made cutting-edge achievements across a range of fields. In 2016, a supercomputer built entirely from processors designed and built in China—the Sunway TaihuLight—topped the global high-performance computing rankings for the first time.[35] China has overtaken the United States in late-stage research and development (R&D) spending and now publishes more scientific papers than any other country.[36] Even feats that drew justified criticism on ethical grounds—such as cloning primates or creating the first genetically edited human babies—show the level of technological sophistication China has achieved.

Technological tools are also a key part of Xi's plans for China's domestic and international security. As one prominent scholar describes it, Xi has worked to build a "techno-security state" in which technological advances are used to promote both national defense and domestic stability.[37] Xi has continued the work of his predecessors to reform and modernize the PLA, with an even greater focus on integrating innovations from the civilian sector into military applications and vice versa, a strategy he calls "military-civil fusion."[38] Domestically, his efforts to enhance internal security have made use of a wide range of new technological tools, giving rise to a new term, "digital authoritarianism," to describe government use of digital technologies to surveil and control citizens.[39]

The rise of digital authoritarianism under Xi looms large in US perceptions of Chinese technological progress, so it merits elaboration here. After decades of debate in Washington about the extent to which political liberalization would follow from Chinese economic reforms, Xi's rule has generated a new consensus in US policy circles that the CCP will stay the authoritarian course. The reasons for this change in perception are wide-ranging but include several technology-related factors. The Chinese Internet, for example, has gone from being a contested space under Xi's predecessor Hu Jintao—far from completely free but with some pockets of relatively open discussion—to being much more tightly controlled and monitored.[40] Crackdowns in 2013 and 2014 on the microblogging site Weibo targeted both large accounts and regular users posting critical commentary, catalyzing a shift to a tamer discourse on the platform and driving many users to instead use WeChat—a then-new app that was less suited to public discussions and was itself subject to increasing censorship.[41] Existing networks of surveillance cameras are being expanded and upgraded to incorporate facial and gait recognition, aided by companies designated as "national AI champions" such as Megvii, Hikvision, and SenseTime.[42] Under the encouragement of the central government, provincial and local leaders are rolling out a wide array of algorithmic tools under the banner of "social credit" programs, aggregating data about the purchasing habits, legal records, and other behavior of their citizens.[43] High-tech tools have been used in an especially concerted way to target and oppress minority populations, most notably Uyghur Muslims in the western province of Xinjiang. A 2018 Human Rights Watch report described how provincial authorities combine low-tech tactics like security patrols and checkpoints with the use of artificial intelligence and big data to "identify, profile, and track everyone in Xinjiang."[44] This tracking has been used to impose sweeping restrictions on the political and religious freedom of Xinjiang's minority residents, including arbitrarily detaining up to 1.5 million Uyghurs and ethnic Kazakhs in so-called reeducation camps, where inmates are allegedly subject to torture and mistreatment.[45] By all indications, the CCP will only increase its use of technology to cement its rule and control its citizens from here.

A final element is China's use of its growing technological capacity to shape its image on the world stage. In Internet governance negotiations, the CCP leans on the idea of sovereignty—a foundational principle of international law—to advocate for the Chinese concept of "cyber sovereignty." In contrast to the bottom-up, globally connected model that has characterized the Internet since its inception, the crux of cyber sovereignty is to make the online world more amenable to state control. Cornerstones of cyber sovereignty include in-country data storage and other technical requirements to ensure that digital services offered in China are compatible with the CCP's surveillance and censorship practices.[46] China has similarly sought to make its mark on the global rollout of fifth-generation (5G) cellular networks. Years of concerted effort from Beijing, including substantial direct and indirect subsidies, have positioned Chinese companies such as Huawei and ZTE well in the lead-up to 5G. Beijing has also coordinated and promoted Chinese companies' engagement in 5G standardization processes.[47] The CCP has further promulgated both cyber sovereignty and Chinese 5G leadership under the auspices of the "Digital Silk Road," the digital companion to the international infrastructure development strategy spearheaded by Xi known as the Belt and Road Initiative (BRI). The Digital Silk Road is a conceptual umbrella for state-supported projects to lay fiber optic cables, install network equipment, establish e-commerce schemes, build data centers, and otherwise advance Chinese technological leadership and CCP interests abroad.[48] US observers describe the Digital Silk Road as a vehicle for China to export its illiberal ideology, especially via sales of surveillance equipment, which are often bundled into "smart city" initiatives. (On the other hand, US exports of surveillance equipment to authoritarian regimes do not seem to be perceived as exporting illiberalism.)[49]

Taken together, China's technological trajectory under Xi has exacerbated US concerns about both the extent and purpose of Chinese technological prowess.

Grappling with a "Near-Peer" Technological Competitor: Obama, Trump, Biden

Xi's assumption of the presidency coincided almost exactly with the beginning of Barack Obama's second term as US president, then continued through the presidency of Donald Trump and the election of Joe Biden. These leaders' approaches to managing technology within the US-China relationship during their presidencies were shaped by the confluence of two trends: broadly, China's overall rise as an economic and military competitor roughly on par with the United States itself, and more narrowly, the critical role of technology in China's plans for international influence and domestic control, as described above. The question of how to navigate the deep technological interconnections between the two countries has emerged as a primary challenge given these trends. Some types of connection—such as IP theft—only advantage China and are thus easily targeted as undesirable. But the vast majority of technological ties—whether in trade, immigration, investment, or other areas—have developed and deepened precisely because they provide at least some substantial benefit to both sides. Simplistic calls to "decouple" from China are premised on a belief that anything that produces benefit to or dependence on China is clearly against US interests. In reality, the administrations of Obama, Trump, and Biden have each grappled with the difficulty of determining which types of technological links with China to prune and which to leave intact. A full accounting of the myriad issues and policies in scope would merit a book-length treatment of its own. What follows is an overview of some of the key themes and battlefields, including areas where US policy since 2012 has been relatively consistent as well as areas of significant disagreement and change.

The long-simmering issue of IP theft and industrial espionage continued largely unabated under Xi and became a clear target for US action as strategic competition intensified. As China matured economically and technologically, the excuse that these practices were a standard part of catch-up development began to wear thin. The Obama administration focused especially on deterring Chinese industrial espionage in cyberspace. In a landmark 2013 report, the US cybersecurity firm FireEye attributed a large-scale, multiyear corporate espionage campaign to a PLA unit based in Shanghai, which the firm designated as "advanced persistent threat 1" (APT1). In May 2014, the Department of Justice indicted five members of APT1—all active-duty PLA members—for cyberespionage against American companies, in the first-ever such charges against representatives of a foreign country. A year later, the White House enacted an executive order to penalize individuals and companies involved in cyber activities including industrial espionage, enabling asset freezes and travel restrictions. This series of initiatives culminated in a bilateral agreement signed by Obama and Xi in September 2015, in which both leaders committed to refrain from supporting cyberespionage against commercial targets. The agreement, which built upon multilateral discussions on cybersecurity norms that had been taking place under the auspices of a United Nations Group of Governmental Experts, represented a more direct acknowledgment of the issue than Beijing had made up to that point. In retrospect, the deal appears to have been a partial success: a 2018 US intelligence report found that Chinese espionage was ongoing but had sunk to "lower volumes than existed before the bilateral September 2015 US-China cyber commitments."[50]

The methods by which China purportedly gains access to US trade secrets are many, however, and most are less blatantly illegal than cybertheft. Xi's promotion of military-civil fusion has intensified US worries that even seemingly innocuous commercial interactions may ultimately benefit the Chinese military. In 2017, a report by the Defense Innovation Unit Experimental (DIUx, since renamed DIU) claimed to have uncovered a systematic, strategic campaign by Chinese investors to make early-stage investments in high-tech US start-ups as a way of gaining access to underlying technological breakthroughs. Researchers and entrepreneurs disputed DIUx's findings,[51] but the report found a receptive audience in Congress and catalyzed the passage of two related bills the following year. These bills sought to update and modernize two key US government tools for preventing technology transfers due to national security concerns: the export control system and the Committee on Foreign Investment in the United States (CFIUS). The first bill, the Export Control Reform Act of 2018 (ECRA), mandated that an interagency process identify "emerging and foundational technologies [. . .] essential to the national security of the United States," then tighten controls on those technologies. ECRA was signed into law on August 13, 2018—the same day as the Foreign Investment Risk Review Modernization Act, which sought to modernize the practices and authorities of CFIUS, an oversight body charged with blocking inbound investment transactions that pose a national security risk. As of early 2022, initial signs from the Biden administration indicate a broadly supportive attitude to measures like these. For instance, the House of Representatives' version of a megabill to promote competition with China includes provisions to introduce CFIUS-like review of outbound investments.[52] Implementation remains a challenge, however, with ECRA's mandated list of technologies for controls still a work in progress nearly four years after the law's passage.

Growing concern about military-civil fusion has also driven criticisms of US technology companies operating in China, on the grounds that if there is no clear distinction between civilian and military technology, any work that involves Chinese employees, researchers, or companies accessing the US firm's technology is tantamount to handing that technology to the PLA. When news leaked in 2018 that Google was considering launching a new censored search engine in China—only months after withdrawing from a controversial Pentagon contract—defense officials were quick to accuse the company of directly aiding the PLA.[53] President Trump himself tweeted that "Google [was] helping China and their military, but not the US[.] Terrible!"[54] Microsoft came under fire for similar reasons in 2019. After the *Financial Times* reported that the company was collaborating with PLA-linked universities in China on AI research that could potentially have applications in surveillance or censorship, Republican senator Marco Rubio described the collaboration as "deeply disturbing."[55] These two cases, and the tech industry's differing responses to them, are a good example of the challenging trade-offs at play. Google engineers overwhelmingly condemned the search engine project, with 1,400 employees signing an open letter in protest.[56] The Microsoft story, on the other hand, prompted significant pushback from the AI research community, disputing the links between the research in question and surveillance or censorship, and affirming the importance of international collaborations for continued progress in basic research. From the tech sector's perspective, the difference seems to come down to the contrast between a reluctance to aid the CCP directly (for instance, via censoring search results) and an undimmed commitment to the value of basic research for the United States and the world at large.

Concerns about military-civil fusion and technology transfer have perhaps been most controversial when it comes to the risks posed by individual students and researchers. The number of Chinese students and scholars working in science and engineering fields in the United States has skyrocketed since 1980, and these individuals now find themselves in the eye of the technology competition storm. Citing the risks of admitting students who may be working on behalf of Chinese intelligence or military organizations, Trump administration officials changed internal guidance on how Chinese visa applications should be screened, leading to longer delays and shorter visas for many applicants in 2018 and 2019.[57] In May 2020, a presidential proclamation formalized this approach, barring entry altogether to students and scholars connected to any organization that "implements or supports the PRC's 'military-civil fusion strategy.'"[58] One group of Republican senators went so far as to propose blocking Chinese students from graduate and postgraduate STEM opportunities altogether.[59] The Biden administration's approach, however, has diverged substantially from Trump's on this issue. Since taking office, Biden has prioritized increasing the number of international students and scholars—including those from China—who can come to the United States to undertake STEM study and research. As of this writing, White House attempts to wrangle Congress into raising green card caps remain a work in progress, but Biden's team did enact a slew of more minor STEM immigration reforms that only required executive branch authority, such as tweaking the requirements to obtain specific types of high-skill visas.[60] Biden's Department of Justice also rolled back a controversial program known as the "China Initiative," which aimed to detect cases of "nontraditional collectors" (for instance, scientific researchers) exfiltrating US technology to China. After a series of these cases had to be dropped due to procedural issues, and in the wake of criticisms that the initiative unfairly targeted scientists of Chinese heritage, the department dropped the program in favor of a broader "Strategy for Countering Nation-State Threats" in February 2022.[61] How to think about the role of STEM researchers and students in strategic competition is likely to remain a challenging topic for US policymakers, given the hard-to-estimate trade-offs between the benefits of a flourishing, open research ecosystem and the risks posed by individual bad actors.

Trade and export controls have become another major battlefield of technology competition. The Trans-Pacific Partnership (TPP), a proposed trade agreement among Pacific Rim countries that was intended to become a keystone of the Obama administration's economic policy in Asia, included protections for patents, copyrights, and trade secrets. These provisions were motivated in part by the hope that China might be incentivized to comply with the terms if a bloc containing many of its closest trading partners was bound by them. The 2016 election doomed that deal, but the Trump administration retained an interest in using trade issues as both carrot and stick to improve Chinese IP practices. Accordingly, IP theft and technology transfer played a part in what became one of the central features of the Trump administration's China policy: the trade war that spanned 2018 to 2020. A Section 301 investigation by the US Trade Representative found in March 2018 that Chinese practices relating to foreign ownership, licensing, investment, and cyberintrusions all placed undue burdens on US commerce. This finding triggered one of the opening salvos in the series of tit for tats that would escalate into the trade war: a presidential memorandum directing that tariffs and investment restrictions be imposed and a case filed with the WTO. Over the following two years, the administration's stated justifications for the trade war consistently included rhetoric about China's illegitimate technology transfer practices alongside complaints about the trade deficit and Chinese industrial policy more broadly. Ultimately, the Phase One deal signed in January 2020 focused primarily on purchase guarantees to reduce the trade deficit. The deal did also include incremental progress on IP protection and technology transfer, though monitoring or enforcement mechanisms were lacking.[62] In theory, many of the core issues related to technology were to be relegated to a Phase Two agreement, but there has so far been little sign of progress toward or interest in such a deal since the 2020 US election.

The momentum behind export control reforms as a tool of strategic competition appears to be more sustained. A particularly interesting case study here is that of 5G since it involves questions of IP theft, questionable trade practices, and military-civil fusion alongside the foundational question of who holds technological leadership in key strategic areas. Telecommunications is an industry where China has competed especially effectively, and accordingly the sector has become ground zero for US government concerns about technology competition. Two of China's largest telecommunications equipment companies, Huawei and ZTE, have been accused of a dizzying array of misdeeds, including stealing trade secrets, violating sanctions, receiving illegal government subsidies, having close ties to Chinese security forces, and being willing to compromise US networks if called upon to do so.[63] Some of these accusations centered around specific offenses that were prosecuted and penalized through the legal system—for example, in the case of a professor at a Texas university charged with passing technology stolen from a Californian company to Huawei.[64]

Other US concerns were broader. In 2012, the House Permanent Select Committee on Intelligence concluded after a yearlong investigation that both firms represented a national security threat to the United States. The unclassified version of the committee's findings revolved not around specific actions by the companies but rather the overall threat posed by having organizations headquartered in China provide US critical infrastructure, given that neither company had proven its independence from the CCP to the committee's satisfaction.[65] In other words, for the first time in living memory, the companies best placed to provide critical infrastructure to the United States and its allies belonged to an economic and military competitor. It wasn't until 2018 that US officials fully realized that China's coordinated strategy to dominate in 5G had worked, but once the realization hit, it sparked a flurry of activity.[66] Part of the

US response focused on preventing Chinese 5G equipment from becoming the default, including rulings to replace infrastructure already installed domestically as well as a State Department–led campaign to persuade allies and partners to shut Huawei out of their networks. But the US reaction also sought to undermine Huawei's ability to compete with US companies more broadly—for instance, by adding the firm and seventy affiliates to the Department of Commerce's Entity List in May 2019, thereby barring them from buying equipment from US suppliers without dedicated licenses.[67]

This marked an early move in an increasing campaign to weaponize the Entity List as a tool of strategic competition. Technically, Huawei's listing was explained by pointing to a January 2019 indictment of the company for providing illegal financial services to Iran. Rhetoric from US policymakers, however, tended to focus less on this procedural justification and more on the desire to take down a rival: in the words of Senator Ben Sasse, the aim was to "effectively disrupt our adversary."[68] From this point on, the addition of Chinese firms to the Entity List accelerated. Some cases, such as the listing of five supercomputing entities in June 2019, were motivated by military ties; others, such as the targeting of eight technology firms connected with surveillance in Xinjiang, cited human rights concerns. Whatever the justification, the net effect was that the Entity List began to play a more prominent role than it had to date. Access to semiconductors (and associated tools and components) soon became a central concern for many of the targeted Chinese companies, given how hard it is to replace US-sourced chips in many technological products. Huawei was hit especially hard after rule changes in 2020 expanded the controls on the company to block its access not only to US products but also to products manufactured abroad if they relied on controlled US-origin components. So far, this newly expansive use of export controls looks set to continue under the Biden administration, which has continued to add Chinese companies to the Entity List at a steady clip.

Taking a big-picture view a little over two years into Biden's tenure, the biggest change in the US approach toward technology competition is perhaps a reorientation toward allies and partners. Where Trump was not known for his talents in building multilateral coalitions, Biden has relied on partnerships in Europe, the Indo-Pacific, and across the world as a core pillar of his technology policy. One example is the formation of the Trade and Technology Council with the European Union, which seeks to coordinate on issues described above including investment screening, export controls, and semiconductors; another example is the incorporation of critical and emerging technologies as a central issue for the partnership known as the Quad (Australia, India, Japan, and the United States).[69] Whether meaningful international coordination on these complex issues will be feasible remains to be seen, but if it can be, it might mitigate some of the downsides of policies that might otherwise risk isolating the United States.

Conclusion

Technology issues are not new to US-China relations, but they have taken on new significance in this era of strategic competition. Early in the relationship, the US approach to technology reflected the highly asymmetric positions of the two countries; later, trade and security played off against each other as China emerged in global markets. Today, strategic competition has become the primary dynamic of the bilateral technology relationship, driven by China's increased ability to rival US technological prowess and the increasingly important role of technology in CCP grand strategy.

How successfully the United States will manage this contest is not yet clear. While Washington has clearly recognized that technology is a key part of its struggle with China, there is little sign of a holistic approach to strategic competition under conditions of globalization. So far, much of the US approach to technology competition has relied on tools and structures that were developed to compete with the Soviet Union, such as export controls, investment restrictions, and immigration limits. But these structures—and the mindset that comes along with them—are poorly suited to the challenges the United States faces today, due to two crucial changes since the Cold War. First, unlike the closed-off Soviet Union, China is one of the United States' largest trading partners, is deeply embedded in the global economy, and is central to multiple technology supply chains. Second, technological innovation has shifted over the last several decades; where much of the most exciting R&D once took place inside the labs of US government agencies and contractors, it has now dispersed to for-profit and academic organizations distributed all over the world. Many US measures rest on the assumption that it is feasible to cut off or significantly slow down China's access to a given technology. In the vast majority of cases, especially in the absence of significant international coordination, this is unlikely to work.

Scholars of technology competition emphasize two elements: protect and promote. If US technology policy centers too much around a "new cold war" paradigm, it risks neglecting and even sabotaging technology promotion at the expense of protection. While trumpeting the importance of fields such as artificial intelligence and quantum computing, the Trump White House repeatedly recommended cuts to basic R&D, undercutting the most fundamental pillar of S&T promotion.[70] Another key ingredient is talent. Supporting STEM education for domestic students will be an important piece of the puzzle, but—given that the United States is competing with a country four times its size—immigration will be crucial too. When only a very small number of Chinese researchers on student or scholar visas deliberately steal technology for China's benefit,[71] designing high-skill immigration policy solely around preventing such cases throws the baby out with the bathwater. The Biden administration has taken some positive steps on both R&D funding and immigration, but it is unclear whether this will be enough to secure US competitiveness going forward.

In shaping technology norms on the international stage, China is pushing at an open door as the United States distances itself from multilateral organizations. China's goal in these fora is to erode the liberal, democratic, and rules-based elements of existing institutions and to prevent the development of new norms that might restrict the CCP, for example, around the use of surveillance technologies. A successful response will not be based on strength alone but on close collaboration with allies to develop—and enforce—a proactive vision of what liberal democratic norms for these new technologies could look like. The greater the focus on US-China bilateral competition, and on brute strength rather than shared values, the more the United States is playing on China's home turf. Biden administration efforts to build technological coordination into US relationships with allies and partners may be a promising start in a better direction, but they have yet to bear substantial fruit.

Ultimately, when it comes to technological competitiveness, the choice the United States faces is whether to lean into the system that led to its success—close alliances, a world order striving toward liberal democratic ideals, and a global scientific enterprise—or to redirect toward China's preferred model, with every country for itself, nationalized scientific research, and a world order based on material power.

Notes

*I am indebted to many friends and colleagues for insights that informed and improved this chapter. Thanks especially to Emefa Agawu, Shazeda Ahmed, Ben Chang, Tarun Chhabra, Rhaina Cohen, Saif Khan, Evan Medeiros, Dahlia Peterson, Matt Sheehan, Paul Triolo, and Remco Zwetsloot for thoughtful comments and discussions.

1. Jonathan D. Pollack, *The Lessons of Coalition Politics: Sino-American Security Relations* (Santa Monica, CA: RAND Corporation, 1984), 39.

2. Chi Su, "U.S.-China Relations: Soviet Views and Policies," *Asian Survey* 23, no. 5 (May 1983): 563, https://doi.org/10.1525/as.1983.23.5.01p00472.

3. Pollack, *Lessons of Coalition Politics*, 47.

4. Harry Harding, *A Fragile Relationship: The United States and China since 1972* (Washington, DC: Brookings Institution Press, 1992), 92; Su, "US-China Relations," 566.

5. Statement by Secretary of Commerce Malcolm Baldrige, quoted in Hugo Meijer, "Balancing Conflicting Security Interests: US Defense Exports to China in the Last Decade of the Cold War," *Journal of Cold War Studies* 17, no. 1 (January 1, 2015): 20.

6. Meijer, "Balancing Conflicting Security Interests."

7. Department of Defense, "Military Sales to China," quoted in Hugo Meijer, *Trading with the Enemy: The Making of US Export Control Policy toward the People's Republic of China* (New York: Oxford University Press, 2016), 60.

8. Meijer, "Balancing Conflicting Security Interests."

9. Xinhua, June 10, 1981, quoted in Harding, *Fragile Relationship*, 120.

10. Harding, 184–86.

11. Meijer, "Balancing Conflicting Security Interests," 28.

12. Meijer, 33.

13. Meijer, 32.

14. Harding, *Fragile Relationship*, 167.

15. Harding, 180.

16. "Trade in Goods with China," United States Census Bureau, accessed November 7, 2020, https://www.census.gov/foreign-trade/balance/c5700.html.

17. H. Asher Bolande, "AT&T's Years of Lobbying in China Yield a Minority Stake in Web Venture," *Wall Street Journal*, June 27, 2001, https://www.wsj.com/articles/SB9935981668657 81749.

18. Meijer, *Trading with the Enemy*, 176.

19. Bill Miller and Vernon Loeb, "U.S. Aerospace Firm Indicted for Sales to Chinese," *Washington Post*, October 20, 1999, https://www.washingtonpost.com/archive/politics/1999/10/20 /us-aerospace-firm-indicted-for-sales-to-chinese/7dd69175-757d-4036-a908-91f2dd40c86e/.

20. Meijer, *Trading with the Enemy*, 222.

21. Meijer, chap. 6.

22. Meijer, chap. 8.

23. *Economic Espionage: Joint Hearing before the Select Committee on Intelligence, US Senate, and the Subcommittee on Terrorism, Technology, and Government Information of the Committee on the Judiciary*, US Senate, 104th Cong. (US Government Printing Office, February 28, 1996), 156.

24. "Second to None: Preserving America's Military Advantage through Dual-Use Technology," National Economic Council, National Security Council, Office of Science and Technology Policy (February 1995), 1; Kathleen A. Walsh, "The Role, Promise, and Challenges of Dual-Use Technologies in National Defense," in *The Modern Defense Industry: Political, Economic, and Technological Issues*, ed. Richard Bitzinger (Santa Barbara, CA: Praeger, 2009), 133.

25. William Reinsch, "Export Controls in the Age of Globalization," *Monitor: Nonproliferation, Demilitarization, and Arms Control* 5, no. 3 (1999): 3–6.

26. "Argentine Charged in Theft of Intel Secrets," *New York Times*, September 25, 1995, https://www.nytimes.com/1995/09/25/business/argentine-charged-in-theft-of-intel-secrets .html.

27. Scott Thurm, "Huawei Admits Copying Code from Cisco in Router Software," *Wall Street Journal*, March 25, 2003, https://www.wsj.com/articles/SB10485560675556000.

28. Del Quentin Wilber, "The Plot to Steal the Color White from DuPont," *Bloomberg*, February 4, 2016, https://www.bloomberg.com/features/2016-stealing-dupont-white/.

29. For useful background on the environment in which the Economic Espionage Act was enacted, see *Economic Espionage*, US Senate, 104th Cong.; Charles Doyle, "Stealing Trade Secrets and Economic Espionage: An Overview of the Economic Espionage Act," Congressional Research Service (2016).

30. See, for example, *1998 Special 301 Report*, Office of the United States Trade Representative, May 1998.

31. *2012 Special 301 Report*, Office of the United States Trade Representative, April 2012.

32. Steve Lohr, "Maybe Japan Was Just a Warm-Up," *New York Times*, January 22, 2011, https://www.nytimes.com/2011/01/23/business/23japan.html.

33. Paul Triolo et al., "Xi Jinping Puts 'Indigenous Innovation' and 'Core Technologies' at the Center of Development Priorities," New America, May 1, 2018, https://www.newamerica.org/cybersecurity-initiative/digichina/blog/xi-jinping-puts-indigenous-innovation-and-core-technologies-center-development-priorities/; Elsa Kania et al., "China's Strategic Thinking on Building Power in Cyberspace," New America, September 25, 2017, https://www.newamerica.org/cybersecurity-initiative/blog/chinas-strategic-thinking-building-power-cyberspace/.

34. *Hearing on The China Challenge: Realignment of U.S. Economic Policies to Build Resiliency and Competitiveness, before the U.S. Senate Committee on Commerce, Science, and Transportation, Subcommittee on Security*, July 30, 2020 (testimony of Rush Doshi), https://www.commerce.senate.gov/services/files/6880BBA6-2AF0-4A43-8D32-6774E069B53E.

35. "New Chinese Supercomputer Named Worlds Fastest System on Latest TOP500 List," TOP500, June 19, 2016, https://www.top500.org/news/new-chinese-supercomputer-named-worlds-fastest-system-on-latest-top500-list/.

36. Hal Sirkin, Justin Rose, and Rahul Choraria, "An Innovation-Led Boost for US Manufacturing," Boston Consulting Group, April 17, 2017, https://www.bcg.com/publications/2017/lean-innovation-led-boost-us-manufacturing.aspx; Jeff Tollefson, "China Declared World's Largest Producer of Scientific Articles," *Nature* 553, no. 390 (2018), https://doi.org/10.1038/d41586-018-00927-4.

37. Tai Ming Cheung, "From Big to Powerful: China's Quest for Security and Power in the Age of Innovation" (working paper, East Asia Institute, 2019), http://www.eai.or.kr/main/english/publication_01_view.asp?intSeq=9973&board=eng_report.

38. "Military-civil fusion" (军民融合) builds on the concept of "military-civil integration" (军民结合), a goal first expressed by Deng Xiaoping in 1978. See Elsa Kania, "In Military-Civil Fusion, China Is Learning Lessons from the United States and Starting to Innovate," *Strategy Bridge*, August 27, 2019, https://thestrategybridge.org/the-bridge/2019/8/27/in-military-civil-fusion-china-is-learning-lessons-from-the-united-states-and-starting-to-innovate.

39. Early usages of the term "digital authoritarianism" include remarks by Sweden's then foreign minister Carl Bildt in May 2011, and Fredrik Erixon and Hosuk Lee-Makiyama, "Digital Authoritarianism: Human Rights, Geopolitics and Commerce," ECIPE Occasional Paper no. 5, 2011, http://hdl.handle.net/10419/174715.

40. Sophie Richardson, "Testimony before the US-China Economic and Security Review Commission," US-China Economic and Security Review Commission, May 4, 2017, 3.

41. Chris Buckley, "Crackdown on Bloggers Is Mounted by China," *New York Times*, September 10, 2013, https://www.nytimes.com/2013/09/11/world/asia/china-cracks-down-on-online-opinion-makers.html; Ian Johnson, "An Online Shift in China Muffles an Open Forum," *New York Times*, July 4, 2014, https://www.nytimes.com/2014/07/05/world/asia/an-online-shift-in-china-muffles-an-open-forum.html.

42. Sarah Dai, "China Adds Huawei, Hikvision to Expanded 'National Team' Spearheading Country's AI Efforts," *South China Morning Post*, August 30, 2019, https://www.scmp.com/tech/big-tech/article/3024966/china-adds-huawei-hikvision-expanded-national-team-spearheading.

43. Shazeda Ahmed, "The Messy Truth about Social Credit," *Logic*, May 1, 2019, https://logicmag.io/china/the-messy-truth-about-social-credit/.

44. "'Eradicating Ideological Viruses': China's Campaign of Repression against Xinjiang's Muslims," Human Rights Watch, September 9, 2018, https://www.hrw.org/report/2018/09/09/eradicating-ideological-viruses/chinas-campaign-repression-against-xinjiangs.

45. Thomas Lum and Michael A. Weber, "Human Rights in China," Congressional Research Service, April 6, 2020, 2, https://crsreports.congress.gov/product/pdf/IF/IF11240; Human Rights Watch, "'Eradicating Ideological Viruses.'"

46. Samm Sacks, "Beijing Wants to Rewrite the Rules of the Internet," *Atlantic*, June 18, 2018, https://www.theatlantic.com/international/archive/2018/06/zte-huawei-china-trump -trade-cyber/563033/.

47. Paul Triolo and Kevin Allison, "The Geopolitics of 5G," Eurasia Group, November 15, 2018, https://www.eurasiagroup.net/live-post/the-geopolitics-of-5g.

48. Thomas S. Eder, Rebecca Arcesati, and Jacob Mardell, "Networking the 'Belt and Road': The Future Is Digital," Mercator Institute for China Studies, August 28, 2019, https://merics .org/en/analysis/networking-belt-and-road-future-digital.

49. A 2019 report by the Carnegie Endowment for International Peace finds that Chinese companies (such as Huawei, Hikvision, Dahua, and ZTE) have sold AI surveillance products to sixty-three countries. By comparison, US companies (such as IBM, Palantir, and Cisco) have sold very similar products to thirty-two countries, including Russia, Egypt, Saudi Arabia, and Turkey. See Steven Feldstein, "The Global Expansion of AI Surveillance," Carnegie Endowment for International Peace, September 17, 2019, https://carnegieendowment.org/2019/09 /17/global-expansion-of-ai-surveillance-pub-79847.

50. "Foreign Economic Espionage in Cyberspace," National Counterintelligence and Security Center, 2018, 7, https://www.dni.gov/files/NCSC/documents/news/20180724-economic -espionage-pub.pdf.

51. Matt Sheehan, "Does Chinese Venture Capital in Silicon Valley Threaten US Tech Advantage?" *Macro Polo*, April 26, 2018, https://macropolo.org/analysis/chinese-vc-silicon-vall ey-threaten-us-tech-advantage.

52. "America COMPETES Act Would Stand Up a Committee to Review Certain Outbound Investment and Offshoring Transactions," Wiley, February 4, 2022, https://www.wiley.law /alert-America-COMPETES-Act-Would-Stand-Up-a-Committee-to-Review-Certain-Outbou nd-Investment-and-Offshoring-Transactions.

53. Idrees Ali and Patricia Zengerle, "Google's Work in China Benefiting China's Military: U.S. General," Reuters, March 14, 2019, https://www.reuters.com/article/us-usa-china-google /googles-work-in-china-benefiting-chinas-military-u-s-general-idUSKCN1QV296.

54. Donald J. Trump (@realDonaldTrump), "Google is helping China and their military, but not the US Terrible! The good news is that they helped Crooked Hillary Clinton, and not Trump. . . . and how did that turn out?" Twitter, March 16, 2019, https://twitter.com/realDon aldTrump/status/1107025689486737410.

55. Kiran Stacey, "Senior Republicans Criticise Microsoft's AI China Work," *Financial Times*, April 10, 2019, https://www.ft.com/content/5f5916fc-5be3-11e9-939a-341f5ada9d40.

56. Kate Conger and Daisuke Wakabayashi, "Google Employees Protest Secret Work on Censored Search Engine for China," *New York Times*, August 16, 2018, https://www.nytimes .com/2018/08/16/technology/google-employees-protest-search-censored-china.html.

57. Jeffrey Mervis, "More Restrictive U.S. Policy on Chinese Graduate Student Visas Raises Alarm," *Science*, June 11, 2018, https://www.doi.org/10.1126/science.aau4407; Emily Feng, "Visas Are the Newest Weapon in U.S.-China Rivalry," NPR, April 25, 2019, https://www.npr .org/2019/04/25/716032871/visas-are-the-newest-weapon-in-u-s-china-rivalry.

58. White House, "Proclamation on the Suspension of Entry as Nonimmigrants of Certain Students and Researchers from the People's Republic of China," May 29, 2020, https://trump whitehouse.archives.gov/presidential-actions/proclamation-suspension-entry-nonimmigra nts-certain-students-researchers-peoples-republic-china/.

59. Tom Cotton, "Cotton, Blackburn, Kustoff Unveil Bill to Restrict Chinese Stem Graduate Student Visas and Thousand Talents Participants," May 27, 2020, https://www.cotton.senate .gov/news/press-releases/cotton-blackburn-kustoff-unveil-bill-to-restrict-chinese-stem-grad uate-student-visas-and-thousand-talents-participants.

60. "FACT SHEET: Biden-Harris Administration Actions to Attract STEM Talent and Strengthen Our Economy and Competitiveness," White House, January 21, 2022, https:// www.whitehouse.gov/briefing-room/statements-releases/2022/01/21/fact-sheet-biden-harr is-administration-actions-to-attract-stem-talent-and-strengthen-our-economy-and-competi tiveness/.

61. Natasha Gilbert and Max Kozlov, "The Controversial China Initiative Is Ending—Researchers Are Relieved," *Nature* 603, no. 214–15 (2022), https://doi.org/10.1038/d41586-022 -00555-z.

62. Virgil Bisio et al., "The US-China 'Phase One' Deal: A Backgrounder," U.S.-China Economic and Security Review Commission, February 2020, https://www.uscc.gov/sites/default /files/2020-02/U.S.-China%20Trade%20Deal%20Issue%20Brief.pdf.

63. Normal Pearlstine, Priya Krishnakumar, and David Pierson, "The War against Huawei," *Los Angeles Times*, December 19, 2019, https://www.latimes.com/projects/la-fg-huawei-timel ine/.

64. Karen Freifeld, "U.S. Charges Chinese Professor in Latest Shot at Huawei," Reuters, September 9, 2019, https://www.reuters.com/article/us-huawei-tech-usa-idUSKCN1VU0J5.

65. Mike Rogers and C. A. Dutch Ruppersberger, "Investigative Report on the U.S. National Security Issues Posed by Chinese Telecommunications Companies Huawei and ZTE," US House of Representatives, 112th Cong., October 8, 2012.

66. Paul Triolo, "The Telecommunications Industry in US-China Context," Johns Hopkins University Applied Physics Laboratory, 2020.

67. David Shepardson and Karen Freifeld, "China's Huawei, 70 Affiliates Placed on U.S. Trade Blacklist," Reuters, May 15, 2019, https://www.reuters.com/article/us-usa-china-huawe itech/chinas-huawei-70-affiliates-placed-on-u-s-trade-blacklist-idUSKCN1SL2W4.

68. Shepardson and Freifeld, "China's Huawai."

69. "U.S.-EU Trade and Technology Council Inaugural Joint Statement," White House, September 29, 2021, https://www.whitehouse.gov/briefing-room/statements-releases/2021 /09/29/u-s-eu-trade-and-technology-council-inaugural-joint-statement; "Fact Sheet: Quad Leaders' Summit," White House, September 24, 2021, https://www.whitehouse.gov/briefing -room/statements-releases/2021/09/24/fact-sheet-quad-leaders-summit.

70. Will Knight, "Trump Proposes a Cut in Research Spending, but a Boost for AI," *Wired*, February 11, 2020, https://www.wired.com/story/trump-proposes-cut-research-spending-bo ost-ai.

71. One retired intelligence officer estimated that "it is unlikely that even one percent [of Chinese students and scholars in the United States] are involved in technology theft." Nicholas Eftimiades, "China's Theft and Espionage: What Must Be Done," *Breaking Defense*, April 19, 2019, https://breakingdefense.com/2019/04/chinas-theft-espionage-what-must-be-done.

PART V

13

Time Horizons and the Future of US-China Relations

David M. Edelstein

What explains the relatively rapid deterioration of US-China relations over the last half decade? While power transitions have long been identified as a source of competition and conflict between great powers, the relationship between the United States and China has followed a notable trajectory, from reasonably cooperative in the early post–Cold War period to the increasing acrimony of recent years. Where is this relationship headed next, and what factors are likely to determine if the relationship develops in a more cooperative or confrontational direction? Over the first year of the Joe Biden presidency, the new administration has sought to manage the strains in the relationship over Taiwan, the South China Sea, and the war in Ukraine while simultaneously promoting cooperation on issues such as climate change. As yet, it is unclear whether the administration cooperation can be sustained without the sources of confrontation undermining it.

Power transitions involve a rising power that is defined by the rise of its material power relative to other declining powers.[1] In the familiar logic, declining powers fear being overtaken by a rising power, so they may pursue a preventive war to defeat the rising power while they still can.[2] Alternatively, rising powers may pursue hegemonic wars in order to establish their claims to being the dominant power in the international system.[3] While the United States and China may not perfectly fit this model, as US capabilities remain substantial and, in many areas, superior to Chinese capabilities, the general dynamic of a rising power threatening a dominant power has been operative over the last few decades. It is the concern China's relative rise provokes that is the source of tension and potential conflict between it and the United States.

Arguments about power transitions, however, often miss that any conflict that occurs between rising and declining powers is frequently preceded by cooperation between those same two states. Such cooperation ranges from economic exchange to political cooperation in the management of international crises. This presents a puzzle: If states can anticipate that they are likely going to have to confront a rising power at some point, why would they not address that threat sooner, when it would presumably be less costly, rather than later? And even more puzzlingly, why would they contribute to the rising power's continued growth? A compelling theory of power transitions must explain cooperation as well as any conflict.

I seek to account for the trajectory of power transitions by noting that such transitions have an essential temporal dimension to them.[4] States act in the present, conscious that power is dynamic and that their short-term behavior may have long-term consequences. The logic of now-or-later dilemmas captures the temporal trade-offs that power transitions present. A declining power's dilemma is between acting now to try to prevent the continuing growth of a rising power with uncertain long-term intentions or waiting until later to act once the rising power's ambitions are clearer. Acting now is costly in the short term but forecloses the possibility of a dangerous long-term threat emerging. Procrastinating saves resources in the short term and makes mutually beneficial cooperation possible, but addressing a threat later may turn out to be much more costly.

The horns of a rising power's now-or-later dilemma are acting now to assert new interests or waiting until later to do so. Claiming territory or resources immediately may have inherent benefits and it may satisfy impatient domestic audiences, but it may also provoke other states into acting more quickly to prevent further aggression. Waiting until later may enable the state to develop the capabilities to be more successful in staking new claims but at the cost of foregone benefits from having asserted new interests earlier. In the next two sections, I explain how both types of states resolve their dilemmas and argue that their resolutions account for patterns of cooperation and conflict. I conclude by suggesting four different scenarios for how Sino-American relations might develop in the coming years.

The Time Horizons of Declining Powers

The time horizons of a relatively declining power like the United States explain variation in strategies from more cooperative to more confrontational approaches. Declining powers generally prefer to procrastinate and address rising great powers later rather than in the present.[5] States in decline rarely have the "geopolitical slack" to expend resources in the short term to address a potential long-term threat.[6] They must attend to immediate threats and seek ways to bolster themselves. Cooperation does not always offer short-term benefits, but economic and political exchange can help a great power post-pone its decline. In the unusual circumstance where a declining power finds itself secure in the short term, it is more likely to focus on addressing long -term threats.

The general focus of a declining power like the United States in the short term suggests a pragmatic approach toward rising powers. Rather than attempting to "strangle the baby in the cradle," the United States has continued to pursue the mutually beneficial economic cooperation that has served US interests in the short term. In general, declining powers are willing to take advantage of short-term opportunities for gain while awaiting further information about the long-term ambitions of a rising power. If a declining power faces another, more significant threat, such as when the United States confronted the threat of transnational terrorism after the attacks of September 11, 2001, the rising power may actually be a useful ally in addressing that threat. Such cooperation is less designed to shape a rising power's intentions, though that would be welcome, than it is simply to produce immediate benefits.[7] When declining powers do shift to more competitive strategies, it is the result of increasing concern about the state's long-term intentions. As China has become more assertive in the South China Sea and elsewhere over the last few years, the United States has become increasingly concerned about the scope of Chinese intentions in the coming decades. The argument suggests an alternative logic to the "shadow of the future." The more aware of—and worried about—the long shadow of the future cast by a rising great power the United States becomes, the more inclined it will be to pursue competitive strategies. A focus on the short term—a muted shadow of the future—makes cooperation more, not less, likely.[8]

Two reasons amplify the inclination of declining powers to focus on short-term opportunities for cooperation. First, uncertainty about the long-term intentions of rising great powers reinforces, rather than undermines, a declining power's interest in short-term cooperation. For as long as Chinese intentions seemed uncertain, the United States was willing to adopt a more cooperative approach toward China. As Jennifer Mitzen and Randall Schweller argue, it is premature certainty, rather than uncertainty, that often leads to competition and conflict.[9] While some international relations scholars claim that states simply assume the worst about a state's uncertain intentions, this argument is both theoretically and empirically dubious.[10] The costs of acting on worst-case assumptions about intentions are likely to be exorbitantly high, and such assumptions are unnecessary for states to protect themselves against potential threats. If the need to act is not as acute, then states with more time to spare might postpone action until they achieve greater clarity about the threat posed by others. Acting in uncertain environments is potentially very costly, with no guarantee that the investment will produce the desired result.

How do states attempt to discern the uncertain long-term intentions of a rising power? That is, how do they calculate the long-term risk posed by a rising power? Information about intentions can be gleaned from the behavioral signals of a rising power, ranging from the acquisition of certain capabilities to the way that state behaves in a territorial crisis.[11] Beliefs about intentions may also be influenced by dispositional attributes, such as the state's regime type or identity.[12] Finally, great powers commonly deploy litmus tests meant to compel a rising power into revealing its true intentions.[13] Framed so as to generate a credible signal of intentions, such tests can lead to misleading results but are nonetheless common among existing great powers. If a rising power's intentions are deemed both credible and threatening, a declining power is likely to become more determined to act sooner rather than later to forestall the rising power's ascension, no matter the short-term cost.[14] The United States has relied on all of these indicators to assess Chinese intentions, from its behavioral signals to its ideological nature. No single indicator has been determinative, but the combination of these indicators has led the United States to become increasingly concerned.

Second, when faced with a possible but uncertain long-term threat, states are reluctant to pursue irreversible strategies. Irreversible strategies are not just costly strategies but strategies that make certain alternatives impossible going forward. Preventive war is costly, but it is also irreversible in the sense that it is difficult to imagine two states going from fighting a war against each other to embracing amity and cooperation shortly thereafter. The pursuit of competitive strategies against a rising power with still-unclear future intentions may generate a self-fulfilling prophecy that makes an adversarial relationship more likely. Declining great powers aim to keep their options open going forward, so they avoid irreversible strategies toward rising powers. Policies that are irreversible have a ratchet effect whereby the intensity can potentially be increased but not decreased.[15] Similarly, behavior in international relations may be irreversible if it fundamentally alters the nature of a relationship in a way that will be difficult to undo regardless of the cost.[16]

Decision-makers are reluctant to pursue irreversible strategies in the face of potential, but uncertain, long-term threats. Thus, the United States would have been wary of adopting a strategy toward China that was irreversible and made future cooperation impossible. Preventive wars are not only costly but likely also have irreversible effects on relations between the warring states.[17] Even a more modest policy, like attempting to cut off a rising power from the global economy, could prove to be irreversible and undesirable if the rising power turns out not to be threatening or if that power pursues alternative partners. Of course, not all irreversible strategies will turn out to have been a mistake, but states cannot know beforehand which will succeed and which will be an error. As a consequence, prudent states are reluctant to commit to such strategies.

Short-term pragmatic cooperation offers immediate benefits, and it also keeps future options open should more worrying information arrive about a rising power's intentions or capabilities.

US strategy toward China in recent years has reflected the caution induced by both uncertainty and irreversibility. In the face of uncertain long-term Chinese intentions, the United States has been reluctant to pursue strategies that would have foreclosed opportunities for mutually beneficial cooperation. For example, while welcoming China into the World Trade Organization (WTO) may have allowed China to continue to prosper and accrue the capabilities necessary for continued military development, the potential economic costs of excluding China from the WTO were substantial and not worth paying, given the continued uncertainty about Chinese intentions and the challenges of reversing course if the decision were made to limit China's participation in the global economy. Rather than acting in more aggressive ways to foreclose China's growth, the United States sustained a strategy of engagement toward China as it awaited more credible information about its intentions. As troubling information about Chinese long-term intentions arrived, US time horizons shifted further into the future with increasing concern. The result has been a more competitive strategy.

The Time Horizons of Rising Powers

Patience is a virtue for rising great powers, and they tend to avoid provocative action if they can. Cooperation with other great powers may help fuel a rising power's growth, and it is certainly preferable to more competitive alternatives. Inasmuch as uncertainty encourages cooperation, rising powers have an incentive to maintain uncertainty about their future intentions. When their interests do expand, rising powers are inclined to do so through "salami tactics," expanding incrementally in a way that may not lead others to sound alarms about their intentions. Rising powers can reasonably expect that their brightest days are ahead, so they have little reason to act sooner rather than later. In the case of China, it certainly benefited from opportunities for economic and diplomatic exchange with other powerful countries, especially when compared to the alternative of possible competitive relations.

But rising powers sometimes lose patience and act aggressively when it would seem premature to do so. There are three explanations for such behavior. First, the leaders of rising great powers may face domestic political incentives to act more aggressively.[18] Nationalist populations may demand that their leaders make use of the increasing capabilities of the rising power. Alternatively, the leaders of rising powers may feel the need to demonstrate the power and potential of their political ideology, whether that be a form of authoritarianism or democracy.[19]

Second, rising powers may require additional resources to continue their rise. Acquiring those resources for themselves may appear a more reliable strategy than relying on having to trade for them. Torn between the desire to maintain uncertainty about future intentions and the imperative to maintain growth, the leaders of rising great powers may find the latter pressure irresistible.

Third, rising powers may be baited into assertive behavior by other states around them. If a neighboring power asserts its own claim to a contested piece of territory, the rising power may not wish simply to accede to that claim. Relinquishing the territory to the other state may be intrinsically costly, and there may be domestic political costs for appearing weak. Smaller powers may, in fact, be tempted to provoke the rising power precisely to test its intentions and draw the attention and commitment of larger allies.

Chinese behavior for much of the post–Cold War period has conformed to the expectations of the argument. During its period of "hide and bide," China refrained from aggressive behavior that might have raised questions about its long-term intentions. Rather than escalating various potential crises, such as the bombing of the Chinese embassy in Belgrade or the EP-3 incident in the summer of 2001, Beijing allowed those situations to fizzle out peacefully. In the wake of the terrorist attacks of September 11, 2001, China indicated an interest in cooperating in counterterrorist operations, even as such a war on terror would benefit China domestically. And, more generally, China signaled a willingness to be a part of cooperative approaches to managing a variety of tense international situations, including with regard to North Korea and Iran.

In the last half dozen years, however, this has largely changed as China has become more assertive in both its own neighborhood and around the globe. What has driven this increasing assertiveness? On the one hand, some have noted an increasingly nationalist Chinese population that is eager to see China capitalize on its increased capabilities. On the other hand, China has also been compelled to react to the behavior of its neighbors, such as Japan and the Philippines. While these other countries may only be asserting their own national interests, their behavior has arguably provoked China into behavior meant to protect its own perceived national interest. The tension of the last several years is likely to culminate in a combination of the increasing assertiveness of a national rising great power and its own perceived need to respond to the behavior of those surrounding it.

Time Horizons and Post–Cold War Sino-American Relations

The argument helps us understand the development of Sino-American relations in the post–Cold War period, in which the United States might be conceived of as the existing great power confronted with the challenge of a rapidly rising power in China.[20]

First, my argument explains the past track record of American cooperation with China. Far from constraining Chinese growth, the United States has been an active contributor to Chinese wealth. For years now, the US trade deficit with China has hovered around $300 billion.[21] While part of this cooperation was undoubtedly motivated by an effort to transform China into a "responsible stakeholder," another rationale for cooperation is that the benefit derived from economic exchange has been as beneficial to the United States as it has to China.[22] While the ability of the United States to interfere with Chinese growth has been limited, skeptics have suggested that the United States ought to have been more aggressive in attempting to constrain China.[23] Cooperation may not have swayed China's future intentions, but the argument herein suggests that cooperation is often motivated more by short-term opportunism than long-term optimism.[24]

Second, as a rising great power, China would be expected to act patiently and await its brightest days ahead.[25] Like other great powers in history, Chinese leaders may have an "optimism bias," expecting the country's growth to continue uninterrupted into the future.[26] As long as the United States valued the short-term benefits from cooperation and China refrained from behavior that might have raised concerns about its long-term intentions, cooperation was mutually beneficial and sustainable. Recognizing this, Chinese premier Deng Xiaoping suggested in 1989, as the Cold War was ending, that China should "hold [its] ground" and "be cool-headed." China must not be "impatient," and instead should "hide [its] capacities and bide [its] time."[27] The growth in Chinese interests has been slow and incremental, seeking to avoid behavior that might be viewed as overly provocative.

Third, the puzzle, then, is what has led to an apparent abandonment of the Chinese grand strategy of patience in recent years.[28] Provocative behavior in the South China Sea has only raised concerns about China's long-term intentions and, by doing so, has made cooperation with China harder to sustain. Growing Chinese nationalism and domestic political pressure to demonstrate China's leadership partly explains China's provocations. In addition, while China carries some fault for the tension in the waters of East Asia, other Asian powers are not blameless. In fact, consistent with my argument, other smaller Asian powers have provoked China perhaps to draw the interest and commitment of the United States to their security.[29]

Fourth, as more immediate threats to the United States perhaps decline, US attention is more likely to shift toward the possible long-term threat posed by China. It has been to the benefit of Sino-American relations that the United States has been occupied by other security concerns in Iraq and Afghanistan. While resolving those other challenges—one way or another—is certainly desirable, the perhaps unwanted consequence is that it is likely to generate more American concern about the continuing rise of China. Prior to the attacks of

September 11, 2001, in the absence of any other short-term threat, the United States started to pay more attention to the long-term implications of the rise of China.[30] After 9/11, the United States became more focused on the immediate threat from transnational terrorism, and the United States and China even found common cause in collaborating to fight terrorism.[31]

In short, temporal dynamics help us understand the cooperative past, the increasingly tense present, and the looming future of Sino-American relations.[32] It would behoove policymakers to consider carefully whether they are wisely weighing the short- and long-term consequences of their behavior and to contemplate whether they can proactively influence how other states value the short term versus the long term. While short-term cooperation may be welcome, the long-term consequences may be regrettable.[33]

Time Horizons and the Future of Sino-American Relations

More specifically, where might Sino-American relations head next? How might time horizons help explain whether the United States and China head deeper into confrontation or find a way to manage their relationship more peacefully? Here, I present four different scenarios reflecting four different combinations of time horizons as indicated in table 13.1.

Scenario #1: Stability Restored

In this scenario, Beijing backs away from its effort to capture short-term rewards and returns to a more forward-looking perspective. Most notably, in this scenario Beijing would send credible signals that it does not intend any short-term effort to invade and incorporate Taiwan. At the same time, a variety of other threats compel the United States to focus on short-term threats to its security rather than any potential long-term threats, including from the continuing rise of China. For this world to take shape would primarily require a shift in the temporal focus of the Chinese government. Economic pressures, as well as continuing concerns with potential threats from Iran, Russia, and, indeed, China, would compel the United States to be intently focused on the short term.

China's shift from its more long-term focus to shorter time horizons was the result of both domestic and international pressures. Domestically, the pressures of increased nationalism along with the political aspirations of President Xi Jinping led Beijing to abandon its earlier patience. Internationally, a desire to access new markets and protect China's perceived territorial interests in the South China Sea has led to increased Chinese assertiveness. A return to longer Chinese time horizons is likely only possible if these domestic and international

Table 13.1 Time horizons and the future of US-China relations.

		United States	
		Short term	Long term
China	Short term	4. increased competition	2. hegemonic war
	Long term	1. stability restored	3. competitive coexistence

pressures are both satisfied, and that seems increasingly unlikely given the escalation in tensions between China, its neighbors, and the United States.

If China were able to extend its time horizons into the future, a more cooperative Sino-American relationship could be restored. The United States would not necessarily become less concerned about future Chinese intentions, but at least Washington might find fewer reasons to be fixated on Chinese behavior in the immediate present. Meanwhile, with a restored focus on the future, China would avoid acting in short-term ways that might only aggravate its relationship with others, including the United States. Sino-American relations in 2025 would come to look more like Sino-American relations in 2005.

Such a world, however, seems increasingly unlikely to emerge. As China grows more powerful, it will see fewer and fewer reasons to put off its efforts to acquire power and resources in the short term. Rising powers focus on the longer term because they believe their brightest days lie ahead, but China may come to see that its brightest days have arrived and that the future may, in fact, not be as bright as now. Once other states become more assertive in their efforts to balance against China, the window for China to succeed without significant opposition may begin to close.

Scenario #2: Hegemonic War

In a second scenario, US time horizons extend into the future, and China's time horizons remain focused on the short term. Interestingly enough, this scenario could facilitate an extension of China's influence and interests across East Asia. By this logic, as the United States considers the long-term future, it becomes more concerned with the implications of continued Chinese growth and aggression. Such a focus would provide an opportunity for China to assert its interests throughout the region, including potentially aggressive action toward Taiwan, with little opposition from Washington, which will conclude that a short-term conflict with China does not serve long-term American interests. Over the long term, such a combination of time horizons is likely to facilitate an acrimonious and dangerous relationship between the two great powers.

What might facilitate such a shift in US time horizons? Washington might shift its attention away from the short-term threat posed by a more assertive China by recognizing that a conflict with China in the short term would be either unwinnable or simply counter to American interests. Essentially, the United States would choose to fold its hand for the moment, waiting until a future day to reengage with China. Such a position could be consistent with more restraint-oriented approaches to US grand strategies. Restrainers generally challenge the value of assertive and engaged grand strategies, arguing that states in these regions can very well take care of themselves. Over the long term, they argue, a more restrained grand strategy would allow the United States to both conserve resources for domestic purposes and address genuine threats to US national interests. At the same time, however, it may allow China to assert its interests, potentially creating dangerous dynamics in East Asia between China and its neighbors. If the United States were to adopt a less active presence in East Asia, China, in this scenario, might see an opportunity to make short-term gains.

Scenario #3: Competitive Coexistence

In a third scenario, both Beijing and Washington adopt long time horizons. This would require both of them to increase their time horizons beyond where they currently are. As suggested earlier, Beijing might extend its time horizons if it perceives that either domestic or international pressures have alleviated. Washington's time horizons might elongate if it senses that short-term competition is not to its benefit. In this scenario, China would back away from any short-term ambitions to capture Taiwan, recognizing that such a move might undermine its long-term potential to become a great power.

While such a combination of time horizons might help avoid short-term competition, it might also set the stage for a sustained long-term relationship that is neither friendly nor conflictual. If both the US and China focus on the long term, they may conclude that the stakes involved are ultimately for hegemony in the international system. Immediate, acute crises will be of less value except insofar as they help determine the longer-term direction of the international system.

Analysts of international politics and grand strategy often place value on political leaders who can see beyond the immediate crisis and focus on the long term. In this case, a combination of long time horizons is likely to feed a lengthy low-level simmer—neither a cooperative relationship nor the most dangerous of possible outcomes. Ultimately, this long-term focus may serve the national interests of both great powers involved, but that does not necessarily mean that it will lead to more peace and friendship in the international system.

Scenario #4: Increased Competition

The fourth and final scenario resembles the situation that has emerged in the last few years. Here, both the United States and China have short time horizons.

That is, they are focused on more immediate costs and benefits while significantly discounting the future. China might, in this scenario, be inclined toward more aggressive action toward Taiwan, but the United States and its allies might also be more inclined to balance against any Chinese aggression. A short-term, tense crisis is the likely result. The consequence of such an interaction is increasingly intense competition in the short term, even if it may have detrimental consequences over the long term. States and their leaders come to value immediate wins even if they may lead, over time, to long-term losses. This scenario is perhaps closest to the model of a new cold war between the United States and China. As with the Cold War between the United States and the Soviet Union, the expectation would be that the United States and China would find themselves competing globally for immediate influence and power.[34]

A continuation of this combination of time horizons would imply a highly competitive relationship between the two countries with the possibility that any disagreement, no matter how seemingly minor, could escalate into a dangerous conflict. Even if the outcome of that conflict does not necessarily benefit either state over the long term, the short-term benefits will be seen as too great to ignore. Unlike the world of hegemonic competition, this world of competition is one in which short-term rewards are valued for their own sake, not because they have long-term implications for the nature of the international system.

In the last few years, the Sino-American relationship has moved in this direction. Washington has had short time horizons for some time now—ever since 9/11—and China has been driven by domestic and international factors to focus more on short-term rewards. The consequence has been increased competition on a range of issues from the South China Sea to trade disputes to environmental regulation, with the looming danger of conflict between the two countries.

Most Likely Outcomes

The current situation, in which both states are focused on the short term, seems most likely to continue. The consequence will be continuing competition over immediate stakes with repeated crises, including over Taiwan, each of which has the prospect of erupting into conflict. The least-likely scenario seems to be a return to the previous, more cooperative world in which China had long time horizons while the US had short time horizons. This is a world in which the two states have mutually compatible interests, and cooperation is in equilibrium. The other two worlds lie somewhere in between. The world in which the US expands its time horizons longer into the future while China remains focused on the short term will occur only if Washington concludes that short-term competition is not in its interests. Instead, Washington would refocus on the long-term future, clearing the way for China to make gains in the short term at the expense of its neighbors. Finally, in the world in which both the US and China become focused on the long term, one can expect a sustained competition to ensue. The time horizons of political actors interact with each other, and as either the US or China becomes more focused on the long term, so will the other.

One final point to make about this analysis is that both the United States and China might try to incentivize each other to shift their time horizons. For the United States, it would be most advantageous if Beijing were more forward-looking rather than seeking to capture immediate rewards. China, too, would prefer if the United States looked more to the future, at least for as long as Beijing prioritizes short-term gains. The challenge is that the steps taken to encourage certain future time horizons may actually wind up creating the opposite scenario. For example, Washington might try to alleviate any international pressure that is compelling Beijing to focus on the short term, but doing so might only create a perception in China that now would be a time to capitalize in an opportunistic way. By trying to discourage the United States from competing in the short term, Beijing may send a signal about its intentions to seek benefits in the short term and, consequently, lead the United States to focus even more intently on the short term. It is difficult enough for states to manage their own time horizons, let alone those of others, and there is no certain way to encourage leaders to focus either more immediately or more forward.

To some, relationships between rising and declining great powers are destined for conflict.[35] But the historical record, including that of the United States and China, suggests a more complicated story. Oftentimes declining powers not only abstain from aggressive strategies that might forestall a rising power's ascent but sometimes contribute to that growth. As two well-regarded Asia scholars and practitioners, Robert Blackwill and Ashley Tellis, have observed about US policy toward China, "Integration, the prevailing U.S. approach toward China and the one followed assiduously since the 1970s, has undoubtedly contributed to China's rise as a future rival to American power."[36] Yet such cooperation usually does not last forever, and over time, competition and conflict become more likely.[37]

To explain these patterns of cooperation and conflict, I have drawn attention to temporal dynamics in international politics. States often face a challenge between acting in the present on both opportunities and threats or postponing those actions until later. Certain combinations of how rising and declining powers resolve these dilemmas lead to more cooperation than some might expect, while other combinations lead to competition. I have also explained why states resolve these dilemmas as they do. Short-term cooperation emerges out of a declining power's pragmatic concern about its survival in the short term and a rising power's hopes for the long term, and that cooperation ends when those foci shift. The argument has both theoretical implications and implications for contemporary and future Sino-American relations.

As with the past of Sino-American relations, the future is likely to be a product of the interaction of the two states' time horizons. As the war in Ukraine unfolds, the choices that both China and the United States make about their involvement in the war will not only reflect their own time horizons but they are also likely to shape the time horizons of the other. In turn, how the crisis develops will undoubtedly have a lasting impact on the relationship between the two countries. Importantly, the time horizons of allies in the region are also likely to be pertinent as they weigh the short- and long-term costs and benefits of opting to cooperate or compete with the United States and China. Ultimately, a return to the cooperation of the first decade of this century is unlikely. China is now too powerful and has illustrated ambitious goals too often to think that cooperation could be recaptured. That said, three scenarios become more likely: unsettled, but generally peaceful, coexistence; the emergence of dangerous competition that could culminate in war; or a significant long-term hegemonic competition between the two states. Which emerges—and how dangerous the situation becomes—will depend on who is myopic and who is farsighted.

Notes

1. Robert Gilpin's analysis of power transitions suggests that they are deeply competitive and often end in war. Robert Gilpin, *War and Change in World Politics* (New York: Cambridge University Press, 1981).

2. For an excellent summary of the logic of wars during power transitions, see Alex Weisiger, *Logics of War: Explanations for Limited and Unlimited Conflicts*, Cornell Studies in Security Affairs (Ithaca, NY: Cornell University Press, 2013), 16–19.

3. Dale C. Copeland, *The Origins of Major War* (Ithaca, NY: Cornell University Press, 2000); Jack S. Levy, "Declining Power and the Preventive Motivation for War," *World Politics* 40 (1987): 82–107; A. F. K. Organski and Jacek Kugler, *The War Ledger* (Chicago: University of Chicago Press, 1980).

4. On time more generally, in the social sciences, see Andrew Abbott, *Time Matters: On Theory and Method* (Chicago: University of Chicago Press, 2001); Barbara Adam, *Time and Social Theory* (Philadelphia: Temple University Press, 1990); Allen C. Bluedorn and Robert B. Denhardt, "Time and Organizations," *Journal of Management* 14, no. 2 (1988): 299–320; Shane Frederick, George Loewenstein, and Ted O'Donoghue, "Time Discounting and Time Preference: A Critical Review," *Journal of Economic Literature* 40 (2002): 351–401; George Loewenstein and Jon Elster, *Choice over Time* (New York: Russell Sage Foundation, 1992). Time has been extensively discussed elsewhere in the social sciences: George Loewenstein, Daniel Read, and Roy F. Baumeister, *Time and Decision: Economic and Psychological Perspectives on Intertemporal Choice* (New York: Russell Sage Foundation, 2003).

5. On alternative strategies toward rising great powers, see Randall L. Schweller, "Managing the Rise of Great Powers: History and Theory," in *Engaging China: The Management of an Emerging Power*, ed. Alastair Ian Johnston and Robert S. Ross (New York: Routledge, 1999), 1–31.

6. On the concept of "geopolitical slack," see Peter Trubowitz, *Politics and Strategy: Partisan Ambition and American Statecraft* (Princeton, NJ: Princeton University Press, 2011).

7. On the socialization of China, see Alastair Iain Johnston, *Social States: China in International Institutions, 1980–2000* (Princeton, NJ: Princeton University Press, 2008).

8. Importantly, I am not the first to suggest that the conventional logic of the shadow of the future does not apply in all contexts. Robert Powell argues that the sequencing and magnitude of costs and benefits affect the degree to which the shadow of the future produces cooperation. If the short-term rewards of defection are large enough, that may cancel out any long-term incentives to cooperate. Robert Powell, *In the Shadow of Power: States and Strategies in International Politics* (Princeton, NJ: Princeton University Press, 1999), 69–73. James Fearon does not quibble with the idea that a lengthy shadow of the future may induce cooperation, but he does argue that such a long shadow is likely to make the initial negotiations over any cooperative agreement more contentious. James D. Fearon, "Bargaining, Enforcement, and International Cooperation," *International Organization* 52, no. 2 (1998): 269–305.

9. Jennifer Mitzen and Randall L. Schweller, "Knowing the Unknown Unknowns: Misplaced Certainty and the Onset of War," *Security Studies* 20, no. 1 (Spring 2011): 2–35.

10. On this point, see the disagreement between Sebastian Rosato, "The Inscrutable Intentions of Great Powers," *International Security* 39, no. 3 (2014): 48–88; and Charles L. Glaser et al., "Correspondence: Can Great Powers Discern Intentions?" *International Security* 40, no. 3 (January 1, 2016): 197–215.

11. James D. Fearon, "Signaling Foreign Policy Interests Tying Hands versus Sinking Costs," *Journal of Conflict Resolution* 41, no. 1 (February 1997): 68–90.

12. On shared identity as the basis of the democratic peace, see Alexander Wendt, "Collective Identity Formation and the International State," *American Political Science Review* 88 (1994): 384–96.

13. Victor D. Cha, "Hawk Engagement and Preventive Defense on the Korean Peninsula," *International Security* 27 (2002): 40–78.

14. For other takes on discerning state intentions, see Zachary Shore, *A Sense of the Enemy: The High-Stakes History of Reading Your Rival's Mind* (Oxford: Oxford University Press, 2014); Keren Yarhi-Milo, *Knowing the Adversary: Leaders, Intelligence, and Assessment of Intentions in International Relations* (Princeton, NJ: Princeton University Press, 2014).

15. Cass R. Sunstein, "Irreversibility," *Law, Probability and Risk* 9, no. 3–4 (September 1, 2010): 227–45. Quote on 237.

16. Irreversibility is similar, but distinct, from path dependence. Whereas path dependence suggests that the options available to a policymaker in the present are deeply influenced by the decisions that have been made in the past, irreversible strategies destroy the path behind the actor as they move along. On path dependence, see Paul Pierson, "Increasing Returns, Path Dependence, and the Study of Politics," *American Political Science Review* 94, no. 2 (June 2000): 251–67.

17. On preventive war, see, among others, Levy, "Declining Power."

18. On nationalist protest in rising China, see Jessica Chen Weiss, *Powerful Patriots: Nationalist Protest in China's Foreign Relations* (New York: Oxford University Press, 2014).

19. Famously making this argument for new democracies is Edward D. Mansfield and Jack Snyder, "Democratization and the Danger of War," *International Security* 20, no. 1 (1995): 5–38.

20. For an analysis of the pragmatic nature of Sino-American relations, see Thomas J. Christensen, *The China Challenge: Shaping the Choices of a Rising Power* (New York: W. W. Norton, 2015).

21. Historical data is available through the US Census Bureau. See https://www.census.gov/foreign-trade/balance/c5700.html.

22. For an analysis of why states may trade with potential enemies, see Hugo Meijer, *Trading with the Enemy: The Making of US Export Control Policy toward the People's Republic of China* (New York: Oxford University Press, 2016).

23. Making the case for a more aggressive strategy toward China is Aaron L Friedberg, *A Contest for Supremacy: China, America, and the Struggle for Mastery in Asia* (New York: W. W. Norton, 2011). Constraining China may be more challenging as it increasingly turns its attention to domestic-based economic growth. See Mark Magnier, "As Growth Slows, China Highlights Transition from Manufacturing to Service," *Wall Street Journal*, January 19, 2016, http://www.wsj.com/articles/as-growth-slows-china-highlights-transition-from-manufacturing-to-service-1453221751; Bettina Wassener, "For China, a Shift from Exports to Consumption," *New York Times*, January 20, 2014, http://www.nytimes.com/2014/01/21/business/international/for-china-a-shift-from-exports-to-consumption.html.

24. For the argument that neither cooperation nor regional balancing appears to have swayed China, see Kurt M. Campbell and Ely Ratner, "The China Reckoning: How Beijing Defied American Expectations," *Foreign Affairs* 97, no. 2 (2018): 60–70.

25. On how rising powers behave toward declining powers, see Joshua R. Itzkowitz Shifrinson, *Rising Titans, Falling Giants: How Great Powers Exploit Power Shifts*, Cornell Studies in Security Affairs (Ithaca, NY: Cornell University Press, 2018).

26. C. T. F. Klein and M. Helweg-Larsen, "Perceived Control and the Optimistic Bias: A Meta-Analytic Review," *Psychology and Health* 17, no. 4 (2002): 437–46; N. D. Weinstein, "Optimistic Biases about Personal Risks," *Science* 246, no. 4935 (1989): 1232.

27. For a discussion of this guidance, sometimes referred to as the "24-Character Policy," see M. Taylor Fravel, *Strong Borders, Secure Nation: Cooperation and Conflict in China's Territorial Disputes* (Princeton, NJ: Princeton University Press, 2008), 134–35; Dingding Chen and Jianwei Wang, "Lying Low No More? China's New Thinking on the Tao Guang Yang Hui Strategy," *China: An International Journal* 9, no. 2 (2011): 195–216.

28. Ting Shi and David Tweed, "Xi Outlines 'Big Country Diplomacy' Chinese Foreign Policy," Bloomberg, December 1, 2014, http://www.bloomberg.com/news/2014-12-01/xi-says-china-will-keep-pushing-to-alter-asia-security-landscape.html.

29. On recent perceived provocations in the South China Sea by nations other than China, see Felipe Villamor, "Duterte Orders Military to Parts of South China Sea Claimed by Philippines," *New York Times*, April 6, 2017, https://www.nytimes.com/2017/04/06/world/asia/rodrigo-duterte-south-china-sea.html; Prashanth Parameswaran "Why Did Indonesia Just Rename Its Part of the South China Sea?" *Diplomat*, accessed August 24, 2017, http://thediplomat.com/2017/07/why-did-indonesia-just-rename-its-part-of-the-south-china-sea/; "Vietnam Goes Bold in the South China Sea," *American Interest*, July 6, 2017, https://www.the-american-interest.com/2017/07/06/vietnam-goes-bold-south-china-sea/; Nobuhiro Kubo, "Japan Warship Takes Asian Guests to South China Sea Defiance of China," ABS-CBN News, accessed August 24, 2017, http://news.abs-cbn.com/overseas/06/23/17/japan-warship-takes-asian-guests-to-south-china-sea-defiance-of-china.

30. For a reminder of the concern about China in the late 1990s, see Michael E. Brown, *The Rise of China* (Cambridge, MA: MIT Press, 2000).

31. Shirley Kan, "U.S.-China Counter-Terrorism Cooperation: Issues for U.S. Policy," Congressional Research Service, December 7, 2004; Shirley Kan, "U.S.-China Counterterrorism Cooperation: Issues for U.S. Policy," Congressional Research Service, July 15, 2010.

32. For the argument that the United States may not be declining relative to China, see Michael Beckley, *Unrivaled: Why America Will Remain the World's Sole Superpower*, Cornell Studies in Security Affairs (Ithaca, NY: Cornell University Press, 2018).

33. On the question of Chinese intentions, see Alastair Iain Johnston, "Is China a Status Quo Power?" *International Security* 27, no. 4 (Spring 2003): 5–56; Jeffrey W. Legro, "What China Will Want: The Future Intentions of a Rising Power," *Perspectives on Politics* 5, no. 3 (September 2007): 515–34.

34. On the new cold war model, see Hal Brands and John Lewis Gaddis, "The New Cold War: America, China, and the Echoes of History," *Foreign Affairs* 100 (2021): 10–20.

35. See the concluding chapter of the first edition of John J. Mearsheimer, *The Tragedy of Great Power Politics* (New York: W. W. Norton, 2001). In the second edition, Mearsheimer backs away from this prediction. See also John J. Mearsheimer, "China's Unpeaceful Rise," *Current History* 105 (2006): 160–61.

36. Robert D. Blackwill and Ashley J. Tellis, "Revising U.S. Grand Strategy toward China," Council on Foreign Relations, accessed April 10, 2015, 18, http://www.cfr.org/china/revisi ng-us-grand-strategy-toward-china/p36371; See also Aaron L. Friedberg, "Competing with China," *Survival* 60, no. 3 (May 2018): 7–64.

37. Anticipating Sino-American conflict is Graham Allison, *Destined for War: Can America and China Escape Thucydides's Trap?* (Boston: Houghton Mifflin Harcourt, 2017).

14

Parsing and Managing US-China Competition

David Shambaugh

The term "competition" has become the leitmotif among American foreign policy specialists for characterizing the American relationship with China. Policy journals are filled with articles on US-China competition, while US government officials and documents increasingly use this terminology.

President George W. Bush was the first to officially describe China as a "strategic competitor" during the 2000 presidential campaign,[1] directly contradicting the second Clinton administration's depiction of China as a "strategic partner," but then the Bush administration largely dropped the term after entering office. Although the term continued to float around among scholars and policy analysts, it then largely went into a sixteen-year hibernation until "strategic competition" became the official centerpiece used by the Trump administration in a variety of official documents and speeches.[2]

The Biden administration has also adopted "competition" as its central intellectual descriptor and policy organizing construct, albeit with different adjectival modifiers. President Biden himself spoke of "extreme competition" in February 2021, but later in the year he used "healthy competition" when speaking with Chinese President Xi Jinping. On various public occasions Biden's National Security Advisor Jake Sullivan has used "intense competition" and "stiff competition," but also "responsible competition." For his part, Secretary of State Antony Blinken has described the relationship as "competitive when it should be, collaborative where it can be, and adversarial where it must be," while Deputy Secretary of State Wendy Sherman has used "stiff competition" "healthy competition," and "responsible competition." Blinken, Sullivan, and Sherman all used "competition" in their face-to-face meetings with Chinese interlocutors during 2021. The Biden administration's Indo-Pacific Strategy described its policy this way: "We will [also] seek to manage competition with the PRC [People's Republic of China] responsibly."[3]

For its part, however, Beijing has categorically and publicly rejected this language. At a meeting in Zurich, Switzerland, in October 2021, Chinese foreign policy supremo Yang Jiechi explicitly told Sullivan, "China opposes defining China-U.S. relations as 'competitive,'"[4] adding that "the U.S. should join Beijing in respecting each other's core interests and major concerns, and follow the path of mutual respect, peaceful coexistence and win-win cooperation between the two countries."[5]

What does it really mean, though, to characterize the US-China relationship as "competitive"? This chapter seeks to unpack and examine this question. It argues that competition has been a consistent feature of the US-China relationship since 1949, even since the 1972 rapprochement, although its nature and intensity have changed over time. It also discusses whether the competitive relationship today (and into the future) qualifies as a "new cold war" (as some assert), and what lessons and tools from Cold War 1.0 may be useful in the current context. Finally, it makes the imperative case for "managing competition" so that the competitive relationship does not become fully adversarial.

Conceptualizing Competition

I think of and describe the relationship between the United States and China today as one of *indefinite comprehensive competitive rivalry*. It is now primarily a competitive relationship in which the existing elements of cooperation are far outweighed by the competitive ones, in which each side seeks to strengthen itself vis-à-vis the other and takes actions and counteractions against the other; it is comprehensive in that it stretches across virtually all functional issue areas and all geographic regions of the world (even into outer space); it has become a classic great power rivalry whereby each increasingly contests the other's presence and influence worldwide; it exhibits the classic reactive and escalatory elements of a "security dilemma"; and it is not time-bound and can be expected to last indefinitely into the future.

It is important to note at the outset, however, that competition is not inherently a negative concept nor is it the opposite of cooperation. "Competition" has a more neutral connotation than (and is to be distinguished from) being "conflictual" or "adversarial." Competition is entirely natural and largely positive in several domains of human activity. Competition is intrinsic in commerce, in innovation and invention, in media, in politics, in sports, in education and the intellectual "marketplace of ideas," among institutions, and in other domains. Competition is not inherently negative nor intrinsically zero-sum. It is often a stimulus for improvement and can bring out the best in various actors. Nor is competition to be thought of as the opposite of cooperation. They can, and do, coexist. Countries, firms, individuals, and various actors can compete and co-operate with each other simultaneously. Thus, when we say that the US-China relationship is primarily competitive, by no means does that imply that there is no scope for pragmatic cooperation (although some commentators, notably in China, falsely juxtapose the two as being mutually exclusive). In a 2013 pub-lication, I was the first to describe this mixed condition as "coopetition,"[6] and I would still argue that this is an accurate term—but with greater emphasis on the latter half of the word today. At that time I also described a "best-case" scenario under these conditions as being one of "competitive coexistence," and I still believe that to be apt today. Competition and cooperation are thus *simultane-ous* conditions—the pertinent question pertains to the *relative balance* between them.[7]

While competition has been a constant feature in the relationship since the 1972 opening, until the past decade it was a secondary feature in a relationship characterized primarily by various efforts to forge a cooperative partnership (see figure 1). Over five decades, cooperative relations primarily characterized seven of ten American administrations.

However, the competitive elements (individually and collectively) have in-creased dramatically since the 2008 global financial crisis. Concomitantly, the areas of bilateral and multilateral cooperation have considerably decreased. As the relationship has become increasingly competitive, it has thus shifted even further toward the left-hand side of the spectrum. Elements of the competition, notably in the security domain, already incline toward the "adversary" end of the spectrum, while other elements such as regional and global geostrategic competition, perceived threats in domestic politics, and technology develop-ment have all become more acutely competitive. Even such areas that were previously predominantly cooperative—such as educational, science, and tech-nology exchanges, and many aspects of the economic relationship—now also exhibit competitive elements. Overall, the center of gravity of the relationship is now squarely on the competition side of the spectrum.

As the broad trajectory of the relationship in recent years has been toward increasing frictions and comprehensive competition and increasing rivalry, simply managing ties so that the competitive dynamics do not bleed into a full adversarial relationship should be the principal goal of both countries; if so managed, it should be seen as a considerable measure of success. While already quite strained, the relationship could get worse—much worse—and it is not im-possible to imagine a *war* breaking out between the two powers (although the waging of a US-China war is quite unimaginable). Given that a conventional conflict (likely triggered offshore) would quickly escalate to attacks on the oth-er's homeland—with a range of conventional, unconventional, even potentially

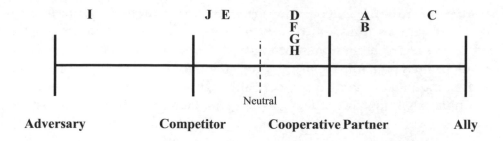

A = Nixon; B = Ford; C = Carter; D = Reagan; E = Bush 41; F = Clinton; G = Bush 43; H = Obama; I = Trump; J = Biden

Figure 14.1 A simple spectrum of US-China relations.

nuclear weapons—such a scenario is to be avoided at all costs. Both sides must have a sober appreciation of this worst-case possibility. That, in turn, requires very deft and careful management of a highly competitive and friction-ridden rivalry. What is particularly concerning is that unlike the Soviet-American Cold War 1.0—which was rather "static" and operated under conditions of "mutual assured (nuclear) destruction" (MAD) and various arms control and other agreements (e.g., the Helsinki Final Act, the Conference on Security and Cooperation in Europe) as well as the overall framework of détente—the US-China competition today is much more fluid and is not conditioned and constrained by such agreements. This makes it particularly unstable. On the other hand, the Soviet-American Cold War had none of the intersocietal interdependencies that characterize US-China relations today. To a significant extent these interdependencies serve as important buffers and anchors. Ryan Hass of the Brookings Institution has thus used the term "competitive interdependence" to describe a multifaceted competitive relationship, but one that is bounded by deep interdependencies that keep the competitive tendencies from becoming fully adversarial.[8]

The mutual goal for both governments should therefore be to deftly manage the multitude of competitive issues in ways that do not progressively "bleed" or inadvertently slide into conflict. Managing fluid competition is like tending a garden: it requires constant attention and proactive management. It can also be thought of as a sporting competition without end—where there is ebb and flow as each contestant advances and retreats on the playing field—but neither side wins or loses. If effectively managed, a certain delicate "equilibrium" can be found and a relationship of "competitive coexistence" can be established.[9] Managing competition will require not only finding issues where cooperative interactions can be forged between the two governments and societies but also building a series of "guardrails," "buffers," and "off ramps" to "bound" the competition so that it does not hemorrhage toward a fully adversarial relationship (recognizing that a competitive relationship is partially adversarial). I discuss this further at the end of this chapter.

Recognizing this fluidity, reviewing the history of US-China relations is also instructive. Over time there has been a repetitive "enchantment-disenchantment cycle" in US-China relations over the past two hundred–plus years. Relations go up and down and pass through repetitive identifiable cycles. Actually, it is not so much a two-stage "love-hate" cycle as it is a multistage enchantment-disenchantment pattern: (1) naive admiration and enchantment; (2) reality intrudes, respective interests assert themselves, difference of opinion and frictions arise; (3) arguments ensue; (4) attempts to find common ground follow; (5) failure to find such common ground leads to (6) estrangement; (7) either conflict *or* a "cold peace" with much friction.[10] Usually, with three exceptions (China's Civil War, the Korean War, the Cold War), when the two sides reach the sixth stage they pull back from the brink (also the case with multiple Taiwan Straits crises). What this chapter argues is that today the sixth stage will be an indefinite, not temporary, condition.

There is also one significant difference today with this historical pattern: China has always been much weaker and the United States far stronger. While, on aggregate, China still remains weaker than the United States, it nonetheless has become a "peer competitor," it possesses a great deal of strength, and it can cause the United States real pain if it so chooses.[11] Beijing also has a powerful sense of enduring grievances against the United States (and the West). China today also has a greater tolerance for friction than has previously been the case. Emboldened by intense domestic nationalism, growing confidence, and hubristic "wolf warrior" public diplomacy, the PRC regime appears much more argumentative, assertive, acerbic, and risk prone.

Adding to the uncertainty and instability is that the relationship is reaching something of a geostrategic threshold—with China's power and influence growing regionally and globally, while America's has been declining relatively. The latter was apparent for several years prior to the COVID-19 pandemic (as a result of Beijing's broadened international footprint as well as the Trump administration's anti-multilateral policies), but it has become even more volatile in the wake of the global crisis. As power transition theorists remind us, this is precisely the most unstable and vulnerable period in relations between established powers and rising powers—when one or the other misjudges its own relative position and takes preemptive actions against the other. This is the so-called Thucydides's Trap.[12]

Since about 2016 the Sino-American relationship has definitely hardened and become more suspicious. There is a mutual animosity, suspicion, and fragility to it today not witnessed since 1989. In that instance the strained relationship was the result of a single event (the June 4 killings in Beijing), whereas today the strains are more structural and systemic, are deeper, are more intractable, and have a long-term indefinite quality to them.[13] A wide variety of variables will all condition the relationship, and these factors mean that the relationship is not entirely in the control of leaders or governments on both sides, as exogenous factors will have a large shaping impact.

Parsing Competition

One way to conceptualize and explore these variables is to break them into distinguishable domains. Drawing on the analytical device of "levels of analysis" first used in the discipline of international relations in the 1960s,[14] for the purposes of understanding the dynamics of US-China relations today and into the future, it is analytically useful to distinguish between five distinct domains of interactions: domestic politics, bureaucratic politics, societies, regional affairs in Asia, and global affairs.

One other caveat concerning the term "strategic competition." I perhaps have a narrower definition of this term than other analysts or the way it is used in this volume. While I accept that powers can compete geostrategically across different regions of the world and different domains—as the United States and China certainly do—I tend to apply the term "strategic" to the security/military domain. Therefore, as discussed above, in this chapter I prefer to use "comprehensive competition" to refer to multiple functional and geographic realms.

Domestic Political Competition

The dramatically different political ideologies and domestic political systems of the United States and China have been at the core of their differences and disagreements ever since the Chinese Communist Party (CCP) came to power and the PRC was established in 1949. Political differences also animate long-standing US support for the Nationalist regime—both on the mainland prior to 1949 and subsequently on Taiwan. The United States did all it could to prevent the CCP from coming to power, and when it did Washington did not officially recognize the PRC as a sovereign state for thirty years. During that lengthy period, differences in political systems and their underlying ideologies fundamentally contributed to the Cold War and led to the American policy of containment against the PRC (from 1949 to 1960 the China containment policy was a subset of the Soviet containment policy, but following the Sino-Soviet split until the Nixon opening, containing China was an independent US policy). It also led to a variety of covert attempts to subvert the communist regime as well as fighting overt hot wars in Korea and Vietnam. Make no mistake: it was precisely the Chinese communist *regime* that the United States objected to on political and ideological grounds—and vice versa, as Beijing viewed "American imperialism" (美帝) as its mortal enemy.

When the two sides pursued their diplomatic rapprochement during the early 1970s it was *not* because they had come to accept each other's political systems (although there was grudging recognition in Washington that after two decades in power the CCP was not a temporary phenomenon); it was *totally* a result of strategic expediency. Both sides had independently concluded that the other was useful in their mutual antagonism against the Soviet Union. But both Beijing and Washington continued to view each other's political system and governing ideology as anathema. They had simply decided to put these differences aside in the context of broader strategic commonality. Subsequently, during the 1980s, when paramount leader Deng Xiaoping, CCP General Secretary Hu Yaobang, and Premier Zhao Ziyang initiated the "reform and opening" policy—which included political reform and liberalization—the United States was supportive (tapping into a long-standing American paternal impulse to liberalize China).[15] The underlying political differences appeared to be narrowing, and the PRC appeared to be moving away from the Leninist regime it had imposed since 1949.

Then came the Tiananmen massacre of 1989 and its aftermath. The common strategic glue had disappeared along with Mikhail Gorbachev's own détente with Beijing and Washington, but now the perception in the United States that China was inexorably moving in a more liberal direction (and the frontal challenge to CCP rule of the 1989 demonstrations) was dashed. From that day until now, the nature of China's political system has returned to be a significant source of America's problems with China. While economic interdependence grew dramatically after the 1990s and pragmatic cooperation was periodically achieved (such as China's admission to the World Trade Organization in 2001 or the 2015 Paris Climate Change Agreement), during the past three decades, fundamentally and deep down, the Chinese communist regime and its repressive rule has been a significant ideological and systemic impediment to ties. The regime appeared to relatively loosen its repression during some of the Jiang Zemin and Hu Jintao eras, but since Xi Jinping came to power in 2012 with his regime of dramatically intensified repression, the nature of China's political system has again risen to the surface as one of the primary problems from the American perspective. Ideologically, a new cold war has begun—or, perhaps more accurately, has simply reemerged into full view after years of dormancy just beneath the surface. The Trump administration (2017–21) made this explicit. Various senior officials explicitly reframed the Sino-American competition as essentially ideological in nature. Former Secretary of State Mike Pompeo's speech at the Nixon Library on July 23, 2020, was an ideological call to arms.[16] As Trump's Deputy National Security Advisor (and top China adviser) Matt Pottinger wrote after leaving office, "The ideological dimension of the competition is inescapable, even central."[17] One aspect of this reframing was that the Trump team took pains to distinguish the Chinese Communist Party from Chinese society, arguing that America's main problem and struggle was with the former, not the latter. The succeeding Biden administration and President Biden himself have similarly cast the Sino-American relationship in politically ideological terms—arguing that the meta competition in world affairs is between democracies and autocracies.[18] Russia and China are exhibits A and B in the minds of President Biden and his administration in the global struggle between democracy and autocracy.

For its part, throughout this long period, Beijing has correctly perceived America's discontent with—and opposition to—its political system. This is not in Beijing's imagination, nor is it "fake news." The CCP regime is well aware of the various covert methods the US intelligence agencies used to try and destabilize its rule from the 1950s to the 1970s. Secretary of State John Foster Dulles publicly proclaimed in a series of speeches during 1957–58 that the United States would pursue a policy of "peaceful evolution" (和平演变) to peacefully evolve communist regimes to become noncommunist and hopefully democratic states. Thereafter, the CCP and government authorities throughout China have been on continual high alert against this American desire and policy. Chinese leader Mao Zedong himself gave a speech in Hangzhou on November 30, 1958, specifically criticizing Dulles's concept, and he rang the alarm bell for the CCP to prepare for such subversion.[19]

The CCP has perceived a wide variety of subversive US mechanisms to have been used by the United States inside China in pursuit of this alleged goal: American foundations, NGOs, media, educational exchanges, religious activists, and covert methods. In the wake of the collapse of the East European communist states and the former Soviet Union in 1989–91, as well as the "color revolutions" of the 1990s (which the CCP attributed, in significant part, to have been the result of Western "peaceful evolution"), the Chinese authorities have been particularly paranoid about such subversion. Xi Jinping has taken the obsessive suspicion to a level unparalleled since the Maoist era, as evident in the infamous CCP Central Committee Document No. 9 of 2013.[20] Since then, the CCP has pursued a variety of programs against so-called Western hostile forces (西方敌对势力).[21] While the CCP has long viewed US "peaceful evolution" as something to be on guard against, under Xi Jinping there appears to be a more existential view of US political and cultural threats to Chinese security and the sustenance of the regime. Xi himself has given multiple speeches, not the least of which was his address to the Twentieth Congress of the CCP in October 2022,[22] concerning the need to prepare for, and engage in, "struggle" (斗争) against such subversive "hostile forces."

Also, following Xi Jinping's speech to the previous Nineteenth Party Congress in 2017, another dimension of the political system variable has arisen with Beijing's touting of its own autocratic system (the "China Option" or 中国方案) as a potential model for other countries to follow.[23] At the Twentieth Congress Xi went further by touting China's own brand of "whole process people's democracy" in contrast to (allegedly) failing "bourgeois democracy." During the Mao era, the CCP regime also pursued such ideological competition against the United States and the West (as well as the Soviet Union post-1960).[24] Compared to Maoist China, Xi and the CCP today are more oblique and less assertive in pushing an alternative model and system, but it is nonetheless a new dimension of competition between the two political systems.[25]

Thus, the two differing political systems have long been—but are even more now—a significant variable and sphere of contention and competition between the two powers. This is not likely to recede unless the CCP regime again reverts to a "softer" and more tolerant form of rule that again appears to be moving in a convergent political trajectory with liberal systems (as was the case from 1980 to 1989 under Deng Xiaoping, Hu Yaobang, and Zhao Ziyang, or 1996 to 2008 under Jiang Zemin and Hu Jintao). From my perspective, the differing political systems are really the core problem in US-China relations. Competition certainly exists in other realms, as explored below, but incompatible political systems lie at the heart of the differences between the two sides. As the US political system has itself displayed multiple signs of dysfunctionality (most notably during the Trump years), Chinese officials have watched with glee and stepped up their criticisms of the American political system and various social maladies.[26]

Bureaucratic Competition

This sphere in US-China competition is different from, but derivative of, the political systemic variable just discussed. This level of analysis entails bureaucratic actors in the two national governments and their institutional "missions." That is, do they pursue missions of cooperation, competition, adversarial confrontation, or some combination thereof toward the other government and country?

From 1949 to 1972 there was, of course, no interaction between the ministries and agencies of the two governments and militaries. As such, by default, they each pursued negative and adversarial missions toward the other side, born of the hostility between the two governments. The propaganda organs in China and the US Information Agency hurled invective at each other. The Voice of America dueled over the airwaves with Radio Peking. The respective intelligence agencies monitored each other from afar, the CIA ran a variety of covert action programs in several parts of China, U-2 overflights monitored China from seventy thousand feet throughout the 1950s and '60s, while China's internal security agencies were on the lookout for spies. The American economic bureaucracies (led by the departments of Treasury and Commerce) enforced the trade embargo and export controls against China,[27] while their Chinese counterparts blocked US goods from seeping in. The US military deployed forces all along China's eastern frontier while maintaining a presence with its ally Taiwan, while the People's Liberation Army (PLA) sought to develop at least minimal deterrents against possible American attacks against the mainland. There were no student or cultural exchanges between the relevant departments and ministries. Absent diplomatic relations, the US Department of State and China's Ministry of Foreign Affairs had no direct interactions (other than the occasional "Warsaw channel"), while each tried to undermine the other in various regions of the world.[28] There were no exchanges between the US Congress or state legislatures and governments and their Chinese counterparts. Science and technology ministries had no contact. And so on. Either the bureaucracy in each country had *no* mission or it had an explicitly *negative* adversarial mission vis-à-vis its counterpart. This is what the Cold War meant in practical bureaucratic terms.

The Sino-American opening of 1971–72 offered the opportunity to forge initial contacts between this range of counterpart bureaucracies for the first time and to turn adversarial missions into cooperative ones. However, two factors impeded this development. First, the two sides were most interested in forging strategic/military cooperation against the Soviet Union rather than forging broad institutional linkages. Second, while the American side was in favor of beginning "familiarization exchanges" at a variety of levels, the Chinese side refused to do so almost in toto (the exception being discussions concerning the Soviet Union). The reason for this, the Chinese side argued, was that such exchanges between governments and societies at all levels were the by-product of normal and formal diplomatic relations. Absent diplomatic ties, Beijing refused to establish such exchanges until 1979.

Moreover, it was not merely a question of deciding to engage in familiarization exchanges with the other side. It was also a question of fundamentally reorienting the mission and mindset of the bureaucracies from a negative one—aimed at countering the other—to a wholly different *positive* approach of cooperating with each other. This also concomitantly involved financial resources. Money that had been allocated toward countering the other now had to be redirected to facilitating positive cooperation with the other. This was not feasible, as adversaries always attract larger resources than partners.

In the United States, a 1971 RAND Corporation study (led by Morton Abramowitz) began the process of conceptualizing how this process of reorientation could be undertaken.[29] Other American China scholars, notably Michel Oksenberg and Richard Solomon, also began to think along these lines. Oksenberg in particular, who was a specialist in Chinese bureaucratic politics, carefully thought through where the potential institutional synergies could be, so that when normalization of full diplomatic relations occurred on January 1, 1979 (and Oksenberg had much to do with it as President Carter's chief China adviser on the National Security Council staff), the US executive branch bureaucracies could spring into action to forge collaborative relationships with their Chinese institutional counterparts, thus attempting to turn negative bureaucratic missions aimed at countering the other into positive cooperative ones. Indeed, in the very first year after normalization no fewer than thirty-five intergovernmental agreements were concluded and initiated. This process Oksenberg described as "marrying bureaucracies."[30]

The reason that this history is relevant to the present is because under the current competitive conditions in US-China relations, the two bureaucracies are now involved in the exact reverse process. They are either engaged in "institutional decoupling," thus breaking off any collaborative relationship, or they are reshaping their positive cooperative missions backward into more negative missions to once again counter the other. One way this is being manifest is simply by not renewing previous agreements and memoranda of understanding (MOUs). A large number have simply lapsed. Many that remain in force have gone dormant. Another method, undertaken by the Trump administration, has been to entirely break off the large-scale Strategic and Economic Dialogue (S&ED) process of the George W. Bush and Obama administrations as well as a number of other dialogues. During the Obama administration there existed just under one hundred bilateral dialogues, under Trump they shrank to less than ten,[31] and only a handful have been continued by the Biden administration. This was unilateral on the American part, as the Chinese side did not seek to do so. China *loves* dialogues (and it causes many foreign interlocutors to complain of "dialogue fatigue"). The ostensible reason the Trump administration terminated the dialogues was that they were viewed as a "trap" to tie the US government up in endless discussions that produced little resolution of issues of concern to the American side, and the implementation of the agreed communiques was normally elusive, while China continued on with its troublesome practices and its accruing of national strength.

Accordingly, many US government departments and agencies have begun programs to scrutinize, curtail, or block exchange programs with their Chinese counterparts. Congress is also playing an active role in this process through passing multiple acts of legislation mandating such scrutiny and reporting requirements. The FBI and other agencies involved in counterintelligence have dramatically stepped up their investigations of different forms of PRC espionage inside the United States. The Department of Justice launched its "China Initiative" in 2018, primarily aimed at curbing PRC economic espionage, "nontraditional" intelligence collection, and "influence operations."[32] Many arrests and prosecutions have been made (and some have been dropped for lack of evidence). The Department of Education, the National Institutes of Health, and other funding agencies have stepped up reporting requirements of American universities involved in collaborative research with China or those that receive grants or gifts from China. The Federal Communications Commission is now more closely policing the operations of Chinese radio and television organs inside the United States, with several Chinese state media organs now being required to register under the Foreign Agents Registration Act (FARA) as "foreign missions." The Department of Defense has curtailed a wide range of interactions it previously undertook with the People's Liberation Army. NASA has been forbidden by law from collaborating with its counterpart, the Chinese National Space Administration (CNSA). Quiet but cooperative work in securing nuclear stockpiles between Sandia National Laboratories and its Chinese counterpart has also slowed (if not stopped).[33] The interagency Committee on Foreign Investment in the United States (CFIUS) has ramped up its scrutiny of Chinese investments, blocking many deals. Congressional exchanges have atrophied, and those between American states and municipalities with Chinese counterparts have come under closer scrutiny by US counterintelligence agencies.[34] As the COVID-19 pandemic revealed, the previous active collaboration between the two countries' Centers for Disease Control (CDC) has become dysfunctional. Even meteorological and weather data are no longer regularly shared.

Chinese bureaucracies have similarly pulled back from their previous interactions with American counterparts. The PRC regime's preoccupation with domestic political stability and security has contributed to the "securitization" of how the regime views cultural, educational, media, and civil society exchanges. All external exchanges now must pass a proverbial "subversion test" before being permitted to proceed. As a result, hundreds of American NGOs have pulled out of China since the passage of the 2017 Foreign NGO Law. The 2015 National Security Law, 2016 Cybersecurity Law, 2017 National Intelligence Law, and (updated) 2021 Counterespionage Law have all sent shivers through the foreign community in China.

This is what "competition" looks like bureaucratically. The two governments are institutionally decoupling, previous agreements have been allowed to lapse, formerly regularized dialogues have been cut off, and normal professional interactions have atrophied. Mutual suspicions are running high, and the two sides are reverting to the negative bureaucratic mission reminiscent of Cold War 1.0.

Societal Competition

Intersocietal interactions have long provided ballast to the US-China relationship. This has been the essence of "engagement."[35] Tens of millions of Chinese students have studied in the United States,[36] and millions have immigrated and become naturalized American citizens. In the pre-COVID period, an average of ten thousand people traveled between the two countries every day. As of 2018 there existed 40 sister state/provinces and 201 sister city relationships. All kinds of businesses have established a presence in the other country, while bilateral goods trade totaled a staggering $656 billion in 2021, according to US government statistics.[37] US committed investments in China totaled $123 billion in 2020,[38] while Chinese foreign direct investment (FDI) in the United States is considerably lower and more fluctuant. Many other indicators illustrate the interconnectedness of the two societies. Thus, the societal level of analysis is the greatest example of Sino-American cooperation. Without it, the frequent strains produced in other spheres would produce even greater frictions and volatility in the relationship.

Yet, even in this domain, "competitive" elements exist. By far, the greatest source of tension is in the trade realm, as demonstrated most notably by the reciprocal tariff and trade war during the Trump administration. But even prior to this unprecedented commercial conflict, there existed a high degree of discontent and frustration among American businesses about the multitude of barriers they faced in China. Competitive commercial frictions also extend to Chinese investments in the United States, particularly into sensitive sectors and locales. Export controls on China have also been significantly strengthened (they always have been tight). These steps have been taken as a result of the increased "securitization" of commercial activities. Thus, it cannot be said that the commercial relationship has been either cooperative or harmonious; indeed, it has grown to rank among the most serious sources of friction in the relationship, despite the gargantuan headline trade numbers. Former President Trump's unprecedented "trade war" against China is Exhibit A in the American commercial frustration with China.

Another element of competitive friction relates to media. American (and other Western) media have long labored under extremely difficult working conditions in China—but with Xi Jinping's crackdown on civil society and stepped-up surveillance and information controls, US media in China have become even more constrained.[39] Conversely, China's media have dramatically broadened their presence in US media markets, commensurate with China's global "great external propaganda" (大外宣) initiative. In 2020 the Trump administration took the step of classifying five Chinese state media organs in the United States as "foreign missions" (the same as foreign embassies and state commercial actors),[40] and it limited the number of accredited employees of these five entities to one hundred and their visas to ninety days. One reason for this action was to institute some closer degree of numerical reciprocity in journalists accredited in each country; by the time of the Trump administration's actions, China had 425 individuals in the United States on journalist visas in 2019,[41] while accredited American journalists in China were around 50 (including wire services like AP, UPI, and economic data providers such as Dow Jones and Bloomberg). The Chinese government responded in kind by expelling almost all employees of the *New York Times*, the *Washington Post*, and the *Wall Street Journal*. This tit-for-tat series of media actions was a significant sign of competitive tensions in this arena, although the Biden administration negotiated a lifting of the ban on these three US media outlets as well as more relaxed reciprocal visa policies.

Both sides' actions are reflective of mutual fears of political subversion. CCP fears of American political subversion were discussed above, but should Americans be concerned about CCP political subversion inside the United States? The answer is yes. In the United States this has become known as PRC/CCP "influence operations" or "united front activities." They are carried out by a broad range of Chinese institutional actors and are targeted against a wide range of domestic American actors, including state and local governments, universities, think tanks, media, corporations, laboratories, and the Chinese diaspora community.[42] China also targets exiled dissidents, Tibetans, Uyghurs, and Falun Gong practitioners. What is occurring in the United States is just part of a global offensive carried out by the Chinese government and CCP actors to influence the international narratives about China. These activities have reached a very serious level in Australia, New Zealand, Europe, and Canada and are increasing in other regions of the world.[43] They have also been discovered inside the United States, and several congressional committees and think tanks have published reports detailing these efforts.[44]

Concerns about China's influence operations have also spilled over into the world of higher education. Here, too, we witness a "securitization" of academic exchanges. The FBI has made a number of arrests—of both American and Chinese nationals—who have been accused (some convicted, some prosecutions dropped) of theft and illicit transfer of intellectual property and know-how from the United States to China. These cases parallel the widespread corporate and cyber espionage against American companies and universities. FBI Director Christopher Wray has indicated that active China-related espionage cases total more than three thousand, while a new case is opened every thirty-six hours.[45] Director Wray has also repeatedly spoken of the need for a "whole-of-society" response to China's "diverse, multilayered, relentless efforts to steal sensitive technology and proprietary information from US companies, academic institutions, and other organizations."[46] The Trump administration started this process, but the Biden administration continued it.

Thus, in the United States, even the world of higher education and universities—which arguably has been among the most cooperative aspects of bilateral relations—now also shows signs of "securitization" and competitive strains. This has carried over into think tank and NGO exchanges, where concerns about Chinese espionage and influence operations have also arisen. Such exchanges, once robust, have significantly atrophied in recent years.[47]

Meanwhile in China, the Xi regime's crackdown against foreign NGOs and the passage of the Foreign NGO Law and related security laws noted above have resulted in the closure and withdrawal of several hundred American NGOs, the termination of a number of educational exchanges, and tourism. Similarly, social science research attempted by American scholars in China has also come under significantly heightened scrutiny and constraints.

Thus, internal security concerns run in both directions and have contributed to a more suspicious atmosphere in each country. It is therefore apparent that "competitive" dynamics extend throughout the societal domain and thus can no longer be counted exclusively on the "cooperative" side of the US-China ledger.

Asian Regional Competition

The Asian region (whether described as the Asia-Pacific or Indo-Pacific) has always been the geostrategic epicenter of US-China multifaceted interactions (military, commercial, cultural, diplomatic).[48] American and Chinese presence and activities in these realms have not always been viewed as explicitly competitive (excepting Taiwan), but this is now predominantly the case.

In terms of security, China has never been happy with the five American alliances, and the US military presence throughout the region, or intelligence gathering near China. While Beijing may have previously tolerated these realities, it has long resented them. Chinese civilian and military leaders have grown more and more opposed and outspoken in recent years. Beijing constantly monitors the alliances for signs of strain and fissures, eager to exploit any. Such has particularly been the case with respect to the alliances with Thailand and the Philippines. In both cases they have drawn away from Washington and closer to Beijing, with China offering a variety of economic inducements to both Bangkok and Manila before the new Marcos administration recalibrated it.

China has long been uncomfortable with the US military forward deployments in the region, which ring China's maritime periphery. Regular US close-in military reconnaissance along China's coastline (just outside its twelve-mile territorial limit) has also been a long-standing (and understandable) irritant for Beijing. American and Chinese ships and planes are having increasing numbers of dangerous close encounters, notably in the South China Sea. US security assistance to Taiwan has always been a particularly neuralgic Chinese concern. While in recent years Beijing has also increasingly expressed its discontent with

US military relationships in Southeast Asia—notably with Singapore, Malaysia, Brunei, the Philippines, Thailand, and Vietnam—it is also extremely critical of the growing US security relationship with India, and Beijing views the development of the "Quad" (the US, Japan, Australia, and India) with deep suspicion. At the 2023 National People's Congress, China's leader Xi Jinping unprecedently and bluntly said: "Western countries led by the United States have implemented all-around containment, encirclement, and suppression of China, which has brought unprecedented severe challenges to our country's development."[49]

For its part, China's military capabilities have steadily improved, and its operations have broadened throughout the region. The PLA Navy is now the largest one in the western Pacific, while its growing inventory of missiles has provided the capacity to reach Guam and attack American targets at long range. China's island building and deployment of military assets in the South China Sea are becoming a real game changer in regional security.

Throughout Southeast Asia, China has increased its presence and influence—diplomatically, commercially, and culturally—and sees itself in clear competition with the United States in the region.[50] The Belt and Road Initiative (BRI) is a significant tool in Beijing's toolbox, as many Southeast and South Asian countries are in dire need of roads, rails, ports, electric grids, hospitals, schools, water treatment, Internet connectivity, and a variety of governance enhancements. But Beijing has also dramatically stepped up its economic aid, cultural presence, public diplomacy, united front activities, and diplomatic presence throughout the Association of Southeast Asian Nations (ASEAN) region and Indian Ocean littoral states. In Australasia, Beijing has combined influence activities with threat of economic penalties against Australia and New Zealand—thus alienating both countries—while ramping up its presence in the South Pacific islands. Similar tactics have been used against South Korea. Meanwhile, the most tension-prone of China's regional relationships—with Japan—remains fragile.

For America's part, the Obama administration prioritized the region with its "pivot" or "rebalance" policy, the Trump administration followed with its "Free and Open Indo-Pacific" initiative, and the Biden administration has focused even greater attention and resources on the region. Under all three administrations, Washington has sought to constrain China's regional position and influence. Overall, while it must be said that China's position and influence has increased relative to that of the United States, the two powers are definitely locked into intensified regional competition.[51] The competition remains fluid, however. There are already apparent signs that Beijing may be overplaying its hand toward a number of countries.[52] In my view, Washington has underplayed its own hand, as the United States has many intrinsic strengths and considerable respect across the region. Without a doubt, Sino-American competition across Asia is intensifying and will be a long-term phenomenon.

Global Competition

As China has "gone global,"[53] so, too, has its competition with the United States.[54] Once geographically limited to Asia and Africa, China is now a true international actor. As it has expanded its presence, interests, and influence on all continents, it has bumped up against long standing American presence and relationships in many parts of the world. This is particularly true in Europe and Latin America (both Central and South America), and increasingly throughout the Middle East and Africa.[55] Some regions and countries have yet to fully grasp the new great power rivalry, while others are beginning to wrestle with the consequences and their policy options.[56]

Simply by virtue of China's newfound presence in these regions, the United States views and defines China as a geostrategic competitor. Hegemons don't like peer competitors, especially those that enter the hegemon's traditional regional spheres of influence.[57] They are thus usually viewed in zero-sum fashion. This need not necessarily be the case, as the two powers' interests overlap in places and they could undertake helpful actions in parallel, such as development assistance, debt relief, Millennium Development Challenge goals, disaster relief, pandemics, counterterrorism, and other areas. Unfortunately, such collaborative thinking is currently lacking in both capitals. Once a "competition mindset" is set in place, it tends to take on an inexorable and reinforcing zero-sum dynamic of its own. Everything is perceived through the prism of contested influence.

This is, for example, the way that Washington has often viewed the BRI, the Asian Infrastructure Investment Bank (AIIB), the New Development Bank (NDB), and the string of China's regional cooperation forums: the Shanghai Cooperation Organization (SCO), China-Arab States Cooperation Forum (CASCF), China–Eastern European Countries (CEEC), Forum on China-Africa Cooperation (FOCAC), China–Community of Latin American and Caribbean States (CELAC), and Pacific Islands Forum.[58] From Beijing's perspective, it sees these institutions as examples of the "new type" of cooperative diplomacy and security—as distinct from the US model of bi- and multilateral alliances—which it seeks to promote in world affairs. From Washington's perspective, they are proof positive of China expanding its spheres of influence.

US-China competition also extends to multilateral international institutions and global governance.[59] Whether correct or not, Washington increasingly views Beijing as a global "revisionist" power that seeks to undermine and overturn the post–World War II so-called liberal international order.[60] Following the Trump administration's intentional erosion of that order, the Biden administration has set it as a top priority to rejoin institutions and reconstruct the normative order. For its part, China's role in global governance has certainly been a work in progress, but it has been a generally positive evolution. Over time China has progressively become an institutional member of international society and gradually assimilated many of the norms and rules of international institutions. Yet it has also long evinced both ambivalence and discomfort with the liberal order it has joined (despite benefiting substantially from it). While China has become more constructively involved and invested in global governance, since Xi Jinping came to power it is now trying to proactively shape the global governance agenda. This, too, puts it at increasing variance with the United States and other liberal states.

Managing Competition

From examining these five distinct arenas of competition, I find China and the United States to be increasingly at odds in each one. In some sectors a clear action-reaction dynamic has emerged, producing an intrinsic zero-sum game. This can be called "hard rivalry." In others, each side takes its own actions not necessarily in response to the other but with a careful eye on the other. This can be called "soft rivalry." As such, many observers still think it too premature to describe the relationship as Cold War 2.0. If that were the case, each side would seek explicitly to counter the other in a tit-for-tat manner in *all* cases and places all the time. That is not (yet) the reality—but it may be fair to characterize this comprehensive competition as Cold War 1.5. To be sure, Sino-American relations certainly exhibit *some* of the action-reaction dynamics (political competition, some aspects of societal competition, and military competition)—but in others (bureaucratic competition, Asian regional competition, and global competition) we see each side unilaterally taking its own actions, driven by their own interests, while carefully monitoring the actions of the other in each sphere. Either way, though, the two great powers are competing for position and influence, using both offensive and defensive means to do so.

Many seasoned former US government officials argue for finding an appropriate "balance" between cooperation and competition.[61] Others, including this author, find the scope for concerted and coordinated cooperation to be very limited, while arguing that full-spectrum competition is reality, is desirable, and is necessary. Such a robust competitive strategy needs to be pursued both offensively and defensively in multiple spatial and functional domains simultaneously. Effective competition with China truly begins domestically by investing in all the tools of comprehensive national power at home. The Biden administration recognizes this and is investing in a wide array of dimensions, from science and education to microchip manufacturing to hard infrastructure. It involves strengthening American democratic institutions and reconstituting the foundations of America's soft power. It certainly involves strengthening

America's hard military power in the Indo-Pacific and investing in next-generation technologies and weapons. It involves strengthening alliances and non-allied partnerships all around the world. It involves countering China's malign behavior inside the United States and around the world (this involves exposing it in the public domain), while using a combination of unilateral, bilateral, multilateral, and media tools to expose and punish Beijing's repressive domestic conduct. The United States should not shrink from pursuing a multispectrum assertive competitive strategy vis-à-vis China.

Under such conditions of intensifying competition, therefore, it is equally necessary and important for both Beijing and Washington to effectively manage their competition,[62] to constrain it, and do what they can to prevent a full-scale multidimensional zero-sum adversarial relationship and military conflict from emerging. It may eventually get to this point, but we are not there yet; it is not inevitable, and it is to be avoided.

Moreover, proactive steps need to be taken to stabilize the competition and create institutions and procedures to actively constrain it. Not surprisingly, many of these lie in the security/military domain: things like "hotlines" and communications frequencies between military authorities at multiple levels in the chain of command, pre-notification of military exercises and large-scale movement of troops or weapons, arms control agreements, "rules of the road" for accidental air and sea encounters, crisis escalation controls (including mutual commitments to "no first use" of nuclear weapons), forbidding cyber attacks on civilian infrastructure, bans on anti-satellite weapons and the placing of kinetic systems in outer space, and convening of a variety of meaningful military-to-military dialogues and civilian dialogues (governmental and Track 1.5 and II) on geostrategic perspectives and policies. There is time and opportunity to try to put in place a variety of confidence-building mechanisms (CBMs) and risk mitigation measures, create channels of communication and crisis-management mechanisms between military and civilian authorities, and plan nonescalatory reactions to anticipated or possible moves by the other side. Such actions are very much needed in an attempt to buffer, bound, and stabilize the escalating competition.[63]

Here, the Cold War offers many poignant lessons, and it is worthwhile to re-open that toolbox and dust off some of the tools.[64] While Cold War 1.0 had differing characteristics from the possible Cold War 2.0, it also exhibits many similarities.[65] The United States and Soviet Union not only had their "tripwires" and "red lines" but they also established a wide variety of conflict-avoidance, confidence-building, and crisis-management mechanisms.[66] US-Soviet détente was a protracted and multilayered set of reinforcing processes. Some involved multiple countries, such as the Conference on Security and Cooperation in Europe (CSCE) and the Helsinki Accords, which could be adapted in the case of

China. Unofficial "Track II" exchanges of experts and the creation of epistemic communities played important roles in the Cold War.[67] These examples from the US-Soviet experience need to be fully reexamined to explore potentially revisable and reusable mechanisms.

One way of thinking about this is to recall the détente framework that President Nixon and Soviet leader Leonid Brezhnev built into the Cold War adversarial rivalry. The détente processes were not mutually exclusive to the geostrategic competition but were supplementary and complementary. In order to defuse tensions, some American scholars believe that a "grand bargain," such as Nixon and Mao struck, needs to be struck between Washington and Beijing—but such overarching schemes are both unlikely and inadvisable in the US-China context today.[68]

If a similar architecture can be constructed between the United States and China in order to "bound" and "regularize" their competition, then catastrophe (war) can be avoided.[69] If this is not done, and buffers are not built between competition and conflict on the spectrum shown in figure 14.1, then there may be an inexorable slide into a fully adversarial relationship. Moreover, other "middle powers" have a strong stake in such "stabilization of competition," and they, too, possess important agency which can contribute to frameworks that can perhaps restrict the intensification of the competition, and perhaps even ameliorate it. Unlike the Cold War, international relations today is not a bipolar system. It is thus well worth the effort of all concerned parties. The future of the world is at stake.

Notes

1. See Thomas Lippman, "Bush Makes Clinton's China Policy an Issue," *Washington Post*, August 20, 1999, https://www.washingtonpost.com/wp-srv/politics/campaigns/wh2000/stories/chiwan082099.htm.

2. Most prominently, see *National Security Strategy of the United States of America*, December 2017, https://trumpwhitehouse.archives.gov/wp-content/uploads/2017/12/NSS-Final-12-18-2017-0905.pdf; *The United States Strategic Approach to the People's Republic of China*, May 26, 2020, https://trumpwhitehouse.archives.gov/wp-content/uploads/2020/05/U.S.-Strategic-Approach-to-The-Peoples-Republic-of-China-Report-5.24v1.pdf; *Elements of the China Challenge*, Policy Planning Staff of the Secretary of State, November 2020, https://www.state.gov/wp-content/uploads/2020/11/20-02832-Elements-of-China-Challenge-508.pdf.

3. *Indo-Pacific Strategy of the United States*, White House, February 2022, 5.

4. "Senior Chinese Diplomat Meets U.S. National Security Advisor," Xinhua, October 7, 2021, http://www.news.cn/english/2021-10/07/c_1310229525.htm.

5. "Chinese and US Officials Hold 'Frank, Constructive' Talks in Zurich," CGTN, October 8, 2021, https://newseu.cgtn.com/news/2021-10-07/Senior-Chinese-and-U-S-officials-hold-frank-comprehensive-talks--149akjhzZQs/index.html.

6. David Shambaugh, "Tangled Titans: Conceptualizing the U.S.-China Relationship," in *Tangled Titans: The United States and China*, ed. David Shambaugh (Lanham, MD: Rowman

& Littlefield, 2013), 4. In recent years senior (and now retired) Chinese diplomat Madam Fu Ying has also used "coopetition" in her speeches and publications, but it is unclear where she learned this term. "Coopetition" is a neologism that has been used in the business world dating back to 1913 and in game theory dating to 1944. See https://en.wikipedia.org/wiki/Co opetition.

7. For a very thoughtful conceptual discussion of these factors, see Harry Harding, "American Visions of the Future of U.S.-China Relations: Competition, Cooperation, and Conflict," in Shambaugh, ed., *Tangled Titans*, 389–409.

8. See Ryan Hass, *Stronger: Adapting America's China Strategy in an Age of Competitive Interdependence* (New Haven, CT: Yale University Press, 2021), chap. 3.

9. As noted earlier, I first used the term "competitive coexistence" in my *Tangled Titans: Conceptualizing the US-China Relationship*. Subsequently, others have as well. See, for example, Kurt Campbell and Jake Sullivan, "Competition Without Catastrophe: How America Can Both Challenge and Coexist with China," *Foreign Affairs* (September/October 2019).

10. While they do not use this typology, both Warren Cohen and John Pomfret have also described this generally repetitive pattern in the history of US-China relations. See Warren Cohen, *America's Response to China: A History of US-China Relations*, 4th ed. (New York: Columbia University Press, 2000); John Pomfret, *The Beautiful Country and the Middle Kingdom: America and China, 1776 to the Present* (New York: Picador Books, 2016).

11. See the discussion in Chas W. Freeman Jr., "China's National Experiences and the Evolution of PRC Grand Strategy," in *China and the World*, ed. David Shambaugh (New York: Oxford University Press, 2020), 54–56. See also Thomas Christensen, "Posing Problems without Catching Up," *International Security* 25, no. 4 (Spring 2001): 5–40.

12. See Graham Allison, "The U.S.-China Strategic Competition: Clues from History," in *The Struggle for Power: U.S.-China Relations in the 21st Century*, eds. Nicholas Burns, Leah Bitounis, and Jonathon Price (Washington, DC: Aspen Institute, 2020), 79–96; Graham Allison, *Destined for War? Can America and China Escape Thucydides's Trap?* (New York: Mariner Press, 2018).

13. I very much agree with Evan Medeiros that the "structural" nature of US-China competition is not only new but qualitatively different from previous periods. See Evan S. Medeiros, "The Changing Fundamentals of U.S.-China Relations," *Washington Quarterly* 42, no. 3 (Fall 2019): 94.

14. See J. David Singer, "The Level of Analysis Problem in International Relations," in *The International System: Theoretical Essays*, ed. Klaus Knorr and Sidney Verba (Princeton, NJ: Princeton University Press, 1961), 77–92; and James Rosenau, ed., *International Politics and Foreign Policy* (New York: Free Press, 1969).

15. On US-China relations during the 1980s, see the superb and insightful study by Richard Madsen, *China and the American Dream: A Moral Inquiry* (Berkeley: University of California Press, 1995). For an excellent account of domestic Chinese politics during the decade, see Julian Gewirtz, *Never Turn Back: China and the Forbidden History of the 1980s* (Cambridge, MA: Belknap Press of Harvard University Press, 2022).

16. Mike Pompeo, "Communist China and the Free World's Future," remarks at the Richard M. Nixon Presidential Library and Museum, Yorba Linda, CA, July 23, 2020, https://sv.use mbassy.gov/secretary-michael-r-pompeo-remarks-at-the-richard-nixon-presidential-library -and-museum-communist-china-and-the-free-worlds-future/.

17. Matt Pottinger, "Beijing Targets American Business," *Wall Street Journal*, March 27–28, 2021.

18. See "Remarks by President Biden in Press Conference," White House, March 25, 2021,

https://www.whitehouse.gov/briefing-room/speeches-remarks/2021/03/25/remarks-by-president-biden-in-press-conference/.

19. See Zhai Qiang, "Mao Zedong and Dulles' 'Peaceful Evolution' Strategy," *Bulletin of the Cold War International History Project*, nos. 6-7 (1995): 227–30.

20. "Document 9: A Chinafile Translation," Chinafile, November 8, 2013, https://www.chinafile.com/document-9-chinafile-translation.

21. See, for example, Chris Buckley, "China Takes Aim at Western Ideas," *New York Times*, August 19, 2013, https://www.nytimes.com/2013/08/20/world/asia/chinas-new-leadership-takes-hard-line-in-secret-memo.html.

22. Xinhua News Agency, "Full Text of the Report of the 20th National Congress of the Communist Party of China," October 25, 2022: https://english.news.cn/20221025/8eb6f5239f984f01a2bc45b5b5db0c51/c.html.

23. See Nadège Rolland, *China's Vision for World Order* (Seattle: National Bureau of Asian Research, 2020).

24. See Julia Lovell, *Maoism: A Global History* (New York: Knopf, 2019); Gregg A. Brazinsky, *Winning the Third World: Sino-American Rivalry During the Cold War* (Chapel Hill, NC: University of North Carolina Press, 2017).

25. Some scholars take exception to this interpretation and argue that China is not trying to export its ideology abroad, and on this basis, they therefore argue, the contemporary US-China struggle cannot be compared to the Cold War. See, for example, Thomas J. Christensen, "There Will Not Be a New Cold War: The Limits of U.S.-Chinese Competition," *Foreign Affairs*, March 24, 2021, https://www.foreignaffairs.com/articles/united-states/2021-03-24/there-will-not-be-new-cold-war. Other leading scholars counterargue that China *is* attempting to export the *means*, if not a holistic model, of authoritarianism abroad. See Elizabeth Economy et al., "China's Role in the World: Is China Exporting Authoritarianism?" (panel discussion, Harvard University, February 9, 2022), https://fairbank.fas.harvard.edu/events/chinas-role-in-the-world-is-china-exporting-authoritarianism/.

26. See David Shambaugh, "A Hot Exchange in Cold Alaska," *China-US Focus*, March 25, 2021, https://www.chinausfocus.com/foreign-policy/a-hot-exchange-in-cold-alaska.

27. See Shu Guang Zhang, *Economic Cold War: America's Economic Embargo against China and the Sino-Soviet Alliance, 1949–1963* (Washington, DC: Woodrow Wilson Center Press, 2001); Hugo Meijer, *Trading with the Enemy: The Making of U.S. Export Control Policy toward the People's Republic of China* (Oxford: Oxford University Press, 2016).

28. See Brazinsky, *Winning the Third World*.

29. Richard Moorsteen and Morton Abramowitz, *Remaking China Policy: U.S.-China Relations and Government Decisionmaking* (Cambridge, MA: Harvard University Press, 1971).

30. I was Oksenberg's assistant on the NSC staff from 1977 to 1978, and this was the terminology he used to describe the process at the time. Much of my work was involved with working with different US executive branch departments and agencies to work through the bureaucratic, legal, and financial dimensions of this process. Oksenberg later described his thinking and actions in two articles: Michel Oksenberg, "The Dynamics of the Sino-American Relationship," in *The China Factor*, ed. Richard Solomon (Englewood Cliffs, NJ: Prentice-Hall, 1981), 48–80; and Oksenberg, "A Decade of Sino-American Relations," *Foreign Affairs* 61, no. 1 (Fall 1982): 196–210.

31. For an analysis of these dialogues, see Bonnie S. Glaser, "The Diplomatic Relationship: Substance and Process," in Shambaugh, ed., *Tangled Titans*.

32. See US Department of Justice, "Information about the Department of Justice's China Initiative and a Compilation of China-Related Prosecutions since 2018," https://www.justice

.gov/nsd/information-about-department-justice-s-china-initiative-and-compilation-china
-related.

33. See Heather Clark, "Chinese Nuclear Security Center Opens with Help from Sandia,"
Sandia Lab News, April 1, 2016, https://www.sandia.gov/labnews/2016/04/01/china/.

34. Mike Pompeo, "Remarks by the Honorable Michael R. Pompeo, Secretary of State,"
National Governors Association winter meeting, Washington, DC, February 8, 2020, https://
www.nga.org/videos/wm2020-pompeo-remarks/.

35. The best single study of "engagement" is Anne F. Thurston, ed., *Engaging China: Fifty
Years of Sino-American Relations* (New York: Columbia University Press, 2021).

36. During the 2018–19 academic year there were 369,548 Chinese students in US universities. These numbers fell to 317,299 in academic year 2020–21 (largely because of COVID-19):
"International Student Data from the 2021 Open Doors Report," Open Doors Data, https://op
endoorsdata.org/data/international-students/all-places-of-origin/. There are also uncertain
numbers studying in American high schools (estimated at eighty thousand).

37. "The People's Republic of China," Office of the US Trade Representative, https://ustr
.gov/countries-regions/china-mongolia-taiwan/peoples-republic-china.

38. Statista Research Department, "Direct Investment Position of the U.S. in China 2000-
2020," Statista, August 4, 2021, https://www.statista.com/statistics/188629/united-states-di
rect-investments-in-china-since-2000/.

39. The deteriorating plight of foreign journalists in China is cataloged in the annual reports of the Foreign Correspondents' Club of China: https://fccchina.org.

40. Xinhua News Agency, China Global Television Network (CGTN), China Radio International (CRI), *China Daily*, *People's Daily*.

41. Sha Hua, "U.S. Puts Limits on Visas for Chinese Journalists," *Wall Street Journal*, May 9, 2020.

42. See Larry Diamond and Orville Schell, eds., *China's Influence and American Interests:
Promoting Constructive Vigilance* (Stanford, CA: Hoover Institution Press, 2019), appendix 1,
"China's Influence Operations Bureaucracy."

43. See Clive Hamilton and Mareike Ohlberg, *Silent Invasion: Exposing How the Chinese Communist Party Is Reshaping the World* (London: One World Publications, 2020).

44. See, for example, Diamond and Schell, *China's Influence and American Interests*; US-
China Economic and Security Review Commission, "China's Overseas United Front Work:
Background and Implications for the United States," 2018; The Hudson Institute, "The Chi-
nese Communist Party's Foreign Influence Operations: How the United States and Other
Democracies Should Respond," 2018; Anne-Marie Brady, *Magic Weapons: China's Political In-
fluence Activities under Xi Jinping* (Washington, DC: Woodrow Wilson Center, 2017).

45. See, for example, Christopher Wray, "Countering Threats Posed by the Chinese Government inside the United States," remarks at the Ronald Reagan Presidential Library and
Museum, Simi Valley, CA, January 31, 2022, https://www.fbi.gov/news/speeches/countering
-threats-posed-by-the-chinese-government-inside-the-us-wray-013122.

46. Wray, "Countering Threats"; see also "Wray Says Whole-of-Society Response Necessary
to Confront China Threat," Homeland Security Today, February 6, 2020, https://www.hsto
day.us/subject-matter-areas/intelligence/wray-says-whole-of-society-response-necessary-to
-confront-china-threat/; Michal Kranz, "The Director of the FBI Says the Whole of Chinese
Society Is a Threat to the US—and That Americans Must Step Up to Defend Themselves," *Business Insider*, February 13, 2018, https://www.businessinsider.com/china-threat-to-america-fbi
-director-warns-2018-2.

47. See Carter Center, *Finding Firmer Ground: The Role of Civil Society and NGOs in U.S.-China
Relations* (Atlanta: Carter Center, 2021).

48. Among many excellent studies, see Avery Goldstein, "U.S.-China Interactions in Asia," in Shambaugh ed.,, *Tangled Titans*, 263–91; Michael Swaine et al., *Creating a Stable Asia: An Agenda for a US-China Balance of Power* (Washington, DC: Carnegie Endowment for International Peace, 2016), http://carnegieendowment.org/files/CEIP_Swaine_U.S.-Asia_Final.pdf.

49. Keith Bradsher, "China's Leader, with Rare Bluntness, Blames U.S. Containment for China's Troubles," *New York Times,* March 7, 2023, https://www.nytimes.com/2023/03/07/world/asia/china-us-xi-jinping.html.

50. See Murray Hiebert, *Under Beijing's Shadow: Southeast Asia's China Challenge* (Lanham, MD: Rowman & Littlefield, 2020).

51. See David Shambaugh, *Where Great Powers Meet: America and China in Southeast Asia* (New York: Oxford University Press, 2020).

52. This is one of the principal arguments in my *Where Great Powers Meet*. Also see Hiebert, *Under Beijing's Shadow*; and Sebastian Strangio, *In the Dragon's Shadow: Southeast Asia in the Chinese Century* (New Haven, CT: Yale University Press, 2020).

53. See David Shambaugh, *China Goes Global: The Partial Power* (New York: Oxford University Press, 2013).

54. See, in particular, Ashley Tellis, Alison Szalwinski, and Michael Wills, eds., *Strategic Asia 2020: U.S.-China Competition for Global Influence* (Seattle: National Bureau of Asian Research, 2020).

55. See David Shambaugh and Dawn Murphy, "U.S.-China Interactions in the Middle East, Africa, Europe, and Latin America," in Shambaugh, ed., *Tangled Titans*, 315–46.

56. With respect to Europe, see, for example, Barbara Lippert and Volker Perthes, eds., *Strategic Rivalry between the United States and China: Causes, Trajectories and Implications for Europe* (Berlin: SWP, 2020); European Think-Tank Network on China (ETNC), *Europe in the Face of U.S.-China Rivalry* (Madrid: Real Instituto Elcano, 2020).

57. John J. Mearsheimer, *The Tragedy of Great Power Politics* (New York: W. W. Norton, 2014).

58. For an analysis of these groupings in China's diplomacy, see Srikanth Kondapalli, "Regional Multilateralism with Chinese Characteristics," in Shambaugh, *China and the World*, 313–42.

59. See Rosemary Foot, "U.S.-China Interactions in Global Governance and International Organizations," in Shambaugh, ed., *Tangled Titans*, 347–70.

60. See Gregory Chin and Ramesh Thakur, "Will China Change the Rules of Global Order?" *Washington Quarterly* (October 2011); Suisheng Zhao, "A Revisionist Stakeholder: China and the Post-World War II World Order," *Journal of Contemporary China* (July 2018); Hoo Tiang Boon, *China's Global Identity: Considering the Responsibilities of Great Power* (Washington, DC: Georgetown University Press, 2019); Jessica Chen Weiss, "A World Safe for Autocracy? China's Rise and the Future of Global Politics," *Foreign Affairs* 98, no. 4 (2019): 92–102; Rosemary Foot and Andrew Walter, *China, the United States, and Global Order* (Cambridge: Cambridge University Press, 2010); David Shambaugh, "China and the Liberal World Order," in Nicholas Burns, Leah Bitounis, and Jonathon Price, eds., *The World Turned Upside Down: Maintaining American Leadership in a Dangerous Age* (Washington, DC: Aspen Institute, 2018).

61. See, for example, Paul Heer, "Why the U.S.-China Strategic Rivalry Has Intensified," *National Interest*, March 22, 2021, https://nationalinterest.org/feature/why-us-china-strategic-rivalry-has-intensified-180843.

62. See Kevin Rudd, "Short of War: How to Keep the U.S.-Chinese Confrontation from Ending in Calamity," *Foreign Affairs*, March/April 2021.

63. In this context, see also the practical and wise policy recommendations in Evan S. Medeiros, "How to Craft a Durable China Strategy," *Foreign Affairs*, March 17, 2021.

64. See David Shambaugh, "As the U.S. and China Wage a New Cold War, They Should Learn from the Last One," *Wall Street Journal*, July 31, 2020.

65. For an excellent discussion of both similarities and differences, see Michael McFaul, "Cold War Lessons and Fallacies for U.S.-China Relations Today," *Washington Quarterly* 43, no. 4 (Winter 2021): 7–39.

66. See, for example, Simon Miles, *Engaging the Evil Empire: Washington, Moscow, and the Beginning of the End of the Cold War* (Ithaca, NY: Cornell University Press, 2020).

67. See Yale Richmond, *Raising the Iron Curtain: Cultural Exchange and the Cold War* (State College: Penn State University Press, 2003).

68. See, for example, Charles Glaser, "A U.S.-China Grand Bargain? The Hard Choice between Military Competition and Accommodation," *International Security* 39, no. 4 (Spring 2015): 49–90; Swaine, *Creating a Stable Asia*; Lyle J. Goldstein, *Meeting China Halfway: How to Defuse the Emerging US-China Rivalry* (Washington, DC: Georgetown University Press, 2019).

69. See Kevin Rudd, *The Avoidable War: The Dangers of a Catastrophic Conflict between the US and Xi Jinping's China* (New York: Public Affairs, 2022).

15

Forecasting the Future of
US-China Relations

Evan S. Medeiros

From the vantage point of early 2023—and the evolving drama of war in Ukraine and instability around Taiwan this past summer—the future of the US-China relationship looks ominous. US-China tensions are running high, driven largely by structural forces and with no end in sight. If inertia takes hold, this trajectory will only worsen, perhaps rapidly. As argued throughout this volume, US-China competition is now broad spectrum in nature, covering security, economics, technology, and governance ideas, and both countries are exploring the boundaries of competition on these issues. The Ukraine war has exacerbated both the immediate and structural tensions at the heart of the relationship.[1] China is now very much a central player in the geopolitics of the war, despite its best efforts to appear "objective and impartial."[2] Beijing's deepening alignment with Russia, as captured in the Xi Jinping March 2023 trip to Moscow and the February 2022 China-Russia joint statement,[3] and its pointed and persistent criticism of the United States and NATO for causing the war have positioned Beijing at odds not just with Washington but with America's allies in both Europe and Asia.[4] And the war has put a greater spotlight on the Taiwan issue and the prospect of Chinese military action. Following Nancy Pelosi's summer 2022 visit to Taiwan, the Chinese military established a new situation of persistent presence around Taiwan, further raising tensions and the risk of an accident or miscalculation. As a result, US-China geopolitical differences and the competitive impulses on both sides are intensifying. The prospects of an East-West divide, albeit different from the past, loom over bilateral relations today.

At the same time, the Ukraine conflict has also highlighted the hard realities facing both China and the United States. Beijing remains a staunch rhetorical proponent of sovereignty and territorial integrity, and China's economy is substantially tied to the United States and Europe. This presents China with an enduring strategic conundrum: how to reconcile competing economic and diplomatic impulses. Perhaps the Chinese will be able to manage the blatant and gnawing tensions between and among its competing interests at a time when the stakes are high and growing. Or perhaps not, leading to an accelerated deterioration in China's ties with Washington and Europe and some hard choices on Beijing's part about its geopolitical alignment in the next decade. The heightened tensions around Taiwan put a fine point on these and other strategic dilemmas facing Beijing right now. Chinese leaders now have to contemplate the possibility of armed conflict with the US over Taiwan, perhaps sooner than desired and during a period of prolonged economic austerity.

Beginning the conclusion of this lengthy volume with a focus on these immediate events, as searing as they are, is more than mere presentism. Today's events highlight the central mission of this volume: understanding the nature of the competition between the United States and China. What are its origins, its core dynamics, and its future trajectory? Will diverging perceptions of each other and the differing interests and visions of global order produce a long-term fracture in US-China ties, leading to a new type of cold war? Or can a political modus vivendi be found for stable, if not mutually beneficial, ties? It is the future that this chapter is focused on.

Drawing on the collective insights of this volume, which cover all of the major dimensions of US-China interactions, an obvious question presents itself: Where is the bilateral competition headed and what specific forces and structural dynamics will drive this evolution? More specifically, can a new strategic modus vivendi be found for a stable relationship of coexistence amid competition, or will the US-China relations simply be a slow devolution into a long-term strategic rivalry, punctuated by bouts of both stability and acrimony? These questions will engage and preoccupy US and Chinese policymakers, business leaders, and scholars for the coming decades. This chapter jumps into this fray by providing a framework for thinking about the future. With no pretense for precision, but with an aspiration for giving structure to this forecast, this chapter seeks to outline the current conditions and future variables that will shape the most consequential bilateral relationship in international relations today.

US-China Relations: Today and Tomorrow

The US-China relationship today has the following core features: it is rapidly evolving, highly uncertain, and increasingly complex. Understanding the nature of these features is essential to forecasting the future—or, at least, to having a better sense of the trajectory of bilateral ties in the coming years. For longtime watchers of US-China relations, these may seem like common observations (i.e., When has the relationship not been complex?), but the reality is that this relationship is an inflection point: much change is occurring, in different forms, and coming fast. The future will be determined by the changing nature of the relationship, the changing nature of both countries, and the choices of both US and Chinese leaders and policymakers in response to the former.

The future of the bilateral relationship is *rapidly evolving* because the nature of international order and the global strategic environment are in deep flux. This is perhaps the most important condition impacting US-China ties today and going forward. The global events of today present US and Chinese leaders with a variety of consequential choices about security alignment and economic interdependence, and it is these choices that will impact the trajectory of US-China ties. Even before the war in Ukraine the structure of the international system was subject to debate, and this has only accelerated since the war. Is the global system still essentially unipolar, transitioning to a US-China bipolar world, or becoming essentially multipolar?[5] The war in Ukraine accelerated this discussion. Following the Russian invasion of Ukraine, many US policymakers now see themselves locked in long-term competition with two major powers, Russia and China, and see, importantly, that this competition is about the core attributes of the global order. Chinese actions accelerated these US perceptions. China positioned itself in opposition to the United States and NATO on Ukraine, accentuating the security and ideological competition with the United States and Europe. Beijing's sympathy for Russian security concerns reinforces the latter and signals a substantial degree of alignment between Moscow and Beijing. Chinese decisions about whether to provide substantial military aid to Russia, whether to circumvent the global sanctions regime, and whether to continue with a coordinated disinformation campaign against the US and European powers will have an outsize influence on US-China ties. So far, Beijing has been careful about not providing major military assistance to Moscow and avoiding widespread violations of sanctions, but questions and concerns in the United States persist. The revival of the transatlantic community and the resurgence of NATO, when combined with Europe's and NATO's growing defense and military ties with key Asian powers, will further accentuate China's insecurities about Western containment of China. All of this accentuates Beijing's anxieties about growing strategic pressure from the United States and its allies in Europe and Asia.

Beyond Ukraine, but also as a result of it, the pressures for deglobalization are accelerating, as countries all over the world now worry about economic linkages as a source of insecurity and vulnerability, not efficiency and prosperity. China, in particular, worries about excessive reliance on the US dollar and being vulnerable to Western sanctions that could cut off its access to critical commodities and technologies, once again subjecting China to blackmail and coercion at the hands of Western power. The choices Chinese policymakers make in reaction to these events will have a defining influence on the trajectory of interactions with Washington—diplomatic, economic, and technological.

Not only are US-China relations rapidly evolving, but they are highly uncertain. The relationship could go in many directions. The trajectory is far from fixed, even for a relationship that has been for decades defined by variability. This uncertainty is not just due to the flux in global order but to the domestic conditions and political forces in both countries. Domestic politics in both countries are having a growing—perhaps outsize—influence on the relationship: on US policies toward China and vice versa. In the United States, favorable public opinion toward China is at historic lows. Key American groups who were once active in and supportive of US-China ties, such as the business community, civil society, and universities, have concerns about operating in China and are feeling more alienated from China as President Xi Jinping has sought to limit their interactions. The global pandemic has accelerated the degree of bilateral disengagement, if not alienation, due to travel restrictions. Moreover, there is a strong bipartisan consensus in Congress supporting greater competition with China, and it has legs in the US political system. Prominent expressions of this include growing restrictions on various bilateral economic interactions (such as foreign direct investment and portfolio investments) and China's movement to the center of US defense planning and procurement.

For China, nationalism is running high, as reflected in Chinese leaders' confidence in their domestic governance choices, which Chinese leaders now call "whole-process democracy."[6] Criticism of Western liberalism is widespread and encouraged in Chinese Communist Party (CCP) circles, with many pointing to the dysfunction of populism in the United States and Europe, and those nations' early failings in dealing with the pandemic (contrasted with China's early successes at containment). These views are reflected in China's public diplomacy, which has become loud and strident in recent years with its frequent and pointed critiques of the United States and others. This is not only popular among nationalists but has now been coined as "wolf warrior diplomacy," in refence to a popular Chinese movie in which a lone Chinese soldier saves the day.[7] As Wu Xinbo notes in chapter 5, Xi actively encourages Chinese officials to embrace a "fighting spirit" and to "dare to struggle." A core driver of this is China's national security apparatus, which views most US policies as a security challenge in light of US criticism of China over Hong Kong, Xinjiang, and Taiwan. Xi's own "national security perspective"—and its priority on ideological security—is driving many of these fears of the United States, viewing most US actions as a threat to political stability and to the CCP itself.[8]

As a result of these domestic perceptions and policies, pressure within China is growing to reduce its reliance on Western capital and technology and, accordingly, to moderate China's economic exposure to the United States. This fear of vulnerability has only become more acute following the international economic sanctions imposed on Russia following its invasion of Ukraine. This is driving a set of policies focused on greater economic and technological "self-reliance." Thus, under Xi, China now appears to have become more determined in opposing Western liberalism and more focused on self-reliance in practical terms, creating greater suspicions and more pressures for disengagement with the United States and other industrialized democracies. A final piece to the domestic puzzle in China is a bureaucratic one. Decisions within China are increasingly made by a small cohort around Xi and within the Central Committee apparatus, allowing these nationalist viewpoints to have greater sway.

In sum, domestic political institutions and political culture on both sides are driving the sense of both geopolitical and ideological competition. As in the past, domestic forces often have a particularly harmful influence on bilateral relations, promoting misinformation, accentuating worst-case assessments, and advocating for the most hard-line policies. The growing influence of domestic forces is unlikely to change in the coming years, absent the intervention and assertion of leadership from either capital or both.

A third feature of the relationship today that will influence its future trajectory is its intensifying complexity. US-China ties have never been simple—far from it—but the emerging dynamics in today's US-China relationship are only making bilateral interaction more complex and convoluted. There are forces pushing the two together and pulling them apart, and the degree to which these are reconciled—or not—will influence the future of the relationship.

On the one hand, US-China linkages and interactions across the relationship remain quite dense, even in the post-COVID era. Representing the two largest economies in the world, which also possess a $700 billion annual goods trading relationship, US and Chinese government policymakers and business leaders interact with each other in regions and venues all over the world and on a diversity of issues. Universities, students, and researchers are still deeply connected. Perhaps most significantly, both countries will remain an important geopolitical reference point for each other and much of the world, even as tensions rise (and maybe because of it). The economic, ecological, technological, and strategic independence among the two is undeniable, as much as policymakers in both countries like to downplay it.

On the other hand, a variety of new and worrisome patterns of interaction are beginning to exhibit themselves. The sources of competition are expanding, intensifying, and diversifying. As noted in this volume, US-China competition now covers security, economics, technology, and even ideas related to domestic and global governance. There is greater tolerance for risk and friction among both US and Chinese policymakers. Both sides are pursuing more confrontational strategies toward the other. There is very little sustained cooperation, even on global issues, and there does not appear to be much interest in remedying this. And perhaps most worrisome, the bilateral communication channels have atrophied, reducing the signal-to-noise ratio at the very time when both sides need clear and credible communication about each other's behaviors and intentions. Collectively, all of this accentuates distrust, reduces restraint, encourages accidents or miscalculation, and diminishes the effectiveness of crisis management.

For US and Chinese policymakers, a core—arguably the defining—challenge in the years ahead will be their ability to reconcile this intensifying competition in all its manifestations, with this existing interdependence in all its manifestations. Will Washington and Beijing find a landing zone that constitutes some form of coexistence, whether uneasy or stable, or will the United States and China find themselves defining a new type of cold war? Several variables will help answer that question.

Key Variables Defining the Future

With so many external and domestic variables affecting US-China relations in flux, assessing the trajectory of US-China ties is a daunting task. One way to narrow the range of options is to highlight those variables that will have an outsize influence on future relations, specifically on the pace, scope, and intensity of US-China strategic competition in the coming years. Four such variables are highlighted below.

First, the policy orientations of the United States and China toward the other will have a defining influence on the trajectory of US-China ties. Does each side treat the other as an implacable adversary engaged in a long-term and hostile competition? Will both sides come to see their contest as an existential one? Or will both sides try to find a strategic modus vivendi for stable relations in which problems are managed, competition is bounded, and economic interactions, while circumscribed, remain substantial? Does coexistence become an acceptable and politically sustainable way to manage US-China ties? As the United States and the Soviet Union did in the 1970s, do both sides settle on a policy that effectively balances competitive and interdependent pressure? On these questions, the domestic politics in both countries will shape the debates and decisions about China's US policy and America's China policy. The US presidential election in 2024 will be just as important as future Chinese leadership transitions, Xi's policy choices, and those of his future advisers. The current trend in the strategy and policy orientations of both sides, as noted earlier, is toward the more competitive end of the spectrum.

Second, the management of the Taiwan issue will be dispositive for the future of the relationship. If it is managed poorly, it will define the future of US-China ties as they descend into highly militarized competition and long-term hostility, and perhaps even confrontation. At the same time, stable cross-strait relations do not guarantee a stable and constructive relationship, but they certainly help. They increase the chances of both sides finding their way to bound competition and toward a coexistence framework. As of today, the Taiwan issue is once again moving to the forefront of the relationship, with military questions now just as prominent as the core political ones at the heart of the Taiwan issue. The current trend lines on Taiwan are worrisome. Perceptions on all three sides of the Taiwan equation—Beijing, Taipei, and Washington—are hardening, and this is driving an expansion of military capabilities on all sides, increasing the risk of an accident or miscalculation. Following the Russian invasion of Ukraine, international attention is more focused on Taiwan than ever before, especially in Europe. Taiwan is rapidly becoming a global issue. China continues to debate the orientation of its Taiwan policy as the election cycle in Taiwan picks up in advance of Taiwan's 2024 elections. Perhaps most ominously, the nuclear shadow is beginning to cast its pall over the Taiwan situation as Beijing accelerates the modernization of its nuclear weapons arsenal.

A third variable to watch will be economics, specifically the structure of the international economy and China's growth prospects. Will global economic forces constrain or enable greater US-China competition? Does global austerity induce caution on both sides, or does it accelerate the pressures for detachment and competition? As of today, regional trade pacts are on the rise, especially in Asia and particularly with China, but the United States is not an active player in them, fostering US perceptions of losing out. At the same time, global events such as the pandemic and the Ukraine war have accelerated the reconsideration of the structure of global trade and investment, reducing the support for complex interdependence (especially for extended manufacturing supply chains). The global focus by multinationals on speed and efficiency is being replaced by a focus on safety, redundancy, and security. Following the voluntary reduction by some one thousand global companies from their operations in Russia, some countries are trying to re-shore manufacturing and/or reduce exposure to uncertain markets like China and Russia. For its part, China faces substantial pressures to reduce exposure to US capital, technology, and markets—previously three of the most prized possessions in US-China interactions.

China's domestic economy is facing unique challenges—striking austerity in 2022—due to a convergence in both structural and cyclical economic challenges. The old drivers of growth are rapidly declining, whereas the new ones aren't providing sufficient impulse. China has made some clear policy errors at home, such as its adherence to a zero-COVID policy that substantially disrupted supply and demand, undermining growth and innovation. Many of China's structural imbalances, such as its debt and demographic changes, are worsening, with no obvious end in sight. The harsh demographic realities, such as a rapidly declining work force and a declining population on a net basis, will set in by the middle of this decade. As these economic challenges accumulate, Xi has prioritized reconfiguring China's economy for greater self-reliance, but its ability to do this remains an open question. Indeed, the consequences of doing so could leave current problems unresolved and therefore lock in lower growth over the long term. In other words, China may face certain unavoidable economic problems if it chooses to pursue a more competitive approach to US-China ties in its economic policymaking. Will China accept austerity at home for the sake of advancing its geopolitical agenda? The answer to this question—and the worsening structural economic challenges—could moderate Beijing's choices about its management of US-China ties.

A fourth and final variable that will have a bearing on the future will be the regional and global reactions to US-China competition. Will other countries tolerate, resist, or encourage it? Current and future tensions in US-China relations now affect countries, regions, and organizations in most regions of the world. To paraphrase the infamous Las Vegas maxim, what happens in US-China relations no longer stays in US-China relations. These responses from countries, regions, and organizations to US-China competition may either constrain or enable the competition. As is commonly stated in capitals all around the world, no one wants to choose between the United States and China, and many fear they will be forced to do so as strategic competition worsens. The responses of these countries will, in turn, influence decisions in Beijing and Washington about the nature of the US-China competition. To date, the concerns of many countries about being drawn into a Cold War–like competition may be creating incentives for restraint in both Washington and Beijing even as distinct groupings form around both the US and China. It was notable that both presidents Biden and Xi said during their first in-person bilateral meeting in Bali in November 2022 that the world expects both countries to manage responsibly such a complex and contentious relationship.

At the same time, these countries, regions, and institutions could become arenas for US-China competition to play out, wreaking havoc on some and offering opportunities to others. It could be a race toward the bottom or, perhaps in some arenas, a race to the top. If history is any guide, for many countries, the former is more likely. US-China competition presents most countries with unwelcome decisions that force them to make choices and trade-offs about their relative political, economic, and national security orientations. This is not to suggest that the world will break up into competing blocks, but some realignments are not only inevitable but already occurring in the wake of the Ukraine war and global economic pressures. The United States and China will likely compete over access to many countries and then use that access to measure their competition, accurately or not. The resulting interaction between US-China tensions, on the one hand, and countries' reactions to US and Chinese moves, on the other, will shape the trajectory of the bilateral competition. Will this dynamic allow for a managed competition or invalidate it as a mode of operation?

These dynamics and the other variables influencing the future of the US-China relationship could play out in many ways. The next section of this chapter provides four scenarios for the future.

Future Scenarios

The current conditions around the relationship—change, uncertainty, and complexity—when combined with the four variables noted earlier make predictions quite difficult. Nevertheless, it is possible to identify a range of general pathways for the future of the relationship. This section outlines four such pathways in the form of scenarios. They are (1) US-China détente, (2) strained but stable relations, (3) a gradual evolution toward an extended rivalry, and (4) an outright geopolitical confrontation.

These four scenarios are simplified, ideal types. They are not meant to be detailed and precise forecasts but rather to capture the different flavors of distinct future outcomes. Also, these four scenarios are not presented as mutually exclusive. The future of the relationship may actually be some combination of these that evolves in different sequences. In fact, it is unlikely that any single scenario will materialize but rather that we will see some combination of the above.

US-China Détente

The prospect of a US-China détente is perhaps the least likely scenario in the next decade. Détente in the US-China context is not a renewal of strategic alignment (such as during the 1970s and 1980s) but rather would constitute a high-level political commitment on both sides to bound competition, manage risks, enhance communication, and, with this base, expand tangible and meaningful cooperation. US-Soviet relations during the 1970s is a useful reference point for this scenario.

A US-China détente would likely have at least three core components. The first one would involve a mutual decision by leaders in Washington and Beijing to bound competition by actively managing the greatest sources of military and security competition; they would do so through both processes and policies. This would manifest in the creation of a variety of high-level channels of communication as well as through the negotiation and implementation of crisis- management mechanisms, confidence-building measures, and perhaps even some limited arms control agreements. This would have to include actions—or inactions—by both to foster a stable situation across the Taiwan Strait but would not necessarily involve formal or explicit agreements. Détente would also require understandings, if not agreements, about China's activities in the East and South China seas and about the disposition of US forces in the western Pacific. These channels of communication would have to extend to bilateral economic and technological relations in order to manage the gathering pressures toward trade and investment disaggregation and the intensifying competition in these aspects of the relationship.

A second component, and a natural extension of the former, would include bilateral agreements to work together on a variety of regional and global issues, especially those issues that have been problematic for the relationship in the past. Bilateral efforts to address challenges such as North Korea's and Iran's nuclear and missile problems would feature prominently. Détente would likely involve expanded cooperation on common translational challenges including climate change, food security, global health, developing country debt, and others. The security concerns associated with these latter issues would be moderated in this scenario, as both sides sought greater advantage in partnership to address such global issues.

A third component of the détente would involve some recommitment to an economic partnership based on reduced barriers to trade and investment and mechanisms to manage the competitive aspects of the US-China economic relationship. Under the conditions of détente, this could involve agreements on agreed-upon sectors for investment that don't touch the national security concerns of either side. Such a limited and targeted expansion of economic ties could manifest as an expression of the fact that both sides have a stake in the other's prosperity and thus contribute to the formation of a broader strategic modus vivendi for the overall relationship. This possibility would also need to include understandings and agreements about US-China global economic interactions in both international economic institutions and third country markets.

Within the next decade, it is difficult to foresee the necessary conditions for the emergence of this kind of détente. Most fundamentally, this scenario would require a shift in the perceptions of existing leaders or a change in the leaders themselves. The current constellation of perceptions and policies in both capitals is taking the relationship in the other direction. With Xi Jinping likely to remain in power for the next five and probably next ten years, a bilateral détente may not even be conceivable until the sixth generation in China emerges. On the US side, given the hardening of views about China (and a corresponding shift in US policies), it is uncertain which future US leaders would want to, or would have the political space to, pursue a détente.

One type of event that could encourage caution and restraint—and function as a stimulant for the emergence of détente—would be a major bilateral security crisis along the lines of the Cuban missile crisis. Such an event would have to sufficiently shock US and Chinese leaders about the risks of armed conflict that they would respond by shifting their focus to managing security competition rather than abetting it. A second type of event that could have such a cata-lytic effect is a period of prolonged Chinese economic austerity, which could aid the emergence of détente. This could produce a decision by Chinese lead-ers to reduce the intensity of their most competitive policies in order to focus on their domestic challenges. To address this austerity, China may recommit to a new round of domestic economic reforms that could include more trade and investment with the United States and other large economies, presumably on the back of the failure of various state-directed development strategies. In other words, given the trajectory of US and Chinese policymaking today, a détente would be conceivable only after a shock to the relationship or a shock to China's domestic order that forced both to question prior assumptions and, thus, open the door to more cooperative strategies—focused on trans-parency, restraint, and cooperation—for the sake of mutual security, stability, and prosperity.

Strained but Stable Relations

A far more likely scenario than a détente is a bilateral relationship defined by strain, tensions, and further competition—but one that is also stable. In es-sence, the United States and China figure out a way to "muddle through" in the current condition of strategic competition without letting the situation tip into crisis or confrontation. In this scenario, Washington and Beijing find a way, more by default than by design, to balance the adversarial, competitive, and cooperative aspects of the relationship. This future would involve some vol-atility but not the risk of outright confrontation or armed conflict. This type of relationship would involve a diversity of dialogue channels, and these would allow for a range of understandings of the greatest source of distrust and risk in the relationship as well as manage the greatest sources of complexity found in economic and technological interdependence.

Also in this scenario, some cooperation would materialize in ways that sig-nal to both countries that they do not see the other as an *existential* threat and implacable foe. The cooperation would more likely be on nontraditional secu-rity issues and outside Asia, where some overlapping interests exist. Similarly in this scenario, both sides reach agreements to bound the most serious security risks, including those related to Taiwan and both sides' military exercises and deployments in the region. This future of "strained but stable" US-China ties would also involve a shared recognition of the value of trade and investment ties; both Washington and Beijing would make efforts to maintain substantial levels of bilateral economic interactions, even as economic and technological decoupling materializes. National security concerns would continue to limit such interactions, but after an initial adjustment a steady state of mutually ben-eficial interaction could be found.

Unlike the détente scenario, this one would not require a shock or crisis in US-China ties or a radical change in leadership on either side. Rather, for this scenario to materialize would require political leadership on both sides to recognize the risks and costs of unrestrained competition and then commit to maintaining stability, even as both sides compete for power and influence in Asia and globally. This outcome is plausible, depending on the results of China's political transition in 2022–23 and the US presidential election in 2024. This scenario does not require a radical change in perceptions or paradigms on either side but rather an active decision *by both leaders* to manage competition, including accepting there are some mutual risks to avoid and mutual interests worth pursuing. In short, this will require active leadership on both sides, including by managing domestic political pressures to see the other as an existential threat and respond in hostile terms.

The current trajectory of elite perceptions and domestic politics in both countries does not make this the most likely scenario, but it does make it possible. For example, a degree of caution could seep into policymaking in both countries after a prolonged period of global economic austerity that diminishes both countries' capabilities or as US allies and partners call for some restraint by Washington and Beijing. China may come to realize the costs of its economic and diplomatic alignment with Russia. In this scenario, domestic politics will play a central role. Given the constraints imposed by domestic politics in both countries, it will be a challenge for US and Chinese leaders to find the political space for a stable but consistent strategic competition. If they don't, the competitive impulses, balancing behaviors, and action-reaction cycles may undermine the ability of both sides to "muddle through" in their pursuit of strategic competition. The emergence of greater nationalist and/or ideological inclinations in either country would rapidly diminish the probability of a protracted period of strained but stable relations. It remains to be seen whether it is possible for either side to create a policy and political framework for the management of strategic competition that does not inevitably produce a deterioration in relations.

Slow Burn toward Rivalry

A third scenario, and perhaps the most likely one, is a slow burn toward rivalry. This scenario involves a continuation of the current dynamics in the relationship, both geopolitical and domestic. The existing constellations of perceptions, policies, and interactive dynamics have set US-China ties on a trajectory of intensifying and comprehensive competition, perhaps marked by occasional bouts of heightened tension or even crises. In this scenario, the US-China security and diplomatic competition lead the way, with a heavy focus on preparing for a conflict over Taiwan. Perceptions on both sides harden as military capabilities improve accordingly. The US and Chinese militaries increasingly come into contact with each other in Asia, raising tensions and the risk of an accident or miscalculation. The Taiwan issue becomes the main driver of both conventional and nuclear arms races, with little interest from Washington or Beijing in managing or limiting the situation. The risk of an accident or a miscalculation remains pervasive. Bureaucratically, only the top levels of the relationship have the ability to take initiatives and drive agendas. Overall, bilateral communication remains limited, and cooperation is sparse.

As the Taiwan issue metastasizes in bilateral dynamics, nuclear weapons move to the forefront of the US-China agenda. China remains determined to expand its nuclear arsenal, which prompts a US response to expand its, bringing the nuclear shadow over most bilateral conversations. High-level bilateral diplomatic communication remains modest, and neither side shows much interest in crisis management, arms control, or related initiatives associated with strategic restraint. China aligns more overtly with Russia, including by expanding defense and intelligence cooperation as well as energy ties. China makes greater efforts to expand its influence in the developing world, especially with countries like Saudi Arabia and Iran, who feel alienated from the United States. Beijing is motivated by a desire to lock up supplies of critical materials invulnerable to Western sanctions and to build political relationships beyond the reach of US power and influence.

Furthermore, the US-China competition takes on a decidedly ideological flavor as both sides see the other as threatening their values and governance choices. Domestic politics in both countries encourage this, especially by framing US-China competition as an overt ideological competition. Both countries become more nationalistic and use threats from the other to advance domestic political agendas. China reorients its economy from its substantial exposure to global demand and technology flows, or at least it tries to do so. China pursues greater self-reliance in capital, commodities, and technologies and privileges state-directed development strategies, with a careful regulation and control of private capital and corporations. Both sides make active efforts to decouple in a limited manner from the other economically and technologically; they do so to reduce vulnerabilities and deny the other key inputs to innovation and growth. Technology becomes a high-profile arena of strategic competition, with a focus on key sectors such as 5G communications, semiconductors, quantum computing, new energy vehicles, and artificial intelligence. Parallel supply chains and distinct technology ecosystems become common throughout the global economy. Both sides struggle with this, given the depth and complexity of interdependence, but such a recognition fails to provide much restraint or even ballast in the relationship. In this scenario, China takes the lead in some key technologies, such as batteries and electric vehicles; in others, such as semiconductors, the competition for technological dominance intensifies. Technology competition assumes a singularly national security rationale.

Finally, in this future, there are regular US-China public confrontations on diplomatic issues, especially at the UN and other multilateral organizations. The Global South becomes an explicit arena for competition, and the latter becomes securitized as China effectively leverages its improved military capabilities to expand its defense relations with others. US and Chinese militaries are regularly bumping into one another in Asia and around the world. The incentives of both sides are to push, probe, and test the boundaries of each other, all with the goal of signaling resolve and capability.

As of this writing, this is the most likely scenario. This scenario is a straight-line projection from current trends, given the political leaders in both countries and their current perceptions and policy orientations (both domestic and external). This scenario assumes a consistent growth in the concerns in both countries about the other's capabilities and intentions. The nuclear dimension of the relationship makes all of this worse. These actions could precipitate an intensifying action-reaction cycle that would manifest in greater attention to military buildup in Asia, a lack of interest in crisis communications or diplomatic cooperation, and the flowering of domestic voices pushing more competitive strategies. A crisis around Taiwan can be expected in this scenario, perhaps by the end of the decade as Taiwan drifts further away and Beijing's anxieties and capabilities grow in unison.

Major drivers of this future would include Xi's remaining in office for the next decade and/or the election of a conservative US political leader who views China as an existential threat. Economic austerity in both countries could be an accelerant of this future rather than induce caution. Assuming the Ukraine war persists and/or China sticks with its alignment with Moscow, US and Chinese alienation will continue, if not worsen. US allies in Europe and Asia are likely to expand their support for this US strategy toward China, fostering Beijing's views that the United States is building a global alliance network to contain it. In this scenario, bilateral relations are defined by geopolitical competition, military rivalry, ideological alienation, and economic and technological disaggregation. It does not take much creativity to get from 2023 to this future scenario. If bilateral inertia sets in, this is where the relationship is headed—an entropy of sorts where both sides let their anxieties and most competitive instincts prevail.

Crisis and Confrontation

The fourth and final scenario is crisis and confrontation. This scenario envisions a relationship that is fundamentally transformed into an overtly hostile one by the searing experience of a military crisis involving armed conflict. This would trigger a rapid and substantial attenuation of cultural and economic ties and the mutual adoption of overtly hostile diplomatic and military postures toward each other. The relevant historical reference point, in general terms, is the military hostility and diplomatic isolation of the 1950s or 1960s, albeit with some obvious differences given the interconnected nature of the global economy and bilateral interdependence today.

This scenario is similar to the previous one in that it begins with a period of acrimony and intensifying competition but then rapidly deteriorates due to a major security crisis in East Asia. This crisis comes to define US-China relations and global politics more broadly, much as the Korean War did in the 1950s. In fact, this bilateral crisis could be the cause of a major geopolitical disjuncture that ushers in a new cold war. Unfortunately, this prospect may be more probable than some of the other scenarios discussed above; if current trends persist, the US-China relationship could be one crisis away from this outcome in the next decade.

There are several pathways to this future. The crisis could involve a major military confrontation, such as over Taiwan or the Korean peninsula, or a more limited one, such as in the East or South China seas involving America's defense of an ally. During this crisis, and especially after armed conflict, both sides would shift from a policy orientation of competition to one of outright hostility. All pretense of balance, managed competition, cooperation, and shared interest would be absent from the thinking in Beijing and Washington. Politicians and the public in both countries would call for a maximalist approach to rivalry and disengagement, especially regarding cultural, economic, and technological ties.

This scenario would have a major impact on both Asia and global security affairs. Washington would lead an effort to fortify its defense presence in Asia and thus pressure US allies, such as Japan, South Korea, and Australia, to similarly fortify themselves for a long-term confrontation with China. If Taiwan were involved in the initial crisis, this scenario could involve the redeployment of US forces on Taiwan, precipitating dramatic changes in US-China ties. The US alliance system in Asia could begin to assume a NATO-like quality of mutual defense commitments *among* its allies, and some NATO allies in Europe could substantially increase their defense presence in Asia, treating China as a strategic rival.

In response, China would adopt a more overtly disruptive and combative posture in Asia to challenge explicitly US alliances and partnership, especially the more vulnerable ones in Southeast Asia. China would likely increase its regional strike capabilities with more missiles and bombers targeting US and allied forces in Asia. China might also push for the rapid creation of regional military bases. An intensive arms race between China and the United States in Asia would be an explicit feature of the regional security situation, as it was in Europe during the Cold War. A nuclear arms race would parallel this. At a global level, China, in concert with Russia, would probably also seek to mobilize a coalition of developing countries to oppose US policies on a host of security, economic, diplomatic, and technological issues. Beijing and Moscow would focus on challenging the most liberal aspects of global rules and norms. US-China competition in regions beyond Asia, like the Middle East, would expand. The global economy and geopolitical alignments would begin to form along an East-West axis, with China and Russia representing the former and the US and all its allies—including some of those in Asia—representing the liberal rules-based order. The East-West axis would be complemented by a North-South axis as the United States and China compete over the alignments of, and access to, the economies of Africa, Latin America, and the Middle East.

From the vantage point of early 2023, this scenario appears a bit too close for comfort. The predicates for it exist. Both sides are increasingly framing their competition in ideological terms, expanding their military capabilities, and probing the boundaries of the other's interests, and they have several proximate disagreements. If these and other trends continue, the relationship becomes one military crisis away from a future of hostility and confrontation. The two most likely candidates for that kind of crisis are Taiwan and the Korean peninsula. Both issues are in flux, the stakes for both the United States and China are substantial, both have military capabilities poised for a future contingency, and, as a result of worsening perceptions, the risks of a crisis are accumulating. In short, there is means, motive, and opportunity for a crisis to emerge.

A corresponding question, then, becomes whether a military crisis could be contained or would escalate in a way that fundamentally changed the relationship and global politics. Given the current atrophy of communication channels, absence of crisis-management mechanisms, worsening domestic politics, and risky behaviors on both sides, the dangers of escalation are substantial. To be sure, there are also risks of a minor security crisis such as a skirmish around the East or South China seas or a military accident at sea or in the air. The latter may not quickly precipitate a dramatic shift in US-China relations but would accelerate the evolution toward the future.

Looking forward, none of these four scenarios are inevitable. There are no laws of physics in international relations, despite the ardent proponents of the Thucydides's Trap argument.[9] Rather, if there is one lesson to take away from US-China interactions over the last fifty years since 1972, it is that agency and contingency matter, for better and for worse. At critical points in the past, leaders on both sides have assumed political and geopolitical risk to stabilize relations. Past leaders have also taken actions that have unmoored the relationship; Xi Jinping's South China Sea strategy and President Donald Trump's trade war come to mind. At the same time, unexpected events within either country and between them have also been a source of instability. The current domestic political debates in both countries about the other and about the Taiwan question, which are increasingly pointed and public, offer notable, if foreboding, examples of this.

Those lessons from history still apply today, even as the circumstances around the relationship and within each country have changed and will continue to do so. Both the United States and China are more ambitious about their roles in Asia and in the world, and to make an obvious point, China is certainly more capable of using, and willing to use, its capabilities to advance its ambitions. This has created new dynamics: the military competition around Taiwan is worsening, and both sides are probing and testing the other's boundaries on other sensitive security issues in Asia. In addition, domestic political forces in both countries are framing the competition in stark and often ideological terms. To be sure, Washington does face some pressures from its allies in Asia and Europe to maintain some sort of US-China equilibrium, even as these allies align more with the United States in this long-term competition.

As these dynamics unfold, the stakes for both Washington and Beijing are quite high given the depth of economic, cultural, technological, and diplomatic ties and the global implications of an openly hostile relationship between the world's two largest economies. In fact, the stakes may actually be rising as China's capabilities expand and improve, as Xi demonstrates a greater tolerance for friction in US-China ties, and as the nuclear shadow looms larger over this relationship. It is at times like this that the role of agency matters more. The US-China relationship works well when leaders on both sides take the reins and assert leadership, either for more stability or a more pointed contest. Such leadership prevents inertia and entropy from taking over, but it also importantly moderates the influence of domestic political currents on the direction of policymaking. More of this is needed today to prevent US-China ties—even as competition intensifies —from becoming defined in exclusively ideological terms and in ways that make coexistence an unwelcome possibility.

The nature of this US-China competition—its scope, its pace, its intensity, and its manifestations—can and should be the provenance of deliberate strategic choice by policymakers in both capitals, regarding both restraint and competition. To do so, it will take an affirmative vision and consistent efforts to prevent the relationship from drifting toward a future that undermines US interests, even as the United States embraces various competitive strategies. As demonstrated throughout this volume, the US-China relationship changes the most—and often unpredictably—when domestic dynamics in one or both countries shift. The arrivals of both Xi Jinping in 2012 and Donald J. Trump in 2016 are prominent examples. Looking forward to the next decade, as new US and Chinese policymakers come online and as the domestic political order in both countries evolves, neither US nor Chinese policymakers should be guided by either their worst fears or their greatest hopes about US-China ties in the twenty-first century.

Notes

1. See Evan S. Medeiros, "The Changing Fundamentals of US-China Relations," *Washington Quarterly* 42, no. 3 (Fall 2019).

2. On China's position on the conflict, see Evan S. Medeiros, "China's Strategic Straddle: Analyzing Beijing's Diplomatic Response to the Russian Invasion of Ukraine," *China Leadership Monitor*, no. 72 (Summer 2022).

3. For an excellent analysis of China-Russia relations since the Ukraine war and the joint statement, see Elizabeth Wishnick, "Strategic Partner or Strategic Player? Russian Asia Experts Assess China's Ukraine Policy," *China Leadership Monitor*, no. 72 (Summer 2022).

4. A notable development in June 2022 was NATO's issuance of a new Strategic Concept document that characterized China as posing "systemic challenges" to NATO and argued that China's "stated ambitions and coercive policies challenge our interests, security and values." See NATO 2022 Strategic Concept, Brussels, Belgium, June 2022, https://www.nato.int/strategic-concept/.

5. For a view on this, see Cliff Kupchan, "Bipolarity Is Back: Why It Matters," *Washington Quarterly* 44, no. 4 (Winter 2021): 123–39.

6. Anatoly Antonov and Qin Gang, "Russian and Chinese Ambassadors: Respecting People's Democratic Rights," *National Interest*, November 26, 2021, https://nationalinterest.org/feature/russian-and-chinese-ambassadors-respecting-people%E2%80%99s-democratic-rights-197165.

7. Peter Martin, *China's Civilian Army: The Making of Wolf Warrior Diplomacy* (New York: Oxford University Press, 2021).

8. Sheena Chestnut Greitens, "How Does China Think about National Security?" in *The China Questions II: Critical Insights into the US-China Relationship,* Maria Adele Carrai, Jennifer Rudolph, Michael Szonyi eds., (Cambridge, MA: Harvard University Press, 2022).

9. Graham Allison, *Destined for War: Can America and China Escape Thucydides's Trap?* (New York: Houghton Mifflin Harcourt, 2017).

Contributors

Richard K. Betts—Leo A. Shifrin Professor of War and Peace Studies, Columbia University

Elizabeth Economy—senior fellow, Hoover Institution; senior fellow for China studies, Council on Foreign Relations

David M. Edelstein—vice dean of faculty and professor in the Department of Government, Georgetown University

Harry Harding—professor of public policy, University of Virginia

Arthur R. Kroeber—founding partner and head of research, Gavekal Dragonomics

Li Chen—associate professor at the School of International Studies, Renmin University of China

Evan S. Medeiros—Penner Family Chair in Asian Studies and the Cling Family Distinguished Fellow in U.S.-China Relations, School of Foreign Service, Georgetown University

James Mulvenon—scientific research and analysis director, Peraton Labs

Phillip C. Saunders—director of the Center for the Study of Chinese Military Affairs, National Defense University

David Shambaugh—Gaston Sigur Professor of Asian Studies and director of the China Policy Program, George Washington University

Helen Toner—director of strategy and foundational research grants, Center for Security and Emerging Technologies (CSET), Georgetown University

Paul Triolo—senior vice president for China and technology policy, Albright Stonebridge Group

Wang Jisi—president of the Institute of International and Strategic Studies, Peking University

Wu Xinbo—dean of the Institute of International Studies and director of the Center for American Studies, Fudan University

Index

Note: Information in figures is indicated by page numbers in *italics*.